HTML & Web Publishing SECRETS®

HTML & Web Publishing SECRETS®

by Jim Heid

with contributions from
Adam Block, Director, Product Development, PC World Online
Roxanne Gentile, Assistant Content Engineer, Macworld Online
Andy King, Webmaster, Webreference.com
Karen Peterson Liberatore, Online Producer, Macworld Online
Dan Shafer, Senior Webmaster, Salon Magazine

IDG Books Worldwide, Inc.
An International Data Group Company

Foster City, CA ♦ Chicago, IL ♦ Indianapolis, IN ♦ Dallas, TX

HTML & Web Publishing SECRETS®

Published by
IDG Books Worldwide, Inc.
An International Data Group Company
919 E. Hillsdale Blvd., Suite 400
Foster City, CA 94404

http://www.idgbooks.com (IDG Books Worldwide Web site)

Library of Congress Catalog Card No.: 96-078229

ISBN: 0-7645-4003-3

Printed in the United States of America

10 9 8 7 6 5 4 3 2 1

1O/QW/QV/2X/FC

Distributed in the United States by IDG Books Worldwide, Inc.

Distributed by Macmillan Canada for Canada; by Contemporanea de Ediciones for Venezuela; by Distribuidora Cuspide for Argentina; by CITEC for Brazil; by Ediciones ZETA S.C.R. Ltda. for Peru; by Editorial Limusa SA for Mexico; by Transworld Publishers Limited in the United Kingdom and Europe; by Academic Bookshop for Egypt; by Levant Distributors S.A.R.L. for Lebanon; by Al Jassim for Saudi Arabia; by Simron Pty. Ltd. for South Africa; by Pustak Mahal for India; by The Computer Bookshop for India; by Toppan Company Ltd. for Japan; by Addison Wesley Publishing Company for Korea; by Longman Singapore Publishers Ltd. for Singapore, Malaysia, Thailand, and Indonesia; by Unalis Corporation for Taiwan; by WS Computer Publishing Company, Inc. for the Philippines; by WoodsLane Pty. Ltd. for Australia; by WoodsLane Enterprises Ltd. for New Zealand. Authorized Sales Agent: Anthony Rudkin Associates for the Middle East and North Africa.

For general information on IDG Books Worldwide's books in the U.S., please call our Consumer Customer Service department at 800-762-2974. For reseller information, including discounts and premium sales, please call our Reseller Customer Service department at 800-434-3422.

For information on where to purchase IDG Books Worldwide's books outside the U.S., please contact our International Sales department at 415-655-3172 or fax 415-655-3295.

For information on foreign language translations, please contact our Foreign & Subsidiary Rights department at 415-655-3021 or fax 415-655-3281.

For sales inquiries and special prices for bulk quantities, please contact our Sales department at 415-655-3200 or write to the address above.

For information on using IDG Books Worldwide's books in the classroom or for ordering examination copies, please contact our Educational Sales department at 800-434-2086 or fax 817-251-8174.

For press review copies, author interviews, or other publicity information, please contact our Public Relations department at 415-655-3000 or fax 415-655-3299.

For authorization to photocopy items for corporate, personal, or educational use, please contact Copyright Clearance Center, 222 Rosewood Drive, Danvers, MA 01923, or fax 508-750-4470.

ABOUT IDG BOOKS WORLDWIDE

Welcome to the world of IDG Books Worldwide.

IDG Books Worldwide, Inc., is a subsidiary of International Data Group, the world's largest publisher of computer-related information and the leading global provider of information services on information technology. IDG was founded more than 25 years ago and now employs more than 8,500 people worldwide. IDG publishes more than 275 computer publications in over 75 countries (see listing below). More than 60 million people read one or more IDG publications each month.

Launched in 1990, IDG Books Worldwide is today the #1 publisher of best-selling computer books in the United States. We are proud to have received eight awards from the Computer Press Association in recognition of editorial excellence and three from *Computer Currents'* First Annual Readers' Choice Awards. Our best-selling *...For Dummies®* series has more than 30 million copies in print with translations in 30 languages. IDG Books Worldwide, through a joint venture with IDG's Hi-Tech Beijing, became the first U.S. publisher to publish a computer book in the People's Republic of China. In record time, IDG Books Worldwide has become the first choice for millions of readers around the world who want to learn how to better manage their businesses.

Our mission is simple: Every one of our books is designed to bring extra value and skill-building instructions to the reader. Our books are written by experts who understand and care about our readers. The knowledge base of our editorial staff comes from years of experience in publishing, education, and journalism — experience we use to produce books for the '90s. In short, we care about books, so we attract the best people. We devote special attention to details such as audience, interior design, use of icons, and illustrations. And because we use an efficient process of authoring, editing, and desktop publishing our books electronically, we can spend more time ensuring superior content and spend less time on the technicalities of making books.

You can count on our commitment to deliver high-quality books at competitive prices on topics you want to read about. At IDG Books Worldwide, we continue in the IDG tradition of delivering quality for more than 25 years. You'll find no better book on a subject than one from IDG Books Worldwide.

John Kilcullen
CEO
IDG Books Worldwide, Inc.

Steven Berkowitz
President and Publisher
IDG Books Worldwide, Inc.

Eighth Annual Computer Press Awards 1992

Ninth Annual Computer Press Awards 1993

Tenth Annual Computer Press Awards 1994

Eleventh Annual Computer Press Awards 1995

IDG Books Worldwide, Inc., is a subsidiary of International Data Group, the world's largest publisher of computer-related information and the leading global provider of information services on information technology. International Data Group publishes over 275 computer publications in over 75 countries. Sixty million people read one or more International Data Group publications each month. International Data Group's publications include: **ARGENTINA**: Buyer's Guide, Computerworld Argentina, PC World Argentina; **AUSTRALIA**: Australian Macworld, Australian PC World, Australian Reseller News, Computerworld, IT Casebook, Network World, Publish, Webmaster; **AUSTRIA**: Computerwelt Osterreich, Networks Austria, PC Tip Austria; **BANGLADESH**: PC World Bangladesh; **BELARUS**: PC World Belarus; **BELGIUM**: Data News; **BRAZIL**: Annuário de Informática, Computerworld, Connections, Macworld, PC Player, PC World, Publish, Reseller News, Supergamepower; **BULGARIA**: Computerworld Bulgaria, Network World Bulgaria, PC & MacWorld Bulgaria; **CANADA**: CIO Canada, Client/Server World, ComputerWorld Canada, InfoWorld Canada, NetworkWorld Canada, WebWorld; **CHILE**: Computerworld Chile, PC World Chile; **COLOMBIA**: Computerworld Colombia, PC World Colombia; **COSTA RICA**: PC World Centro America; **THE CZECH AND SLOVAK REPUBLICS**: Computerworld Czechoslovakia, Macworld Czech Republic, PC World Czechoslovakia; **DENMARK**: Communications World Danmark, Computerworld Danmark, Macworld Danmark, PC World Danmark, Techworld Denmark; **DOMINICAN REPUBLIC**: PC World Republica Dominicana; **ECUADOR**: PC World Ecuador; **EGYPT**: Computerworld Middle East, PC World Middle East; **EL SALVADOR**: PC World Centro America; **FINLAND**: MikroPC, Tietoverkko, Tietoviikko; **FRANCE**: Distributique, Hebdo, Info PC, Le Monde Informatique, Macworld, Reseaux & Telecoms, WebMaster France; **GERMANY**: Computer Partner, Computerwoche, Computerwoche Extra, Computerwoche FOCUS, Global Online, Macwelt, PC Welt; **GREECE**: Amiga Computing, GamePro Greece, Multimedia World; **GUATEMALA**: PC World Centro America; **HONDURAS**: PC World Centro America; **HONG KONG**: Computerworld Hong Kong, PC World Hong Kong, Publish in Asia; **HUNGARY**: ABCD CD-ROM, Computerworld Szamitastechnika, Internetto online Magazine, PC World Hungary, PC-X Magazin Hungary; **ICELAND**: Tolvuheimur PC World Island; **INDIA**: Information Communications World, Information Systems Computerworld, PC World India, Publish in Asia; **INDONESIA**: InfoKomputer PC World, Komputek Computerworld, Publish in Asia; **IRELAND**: ComputerScope, PC Live!; **ISRAEL**: Macworld Israel, People & Computers/Computerworld; **ITALY**: Computerworld Italia, Macworld Italia, Networking Italia, PC World Italia; **JAPAN**: DTP World, Macworld Japan, Nikkei Personal Computing, OS/2 World Japan, SunWorld Japan, Windows NT World, Windows World Japan; **KENYA**: PC World East African; **KOREA**: Hi-Tech Information, Macworld Korea, PC World Korea; **MACEDONIA**: PC World Macedonia; **MALAYSIA**: Computerworld Malaysia, PC World Malaysia, Publish in Asia; **MALTA**: PC World Malta; **MEXICO**: Computerworld Mexico, PC World Mexico; **MYANMAR**: PC World Myanmar; **NETHERLANDS**: Computer! Totaal, LAN Internetworking Magazine, LAN World Buyers Guide, Macworld Netherlands, Net, WebWereld; **NEW ZEALAND**: Absolute Beginners Guide and Plain & Simple Series, Computer Buyer, Computer Industry Directory, Computerworld New Zealand, MTB, Network World, PC World New Zealand; **NICARAGUA**: PC World Centro America; **NORWAY**: Computerworld Norge, CW Rapport, Datamagasinet, Financial Rapport, Kursguide Norge, Macworld Norge, Multimediaworld Norge, PC World Ekspress Norge, PC World Nettverk, PC World Norge, PC World ProduktGuide Norge; **PAKISTAN**: Computerworld Pakistan; **PANAMA**: PC World Panama; **PEOPLE'S REPUBLIC OF CHINA**: China Computer Users, China Computerworld, China InfoWorld, China Telecom World Weekly, Computer & Communication, Electronic Design China, Electronics Today, Electronics Weekly, Game Software, PC World China, Popular Computer Week, Software Weekly, Software World, Telecom World; **PERU**: Computerworld Peru, PC World Profesional Peru, PC World SoHo Peru; **PHILIPPINES**: Click!, Computerworld Philippines, PC World Philippines, Publish in Asia; **POLAND**: Computerworld Poland, Computerworld Special Report Poland, Cyber, Macworld Poland, Networld Poland, PC World Komputer; **PORTUGAL**: Cerebro/PC World, Computerworld/Correio Informático, Dealer World Portugal, Mac*In/PC*In Portugal, Multimedia World; **PUERTO RICO**: PC World Puerto Rico; **ROMANIA**: Computerworld Romania, PC World Romania, Telecom Romania; **RUSSIA**: Computerworld Russia, Mir PK, Publish, Seti; **SINGAPORE**: Computerworld Singapore, PC World Singapore, Publish in Asia; **SLOVENIA**: Monitor; **SOUTH AFRICA**: Computing SA, Network World SA, Software World SA; **SPAIN**: Communicaciones World España, Computerworld España, Dealer World España, Macworld España, PC World España; **SRI LANKA**: Infolink PC World; **SWEDEN**: CAP&Design, Computer Sweden, Corporate Computing Sweden, Internetworld Sweden, it.branschen, Macworld Sweden, MaxiData Sweden, MikroDatorn, Nätverk & Kommunikation, PC World Sweden, PCaktiv, Windows World Sweden; **SWITZERLAND**: Computerworld Schweiz, Macworld Schweiz, PCtip; **TAIWAN**: Computerworld Taiwan, Macworld Taiwan, NEW ViSiON/Publish, PC World Taiwan, Windows World Taiwan; **THAILAND**: Publish in Asia, Thai Computerworld; **TURKEY**: Computerworld Turkiye, Macworld Turkiye, Network World Turkiye, PC World Turkiye; **UKRAINE**: Computerworld Kiev, Multimedia World Ukraine, PC World Ukraine; **UNITED KINGDOM**: Acorn User UK, Amiga Action UK, Amiga Computing UK, Apple Talk UK, Computing, Macworld, Parents and Computers UK, PC Advisor, PC Home, PSX Pro, The WEB; **UNITED STATES**: Cable in the Classroom, CIO Magazine, Computerworld, DOS World, Federal Computer Week, GamePro Magazine, InfoWorld, I-Way, Macworld, Network World, PC Games, PC World, Publish, Video Event, THE WEB Magazine, and WebMaster; online webzines: JavaWorld, NetscapeWorld, and SunWorld Online; **URUGUAY**: InfoWorld Uruguay; **VENEZUELA**: Computerworld Venezuela, PC World Venezuela; and **VIETNAM**: PC World Vietnam.

3/24/97

Credits

Acquisitions Editor
Nancy Dunn

Development Editor
Amy Thomas

Technical Editors
Dennis Cohen
Dennis Cox

Copy Editors
Katharine Dvorak
Suki Gear

Project Coordinator
Katy German

Graphics and Production Specialists
Tom Debolski
Renée Dunn
Mark Schumann
Elsie Yim

Quality Control Specialist
Mick Arellano

Proofreader
Annie Sheldon

Indexer
Steve Rath

Book Design
Draper and Liew, Inc.

About the Author and Contributors

Jim Heid is an award-winning columnist for *Macworld* magazine, where his "Media" column covers Web-development issues and technologies. The author of numerous bestsellers on Windows and Mac OS computing, he also writes about online and multimedia technologies for *PC World* magazine.

Heid is also a regular contributor to *Macworld*'s features and reviews sections, where he specializes in multimedia production and Web publishing — a mix that exploits his background as a typographer, musician, videographer, and audiophile. (He worked in his father's recording studio, which was Pittsburgh's first.) He has also taught electronic publishing and fine typography at the Kodak-founded Center for Creative Imaging in Camden, Maine.

Heid has been working with and writing about personal computers since the late 1970s, when he computerized his home-built ham radio shack with one of the first Radio Shack TRS-80s and a 300 Bps modem. In the early '80s, he was Senior Technical Editor for *Microcomputing* magazine, where he wrote about Windows 1.0 and the original 128K Mac, not to mention MS-DOS and CP/M. His 1,200-page *Macworld New Complete Mac Handbook, 4th Edition* (IDG Books Worldwide, 1995) is a four-time winner of the BMUG Choice award for best general Macintosh book.

Jim Heid is a popular speaker at user group meetings and conventions, and has appeared as a guest on numerous computer-related TV and radio programs. He and his wife live on California's scenic Mendocino coast.

Adam Block is Director of Product Development for PC World Online, where his responsibilities include leading the research and development of new Web sites and electronic publications. He's particularly interested in issues of user interface design and site navigational structure. Adam also coteaches a class in new media journalism at the University of California at Berkeley Graduate School of Journalism. He asserts that each time they've taught the course, the instructors have learned as much as the students. In his scarce free time, Adam enjoys jai-alai, Bonsai trimming, and the caber toss.

Roxanne Gentile produces editorial content in her role as Assistant Content Engineer for Macworld Online (`http://www.macworld.com/`). She also writes articles and reviews for *Macworld* magazine and is a recipient of the American Business Publishers' Jesse H. Neal Editorial Achievement award for her work at Macworld Online.

Andy King has been creating Web sites since 1993 and is the Webmaster at Athenia Associates, creators of webreference.com and coolcentral.com. Webreference is devoted to teaching people the art of Web development and has won over 60 awards. Andy edits, oversees, and writes for Webreference, and has also written for *MacWeek* and *Web Techniques*. Contact him at aking@webreference.com, or visit his Web site at `http://www.webreference.com/`.

Karen Peterson Liberatore is a producer and editor at Macworld Online (`http://www.macworld.com/`), where she creates Web-specific content. She is also editor of Macworld's electronic newsletter. Liberatore got her start in the online realm in the late '80s by cruising every bulletin board system she could find. A former newspaper journalist, she has worked variously as a daily news reporter, feature writer, feature editor, and editor of a community weekly. While on the staff of the *San Francisco Chronicle*, Liberatore worked in the Editorial Systems Department where her specialty was telecommunications. She recently received a Jesse H. Neal Award from the Association of Business Publishers for her work at Macworld Online. Her analog interests include gardening and California history.

Dan Shafer is the Director of Technology and Senior Webmaster for Salon Magazine (`http://www.salon1999.com/`), one of the most critically acclaimed online publications on the Web. He writes and speaks frequently about the Web and related technologies. He has written extensively about JavaScript, including the popular book *JavaScript and Netscape Wizardry*. The best-selling author of more than 50 books about high technology and computers lives near San Francisco with his wife, Carolyn.

To Maryellen and to my mother, and to the memory of George Heid, my father and a radio and TV pioneer who would have loved the twentieth century's latest communications medium

Foreword

Oh no, you say. Not another book on HTML and Web publishing. As you glance down the many feet of books available on this topic, why should you read this one?

No one can deny that the Web has taken off like a rocket. Just about everyone these days has either his or her own Web site at theirowncompanyname.com or a home page on America Online, CompuServe, or some other shared plot of cyberspace. URLs are now found on everything from bus shelters to cereal boxes, and we think nothing of e-mailing our neighbors, relatives, and friends. The Web is completely out of control, but it's a boon for those of us who try to provide clarity and cut through the confusion. Or at least I hope we are able to.

The Web Explosion has also seen hundreds of Web-related books, not to mention over a hundred different Web servers and hundreds more Web-oriented products. Even though many of these products are freely available over the Internet, you still will need to take time to just figure out what software makes the most sense for you to use. Here's where this book can help provide guidance in picking the right products.

Writing HTML and publishing a Web site is easy. If I can do it, with my better programming years in my very distant past, anyone can. All it takes is a text editor, the ability to learn a few commands, and some quiet time to experiment.

Writing good HTML that can be viewed by many different visitors under many different circumstances and equipment configurations is much harder. If you know enough HTML to put up a half-way decent Web page and don't have time to do much more, then put down this book and move on to something noncomputer related. If you want to learn the subtleties and understand the new developments, such as style sheets and how to get the most out of the tags you don't know, then this book is for you.

The same goes for running a good Web site. I put up my first Web server in the fall of 1995 — it seems so long ago. Back then, it was hard to find an Internet provider that would host a Web site on anything other than UNIX, and most providers were reluctant and expensive at that. Now you have a lot of choices among providers, and many will bundle in other services, such as log analysis and link tracking (tools used to help you fix errors and broken links).

Most Web sites today are just pages of text that haven't changed for many months. Transforming these sites into living, breathing entities will take a lot of work and require you to learn some new tools and techniques. Where do you go for help to take your Web site to these new heights? Right here.

For example, have you ever tried to create your own animated GIFs? They can be a lot of fun and, if done properly, add value to your pages. If done poorly, they can annoy your visitors and contribute to motion sickness.

I love to learn new things. One of the great opportunities about the Web is also its greatest challenge: there is so much to learn every day. The Web is also a great teacher. I can't count the number of times I wanted to understand how a page was constructed and would download it to my disk and pick it apart.

Try something new on the Web today.

David Strom
Publisher of Web Informant, http://www.webinformant.com
david@strom.com

Preface

I'm going to start this book with a confession: Until fairly recently, I wasn't that excited about the Internet.

"Ah, an antivisionary," you say. "You've probably said 'VCRs will never catch on' and 'Madonna's records will never sell,' too."

Not true. (Well, Madonna's success has surprised me a little.) It isn't that I thought online communications didn't have anything to offer — far from it. I bought my first modem, a 300-baud, manual-dial dinosaur, in 1980. It was connected to a Radio Shack TRS-80 Model I that I had in my bedroom, and because my room had a phone jack but no phone, I had to yell downstairs and ask my mom to dial bulletin board numbers for me. Talk about workgroup computing.

The reason I wasn't initially fired up about the Internet is because there wasn't much you could do on the Net that you couldn't do — and do much easier — on a commercial online service. Sure, the Net had bigger discussion boards, larger software libraries, and was kinda-sorta free, but the user interface was ugly and the connection tribulations were titanic.

Then the World Wide Web came along. The Web supported hyperlinks — click something and jump somewhere else, maybe to a different part of a document, maybe to a different part of the world. The Web supported inline graphics: instead of ugly pages of nothing but text, we could have ugly pages containing text and graphics.

As the Web evolved (I almost said "matured," but we're not there yet), its capabilities as a communications medium have grown exponentially. Besides text and graphics, Web sites can now provide live audio, video, 3D virtual reality scenes, and richly formatted documents. The Web has become a major communications medium, one that combines the power and potential of print, radio, and television.

I'm excited now. For me, the Web is a dreamland that gives me the opportunity to employ all of the vocations and avocations I've had over the years: writing, typography and design, audio and video production, programming, and publishing. Many Web publishers have similarly diverse backgrounds. Now we get to apply our experience in one place: at our computers, strong coffee at our sides, wrist braces on our arms. Is life sweet, or what?

Why You Should Read This Book

HTML & Web Publishing SECRETS shows you how to use a Windows or Mac OS computer to design, develop, serve, and maintain a next-generation Web site for publishing on the Internet or on a company-wide intranet.

If you've browsed the bookstore shelves — maybe you're doing that right now — you've probably noticed that there isn't exactly a shortage of books on this subject. So what's so different about this book? Several things.

***HTML & Web Publishing SECRETS* isn't obsessed with teaching you HTML.** The first generation of Web books concentrated on teaching you how to write Hypertext Markup Language (HTML) code, the formatting language that describes the structure of Web pages. There was a good reason for this: When these books were published, the only way to create a Web page was to hand-peck codes such as `<A HREF>` and `<IMG SRC>`.

Today, there are over a dozen free and commercial products that enable you to create Web pages without pecking codes. Some operate much like a desktop publishing program: they import text and graphics, drag them around, and then save your work as an HTML page. Other products are designed to convert existing documents — publications, word processor files, even presentations — into HTML format.

In short, we're out of the HTML stone age. In recognition of that, this book will guide you to the best Web page design programs and pass along the secrets for making them sing.

***HTML & Web Publishing SECRETS* covers the latest in HTML and covers it smartly.** Now wait. I just said this book isn't obsessed with HTML, and now I'm saying it covers the latest. Let me explain. As useful as today's Web-design software is, you *must* know enough about HTML to streamline and optimize your pages so that they load quickly and look good on different machines and on different Web browsers.

What's more, some of the very latest developments in HTML, such as *style sheets,* that give Web publishers more control over the appearance of a page, aren't supported by the current crop of Web-design software. *HTML & Web Publishing SECRETS* covers these latest HTML developments in detail, and covers HTML from the perspective *today's* Web publishers need: how to understand and tweak the code produced by a Web-design program.

***HTML & Web Publishing SECRETS* is multimedia-aware.** Some multimedia elements have been available on the Web for some time — audio files that Web surfers can download, for example. But recently, the Web has experienced a multimedia revolution: Real-time audio and even video are becoming common, as are animations, virtual reality, and sophisticated user interfaces that used to be the province of CD-ROMs. I write about these topics monthly in my "Media" column in *Macworld* magazine, which covers multimedia production and Web site development. So it's a pleasure to be able to cover them here, and with a degree of detail that other Web publishing books do not.

***HTML & Web Publishing SECRETS* is intranet-aware.** While the Internet has drawn the attention of everyone from TV news correspondents to myopic legislators, another Web revolution has been taking place in businesses and institutions: intranet web sites, ones that operate within an organization's network and serve as libraries, bulletin boards, and water coolers. Intranet web development is hot, and for good reasons. For one thing, intranet-based services are relatively easy to implement — far easier than writing custom applications in languages such as Visual Basic. For another, intranets put a familiar interface — that of the Web — on a custom application. If your employees surf the World Wide Web, they will immediately feel familiar with an intranet-based application. And finally, intranets have the advantage of platform independence: an intranet web can reach any employee with a computer, whether the machine is a Windows box, a Mac OS machine, a network computer, or a UNIX workstation.

You won't find one particular chapter in this book that deals with intranets. Instead, you'll find "Intranet Angle" sidebars and icons throughout the book that describe how a given topic relates to intranet development. After all, the only major difference between intranet web sites and Internet Web sites is the wire on which they travel.

***HTML & Web Publishing SECRETS* contains server details.** So many Web publishing books tell you about HTML, show how to optimize graphics, and maybe even introduce you to forms and Common Gateway Interface (CGI) concepts. But at some point, the vast majority of them leave you hanging by not covering the actual server software that dishes out your Web pages. To me, this is like a cookbook that tells you what ingredients you need and shows how to mix them, but doesn't tell you how long to cook the dish and at what temperature.

Because servers are such an important part of the Web equation, this book contains an entire section about them. And you'll get your advice from battle-scarred veterans: Adam Block and Dan Shafer, two gentleman who are in the trenches of high-end, high-volume Web serving. Adam helps run the servers at PC World Online, while Dan runs the Mac OS-based servers at Salon Magazine, 1996's Cool Site of the Year.

***HTML & Web Publishing SECRETS* is authoritative.** Web development is a broad field that encompasses everything from design to writing to programming. I can't begin to claim to be a master of all these trades, so I sought out contributions from people who are. Several of this book's chapters contain contributions by the people behind some of the best sites on the Web: PC World Online, Macworld Online, Salon Magazine, and Webreference.com.

***HTML & Web Publishing SECRETS* covers both the Windows and Mac OS platforms.** The Macintosh is a major force in Web publishing. Many Web developers, myself included, have migrated to the Web from the worlds of publishing and multimedia development — two Mac strongholds.

But the Windows platform has something of an installed base, too. That's one of the reasons this book covers Web development issues from both platforms' perspectives. The larger reason is that Web developers must consider multiple platforms when creating their sites: your site's visitors might be using Macs, Windows machines, UNIX iron, or maybe even newfangled Web adapters connected to TV sets.

In other words, the Web world is no place for platform bigotry. If you're a Mac loyalist who has a "Pentium Happens" bumper sticker, or a Windows fiend who dismisses the Mac as a non-player, you'll just have to skip over the sections that cover whichever platform you hate. But if you're smart, you'll read everything, because the Web is the ultimate platform-independent medium, and because the best weapon against bigotry is knowledge.

So you Mac zealots: read the stuff about Windows; there are some mighty fine products Over There. And you Windows fiends, read the sections about Mac OS products; the Mac commands a disproportionately large segment of the Web development and Web surfing worlds, and you might find that the tool you've been searching for runs a computer that smiles when you switch it on.

Who Should Read This Book

HTML & Web Publishing SECRETS is for anyone who is involved or wants to be involved with any aspect of Web site development, from conceptualizing the site's content and structure to creating its pages and graphics to implementing multimedia elements to setting up and maintaining the server.

You might be a professional Web site developer or a publisher or multimedia producer who's making the transition to the Web. You might be a corporate developer who's been assigned to set up an intranet site. Or you might be a Web surfer who wants to set up your own home page to showcase your kid's birthday photos.

Whoever you are, this book assumes you know Web basics: you know what hypertext links are, you know what a browser is. (That's right — it's a machine for making 24-year-old millionaires.) You might even be operating a Web site now, although that certainly isn't a prerequisite.

A Closer Look Inside

There are four parts to *HTML & Web Publishing SECRETS.*

Part I: Webmaster Secrets, begins by addressing the nuts and bolts behind site development: how to determine what to publish, how to write effective hypertext, how to create and optimize Web pages and graphics. The part wraps up with an advanced look at the latest HTML developments and ways to add immediacy to your site — from setting up a Web cam to uploading digital camera images from remote locations.

Part II: Advanced Interactivity Secrets, shows you how to make your Web site more interactive by enabling visitors to search for content, post messages for each other, conduct real-time chats, and access databases. As the Web evolves, Web surfers are becoming a more-demanding lot — they want more than hypertext links. Adding the kind of interactivity I've just described will draw visitors to your site and entice them to keep coming back.

Part III: Web Multimedia Secrets, looks at techniques and technologies for adding audio, video, animation, and virtual reality to your site. This section examines and compares today's leading Web multimedia technologies and shows you how to use them — and how to use them to add genuine value, not just novelty, to your site.

Part IV: Web Server Secrets, assesses several of the leading servers that are available for the Windows 95, Windows NT, and Mac OS platforms. You'll also find tips on how to optimize a server's performance, how to keep it running, and what to do when it crashes during the middle of the night. And because not everyone can justify or afford a dedicated Web server, this section also shows how to set up a site with an Internet service provider — and how to find a provider who you can count on.

Finally, two appendixes provide quick reference to HTML and describe the contents of the *HTML & Web Publishing SECRETS* CD-ROM that accompanies this book.

Conventions Used in This Book

This book contains several types of sidebars, each of which presents a certain kind of information. These sidebars are labeled with icons, which also appear in the page margins.

If a particular topic contains relevant software on the *HTML & Web Publishing SECRETS* CD-ROM, this icon will tell you so.

The Secrets boxes and icons highlight tips and techniques relating to the topic at hand.

The Backgrounder boxes provide the big picture of how a given technology works or describe a technical concept in more detail.

The Intranet Angle icon highlights tips and secrets specific to intranet site development — they put an intranet spin on whatever topic is being discussed in the surrounding pages.

Read the Book, Visit the Site

This book covers a lot, but it doesn't cover tomorrow. The Web is evolving at a frantic pace, and there's only one medium that can keep up: the Web.

Which is why this book has its own Web site. You'll find it at `http://websecrets.heidsite.com/`. As a reader of this book, you're invited to join a members-only area containing news and updates, links to relevant information sources, additional examples, a conferencing and chat area, downloadable software, and much more. Visit the address above to learn more.

After you've signed up, stop into the conference area and say hello. I invite your questions as well as your comments on this book and suggestions for how to improve it.

Thanks for reading *HTML & Web Publishing SECRETS.*

Jim Heid
Albion, California
(see http://www.heidsite.com/weathercam.html)

Acknowledgments

This book was supposed to take about four months to write. It took nearly a year. It's for this reason that my acknowledgments begin with the folks at IDG Books Worldwide, who showed more patience than Job in putting up with this book's, um, extended gestation period.

Topping that list is Amy Thomas, who as this book's development editor, shepherded chapters through the long and winding publishing process, gently prodding me and my coauthors toward the finish line, listening to my answering machine far more than she wanted to, and always maintaining a even-keeled, pleasant and professional demeanor. As I write this, Amy and I have been working together for almost a year — and have yet to meet. Such is life in cyberspace. We will meet one of these days, Amy, and when we do, the drinks are on me. Thank you.

I'm also indebted to acquisitions editor Nancy Dunn. Nancy helped develop this book's initial table of contents, she helped line up our stunning stable of coauthors, and she handled innumerable chores relating to software licensing. I *have* had the pleasure of meeting Nancy — she was an editor at *Macworld* magazine during my formative years as a computer magazine columnist, and was instrumental in getting my first column off the ground. I look forward to the next time our paths cross.

My thanks also go to all the production artists at IDG Books Worldwide who toiled over a hot T-square (okay, a publishing program) to turn a manuscript into the book you're holding now. I doff my printer's visor to Katy German, Tom Debolski, Mark Schumann, and Elsie Yim. And without the skills of IDG Books Worldwide's marketing and publicity staff, there's a good chance you wouldn't know that this book even existed.

While I'm on the subject, this book *wouldn't* have existed without the contributions of several coauthors: Adam Block, Roxanne Gentile, Andy King, Karen Liberatore, and Dan Shafer. Each of these folks is an expert in his or her field; the list of sites they work on reads like a "Who's Who" — PC World Online, Macworld Online, Webreference.com, and Salon Magazine (1996's Cool Site of the Year). Each of these gurus has been generous in sharing his or her expertise with the rest of us. I'm thrilled to have had the opportunity to work with each of them; I've learned from them, and I know you will, too.

When you write a book about Web publishing, it helps to have good connections. I have a great connection: a 24-hour Centrex ISDN line. Measured against all the T1 and T3 lines of the world, that may not seem like a very big deal. But my particular line winds its way across and beneath a couple of hundred acres of wind-swept coastal grassland, and then threads through nine miles of rugged ridges and redwoods. And then it enters a small building tucked behind a high school: the home of Mendocino Community Network (`http://www.mcn.org/`), a not-for-profit service provider that brings the information superhighway to a region that is roughly 60 miles away from the nearest concrete superhighway.

MCN makes it possible for me to do what I do where I do it, and I'm eternally grateful to everyone associated with it, particularly the incredibly dedicated Rennie Innes, Dave Martin, Barbara Chase, and Mark Morton. And while I'm at it, Carl, Terry, and all the other local heroes at Pacific Bell have my thanks for successfully bringing ISDN to my windy bluff and for keeping the line humming.

I also want to thank my colleagues at *Macworld* magazine for permitting me to adapt portions of my *Macworld* articles for use in this book. And a special thank you to Kate Ulrich, my column editor, for not only being such a pro and a pleasure to work with, but for putting up with too many, shall we say, deadline adjustments as this book came together.

And finally, here at Heidsite, my undying love and gratitude go to my wife and best friend, Maryellen Kelly. You give me purpose, inspiration, and delight, and even when you're complaining about my Internet expenses, I can't imagine life without you. Or without Trixie, the Heidsite mascot (`http://www.heidsite.com/trixie.html`), my safety valve, my brown clown — who still knows when it's time for a squeak-squeak break.

Contents at a Glance

Table of Contents

Part I

Webmaster Secrets

Chapter 1

Site Strategies

In This Chapter

- Deciding what to publish: taking advantage of the Web's strengths
- Are you prepared to publish? It's more work than you may think
- The intranet angle: web-weaving at work
- Deciding between your own server or a service provider: expense and hard work versus less control

To create a good Web site, you have to open your eyes — to the possibilities of Web publishing, to the effort required to set up and maintain a site, and to the thorny issues behind serving a site.

This chapter's job is to pry those eyelids open and cast some bright light on the realities of Web publishing. If you haven't set up a site yet, this chapter will give you a few things to think about as you stare at the ceiling at night. If you're already creating Web sites, you still may want to browse this chapter and compare its advice to your own experiences.

Why Publish on the World Wide Web?

One of the things you often hear about publishing on the World Wide Web is that it enables you to reach a huge audience relatively cheaply. The Web audience numbers in the millions. Generally, you can put more information in front of this audience for less money than you would spend in the print or broadcast media.

How many people surf the Web, anyway?

The number of people surfing the Web depends on who you ask. In an attempt to quantify the Web-surfing population, demographers, advertisers, and researchers have conducted numerous surveys.

In 1995, CommerceNet (`http://www.commerce.net`), a consortium of 130 companies interested in Internet commerce, commissioned Nielson Media Research to size up the Web-surfing audience. After conducting a telephone survey, Nielson initially reported that the United States had 22 million adult Internet users.

Several professors soon disputed these numbers, and after analyzing Nielson's own data, estimated the audience to be 16.4 million — 5.6 million fewer Internet users than Nielson's original census.

Nielson fired up the calculators again and came up with a revised number: 19.4 million Internet users, 14.6 million Web users, and 1.9 million people who had made a purchase online.

Do these variances matter? To statisticians, maybe. To people who are trying to sell advertising on the Web and need to provide specific numbers to their prospects, definitely. What matters is the Web audience is big and getting bigger. In an article on the Nielson debate in the *New York Times,* Xerox's Mark Resch summed it up: "We're in a hurricane, and they are arguing about whether the wind is blowing 150 miles an hour or 130 miles an hour."

In March of 1997, the storm winds kicked up again when CommerceNet released its latest survey results. Web use had more than doubled from the previous survey, and 23 percent of all persons in United States and Canada over 16 years of age had used the Internet within the previous month. The report also found a larger percentage of women on the Internet — 42 percent compared to 34 percent in the 1995 survey.

The 1997 survey also indicated that the Internet is on its way toward being a mainstream medium. The 1995 survey classified 50 percent of Internet users as "professionals" or "managers" (and as a Dilbert reader, I find it interesting that the survey drew a distinction between being a professional and being a manager). In the 1997 survey, that figure dropped to 39 percent, indicating that more ordinary folks — or unprofessional managers — are tapping into the Internet.

And perhaps best of all for people who see dollar signs in their URLs, the 1997 survey showed that a dramatically larger number of people are using the Web to make purchases or to make purchase decisions. Nearly three-quarters — 73 percent — of all Web users in the survey had used the Web to search for information about a specific product or service. In the 1995 survey, only 55 percent of Web users reported using the Web for shopping.

But the number of Web surfers who actually purchase products online is still relatively small. In the survey, only 15 percent reported actually purchasing a product online. That's 5.6 million people, but it's clear that far more people are using the Web to learn about products than to buy them — and that brings new meaning to the term window shopping.

Where are they surfing?

Table 1-1 shows how one yardstick, the number of Web sites listed on Yahoo! and other indices, measured the ten most wired countries, U.S. states, and U.S. cities as of May 1996. More current statistics aren't available, but the bottom line is clear (and, when you think about it, pretty darn obvious): the most wired countries and communities are those known for having technology and business centers.

Table 1-1 The ten most wired list

Ten Most Wired Countries	*Ten Most Wired U.S. States*	*Ten Most Wired U.S. Cities*
United States	California	New York City
Canada	Texas	Seattle
United Kingdom	Florida	Atlanta
Australia	New York	Chicago
Germany	Massachusetts	San Francisco
Italy	Pennsylvania	Los Angeles
Japan	Washington	Houston
Netherlands	Illinois	Boston
France	Ohio	Washington
Ireland	Virginia	Austin

Source: Pax Communications. Based on number of Web sites listed in Yahoo! and other indices, as of May 1996.

Other ways to measure the Web's growth

Another way to assess the size of the Internet and World Wide Web is to look at how the numbers of Web servers and registered domain names have climbed.

- The number of commercial domain names (ones whose names end in .com) is increasing by several hundred percent a year, according to InterNIC Registration Services (`http://www.internic.net/`).
- WebCrawler, the search service operated by Global Network Navigator, reported it had counted 145,166 servers in April 1996 — and that's servers, a vast number of which are dishing out multiple sites. In WebCrawler's words, "These numbers reflect only servers with actual working IP addresses, and do not account for the larger number of logically distinct sites that often coexist on a single host." Figure 1-1 illustrates how the number of servers indexed by WebCrawler has increased.

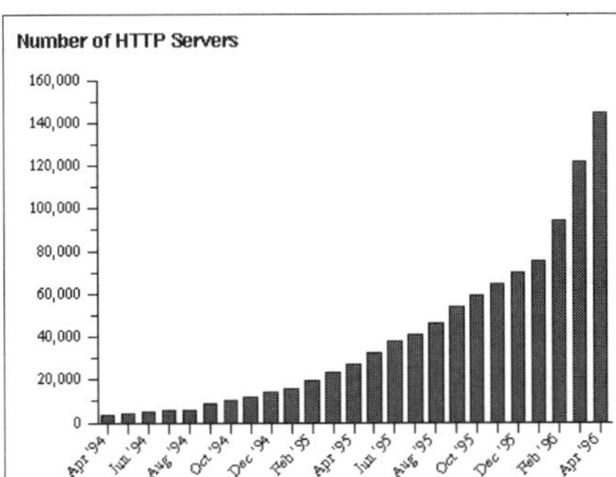

Figure 1-1: Is the Web a growing communications medium? You bet. Source: WebCrawler (http://www.webcrawler.com/).

Finding Web Statistics on the Web

Here are a few places to find current Web statistics and demographics. You can find links to these and more demographic and statistics sites on my Web site at `http://websecrets.heidsite.com/`.

- `http://www.cc.gatech.edu/gvu/user_surveys/` — The Graphics, Visualization, and Usability Center of the Georgia Institute of Technology's College of Computing conducts surveys at regular intervals and posts the results and summaries here.
- `http://webcrawler.com/WebCrawler/Facts/Size.html` — This page contains WebCrawler's latest statistics, including the latest version of the graph in Figure 1-1.
- `http://www.nw.com/` — Network Wizards's Mark Lottor has written software that he uses to estimate the size of the Internet. His regularly updated results appear here.
- `http://www.yahoo.com/Computers_and_Internet/Internet/World_Wide_Web/Statistics_and_Demographics/` — This Yahoo! page contains links to sites containing Web statistics and demographic information.

Money isn't everything

Low cost isn't the best reason to publish on the Web, and for a simple reason: the Web isn't always a cheaper medium than print or broadcast. In fact, the opposite can be true (see the Backgrounder sidebar "Web Publishing: Redefining 'Black Hole'?"). It takes a lot of work and equipment to produce, maintain, and serve a large Web site, and a great many companies — even ones whose sites are hot enough to support advertising — are sowing more cash than they're reaping.

The best reason to publish on the Web is to take advantage of the unique capabilities of this medium.

The Web can be timely

Only the broadcast media can deliver information as quickly as the online world. Many print publishers are taking advantage of this to supplement their coverage with updates that are posted daily or even several times a day.

Notice I said the Web *can be* timely — whether it actually is depends on how much work you devote to updating a site. A site doesn't have to be updated hourly to be a good Web site, but you should update it frequently enough to encourage repeat visits.

The Web allows for easy revision

You can't beat the online world when it comes to publishing information that requires frequent updating: current news, price lists, sports statistics, the number of times Liz Taylor has tied the knot. The Web is an ideal publishing medium for fast-changing information.

Web Publishing: Redefining "Black Hole"?

Is it cheaper to publish on the Web than in other media? Ask Don Logan. Logan is the president and chief executive officer of Time Inc., whose gargantuan Pathfinder site (`http://www.pathfinder.com`) is the online presence for many Time-Warner magazines, including *Time, Life, Money, People,* and *Sports Illustrated,* as well as a promotional outlet for Time-Warner's book-publishing and movie-making ventures.

In April 1996, Time-Warner announced that it would be launching a subscription-based Pathfinder news site, saying that advertising revenue alone wasn't enough to support the high startup costs of operating Pathfinder. Several months prior to the announcement, Time's Don Logan described Pathfinder as "giving new definition to the term 'black hole.'" According to an article in the *New York Times,* he later said he regretted having made the remark.

Time Inc.'s announcement follows similar moves by many large-scale Web publishing ventures. The *Wall Street Journal* and the *San Jose Mercury News* charge subscription fees for their sites; more will follow. It isn't surprising: the amount of advertising on Web sites is growing, but it's a rare site that earns a profit from ad revenues alone. It's a rare site that earns a profit, period.

So why are so many companies pouring time and money into the Web? No, it's not just because their competitors are. It's because the Web is the first new communications medium to come along since television, and it's an exciting one. It's because the demographics of Web surfers are appealing to anyone with products to sell. And it's because technology is gradually coming together that promises to ease making money serving a Web site. Experience now will pay off later — hopefully.

The Web is interactive

A good Web site uses hypertext and hot spots to enable visitors to branch off to areas that entice them. At its worst, this is the Web's answer to channel surfing: the mouse potato. But at its best, hypertext gives visitors the freedom to chart their own courses, to explore topics in greater levels of detail, and to jump to related topics.

On the Web, *interactivity* can have additional meanings. It may mean enabling visitors to search a large database — your product catalog or that list of Liz's hubbies. It may mean enabling visitors to interact with you through a feedback page or a guestbook. And it may mean enabling visitors to interact with each other — through message boards or real-time chats.

The Web crosses platform borders

The same Web site can reach any computer with a browser and a connection: Windows, Mac OS, UNIX, Oracle Network Computer, Apple Newton, WebTV — you name it. (Whether the site will look good on all of these platforms isn't guaranteed, however — more on that later.) The Web doesn't destroy the platform barrier, but it lowers it more than any other digital publishing medium to date.

The Web allows for dynamic data

By *dynamic data*, I mean audio, video, and animation. This is the aspect of the Web that I find most exciting. No other publishing medium on the planet can combine the depth and scope of print, the interactivity of CD-ROMs, and the immediacy, timeliness, and audio-visual potential of broadcasting.

And that is the best reason to publish on the Web.

What Are You Going to Publish?

The answer to this question should be influenced by each of the Web advantages I've just discussed. Several questions should always be on your mind as you plan, develop, and maintain sites.

- **How can I take advantage of the Web's potential for timeliness and immediacy?** It might be by updating a portion of your site at regular intervals — a daily or weekly news area (as shown in Figure 1-2). Or it might be by occasionally posting information from a remote location — for example, a report from a tradeshow or conference or a digital postcard from a camping trip. Think about ways to make your site a place people will want to visit more than once.

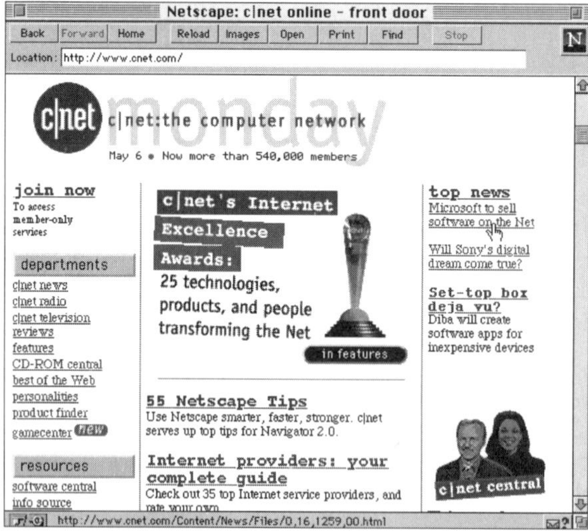

Figure 1-2: The popular c|net Web site (http://www.cnet.com/) offers daily news in both text and audio formats, taking advantage of both the Web's potential for immediacy and its support for dynamic media.

- **How can I take advantage of hypertext and linking?** The answer may be to provide links to other Web sites that provide additional information (as shown in Figure 1-3). To build on the examples I used previously, you might add links to sites that cover the city where the convention is being held. You might create a map of the tradeshow floor and have hot spots that link to your company's booth. You might create a map of the state park where the family set up camp, with hot spots that link to information on the lake, the mountain trail, the place where the dog got skunked. Think about how the information on your site relates to other information both on your site and elsewhere, and then create links that weave this information together.

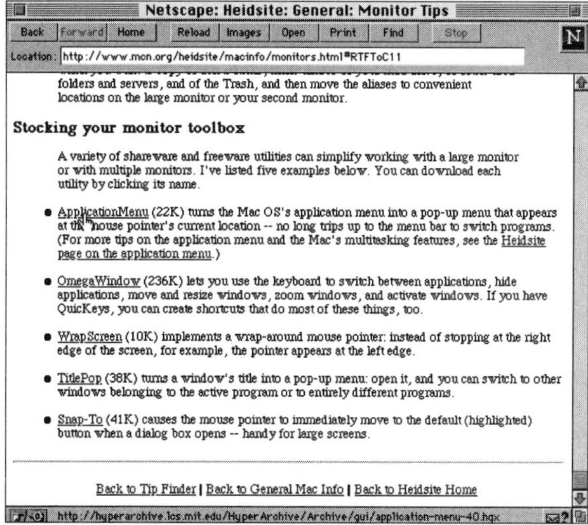

Figure 1-3: A simple example of how links can enhance a Web page. This page on my site contains an excerpt from my *Macworld New Complete Mac Handbook* (IDG Books Worldwide, 1995), describing some interesting shareware utilities. Rather than just posting the text as it appeared in the book, I added links to a shareware library, enabling visitors to actually download the programs described.

- **How can I apply the other aspects of Web interactivity?** One answer might be a form that enables visitors to ask questions or provide feedback. Message boards, guestbooks, and real-time chats (such as those shown in Figure 1-4) provide higher levels of interaction. An intranet Web might have message boards that enable employees to make suggestions, ask questions, and trade ideas. Think of ways to turn the site into a meeting place for people with similar interests.

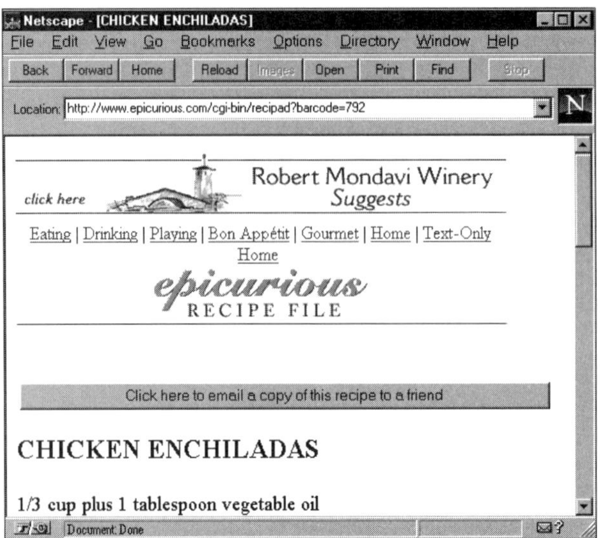

Figure 1-4: Epicurious (http://www.epicurious.com/) is the online presence for *Gourmet* and *Bon Appetit* magazines. This site contains numerous areas for visitor interaction, including a daily poll, message boards for swapping recipes and cooking tips, and a feature that lets you e-mail a copy of a recipe to a friend.

- **How can I exploit the Web's multimedia potential?** At the simplest level, exploiting the Web's multimedia potential means using graphics as well as text. At a more sophisticated (and more complicated) level, it means employing audio, video, and animation: interviews with customers or employees or tradeshow attendees who visited your company's booth; video clips that illustrate how a product works; a virtual reality tour of your factory, of the tradeshow floor, or of the family's campsite; or animations showing how a new factory process works or how a game-winning basketball play took place (as shown in the Figure 1-5 example). Think beyond words and still pictures and consider how dynamic media might make your site more informative, educational, enriching, or fun.

The best Web sites exploit each of these advantages; the worst ones are simply electronic brochures or adapted versions of existing product propaganda.

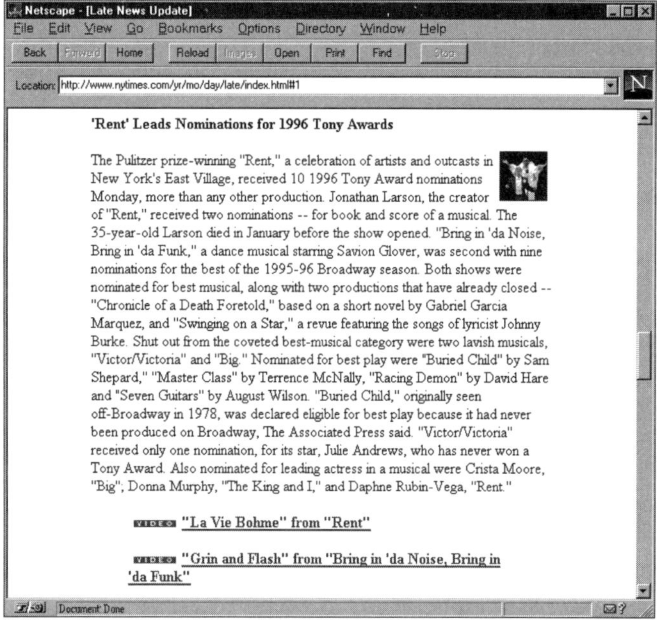

Netscape - [Late News Update]

File Edit View Go Bookmarks Options Directory Window Help

Back Forward Home Reload Images Open Print Find Stop

Location: http://www.nytimes.com/yr/mo/day/late/index.html#1

'Rent' Leads Nominations for 1996 Tony Awards

The Pulitzer prize-winning "Rent," a celebration of artists and outcasts in New York's East Village, received 10 1996 Tony Award nominations Monday, more than any other production. Jonathan Larson, the creator of "Rent," received two nominations -- for book and score of a musical. The 35-year-old Larson died in January before the show opened. "Bring in 'da Noise, Bring in 'da Funk," a dance musical starring Savion Glover, was second with nine nominations for the best of the 1995-96 Broadway season. Both shows were nominated for best musical, along with two productions that have already closed -- "Chronicle of a Death Foretold," based on a short novel by Gabriel Garcia Marquez, and "Swinging on a Star," a revue featuring the songs of lyricist Johnny Burke. Shut out from the coveted best-musical category were two lavish musicals, "Victor/Victoria" and "Big." Nominated for best play were "Buried Child" by Sam Shepard," "Master Class" by Terrence McNally, "Racing Demon" by David Hare and "Seven Guitars" by August Wilson. "Buried Child," originally seen off-Broadway in 1978, was declared eligible for best play because it had never been produced on Broadway, The Associated Press said. "Victor/Victoria" received only one nomination, for its star, Julie Andrews, who has never won a Tony Award. Also nominated for leading actress in a musical were Crista Moore, "Big"; Donna Murphy, "The King and I," and Daphne Rubin-Vega, "Rent."

VIDEO "La Vie Bohme" from "Rent"

VIDEO "Grin and Flash" from "Bring in 'da Noise, Bring in 'da Funk"

Document: Done

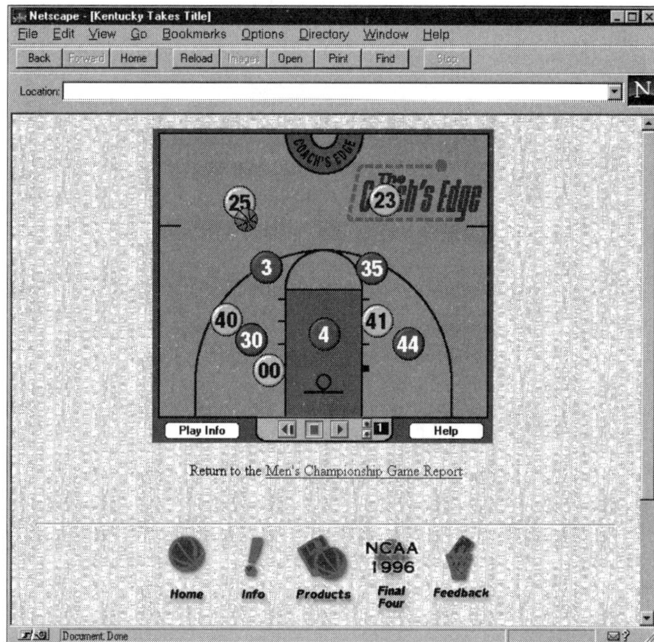

Figure 1-5: The *New York Times* Web site (http://www.nytimes.com/) often enhances stories with audio and video clips (top). The Coach's Edge site (http://www.coachesedge.com/) uses animations to illustrate basketball plays. Through animation, you can see the ball move from player to player, the players jockey for position on the court, and the ball entering the hoop (bottom).

What to Put on an Intranet Web Site

Here are just some of the things you may find — or may put on — an intranet Web site. Later chapters contain additional details on many of these applications.

- *Directories:* Personnel, branch offices, local pizza joints. In searchable form, they can put often used (and often revised) information at employees' fingertips.
- *Internal publications:* Newsletters, employee handbooks, benefits guides, policy papers. With hypertext links, online publications can be easier to navigate than paper documents. And when the inevitable revisions are required, you won't have to toss any outdated copies.
- *Training programs:* Courseware for employee education, complete with audio and video clips and animations.
- *Forms:* Health insurance claim forms, expense forms, requisition forms. Put them in Adobe Acrobat Portable Document Format, and employees can print a form whenever they need one. No need to stockpile paper versions or to throw out reams of outdated forms.
- *Schedules:* Project schedules, work-shift schedules, company softball team practice schedules, carpool schedules.
- Maps: Directions to branch offices, supply houses, customer sites.
- *Advertisements:* Not cola commercials, but employee-to-employee classified ads — roommate wanted, used car wanted, carpool companion wanted, for example.
- *Bulletin board stuff:* Letters of praise from happy customers, letters of rage from unhappy ones, job postings, jokes, lost-and-found notices.
- *Real-time video:* Frequently updated displays of the company day-care center or the factory floor, courtesy of a Web cam (described in Chapter 8).
- *Client-server applications:* Although intranet sites are most often used to publish information, some are used as client-server applications that enable employees to fill out expense reports or enter and retrieve database information. Such Web applications can be easier to develop than stand-alone applications, and they have the advantage of the familiar Web interface.

Are You Prepared to Publish?

Not all Web publishers would agree with Time Inc. president and CEO Don Logan's use of the phrase "black hole" to describe a Web publishing venture. But many will admit that a large Web site can suck time, money, and personnel into its gravitational pull. Even a small site like mine tugs at time and energy.

I'm not trying to discourage you — far from it. But you should know what you're getting into.

Content development

One of the biggest and costliest jobs can be developing your site's content: the stuff you're going to publish. A great many Web sites — according to some critics, too many of them — are adapting existing content for their sites. (The industry even has an ugly jargon term for it: *repurposing.)* As later chapters describe, a variety of programs enable you to convert existing documents into HTML form.

These conversion programs aren't repurposing panaceas. You can still expect to spend time tweaking the resulting files to fix formatting problems. And if you're asking yourself those all-important questions I just outlined, you will spend at least as much time enhancing the converted documents with hypertext links and multimedia elements.

Content maintenance

You've put in the long hours, pumped the caffeine, and worked your wrists sore, but you've done it — your site is up. Guess what? Your job has just started. If you're serious about taking advantage of the Web's potential for timeliness and immediacy, you will have to update and revise the site at regular intervals. If you don't, you'll earn the Web world's term of derision for an outdated site: a *cobweb site.*

Content maintenance means not only posting new material to encourage repeat visits and keep up with the times but also updating existing material. You've probably wandered into part of a site and found outdated information that contradicts newer information elsewhere on the same site. It's easy to fall into this trap and forget that a brand-new page may contradict an older one.

If your site contains links to other sites, content maintenance takes on a third dimension: making sure those links still work. Web sites and Web pages come and go faster than fads. If your site has a link to a site or a page that's no longer available, visitors will see a frustrating error message when they click on the link.

Testing the many links that may be present on a large site is time-consuming drudge work. Fortunately, many programs are available that will do the work for you. I examine the best of them in Chapter 4.

Visitor services

I mentioned earlier that a good Web site enables visitors to interact with each other and with you. At the risk of stating the obvious, interaction is a two-way street: if you encourage visitors to send you e-mail or ask questions on a message board or in a guestbook, you had better be prepared to spend time reading and answering them.

As I've found with Heidsite, this can be another major time consumer. I encourage questions and feedback, but answers are often delayed by deadlines and, well, paying jobs. The volume of e-mail and questions has gotten so large that my site now contains a disclaimer stating that replies may not always be prompt. If you're going to be late, at least tell people you're going to be late.

Server setup

The expenses I've discussed up to now have been mostly time and labor oriented. Here's one that isn't: the Web server itself, the computer that will dish out your pages and content to the Web surfers of the world or to your intranet's users. Besides the computer, you'll need Web server software as well as networking and communications hardware that will link your server to your intranet or the Internet.

For an Internet Web site, there's another alternative: paying an Internet service provider (ISP) to host your site using its computers. There's a lot to be said for this approach, but it has its drawbacks, too. In fact, there's so much to say about site serving that it deserves a closer look. Chapter 15 explores the "serve or be served" issue in detail; here's an overview to set the stage.

Site-Serving Strategies

The serve-it-yourself versus ISP dilemma often boils down to a choice between control, convenience, and cost. When you serve a site yourself, you have much more control over what you can put on the site (I'll describe why shortly). When you have an ISP host a site, you have less control but also less initial expense and, assuming you have a reliable service provider, fewer headaches.

Keep in mind this entire discussion applies primarily to Internet World Wide Web sites, not to intranet webs. If you're setting up the latter, you'll always be serving the site yourself, or maybe with the help of a corporate information services department.

Serving it yourself: the pros

The biggest arguments for operating your own server are that you have the freedom to fine-tune its performance and that you have the flexibility to add special features to your site.

Control, control, control

As we'll see in later chapters, adding many features to a Web site — for example, real-time audio, certain types of animations, and interactive forms — requires installing special software and tweaking the Web server software. ISPs will generally do this work for you (for a price, of course), but when you operate your own server, you can add or change these features more quickly and monitor them more closely.

Knowledge is power

Another advantage to serving the site yourself is you can have up-to-the-minute statistics on who's visiting your site. Every Web server software package keeps a digital diary, a connection log that details which pages were visited, how often, and by what kind of computer and browser program. Oftentimes, you can even track the visits of individual users from these logs.

All of this information can help you to fine-tune your site's content: Which pages are the most popular? Which ones are getting dusty? What percentage of your visitors are browsing with Netscape Navigator? What percentage are arriving through America Online or another commercial online service? Information like this is priceless, and an ISP may not be able to provide you with all of it. And even if it can, chances are you won't get it on a minute-by-minute basis.

Serving it yourself: the cons

The biggest drawbacks to operating your own server are that it adds yet another burden to your job and that it can be costly.

More work for you

When an ISP hosts your site, the ISP's technicians have to grapple with the nitty-gritty details of server setup and maintenance. They're the ones who have to sweat when a server's hard drive crashes, when the power goes out, or when the phone lines act up. When you host the site yourself, it's your sweat glands that are always on call.

As you'll see in Part IV, it isn't particularly difficult to configure and operate Web server software, but configuring the hardware and the network connections can quickly turn someone with Howard Stern's haircut into someone with Sinead O'Connor's.

More expense for you

Most ISPs charge a monthly fee for hosting a site — a large site can cost hundreds of dollars or more per month to host, but you can put a small site on the Web for about $30 a month. If you use a commercial online service to host a small site, you can spend even less.

If you want to operate your own server, however, get out your checkbook for:

- A computer to do the serving
- A fast, preferably continuous connection to the Internet
- A backup power supply to get you through brief outages
- Software for serving, for server maintenance, for adding special interactivity features, and perhaps for security

Later chapters will examine each of these money pits in more detail, but you don't have to skip to them now to realize you can spend a healthy dime serving up a site yourself.

ISP hosting: the pros

The best arguments for paying an ISP to host your site are based on convenience and, ideally, reliability.

Instant on-ramp

When an ISP hosts your site, all you have to do is upload your Web pages to its computers. The ISP deals with the Internet connection headaches and with the responsibilities of keeping the server up and running. And in a world of power outages, brown-outs and surges, and flaky Internet connections, these are big responsibilities.

Potentially faster performance

Unless you're well-heeled or you have access to a high-speed connection in a business or educational institution, an ISP is likely to have a faster connection to the Internet than you may be willing or able to spring for if you're operating your own server. Most ISPs have at least one high-speed T1 phone line, and many have multiple T1s or better. (You'll learn more about the site-hosting option in Chapter 15.)

Chances are that your ISP will also have faster server computers, too. Again, this may not be the case if you're setting up a major-league site with major-league money behind it. It may also not be the case if you live in a rural area and are using a small ISP. That's my situation: my ISP is a nonprofit business operated by the local school district, and its primary servers are a bank of Macintoshes — some of which are slower than the machines on my desk.

And this is just one of the reasons the previous subhead reads *"Potentially* Faster Performance." Another reason is the fact that your ISP is probably using the same computer that hosts your site to serve numerous other sites. In this case, each site's performance depends in part on how much action the other sites are getting. If the server is a fast, workstation-class machine and all the sites are seeing only moderate traffic, this won't be a problem. If the server isn't a cheetah and one of the sites is the Web's latest hot spot, your site's performance will suffer.

ISP hosting: the cons

I've already described two key cons: less control over content and performance, and fewer statistics. Here's another one.

Uncertain reliability

If you've spent any time on the Web, you probably know that ISPs aren't exactly the objects of universal adoration. Complaints about reliability, performance, and customer service abound. If you've had problems with an ISP from a Web *surfing* standpoint, you may have nightmares from a Web *serving* standpoint.

Now there are fine ISPs, both large and small. But the bottom line is that having a site hosted by an ISP doesn't guarantee rock-solid reliability — not by a long shot.

Combination platters: combining your own server with an ISP's

Here's an interesting twist on this entire dilemma that I haven't seen covered all that much. It's possible, and in fact pretty easy, to combine both serving approaches: that is, to have an ISP serve most of your site but to serve some portions of the site yourself.

Here are some examples of how I use this approach with Heidsite.

The Weathercam page

My site has a Weathercam, a video camera that provides a continuously updated view of the world outside my office window. Because of the hardware involved in doing this — in my case, a video camera is connected to a Macintosh containing video-digitizing hardware — the Weathercam page *has* to be served from a computer located in my office. It would be far more complicated to have a Weathercam page served by a remote ISP.

Most of my site is served by an ISP. However, the Weathercam link on my home page refers to a page located on my local server. When someone clicks on that link to peer through the Weathercam, my local server kicks in and dishes out the page. Visitors don't know or care that the Weathercam page is coming from a different server.

The conferencing area

Heidsite also contains a conferencing so that visitors can leave comments and ask questions. The conferencing area is handled by a special program called a *CGI,* short for *Common Gateway Interface*. (Later chapters discuss CGIs in detail.) Rather than asking my ISP to install a specialized CGI on its server, I serve the guestbook pages using my local server.

Summing up the combination-platter benefits

This combination-platter approach has several advantages.

- Most of my site is served by my ISP's fast server connected to a T1 phone line, giving visitors the fast, reliable response that's so important. The few portions of my site that I serve myself go out over an ISDN line, which isn't as fast as a T1, but is still quite adequate.
- By having my ISP serve most of my site, I avoid bogging down my ISDN line with traffic that would slow my own Web-surfing endeavors.
- If my own local server goes down for any reason — the power fails, the system crashes, or I need to temporarily commandeer the machine for a different project — the majority of my site remains available.

- I'm able to provide those features and media elements that require server tweaks or special software, while still enjoying the benefits of having an ISP host my site.

The Combination-Platter Approach for Misers

Here's a way to apply this combination-platter serving strategy if you don't have a 24-hour connection to the Internet. Say you have a dial-up modem connection or an ISDN line for which you pay per-minute connect charges during prime-time hours. Simply inform visitors that portions of your site (the portions you serve locally) are only available during certain hours, for example, "This site's RealAudio clips are available between the hours of 5 p.m. and 6 a.m. Pacific time."

This isn't the optimum way to serve a site, of course (ideally, all of your content is available all of the time). Visitors who can't tell time all that well may still click on a link that isn't available, earning themselves an annoying delay followed by a browser error message. But at least you can warn them and minimize this risk. And it's an economical alternative to a full-time connection.

Summary

- Publishing on the World Wide Web can enable you to reach a large audience economically, but a large-scale Web site requires a big investment in time, labor, equipment, and money.
- The best reasons to publish on the World Wide Web are to take advantage of the medium's unique capabilities: hypertext, audio, and video, and the way the Web combines the depth and scope of print with the immediacy and media-richness of the broadcast media.
- When developing and maintaining a site, always ask yourself how you can take advantage of the Web's strengths — don't just create on-screen versions of print material.
- The work involved in developing and operating a site includes content development, content maintenance, visitor services, and server maintenance.
- The choice between serving a site yourself and having a service provider host it often boils down to a decision between control and convenience. But you can combine both serving approaches and have the best of both worlds.

Chapter 2

Site Design Secrets

In This Chapter

- Structuring a site for efficient navigation: from the big picture to the window titles
- Dealing with browser compatibility issues, Part 1
- Work in progress: What's the right way to be "under construction"?
- The intranet angle: creating bookmarks for your intranet sites

Before the cameras roll in Hollywood, movies are planned on storyboards. Before the hammers pound at a construction site, plans are drawn. Before a jet's tires leave the runway, a flight plan is filed. Before the shopping cart hits the aisles, a list is made.

You can probably see what I'm getting at here.

Advance planning is essential for major endeavors, and it doesn't hurt to plan for minor ones either. This chapter's job is to stress the importance of planning in Web publishing: planning the overall structure of a site, planning how visitors will navigate its pages, and planning for updates and revisions.

In some ways, this is a chapter about user interface design. Web site development has something in common with software development: Both require a system of controls and an on-screen presentation that make it easy for users to figure out how to use what you've given them. Make it easy, and they'll enjoy themselves and visit often. Make it hard, and they'll bail out and never come back.

As I researched this book, I noticed that only a few Web publishing books discuss the issues behind site design and navigation, and these discussions tend to be buried in the back somewhere, long after the nitty-gritty chapters on HTML, graphics, and server setup. But the time to think about site design issues is at the beginning — before you write a single HTML tag or create a single image file.

The Big Picture: Site Structure

Whether you're talking libraries, department stores, or the Web, organization and structure are essential. Without them, it's difficult for visitors to find what they came for, and it's easy for them to get lost — and frustrated.

The tree chart structure

You've seen a company organizational chart, those tree-like diagrams that depict the pecking order from the Big Cheese on down. An organizational chart is a type of *tree chart*, and it does a great job of depicting a hierarchy. Just about any highly structured entity can be represented in this same format — including a Web site (as shown in Figure 2-1).

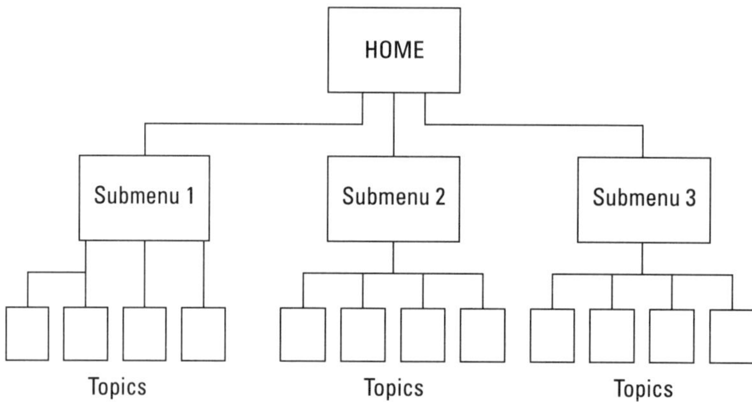

Figure 2-1: An organizational chart applied to a Web site

Because of the way visitors use a Web site — arriving at a home page and then branching off into topics and subtopics — drawing a tree chart of a site is a good way to plan its structure. For easier revision, use a program that provides features for drawing tree charts, such as Claris Impact, Adobe Persuasion, Microsoft PowerPoint, CorelFlow, or DeltaPoint's DeltaGraph. I've heard some designers plan sites by attaching sticky notes to their office walls.

Shaping your tree

Some trees' shapes are more pleasing than others. An important aspect of Web site design involves shaping the site's tree hierarchy so it's neither too shallow nor too deep.

Don't be shallow

In a shallow tree hierarchy, there isn't enough structure beneath the home page. Rather than leading to a list of several subtopics from which visitors can branch, the home page leads to dozens of individual pages. This lack of structure turns the home page into a huge collection of unrelated topics (see Figure 2-2).

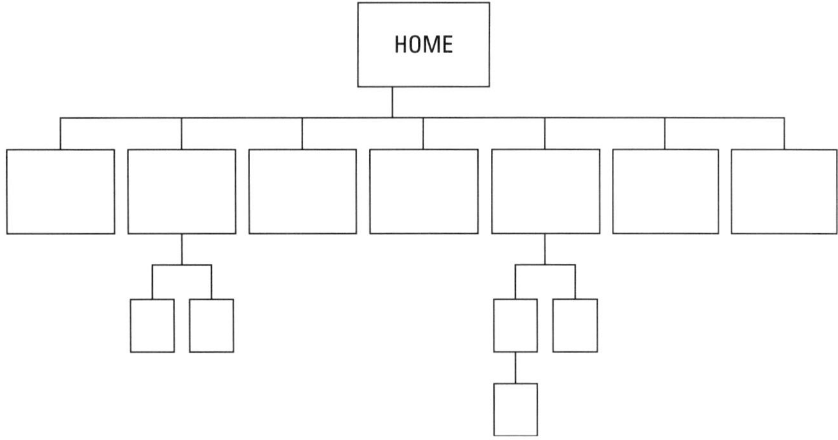

Figure 2-2: A shallow tree hierarchy lacks sufficient organization; the home page is a large list of unrelated topics.

In an overly shallow site structure, visitors have to do too much scrolling, clicking, and searching to find the information they're interested in.

Don't get deep

It's possible to have too much of a good thing — to take the tree structure too far, with each menu page leading to another menu page, which leads to yet another. Figure 2-3 shows this obsessive approach.

A second problem with an excessively deep menu hierarchy is that, in your zeal to pigeonhole and categorize, you often end up with individual pages containing only two or three options.

Finally, excessively deep hierarchies cause problems for Web *robots,* programs that traverse the World Wide Web automatically to perform tasks such as ensuring the accuracy of site links and indexing the contents of a site for a search service. Examples of Web robots include WebCrawler, Lycos, MOMSpider, and the World Wide Web Worm. (See Chapter 8 for more details on robots and the effects they can have on a Web site, and Chapter 10 for details on setting up a robot on your site.)

Two or three clicks: just right

In Figure 2-4, my example site is reorganized yet again, this time grouping the pages into logical categories that enable visitors to find information efficiently. Notice that no single page is more than three clicks away.

Try to avoid making visitors click more than two or three times to reach the page they want.

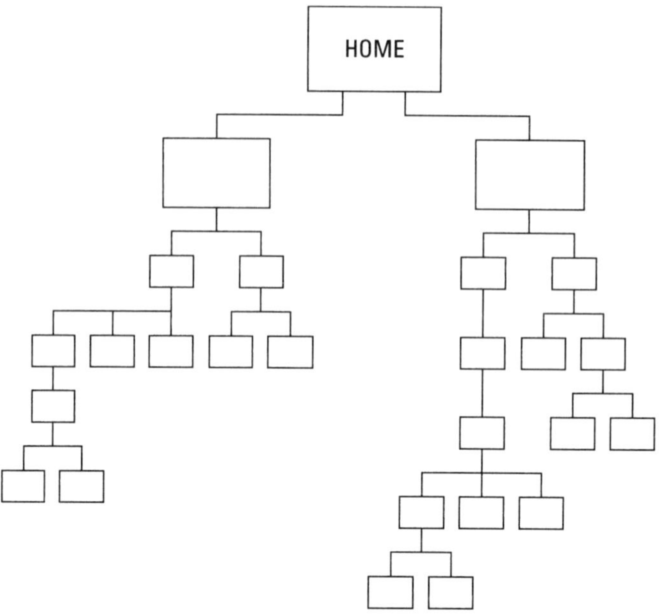

Figure 2-3: A deep tree hierarchy requires too many clicks to get to a particular page.

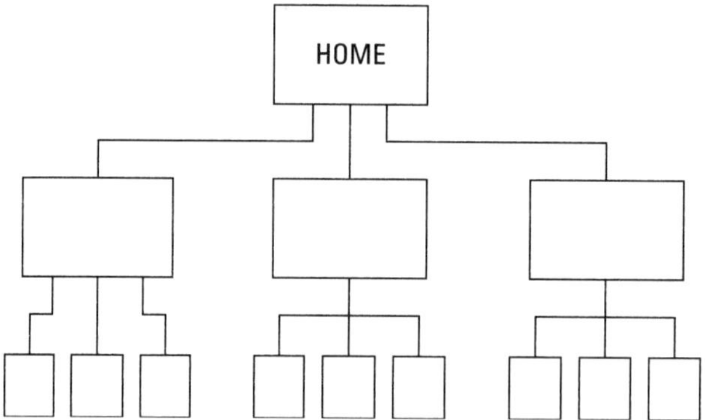

Figure 2-4: In general, two to three clicks should take visitors where they want to go.

The hypertext angle

If you're linking related pages on your site together — and you should be — your tree's branches aren't going to look like the ones in the previous figure. Instead, some pages will have tunnels leading to other pages, which may be in completely different areas of a site (as shown in Figure 2-5).

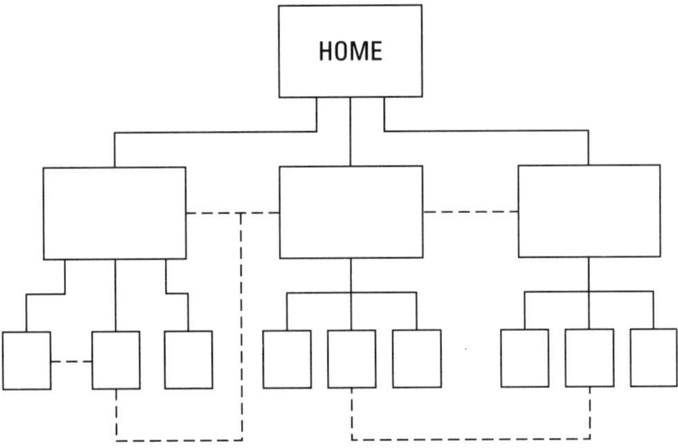

Figure 2-5: Hypertext links enable visitors to navigate based on content.

In a site about animals, for instance, the pages on cats and dogs may have sections called "Typical Adversaries in Warner Brothers Cartoons," with each section containing a link to the other animal's page.

This may seem to defeat the purpose of a tree-like structure, but it actually provides a secondary layer of structure and organization, one that kicks in as a visitor explores your site: Hypertext links enable visitors to navigate not by choosing menu options, but by following paths to related information.

SECRET

Use the tree structure to enable visitors to navigate quickly, and use hypertext links so they may explore paths of related information.

Outlining: another way to think about structure

Another way to think about and plan the structure of a site is to use the classic outline format, in which headings and indented subheadings show the relationships between topics and subtopics. Many high-end word processors have outlining features; you can use them to flesh out the structure of a site (see Figure 2-6).

Outlines work so well for mapping out a site's structure that some site design programs provide outline modes for working with pages. NetObjects' Fusion, discussed in Chapter 4, is one example; UserLand's Frontier, discussed in Chapter 16, is another.

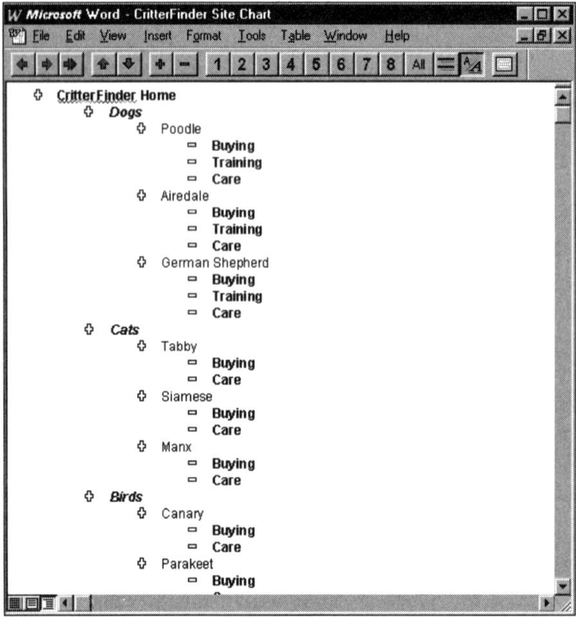

Figure 2-6: A site about pets as seen in Microsoft Word's outline view

Navigation Scheme Secrets

Once you've developed a structure for a site, it's time to develop the devices that will make that structure obvious and easy to use. This is an important point: Even a well-structured site won't be easy to navigate unless you give visitors consistent, easy-to-follow navigation devices.

Consider the interstate highway system, certainly a well-structured entity. But imagine if every exit sign was a different color. Or imagine if a highway's number changed when you crossed a state line. Fortunately, things aren't this way. You can fly into any city, hop into a rental car, and know how to navigate because the signposts are *consistent.*

Here's another example: a typical fast-food empire. Say what you will about the nutritional value of their chow, but you can't argue that fast-food chains aren't well-structured entities, with a specific range of offerings prepared in the same way whether you're in Manhattan or Moscow. Now look at the navigation system: Menus are always above and behind the counter, and the drive-through menu and window are always in similar locations. You can go into any chain's outlet and know exactly how to clog your arteries because the user interface is *consistent.*

There are several navigation devices you can employ for a Web site: banners across the top of each page, navigation buttons or labels on the top or bottom of each page, and the titles that appear in the Web browser's window. The following section describes each device and shows examples of sites that use it effectively.

Page banners

Page banners are the Web page equivalent to the running headers that appear on each page of a book or magazine — they provide reference points that remind visitors where they are. Figure 2-7 shows some text-based and graphical banners.

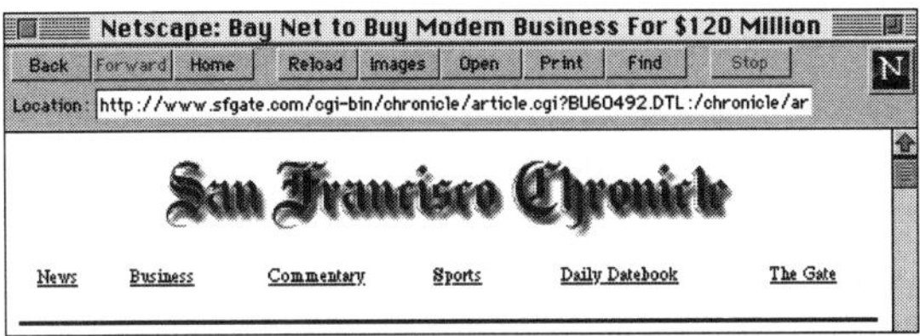

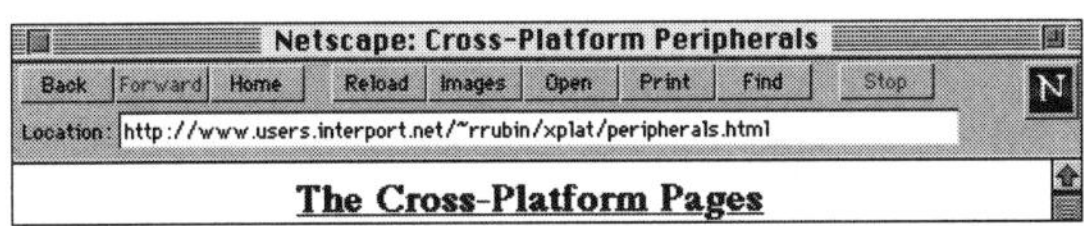

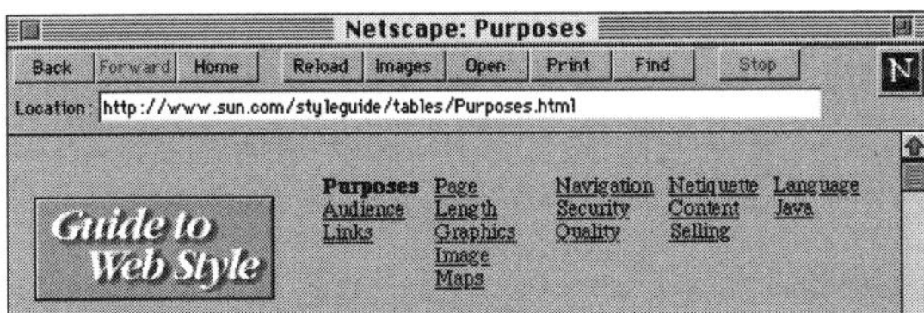

Figure 2-7: Web page banners can be flashy or simple, as shown in this sampling. From top to bottom: The *San Francisco Chronicle*, Yahoo!, Ross Scott Rubin's Cross-Platform Pages site, and Sun Microsystems's Guide to Web Style.

Another important objective for creating page banners is to associate each page with the site to which it belongs: There's no guarantee a Web surfer will arrive at a particular page by following your hierarchy. He or she could get there in one fell swoop by clicking a link in a different site.

SECRET

When creating a page, work on the assumption that it will be the first part of your site a visitor will see, and give the page a clear identity associating it with the site.

Glitzy, graphical banners

Figure 2-8 shows a particularly clever implementation of page banners. This example is from the Web site for Studio Archetype, formerly Clement Mok designs (`http://www.cmdesigns.com/cmd.htm`). This award-winning studio has done print and interactive design for many major companies, including Adobe Systems, Sony Entertainment, HarperCollins Publishers, and Twentieth Century Fox.

The Studio Archetype Web site's page banners are separate graphics that, when viewed together, not only show you where you are, but indicate the path you took to get there. Very smart.

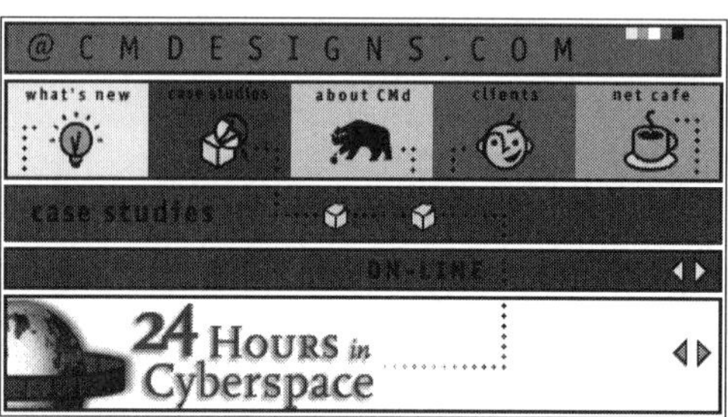

Figure 2-8: Studio Archetype's page banners in action

The topmost graphic in the figure represents the site's home page. The graphic below it contains a strip of icons that lets you navigate to each of the site's primary areas. When you choose an area, another graphic appears below the icon strip that identifies the area you've entered and, in some cases, enables you to choose additional options. Notice how the dotted lines within each graphic connect to form a pathway that shows you where you are and where you've come from.

Simple text banners

Figure 2-9 shows how tried-and-true text can be just as effective as glitzy graphics. This example is from Sun Microsystems's Guide to Web Style site (`http://www.sun.com/styleguide/`) — a wonderful site that should be on any Web developer's bookmark list.

As the figure shows, these banners work double duty, also serving as navigation devices. It's a smart, efficient use of screen space: One glance not only tells visitors where they are, but where they can go. And because it's all done with good, old-fashioned text, it's even fast on slow modem connections.

The banners' text, by the way, is formatted using HTML tables. Chapter 7 contains all the details, and the *HTML & Web Publishing SECRETS* CD-ROM contains some page templates you can use to create similar navigation banners.

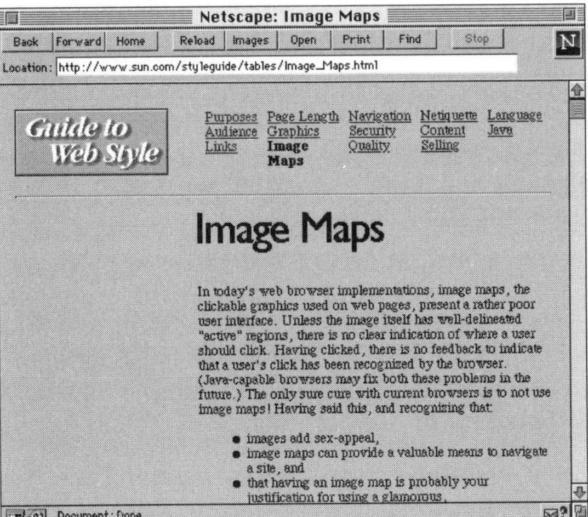

Figure 2-9: The text-based banners on Sun Microsystems's Guide to Web Style site. The underlined headings represent other sections of the site, while the bold heading tells visitors, "You are here."

Navigation bars

The Sun style guide banners make an ideal segue into the next navigation device on the tour: *navigation bars*. Sun's site notwithstanding, navigation bars are usually different from page banners. Banners are generally signposts that let visitors know where they are, while navigation bars are controls that let visitors move from section to section.

Text or graphics? Or both?

Graphical navigation bars are common. Many a site's pages contain little rows of icons for moving from section to section (see Figure 2-10).

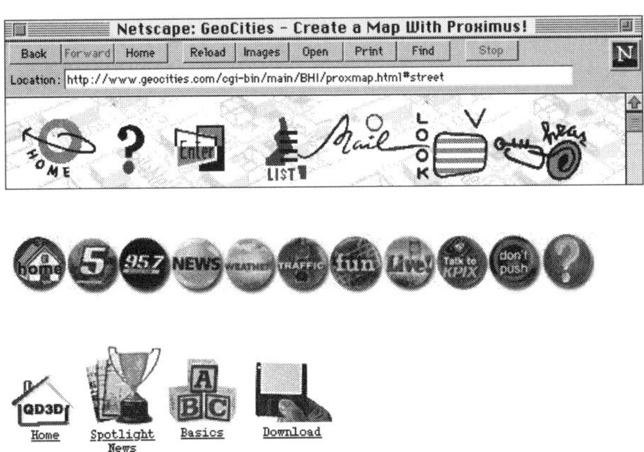

Figure 2-10: Icons everywhere! A sampling of some graphical navigation bars.

The advantage of icons is they aren't specific to any particular language. On the *World Wide* Web, that can be a real plus.

But there are serious drawbacks to icons, too.

- **Icon meanings aren't always clear.** In his or her zeal to squeeze an entire row of icons onto a page, a designer may create tiny pictures whose meanings are vague.
- **Icon images aren't consistent across Web sites.** Are visitors really going to spend enough time in your site to memorize the meanings of your navigation icons? Or are they going to arrive at your site through a different site, which might have its own iconic language? Forcing visitors to memorize your own private sign language means making them work harder to navigate your site — a bad idea.

These drawbacks are why I prefer text-based navigation bars. Now, by *text-based,* I don't necessarily mean HTML-generated text. A navigation bar can be comprised of "pictures of text" — that is, of graphics containing text created in a program such as Adobe Photoshop. Figure 2-11 shows the text-based navigation bars that Adobe uses on its Web site (`http://www.adobe.com/`).

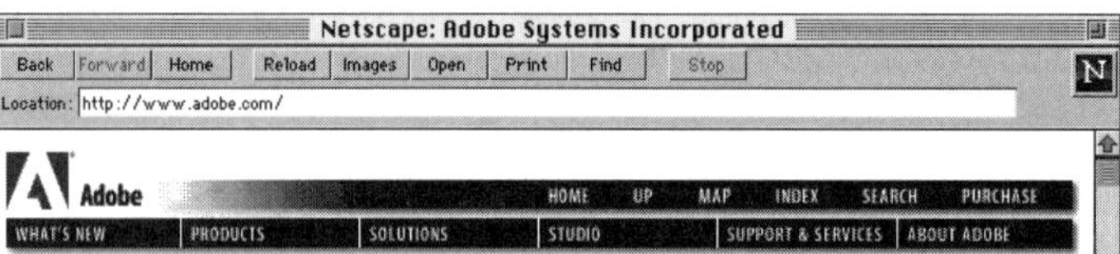

Figure 2-11: Adobe's navigation bars

Notice that Adobe's navigation bars perform the same dual-purpose role as the banners in Sun's Web style guide: letting you know not only where you can go, but where you are at the moment. In Adobe's case, the text button corresponding to your current location appears in a different color.

If you just *have* to have icons on a navigation bar, at least supplement them with text labels, like those shown in Figure 2-12.

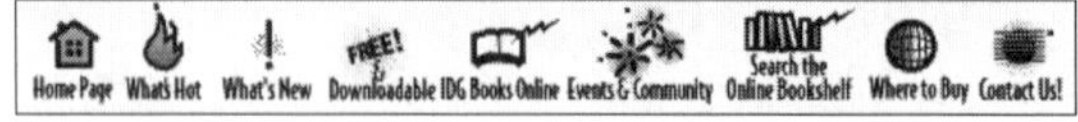

Figure 2-12: Text labels help to clarify icons, whose meanings aren't always obvious — as you can see in this navigation bar from, ahem, an early version of IDG Books Worldwide's Web site (http://www.idgbooks.com). I'm happy to report that the site now sports a much nicer happy to report scheme — with no icons!

BACKGROUNDER

Graphics and Web Servers: A Preview of Coming Discussions

This chapter deliberately avoids discussing nitty-gritty implementation details; its goal is to get you thinking about the overall structure of a Web site and about the navigation devices you will provide to make it easy to use.

But where navigation bars are concerned, there are important implementation issues to consider at the beginning. These issues have a direct effect on how fast your Web site is and how hard your Web server has to work to dish out your pages.

There are two basic ways to implement a graphical navigation bar. (And remember, by graphical, I mean a bar containing icons or graphical text created in a program such as Photoshop.) I discuss the details behind each technique in Chapter 6. Until then, here's an overview of each graphical navigation technique and its advantages and disadvantages.

- You can create an *image map,* a single graphic containing the entire navigation bar.
- You can create each button or icon as a separate graphic and display them alongside one another to provide the illusion of a continuous bar.

The advantage of an image map is its graphic will generally load more quickly than will the numerous separate graphics required with the second technique. The downside of an image map is it isn't as easy to create the "you are here" effect illustrated in Figure 2-11.

The advantage of using separate graphics is they *do* make it easier to create that "you are here" effect. The disadvantage, however, is placing a large number of separate graphics on a page can significantly slow your Web server, especially if your site is popular. I get into the technical reasons behind this in Chapter 6 and in Part IV. For now, keep in mind that placing more than four to six graphics on a page can bog down a busy Web server.

Top of page or bottom? Or both?

Where should navigation bars go: at the top of each page, at the bottom, or at the top *and* bottom? There's no cast-in-stone rule on this one. In fact, there are good arguments in favor of each option.

- Putting the bars at the top of each page enables visitors to jump around within the site without having to scroll to the bottom of the page.
- Putting the bars at the bottom of each page enables visitors who have explored a given page to jump elsewhere without having to scroll back to the top of the page.

And after reading these two bullet points, you don't have to be Albert Einstein to know that...

- Putting the bars at the top *and* bottom of each page combines both of the aforementioned advantages: quick navigation for surfers and convenient navigation for explorers.

How do the sites I've been looking at in this chapter handle this placement issue? The Sun Web style guide places its banner/navigation bar hybrids on both the top and bottom of each page. Adobe's Web site places its primary navigation buttons along the top of each page — but most of the site's menu pages fit entirely on one screen, so scrolling isn't a problem.

Using frames for navigation bars

Here's yet another option for positioning navigation bars: Place them within a *frame,* that unique split-window pane device that debuted with Netscape Navigator 2.0. When you place navigation buttons within a frame, they remain visible at all times (as shown in Figure 2-13).

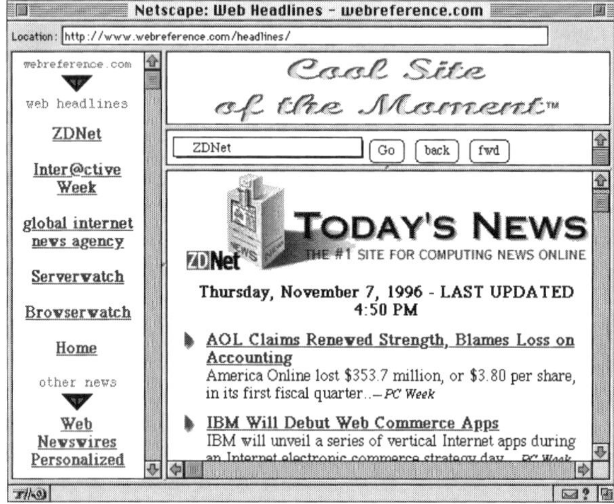

Figure 2-13: On Webreference.com, navigation links live within a frame — at least on browsers that support frames.

There are some big drawbacks to the frame approach. For one thing, as of early 1997, only Netscape Navigator 2.0 and Microsoft Internet Explorer 3.0 (and later versions of both) support frames. If you use frames, you need to develop additional HTML code to support frame-ignorant browsers. (Chapter 7 contains examples.)

Frames also eat up valuable screen real estate. It's convenient to have navigation buttons handy when you're speed-surfing, but when you're taking an in-depth trek through a site, they can get in your way and take up space. And as Chapter 7 describes, frames create complex user-interface issues that few sites address correctly.

I'm not a big fan of frames, but a great many Web developers — and Web surfers — are. In the end, you need to weigh the advantages of frames against their drawbacks and then factor in your own tastes. If you decide to frame your Web site, be sure to read the tips in Chapter 7— and consider providing a frame-free version of your site for those visitors who can't or won't use frames.

The right way to go back and home

It's common for Web pages to include buttons or hypertext links labeled Back and Home, which when clicked, take a visitor up one level in your site hierarchy (the Back button) or to the top level (the Home button).

The problem with this naming scheme is it assumes a visitor entered a given page from either the home page or from the page above the current page. On the Web, there's no guarantee of this: Because one site can be linked to another, a visitor can click a link in Site A that puts him or her deep within the hierarchy of Site B. In this scenario, a button or link labeled Back is misleading. If the visitor clicks it, he or she won't go *back* to the page on Site A — which is what the word Back certainly implies. Instead, he or she will go up one level in *your* hierarchy.

You can probably see how this applies to the word Home, too. A visitor who was instantly teleported to a page deep within your site, instead of arriving there through your hierarchy, won't know where Home is.

There's a simple solution. For pages that might be linked by other sites, avoid the ambiguous Back or Home and be specific: Back to CritterFinder Home or simply CritterFinder Home would be better alternatives in this case.

In a related vein, some sites also use buttons or labels named Up or Up One Level, but these are ambiguous: Why should visitors click something named Up? Where will that take them? These labels are also needlessly technical — they put too much stress on the hierarchical nature of a site.

SECRET

Make the wording of your navigation buttons clear and unambiguous. Don't assume that a visitor arrived at a certain page by burrowing through your hierarchy, because it's possible that he or she got there in one click from a link on another site.

A table of contents or site map

Another useful navigation device is a table of contents page, often called a *site map*. This is a page that provides an at-a-glance view of the site's structure. As Figure 2-14 shows, it can be text based or graphical.

The text-based map in Figure 2-14 is very detailed: It goes all the way down to individual pages within each part of the site. The graphical map, on the other hand, provides only a broad overview of the site's structure. Neither approach is inherently superior; each succeeds in its job, which is to provide the big picture of how a site is structured.

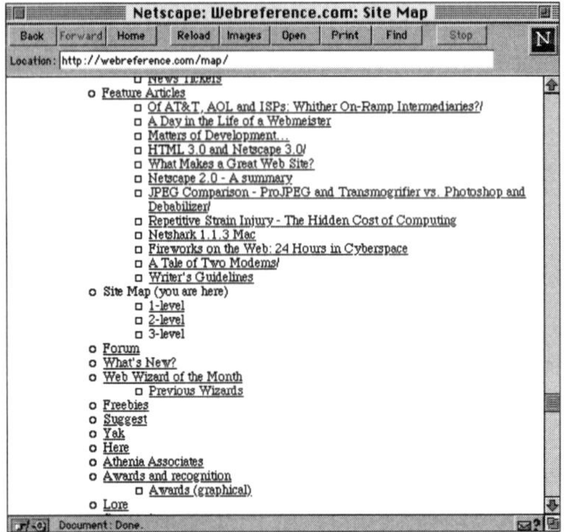

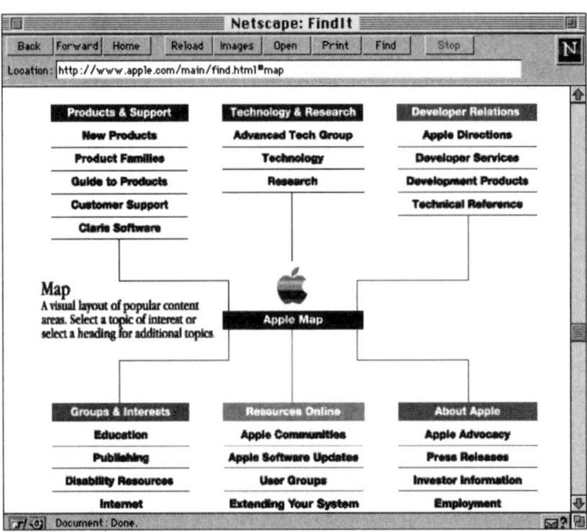

Figure 2-14: Two site maps in action. Top: This text-based map is for Webreference.com (http://webreference.com/), an excellent Web developer's site. Bottom: This graphical map is of Apple's Web site (http://www.apple.com/). Visitors can jump to any section by clicking the appropriate area of the map. (©Apple Computer, Inc. 1997. Used with permission. Apple® and the Apple logo are registered trademarks of Apple Computer, Inc. All rights reserved.)

Tables of contents within pages

If your site contains lengthy text pages such as articles or technical reports, consider giving each text-heavy page its own small table of contents that enables visitors to jump to sections within the page. Use the subheadings in the text as the entries for the table of contents, create an HTML anchor for each subhead, and then link each entry in the table of contents to its appropriate anchor. If you use multiple levels of subheads in your text-heavy pages, indent the mini table of contents appropriately to emphasize the levels (as shown in Figure 2-15).

Figure 2-15: Heidsite contains many excerpts from my books (including the one you're reading now). To make each excerpt easier to navigate, each page contains a mini table of contents.

Miscellaneous Site Secrets

To wrap up this chapter, here is a collection of site-design tips, rants, and philosophical ramblings.

Window titling tips

Every single Web page has a perfect location for a road sign that shows visitors where they are. It doesn't eat up any additional screen space. Its bandwidth requirements are practically nonexistent. And yet a surprising number of otherwise great Web sites don't take full advantage of it.

I'm referring to the *window title* — the text that appears at the top of a browser window. It's the text that, in an HTML document, is tucked in between the `<TITLE>` and `</TITLE>` tags.

At the very least, a window title should be *meaningful:* it should state, in as few words as possible, the page's purpose. Here are a few examples:

Bad: Welcome to My Home Page

Good: The Bill Gates Home Page

You never see a road sign at a town line that says "Welcome Here" — yet you do often see the equivalent in Web page titles. Here's another good reason for meaningful titles: When a visitor bookmarks a page, a Web browser uses the page title as the bookmark name. Phrases like *Welcome to* look kind of strange in a list of bookmarks or favorites.

Tell visitors where they are, and phrase the title so it makes sense in a bookmark list.

Bad: Price List

Good: Acme Products Price List

A visitor may arrive at your page through a link on a different site. Work on the assumption that a given page may be the first thing a visitor sees on your site, and title the page accordingly.

Window titling at Heidsite

For my site, I use a window-titling scheme that not only tells visitors where they are, but also shows the path that led them there. I do this by spelling out the path to the current page, as shown in Figure 2-16.

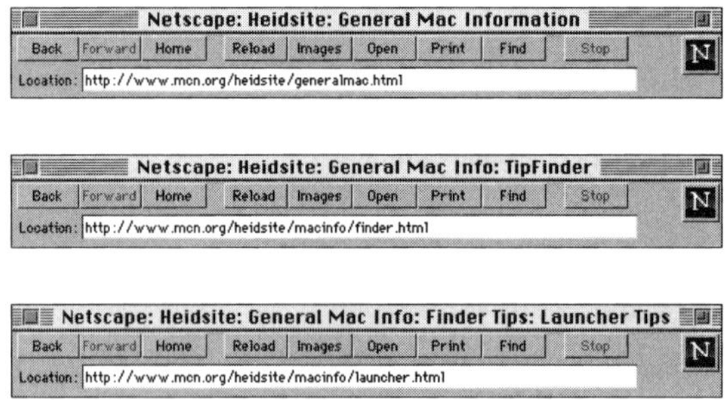

Figure 2-16: Heidsite's window titling in action

The preceding figure shows how the window title changes as visitors tunnel their way from the home page to a specific set of tips. Spelling out the path to the current page helps reinforce the site's structure.

A word about being "Under Construction"

Every online Web style guide warns you not to use the trite phrase "Under Construction" and its silly digging construction worker sign. So why does this nonsense still pollute site after site? Probably because not enough people take the time to read Web style guides. It is for this reason — and I apologize to readers who *have* read online Web style guides — that I repeat the rule here: Don't use the phrase "Under Construction" on your site, and don't use the dorky little construction worker sign. A good Web site is *always* under construction.

I feel better now.

Is it okay to say "Road Work Ahead"?

Having vented my spleen, I realize there are times when a certain page or area won't be complete, but you can't bear to delay the site's debut until it is. There's a right way and a wrong way to handle this situation.

The wrong way: Simply post pages as you complete them. When visitors activate a link that will work someday but doesn't now, a server error message appears (as shown in Figure 2-17).

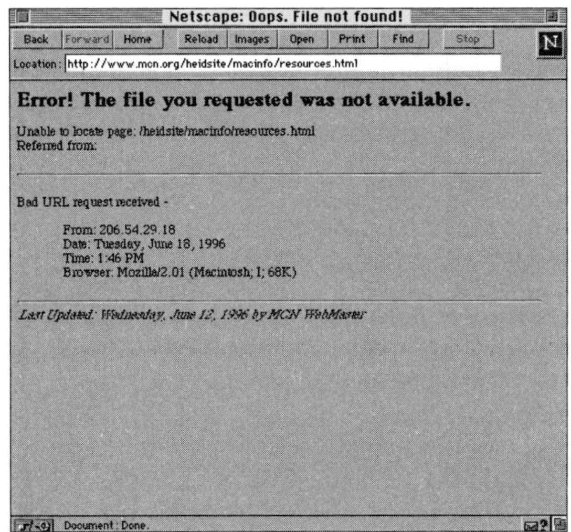

Figure 2-17: The wrong way (top) and the right way (bottom) to handle an unfinished site.

The right way: For each unfinished page, create a place-holder page that explains that this particular page isn't finished yet. If possible, provide the date when the page will be finished — ideally, at least some visitors will return to see it.

This approach takes a bit more effort than simply doing nothing, but it has two advantages:

- It avoids jarring your visitors with a Web server's "not found" error message — a message that could just as easily mean a bad link or an incompetently designed site as it could an unfinished page.
- It helps you flesh out the overall structure of the site. You can create accurate maps of your site using programs such as Adobe SiteMill, Microsoft FrontPage, and NetObjects Fusion. And when you're ready to finish a given page, you can open the placeholder page and use it as your starting point.

Avoid the "best viewed with..." syndrome

You see them everywhere: "This site best viewed with Netscape Navigator 2.x or later." "This site looks best with Microsoft Internet Explorer 2.x or later."

Try to avoid fouling your sites with messages like these. One reason is they're tacky — they're blatant advertisements for other companies' products.

But the larger reason is you alienate visitors who aren't using your blessed browser. If you're trying to reach as many people as possible, you shouldn't restrict yourself to only those folks who use a certain browser — no matter how popular that browser is.

Now this doesn't mean you should design bland, generic-looking pages. It's possible to develop a site that takes full advantage of Netscape's or Microsoft's HTML extensions but also looks good on other browsers. Sometimes you can do some clever HTML coding to accomplish this within a single page. (Chapter 7 describes some techniques.) Other times, you may have to create entirely separate pages and then route visitors to the appropriate ones using special software running on your server. (Section IV contains the details.)

SECRET

The bottom line is that good Web developers don't force visitors to use specific products in order to explore their sites.

The problem with plug-ins

Here's a related issue. Many of today's hot Web development technologies require that visitors download and install plug-in modules (software add-ons that extend a browser's capabilities) — to enable the browser to play audio files or animations, for example.

Too many Web developers make the mistake of employing these technologies in home pages — the first pages that visitors see when they hit a site. The problem with this approach surfaces when visitors don't have the required plug-ins. Instead of seeing a cool animation or hearing a soundtrack, they see browser error messages and missing plug-in icons (see Figure 2-18).

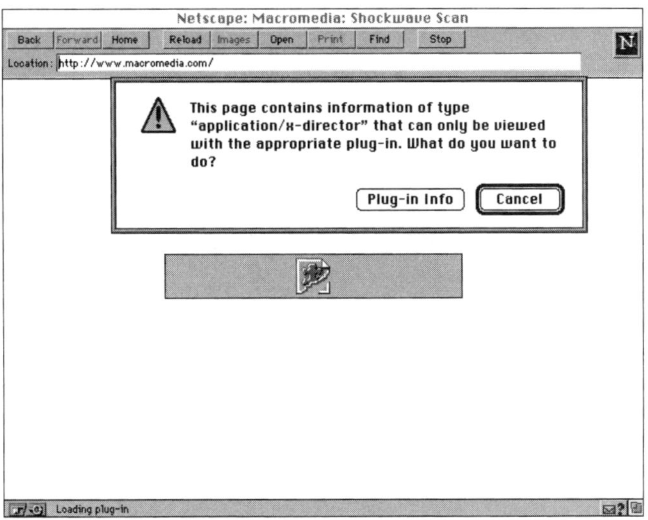

Figure 2-18: This is progress? No — it's what happens when you hit a plug-in crazy site without the required plug-ins.

SECRET

To avoid these error messages, don't use any plug-in-based technology on a site's home page. Instead, include a message on the home page informing visitors they may need to download some plug-ins or helper applications in order to experience the site in all its glory. You don't have to list everything they need; you might simply have a message that says, "To get the most out of this site, we recommend several plug-ins and helper applications." Link the phrase "plug-ins and helper applications" to another page that lists the specifics and provides links to the Web pages containing the software that visitors will need to download.

Another alternative is to make the home page a *front door* — a page that welcomes visitors and provides options that let them branch to either a plug-in-enhanced version of the site or to a "straight" version (see Figure 2-19).

Detecting plug-ins with Navigator 3

ON CD-ROM

For Navigator 3, Netscape enhanced the JavaScript language, so now developers can write JavaScript scripts that detect whether a visitor has a given plug-in. Chapter 14 shows some example scripts, which are also included on the *HTML & Web Publishing SECRETS* CD-ROM.

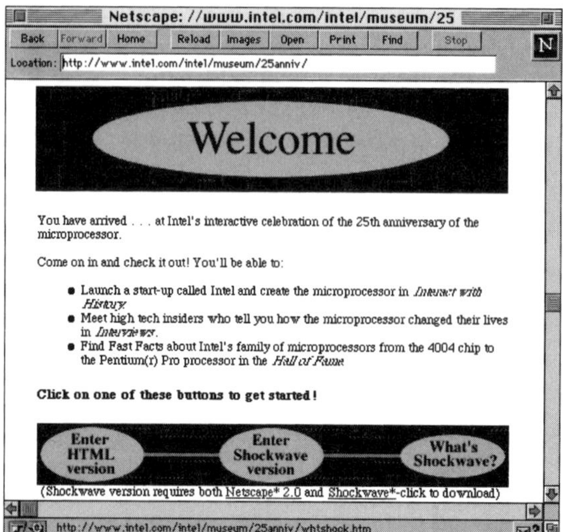

Figure 2-19: A front-door home page enables visitors to enter the site in the way that suits them and their system configuration.

Creating a low-bandwidth version of a site

A variation of the front-door approach can also be useful if you want to create a site that relies heavily on graphics for navigation. It's common to use relatively large graphics on the first few levels of a site — for example, on its home page and on the subtopic pages just beneath it. The problem, of course, is that these graphics are likely to scare away visitors with slower modems. And they don't do anything to ease the problem of Internet congestion.

The solution: Create low-graphics versions of the primary navigation pages, and then create a front-door home page that gives visitors the opportunity to use the low-bandwidth version. You can see this approach in action at the *Epicurious* Web site (shown in Figure 2-20).

Site structuring from the intranet perspective

The vast majority of this chapter's concepts and diatribes applies to World Wide Web sites and intranet Web sites alike. But intranet sites provide a couple of unique wrinkles and opportunities.

Navigation differences

Elsewhere in this chapter, I recommend against using vague terms such as "Back" as well as against using icon-based navigation schemes. Both recommendations are based on the fact that, on the World Wide Web, a visitor may enter a site from a link on a different site, in which case terms like Back are inaccurate. As for icons, unless accompanied by text labels, their meanings are likely to be unclear to occasional visitors.

Figure 2-20: Choose your bandwidth: The Epicurious home page (http://www.epicurious.com/) provides a text-only home page option.

On a closed intranet site — one that is isolated from the World Wide Web — these points don't necessarily apply. If you can be sure a person will only enter a page through your own hierarchy, then navigation terms such as Back aren't as vague. And for a corporate site that will be used on a day-in, day-out basis, there's nothing wrong with creating an icon-based navigation scheme. Your users will probably memorize the icons quickly. (Supplementing icons with text labels is still a good idea, however; it will help new and temporary employees, not to mention those folks with less than elephantine memories.)

Browser and plug-in compatibility

This chapter spends a fair amount of space discussing browser compatibility and plug-in issues: creating pages that work with as many browsers as possible, and providing front-door pages that let visitors know which plug-ins and helper applications they'll need to use a site or section before they get there.

In an institutional setting, you probably — or at least you hope to — have more control over visitors' system configurations. If Netscape Navigator is the company standard and everybody has it, there's no need to spend the extra effort developing an intranet site that will look good on other browsers.

Similarly, if you can be sure everyone will have a fixed set of plug-ins and helper applications, there's no need for front-door pages. But because individual configurations can vary as users tinker with their machines, it's still a good idea to at least have a help or troubleshooting page that summarizes what's required to use a site.

Navigation aids, Part 1: custom bookmark files

If you use Netscape Navigator, a great way to supplement an intranet site's own navigation features is by creating a bookmark file for the site and then distributing the file to everyone who uses the site. By taking advantage of the hierarchical bookmark features provided by Navigator 2.0 and later versions, you can provide a convenient launching pad to all areas of the site.

To install the bookmarks for the Windows version of Navigator, copy the bookmark file to the same directory that contains the Navigator program. On the Macintosh, place the bookmark file in the folder named Netscape f, which is within the System Folder's Preferences folder.

Navigation aids, Part 2: custom directory buttons

With Netscape Navigator 3.0 and later versions, you can customize the directory buttons that appear at the top of the browser window. Instead of the Netscape standard — What's New?, What's Cool?, and so on — you can create directory buttons that take users to various spots on your intranet site: Human Resources, Price Lists, Company News, and so on.

To customize Navigator's buttons, you need an add-on utility: the Netscape Administration Kit. The Administration Kit also enables you to add custom menu items to Navigator's Directory menu and even customize the browser window animation — replace the standard Navigator meteor shower with an animated version of your company logo, for example.

For the scoop on the Netscape Administration Kit, visit Netscape's Web site at `http://home.netscape.com/`.

Navigation aids, Part 3: custom menus

On the Macintosh side, a terrific shareware program called URL Manager Pro enables you to create custom menus for Netscape Navigator. You might use these to create a custom menu bar that enables employees to navigate your company's intranet sites. (You can download URL Manager Pro from most shareware sites or from the author's site, at `http://www.xs4all.nl/~alco/urlm/`.)

Summary

- A good way to design a Web site's structure is to create a hierarchical tree chart.
- A site's hierarchy should be neither too shallow nor too deep; as a general rule, a visitor should be able to access any page with two or three mouse clicks.
- A Web site's navigation devices should be unambiguous and consistent from page to page.
- Page headings, or banners, are a good way of saying "You are here" — reminding visitors of where they are within your site.
- Navigation bars are controls that enable visitors to move within a site. They can be text-based or graphical. They can be located at the top of each page, at the bottom, or to minimize scrolling on long pages, at the top *and* bottom.
- Avoid vague button or link names such as "Back." Instead, make the names clear and unambiguous.
- A table of contents, or site map, is a great way to provide the big picture of a site's structure.
- On lengthy text pages, include a mini table of contents that enables readers to jump to key sections without having to scroll.
- Use HTML's `<TITLE>` tag to create clear window titles that also hint at the site's structure.
- For an incomplete Web site, create placeholder pages for pages that aren't complete. Never have a link to a nonexistent page.
- Rather than giving a company a free advertisement with a "best viewed with" message, try to design a site so it takes advantage of the latest browser developments while still looking good in other browsers.
- If you use plug-in-based technologies such as Shockwave, provide a front door or message that lets visitors know what they'll need to view the site or page.
- If you use a graphics-intensive navigation scheme for upper levels of a site, consider creating a text-only path for visitors with slow connections.

Chapter 3

HTML Truths and Tidbits

In This Chapter

- Understanding HTML's approach to formatting
- Dealing with browser compatibility issues, Part 2
- A field guide to HTML standards (official and otherwise)
- Sticking to the standard: HTML validation, and why you may (or may not) use it
- What's ahead for HTML?

The wonderful thing about the HyperText Markup Language (HTML) is that it gives Web developers complete control over the appearance of a page. With just a few codes, you can specify fonts and sizes, control the position of text and graphics down to a single-pixel level, and make pages that rival anything a print publisher can create. HTML is a designer's dream.

And if you believe any of that, I'm taking offers on a certain bridge in Brooklyn.

The fact is, there's nothing dreamy about HTML from a designer's standpoint. HTML provides little control over the fine details of page formatting.

But as programmers say, that isn't a bug — it's a feature. HTML was *designed* not to represent nitty-gritty formatting details. In fact, for reasons I describe shortly, HTML's approach to formatting is one reason the World Wide Web has become the mass medium that it is.

This chapter contains some general background on HTML — information that sets the stage for subsequent chapters' details on HTML editors and tips. This chapter *isn't* a primer on HTML. As I mentioned in the preface, I assume you have at least a basic familiarity with HTML. If you're an absolute beginner — if terms such as *tag* are new to you — you may want to refer to Appendix A for an HTML overview and quick reference.

Function over Form

I often hear graphic designers bemoaning the lack of formatting control that HTML provides: You can't specify margin widths, line spacing, or particular fonts. You can't precisely position elements on a page. After running down the list of HTML's limitations, graphic designers often conclude by saying they hope future versions of the HTML standard will provide the kind of control they get from print publishing programs.

I disagree at this point: I hope that future versions of HTML *don't* provide this degree of control. I sympathize with the designer's plight — my first full-time job was as a typographer at a top-flight type house, so I understand and appreciate a designer's need for control. It's just that HTML is not the ideal route to that control.

Structure versus format

SECRET

HTML isn't a designer's dream because it wasn't created to be one. HTML was designed to represent the *structure* of a document: its headings, its body text, its bulleted lists, and so on. To explain it in conversational form, HTML wasn't designed to say things like, "This sentence is 24-point Palatino Bold with one-inch margins," but to say, "This sentence is a heading." It's up to the browser to decide how to render that heading.

So why is this approach good?

- **It's platform- and machine-independent.** HTML's emphasis on structure rather than format is what enables a page to be viewed on any Web platform, regardless of its screen size and its graphic and typographic capabilities. Because HTML pages are not tied to a specific font or a specific brand of computer, they can be displayed by any device with a Web browser — a Mac, a UNIX box, a Windows machine, an aging Amiga, a network computer connected to a TV set, or a palm-top computer such as an Apple Newton MessagePad.
- **It's compact.** It takes fewer commands to describe a document's structure than it does to describe low-level formatting details. Even the conversational sentences a few paragraphs above illustrate this point: It took fewer words to say "This is a heading" than it did to say "This sentence is 24-point Palatino Bold with one-inch margins." HTML's compactness translates into faster transfers, something that's important to any Web surfer.
- **It's simple.** HTML is easy to learn and use. An afternoon is all it takes to learn how to create pages that mix text and graphics and contain hypertext links. It isn't until you get into the advanced formatting aspects of HTML — tables, frames, and other extensions — that the language becomes a bit tricky. See that? HTML only becomes complex when advanced formatting enters the picture.

What's a control freak to do?

It's possible, and indeed easy, to create simple, good-looking pages using only HTML's standard features. But if you're after more — the ability to specify a certain font, for example, or to finely control line spacing and line endings — you have two basic options.

Push HTML to its limits

With some clever tricks, you can control line spacing, create multiple-column pages, and much more. Some of these tricks are easy; others are time consuming and may be more trouble than they're worth. Some rely on broadly supported HTML features such as tables; others require newer HTML features such as style sheets, which are discussed in Chapter 7. Still others involve offbeat techniques, such as using tiny, one-pixel graphics to act as spacers. Chapter 5 contains details on the range of hoops through which you can make HTML jump.

Turn to a portable document technology

Technologies such as Adobe Acrobat enable you to distribute richly formatted documents on the Web. You can use a page-layout program to create an elaborately formatted, full-color document, and then use Acrobat to put it in electronic form, complete with hypertext links and hot spots. Acrobat and other portable document technologies have their own drawbacks, but they're currently the Web developer's best tools for advanced formatting.

Use a Java- or plug-in based layout technology

As Chapter 4 describes, layout tools that rely on Java applets or plug-in modules to present page content are becoming available. The most notable example from the Java camp is Random Noise's Coda. In the plug-in arena, there's Quark, Inc.'s QuarkImmedia. These and similar products work around HTML's limitations by bypassing it completely. Their downsides: limited browser compatibility and reliance on plug-ins.

The Levels and Dialects of HTML

One of the biggest issues that Web developers bump their heads into every day is compatibility, creating pages that render well within the numerous browsers that are in use: the very latest version of Netscape Navigator, Microsoft Internet Explorer, NCSA Mosaic, Spyglass Mosaic, the old America Online InterCon browser, and the Lynx text-only browser, for example.

Why would the numerous browsers out there cause compatibility problems? After all, there are numerous brands of TV sets, but every TV can show the same programs. Here's why:

- HTML has evolved over the years — new formatting tags have been added to the language and not all browsers support the latest incarnations.

- In their zeal to remain (or become) leading players in the Web world, some companies — okay, Netscape Communications and Microsoft — have added tags and formatting features that the competition doesn't provide.

So, the browser compatibility issue results from a combination of an evolving standard and complete divergence from the standard. In other words, the rules keep changing and people keep making up their own rules.

Should you really worry about browser compatibility?

Just how important is it to be compatible with the entire universe of Web browsers? I addressed this question briefly in the previous chapter, but it's such an important issue for Web developers that it's worth revisiting.

Take a look at Table 3-1 — it shows a breakdown of the browser market share as measured by Interse Corporation (`http://www.interse.com/`), a developer of Web-analysis software, now owned by Microsoft.

Table 3-1 One company's gauge of browser market share in 1996

Month	*Netscape Navigator (%)*	*Microsoft Internet Explorer (%)*	*Other (%)*
December	54.4	33.0	12.6
November	59.9	31.2	9.0
October	61.5	30.0	8.5
September	52.3	39.1	8.6
August	62.7	29.1	8.1
July	72.6	15.8	11.5
June	78.2	8.3	13.6
May	83.2	7.0	9.8
April	82.2	7.0	10.7
March	80.5	6.5	13.0
February	77.0	8.3	13.8
January	81.3	5.5	13.3

Source: Interse Corporation (http://www.interse.com/)

You don't have to be a statistician to see that Netscape Navigator has a, shall we say, commanding lead. But some additional points are in order.

The table doesn't break Navigator's share into version numbers. At present, Navigator is up to version 4.0. Each version introduces new HTML tags and features, but the Web-browsing public doesn't always upgrade immediately (or at all). Take a look at Table 3-2, which shows a breakdown of the Netscape Navigator versions that accessed the servers at the University of Illinois at Urbana-Champaign on one day in early 1997.

Table 3-2 Enhanced for which Netscape?

Netscape Version	*Accesses (%)*
3.x	65.9
2.x	27.1
1.x	5.1
4.x	1.8
Other	.1

Source: University of Illinois at Urbana-Champaign Browser Statistics page (http://www.cen.uiuc.edu/bstats/latest.html)

The point: Even if you're developing an "enhanced for Netscape" site, you're going to have to jump through some hoops to ensure that *all* Netscape Navigator users will be able to see your pages. Or you'll have to decide to enhance for a particular version and either leave some visitors out in the cold (if you choose the latest version), or not take advantage of the latest Netscape innovations (if you choose an earlier version). More on this in Chapter 7.

Microsoft Internet Explorer is coming on strong. In a survey conducted in May 1996, Dataquest (`http://www.dataquest.com/`) found that Internet Explorer had seven percent of the browser market. By early 1997, that figure had jumped to as high as 33 percent, depending on whose numbers you trust.

The point: Internet Explorer may still have a smaller piece of the browser pie, but 30 percent isn't chicken feed. (Pardon my mixed culinary metaphors.) And Microsoft is determined to increase its market share — as if you need me to tell you that.

Combined, even the minor players are significant. The market share percentages of other browsers, such as America Online and Spyglass Mosaic, are in the single or low double digits. But that represents an audience of a few million Web surfers. Do you really want to ignore an audience that large?

The point: As I said in the previous chapter, the best development approach for the World Wide Web is to either create a site that works in as many browsers as possible, or implement server technology that detects which browser a visitor is using and dishes out appropriate pages. For intranet sites where you can be certain all visitors will be using a specific browser, feel free to go crazy and use browser-specific features.

Let's take a closer look at each edge of the HTML sword.

The levels of the HTML standard

As of early 1997, there are four major levels of HTML.

Level 0

Yes, there is an HTML 0.0! This level specifies only the most basic HTML capabilities: headings, lists, anchors, and so on. Level 0 doesn't allow for images or rudimentary character formatting such as boldface (the `<STRONG>` tag). Text-only browsers such as Lynx generally conform to the Level 0 specification.

Level 1

Level 1, or HTML 1.0, is a mandatory level for all graphical Web browsers. Level 1 adds support for images, emphasis, and text highlighting.

Level 2

Level 2's primary enhancement involves support for on-screen forms that visitors can fill in and submit (to sign a guestbook, for example, or complete a survey).

Level 3.2

Level 3.2 adds support for many of the things we now take for granted on Web pages. Most of these enhancements were pioneered and popularized by Netscape Communications. Now they're part of the HTML specification, and they include:

- columnar tables such as those used to show baseball standings or stock market data and create multiple-column pages
- mixed font attributes such as bold and italic
- centered and right-aligned text
- text that flows around images and figures
- mixed font sizes, including support for superscript and subscript characters
- support for client-side image maps (discussed in Chapter 6)
- support for Java applets, which are small programs written in the Java programming language (covered in Chapter 14)

You may be more familiar with something called HTML 3.0, but in the hallowed halls of the Web standards organization — the World Wide Web Consortium, or *W3C* — there's no such beast. The specification for HTML 3.0 expired before ever being approved. The W3C abandoned the HTML 3.0 spec in favor of 3.2.

Free enterprise meets HTML

Standards groups such as the W3C are important, but what often drives the evolution of any technology is private industry and good, old-fashioned competition. This has certainly been the case with HTML: Netscape Communications was largely responsible for the widespread adoption of such HTML 3.2 enhancements as tables and text that flows around images.

Netscape has company now: Microsoft is working hard to not only increase its market share in the browser and server fields, but also to drive the evolution of HTML.

This section summarizes the key extensions both companies have made to HTML. Some of these extensions have been incorporated into working drafts of the HTML specification; others remain specific to either Netscape Navigator or Microsoft Internet Explorer. Each company is talking out both sides of its mouth, claiming a commitment to open standards while also introducing its own extensions to HTML. Welcome to world of free enterprise, World Wide Web style.

Navigator 3 HTML extensions

As Part III describes, many of Navigator 3's biggest enhancements are in the multimedia areas: Navigator 3 supports embedded audio and video clips and virtual reality models. Many of the new tags supported by Navigator 3 relate to these elements.

Navigator 3 also adds new capabilities to the JavaScript scripting language. Among other things, JavaScript's enhancements make it possible to detect which software plug-ins a Navigator user has installed — a capability that becomes very important when you start using plug-in technologies such as Macromedia's Shockwave for Director. Chapters 7, 8, and 11 show JavaScript in action.

Netscape also expanded Navigator 3's HTML vocabulary to support little formatting niceties, such as the ability to format table cells in various colors and have multiple columns of text on a page. Netscape also added support for the `<FONT FACE>` tag — originally introduced by Microsoft for its Internet Explorer browser — which enables you to place text in a specific typeface. And a new `<IMG>` tag provides more control over white space by enabling you to add extra horizontal or vertical space. (These and other formatting-related tags are discussed in Chapter 5.)

As this book was going to press, Netscape was working on version 4.0 of Navigator, which introduces still more extensions to HTML. Some of these extensions are covered in Chapter 7. You can learn more details about them on Netscape's Web site (`http://www.netscape.com/`) and on this book's Web site (`http://websecrets.heidsite.com/`).

Microsoft Internet Explorer HTML extensions

In its zeal to show the world it could influence the direction of the Web (or at least try really hard to), Microsoft introduced a whole flock of HTML extensions when it shipped version 2.0 of Internet Explorer. The trend continued with Internet Explorer 3.

The Internet Explorer extensions span the spectrum from basic presentation enhancements (colored table cells, line spacing and margin controls, and so on), to advanced presentation elements (support for frames and style sheets, discussed later), to multimedia (embedded audio and video clips), to advanced interactivity (support for Microsoft's ActiveX controls).

Some of the Internet Explorer 3 additions are aimed at keeping up with Netscape, including support for animated GIF graphics (discussed in Chapter 13) and support for frames.

Why am I telling you all this?

I've provided this overview to hammer home a point I've been making in this chapter and previous ones: The Web world's evolving standards provide opportunity for innovation in Web site design, but they also introduce compatibility headaches you must consider if you want your site to look good in most browsers.

Test your browser

SECRET

The Web Resources Group at the University of Arkansas has created a Web test-pattern site that enables you to see how various browsers handle various levels of HTML and HTML extensions. You can perform compliance tests for HTML 2.0 and HTML 3.x as well as the Netscape Navigator and Microsoft Internet Explorer sites. The site is called WWW Test Pattern, located at `http://www.uark.edu/~wrg/`. It's a worthwhile visit.

Web Proofreading: HTML Validators

Let's turn from the anarchic world of competing browsers back to the rigid world of HTML standards. HTML is often described as a programming language — it's common to hear people say they "program in HTML."

HTML isn't a programming language, it's a markup language (as the name denotes). I can understand why someone wouldn't want to say, "I mark up in HTML," but that's what an HTML-smith does.

I'm rambling down this path as a prelude to discussing the importance of creating HTML that adheres to the HTML standard you've adopted for a given Web site. Because although HTML isn't a programming language, it does have something in common with programming languages: the arrangement of symbols and tags — the *syntax* — of an HTML page must be accurate. If the syntax isn't correct, bad things happen; the page doesn't display properly, links don't work, and so on.

In HTML coding and in computer programming, it's possible to create a sloppy end product that still works. In the programming world, this may mean an inefficiently written program that runs slowly and devours memory, but still performs its intended function. (Too many software companies are pretty good at creating these monsters.) In the HTML world, it may mean creating a page that uses HTML's tags in a sloppy, nonstandard fashion, but still renders properly in most browsers. In programming and in HTML, there's room for slobs.

Or is there? Companies that ship slow, bloated software are rightfully criticized. And HTML coders who create sloppy pages earn the ire of visitors whose browsers have trouble deciphering poorly written HTML. Precision pays.

Validation sites

Where HTML is concerned, there's hope for the sloppy. Numerous sites exist that perform HTML *validation* — a special program at the validation site proofreads your pages and points out places where they diverge from the HTML standard. With most validation sites, you can choose which level of HTML you want your pages to conform to; you can even choose the de facto standards such as Microsoft Internet Explorer or Netscape Navigator.

How validation sites work

Every validation site works in a similar way. You begin by supplying the address (the Uniform Resource Locator, or URL) of the Web page you'd like to validate and the level of HTML you want to check against. The site attempts to access the page at the address you specified. If it's successful, a special program called an *SGML parser* kicks in and scans the page, looking for out-and-out HTML errors (such as a missing tag in a hyperlink) and any HTML coding that varies from the standard you've chosen. The end result is a report listing any problems found, as shown in Figure 3-1.

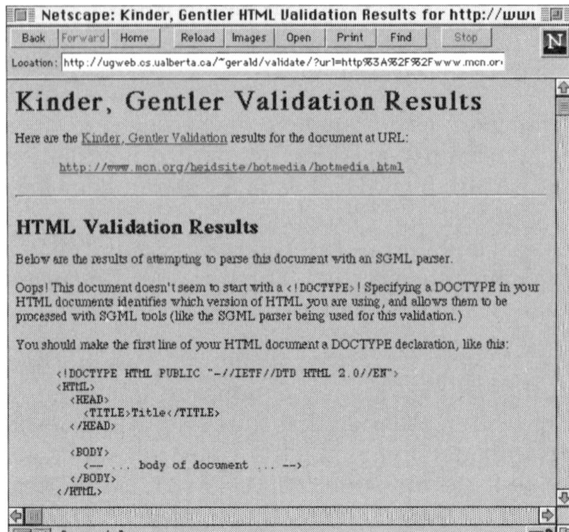

Figure 3-1: Houston, we have a problem: a typical HTML validation site's report

Am I really that bad?

Your first experience with an HTML validator is likely to be a sobering one: Pages that work perfectly in every browser you own can still generate a flock of errors. Pages created by a Web-development package such as Adobe PageMill can also send the penalty flags flying.

Before you get depressed and head for the tequila shooters, keep in mind that HTML validators tend to be extremely strict. It's their job. As Sergeant Friday used to say, "We don't make the laws, ma'am, we just enforce them."

Web browsers, on the other hand, are very forgiving of little departures from the HTML standards. As long as a page doesn't contain serious problems, such as missing quotes at the end of a hypertext link, most browsers are able to render it correctly.

So why bother with HTML validation?

If you've checked your pages in all the current browsers, is it really necessary to run them through an HTML validator?

Absolutely not. But what about future browsers? What about future HTML layout tools? There's no guarantee that future browsers or HTML editors will be as forgiving as today's. And if they aren't, you've got problems — you might find out that hundreds of pages don't render correctly in Netscape Navigator 2000 or can't be opened by SuperPageMill 99.

SECRET

If your pages adhere like Crazy Glue to a published HTML standard, they have a better chance of withstanding the test of time. If they're only "close enough to render correctly in most browsers," they're at risk of being incompatible with future Web browsers or tools.

Going beyond HTML validation

Most validation Web sites now go beyond just HTML validation to perform other site-checking tasks. Some check the links on the page you specify to make sure the links are active. Some check to make sure you've included alternate text (the `alt` attribute) in image tags. (Chapter 6 describes why it's important to do so.) Some even whine if you use the text "click here" in a link. (Chapter 5 describes why this is a no-no.)

Table 3-3 lists the top HTML validation sites.

Table 3-3 Get your HTML validated here: my favorite HTML validation sites

Site Name	*URL*
Doctor HTML	`http://imagiware.com/RxHTML/`
WebTechs Validation Service	`http://www.webtechs.com/html-val-svc/`
A Kinder, Gentler HTML Validator	`http://ugweb.cs.ualberta.ca/~gerald/validate/`

Do-it-yourself HTML validation

All HTML validation sites have one requirement: The pages you want to check must already be available on a Web server. In day-to-day production, however, it's useful if you validate pages *before* posting them on a site. After all, if a page has errors, you don't want it available to the world.

A variety of SGML parsers and HTML validation programs are available in the UNIX world. A growing number are also available for Windows. Some of the best include:

- Cerebral Systems Development's Webber, a powerful yet inexpensive HTML editor
- Albert Wiersch shareware HTML Validator
- Talicom's HTML PowerAnalyzer, part of the HTML PowerTools package, a slick set of HTML validation, formatting, and tweaking tools
- SoftQuad's HoTMetaL Pro 3.0 HTML editor

A trial version of HTML PowerTools is included on the *HTML & Web Publishing SECRETS* CD-ROM.

On the Mac OS side, there's SoftQuad's HoTMetaL Pro 3.0. And users of Bare Bones Software's BBEdit, a popular text editor among HTML gurus, can perform HTML validation using Lindsay Davis's free BBEdit HTML Extensions (`http://www.york.ac.uk/~ldl1/BBEditTools.html`). An enhanced version of his extensions is included with BBEdit 4.x.

And then there are Perl-based validators. Many HTML validation sites use parsers written in Perl, a programming language commonly used in Web development. Perl originated (and is still most popular) on UNIX computers, but versions of Perl have long since been created for the Mac OS and Windows (as well as for OS/2, Amigas, Ataris, and other operating systems). You can install a version of Perl for your operating system and then use it to run an HTML validator on your pages.

For more information on Perl, you may want to visit the Perl home page at `http://www.perl.com/perl/`. You'll find versions of Perl for numerous operating systems as well as links to sites containing Perl programs (called *scripts)* that you can download and adapt for your site. But note the word *adapt:* You generally have to perform at least minor modifications to a Perl script before it works with your system. If you don't have any programming experience, you may want to pass on Perl.

Parting thoughts on HTML validation

If the present is more important than the future — and in the Web world, it often is — don't obsess over HTML validation. Many sites change so quickly that it doesn't really matter whether a page will work years or even months down the road. In the transitory, time-sensitive world of the Web, what often counts most is that a page works *now* and is available *now.*

But you owe it to yourself to experiment with some HTML validation sites, particularly the wonderful Doctor HTML site (`http://imagiware.com/RxHTML/`). Chances are you'll learn something about HTML that will make your pages better. And that alone is worth the visit.

What's Ahead for HTML?

It's obvious: more standardization, more consistency from one browser to the next, and a simpler, streamlined set of tags.

And if you believe any of that, might I interest you in a parcel of marsh in the Sunshine State?

As Andy King describes in Chapter 7, HTML is being balkanized as browser vendors — okay, as Microsoft and Netscape — continue to add their own tags, tag variations, and unique features in the hopes of winning over Web developers and surfers alike. The balancing act between compatibility and innovation isn't going away any time soon.

And as HTML evolves, it will become more complex. The basic set of HTML tags is so simple that most people can create their first page in a few minutes. But it isn't quite as easy to create elaborately formatted pages and take advantage of formatting and user interface options such as tables and frames. And as designers demand greater control over document presentation — and browser developers accede to their demands — the full HTML learning curve will become steeper.

But as we head into the trenches to examine HTML editing tools and techniques in the next chapters, there's good news too: HTML's bifurcation and increasing complexity are problems only if you allow them to be. Compose your pages with compatibility and simplicity in mind, and you'll enjoy all those benefits — platform independence, performance, and elegance — that have made HTML so popular to begin with.

Summary

- HTML stresses structure over presentation, and as such, doesn't provide the precise formatting controls that many designers want.
- HTML's structure-oriented approach makes it platform- and machine-independent, compact, and easy to learn.
- It's possible to create relatively sophisticated on-screen layouts using HTML, but portable document technologies such as Adobe Acrobat or Java-based layout tools such as Random Noise's Coda are better for applications requiring fine control over presentation.
- There are several official HTML standards, ranging from Level 0 to Level 3.2. However, HTML's evolution is being driven largely by Netscape Communications and Microsoft.
- HTML validation sites enable you to check your Web pages to determine how well they adhere to a given HTML standard. Because browsers tend to be forgiving of variations and imprecise coding, it isn't essential to validate your pages. However, doing so will improve the chances that your pages will work properly in future browsers and HTML development programs.

Chapter 4

Making Pages

In This Chapter

- A survey of HTML creation programs — which is best for you?
- Converting existing documents with HTML converters
- Tips and secrets for PageMill, Home Page, HoTMetaL Pro, and more
- Optimizing your HTML — performance versus legibility?
- A grab bag of HTML tricks and secrets

HTML may be relatively easy to learn, but it definitely isn't fun to type. Typing a single tag is a workout for your digits: Shift-comma to get the < bracket, type the tag (careful — don't make any mistakes), Shift-period to get the > bracket. Sometimes it seems like an HTML author does more shifting than a truck driver.

Thanks to an entire industry of HTML editors and converters, it's no longer necessary to hand-peck HTML tags into a text editor. Some programs enable you to create pages by clicking and dragging text and graphics — much as you would in a publishing program. And like a publishing program, these HTML layout programs provide what-you-see-is-what-you-get (WYSIWYG) displays that enable you to see how your pages will look. (Although as I describe later, it's still essential to test your pages in a variety of browsers.)

Have a collection of existing documents you want to publish? Use one of the many HTML converters, programs that translate existing documents — word processor files, desktop publications, even presentations — into HTML form. Stuck with a pile of paper that must go on the Web? The latest optical character recognition (OCR) programs will scan your pages and create HTML documents of the results.

As useful as they are, HTML editors and converters can't replace skilled hand-coding. But they can give you a tremendous head start in creating pages. Many Web developers use these programs to rough out pages that they then tweak by hand. It's a smart approach that provides the best of both worlds — and saves you from typing every single tag on a page.

I begin this chapter by surveying the top HTML tools and providing tips for using them. Some of the programs described here are included on the *HTML & Web Publishing SECRETS* CD-ROM, found in the back of this book. (For a complete list of the programs on the CD-ROM, see Appendix B.) I wrap up the chapter with a grab bag of HTML tricks and secrets, some of which set the stage for subsequent chapters.

A Field Guide to Page Makers

Many types of programs are available for creating HTML pages. To help you choose software based on your needs and your desire to get your hands dirty with HTML, this section outlines each category and spotlights some of the individual programs.

This section isn't a complete guide to every HTML page-creation program, however. New programs and new versions appear constantly. You can find updates on the latest HTML creation tools at my Web site, `http://websecrets.heidsite.com/`.

WYSIWYG editors

If the graphical user interface era has a mantra, it's "What you see is what you get." From word processors to publishing programs to presentation packages, WYSIWYG displays have taken much of the guesswork out of document formatting. Put another way, you youngsters don't know how lucky you are — why, when I was your age, formatting a document meant typing codes that looked...well, a lot like HTML.

On CD-ROM

Try These Page Makers For Yourself

Whether you use a Mac OS or Windows machine, the *HTML & Web Publishing SECRETS* CD-ROM contains a full spectrum of HTML editors, converters, and utilities.

Claris Home Page (Mac OS and Windows). Claris Home Page is a first-rate HTML layout program that combines a straightforward and approachable user interface with support for the most popular HTML extensions.

HTML Power Tools (Windows). OppoSite Software's toolbox of HTML utilities will help you clean up, analyze, and convert your HTML code. And because you have the exquisite taste to be an *HTML & Web Publishing SECRETS* reader, you can upgrade from the demonstration version to the full version for a discounted price. For details, see OppoSite's advertisement page at the back of the book.

Myrmidon (Mac OS). This clever utility from Terry Morse Software enables you to convert just about any document to HTML. Try the trial version, then buy the full product at a discount (see the Terry Morse Software advertisement at the back of the book).

RTFtoHTML (Mac OS and Windows). This shareware gem converts Rich Text Format (RTF) files into HTML.

Fortunately, WYSIWYG editors have taken a lot of the guesswork out of creating HTML pages. These programs include Adobe PageMill; Claris Home Page; Symantec's VisualPage; Netscape Composer (formerly Navigator Gold); Microsoft FrontPage; NetObjects Fusion; and Macromedia Backstage.

All WYSIWYG editors have a few things in common, including the following:

- **They're interactive and, yes, WYSIWYG.** You format text and position page elements by choosing menu commands, clicking toolbar icons, and in some cases, by clicking and dragging as you would in a publishing or drawing program. At all times, the screen shows how the page will appear in a Web browser (see Figure 4-1). This eliminates the need to load a page in-progress into a browser just to see how it's coming along.
- **You can drag and drop until you drop.** Most WYSIWYG editors enable you to import text and graphic elements by dragging and dropping them from other programs or from the Macintosh Finder or the Windows desktop or Explorer.
- **You don't see HTML codes unless you want to.** Because you do most of your work in the program's WYSIWYG window, you're shielded from the ugly world of HTML tags and attributes. But because a smart Web developer will also hand-tweak pages where necessary, many WYSIWYG programs also enable you to view and edit the HTML tags that lie behind a page design.

- **They'll mislead you if you let them.** The primary problem with WYSIWYG editors is that what you see — or more precisely, what your site's visitors will see — will depend on the browser used to view the final pages. A WYSIWYG editor's preview mode may not render a page in the same way a browser will under real world conditions. For this reason, you should think of WYSIWYG editing as "what you see is probably pretty close to what you get." And you should obsessively test your pages with as many browsers as you can get your mitts on — or at least with the browsers you explicitly intend to support.

WYSIWYG adapters

The programs I discussed so far in this chapter were built from the ground up for WYSIWYG HTML editing. But there's another breed of WYSIWYG editor: programs that weren't designed for HTML editing but have had HTML editing features grafted onto them.

The two most notable examples of this group are Microsoft Word and QuarkXPress. Microsoft's Internet Assistant turns Word into a WYSIWYG editor: you can create tables, format and position text and graphics, and prepare a document using Word's standard formatting features. You can browse the Web, add hypertext links, and assign styles. When you're done, you can save the document as an HTML file.

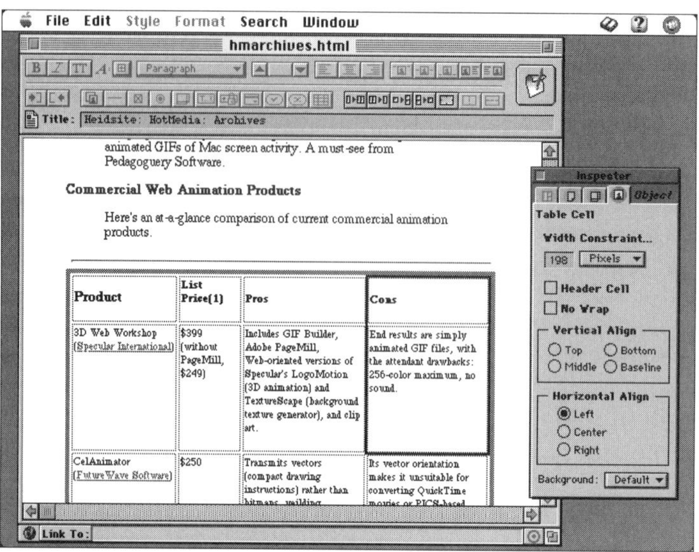

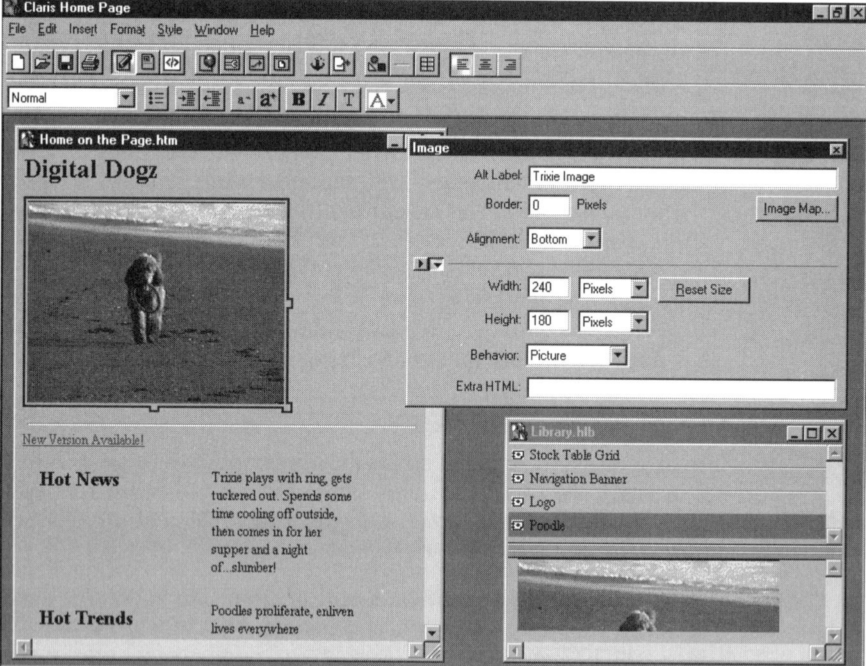

Figure 4-1: WYSIWYG editing at its best: Adobe PageMill (top) and Claris Home Page (bottom)

The Internet Assistant is available for both the Macintosh and Windows versions of Word; it's free and available for downloading from Microsoft's Web site, at `http://www.microsoft.com/`. (An enhanced version is included with Microsoft Office 97.) You'll find secrets for the Internet Assistant family later in this chapter.

QuarkXPress gains WYSIWYG editing skills from a third-party product, Astrobyte's BeyondPress. BeyondPress is an extension that weaves itself into QuarkXPress and adds HTML-editing features. The combination of QuarkXPress's page-layout power and BeyondPress's support for the latest HTML features forms a much more sophisticated editing environment than that formed by Microsoft's Internet Assistant for Word (see Figure 4-2).

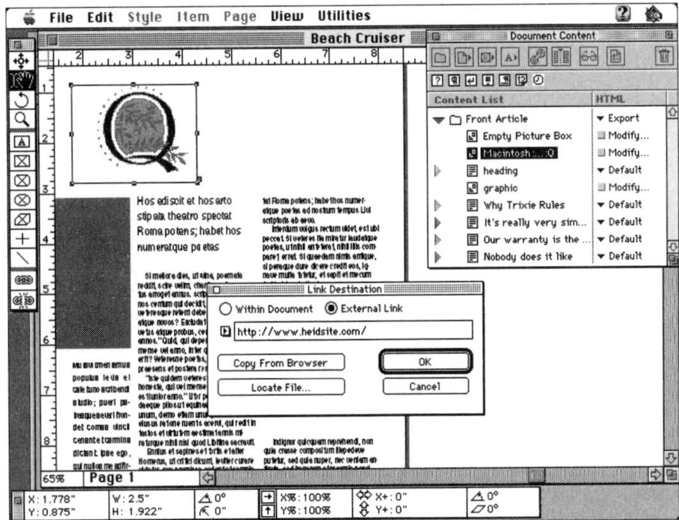

Figure 4-2: Astrobyte's BeyondPress combines with QuarkXpress to form a sophisticated WYSIWYG editing environment.

HTML editors

This class of program puts more emphasis on enabling you to manipulate HTML tags than on providing WYSIWYG editing. HTML editors (sometimes called tag editors) include SoftQuad's HoTMetaL family (Mac OS and Windows), Optima System's PageSpinner (Mac OS), Bare Bones Software's BBEdit (Mac OS), Sausage Software's HotDog series (Windows), and Nesbitt Software's WebEdit Pro (Windows).

There's common ground among HTML editors, too, such as the following:

- **They provide pop-up access to tags.** HTML editors may not insulate you from HTML tags, but they eliminate the need to type them. Most editors provide pop-up menus containing HTML tags organized according to category: choose a tag, and the editor inserts it into the page for you (see Figure 4-3).

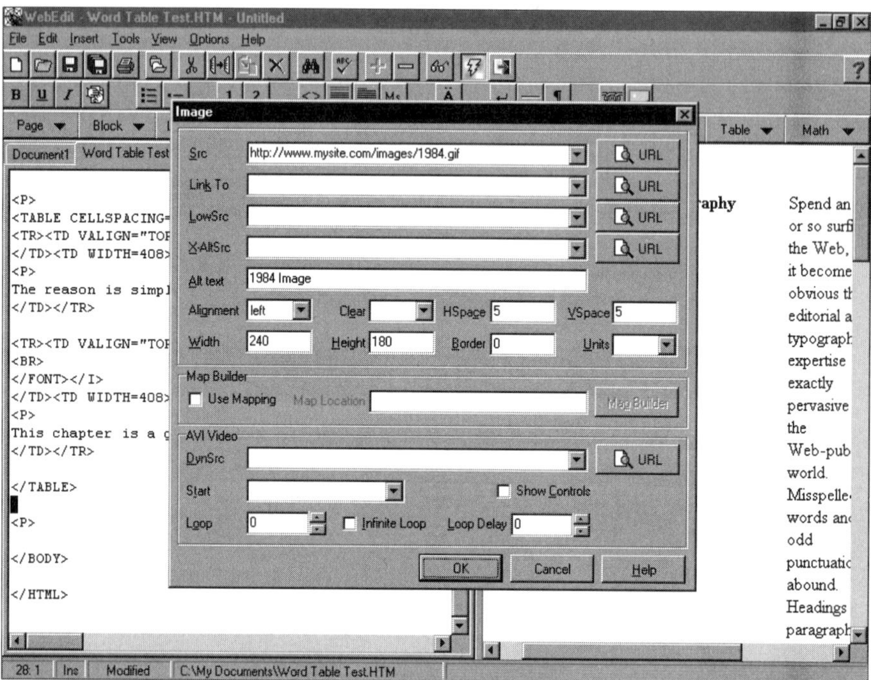

Figure 4-3: Pick a tag, any tag. Editing a page in Nesbitt Software's outstanding WebEdit Pro

- **They provide a fill-in-the-box approach to building tags with many attributes.** Many HTML tags accept numerous attributes. For example, the `<IMG>` tag, which displays a graphic, accepts optional attributes that specify the size of the graphic, its alignment, whether or not you want a border around the graphic, and more. Most HTML editors enable you to build these complex tags within dialog boxes that provide convenient access to all of the tag's attributes (see Figure 4-4).
- **They provide preview features.** Even HTML editors eventually let you see how a page will actually look. Some programs provide a preview feature that opens the page you're working on in the browser of your choice. Other programs provide a built-in preview function that displays a page in a separate window or alongside the HTML window. Still other programs provide both features.

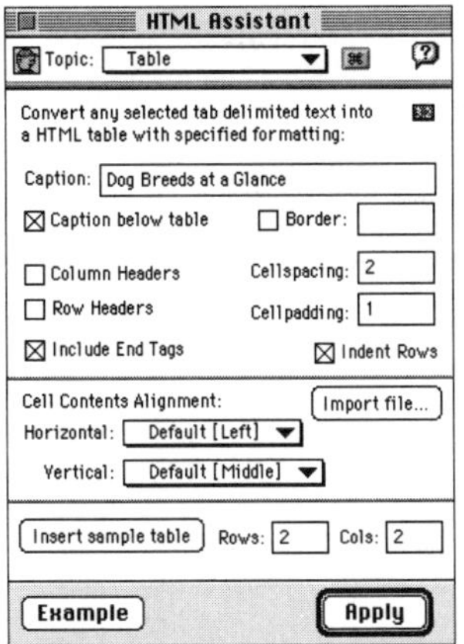

Figure 4-4: Building a tag in PageSpinner, an HTML editor for the Mac

HTML converters

HTML converters are designed to convert existing documents into HTML form. If you have a large number of documents that you want to adapt for the Web, or if you want to create Web pages using a program you've already mastered, an HTML converter is for you — provided you realize that your converted pages will probably need some tweaking in an HTML editor, and that an HTML converter doesn't support the broad range of advanced HTML formatting tags.

HTML converters come in several flavors, discussed in the sections that follow.

Export filters or plug-ins

Some HTML converters work within existing programs. As I mentioned earlier, Microsoft's Internet Assistant for Word turns Microsoft Word into an HTML-layout program. Microsoft also offers an Internet Assistant for its Excel spreadsheet program (Mac OS and Windows), and for its Access 97 database manager and Schedule+ calendar program (both for Windows only). The Internet Assistant for Access 97 is discussed in Chapter 10.

Adobe PageMaker's HTML Author plug-in module adds similar capabilities to PageMaker (see Figure 4-5), while Adobe's HoTaMaLe adds HTML export features to Adobe's document publishing program, FrameMaker. ClarisWorks, the popular Mac and Windows integrated software package from Claris, also includes HTML export features.

The pros

HTML export filters enable you to take advantage of your familiarity with a given program — and of the documents you've created with it. Rather than learning a new program, you can use all the commands and features you're familiar with to create new HTML pages and to convert your existing documents into HTML form.

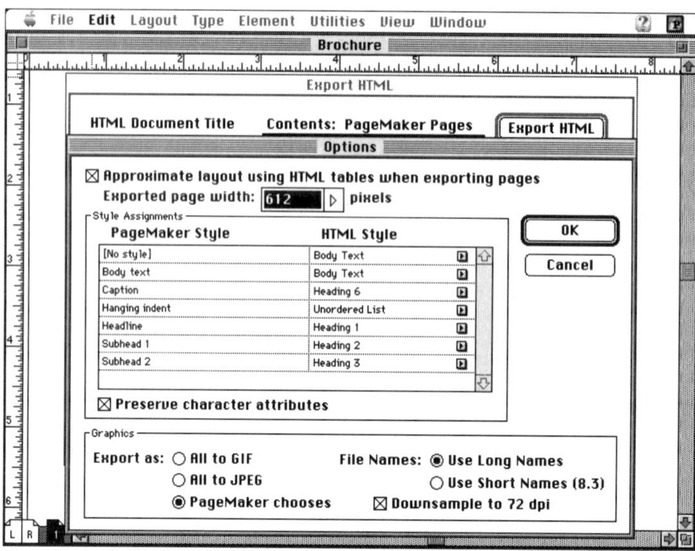

Figure 4-5: The HTML Author plug-in module enables a PageMaker publication to be converted to an HTML document.

Another advantage of HTML export filters is that they enable you to take advantage of the other features your application programs provide: features such as spelling checkers and file-format conversion. Goodies like these are often missing or limited in WYSIWYG and HTML editors, but they're common in word processors and publishing programs.

The cons

HTML export filters can be time-savers, but there are some serious drawbacks. For instance, you generally can't use the program within which you run the filter to edit the resulting HTML. You can't, for example, convert a PowerPoint presentation into HTML and then use PowerPoint to fine-tune the code. (As I show later, this drawback doesn't apply to Microsoft's Internet Assistant for Word, which does provide some powerful HTML-editing features.)

Also, HTML export filters operate within programs that contain much richer formatting capabilities than what HTML can support. You may be disappointed with the way a document with complex formatting looks after it's been converted into HTML. By comparison, a WYSIWYG or tag editor won't let you create any formatting that isn't supported by HTML.

And finally, export filters and converters don't provide the rich formatting and site-management features that you find in programs such as Adobe PageMill and SiteMill, Claris Home Page, NetObjects Fusion, or SoftQuad's

HoTMetaL Pro. Microsoft's Internet Assistant for Word, for example, doesn't let you specify the hot spots in a clickable image map, and no HTML plug-in enables you to track and update the hundreds of links present in a large site.

Stand-alone converters

This is an interesting breed of beast. Numerous programmers have created free or shareware programs that convert documents into HTML form. Many stand-alone converters operate on word processing documents, such as Microsoft Word files or WordPerfect files. Others convert documents saved in Rich Text Format (RTF), a format that many word processors and publishing programs can create. Still others convert PostScript files. Regardless of the input file formats they support, HTML converters all work in a similar manner: they read a file and translate its formatting into equivalent HTML.

Many stand-alone converters have special features that go beyond simple format conversion. For example, consider the shareware converter called RTFtoHTML, by Chris Hector. (It's included on the *HTML & Web Publishing SECRETS* CD-ROM and is also available at `http://www.sunpack.com/RTF/`.) If you format your RTF files in a specific way, the poetically named RTFtoHTML will automatically create a table of contents for the headings in a given document — a big time-saver.

Faster Formatting with RTFtoHTML

The RTFtoHTML utility automatically retains formatting elements such as bold, underlining, and italics. But the utility can do so much more — if you take a bit of time to prepare the files you want to convert.

The secret to automating formatting with RTFtoHTML is to use your word processor to assign style sheets to the elements of the document you want to convert. For example, all versions of Microsoft Word provide predefined styles called Heading 1, Heading 2, Heading 3, and so on. (Word uses these styles in its outline view.) If you assign these styles to the headings in your text files, RTFtoHTML will create a separate HTML file that contains a table of contents for the document you're converting (see Figure 4-6). You can then combine this table-of-contents file with the converted HTML file, or you can keep it separate.

Customizing RTFtoHTML

RTFtoHTML includes a special translation file that tells it how to translate paragraphs that have style sheets assigned to them. In the Windows version of RTFtoHTML, this translation file is named html-trn; in the Mac version, it's named html-trans. Regardless of its name, it works identically, and you can use any word processor or text editor to fine-tune the way RTFtoHTML performs its magic.

RTFtoHTML uses additional settings files that control other aspects of the translation process, such as how special characters (such as bullets) are translated. You'll find all the details in the program's online documentation.

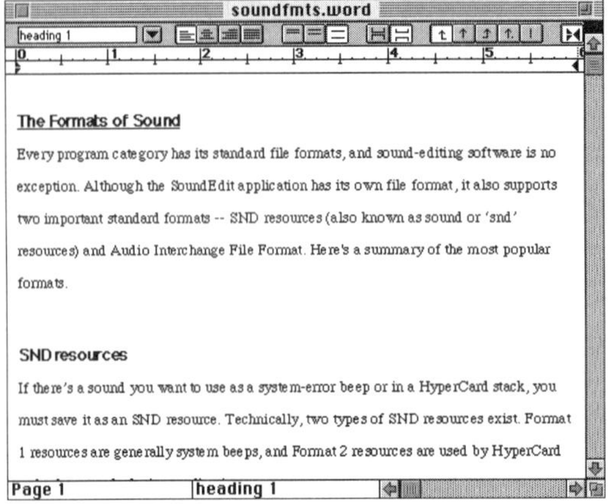

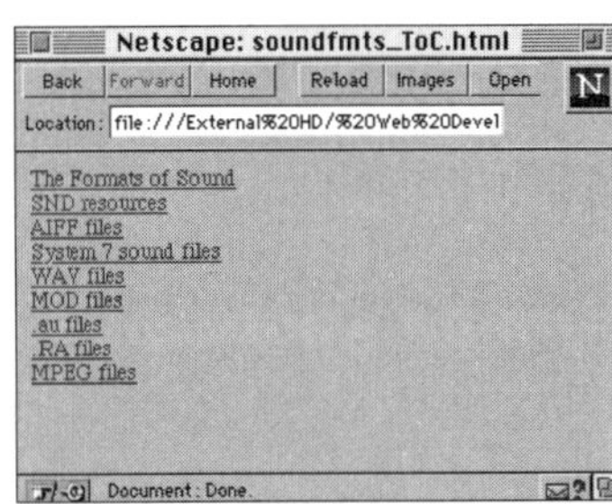

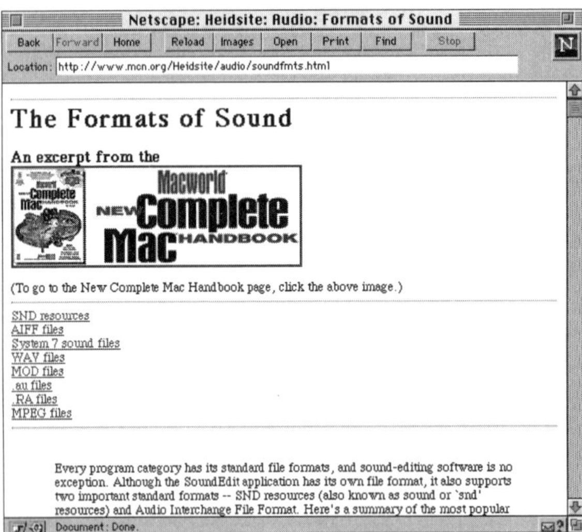

Figure 4-6: A typical RTFtoHTML session. Top: This Microsoft Word document contains headings formatted in Word's Heading styles. Middle: RTFtoHTML creates a separate HTML file containing a table of contents for each heading. Bottom: By combining the two files using the HTML editor of your choice, you can add a table of contents to the beginning of a lengthy page.

Printing to HTML: the amazing Myrmidon

If you use a Mac OS machine, there's a unique HTML converter you should know about: Terry Morse Software's Myrmidon (`http://www.terrymorse.com/`). Myrmidon can create an HTML page from any application that has a Print command — and it does a remarkably good job of preserving the document's formatting.

Myrmidon operates much like a printer driver. After installing it, select its icon in the Chooser. Next, go into any application program and use its Page Setup and Print commands to create an HTML page. The Page Setup dialog box enables you to customize Myrmidon's conversion settings; for example, you can tell Myrmidon to preserve the color of text and you can match point sizes to HTML `<FONT>` tag sizes. You can also have Myrmidon generate a linked table of contents and place it at the top of the HTML page.

When you choose an application program's Print command, the application thinks that it's sending a document to a printer. In reality, Myrmidon swings into action, converting the formatting data being generated by the application into HTML code. If the document contains graphics, Myrmidon converts them into GIF images and creates links to them.

ON CD-ROM

The *HTML & Web Publishing SECRETS* CD-ROM that accompanies this book contains a trial version of Myrmidon. Put it through its paces — you'll find it's a terrific way to quickly convert just about any document into HTML.

Oh, and what's up with the name? My Microsoft Bookshelf dictionary says *Myrmidon* is pronounced "meer-meh-don," and defines it as follows:

1. Greek Mythology: A member of a warlike Thessalian people who were ruled by Achilles and followed him on the expedition against Troy.
2. Myrmidon: A faithful follower who carries out orders without question.

I'm guessing that Terry Morse had the second definition in mind.

Optical character recognition programs

Converters are convenient when you want to adapt existing electronic files to the Web, but what about those reams of paper documents that you want to put on a site? You have to hire a typist to peck them into a word processor, and then convert the files into HTML, right?

Wrong. If you have a scanner, you can choose between two OCR programs that support HTML: Caere Corporation's OmniPage Pro (Windows and Mac OS) and Xerox's AccuText (Windows and Mac OS). Both programs can scan formatted pages and generate HTML files from them, keeping the same formatting. For example, text that's bold in the paper document is formatted in bold in the HTML file, as shown in Figure 4-7.

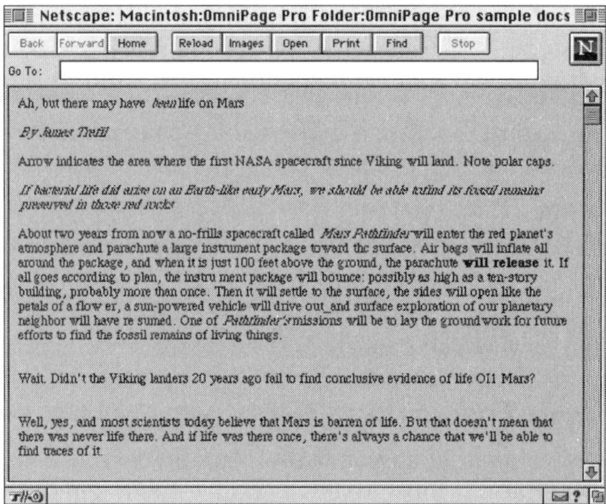

Figure 4-7: From paper to pixels — a paper document (top) and its Web page (bottom), generated by Caere's OmniPage Pro

OCR programs aren't Web-publishing panaceas. You'll want to set aside time to carefully proofread the text the programs generate, as OCR packages are prone to subtle mistakes that typists don't make — such as interpreting the letter *S* as the numeral *5*. What's more, OCR programs generally don't support advanced HTML formatting, such as tables.

But these drawbacks aside, if you have a stack of paper that wants to ride the Web bandwagon, OmniPage Pro and AccuText will give you a big head start.

Site-building tools

HTML layout programs, editors, and converters are great for creating single pages, but a Web site might consist of dozens or hundreds of pages or more, all linked to each other and to external sites. As terrific as HTML layout and editor programs are, they don't help with the larger picture of site management: keeping track of the links on a large site, checking external links to verify that those pages are still available, and making it easier to obtain consistent navigation and design schemes across many pages.

For jobs like these, you might consider a *site-building* program. Site builders provide HTML-layout features for designing individual pages, but they also provide the types of site-management features that I just described. Some of the features you might find in a site-building program include the following:

- **Hierarchical site displays.** You can view your site as a list of pages. Some programs, such as Adobe SiteMill, organize a site in outline form; others, such as NetObjects Fusion, display a site as a tree chart (see Figure 4-8).
- **Internal link management.** If you change the name of a page or move it to a different directory, the program updates other pages containing links to it.
- **External link management.** You can have the program attempt to contact remote Web sites to which you've created links. If the program is unsuccessful, you can choose to remove or correct the link.
- **Global formatting and editing.** Some programs enable you to define standard navigation elements that appear on all pages. If you change the element, the program automatically updates it on all pages where it appears — a tremendous time-saver. Some programs also provide search-and-replace features that work across an entire site: great for when your company changes its name.
- **Advanced publishing features.** Some site-building programs also provide advanced features, such as built-in database managers that hold frequently changing information, or the ability to connect to external database managers such as Microsoft Access, or wizards that enable you to create conferencing systems (further discussed in Chapter 9).
- **File-uploading features.** Most programs enable you to automatically transfer your site — or just those pages that you've changed since the last update — to a service provider.

In this section, I spotlight a few site-building programs and contrast their features and differences in approach.

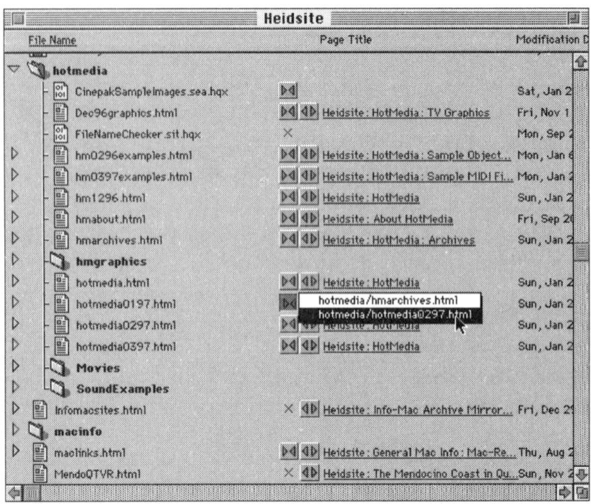

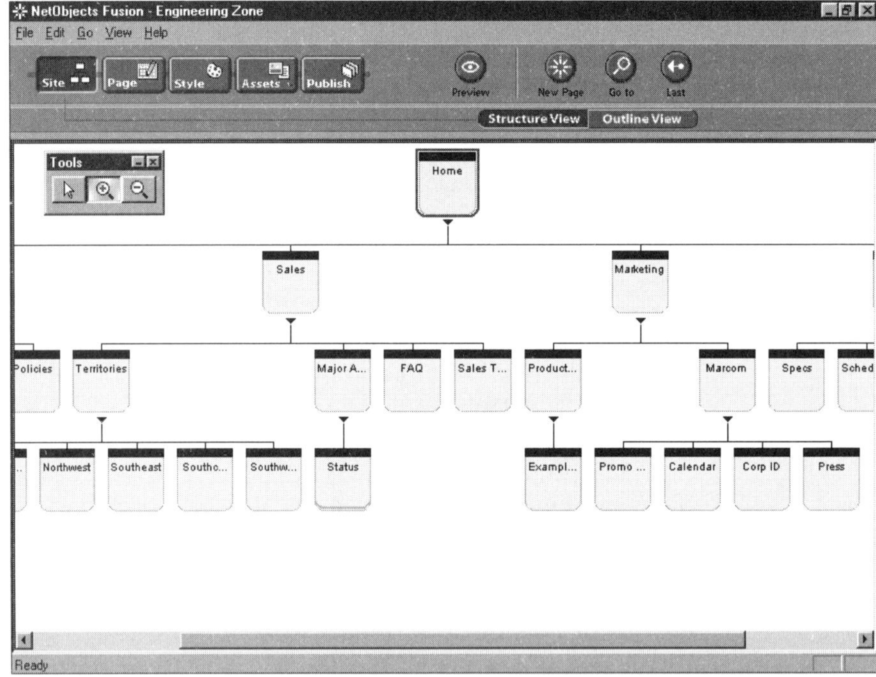

Figure 4-8: The big picture: A Web site as seen through Adobe SiteMill (top) and NetObjects Fusion (bottom)

Adobe SiteMill

Adobe SiteMill, available for only the Mac OS at this writing, concentrates on managing links and transferring pages to a Web server. SiteMill doesn't provide global formatting aids or built-in database publishing tools; indeed, SiteMill 2.x doesn't even provide HTML-layout features. SiteMill 1.x provided layout features identical to those of PageMill 1.x, but Adobe removed these features in SiteMill 2.x, instead adding a link feature that enables you to launch your favorite HTML editor when you double-click on a page in SiteMill.

SiteMill 2.x is also tightly integrated with PageMill 2.x — you can drag URLs between the two programs and drag page icons from SiteMill into PageMill. This division-of-labor approach makes sense: use PageMill to build your pages, and SiteMill to manage the big picture.

SiteMill does a good job of verifying external links. An External URLs window shows all the external links in a site, and you can verify them all at once or one by one (see Figure 4-9).

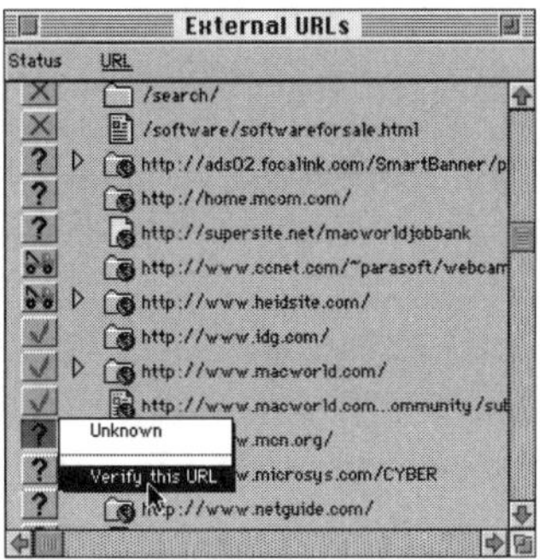

Figure 4-9: SiteMill's External Links window. The icons adjacent to the links indicate whether the link is still valid, broken, or unchecked.

With SiteMill's site window, you can view the structure of a site; icons next to each page indicate whether that page has internal links, external links, or both. The icons are actually pop-up menus: click on one and hold down the mouse button, and a list of linked pages appears.

Microsoft FrontPage 97

FrontPage 97 is an ambitious site-building package that combines HTML layout and link management with advanced server options for database publishing and conferencing. (FrontPage 97's database publishing features are discussed in Chapter 10.)

FrontPage 97 relies heavily on wizards that walk you through the process of creating sites. The program includes wizards for building a variety of common types of sites and pages: a personal site, a site for scheduling projects, a registration system for conferences, a guestbook page, and more. For processing forms and handling tasks such as database access, FrontPage 97 includes server extensions that work with all popular Windows and Mac OS servers. (Both the Windows and Mac OS versions of FrontPage 97 also include personal Web servers.)

SECRET

No Missing Links: Link-Checking Utilities

One of Adobe SiteMill's strengths is its ability to check and verify not only links within a site, but also links to external sites. Link-checking, also called *link-verification,* eliminates the need for you to manually click on every link in your site — a chore that ranks between flossing and rotating your car's tires on the Fun Things to Do scale.

Besides SiteMill, several link-checking utilities are available, including the following:

- HTML Power Analyzer (Windows), part of the HTML Power Tools package from OppoSite Software (`http://www.opposite.com/`). A trial version of HTML Power Tools is included on the *HTML & Web Publishing SECRETS* CD-ROM that accompanies this book.
- InfoLink Link Checker (Windows), from Biggbyte Software (`http://www.biggbyte.com/`).
- SiteCheck (Windows and Mac OS), from Pacific Coast Software (`http://www.pacific-coast.com/`).
- HTML Link Checker (Mac OS), from Nisseb Software (`http://www.calles.pp.se/nisseb/html_linkchecker.html`).

Broken links annoy visitors and reflect poorly on your site. If you frequently reorganize or add to your site — and particularly if your site contains a lot of links to external sites — run a link checker regularly.

In FrontPage 97, your work is divided between the FrontPage Explorer, which depicts the overall structure of a site; and the FrontPage Editor, which enables you to create and edit individual pages (see Figure 4-10).

FrontPage 97 can import a much larger array of file formats than most HTML tools. Besides enabling you to import and convert several word processor formats, FrontPage 97 can import graphics in TIFF, BMP, EPS, and other formats and convert them to GIF or JPEG files. (For the lowdown on Web graphics, see Chapter 6.) FrontPage 97 also includes a library of clip art and a graphics package, the Microsoft Image Composer, that enables you to create collages and optimize graphics for fast downloading.

SECRET

FrontPage 97 is available for both the Windows and Mac OS platforms (the Mac OS version was in beta testing at this writing), but the Windows version is the better program. The Mac OS version is hampered by its reliance on Microsoft's Object Linking and Embedding (OLE) technology, which lets you drag and drop text and graphics between Microsoft applications — but that's all. You can't, for instance, drag and drop links from Netscape Navigator or even from Microsoft's own Internet Explorer, which uses the Mac OS's drag-and-drop technology. You can learn more about FrontPage 97 at `http://www.microsoft.com/frontpage/`.

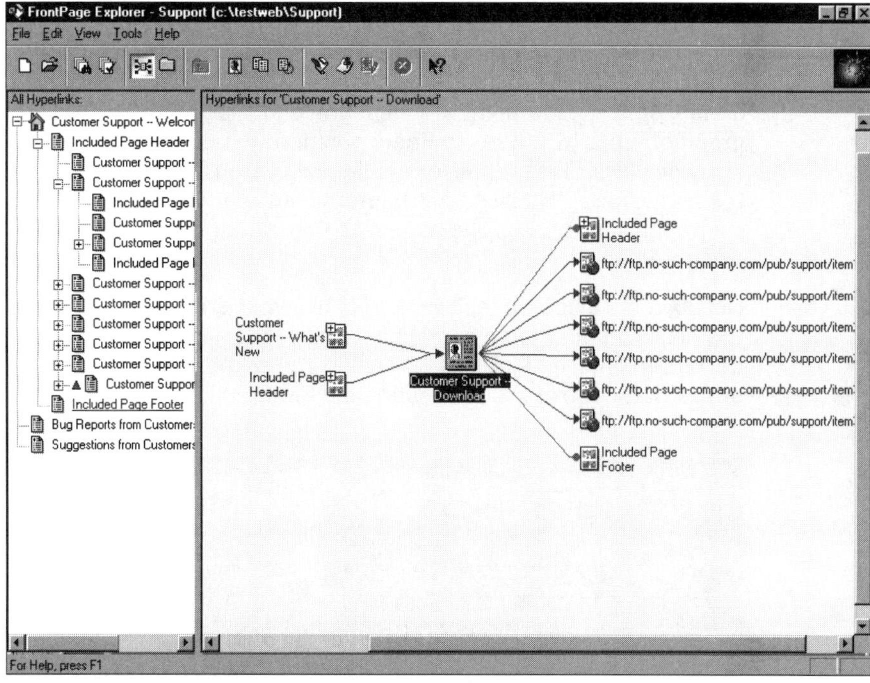

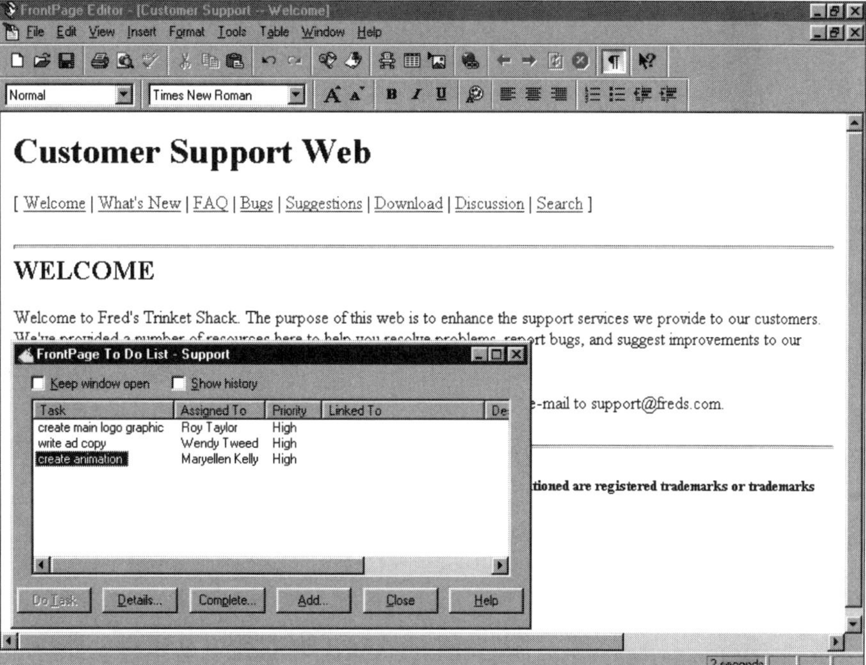

Figure 4-10: The Microsoft FrontPage Explorer (top) and FrontPage Editor (bottom)

NetObjects Fusion

Every HTML layout tool I've described so far provides a word-processor-like interface. That is, when you create a new HTML page, you're presented with a blinking insertion point at which you can type, create a table, or insert a graphic. When you want to finely position text or graphics, you must struggle with HTML tables or single-pixel GIFs (both of these spacing-control techniques are discussed in Chapters 5 and 6). You can't drag blocks of text or graphics around on the screen as you can in a publishing or drawing program.

ON CD-ROM

NetObjects Fusion doesn't have this drawback. Fusion is the first program that lets you position elements by simply dragging them to their destinations (see Figure 4-11). Behind the scenes, Fusion creates HTML tables that control the elements' positioning.

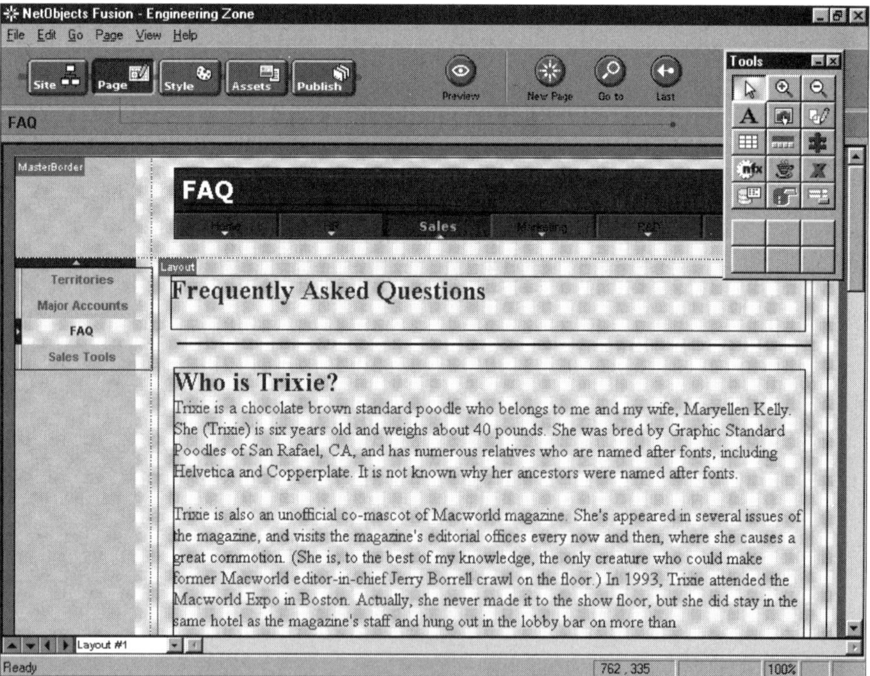

Figure 4-11: Click and drag HTML layout with NetObjects Fusion

Fusion's MasterBorder feature makes it easy to create consistent page banners and navigation elements. Like the header and footer of a word processor, the MasterBorder area of the Fusion layout window holds elements that you want to repeat on each page. But unlike any word processor, Fusion extends the concept to include the left margin of the page, making it easy to create, say, a navigation bar that runs down the left edge of each page.

Fusion's talents don't end with page layout. You can create *site styles* — templates that control the appearance of banners, buttons, links, and page backgrounds — or choose one of the more than 50 styles included with Fusion (many of which are corny looking, sad to say).

With Fusion's Assets window, you can keep track of the graphics, movies, sounds, and other media elements used in your site. And you can update them. If the company logo changes, for instance, just replace its graphic in the Assets window, and Fusion updates all pages in which the logo appears. Fusion also provides thorough site-management features, including external link checking, built-in file uploading, and an attractive hierarchical site map (see Figure 4-12).

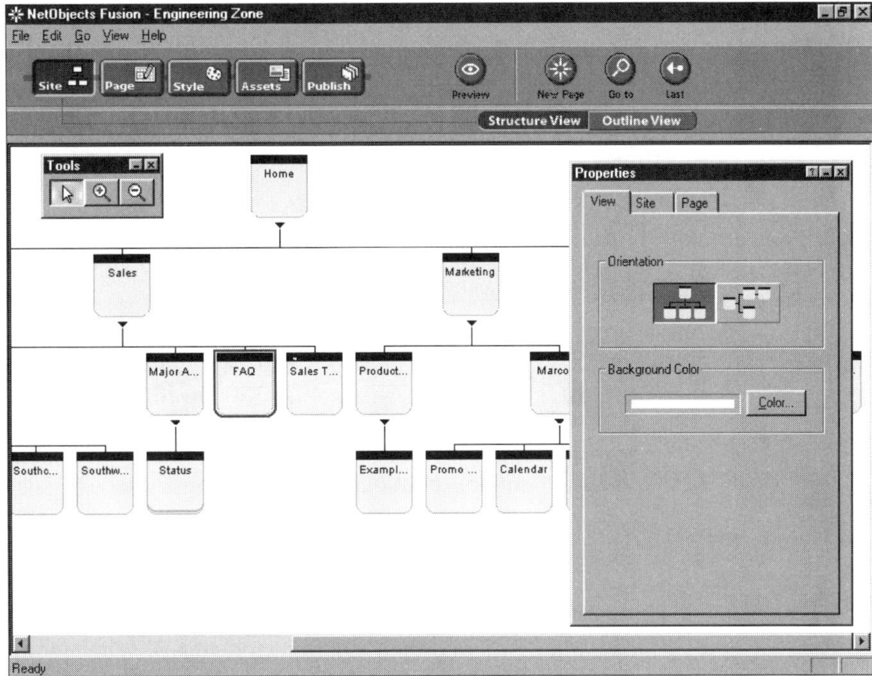

Figure 4-12: The big picture: NetObject Fusion's site map display

Fusion also contains excellent database publishing features. You can use a built-in database to store text and graphics, or tap into external databases such as Microsoft Access. See Chapter 10 for a look at database publishing with Fusion.

You'll find some more coverage of Fusion in Chapter 10. To learn more about the program, visit NetObjects' Web site at `http://www.netobjects.com/`.

Other contenders

Some additional site-building tools you might want to investigate include the following:

- **Macromedia's Windows-based Backstage family** (`http://www.macromedia.com/`) provides strong database-publishing features and the ability to create discussion groups, forms-handling routines, and display dynamic content such as page counters and the current date and time.
- **HAHT Software's Windows-based HAHTsite** (`http://www.taht.com/`) combines visual HTML editing with strong database publishing, dynamic page generation, and scripting features.
- **DeltaPoint's QuickSite** (`http://www.deltapoint.com/`) relies on templates and page wizards to provide consistent navigation schemes and painless page building. QuickSite doesn't provide WYSIWYG page editing; you build pages by choosing options in dialog boxes. If you prefer to be able to manipulate page elements in a more direct manner, QuickSite isn't for you. QuickSite is available for Mac OS and Windows machines alike.
- **GoLive Systems' Mac OS-based CyberStudio** (`http://www.golive.com/`) provides five modules in which you can drag and drop elements; view HTML in an outline mode; create JavaScripts; and view graphical maps of a site's structure.
- **Corel's Windows-based WebMaster Suite for Windows** (`http://www.corel.com/`) includes Corel's WEB.DESIGNER, which provides solid layout HTML layout features. Also included in this impressive bundle is O'Reilly & Associates's outstanding WebSite server software (discussed in Chapters 10 and 17); Corel WEB.DATA, a database-publishing package; and a massive collection of clip art.

The bad news about site-building programs

Although most site-building tools provide a broad range of features, these features often don't go as far as their counterparts in stand-alone programs. And you may find a site-building program's obsessive reliance on structure to be constraining. Too many site-building programs effectively say, "Do things my way or not at all."

If your HTML and graphic design experience is limited, a site-building program such as NetObjects Fusion might be perfect. But if you sleep with a T-square and dream in HTML — or if you're part of a Web-development team consisting of designers, HTML coders, and server managers — you might prefer to assemble your own site-building toolbox, picking and choosing the best HTML editors, link-management utilities, database publishing add-ons, and so on.

Assembling your HTML toolbox

A well-stocked HTML toolbox combines programs from each of the categories I've described. In the course of a typical project, you might do any of the following:

- Create the initial design of a page in Adobe PageMill, and then hand-tweak its code in BBEdit or WebEdit Pro
- Save a collection of word processor files as RTF documents, translate them into HTML with an RTF-to-HTML converter, and then open the results in HoTMetaL Pro or another HTML editor for final tweaking
- Convert a document into an HTML page using Myrmidon, and then apply advanced formatting using Claris Home Page
- Scan paper documents, convert their text into HTML using OmniPage Pro, and then import that HTML file into NetObjects Fusion

No single HTML tool can meet every page-creation challenge. Smart Web developers combine tools from every category to take advantage of each tool's strengths.

Online Resources for HTML Tools

As you might expect, the online world is a goldmine for information about the HTML tools discussed in this chapter. Here's a summary of some of the best online information sources for popular programs.

Adobe PageMill. The PageMill-Talk mailing list, operated by Blue World Communications, is where PageMill users exchange tips and techniques. Representatives from Adobe join in frequently to respond to questions and criticism. To join, visit `http://www.blueworld.com/lists/pagemill-talk/`.

Claris Home Page. Blue World Communications also operates a mailing list devoted to Home Page. To join, aim that browser of yours to `http://www.blueworld.com/lists/homepage/`.

HoTMetaL Pro. SoftQuad offers an array of support services for its HoTMetaL Pro editor — but to use them, you must register the software first. (You can do so online or the old-fashioned way: by sending in your registration card.) Once you've registered, you can enter the HoTMetaL Pro support area by going to `http://www.sq.com/supportcentre/support.htm`. There you'll find tips, frequently asked questions, software updates, and the Metalworkers Forum, a discussion area where you can trade questions and answers with fellow, um, metalworkers.

Microsoft FrontPage. Microsoft's Web site contains an extensive support area for FrontPage, which is located at `http://www.microsoft.com/frontpage/`.

NetObjects Fusion. NetObjects operates several newsgroups where you can post questions about NetObjects Fusion and read about other users' experiences with the program. You can get to the newsgroups and to other sources of support for Fusion by going to the NetObjects home page at `http://www.netobjects.com/` and then clicking on the Support button.

Different strokes: Coda and QuarkImmedia

As designers clamor for more control over the appearance of Web pages, new products are emerging that bypass HTML entirely and take their own approach to page presentation.

RandomNoise's Coda

One such product is Coda, from RandomNoise (`http://www.randomnoise.com/`). Coda is the first Web-design tool constructed completely in Java: you run Coda's design application within Netscape Navigator or Microsoft Internet Explorer. Coda provides far more control over page design and user interface elements than does HTML. You can create animated buttons that flash when the mouse pointer moves over them and that play sounds when a user clicks them. You can create flipbook-style animations that go well beyond the capabilities of an animated GIF file (discussed in Chapter 12). And you can position text and graphics with precision (see Figure 4-13).

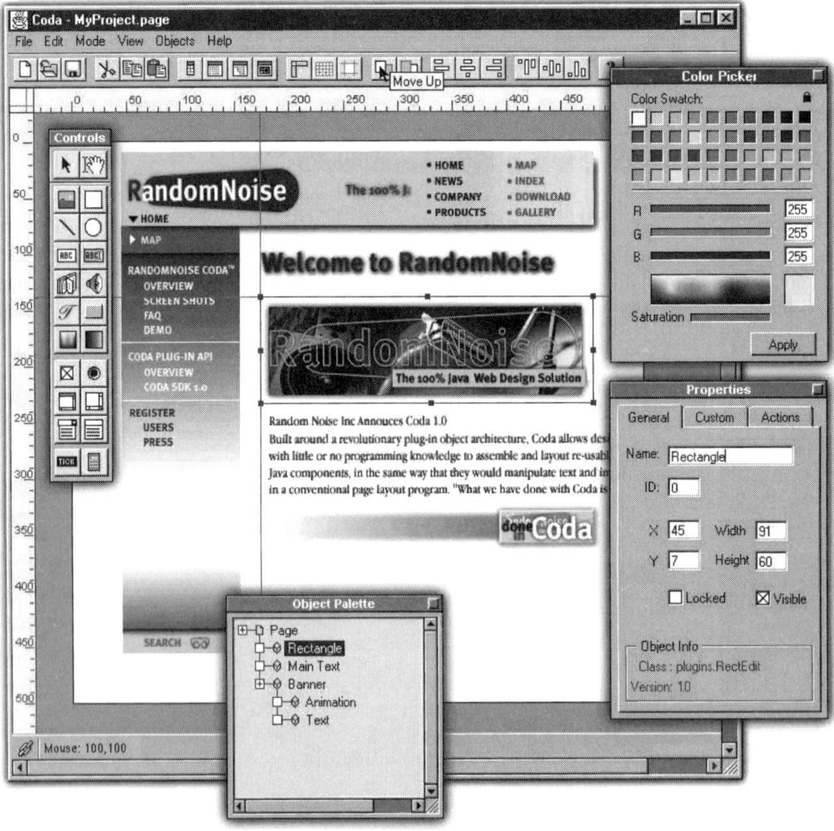

Figure 4-13: A new way to build pages — RandomNoise's Coda

The end result of a session with Coda is a Java applet that runs on any Java-supporting browser. That's right: The Coda design program runs under Java, and so do the pages that you create with Coda. Coda (and the pages you create with it) run on any Java-supporting platform. It's a cool new approach and it shows a lot of promise.

Coda takes advantage of Java's object-oriented nature by being extensible. You can add authoring features by dropping in new Java objects. New objects are automatically added to Coda's Control palette.

Coda is clearly pushing the envelope — alas, the envelope is pushing back a bit. Although Java is platform-independent language, it runs better on some platforms than on others. At this writing, Windows provides better Java support than does the Mac OS (this will hopefully change over time as newer browsers appear and as Apple continues to integrate Java into the Mac OS).

And even on Windows, there's variation among browsers. As of early 1997, Microsoft Internet Explorer is a better browser for viewing Coda-built sites; it's able to cache the Java run-time software that's necessary to view Coda-built pages. With Netscape Navigator 3.x, a visitor must either download the run-time each time (which takes about a minute on a 28.8Kbps modem), or run a special installer program.

But these drawbacks are side effects of Java's relative immaturity. As it evolves, Coda stands a chance of becoming a major player in Web authoring.

Quark's QuarkImmedia

If you have any print publishing experience, you're undoubtedly familiar with Quark Inc.'s QuarkXPress publishing program. QuarkImmedia extends QuarkXPress to the Web.

QuarkImmedia is an extension for QuarkXPress that adds multimedia authoring features. With QuarkImmedia installed, you can use QuarkXPress to create interactive productions containing movies, sounds, and animations as well as buttons and hot spots that play multimedia elements and branch to other screens when clicked. QuarkImmedia also enables you to create hybrid CD-ROM/Web projects: you can use QuarkImmedia to create an interactive CD-ROM that contains links to content stored on Web sites. And you have all the wonderful typographic control that QuarkXPress is known for — and that HTML lacks.

The primary drawback to QuarkImmedia is that visitors must download the QuarkImmedia Player, a browser plug-in, before they can view any sites created with QuarkImmedia. This is where RandomNoise's Coda has a real edge: once the various Java-related wrinkles I mentioned are ironed out, any visitor whose browser supports Java can view Coda-built pages without first having to download a plug-in.

Still, QuarkImmedia is a powerful package well worth investigating, particularly if you're a QuarkXPress user and need that program's legendary typographic control. You can download a trial version of QuarkImmedia from Quark's Web site, at `http://www.quark.com/`.

HTML Tool Secrets

This section is a collection of tips and secrets for the top HTML editing tools. These tips relate to the overall operation of each program. For tips on using these programs for specific tasks — creating image maps, working with frames and tables, modifying graphics, and so on — see the chapters that discuss these topics specifically, or just look for the product's name in the index at the back of this book.

Adobe PageMill secrets

PageMill was the first WYSIWYG HTML editor, and it remains one of the best. Unless otherwise noted, the following tips apply to all versions of PageMill.

Duplicating elements

If you've crafted a complex set of elements and you want to create a similar set elsewhere on the page (or on a different page), you can duplicate the elements by selecting them and then pressing the Option key (Mac) or Ctrl key (Windows) while dragging the elements.

Don't forget the pasteboard

PageMill's pasteboard is a work area that can hold just about anything: text (with or without links), graphics, tables (PageMill 2.x only), and any combination of the above.

The pasteboard is a great place to store items that you use on multiple pages — such as navigation bars or frequently used links. To put something on the pasteboard, select it and then drag it to the pasteboard. To move an item from the pasteboard into a page, select the item and drag it to the spot you want it to appear. If you'd like to keep a copy of the item on the pasteboard — perhaps to insert elsewhere — press Option (Mac) or Ctrl (Windows) and then drag.

Creating a "super pasteboard"

You can also use a PageMill document as a pasteboard. Just choose New Page from the File menu, and you get a blank, untitled document in which you can stash items. Want another super pasteboard? Choose New Page again. The advantage of this approach is that you can have multiple virtual pasteboards open at once and save each one on disk.

Extracting links from your bookmarks file

The previous tip combines nicely with this one. Say you've been surfing the Web as a prelude to putting together a page of links, and you've created bookmarks for the sites that you want to link to. Open up your browser's bookmarks file in PageMill, and then drag the links to the page you're constructing — no retyping, no copying and pasting, no inaccurate links. (*Note:* Don't edit or save your bookmarks file using PageMill; doing so may alter it in a way that will prevent your browser from reading it.)

Opening pages in edit mode (2.x)

Want PageMill to be in its editing mode when you open a page? Choose Preferences from the File menu and, from the Open Pages In pop-up menu, choose Edit Mode.

PageMill and pretty printing

Later in this chapter, I discuss the advantages of pretty printing — formatting your HTML code to make it more legible. If you're a PageMill user, don't bother taking the time to pretty-print your HTML; when you save a page, PageMill discards extra spaces, tabs, carriage returns, and the like, and formats the page's HTML in its own, rather bland way.

Another way to create tables (2.x)

PageMill 2.x contains features for creating HTML tables (discussed in more detail in Chapter 7), but if you're a Microsoft Excel veteran, there's another way to make tables: create them in Excel and then paste them into PageMill. In Excel, copy the range of cells you want to transfer, and then choose Copy from the Edit menu. Then, switch to PageMill, position the blinking insertion point where you want the table to appear, and choose Paste.

Note that PageMill doesn't retain cell formatting, such as bold type or bordered cells. To transfer Excel tables *and* retain formatting, you might want to use Microsoft's Internet Assistant for Excel, which is described later in this chapter.

PageMill and plug-ins (2.x)

One of the many breakthroughs in PageMill 2.x includes support for Netscape Navigator plug-ins, those software expansion modules that enable Navigator (and plug-in compatible browsers, such as Microsoft Internet Explorer) to work with new data types, such as QuickTime movies, virtual reality models, Macromedia Director Shockwave projects, and much more. This enables to you work with these next-generation data types using the same drag-and-drop simplicity that PageMill applies to simple text and graphics. Just copy the plug-ins you need to the folder called Browser Plug-ins (it's located within the Plug-ins folder, which lives inside the PageMill folder).

It's worth noting that PageMill supports more than just Netscape plug-ins. PageMill 2.0 introduced a PageMill plug-in format designed to enable developers to extend PageMill's features. The Macintosh version of PageMill 2.x includes a plug-in that simplifies creating tags for use with Maxum Development's NetCloak software (discussed in Chapter 16). Check Adobe's Web site at `http://www.adobe.com/` for information about plug-ins that are currently available.

URL entries made easier (2.x)

When you're typing a URL into the link bar at the bottom of the document window, PageMill cuts down the number of keystrokes by completing parts of the URL for you. Type the first letter of the URL's protocol (for example,

h for http or **f** for ftp) and press the right-arrow key, and PageMill completes the protocol for you, all the way down to the double-slashes. Press the right arrow again, and PageMill adds the *www* prefix to the domain name.

PageMill can also add a suffix (com, org, net, edu) to a URL. Type the period that precedes the suffix and then press right arrow, and PageMill adds the com suffix. If you want a different suffix, press right arrow until the desired suffix appears.

This all sounds complicated, but it's easy. Here's how you might use the shortcut feature to create a link to `http://www.heidsite.com`:

1. Type **h** and then press the right arrow key twice.
2. Type **heidsite** and a period (.), and then press the right arrow key again.

That's all there is to it.

Just what is a naturalsizeflag?!

If you've examined the HTML that PageMill creates, you've probably seen the `naturalsizeflag` attribute, which PageMill includes in every single `<IMG>` tag. What's the story behind it? The following description was posted by the PageMill product manager on the wonderful PageMill-Talk mailing list, a list every PageMill user should subscribe to. (For details on this and other lists relating to HTML editors, see the Secrets sidebar, "Online Resources for HTML Tools," earlier in this chapter.)

> This tag is used only by PageMill, and our testing shows it to be benign in browsers and many parsers. The use of this tag stems from the fact that PageMill always writes out height and width attributes on every image, because it makes the browser run faster if your HTML file declares the width and height (the browser can lay out the page without having to wait for the image to be loaded). The problem comes with this scenario:
>
> 1. Drag image onto page. You choose not to scale or resize it.
> 2. Save. PageMill writes out the explicit height and width of the image.
> 3. Update the image in an image editor or switch files in the finder, so the image dimensions change.
> 4. Reopen the file in PageMill.
>
> Here's the question — which dimensions should it display the new logo file with? Should PageMill use the explicit dimensions that were written out with the file, or should it change the dimensions to prevent squishing the image?
>
> HTML doesn't make a distinction between "here's the exact height and width that I want this image to be scaled to" and "here's the image's natural height and width just as a hint to make the browser run faster." However, people use the height and width ability of HTML to serve both purposes.
>
> The `naturalsizeflag` makes that distinction. It tells PageMill whether you explicitly set that dimension (either through the attribute inspector or by interactively resizing the image), or whether PageMill wrote out the height and width

for browser speed. If you scaled the image, then PageMill will force the updated image into the dimensions indicated in the HTML file; if not, we'll resize the image and write out new height and width values.

`naturalsizeflag` can have four values:

0 — user explicitly set height and width; use those numbers (squish)

1 — user set height explicitly, width can change freely

2 — user set width explicitly, height can change freely

3 — user hasn't set and specific size, both dimensions can change.

Typically, you'll see just 0 or 3.

Claris Home Page secrets

For a while, Adobe PageMill had the drag-and-drop, WYSIWYG editing field all to itself. Claris Home Page changed that. Home Page provides solid support for HTML 3.2 extensions such as tables, and also supports frames. Here are some general Home Page tips and secrets. Check the index at the back of the book to find Home Page secrets for specific Web chores, such as working with graphics or tables.

SECRET

File Naming Tips for All HTML Editors

Regardless of the HTML editor you use, to ensure that your pages' file names are compatible with any computer platform and server, follow these rules for file naming:

- **Use only alphanumeric characters.** For example, use a-z, A-Z, 0-9 and the underscore. Don't use spaces, quote marks, or special characters such as ü.
- **Use consistent uppercase and lowercase spelling for filenames.** UNIX-based servers are case-sensitive: they'll interpret Alpha.html and alpha.html as different files. If you're using a program such as PageMill that enables you to create links by dragging and dropping, you won't have to worry, because the program will supply the name exactly as it's stored on disk. But keep this rule in mind if you embark on a file-renaming chore. In general, it's best to stick with all-lowercase letters in your HTML filenames.
- **Keep filenames relatively short — under 30 or so characters.** (If you're using Windows 3.1, follow the 8 by 3 convention; for example, filename.htm).
- **Always use the appropriate file extension.** Use html for HTML pages (for Windows 3.1 servers, use .htm); gif for GIF images; and jpg for JPEG images. You'll find naming tips for other file formats, such as audio and digital video clips, in later chapters.

After you've begun creating links to files, don't move them to other folders, rename, or delete them. Doing so will break links, and your site's visitors will see annoying "Error 404 — file not found" error messages. (Note that site-management and link-checking software such as Adobe SiteMill can check and often fix problems such as these.)

Duplicating items

As in Adobe PageMill, you can duplicate one or more items by selecting it or them and then pressing Option (Mac) or Ctrl (Windows) while dragging the item or items.

Object Editor secrets

Chances are you spend a lot of time in Home Page's Object Editor window (where you specify such attributes as image size and alignment, table dimensions, horizontal rule dimensions, and form elements).

To display the Object Editor to modify an item, double-click the item you want to modify. You don't have to close the Object Editor when you've finished editing an object. Just click elsewhere in the page you're editing, and the Object Editor window shrinks to a smaller size. You might drag it off to an unused corner of your screen, or, if you have a Mac OS machine equipped with multiple monitors, to an adjacent monitor. When you want to edit another object, double-click the object, and the Object Editor window expands to reflect that object's characteristics.

Visiting the library

Home Page's answer to PageMill's pasteboard is the *library* — a special type of document in which you can stash frequently used items. Several attributes make Home Page's library feature much more convenient and powerful than PageMill's pasteboard feature, such as the following:

- **Naming items.** When you drag an item into the library window, Home Page gives it a name that begins with "untitled." Select the name and type a descriptive label for the item, such as "logo graphic" or "navigation table." This makes it easy to find and retrieve items.
- **Working with multiple library files.** You can create as many library files as you like and switch between them using the File menu's Open command. You might create one library file for often used graphics, another for often used text items, and still another for frequently used links. You can move an item from one library into another by dragging it to the destination library.
- **Editing within the library window.** You can create new page elements directly within the library window: choose New Entry from the Library menu, and then use Home Page's editing and formatting features as you normally would.
- **Swapping libraries across platforms.** If you use both Mac OS and Windows machines, you'll be glad to know you can swap libraries between the Mac OS and Windows versions of Home Page. But there's an important caveat to keep in mind if you use libraries to hold images: Home Page doesn't actually store an image in a library; rather, it stores a *link* to the image. If you transfer a library file to a different machine, Home Page won't actually transfer the image.

Sanitizing Home Page's HTML

Like Adobe PageMill, Claris Home Page adds a variety of HTML comments and specialized tags to your pages. These comments won't cause problems in browsers, but they can cause an HTML validation program to raise its red flags.

If you'd prefer to omit Home Page's comments and tags, choose Preferences from the Edit menu and then click the HTML Output tab. Then, uncheck the box labeled Generate X-SAS Tags. To fine tune (or remove) the HTML comment that Home Page puts in a page's header area, use the Header Comment pop-up menu.

Symantec Visual Page secrets

Visual Page arrived late to the HTML layout party, but it turned a few heads when it got there. For starters, Visual Page provides more powerful table-editing features than either PageMill 2.x or Home Page 2.0 — and as Chapter 5 describes, tables are popular devices for page formatting. Visual Page enables you to apply formatting changes to all cells of a table at once. And I love the way it reformats line endings on the fly as you resize a table or frame.

I also like the way Visual Page lets you display both a WYSIWYG editing window and an HTML editing window at the same time, rather than having to toggle between them as you must in PageMill or Home Page. While Visual Page 1.0 lacks site-management features such as link checking, it does provide a handy Site Window that shows the hierarchy of a site and enables you to open a page or graphic by double-clicking its name. And it has first-rate FTP upload and download features.

Enough raving — here's a collection of tips for Visual Page.

The ultimate View Source command

HTML coders do it all the time. You see a great-looking page and use your browser's View Source command to see how it was done. Visual Page lets you go a step further and actually download an HTML page — including its graphics — from any remote Web site. Just choose Download Remote File from the File menu, and type the file's URL in the dialog box that appears. If the file is a home page, just type the domain name — for example, `http://www.nytimes.com/`. (And as with most browsers, you can omit the http:// part and just type `www.whatever.com`.)

After you type the URL and press Return, Visual Page presents a Save dialog box. Type a name for the file, press Return, and sit back. After the download is complete, Visual Page opens a new document window containing the page; its graphics are saved in the same folder where you saved the page itself.

Keep in mind that you've downloaded copyrighted material. Go ahead and scarf up your favorite pages to see how they were done, but don't go posting someone else's efforts on your site.

By the way, the ability to download a remote file is also handy when you're on the road and need to update a specific page on your own site. Just download it, make your changes, and then repost it.

The hints in hard copy

Visual Page adds a Hints command to the Apple menu. Choose it, and a window appears containing useful, if awkwardly written, tips. One problem: You can't try out the tips unless you close the window, and Visual Page doesn't include the tips in printed form.

So, it is with great pleasure that I present Table 4-1, which presents the best hints in an easy to read form — *on paper!*

Table 4-1 Visual Page hints

To Do This	*Do This*
Open a document referred to in a URL	Press Control and click on the link
Display a pop-up menu containing a list of the anchors on a page	Press Control and click on a selected (but not linked) text or image
Select all of a link	Triple-click on it
Move the insertion point between the Link edit field and the page	Press Command-Tab
Update the WYSIWYG view after making edits in the HTML source window, or vice-versa	Press Enter
Suppress real-time line-break adjustment and image resizing when resizing a frame or table	Press Option and then resize
Open an image	Press Option while double-clicking the image
Duplicate selected text or graphics item	Press Option while dragging the selection

Make your own pasteboard

Visual Page doesn't provide a pasteboard or library feature as do PageMill and Home Page, but you can make your own: just create a new, untitled document and use it to store frequently used elements. Visual Page also supports the Mac OS's drag-and-drop features, so you can drag items from clippings files or the Scrapbook directly into your pages.

SECRET

Cleaning Up After a WYSIWYG Editor

If you use a WYSIWYG editor and you've viewed the HTML source behind the files they create, you've probably seen some tags and attributes that don't look familiar: things such as `naturalsizeflag` and X-SAS. Maybe you've even tried in vain to look some of them up in an HTML reference manual.

The reason you didn't find those bizarre tags and attributes is that they don't exist. That is, they aren't actually part of any HTML standard, but instead, are custom tags added by a WYSIWYG program and used by the program for various housekeeping tasks.

I described PageMill's `<NATURALSIZEFLAG>` tag and how it works earlier in this chapter. Both PageMill and Home Page also use a variety of HTML comments to store various tidbits of housekeeping information, such as a location of an editing window on the screen.

If you want to tighten up your completed HTML pages — or if you don't want an HTML validator to go into meltdown reporting on bizarre nonstandard tags — you can manually remove these tags and comments. If you use a Macintosh, you can also use Bare Bones Software's wonderfully powerful BBEdit to clean up and reformat your HTML. BBEdit includes a tool named PageMill Cleaner that does exactly what the name implies — exorcises all those nonstandard PageMill tags from your pages.

One final caveat: Think twice about cleaning up a page that you may want to edit in PageMill or Home Page again. If you modify a cleaned-up page in PageMill or Home Page, the program will dirty the page up all over again — that is, it will put the nonstandard tags back in. (This drawback doesn't apply to Home Page if you use the program's Preferences command to specify that non-standard tags be omitted, as described in the previous section.)

HoTMetaL Pro 3 secrets (Windows)

SoftQuad's HoTMetaL Pro has become one of the most popular commercial HTML editors for Windows. (HoTMetaL Pro is also available for the Mac OS, but hasn't established as large a following on the Mac OS platform, thanks largely to the popularity of Adobe PageMill and Bare Bones' BBEdit.) This section contains some secrets for HoTMetaL Pro 3, which is available in both Mac OS and Windows versions.

Minimizing mouse movements

With HoTMetaL Pro's keyboard shortcuts, you can insert elements without using the mouse. Type Control-I (Windows) or Command-I (Mac OS) to display the Insert Element dialog box, and then type the first few letters of the element you want to insert (for example, **BLO** for `BLOCKQUOTE`), or keep pressing a letter to cycle through the elements whose names begin with that letter (for example, typing Control- or Command-I, S, S, S... cycles through S, `SAMP`, `SMALL`, `SPAN`, and so on). Press Return or Enter, and HoTMetaL Pro inserts the element and positions the blinking insertion point within it. One more slick feature: HoTMetaL Pro is smart enough to show in the Insert Element dialog box only those elements that you can legally insert at the current location of the insertion point.

Element selection strategies

You can select an entire element by clicking its opening or closing tag. For example, to select a paragraph, click the <P> or </P> tag. To select the entire body section of a page, click the <BODY> or </BODY> tag.

Drag-and-drop secrets

Fast duplication

To make a duplicate of an element, press the Ctrl key (Windows) or Option key (Mac) and then drag the element. This drag-and-drop duplication works within a document or across documents.

One-click links

You can create a link to a file by simply dragging and dropping the file's icon from the desktop, from a folder, or from the Windows Explorer or Mac OS Finder. Then, position the blinking insertion point to the left of the </A> tag and then type the text or insert the image that you want to activate the link. To avoid breaking the link, don't move the file after using this technique.

How to end a paragraph

In many HTML editors, including PageMill and Home Page, you can force a line break by pressing the Return key. Not so in HoTMetaL Pro. To end a paragraph, you must click the paragraph symbol (¶) in the toolbar.

Use that right-hand mouse button (Windows)

When you select an element and then right-click, a shortcut menu appears with options that enable you to work with whatever you've selected. For example, if you right-click inside an image, the shortcut menu's options enable you to view or edit an image file or launch the image map editor. If you right-click in an area of text, you can cut, copy, or paste. Regardless of what you right-click, the shortcut menu always contains an Insert Element command that enables you to, well, insert an element.

Searching and replacing elements

With HoTMetaL Pro's search-and-replace features, you can change one element into another type of element. This works best for elements that are of the same type — for example, character-formatting tags. Say you want to change all the <I> (italic) elements in your Web document to <EM> (emphasis). Here's how: Position the insertion point at the beginning of the page and choose Find and Replace from the Edit menu. In the Find and Replace dialog box, type <I> in the Find field and <EM> in the Replace field, and click Replace All. All of the <I> tags in the page will change to <EM> tags.

Importing formatted text from word processors

HoTMetaL Pro can import formatted text files created in all popular word processors, automatically converting the files into HTML. HoTMetaL Pro does a reasonably good job of retaining a file's contents. For example, if you use Microsoft Word to assign heading styles to the headings in a document, HoTMetaL Pro converts those headings into HTML headings. HoTMetaL Pro also retains basic character formatting such as bold and italic text. I've even had success at converting tables created in Microsoft Word for Windows 95.

Secrets for Microsoft's Internet Assistant family

A forest of pages has been written about how Microsoft reinvented itself as an Internet-savvy company. There's one aspect of this reinvention, however, that doesn't get a great deal of attention: the company's family of Internet Assistants, which are available for Word, Excel, PowerPoint, Access, Schedule+, and Outlook. (On the Mac, the selection is limited to Internet Assistants for Word and Excel; look for this to change later in 1997, when Microsoft ships the Mac OS version of Office 97.) With these add-ons, Microsoft managed to graft HTML features onto the most popular application programs in the industry. And in the Office 97 family, each program's toolbar sports an Insert Hyperlink button that enables you to insert live links into any document.

What's equally remarkable about the Internet Assistants is that they're actually pretty good. Each one extends the native talents of its companion program in clever ways. This section contains some examples.

How to Excel at tables

Excel's row-and-column orientation makes it a great tool for creating tables, which can be tricky to create with HTML, even in WYSIWYG tools such as PageMill and Home Page. The Internet Assistant for Excel lets you apply Excel's table-editing and table-formatting talents to your HTML endeavors. You can use the Internet Assistant to create an entirely new document containing a spreadsheet table. You can also use it to add a table to an existing HTML document. It's this second feature that's particularly useful, however. The Internet Assistant for Excel enables you to create an HTML page using your favorite HTML tool, and then insert a table created in Excel.

Here's how:

1. In the HTML document, insert a comment tag that reads `<!--##Table##-->` at the point where you want the table to appear. The Internet Assistant for Excel will search for this comment and insert the table at that point.
2. Use Excel to create and format your table.
3. When you've finished, choose Internet Assistant Wizard from the Tools menu. If you're using Excel 97, choose Save as HTML from the File menu. If you don't see either command, be sure the Internet Assistant is installed properly. Its file must be in the Library folder, and you must activate it by choosing Add-Ins from the Tools menu and then checking the Internet Assistant Wizard box.

The Internet Assistant uses a typical Wizard-style dialog box that walks you through the rest of the process, as shown in Figure 4-14 and outlined, step by step, in the following paragraph.

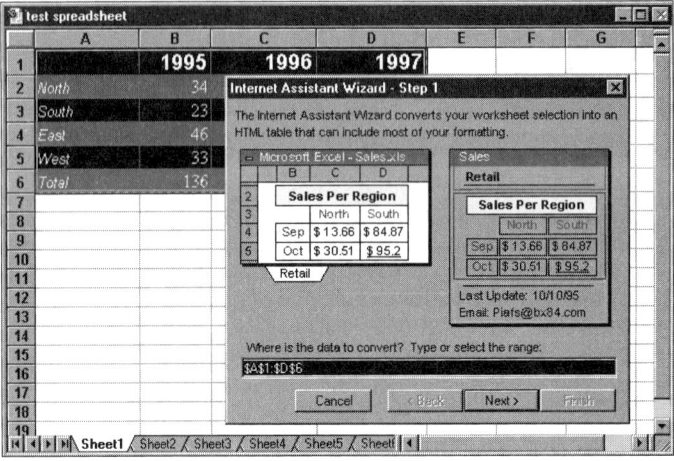

Figure 4-14: Converting a table using the Internet Assistant for Excel

In Step 1, you specify the cell range to be converted. In Step 2, you specify whether you want to create a new HTML page or insert a table in an existing page. (For this discussion, you should choose the option that reads "Insert the Converted Table to an Existing HTML File.") In Step 3, you tell the Wizard which file you want to modify — specify the file containing the `<!--##Table##-->` comment.

Step 4 is an interesting one — it lets you specify whether you want to retain the table's formatting or convert only the table's data. The Internet Assistant Wizard can convert most of the formatting that Excel supports, including font, size, and cell colors.

Finally, Step 5 lets you supply a name for the completed page. Alas, you can't just update the page you started with; you have to create an entirely new page.

How to make your PowerPoint

What in the world does PowerPoint, a presentation program, have to do with HTML and the Web? Well, think about it. A PowerPoint presentation is a series of screens, which can contain text, graphics, video, and sound. Each screen can also contain hot spots that enable you to navigate through the screens.

Sounds a bit like a Web site, doesn't it?

Unlike the assistants for Word and Excel, the Internet Assistant for PowerPoint doesn't turn PowerPoint into a Web authoring tool. Instead, it lets you easily adapt — yes, repurpose — a PowerPoint presentation so that you can post it on a Web site or distribute it on a floppy disk or CD-ROM.

Installing the Internet Assistant for PowerPoint adds a new command to PowerPoint's File menu, Export as HTML. In PowerPoint 97, this command is named Save as HTML. Both commands cause the Internet Assistant to swing into action and perform an array of tricks, including the following:

- It creates an index page that acts as a table of contents for the presentation.
- It generates a separate HTML page for each slide in the presentation. Each page contains an image of its slide as well as navigation buttons that enable you to step to the next and previous slides and also view text-only versions of the slides.
- It also creates a separate, text-only HTML page for each slide in the presentation.
- For slides containing interactive hot spots created using PowerPoint's Interactive Settings command, the assistant creates a clickable image map and the appropriate code so that users can jump between slides by clicking the hot spots. (The image map is a client-side map, which is further described in Chapter 6.)

The assistant stores all of these files in a new folder directory, which it also creates. In all, it's a pretty impressive feat. See Figure 4-15 for an example.

Here are a few tips and secrets for the Internet Assistant for PowerPoint:

- **Adding a link to a hot spot.** You can set up a hot spot to act as a link to a Web site. In PowerPoint, select the hot spot's button or art, and choose Interactive Settings from the Tools menu. Click the Run Program button, and in the adjacent text area, type the full URL of the Web page you want to link to (for example, `http://www.heidsite.com/`). Click OK. The Internet Assistant supports other common protocols and commands, too, including `ftp`, `mailto`, and `file`.
- **Creating a framed presentation.** If you want to overwhelm your visitors with more information and navigation options than they may be able to handle, use the Internet Assistant's Framed Slideshow option. In a framed presentation, the Slide frame contains the slide image itself. The Navigation frame contains slide navigation controls that enable viewers to see the next and previous slides. The Notes frame displays any speaker notes for the associated slide, while the Outline frame displays the outline for the entire presentation. Viewers can click headings to jump to a particular slide or Web page. The Outline Controls frame contains Expand and Collapse buttons that enable viewers to control the way the outline in the Outline frame is displayed. Whew.

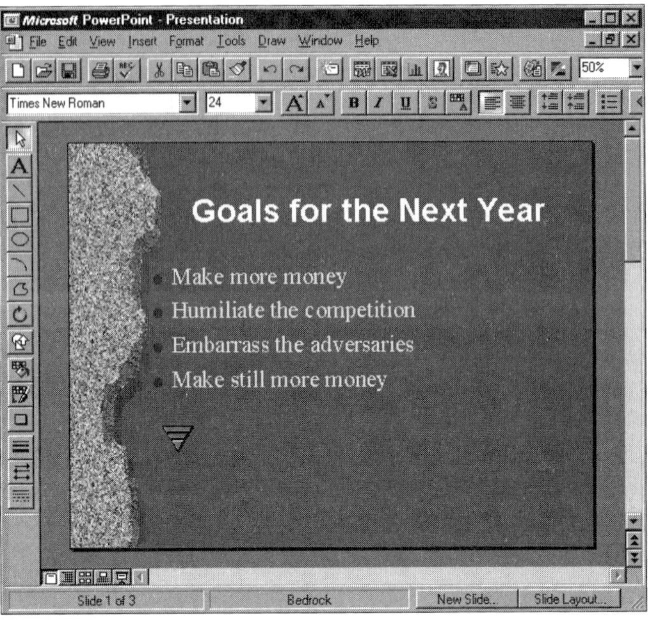

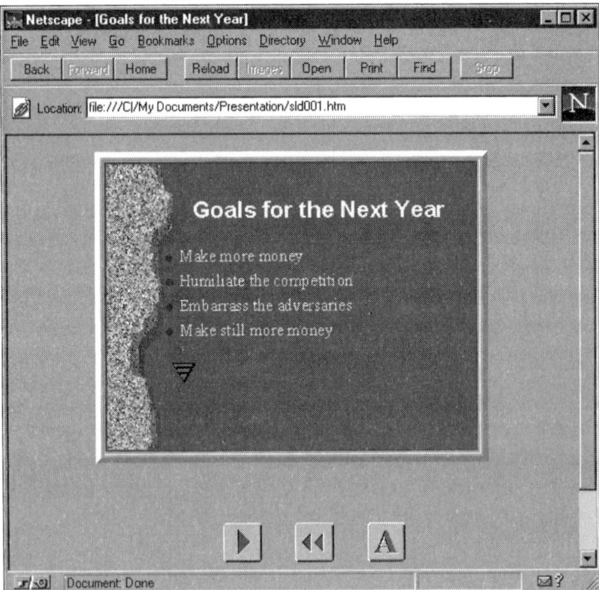

Figure 4-15: From conference room to Web: a slide from a PowerPoint presentation (top) and its Web page (bottom).

- **Controlling image size.** Strangely, the size of the slide images that appear on each Web page is determined by the resolution setting of your monitor. For example, if your monitor is set to 640×480 pixels, each slide image will be larger than if it was set to 800×600 pixels. You'll need to experiment to find the monitor settings that yield the ideal image size: a size that is big enough so that your slides' text is readable, but not so big as to cause lengthy downloads.

  And don't forget to choose the correct file format for each image. Use GIF if your slides contain primarily solid colors; JPEG if they contain photographic images. See Chapter 6 for all the details on GIF versus JPEG decisions.

HTML Tricks and Secrets

We've looked at HTML tools of every stripe, and we've seen where they sing and where they sink. Now let's look at a few things you might try with them. This section is a grab bag of HTML tricks and secrets — little things that can enhance your pages, big things that can save astronomical amounts of time, and medium-sized things that are just plain worth knowing.

If you're an HTML newbie, you might want to refer to Appendix A for an HTML primer and an overview of the structure of Web pages.

Directory structures and references (or, about those URLs in your <HREF>s...)

Let's start with a Big Thing: the way you spell out the uniform resource locators, or URLs, in tags that refer to other files (for example, `<HREF>` tags and `<IMG>` tags). There are a couple of ways of doing it, and each method has its good points and bad ones.

Absolute references

The most explicit way of spelling out a link's destination is to spell it out; that is, to provide the full address of the page that the link points to — for example, `<a href="http://websecrets.heidsite.com/ch4/tools.html">`. This is an absolute reference, also called an absolute URL. (There's a vodka advertisement in there somewhere.)

Relative references

No, a relative reference is not a snide comment you make about your in-laws. It's a shorter way of writing a link's destination: instead of spelling out the full address of the destination, you spell out the address relative to the current address. A relative reference is also often called a relative URL.

For example, say I'm working on the page that will be located at `http://websecrets.heidsite.com/ch4/tools.html`, and I want to have a link to a page called `tips.html` that will be located in the same directory (ch4). Instead of spelling out the full address of the page, I can simply write `<a href="tips.html">`.

When a browser program encounters a relative URL, it fills in the blanks — that is, it completes the address by combining the relative URL with a base address, which is normally the address of the page containing the relative URL. (I say "normally" because you can change the base address using the `<BASE>` tag; more on this shortly.) The following table illustrates how a relative URL and the base address combine to form a full address.

Table 4-2 How relative references work

Base URL	`http://www.yoursite.com/`
Relative URL	`features/hotstuff.html`
Complete URL	`http://www.yoursite.com/features/hotstuff.html`

Comparing absolute and relative references

The advantage of an absolute reference is that there's no ambiguity — you're spelling out the entire address of the destination link, down to the last virtual street sign. The disadvantage is that the address is carved in stone: If you need to move a set of pages to a different server or directory, you have to edit each reference.

After reading the previous sentence, you can probably guess that the advantage of a relative reference is portability. Relative references enable you to move an entire set of pages from one server to another without having to laboriously edit every single reference.

Relative references also make it possible to develop and test a Web site on a local hard drive before putting it up on a server. If you used absolute references for files stored on a local hard drive — for example, if you wrote `<a href="file:///harddrive/myfile.html>` — you would have to edit every reference before you could post the site on a server.

It's relatively easy

Fortunately, most HTML editors create relative references when you use their link-creation features. For example, when you create a link by dragging and dropping a page icon in Adobe PageMill, PageMill creates a relative reference.

There may be exceptions — HTML programs or converters that foolishly create absolute references instead of relative ones, for example — but generally, the most common way of creating absolute references is by typing them yourself. So when you're hand-tuning some HTML, train yourself to create relative references and not absolute ones.

Relative References and CD-ROM Distribution

An additional benefit of using relative references is that they make it easy to create a CD-ROM version of a Web site. Why would you want to distribute a Web site on a CD-ROM? CD-ROMs are an ideal medium for distributing Web sites to people who don't have an Internet connection. Put your company's Web site on a CD and distribute it at a trade show. Or if you've spent time converting company manuals to HTML for an intranet site, zap them onto a CD and send it to your field offices.

Recipients can use their own Web browsers, to explore your content, or you can license a browser and include it on the CD. Microsoft offers a terrific free licensing program for Internet Explorer; see `http://www.microsoft.com/ie/ieak/`.

Creating a Web site that runs entirely from a CD-ROM isn't too different from creating an ordinary site. But you need to follow a few rules. Here are some tips for creating a Web site that can run from a local CD or from a Web server.

- Use relative references rather than absolute references in all URLs.
- Use client-side image maps. Server-side image maps don't work when there isn't any server, so be sure all your image maps have client-side support. For details on client-side image maps, see Chapter 6.
- Omit pages that rely on Common Gateway Interfaces. If parts of the site rely on CGIs for processing — for example, a search page, a guest book, a shopping cart — omit those portions from the CD-ROM, where CGIs don't work.

Controlling relative references with <BASE>

You might have noticed that I said the base address — the address the browser combines with a relative reference — is usually the address of the page on which the relative reference appears. I said usually because you can change the base address using the `<BASE>` tag.

The `<BASE>` tag must appear within the page header; that is, between the `<HEAD>` and `</HEAD>` tags. The `<BASE>` tag accepts just one attribute: `href`, and this attribute must be a valid URL. Here's an example of a `<BASE>` tag:

```
<html>
<head>
<title>Welcome to the Digital Doghouse</title>
<base href="http://www.mysite.com/">
</head>
(...rest of page here)
```

The previous example tells the browser that any relative addresses in this page are relative to `http://www.mysite.com/`, regardless of the address from which the page was actually retrieved.

Creating <BASE> tags in some popular programs

One way to create a <BASE> tag is obvious: hand-peck it into your favorite HTML or text editor. But many HTML editors also provide a dialog box option that enables you to specify a page's base address. Here are some examples:

- **Bare Bones Software's BBEdit.** The New Document dialog box that appears when you click the New Document button in the HTML Tools palette enables you to specify a base address.
- **Claris Home Page.** Choose Document Options from the Edit menu, be sure the General tab is active, and then type the base URL in the Base Document URL field.
- **Symantec's Visual Page.** Click the Document Settings icon in the toolbar, and then enter the base URL in the URL Settings area of the Document Settings dialog box.
- **Nesbitt Software's WebEdit.** Open the Insert menu, and then open the Page Structure Tags submenu and choose Base. Specify the base URL in the dialog box that appears.

The <BASE> tag and frames

If you're using frames, you can also use the <BASE> tag to specify which frame or window the browser should use to display a linked document. For more details on this use of <BASE>, see Chapter 7.

Formatting your HTML

As I mentioned in the previous chapter, HTML's emphasis on structure over content makes it inherently compact. Create sensibly-sized HTML documents — ones with a reasonable amount of text and optimized graphics — and your site will load quickly, even over slow modem connections. (Chapter 5 describes what a "reasonable" amount of text is, and Chapter 6 shows how to optimize graphics for fast loading.)

You can take advantage of HTML's compactness to format your pages so that they're easier to read and modify. By format, I don't mean the formatting that visitors will see when they arrive at a page, but the format of the HTML tags that you see when you create and edit the page.

Format for legibility

In the programming world, it's common practice to indent lines of related code and, in general, format them in a way that makes the code easier to read and understand. Programmers have a jargon term for this friendly formatting: pretty printing.

You can apply the concepts behind pretty printing to HTML code to make your pages easier to understand. If you have to modify a page a few months after creating it, it's a lot easier to remember what you did and how you did it when you can easily decipher the page's HTML.

Applying this formatting to your HTML is easy, too. Just follow a few simple rules.

Use returns liberally

As you probably already know from working with HTML, a Web browser wouldn't know a return if it tripped over it. For example, if you're working directly with HTML code in an HTML editor, you can't force a line break or even end a paragraph of text by pressing the Return key. If you try, the line or paragraph appears to end properly in your HTML listing, but a browser blindly ignores the return and runs one line into the next. (The solutions in these examples are to use the `<P>` and `</P>` tags to define the start and end of paragraphs, respectively, and the `<BR>` tag to force a line break.)

The fact that browsers are ignorant of returns means you can use line breaks to improve your HTML's legibility. Simply use a text editor — or the text-editing mode of a WYSIWYG text editor such as Adobe PageMill or Claris Home Page — to insert a return before any tag that you want to appear on a line by itself.

Indent related lines

Using returns liberally is only half of the pretty-printing equation; the other half involves indenting related lines of code — for example, the code that describes a row of data in a table.

To indent a line of code, position your editor's blinking insertion point before the tag and then press the spacebar until the tag is where you want it. Depending on your HTML editor, you may also be able to use the Tab key — a faster approach and the one you're probably used to using in your word processor. Some editors, however, lock out the Tab key. (Claris Home Page 1.x is one of them, although version 2.x's HTML-editing window does enable you to indent by using the Tab key.) If pressing the Tab key gets you nowhere, use the spacebar.

Pretty printing in action

The best way to understand and appreciate the benefits of pretty printing is with an example. Figure 4-16 shows the same chunk of HTML formatted with and without pretty printing. Which would you prefer to stare at for hours on end?

It's worth noting that some HTML editors apply some pretty printing automatically. Claris Home Page, for instance, indents table tags. I'd like to see more programs adopt this approach.

Automatic pretty printing with BBEdit (Mac OS only)

Bare Bones Software's BBEdit editor includes an extension called Format HTML that does a great job of pretty printing. If you have an older version of BBEdit that didn't include Format HTML, you can download the extension from the Bare Bones Web site, at `http://www.barebones.com/`.

default.compact.html

```
<HTML><HEAD><TITLE>Heidsite: Jim Heid's Mac and Multimedia
Hangout</TITLE></HEAD><BODY BGCOLOR="#ffffff"><P><CENTER><IMG
SRC="Graphics/Heidsite.gif" WIDTH="475" HEIGHT="99" ALIGN=bottom ALT="H E I D S I T E
- Jim Heid's Mac and Media-Production Hangout"><HR><B>Welcome to Heidsite!</B><BR>Have
a question? Want to comment?<A
HREF="http://www4.heidsite.com/HTMLpages/guestBook.html">Visit the guest
book</A><BR><B>New! Free stuff! Shareware! Visit <A HREF="downloadzone.html">The
Download Zone</A><BR>New! Looking for something? Heidsite is now fully <A
HREF="http://www4.heidsite.com/eg.acgi">searchable</A></B><BR>What's it like outside?
Visit the <A HREF="http://www4.heidsite.com/weathercam.html">Heidsite Weathercam</A>
-- now with QuickTime VR<BR><HR><B>N e w s / V i e w s<BR></B><a
href="/heidsite/hotmedia/hotmedia.html">HotMedia</a> for my July 1996 column is now
available.<br>Apple launches new <a href="http://www.macos.apple.com/macos8/">Web
site</A> for Mac OS 8 (aka Copland)<BR>4/18: <a href="audio/qt22.html">New QuickTime
versions</A> to bring better MIDI, pro video support<BR>Apple ships beta versions of new,
easier <A HREF="qtvrtools.html">QuickTime VR tools</A><BR><B>How does MIDI work?
</B><A HREF="audio/MIDIfrontdoor.html">Find out</A> in the new Shockwave for FreeHand
tutorial<BR>Adobe posts <A
HREF="http://www.adobe.com/Software.html#updts">Premiere4.2.1 updater</A> on its
Web site -- update fixes sound-sync, other bugs<BR></CENTER><HR><BR><MAP
NAME="mainmap"> <AREA SHAPE="RECT" COORDS="366,50,436,144"
HREF="AboutHeidsite.html"> <AREA SHAPE="RECT" COORDS="245,56,320,143"
HREF="handbook.html"> <AREA SHAPE="RECT" COORDS="124,56,189,143"
HREF="audio/audio.html"> <AREA SHAPE="RECT" COORDS="2,56,74,146"
HREF="video/video.html"> <AREA SHAPE="RECT" COORDS="261,2,407,40"
HREF="hotmedia/hotmedia.html"> <AREA SHAPE="RECT" COORDS="35,1,165,38"
HREF="generalmac.html"></MAP><CENTER><A
HREF="http://www.mcn.org/imagemap/imagemap.cgi$mainmap"> <IMG
SRC="graphics/mainmap.gif" WIDTH="437" HEIGHT="148" BORDER="0" ALT="No graphics?
Click the text labels below instead." ISMAP USEMAP="#mainmap"
ALIGN=bottom></A><BR><HR><A HREF="generalmac.html">General Mac Info</A><B> | </B><A
HREF="hotmedia/hotmedia.html">HotMedia</A><B> | </B><A
```

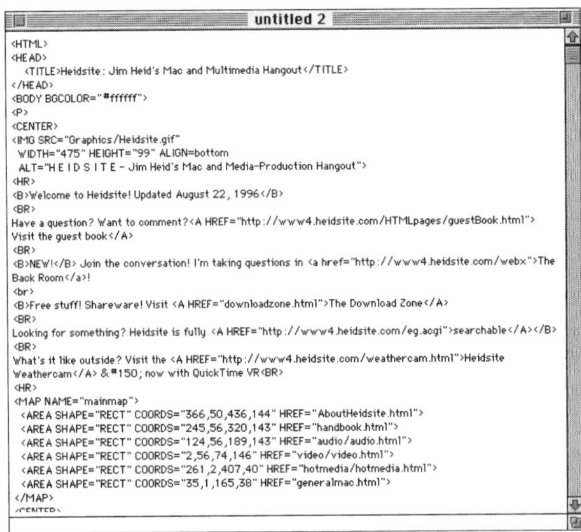

untitled 2

```
<HTML>
<HEAD>
  <TITLE>Heidsite: Jim Heid's Mac and Multimedia Hangout</TITLE>
</HEAD>
<BODY BGCOLOR="#ffffff">
<P>
<CENTER>
<IMG SRC="Graphics/Heidsite.gif"
 WIDTH="475" HEIGHT="99" ALIGN=bottom
 ALT="H E I D S I T E - Jim Heid's Mac and Media-Production Hangout">
<HR>
<B>Welcome to Heidsite! Updated August 22, 1996</B>
<BR>
Have a question? Want to comment?<A HREF="http://www4.heidsite.com/HTMLpages/guestBook.html">
Visit the guest book</A>
<BR>
<B>NEW!</B> Join the conversation! I'm taking questions in <a href="http://www4.heidsite.com/webx">The
Back Room</a>!
<br>
<B>Free stuff! Shareware! Visit <A HREF="downloadzone.html">The Download Zone</A>
<BR>
Looking for something? Heidsite is fully <A HREF="http://www4.heidsite.com/eg.acgi">searchable</A></B>
<BR>
What's it like outside? Visit the <A HREF="http://www4.heidsite.com/weathercam.html">Heidsite
Weathercam</A> &#150; now with QuickTime VR<BR>
<HR>
<MAP NAME="mainmap">
 <AREA SHAPE="RECT" COORDS="366,50,436,144" HREF="AboutHeidsite.html">
 <AREA SHAPE="RECT" COORDS="245,56,320,143" HREF="handbook.html">
 <AREA SHAPE="RECT" COORDS="124,56,189,143" HREF="audio/audio.html">
 <AREA SHAPE="RECT" COORDS="2,56,74,146" HREF="video/video.html">
 <AREA SHAPE="RECT" COORDS="261,2,407,40" HREF="hotmedia/hotmedia.html">
 <AREA SHAPE="RECT" COORDS="35,1,165,38" HREF="generalmac.html">
</MAP>
```

Figure 4-16: HTML without pretty printing (top) and with it (bottom)

Parting thoughts on pretty printing

There are no carved-in-stone rules that dictate how or whether you should pretty-print your HTML. Use whatever formatting technique makes your pages easier for you to read and understand. You might decide, for example, that indents don't provide any significant legibility advantage and use only returns. And don't feel obligated to spend hours pretty-printing your pages.

Oh, and one more thing. All those extra returns, spaces, and tabs may not mean diddly to a browser, but they do mean diddly to the Internet. That is, they do make your pages larger, which means they take longer to transfer. Is the size difference significant? Generally, no — a pretty-printed page might be a hundred or so bytes larger than a page whose tags are squished together like subway commuters. And the benefit in legibility is worth the extra bytes.

Making a case for lowercase

One more HTML-formatting point concerns case: should you capitalize your HTML (<A HREF="address">) or format it in lowercase (<a href="address">)? HTML editors generally capitalize HTML tags, but if you're typing tags by hand using a text editor, don't feel obligated to your Shift key. Lowercase tags work just fine in all modern browsers, and they're easier to type and read.

Summary

- A wide selection of HTML tools exists, ranging from WYSIWYG layout programs such as Adobe PageMill, Symantec's Visual Page, Claris Home Page; to HTML editors such as SoftQuad's HoTMetaL Pro, Bare Bones Software's BBEdit, and Nesbitt Software's WebEdit Pro; to HTML adapters such as Astrobyte's BeyondPress for QuarkXPress and Microsoft's Internet Assistant series; to standalone converters such as RTFtoHTML.
- Site-building programs such as NetObjects Fusion provide not only HTML layout features, but also features for managing an entire site.
- A smart HTML author uses tools from every category to exploit the strengths of each.
- Using relative rather than absolute references in your hyperlinks makes your Web site more portable — easier to move from one server to another.
- Pretty printing your HTML — using returns and indenting to indicate the structure of a page — makes a page's HTML source easier to read and understand.

Chapter 5

Web Writing and Typography

In This Chapter

- The special considerations behind writing for the Web
- Punctuation and Spelling 101: a quick refresher
- Secrets for improving your Web typography
- Advanced formatting options: fonts and tables
- The future of Web typography

Spend an hour or so surfing the Web and it becomes obvious that editorial and typographic expertise aren't exactly pervasive in the Web-publishing world. Misspelled words and odd punctuation abound. Headings and paragraphs are plagued with bizarre formatting, inducing headaches after a few sentences.

The reason is simple: most small Web sites are operated by people who don't have editorial and typographic training or experience. Editorial and typographic standards suffered when desktop publishing made it possible for anyone with a computer to produce printed materials. The Web's democratization of online publishing is only furthering the trend.

What's more, the Web's hypertext and screen-oriented characteristics introduce unique issues, ones that don't surface in the traditional world of print. And HTML's relatively limited formatting capabilities can frustrate print or multimedia designers who are used to having full typographic control.

This chapter is a guide to Web editorial and typographic issues. You'll find tips and secrets aimed at improving the appearance and readability of your pages' text, as well as details on some of the latest HTML text-formatting options.

ON CD-ROM

Add These Formatting Tools to Your Toolbox

The single-pixel GIF. The handy spacing tool discussed in this chapter, along with example files that illustrate its use.

Table-formatting example files. Several HTML files that illustrate the use of tables for advanced formatting applications.

Small-capitals examples. Several HTML files that show how to use the `<FONT SIZE>` tag to simulate small capitals.

Web Writing Secrets

Before we look at Web text-formatting issues, let's take a look at the text itself. This section is a collection of observations and secrets for some of the most common Web writing issues and errors.

"Click here" — is it really evil?

You see it all the time in Web style guides: "Never write 'click here' to indicate a hyperlink — it's bad form." I'm not as vehement. "Click here" is fine for some contexts, bad for others. Here's my take:

The anti-"click here" contingent recommends against the phrase for two reasons: some people are using text-only browsers and therefore don't have a mouse with which to click, and "click here" doesn't make much sense when a Web-based document is printed.

Both objections are valid, although the population of text-only browser users is small and getting smaller. As for the second objection, the anti-"click here" crowd's alternative wording is often no better. Many style guides suggest doing something like this:

Supposedly wrong: For more information on dogs, click here.

Supposedly right: More information on dogs is available.

Is available? Why is that better than *click here,* especially when the document is printed? *Is available* tells people reading hard copy that more information is out there somewhere, but it gives them no indication where. Here's my suggestion:

SECRET

When you expect that a page will be printed, include the URL of the linked page in the link itself, for example:

For more information on dogs, see http://www.dogs.com/moreinfo.html.

Now, I'll be the first to admit that this can lead to long, ugly hyperlinks, especially for pages that are buried within multiple directories. But it does have the advantage of being versatile and explicit. The link works fine in an on-screen context, and it conveys essential information even when committed to paper.

What about small blurbs in pages that you don't expect to be printed, such as home pages or lists of links? Go ahead and use *click here.* It's strong and it's direct. And you know what? I bet that small minority of people who use text-only browsers will figure out what to do.

The mailto variation

The `<HREF>` tag's `mailto` attribute is a variation on the "click here" theme, enabling surfers to activate their browsers' e-mail features and drop you a line. It's a good idea to include `mailto` throughout a Web site — doing so encourages visitors to interact with you. But on pages that may be printed, include your actual e-mail address as well. For example:

Typical: Questions or comments? Please write.

Better: Questions or comments? E-mail jim@heidsite.com.

There's one other advantage to this style: some browsers don't have built-in e-mail features, and explicitly spelling out your e-mail address enables users of those browsers to reach you.

Don't go overboard with links

Just because hypertext enables you to create links throughout a series of pages doesn't mean you should take every opportunity to do so. One example of what *not* to do is on the otherwise outstanding space shuttle site operated by NASA. In the section describing the shuttle's workings, each page is polluted with links to a document that contains definitions of various components. By itself, that isn't so bad, except that *every occurrence* of a given word is linked to its definition. The result is a visual mess (see Figure 5-1).

Not only does this hyperactive approach to hyperlinks lead to a sloppy-looking screen, it dilutes your message. Rather than concentrating on your text, visitors are subconsciously wondering what's behind each link and debating whether or not to find out.

A cleaner and more effective solution would be a list of terms at the bottom of the page, with each term linked to its glossary entry. At the top of the page, include a link that says something like, "Find an unfamiliar term? Click its entry in the glossary." Link the word "glossary" to an anchor located at the bottom of the page, just before the list of terms.

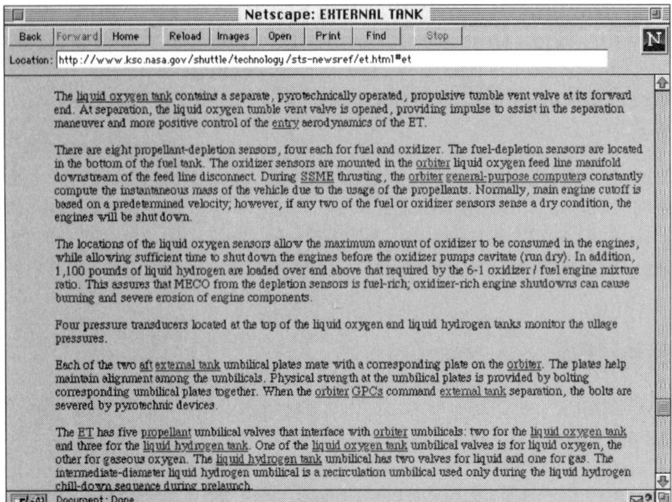

Figure 5-1: Too much of a good thing: link mania on NASA's space shuttle site (http://shuttle.nasa.gov/).

How long should a Web page be?

User interface studies have shown that people don't like to scroll much and that they're unlikely to scroll unless they're really interested in a page's subject.

Some people have compared the bottom of the screen to the fold in a newspaper — just as the most important stories in a newspaper appear above the fold, the most important information on a Web page should fit within a single browser window.

What about lengthy reports or articles? One school of thought says you should divide such pieces into multiple pages, each of which fits on a single screen, and create Next and Previous links for visitors to page through the article. The other school says that it's best to keep a lengthy passage on one page.

I'm from the second school — I dislike reading stories that are split across multiple pages. The delay that occurs when my browser hunts down and retrieves the next page is distracting and can be several seconds long. And of course, it's cumbersome to print or save a story that is split across multiple pages.

If a document is *really* long — more than four or five screenfuls of text — consider splitting it across two or three screens. But for those folks who want to print the document, consider providing a link to a file containing the page's text, perhaps in Adobe Acrobat Portable Document Format (PDF). (For details on Adobe Acrobat, see `http://www.adobe.com/acrobat/main.html`.)

Provide navigation devices within large pages

I mentioned this tip in Chapter 1. To enable visitors to navigate a long page without scrolling, put a table of contents at the top of the page, with each entry linking to an anchor adjacent to its corresponding subhead. Many Web developers also place a link or button near each section subhead, which enables visitors to jump back to the top of the page (see Figure 5-2).

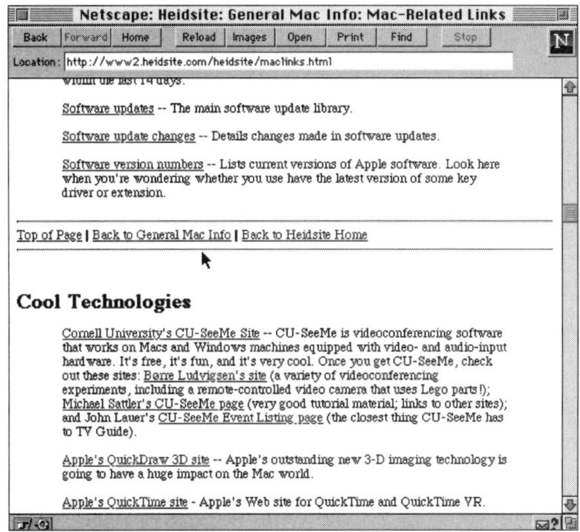

Figure 5-2: Navigation aids within a page

Write with search engines in mind

Search engines such as Digital's AltaVista (`http://altavista.digital.com/`) usually include the first few sentences of a page's text in their search results, which is another good reason to place a page's most important content up front.

Write tight

A person's reading speed is about 25 percent slower when he or she is reading from a screen. As a result, it's important to keep your writing concise. And because you're trying to hook the reader before he or she clicks off to a different page, avoid long-winded introductions. Enough said.

Think globally: international issues

In World Wide Web sites, it's important to be sensitive to the obvious fact that your pages may be read by visitors around the world. That means making the effort to avoid confusion in several areas.

Dates

Different countries format dates in different ways. In the United States, 8/12/60 refers to August 12, 1960, but in many European countries, it's interpreted as December 8, 1960. To avoid confusion, be explicit.

Wrong: 8/12/60

Right: 12 Aug 1960 or August 12, 1960 or Aug 12, 1960

Currency

Americans may be fond of the almighty dollar, but Canadians and Australians use the dollar sign ($) symbol, too. If you're publishing price information to an international audience, you may want to be explicit about whose dollars you're referring to.

Wrong: For only $19.95, you can be beautiful.

Right: For only $19.95 (US), you can be beautiful.

Alternate: For only $US 19.95, you can be beautiful.

Getting it right: its versus it's

Here's one that is by no means limited to the Web, but flourishes online nonetheless: the hideous misuse of "it's" and "its." They're two different words, and they aren't interchangeable. (There's historical proof that this problem is not Web-specific. An *it's* versus *its* discussion appears on page 1 of Strunk and White's legendary *The Elements of Style,* which was published in 1959 and remains available today. This little book, published by Macmillan Publishing Company, Inc., should be on every Web writer's bookshelf.)

It's is a contraction for the words *it is*. Some examples are: *It's a party. It's too late. It's going to rain.* On the other hand, *its* is a possessive — it refers to possession or to the object of an action. Some examples are: *The dog chased its ball. Its tires are flat. The play closed shortly after its premiere.*

Forget trying to remember parts of speech and just remember this trick: try the sentence with the words *it is* and see if the sentence still makes sense. If it does, use *it's*; otherwise, use *its*.

Punctuation quick reference

The incorrect use of common punctuation also makes Web-surfing proofreaders wince. Here are the most important rules:

- Add one space, not two, after a period or other punctuation symbol.
- Periods and commas go within quotes.

  Wrong: It's a little too "cute".

  Right: It's a little too "cute."

- Colons and semicolons go outside quotes.

  Wrong: And it's "right;" but is it?

  Right: And it's "right"; but is it?

- If a parenthetical phrase is a complete sentence, its period goes before the closing parenthesis. If the phrase isn't a complete sentence, the period follows the closing parenthesis.

  Wrong: I'm positive (Of course, I could be wrong).

  Wrong: I'm positive (Of course, I could be wrong.).

  Right: I'm positive. (Of course, I could be wrong.)

SECRET

For More on Web Writing and Typography, Click Here

Several Web sites address Web writing issues and should be on every Web developer's bookmark list.

- **David Siegal's Web Wonk page** (`http://www.dsiegel.com/tips/index.html`). Tips on Web writing and typography. I also recommend Siegal's book, *Creating Killer Web Sites* (Macmillan Computer Publishing, 1995), and its companion Web site, `http://www.killersites.com/`. Siegal tends to obsess on design issues more than most Web developers would — and, in some cases, should. But that's a good thing.
- **Microsoft Typography** (`http://www.microsoft.com/truetype/`). Given that Microsoft introduced the `<FONT FACE>` tag and was the first major browser vendor to support Cascading Style Sheets, it isn't surprising that the company has a Web site devoted to Web typography. This must-visit site also contains free TrueType fonts for the Mac and Windows platforms. (These fonts are discussed elsewhere in this chapter.)
- **Sun Microsystems' Guide to Web Style** (`http://www.sun.com/styleguide/`). I've mentioned this in previous chapters, but it's worth pointing to again.
- **Interface Design for Sun's WWW Site** (`http://www.sun.com/sun-on-net/uidesign/`). The fascinating tale behind Sun Microsystems's Web site, written by Sun's Jakob Nielsen.
- **What Is Good Hypertext Writing?** (`http://kbs.cs.tu-berlin.de/~jutta/ht/writing.html`). A fine introduction to writing hypertext documents by Jutta Degener.
- **William Strunk's The Elements of Style** (`http://www.cc.columbia.edu/acis/bartleby/strunk/`). Not the Strunk and White version I recommended earlier in this chapter, but the original — now in hypertext form, thanks to Columbia University.

Web Typography and Formatting Secrets

Given HTML's deliberately limited formatting capabilities, the phrase "Web typography" is almost a contradiction in terms. It isn't easy to create a typographically beautiful Web page, but there are some tricks you can employ to gain more control over line and character spacing, multicolumn layouts, and the like. And there's a great deal you can do to make sure your text is legible and easy to read.

Unless otherwise noted, all the tips in this section work with any browser that supports tables and the `<IMG>` tag's extended attributes (`height`, `width`, `vspace`, and `hspace`).

Spacing secrets: the single-pixel GIF

Typographers and designers are used to having fine control over the amount of vertical spacing — the leading — between paragraphs and between subheads and paragraphs. They're also used to being able to indent the first line of a paragraph by a specific amount, often an *em space*, which is a fixed unit of space equal to the width of a capital *M* in the current font.

HTML doesn't provide this kind of spacing control. You can get an extra line space by including a blank paragraph or by using the `<BR>` tag (see Figure 5-3), but you can't specify that there be, for example, 24 points of extra space after a paragraph and before a subhead.

HTML also doesn't provide control over paragraph indents. In fact, it doesn't provide for paragraph indents at all.

Cascading Style Sheets, discussed in Chapter 7, do support indents and other advanced formatting controls, but Cascading Style Sheets probably won't be widespread for some time. Even then, you'll want to think twice about relying exclusively on them, because older browsers, including Netscape Navigator 3.0 and Microsoft Internet Explorer 2.0, don't support Cascading Style Sheets. (The techniques I cover in this section work in all versions of all popular browsers.)

Experienced Web developers work around HTML's spacing limitations with a small but powerful weapon: the single-pixel GIF. This is a GIF-format image file that contains — yes, that's right — a single pixel. The file is tiny — less than 50 bytes. By using it along with the `<IMG>` tag's extended attributes, you can create a lean, mean, spacing machine.

The secret to the single-pixel GIF lies in the `<IMG>` tag's `hspace` and `vspace` attributes, which enable you to add extra horizontal and vertical space around an image.

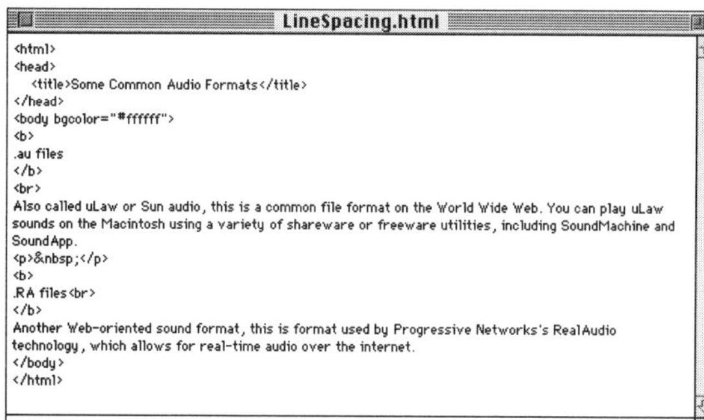

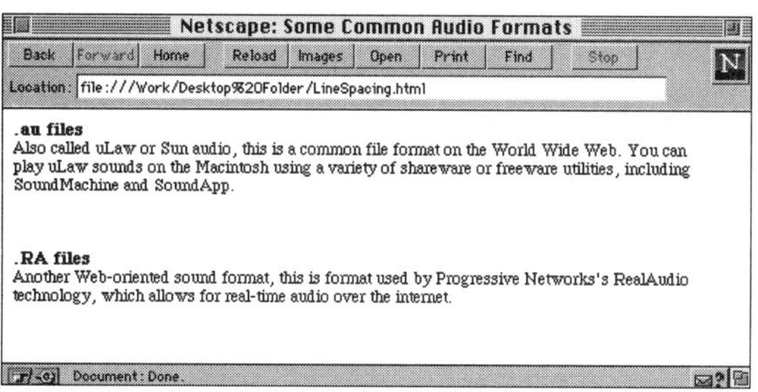

Figure 5-3: Bare-bones spacing control with the <P> tag. Top: The source HTML. The nonbreaking space (represented by the   code) ensures that the "paragraph" renders properly in all browsers. Bottom: The results.

- To add extra vertical space, include a `vspace` attribute listing the amount of extra space you want. For example, `vspace=10` gives you ten extra pixels of space.
- To add extra horizontal space, include an `hspace` attribute listing *half* the amount of extra space you want. For example, to create a 20-pixel paragraph indent, use `hspace=10`. (You have to specify half the amount you want because `hspace` adds the specified amount before *and* after the image.)

As mentioned in the "On the CD-ROM" sidebar at the beginning of this chapter, you'll find a single-pixel GIF file and example files that illustrate its use on the *HTML & Web Publishing SECRETS* CD-ROM. (See Appendix B for more details on what is on the CD.)

Adding vertical spacing

To use the single-pixel GIF to add vertical spacing, use the `<IMG>` tag's `vspace` attribute to specify the number of pixels you want to add (see Figure 5-4).

```
<html>
<head>
<title>
Leading Example
</title>
</head>
<body bgcolor=#ffffff>
<font face="Impact" size=6>
Leading. It rhymes with shedding.
<br>
```

```
</font>
<b>
<IMG SRC="dot_clear.gif" vspace=20>So what's the deal behind this
tiny little GIF file, anyway?<br>
</b>
<IMG SRC="dot_clear.gif" vspace=10>Experienced Web developers work
around HTML's spacing limitations with a small but powerful weapon:
the single-pixel GIF. This is a GIF-format image file that contains
&#150; yes, that's right &#150; a single pixel. The file is tiny:
less than 50 bytes. By using it along with the &lt;img&gt; tag's
hspace and vspace attributes, you can create a lean, mean, spacing
machine.<BR>
</body>
</html>
```

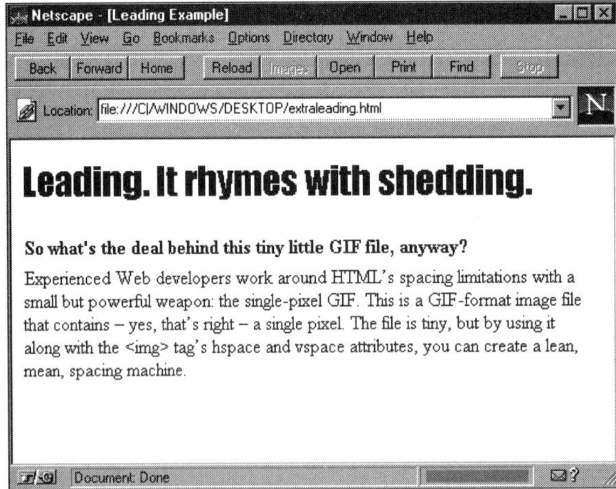

Figure 5-4: Adding vertical space with a single-pixel GIF. Top: The source HTML. Here, extra space is being added above and below the bold subhead. Bottom: The results.

By inserting a single-pixel GIF between *every line* in a paragraph, you can open up its line spacing to create an airy look, as shown in Figure 5-5.

```
<html>
<head>
<title>
Wide Leading Example
</title>
</head>
<body bgcolor=#ffffff>
<font face="Impact" size=6>
Leading. It rhymes with shedding.
<br>
</font>
<b>
```

```
<IMG SRC="dot_clear.gif" vspace=24>So what's the deal behind this
tiny little GIF file, anyway?<br>
</b>
<br>
Experienced Web developers work around HTML's spacing limitations
with a<br>
<IMG SRC="dot_clear.gif" vspace=16>small but powerful weapon: the
single-pixel GIF. This is a GIF-format image file<br>
<IMG SRC="dot_clear.gif" vspace=16>that contains &#150; yes, that's
right &#150; a single pixel. The file is tiny, but by using it<br>
<IMG SRC="dot_clear.gif" vspace=16>along with the &lt;img&gt; tag's
hspace and vspace attributes, you can create a lean,<br>
<IMG SRC="dot_clear.gif" vspace=16>mean, spacing machine.<br>
<IMG SRC="dot_clear.gif" vspace=16>
</body>
</html>
```

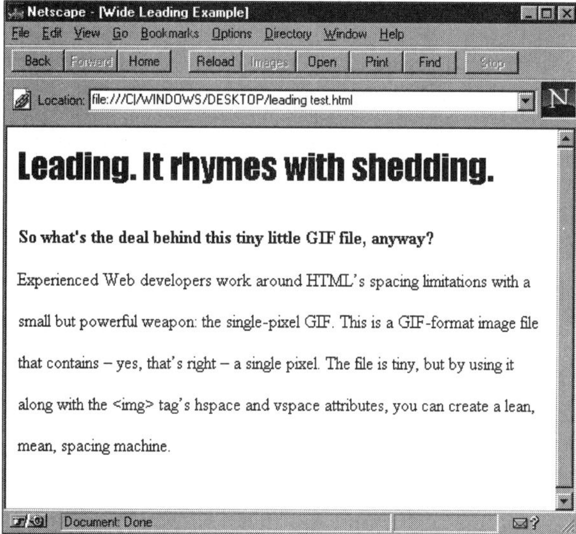

Figure 5-5: Opening up line spacing with the single-pixel GIF. Top: The source HTML. Bottom: The results.

It's important to format your HTML exactly as I have in the previous figure. In specific terms, don't put an extra return after the `<IMG>` tag. If you do, you wind up with a little bit of extra horizontal space before the first character of the following sentence.

Adding horizontal spacing

To use the single-pixel GIF to add horizontal spacing — most commonly, a paragraph indent — use the `<IMG>` tag's `hspace` attribute to specify the width of the indent (see Figure 5-6).

```
Experienced Web developers work around HTML's spacing limitations
with a small but powerful weapon: the single-pixel GIF. This is a
GIF-format image file that contains &#150; yes, that's right &#150; a
single pixel. The file is tiny, but by using it along with the
&lt;img&gt; tag's hspace and vspace attributes, you can create a
lean, mean, spacing machine.<BR>
<img src="dot_clear.gif" hspace=10>To use the single-pixel GIF to add
horizontal spacing &#150; most commonly, a paragraph indent &#150;
use the &lt;img&gt; tag's hspace attribute to specify the width of
the indent.
```

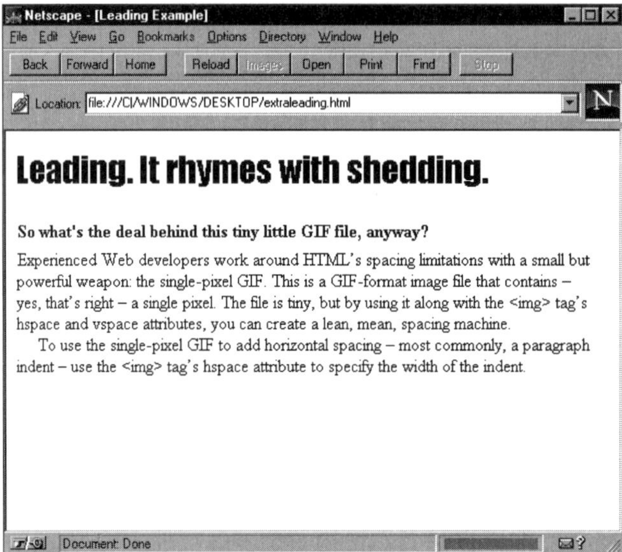

Figure 5-6: Creating a paragraph indent with a single-pixel GIF. Top: The partial HTML source showing a 20-pixel indent. Bottom: The results.

Creating an indent with nonbreaking spaces

There's another technique for creating a paragraph indent, and it doesn't require the use of the single-pixel GIF. Simply begin a paragraph with two or three nonbreaking spaces, which you can get with this code:

```
 
```

A full indent may look something like:

```
   This is the first sentence...
```

Use the single-pixel GIF liberally

You can use the single-pixel GIF as many times as you like with no real performance penalty. A visitor's browser downloads the GIF just once, retrieving every other occurrence from the browser's cache.

Making — and using — dashes

Typists use two hyphens to create a dash - - like those. Typographers use a true em dash — like that one. There isn't a standard way to generate an em dash with HTML, but there is a nonstandard way — and fortunately, it's supported by Microsoft's Internet Explorer and Netscape Navigator.

This is the code: `–`. Figure 5-7 shows it in action.

```
Leading &#150; it rhymes with shedding.
```

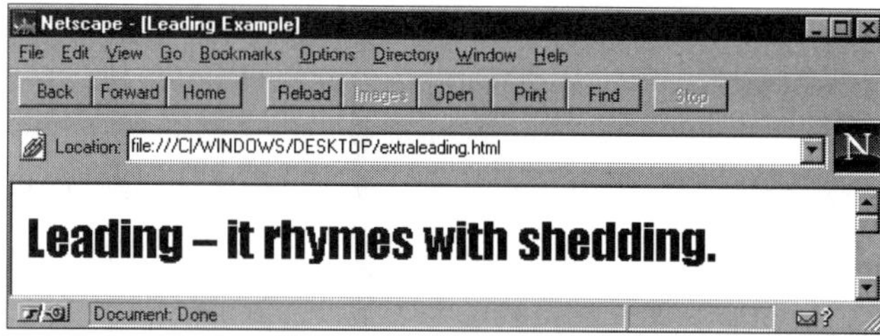

Figure 5-7: Making an em dash. Top: The HTML source. Bottom: The result.

Should you put a space on either side of the dash? That's up to you. In print, I prefer no space. (As you can see from these pages, at IDG Books Worldwide, designers disagree). On the screen, I think a space on either side of a dash helps.

What about en dashes?

There's a lesser-known dash called the *en dash,* which is used to represent the word *to,* as in: George Bush was president from 1988–1992. You can get an en dash with this code:

```
&#151;
```

Should you put a space on either side of an en dash? I prefer my en dashes closed (that is, with no space around them), but preferences vary. What's important — and this applies to spaces around em dashes, too — is that you're *consistent* throughout a page and, for that matter, a site.

Line length issues

Studies show that the optimum line length for body text allows for roughly 8 to 12 words per line. Extremely narrow measures can be tiring to read, especially on the screen (and they lead to excessive scrolling). Extremely wide measures are just as bad: the reader's eye often skips to the beginning of the same sentence, a phenomenon called *doubling.*

Alas, ensuring an ideal line length isn't easy on the Web. Several factors are working against you:

- HTML 3.2 doesn't permit you to specify an exact line length. (Although you can obtain some degree of control by using tables, as described shortly.)
- Web surfers can change your pages' margins by simply resizing their browser windows.
- Web surfers can change the font and type size in which your pages' text appears.
- Font sizes differ across platforms — Mac OS fonts are generally smaller than their Windows equivalents, so on a Mac OS machine, more words appear on each line.

As a Web page designer, you have to resign yourself to the fact that some aspects of a page's final appearance are out of your hands. Still, there are a few things you can do to regain at least some control.

Specifying the font and size

Both Netscape Navigator 3.x and later and Microsoft Internet Explorer 2.x and later support attributes to the `<FONT>` tag that enable you to specify a specific font and font size. (For more details, see the section "Specifying font sizes, typeface, and color" later in this chapter.)

Suggesting a browser window width

If your line lengths depend on a visitor's browser window being a certain width, include on your home page a graphical gauge that instructs visitors to size their windows appropriately. Figure 5-8 shows the gauge used by the *New York Times* Web site (`http://www.nytimes.com/`).

Figure 5-8: The New York Times home page and its browser-width gauge

Don't make assumptions on text fit

Don't create a page on the assumption that its text will fit within a specific space. This is especially important if you're running a text block around a graphic using the `<IMG ALIGN=LEFT>` tag, described in the next chapter. Figure 5-9 illustrates how the size of a text block can differ between the Mac and Windows platforms.

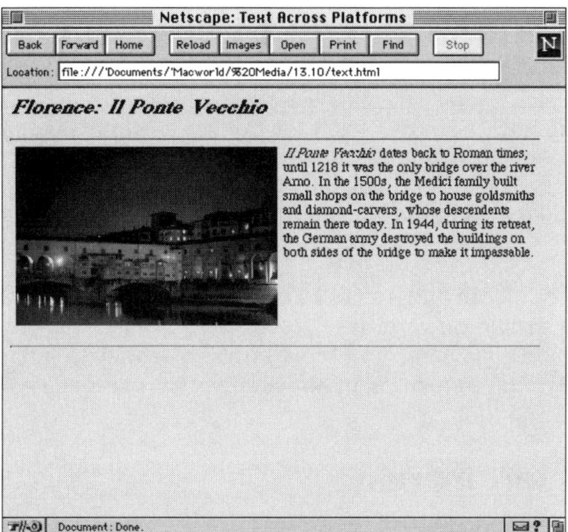

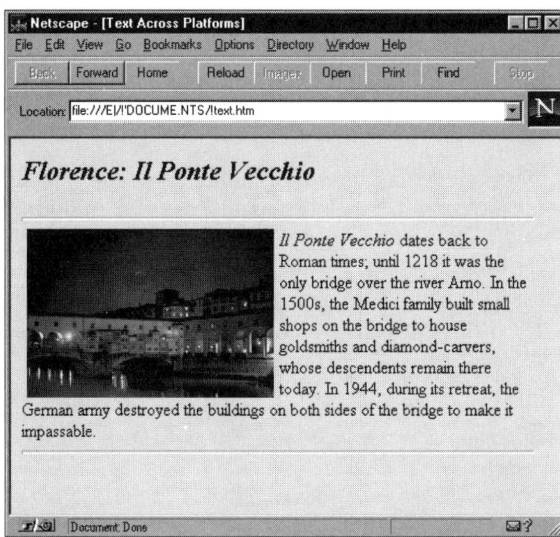

Figure 5-9: The identical HTML page viewed with the same font (Times) and same browser window width, but on different platforms: the Mac (top) and Windows (bottom). Windows fonts tend to be larger than their Mac equivalents.

Use graphic text when you want full control

If you must have total control over the appearance of a piece of text, use a "picture of text." Create anti-aliased text in a graphics program such as Adobe Photoshop, save the text as a GIF file, and then use an `<IMG>` tag to refer to the graphic text. (The next chapter contains details on creating anti-aliased graphic text.)

Using borderless tables to create columns and sideheads

HTML tables may have been designed for tabular material such as sports standings and financial data, but they also make excellent layout tools. Here are a few ideas to get your creative juices flowing. You'll find example files that illustrate these techniques on the *HTML & Web Publishing SECRETS* CD-ROM.

Note that this section heading refers to *borderless* tables — ones whose border has been turned off with the `<TABLE>` tag's `border=0` attribute. In general, you should always turn off table borders — they're junky looking. But it's especially vital to turn them off when you're using tables as advanced formatting tools.

Creating a left margin

HTML text is normally crammed up against the browser window's left edge — not terribly attractive. One way to create a left indent is with the `<BLOCKQUOTE>` tag: use `<BLOCKQUOTE>` before the text you want to indent and `</BLOCKQUOTE>` after it.

The problem with `<BLOCKQUOTE>` is one browser may render it differently than another. Some browsers even format `<BLOCKQUOTE>` text in italics.

A better way to create a left margin is by placing the page's contents within a table, one whose leftmost column serves as a spacer (see Figure 5-10).

```
<HTML>
<HEAD>
   <TITLE>Using a Table as an Indent</TITLE>
</HEAD>
<BODY BGCOLOR="#FFFFFF">
<TABLE BORDER=0>
   <TR>
      <TD width=70> </TD>
      <TD valign=top width=450>
      HTML tables may have been designed for tabular material such
as sports standings and financial data, but they also make excellent
layout tools. Here are a few ideas to get your creative juices
flowing. You'll find some example files that illustrate these
techniques on the <i>Web Publishing Secrets</i> CD.<BR></TD></TR>
</TABLE>
</BODY>
</HTML>
```

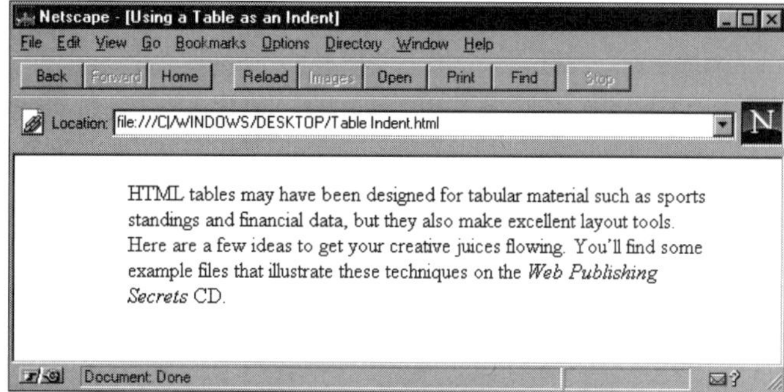

Figure 5-10: Using a table's first column as a spacer. Top: The HTML source. Bottom: The result.

Note that this simple table has just one row, with two cells.

Add a `bgcolor` attribute to the leftmost column, and you can even create a colored bar to the left of the text (see Figure 5-11). The `bgcolor` attribute for table cells is supported by Microsoft Internet Explorer 2.x, Netscape Navigator 3.x, and later versions of both. (See Chapter 7 and Appendix A for more details on `bgcolor`.)

```
<TABLE BORDER=0 cellpadding=5>
   <TR>
      <TD width=70 bgcolor=blue> </TD>
      <TD valign=top width=450>
      HTML tables may have been designed for tabular material such
as sports standings and financial data, but they also make excellent
layout tools. Here are a few ideas to get your creative juices
flowing. You'll find some example files that illustrate these
techniques on the <i>Web Publishing Secrets</i> CD.<BR>
</TD></TR>
</TABLE>
```

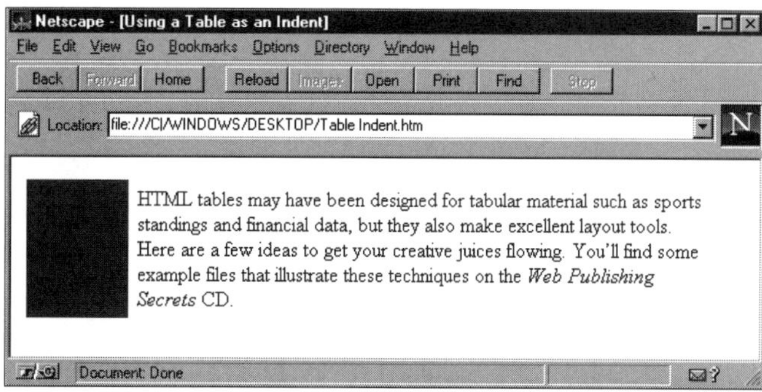

Figure 5-11: Adding color to a table's spacer column. Top: The HTML source. Note the addition of a cellpadding value to put some space between the color and the text. Bottom: The result.

A more common way to create a margin bar like this one is with a background graphic; the next chapter contains all the details.

Creating multicolumn layout grids

Tables are equally useful for creating multicolumn layout grids. A great many Web sites use tables in this way (see Figure 5-12).

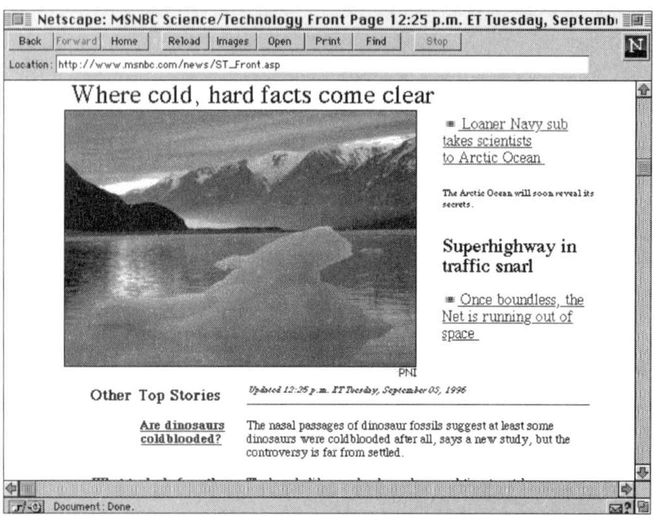

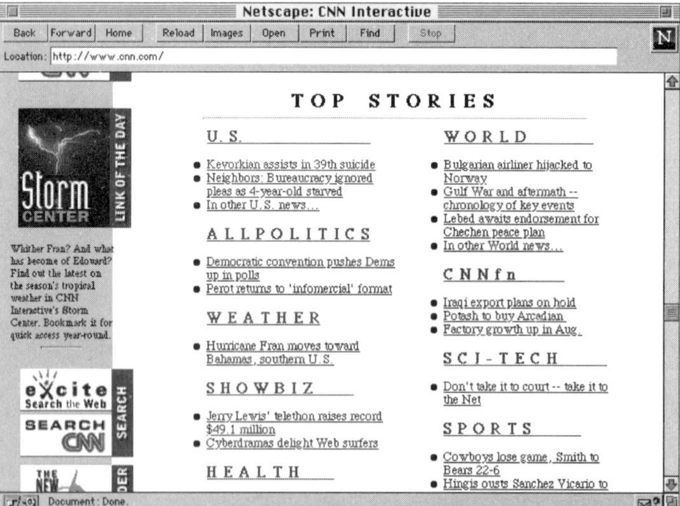

Figure 5-12: Borderless tables are in the news, creating the multicolumn grids used on MSNBC's site (top) and CNN's (bottom).

Creating sideheads

A *sidehead* is a subhead that appears in the left margin, adjacent to the body text it references. Tables are great for these, too (see Figure 5-13).

```
<HTML>
<HEAD>
   <TITLE>Sidehead Example</TITLE>
</HEAD>
<BODY BGCOLOR="#FFFFFF">
<TABLE BORDER=0 CELLPADDING=1>
   <TR>
      <TD width="75" VALIGN=top>
         <FONT SIZE=4><b>Future Directions</b></FONT>
      </TD>
      <TD width="300" VALIGN=top>
         <P>Cascading Style Sheets, discussed in Chapter 7, do
support indents and other advanced formatting controls, but they
probably won't be in widespread use until sometime in 1997. Even
then, you'll want to think twice about relying exclusively on them,
since older browsers, including Netscape Navigator 3.0 and Microsoft
Internet Explorer 2.0, don't support them.<BR>
      </TD></TR>
</TABLE>
</BODY>
</HTML>
```

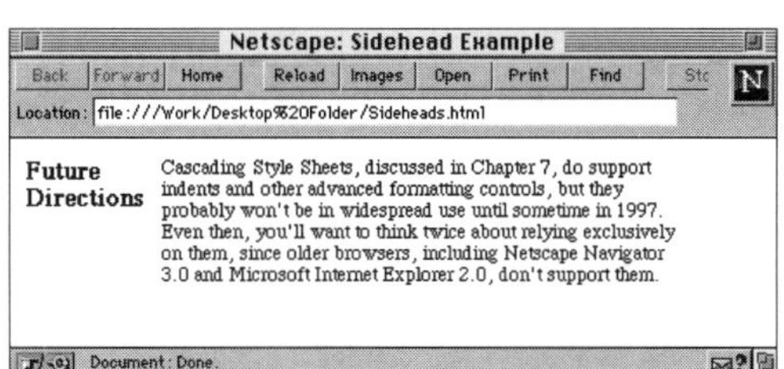

Figure 5-13: Using a table to create sideheads. Top: The HTML source. Adjust the cellpadding value in column one as required. Bottom: The results.

If you want to place multiple sideheads, each one adjacent to the section it introduces, begin a new table row for each new sidehead.

Positioning in-margin graphics

You can use the technique I just described to position a graphic in the margin, as shown in Figure 5-14.

```
<HTML>
<HEAD>
   <TITLE>In-Margin Graphic Example</TITLE>
</HEAD>
<BODY BGCOLOR="#FFFFFF">
<TABLE BORDER=0 CELLPADDING=1>
   <TR>
      <TD width="75" VALIGN=top>
         <img src="Speaker.gif">
      </TD>
```

```
        <TD width="300" VALIGN=top>
            <P>Cascading Style Sheets, discussed in Chapter 7, do
support indents and other advanced formatting controls, but they
probably won't be in widespread use until sometime in 1997. Even
then, you'll want to think twice about relying exclusively on them,
since older browsers, including Netscape Navigator 3.0 and Microsoft
Internet Explorer 2.0, don't support them.<BR>
        </TD></TR>
</TABLE>
</BODY>
</HTML>
```

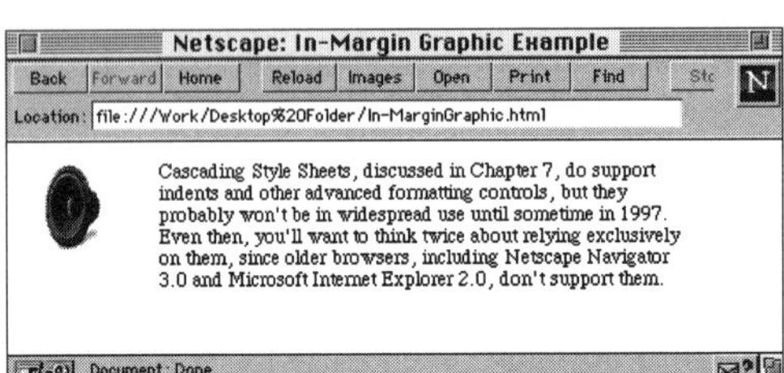

Figure 5-14: Using a table to position a graphic in the margin. Top: The HTML source. Bottom: The results.

Specifying font sizes, typeface, and color

Little by little, Web authors are getting more control over Web typography. Some of the most important developments revolve around specifying the size and color of text and the font in which it appears. The tips in this section work in both Netscape Navigator 3.x and later and Microsoft Internet Explorer 2.x and later.

What Are the Best Tools for Table Tricks?

Most HTML tools support HTML tables, but some are better than others for the formatting tricks I've described in this chapter.

The current versions of all WYSIWYG layout tools — for example, Adobe PageMill, Claris Home Page, NetObjects Fusion, and Symantec's Visual Page — all provide solid table-editing features. All enable you to resize table columns by dragging their boundaries, and all enable you to mix and match column width — an essential capability for many formatting tasks. I'm particularly fond of the way Visual Page adjusts line breaks dynamically as you resize table borders.

I'm also pleasantly impressed with Microsoft's Internet Assistants for Word and Excel. Word and Excel have excellent table-editing features, and their respective Internet Assistants do an excellent job of translating these features into HTML.

Specifying font color with <FONT COLOR>

The <FONT COLOR> tag enables you to specify the color in which type appears. You can use hexadecimal values to specify color or you can use the color names that Netscape Navigator and Internet Explorer support. For example, the following text would appear in blue:

```
<font color=blue>
Singin' the blues.
</font>
```

See Appendix A for details on color specification in HTML.

Controlling font size with <FONT SIZE>

One crude way to specify font sizes is with the HTML heading tags, such as <H1> and <H2>. A better way is to use the <FONT SIZE> tag, which lets you choose one of seven font sizes. (Alas, you can't choose a specific point size, such as 14-point.)

In the world according to <FONT SIZE>, text normally appears in a default size of 3. You can create text that's larger or smaller than this default size in either of two ways:

- **Specifying an absolute size.** For example, <FONT SIZE=7> gives you the biggest possible text.
- **Specifying a relative size.** For example, <FONT SIZE=+1> changes the size to whatever the default size is plus one.

Changing the default size with <BASEFONT>

You can change the default size from 3 to any other value by using the <BASEFONT> tag, like so:

```
<basefont size=5>
```

Should you use relative or absolute sizes?

SECRET

Using <BASEFONT> in combination with relative font sizes (instead of absolute ones) gives you the flexibility to change a page's sizes in one fell swoop. If you use relative sizes, simply change a page's <BASEFONT> tag, and all the sizes within that page change accordingly — but still retain their relative size characteristics. On the other hand, if you use absolute sizes throughout a page, making size changes requires you to manually edit each and every occurrence of the <FONT SIZE> tag.

Simulating small caps with <FONT SIZE>

Small capitals, also called small caps, are capital letters whose height matches that of the lowercase letters in a type font. Small caps are typically used for abbreviations, such as A.M. and P.M, or for acronyms, such as NASA or RAM. When set in small caps, these bowls of alphabet soup don't overwhelm the surrounding text as normal, full-size capitals often do.

When desktop publishing caused many high-end type houses to become boarded up, the use of small caps declined dramatically — many desktop publishers didn't know what they were. Even when they learned, the results weren't always pretty: most digital fonts lack true small caps, and programs that provide a small caps formatting option simulate them by using a smaller font size.

And that's where this tip comes in. Using the `<FONT>` tag's `size` attribute, you can simulate small caps. Figure 5-15 shows how.

```
<HTML>
<HEAD>
   <TITLE>Small Caps Example</TITLE>
</HEAD>
<BODY BGCOLOR="#FFFFFF">
<P><TABLE BORDER=0>
   <TR>
      <TD width="75" valign=top>
       
      </TD>
      <TD width="300" VALIGN=top>
      <font size=-1>SMALL CAPITALS</font> are typically used in body
text for acronyms such as <font size=-1>NASA</font> and for
abbreviations such as <font size=-1>A.M.</font> You might also use
them as a design element &#150; to set off the first words of a
paragraph, as shown in this example.
      </TD></TR>
</TABLE>
</BODY>
</HTML>
```

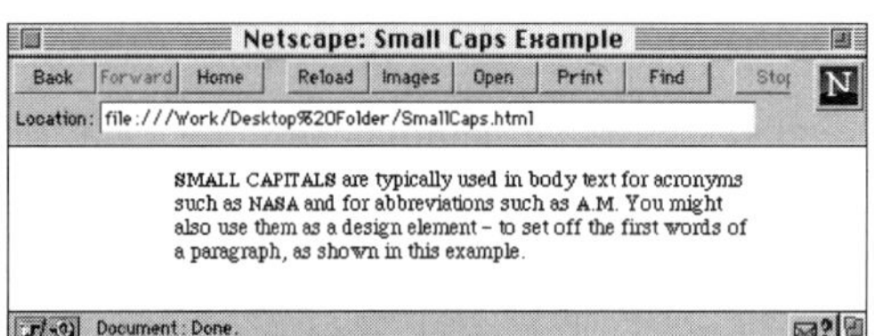

Figure 5-15: Simulating small caps with <FONT SIZE>. Top: The HTML source. Bottom: The results.

A size value of -1 works well for simulating small caps in body text, and the results look quite good.

As Figure 5-16 shows, you can employ this technique to simulate the mixing of conventional caps with small caps. For the small caps, use a font size one size below that of the full-size caps. For example, for full-sized caps formatted using `<FONT SIZE=5>`, use small caps formatted using `<FONT SIZE=4>`.

```
<HTML>
<HEAD>
   <TITLE>Small Caps Example</TITLE>
</HEAD>
<BODY BGCOLOR="#FFFFFF">
<P><TABLE BORDER=0>
```

```
    <TR>
        <TD width="100" valign=top>
        <font size=5>S</font><font size=4>MALL <font
size=5>C</font><font size=4>APITALS</font>
        </TD>
        <TD width="300" VALIGN=top>
        <font size=-1>SMALL CAPITALS</font> are typically used in body
text for acronyms such as <font size=-1>NASA</font> and for
abbreviations such as <font size=-1>A.M.</font> You might also use
them as a design element &#150; to set off the first words of a
paragraph, as shown in this example.
        </TD></TR>
</TABLE>
</BODY>
</HTML>
```

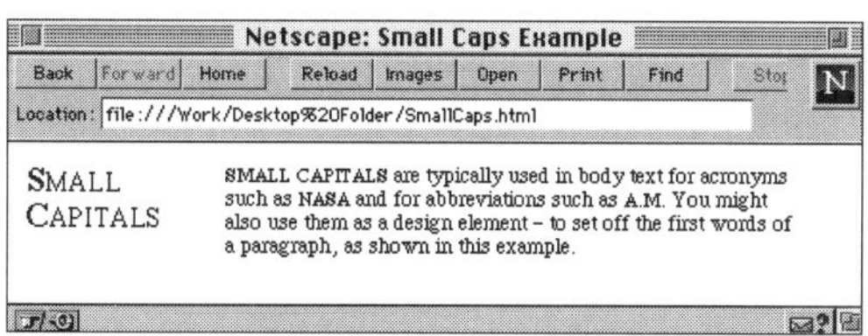

Figure 5-16: Simulating full-size and small caps with <FONT SIZE>. Top: The HTML source. Bottom: The results. Notice how the differing character weights can clash.

Depending on the specific font sizes you use, you may see a jarring visual problem: the full-sized capitals appear to be considerably bolder than the small caps. A work-around to this problem is to use the `<B>` tag to format the small caps in bold. This fattens up the stem weights of the small caps, causing them to more closely approximate the weight of the full-sized capitals.

The *HTML & Web Publishing SECRETS* CD-ROM contains some example files that illustrate the use of `<FONT SIZE>` for simulating small capitals.

Specifying fonts with <FONT FACE>

Thank you, Microsoft! That isn't a phrase I utter every day — except where Web typography is concerned. Microsoft has done more to further the cause of good typography on the Web than almost any other company.

One of Microsoft's gifts to the Web designer is the `<FONT FACE>` tag, now also supported by Netscape Navigator. The `<FONT FACE>` tag enables you to specify the fonts in which a page's text appears. And because not all Web surfers have the same set of fonts, you can specify what I call *fall-back fonts:* ones that are used instead of your first choices.

The `<FONT FACE>` tag works in Netscape Navigator 3.0 and later and in Microsoft Internet Explorer.

The <FONT FACE> tag in action

Using the `<FONT FACE>` tag is easy. Just surround the text to be formatted like the following code:

```
<font face="font name,second choice,third choice">
Your text here
</font>
```

Figure 5-17 shows some examples.

```
<html>
<head>
<title>
Font Face Example
</title>
</head>
<body bgcolor=#ffffff>
<font face="Impact,Helvetica" size=6>
Fonts. Use them wisely &#150; or else.
</font>
<br>
<br>
<font face="Times New Roman,Times" size=5>
<b><i>ultra</i></font><font face="Arial,Helvetica" size=6><b>Cool</b>
</font>
</body>
</html>
```

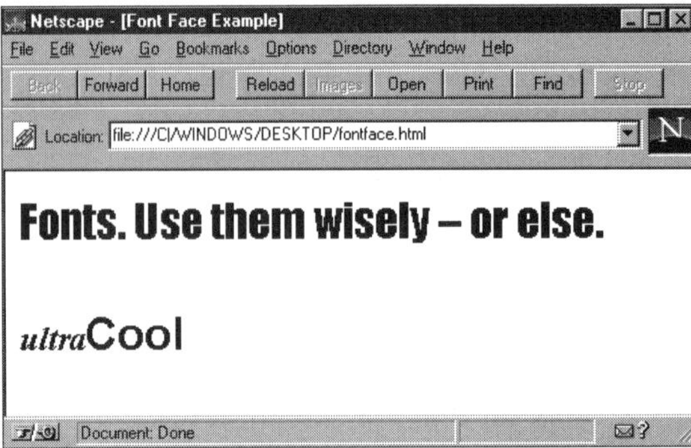

Figure 5-17: <FONT FACE> in action. Top: The HTML source. Bottom: The results.

You can also combine `<FONT FACE>` with values for color and size.

One great thing about `<FONT FACE>` is that it enables you to specify alternatives if your first choice isn't installed on a user's system. (If none of the fonts you specified are available, the text appears in the browser's default font, which is usually Times.) Here are a few ways you can take advantage of `<FONT FACE>`.

- **Compensate for platform differences.** On Windows systems, a Helvetica look-alike called Arial is a standard font; on Macs, Helvetica is a standard font. Similarly, the Mac OS's monospaced font Courier has a Windows equivalent named Courier New. By using the tag `<FONT FACE="Arial,`

`Helvetica">` or `<FONT FACE="Courier,Courier new">` you can take these name differences into account and still get the desired results.

- **Ensure that at least similar fonts are used.** Maybe you have a headline that you want to appear in Impact (a free Microsoft TrueType font discussed shortly). If a user doesn't have Impact installed, do you really want the headline to appear in Times, which is about as different as you can get? A better approach is to specify a similar substitute, in this case Arial:

```
<font face="Impact,Arial">
```

  Arial isn't exactly a dead ringer for Impact, but it's a lot closer than Times.

TrueType versus PostScript

The `<FONT FACE>` tag doesn't discriminate between these popular font formats. You can specify any font you like, and if it's installed on a visitor's system, it will be used.

Still, there is an argument for preferring TrueType fonts: TrueType is built into the Mac and Windows platforms, but automatic support for Type 1 PostScript fonts is not. To be more specific, the Mac OS and Windows can't automatically generate any size of Type 1 PostScript font unless you have the Adobe Type Manager (ATM) utility installed. ATM is an extremely popular utility, but if you want to be absolutely safe, specify only TrueType fonts.

Which Fonts Are Visitors Most Likely to Have?

If you want to specify fonts that most people are likely to have, which ones should you use? Table 5-1 lists the most common bundled fonts in the Windows and Mac OS worlds. I've organized this table so the fonts that most closely match each other are listed in adjacent columns.

Table 5-1 The most common Windows and Mac OS fonts

Windows	***Mac OS***
Arial	Helvetica
Arial Narrow	N Helvetica Narrow
Bookman Old Style	Bookman
Century Gothic	Avant Garde
Century Schoolbook	New Century Schlbk
Courier New	Courier
(no common bundled equivalent)	Palatino
Times New Roman	Times

Free fonts! The Bill Gates Collection

Microsoft's Web Typography site (`http://www.microsoft.com/truetype/`) contains a versatile set of TrueType fonts that you can download for free. Better yet, fill out an on-screen registration form, and you can post some or all of these same fonts on your Web site for others to download. Microsoft's strategy is to have a standard set of fonts on both Macs and PCs that Web designers can summon in their pages.

It's likely that someday soon fonts such as Impact and Verdana will become trite and despised, as overused as Times and Helvetica were in the early days of laser printing. But for now, seeing the occasional heading formatted in one of these fonts is a breath of fresh air in a typographically stale world.

Accessing bold, italic, and bold italic

You can't access the bold, italic, or bold italic version of a font by including its name in the `<FONT FACE>` tag. For example, `<FONT FACE="Helvetica Bold Italic">` doesn't work. To access these stylistic variations, use the `<B>` and `<I>` HTML tags. For example, use the following for Helvetica Bold Italic.

```
<font face="Helvetica">
<b>
<i>
This is Helvetica Bold Italic.
</i>
</b>
</font>
```

Of course, you can scrunch the `<B>` and `<I>` tags together; you don't have to place them on separate lines as I did in this example.

The trouble with italics

Speaking of italics, it's worth noting that some fonts don't include true italics, substituting instead a slanted, or *oblique* version of the font. These pseudo-italics are *ugly,* especially those derived from serif fonts such as Times. Some fonts include true italic versions, but it's up to an individual user to install them on his or her system. (As an aside, it's worth noting that some sans-serif typefaces *include* an oblique style. So if you see a font on your system whose name ends in Oblique, don't feel obligated to delete it!)

As a Web developer, there's nothing you can do about a visitor's lack of a true italic. Your choices boil down to:

- **Not using italic in your pages.** This isn't a very appealing choice. Italic type has its place — for introducing new terms, for emphasizing a word or phrase, or for denoting the title of a book or magazine, such as *HTML & Web Publishing SECRETS* or *Boy's Life.*
- **Creating a "what we recommend to view this site" page.** This isn't a thrilling alternative, because it calls attention to the mechanics and the relative crudeness of the Web. You don't see a "what you need" page at

the beginning of a book. (Can you imagine it? "This book is optimized for a light bulb of at least 75 watts, a pair of reading glasses, a comfy chair, and a dry red wine — preferably, a Merlot.") But crude the Web is, and as Web developers, if we want visitors to see our sites the way we want them to appear, it doesn't hurt to provide a list of recommended surfing equipment. And if you take advantage of Microsoft's free TrueType font collection by posting it on your Web site, being able to offer a few free fonts that visitors can use in all their applications is a nice incentive.

Watch your text colors and backgrounds

If you've read this far, you obviously have such exquisite typographic taste that you don't even need to read this tip. But just in case you've accidentally opened the book to this page and you haven't read the preceding portions of this chapter, here it is.

To ensure that your pages are readable and legible, be sure you have lots of contrast between the text color and the background color (or pattern, if you're using a background image as described in the next chapter). By *lots of contrast*, I mean a combination such as black type on a white or slightly off-white background — a combination that readers are used to seeing in print.

Whatever you do, don't use dark-colored text against a dark background. I've seen too many a page formatted in barely readable color schemes, such as dark blue type against a black background. It's hard to believe that some Web publishers would be so typographically tasteless — don't they read their own pages?

Reverse type — white type on a dark background — is a common typographical device in the print world. It doesn't always translate well to the Web, however, because cheaper monitors don't display it well. The white characters tend to bleed into the background. I recommend avoiding reverse type for lengthy passages of text. In fact, that's a good rule of thumb for the print world, too.

And if you *must* use background graphics, choose graphics with subtle patterns. The next chapter contains more advice on graphics and patterns. In the meantime, remember: less is best.

What's Ahead for Web Typography

With the HTML extensions and the work-arounds I've described in this chapter, you can go a long way toward creating typographically attractive documents. And fortunately, more control will soon be possible.

One coming trend will be the adoption of Cascading Style Sheets, which you can learn about in Chapter 7. Style sheets provide more of the typographic control that designers need without sacrificing HTML's structured qualities.

Another welcome development is the OpenType standard, which is a collaborative effort of Adobe and Microsoft. OpenType will enable font embedding: rather than just being able to specify a font and hope that it exists on a user's system, you will be able to embed a specific font so it downloads along with a given page. Won't this dramatically increase the size of Web pages? OpenType's creators say no. According to its proponents, OpenType will compress fonts and embed only those font weights and even characters that are required for a given page.

Ultimately, however, it will be some time before these enhancements become as ubiquitous as single-pixel GIFs, borderless tables, and `<FONT>` tags. These humble tools are supported by the largest array of browsers. Fortunately, when used carefully, they can deliver fine results — not the drop-dead-gorgeous typography that high-end designers crave, but better looking pages than traditional online services have offered so far.

Summary

- Good writing and accurate punctuation aren't always in generous supply on Web sites. But following a few simple rules and investing in (and reading) a couple of good style guides will go a long way toward improving your site's copy.
- Watch your page length: People don't like to scroll, and it's important to design a page so important information appears on a single screen.
- HTML doesn't provide for common devices such as paragraph indents and variable line spacing, but you can obtain them by using a single-pixel GIF file along with the `<IMG>` tag's `hspace` and `vspace` attributes.
- You can use borderless tables to create margins, sideheads, in-margin graphics, and multiple-column layout grids.
- The `<FONT>` tag's `face` attribute enables you to specify the fonts in which a page's text appears.
- The `<FONT>` tag's `size` attribute provides control over the size in which text appears. You can use the `size` attribute to create headings and to simulate small capitals.

Chapter 6

Graphic Themes

In This Chapter

- Optimizing Web graphics for efficiency and performance
- GIF? JPEG? Something else? Choosing the right format for your Web graphics
- Secrets of the graphics-related HTML tags
- Creating cool graphical navigation schemes
- Server-side versus client-side image maps

One of the biggest reasons the Web is so popular is its support for graphics. Attractive graphics can dress up Web pages, as well as convey information and serve as navigation guides. But preparing graphics for the Web isn't straightforward — you must consider several basic computer-graphics issues, such as file formats, resolutions, and color palettes. There are also special, graphics-specific HTML tags to contend with and subtle technical issues. For example, the way you use graphics on a site can have a significant impact on the performance of your Web server.

Your ability to address these issues is a major factor in determining the performance and usability of your sites. This chapter is a guide to graphic themes, including the underlying concepts and issues you need to know when creating Web graphics, and tips and secrets for creating great graphics in today's most popular graphics program, Adobe Photoshop.

Optimizing Graphics

The Bandwidth Conservation Society wants you to slim down. The BCS is, in its own words, a "loosely knit group of Web developers that disagree on nearly everything" except the need to keep World Wide Web graphics as small as possible — in order to use less server space and processor time, to impose less traffic on an increasingly crowded Internet, and most important, to deliver faster performance to Web surfers.

The idea is simple, really. When you keep Web graphics small, you use network bandwidth more efficiently, enabling visitors to enjoy a more satisfying performance. By *small*, I don't mean matchbook-sized graphics. From the Web's perspective, small graphics are graphics whose resolution and color depth have been reduced to use the least amount of space while preserving image quality.

On CD-ROM

Tame Your Graphics with These Tools

There's a full palette of terrific graphics utilities, samples, and ready-to-use art on the *HTML & Web Publishing SECRETS* CD-ROM. See Appendix B for a complete listing of the CD-ROM contents and look for the CD-ROM icons throughout this chapter. In the meantime, here's a summary:

Ulead PhotoImpact with Web Extensions. A trial version of Ulead's outstanding image editor and its Web-graphics extensions.

RGB-hex converters. Mac OS and Windows utilities for converting color values between RGB and hexadecimal.

Ready-to-use art. Both the Claris Home Page and the Ulead PhotoImpact trial versions include extensive art libraries. I've also thrown in a collection of my own colored, single-pixel GIF files and border graphics.

Netscape color swatches. If you load this into Photoshop and use it to choose colors, your graphics will never be undesirably dithered again.

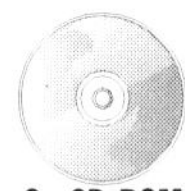

On CD-ROM

You can employ a variety of techniques and tools to help graphics look their best and use the least amount of bandwidth. I discuss these tricks in this section and pass along some advice for choosing file formats for Web site graphics. You'll find some sample images and a large collection of graphics utilities and add-ons on the *HTML & Web Publishing SECRETS* CD-ROM (see the "On the CD-ROM" sidebar at the beginning of this chapter).

Which format for Web graphics?

One of the most basic decisions you must make when preparing Web graphics is choosing a file format.

GIF

The Graphics Interchange Format (GIF) is the most popular format for Web graphics. *Interlaced GIF* files are files whose data is arranged in such a way as to allow what is perceived to be a faster display. In other words, instead of oozing onto the screen from top to bottom, an interlaced GIF appears in a coarse form almost immediately, and then gets progressively sharper. GIF files also support *transparency,* an attribute that enables an image to blend with the Web page's background color. For details on interlacing and transparency, see "GIF secrets" later in this chapter.

You can create interlaced GIFs with the Adobe GIF89a plug-in for Photoshop (available at `http://www.adobe.com`). PhotoGIF, from BoxTop Software (`http://www.boxtopsoft.com`), is another excellent Photoshop plug-in for creating GIF files. Version 1.6 of Equilibrium's must-have DeBabelizer utility can also create interlaced GIFs.

BACKGROUNDER

Graphics Jargon: Bit Depth and Dithering

One of the most important aspects of slimming down Web graphics is choosing an appropriate bit depth. You may hear that phrase all the time, but what does it *mean*?

Bit depth refers to the number of bits assigned to each screen dot, or pixel, of an image. In a computer's video memory, the bits that represent each pixel can be on (assigned a value of 1) or off (assigned a value of 0) in different combinations.

For example, when two bits are assigned to each pixel, four on-off combinations exist — both bits on; both bits off; one bit on, second bit off; and second bit on, first bit off. So a two-bit graphic can contain up to four colors.

When four bits are assigned to each pixel, you get 16 on-off combinations, or a maximum of 16 colors. With eight bits per pixel, you get 256 combinations — and colors. Internally, Windows and Mac OS machines use 32 bits to describe colors, giving them the capability to create more than 16 million different hues. But remember, the number of colors that can actually be displayed at once depends on the type of graphics circuitry a computer has.

Dithering refers to the process of simulating colors by arranging colored pixels in a pattern. Look closely at any color image printed in a magazine, and you'll see one example of dithering. With computer graphics, dithering makes it possible to simulate colors that can't directly be displayed.

Dithering is a mixed bag where Web graphics are concerned. On one hand, it can be extremely useful for slimming down the size of a photograph while maximizing its image quality. But for the colors you *want* to appear solid — perhaps a company logo or a horizontal bar — dithering is A Bad Thing. See the section called "Steps to smaller graphics" later in this chapter for more details on when and how to use dithering — and when and how to avoid it.

JPEG

GIFs are limited to a color depth of 8 bits — 256 colors. For photographs, JPEG (Joint Photographic Experts Group) tends to deliver better results as well as smaller files. But due to differences in the way GIF and JPEG formats compress image data, GIF delivers better results and smaller files for line art and solid colors. GIF is also better for images that contain sharply contrasting borders, such as a black line adjacent to a white one. JPEG, however, can introduce undesirable artifacts, particularly where high-contrast areas meet. (Later sections of this chapter contain more details on GIF and JPEG graphics.)

File formats and browser compatibility

As you can see, the nature of your images is a major factor behind your choice of a file format. Another factor is your destination browser. Many older Web browsers can't display JPEG files alongside text and other page elements. If you want your graphics to reach every possible browser, GIF is currently your best bet.

Progressive JPEG, PNG, and beyond

Two up-and-coming graphics formats mean more choices. One is the *progressive JPEG* format, which provides an interlaced GIF-like effect in that an image appears in crude form quickly and gradually sharpens into view. Progressive JPEGs also tend to be slightly smaller than conventional, or *sequential,* JPEG files. You can create progressive JPEGs using Adobe Photoshop 4.0. The current versions of the most popular browsers can display progressive JPEGs, including Netscape Navigator 2.0 and later; Microsoft's Internet Explorer; and Spyglass's Enhanced Mosaic 2.1.

Another promising newcomer is the Portable Network Graphics, or PNG (pronounced *ping*) format. PNG supports 24-bit images as well as an impressive interlacing scheme. Unlike JPEG, which sacrifices image quality, PNG also provides lossless compression.

Several graphics-conversion utilities, including Equilibrium Technologies' DeBabelizer 1.6.5 and Lemke Software's GraphicConverter 2.2.2 (a shareware utility; 100102.1304@compuserve.com) can create PNG files. Alas, PNG support among browsers remains spotty. Netscape Navigator doesn't directly support it, although there are plug-in modules that add PNG support. One such plug-in is the amazing Quick View Plus, from Inso Corporation (`http://www.inso.com/`). Quick View Plus supports not only PNG graphics, but also roughly 200 other file formats for opening word processor, spreadsheet, database, and graphics files. Another PNG plug-in is PNG Live, a free Navigator and Internet Explorer plug-in from Siegal & Gale. PNG Live is available for Windows 95 and NT, and Power Macintosh; for more information, go to `http://speedy.siegelgale.com/solutions/png_index.html`.

A lot of smart people are developing ways to crunch images down to sizes smaller than you might have thought possible not long ago. Iterated Data Systems (`http://www.iterated.com`) has developed a fractal-based compression scheme and a Netscape plug-in called Fractal Viewer to support it. Ultimately, though, whether this and other futuristic formats take off depends on how many browsers support them directly — without plug-ins. Until that happens, GIF and JPEG are the formats of choice.

Bit depths: fewer bits buy better performance

It'd be wonderful to create a Web site filled with 24-bit color images. But 24-bit color images devour storage space — a full-screen (640×480 pixels), 24-bit color image requires 900K of disk space. Images this large would choke a modem and bog down a server.

What's more, many Macs and Windows machines are limited to displaying only 256 simultaneous colors — a few hues short of the 16 million that 24-bit color makes possible. When your gorgeous 24-bit images load on a 256-color machine, their subtle color shifts will turn into jarring bands and speckles.

To get better performance and work within the 256-color constraints of most computers, reduce the bit depth of graphics. Won't this introduce speckles and color banding? Yes, but you can minimize the degradation. In other words, by carefully reducing the image's quality yourself, you can prevent it from looking even worse. Call it controlled degradation.

If you're creating GIF files, reduce your graphics to the lowest depth that still provides acceptable image quality. Again, simple images can reduce to 4-bit color with little quality degradation.

For JPEG files, experiment with different compression settings to arrive at the optimum balance between image quality and file size.

Steps to smaller graphics

When a full-color image is displayed on a 256-color computer, the computer must simulate the colors that it can't actually display. It does so by dithering: combining pixels in patterns that simulate other hues.

But which 256 colors does the computer use to do its dithering? The answer lies within an internal data table called a *color palette* or *color look-up table.* This is basically a digital version of a paint store's color-mixing chart: it contains a series of 256 entries, each with a corresponding formula for a specific color.

The standard color palette — the one defined by the computer's operating system — is called the *system palette.* The system palette contains a wide range of hues and gray shades.

But in recognition of the fact that one palette might not fit all images, Windows and the Mac OS can also work with *custom color palettes* — ones whose 256-color recipes are fine-tuned to match those in a particular image. A custom palette is also often called an *adaptive palette,* because its contents have been adapted to meet the color needs of a specific image.

SECRET

How to Scan for the Screen

Graphics destined for the screen have a resolution of 72 dots per inch (dpi). You can scan photos or artwork at 72 dpi, but you may get better quality by scanning the photos at a higher resolution and then using Adobe Photoshop to downsample the images to 72 dpi. Generally, scanning at 150 to 200 dpi delivers fine results.

To downsample a high-resolution image scan to screen resolution in Photoshop, choose the Image command and type 72 in the Resolution text box. Apply the Unsharp Mask filter after downsampling to sharpen up a resampled image.

You can manipulate color palettes with an image-editing program such as Adobe Photoshop. (Photoshop is the program I use for all of the examples in this chapter.) You can also use a graphics utility such as Equilibrium DeBabelizer. As I describe shortly, manipulating color palettes to provide the best image quality on 8-bit displays is a vital stage in the production process. (*Warning:* It also contributes to self-induced baldness among Web publishers.)

System versus adaptive palettes

As I mentioned previously, the standard system palette contains a wide range of hues, many of which may not be required by a given image. Similarly, the system palette may not contain hues that an image *does* require. As a result, if you dither an image to a system palette, the resulting image often contains excessive dithering and has a speckled look. See Figure 6-1 for an example of an image dithered to both a system palette and an adaptive palette.

Figure 6-1: The same image dithered to a system palette (top) and an adaptive palette (bottom)

When you use an adaptive palette, Photoshop creates a palette tuned to the actual hues present in the image. The result is less dithering and a more pleasing image.

The bad news about adaptive palettes

Unfortunately, the system palette can sometimes be the best choice for Web graphics — not always, but sometimes. Here's the deal. On 256-color displays, a Web browser imposes its *own* built-in color palette, which is very similar to the standard system palette. If you prepare images with an 8-bit adaptive palette, they can look horrible when displayed on 256-color monitors — the colors become all splotchy and look, well, weird.

An image's adaptive palette will, however, kick in on monitors set to display thousands (16-bit) or millions (24-bit) of colors.

This palette paradox distills into a simple rule: If you require your site's visitors to have 16- or 24-bit displays and you want compact, fast-loading graphics, dither to an 8-bit adaptive palette. Then examine the image on an 8-bit display. If it looks lousy, you might want to dither to an 8-bit system palette instead of an adaptive palette. Or, you might want to dither to the palette of the browser you expect most people to be using. For details on this option, see "GIF secrets" later in this chapter.

Reducing bit depths in Adobe Photoshop

To reduce an image's bit depth in Adobe Photoshop, choose Indexed Color from the Mode menu. In the Indexed Color dialog box, choose the appropriate options, as shown in Figure 6-2.

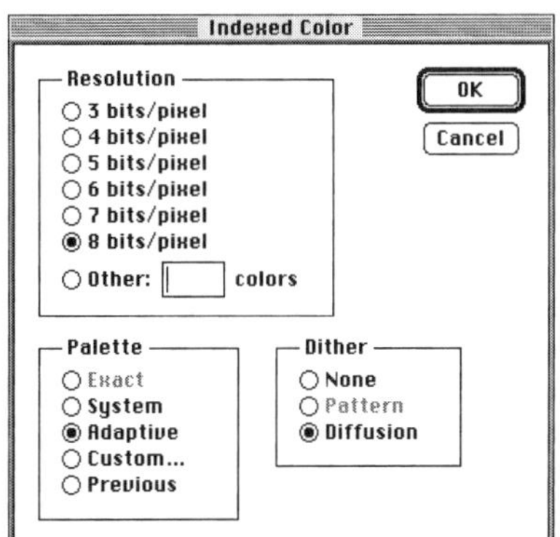

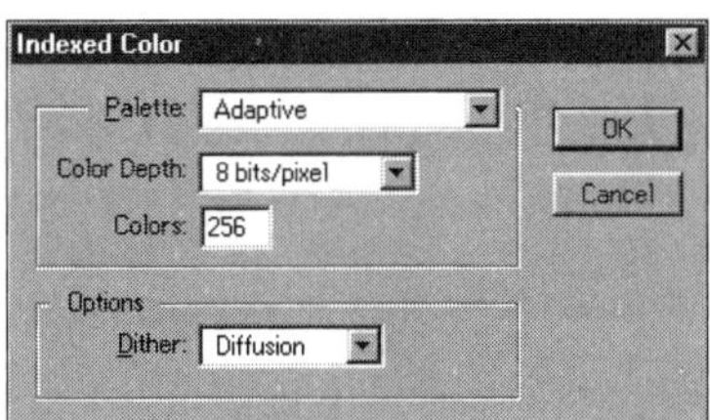

Figure 6-2: Reducing bit depths in Adobe Photoshop 3.0 (top) and 4.0 (bottom)

So how low can you go? The following are some tips for bit-depth reduction:

- For simple images — line art or images containing nothing but anti-aliased text — bit depths as low as 4 bits per pixel can deliver good results.
- For photographs, 8 bits per pixel is often the best choice, although 7 bits per pixel may be adequate for some images.
- Diffusion dithering usually provides the most pleasing appearance for low bit-depth images. Unfortunately, it leads to larger GIF files because GIF's compression scheme is most efficient with areas of solid colors, which dithering, by definition, removes.

Anti-Alias Your Graphics' Text

Chances are some of your images will contain text: captions, call-out labels, navigation options. Text looks better when it's anti-aliased — its edges, rather than appearing jagged, appear smoothed by a faint row of dimmer pixels.

If you're creating text in Adobe Photoshop, be sure the Anti-Aliased box is checked in Photoshop's Type Tool dialog box. If you need to add text to an image scanned at a high resolution, create the text *after* resampling the image to 72 dpi. Downsampling anti-aliased text can introduce ugly artifacts.

Photoshop can also apply anti-aliasing to line art, such as a logo. To anti-alias an illustration created in Adobe Illustrator, choose General from Photoshop 4's Preferences submenu (in the File menu) and be sure the Anti-alias PostScript Box is checked. On the Mac OS side, you can also open and anti-alias a PICT image using the Anti-Aliased PICT command in the File menu's Import submenu.

Need top quality? Provide alternatives

With good source images, careful palette manipulation, and the right file formats, you can shoehorn remarkably good-looking graphics into a small file. Still, there may be times when you just have to have 24-bit quality — in a title or site on fine art, for example.

For these cases, provide your graphics in two versions and let users choose the one that meets their quality requirements and hardware. Have your title or Web site display the low-quality images by default, and provide a way to get to the high-quality versions — by clicking on a low-quality image, for example.

If you take this approach, be sure to let visitors know how large the high-quality versions are: include the file size in the link or in a caption adjacent to the low-quality version.

GIF secrets

This section is a collection of tips and secrets for making GIF files. This section doesn't cover animated GIFs; for details on these puppies, see Chapter 13.

When to use GIF files — and when not to

GIF files are best for the following:

- Complete compatibility with all browsers
- Small graphics, such as navigation icons or image thumbnails
- Graphics containing mostly solid colors

On the other hand, you might consider a different format — particularly JPEG — for the following:

- Large photographs or other continuous-tone images
- Graphics containing a large number of colors
- Graphics in which a GIF version would be larger than its JPEG equivalent

GIF basics, Part 1: interlacing

As mentioned at the beginning of this chapter, a GIF file can be interlaced, that is, saved in a way that makes it appear to load faster. You can use a variety of programs to create interlaced GIFs, starting with Adobe Photoshop. For Photoshop 3.x and 4.x, Adobe offers a plug-in export module called GIF89a Export, that provides an interlacing option and some basic bit-depth reduction features. Figure 6-3 displays the GIF89a Export Options dialog box.

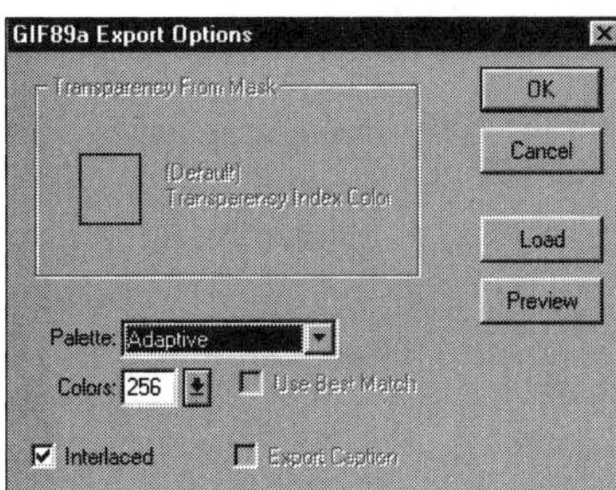

Figure 6-3: Photoshop's GIF89a Export plug-in

Third-party GIF plug-ins, including Digital Frontier's HVS Color (discussed shortly) and BoxTop Software's PhotoGIF, can create interlaced GIFs. A variety of shareware graphics programs, including Graphic Converter (Mac OS) and LView (Windows), also can. Many of these tools are included on the *HTML & Web Publishing SECRETS* CD-ROM (see the "On the CD-ROM" sidebar at the beginning of this chapter).

Many Web authoring packages can also convert conventional GIFs into interlaced GIFs. Two examples:

- SoftQuad's HoTMetaL Pro includes a basic image editor, called MetalWorks, which can interlace GIFs (and also perform bit-depth conversion and many of the other chores discussed in this chapter).
- Adobe PageMill has a built-in interlacing feature. To interlace an image in PageMill 2.x, press the Command (Mac OS) or Ctrl (Windows) key while double-clicking the image. Click the interlace icon (it's the tiny disk superimposed over an image), and then save. In PageMill 1.x, simply double-click the image and then click the interlace icon — you don't have to Command-click the image.

Interlacing is particularly useful for large graphics, as it enables visitors to get an idea of what the graphic looks like before it has completely loaded. If the graphic is a navigation element such as an image map (discussed later in this chapter), visitors can even click on appropriate hot spots as soon as the hot spots come into view. Interlacing is less useful for tiny graphics such as buttons or logos, however. These load fast enough to satisfy even the most impatient surfer.

GIF basics, Part 2: transparency

GIF transparency is an extremely useful attribute that enables an image to blend with the page's background. Figure 6-4 illustrates how an image with and without transparency interacts with the rest of the page.

Figure 6-4: An image without transparency (left) and with it (right)

Without transparency, an image is displayed exactly as it's stored: within a rectangle whose dimensions enclose the entire image. With transparency, that rectangle disappears and only the actual image appears. It's clear — no pun intended — that applying transparency is an essential technique when you have graphics that must blend with the page.

All of the GIF export plug-ins I discussed in the previous section support transparency, as do many Web authoring tools and shareware image editors.

When applying transparency, you essentially say, "Any portion of this image that is white (or gray or turquoise or whatever) is to be treated as though it were transparent. Instead of displaying the white (or gray or turquoise or whatever) in the image, display the page background instead."

You can designate only one color as the transparent color. Most transparency tools enable you to select this color by simply clicking on it.

One problem with transparency appears in graphics that contain anti-aliased (smooth-edged) text or line art. Anti-aliasing smoothes jagged edges by using a row of dimmer pixels. Those dimmer pixels often stick out like sore thumbs in a transparent graphic, as shown in Figure 6-5.

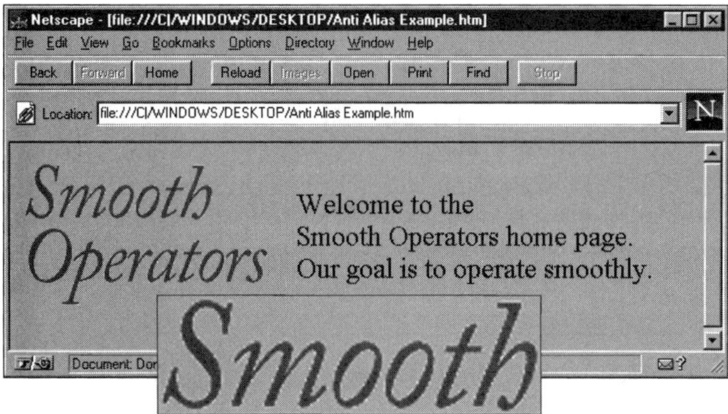

Figure 6-5: Anti-aliasing and transparency don't always get along. This anti-aliased text doesn't look so smooth when the graphic is made transparent and then displayed over a colored background. Note the artifacts at the character edges (see magnified inset).

One solution in this case is to not use transparency, and instead make the background of the graphic the same color as the background of the page (see Figure 6-6).

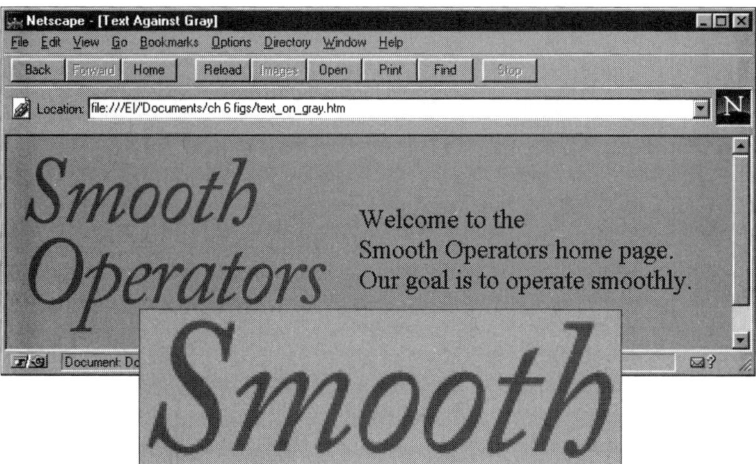

Figure 6-6: When the graphic's background is the same color as the page background, transparency isn't needed — and its negative effects are avoided.

By the way, you may hear GIF files with transparency referred to as GIF89a files. GIF89a is a more recent version of the GIF format. This version added support for transparency. (It also added support for animation, as discussed in Chapter 12.) The original version, GIF87a, didn't support transparency.

HVS Color: a graphics miracle worker

If you're obsessed with getting the best combination of file size and image quality in your GIF files, you need Digital Frontier's HVS Color, a plug-in for Adobe Photoshop and Equilibrium DeBabelizer. Using sophisticated color-analysis techniques, this miracle-worker can convert a 24-bit image to 8-bits or fewer with little discernible difference in quality (see Figure 6-7). HVS Color doesn't do any dithering, either, so GIF files remain compact. (HVS, by the way, stands for *Human Visual Systems.)*

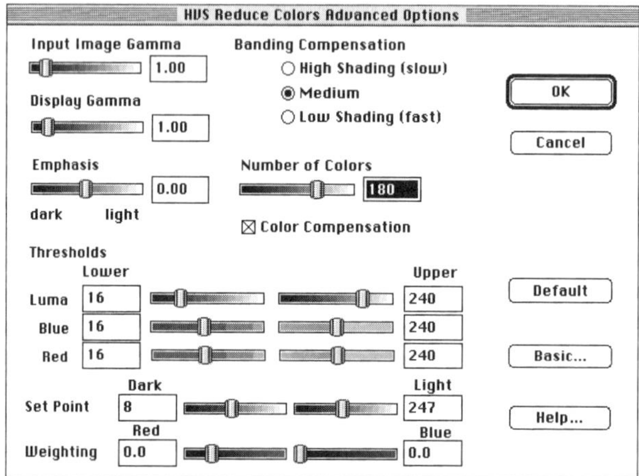

Figure 6-7: Top: HVS Color in action. Middle: An image before processing (file size: 214K). Bottom: The same image after processing (file size: 54K).

ON CD-ROM

These black-and-white reproductions don't do justice to HVS Color's talents. You have to see this plug-in in action to appreciate it. Fortunately, you can — a demonstration version is available from Digital Frontiers' Web site, at `http://www.digfrontiers.com/`.

Using HVS Color is easy. Open the file you want to convert, choose HVS Color from Photoshop's Export submenu, specify a name for the altered file, and then choose the desired options from HVS Color's dialog box. (The preset settings work well for most images.)

After you okay the dialog box, HVS Color works its magic and saves the file as a PICT file. That's right — PICT. To create a GIF file, open the newly created PICT and save it as GIF file.

One more thing: HVS Color likes memory and plenty of it. If you plan to reduce large files, prepare to allocate at least 14MB to Photoshop, and preferably 20MB or more.

Ulead's PhotoImpact SmartSaver

If you're working in Windows, another outstanding choice for graphics optimizing is Ulead Systems' PhotoImpact SmartSaver. This is a plug-in module that operates with Ulead's PhotoImpact image-editing program as well as with programs that use Photoshop-compatible plug-ins, including, of course, Photoshop itself. Even if you don't have an image editor, you can use SmartSaver by running it directly from the Windows Explorer.

SmartSaver supports both GIF and JPEG optimizing. The program provides several terrific advantages over Photoshop's built-in features, including the capability to reduce the bit depth of an RGB formatted image without having to first convert the image to indexed color. Best of all is SmartSaver's real-time preview feature, which shows the effects of your tweaks as you make them: you don't have to go through the chore of repeatedly making changes and then undoing them until you find the best settings, or of saving multiple versions of a file, as you must do with HVS Color. SmartSaver is the fastest, most convenient way to optimize graphics (see Figure 6-8).

ON CD-ROM

A fully functional, 30-day trial version of SmartSaver is included on the *HTML & Web Publishing SECRETS* CD-ROM, along with many other goodies from Ulead Systems.

Dithering to the Netscape or Internet Explorer palette

In the section "The bad news about adaptive palettes," earlier in this chapter, I mentioned that a browser imposes its own palette on monitors that are set to display 256 colors. I also mentioned that this browser palette is similar, but not identical, to the computer's system palette. And I said that for the best color fidelity on 256-color monitors, you might want to dither to the palette of the browser you expect most of the visitors to your site to use.

Figure 6-8: Ulead's PhotoImpact SmartSaver. The Before and After display shows the effects of your settings — note the file-size information above the image.

The easiest way to do this is with the wonderful Ulead PhotoImpact SmartSaver utility that I discussed in the previous section. It provides options that enable you to dither to the Netscape or Microsoft Internet Explorer palette as well as to the Windows system palette.

To access these options, click the Color Reduction tab. Then, choose the desired palette from the Palette pop-up menu, as shown in Figure 6-9. While you have the Color Reduction options in front of you, consider reducing the number of colors in the Colors area to further shrink the final file.

Figure 6-9: Choosing a palette in Ulead's SmartSaver

You can also dither to the Netscape or Internet Explorer palette using Adobe Photoshop. In Photoshop 3.x, the Indexed Color dialog box lets you load a palette file that's stored on disk. Simply click the Custom button, and then click Load in the dialog box that appears. Locate the palette file in the Open dialog box, load it, and then click OK. To load a custom palette in Photoshop 4.x, choose Color Table from the Image menu's Mode submenu.

So where do you find the Netscape and Internet Explorer palette files? Why, on the *HTML & Web Publishing SECRETS* CD-ROM, of course. (And note that Photoshop 4 also lets you dither to a generic, 216-color "Web palette" without having to load a custom palette file. In the Indexed Color dialog box, choose Web from the Palette pop-up menu.)

The ProGIF plug-in included with Digital Frontier's HVS WebFocus (see the "Digital Frontiers' HVS WebFocus" section later in this chapter) also provides built-in dithering to the Netscape palette.

Avoiding dithering entirely

If you're creating a graphic — some colored text, such as a logo, or simply some bullets or bars — you can avoid dithering entirely (or at least in Netscape Navigator) by using only the colors that exist in the Netscape color palette.

How do know which colors those are? Easy. On the *HTML & Web Publishing SECRETS* CD-ROM is a file called *Netpal.ACO.* This file contains the 216 colors in the Netscape palette, stored in Photoshop's swatches format. You can load these colors into Photoshop, and then choose from them when you're creating your graphics. See the "Loading the Netscape Palette into Photoshop" steps for directions how.

STEPS

Loading the Netscape Palette into Photoshop

Step 1. In Photoshop, open the Swatches palette by choosing Show Swatches from the Window menu.

Step 2. Open the Swatches palette's menu (click the triangle near the upper-right corner of the palette) and choose Load Swatches.

Step 3. Locate the file `Netpal.ACO` and double-click its name.

That's all there is to it. Now you can choose colors from the Swatches palette and rest assured that Netscape Navigator won't dither them.

Photoshop saves the current set of swatches, so you don't need to repeat these steps unless you reset the swatches or load a different set. Just in case you do have to reload the swatches, you might want to copy the `Netpal.ACO` file to your Photoshop folder.

JPEG secrets

JPEG remains the best format for photographic and other continuous-tone images. Here are some secrets for getting the best results.

How much compression should you use?

Photoshop and many other image editors provide several quality options for JPEG files, which generally appear when you save the file. Photoshop provides four quality options: Low, Medium, High, and Maximum. Which should you use?

Generally, the Medium setting yields excellent results. If your image contains sharply contrasting areas — a bright yellow beach umbrella against a blue sky, for example — you might find it better to use the High setting to avoid compression artifacts where the contrasting areas meet. Figure 6-10 shows the effects of several compression settings on image quality and file size.

Original image (290K)

Quality setting: High (31K)

Quality setting: Medium (22K)

Quality setting: Low (18K)

Figure 6-10: JPEG in action

JPEG optimizing with Ulead's SmartSaver

For optimizing JPEG files, a variety of utilities and plug-ins exist. Ulead's PhotoImpact GIF/JPEG SmartSaver is one example. I introduced this terrific utility in the "GIF secrets" section of this chapter. SmartSaver's JPEG-related features are just as impressive. As Figure 6-11 shows, SmartSaver gives you far more control over JPEG output than what Photoshop's simple low-medium-high dialog box provides.

SECRET

Following are some tips for using SmartSaver's JPEG options.

Smoothing

If your image has a large, indistinct background — such as the ocean or sky — applying some smoothing can improve compression with minimal loss in image quality.

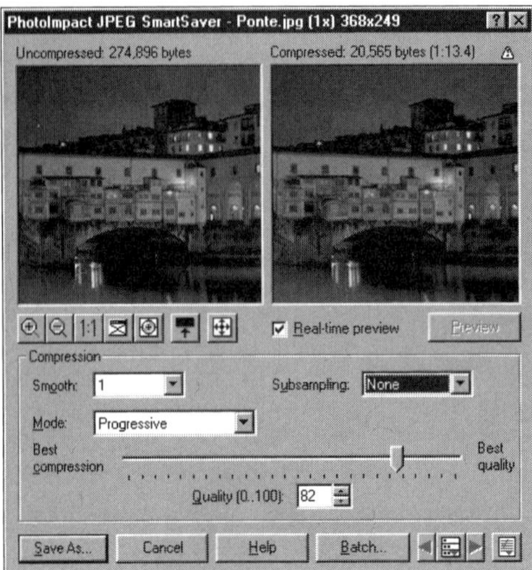

Figure 6-11: Ulead PhotoImpact SmartSaver's JPEG mode

Subsampling

SmartSaver's Subsampling pop-up menu lets you choose between two methods of compressing the color information in a JPEG image. YUV411 compression provides the smallest file sizes. YUV422 provides less compression but better color fidelity. (If you're interested in the technical details behind these compression schemes, see SmartSaver's online help.)

"Just make it small"

When you're optimizing a JPEG image, you don't really start out thinking, "Gee, I really want slight smoothing with YUV411 subsampling." You start out thinking something like, "I sure wish I could get this picture to be under 35K."

Ulead's PhotoImpact SmartSaver provides one more terrific feature that addresses this need. Choose its Compress By Size command, and a dialog box appears into which you can enter a desired size for the graphic. Enter the desired size, click OK, and watch SmartSaver do its thing. If you aren't happy with the results, try a different size.

Digital Frontier's HVS WebFocus

HVS WebFocus is a set of plug-ins for the Macintosh and Windows versions of Adobe Photoshop and plug-in compatible programs. HVS WebFocus adds two file-format modules to Photoshop: ProGIF and ProJPEG. (I'll leave it up to you to guess which one handles which file format.)

Both ProGIF and ProJPEG do a solid job of GIF and JPEG optimizing, and provide more options than Photoshop's built-in GIF and JPEG support. ProJPEG, in particular, provides an advanced set of JPEG-optimizing tools as well as a preview window that shows the results of your tweaks. If you're using the Mac OS, it's the best JPEG-optimizing tool available. If you're using Windows, though, check out Ulead's PhotoImpact SmartSaver, too.

Parting thoughts on graphical dieting

No matter how careful you are, there's no escaping the fact that graphic compression has a negative impact on image quality. Watching an image's quality degrade as you put it through a weight-loss program can be depressing. Hey, no one ever said dieting was fun — not even the Bandwidth Conservation Society, whose Web site contains lots of graphical diet plans and examples. It's at `http://www.infohiway.com/faster`.

Graphics HTML Secrets

In keeping with this book's assumption that you already have a basic familiarity with HTML, I don't discuss the basics of including images in HTML pages here. I assume you're already familiar with basics behind the `<IMG>` tag. If you aren't, see Appendix A for a quick reference to HTML.

In this section, I describe some of the finer points of the graphics-related HTML tags and attributes. Many of the tags or attributes described here originally debuted in Netscape Navigator, but are now widely supported among browsers.

A reminder to use height and width

The `<IMG>` tag's `height` and `width` attributes specify — you got it, Einstein — the height and width of the image referenced in the tag. One way to use these attributes is to stretch or scale an image to a specific size; I presented an example of this in Chapter 5's discussion of single-pixel GIF tricks, and I'll illustrate another example later in this chapter.

But using height and width is also valuable even when you aren't scaling an image — in fact, it's one of the easiest and most important things you can do to improve the perceived performance of a Web site.

The reason: most browsers read the `<HEIGHT>` and `<WIDTH>` tags and then lay out the page appropriately, positioning text, tables, and other elements correctly even before the images on the page have finished loading. You can see this for yourself by loading a page that uses `height` and `width` attributes — try my Weathercam page at `http://www4.heidsite.com/weathercam.html`. You'll notice that the text below the cam's image appears before the image has finished loading. If I hadn't used the `height` and `width` attributes, the text below the image wouldn't appear until the image had finished loading — because the browser wouldn't have known how large the image was. In other words, using `height` and `width` enables the browser to know an image's size ahead of time, and to lay out the rest of the page appropriately.

By the way, you may notice that I haven't used the `height` and `width` attributes in most of this chapter's HTML examples. I've left them out in the interest of space, and because I didn't want to detract from the concepts showcased in each example. In the real world, I wouldn't think of writing an `<IMG>` tag that didn't contain `height` and `width` attributes.

Determining image dimensions

So how can you find out an image's dimensions? If you use an HTML authoring tool, you don't have to bother. Every tool I know of automatically uses the height and width tags when you include an image in a page. If you're hand-coding some HTML, you can use an image editor to determine image dimensions. In Adobe Photoshop, for instance, open the image and then choose Image Size from the Image menu. If necessary, choose Pixels from the Width and Height pop-up menus. Your image's dimensions appear here.

If you're using the Mac OS, there's an easy way to determine an image's dimensions: paste it into the Mac's Scrapbook desk accessory. The Scrapbook window displays the image's dimensions.

A reminder to use alt

The `<IMG>` tag accepts an optional attribute, `alt`, that can contain text that appears instead of the image, like the following:

```
<img src="poodle.gif" alt="Poodle picture">
```

The most common use of `alt` is to provide text that appears for visitors who turned off their browser's automatic graphics-loading feature (or those visitors who are using the Lynx text-only browser). This is particularly important if you're using graphical navigation buttons; providing `alt` text enables visitors to see the navigation options that the buttons represent.

Another good reason to provide `alt` text is because a growing number of browsers, including Netscape Navigator 3.0 and Microsoft Internet Explorer 3.0, display `alt` text before an image loads. This gives you the opportunity to convey information about what the image represents.

lowsrc secrets

The `lowsrc` attribute to the `<IMG>` tag enables you to boost the perceived performance of a page by causing a low-resolution version of an image to appear first, followed by a high-resolution version. But `lowsrc` has some subtle uses, too — including simple animation. The `lowsrc` attribute is supported by Netscape Navigator 2.0 and later; it is not supported by Microsoft Internet Explorer 3.0.

First, the basics. Say you have a page containing a big JPEG file and you'd like to improve the page's perceived performance by providing a low-res version of that JPEG file. Here's how to make one in Adobe Photoshop:

Open the high-res version of the image and choose Grayscale from the Mode menu (in Photoshop 4.x, the Mode submenu in the Image menu). Then, when asked "Discard color information?", click OK. Next, choose Bitmap from the Mode menu (in Photoshop 4.x, the Mode submenu in the Image menu). In the Bitmap dialog, be sure the resolution is 72 dpi and that the Diffusion Dither radio button is active. Click OK, and you get an image that looks decidedly low-res (see Figure 6-12).

Figure 6-12: A low-res image is born. Left: The original image. Right: The low-res version.

Next, save the low-res version *under a different name* and as a GIF file. Choose Save As, choose CompuServe GIF from the Format pop-up menu, and then name the file. For simplicity's sake, you'll probably want to store the file in the same directory as its high-resolution sibling; this creates an `<IMG>` tag that is easier to read.

Speaking of the `<IMG>` tag, adding a `lowsrc` attribute is a simple matter of referring to the low-res image you created, like so:

```
<img src="bigpicture.jpeg" lowsrc="smallpicture.gif">
```

The `lowsrc` attribute can go anywhere within the tag — before or after the all-important `height` and `width` attributes, for instance.

Graphics file formats and lowsrc

In the preceding example, I used a black-and-white GIF file for the low-res version and a JPEG file for the high-res version. But there's no law prohibiting you from using other file-format combinations. You might, for example, use a heavily compressed JPEG for the low-res version and an only slightly compressed JPEG for the high-res version. Experiment with different combinations of formats, color palettes, and compression schemes to find one that provides the best results.

Cool ways to use lowsrc

The `lowsrc` version of an image doesn't have to be the same image as the high-res version — in fact, it doesn't even have to be a low-res image. In other words, you can use `lowsrc` to have a browser successively load *any* two images.

You might use `lowsrc` to create a simple, two-image animation. (You can even use JPEG files for this — something animated GIFs, discussed in Chapter 12, obviously don't permit.) Or you might even use `lowsrc` to switch from one image to a second image that isn't even the same size. (In this case, the second image is scaled to the height and width of the `lowsrc` image — or to the `height` and `width` attributes, if you've included them.)

You can probably think of even more clever ways to use `lowsrc`. Just keep in mind that many browsers, including Microsoft Internet Explorer, don't support it. In these browsers, only the image referenced by the actual `<IMG SRC>` tag is displayed.

Will lowsrc slow your server?

There is one potential drawback to `lowsrc`. Using it means that a visitor's browser will make two connections to your server rather than just one. (The first connection retrieves the low-resolution graphic and the second retrieves the full-resolution graphic.) If your site is very busy, this could unnecessarily bog down your server. And even on lightly used sites, this could make your site seem sluggish to load. If you're concerned about performance — and any Webmaster should be — you might want to try hitting your site with a slow modem to judge the effect `lowsrc` has on it.

Running text around graphics

Previous chapters have beaten to death the message that HTML isn't designed for precise layout control — but these chapters also pointed out the fact that you can still accomplish a lot with HTML, especially with the latest HTML extensions.

One extremely useful extension (now part of the HTML 3.2 specification) enables you to run text around a rectangular graphic. I'm referring to the `align=left` and `align=right` attributes of the `<IMG>` tag. Figure 6-13 illustrates `align=left` in use.

```
<HTML>
<HEAD>
    <TITLE>Text Across Platforms</TITLE>
</HEAD>
<BODY BGCOLOR="#eaeaea">
<h2><I>Florence: Il Ponte Vecchio</I></h2>
<HR>
<IMG SRC="Ponte.JPG" WIDTH="227" HEIGHT="151" ALIGN=left hspace=5>
<i>Il Ponte Vecchio</i>
dates back to  Roman times; until 1218 it was the only bridge over the
river
Arno. In the 1500s, the Medici family built small shops on the bridge to
house goldsmiths and diamond-carvers, whose descendents remain there today.
In 1944, during its retreat, the German army destroyed the buildings on
both sides of the bridge to make it impassable.<BR clear=left>
<HR><BR>
</BODY>
</HTML>
```

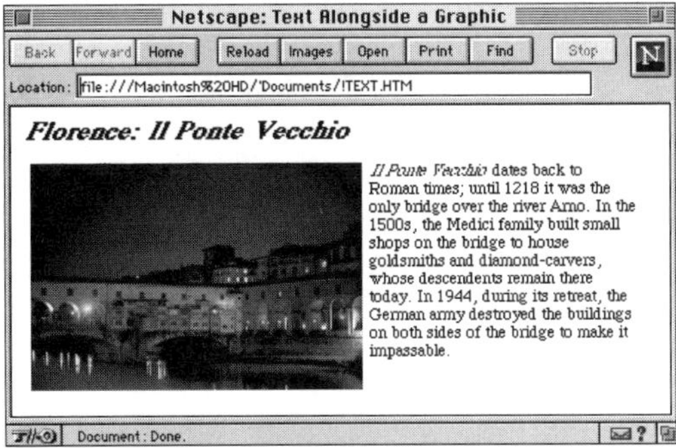

Figure 6-13: The text wraps around the graphic.

Use hspace and vspace for extra space

In the HTML examples in this section, notice I also use the `hspace` and `vspace` attributes to add several pixels of extra space around an image. Without these attributes, text would cram up against the image — a design sin if ever there was one.

Formatting captions and using <BR CLEAR>

You can use `align=left` or `align=right` to format a caption so that it appears alongside a graphic, and so that the text following the caption resumes at the left margin. The key to the latter is the `<BR CLEAR>` tag, as shown in Figure 6-14.

```
<HTML>
<HEAD>
<TITLE>Text Alongside a Graphic</TITLE>
</HEAD>
<BODY BGCOLOR="#ffffff">
<H2><I>Florence: Il Ponte Vecchio</I></H2>
<IMG SRC="Ponte.JPG" WIDTH="227" HEIGHT="151" ALIGN=left hspace=5>
<I>Il Ponte Vecchio</I> dates back to Roman times; until 1218
it was the only bridge over the river Arno. In the 1500s, the
Medici family built small shops on the bridge to house goldsmiths
and diamond-carvers, whose descendents remain there today. In
1944, during its retreat, the German army destroyed the buildings
on both sides of the bridge to make it impassable.
<br clear=left>
<br>
<a href="home.html">Go Home</a> | <a href="more.html">See More</a>
</BODY>
</HTML>
```

Figure 6-14: The align attribute is used to format a caption, and <br clear=left> is used to have the body text resume at the left margin.

Running text between two graphics

By using `align=left` *and* `align=right`, each in its own `<IMG>` tag, you can cause text to run between two graphics, as shown in Figure 6-15.

```
<HTML>
<HEAD>
<TITLE>Text Between Two Graphics</TITLE>
</HEAD>
<BODY BGCOLOR="#ffffff">
<H2><I>Florence: Il Ponte Vecchio</I></H2>
<IMG SRC="Ponte.JPG" WIDTH="227" HEIGHT="151" ALIGN=left hspace=5>
<IMG SRC="Ponte.JPG" WIDTH="227" HEIGHT="151" ALIGN=right hspace=5>
<I>Il Ponte Vecchio</I> dates back to Roman times; until 1218
it was the only bridge over the river Arno. In the 1500s, the
Medici family built small shops on the bridge to house goldsmiths
and diamond-carvers, whose descendents remain there today. In
1944, during its retreat, the German army destroyed the buildings
on both sides of the bridge to make it impassable.
<br clear=left>
<br>
<a href="home.html">Go Home</a> | <a href="more.html">See More</a>
</BODY>
</HTML>
```

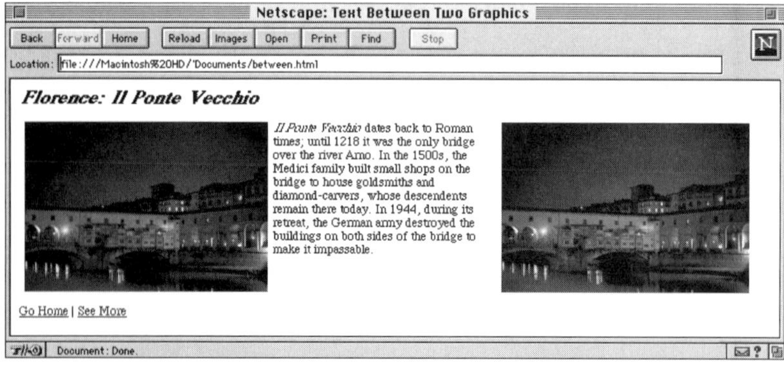

Figure 6-15: Use align=left *and* align=right to sandwich text between two graphics.

Don't forget tables

If you need to precisely position text relative to graphics, don't forget about the table-layout techniques I described in the previous chapter. They can provide better, more consistent results than simply using `align=left` or `align=right`.

Graphics Secrets

I've talked about the mechanics of choosing graphics formats, optimizing graphics, and spewing them onto a page. This section is a cookbook of ideas and secrets for applying graphics in cool and creative ways.

Removing the hex on your color

For some not-so-wonderful reason, you have to specify colors in HTML using hexadecimal notation — base 16! The specific format is #RRGGBB, where RR is the red value, GG is the green, and BB is the blue. For example, the tag: `<BODY BGCOLOR="#FFFF00">` yields a bright yellow. Tags for specifying font color and table cell colors work similarly (see Appendix A for more information).

This scheme complicates life if you want to create a graphic with a color that matches the color of the background or of some text. Last time I checked, no graphics programs enabled you to specify colors by using hexadecimal notation. So how do you ensure that the colors in the graphic match the colors of the page or its text?

There are a few ways to do this. All graphics programs and a great many HTML layout programs let you specify colors by entering the red, green, and blue values into a dialog box that's often called a *color picker.* You can take advantage of this feature to calculate the hex equivalents for a particular color.

Here's how: If you're working in a graphics program, open the program's color picker and choose the color you want — either by clicking on the color or by typing precise values into its text boxes. Before you okay the dialog box, jot down the red, green, and blue (RGB) values of the color. (If you're using the Mac OS and you don't see RGB text boxes, do the following: click on the color picker's More Choices button, and then click the Apple RGB option. Now you should see red, green, and blue sliders, each with a text box to its right.)

After you've jotted down the RGB values for the color, you can go into your HTML program and use *its* color picker to specify those values for your background color, for the text, or for whatever element you want to color. If you view the HTML source after you've specified the color, you'll see that your HTML editor has done the ugly conversion into hex for you.

RGB-hex conversion utilities

If you're hand-coding your HTML or if your program doesn't provide its own color picker, you can obtain the hex values with an RGB-hex converter utility.

On the Windows side, Patrick Stepp's shareware QuickColor lets you enter RGB values and displays their hex equivalents. You can also do the opposite: enter the hex values and get their RGB equivalents. That can be handy if, say, you want to recreate a certain color that you've seen on another Web site. QuickColor is included on the *HTML & Web Publishing SECRETS* CD-ROM.

As for the Mac OS, there are a couple of RGB-hex converters. One is John Cope's free HTML ColorMeister, which lets you choose colors and then generate the appropriate HTML. ColorMeister is also included on the *HTML & Web Publishing SECRETS* CD-ROM. Another is David Christensen's shareware program, HTML ColorPicker.

Cache and carry: reusing graphics

You probably know that all of today's browsers *cache* graphics: they store the graphics temporarily on a visitor's hard drive in case the graphics are called for again. If a cached graphic *is* needed again — because it appears elsewhere on a page or even on a different page — the browser retrieves it from the cache instead of over the network. The result: the graphic appears much faster, the Web server has one less thing to do, and the stream of bits blasting across the network is that much smaller.

You can take advantage of graphics caching to boost the performance of your site and lighten the load on your server and network by simply reusing graphics within a page and across multiple pages. If you use graphical borders or buttons, you're probably doing this already. But there are also some subtle applications of graphics caching. For example, in Chapter 2, I talked about the importance of establishing an identity for a Web site by placing a banner of some kind at the top of each page. Let's say you have a banner arrangement similar to that of Figure 6-16 — a logo that appears on every single page, and a graphic or some anti-aliased text that identifies the specific area of a site.

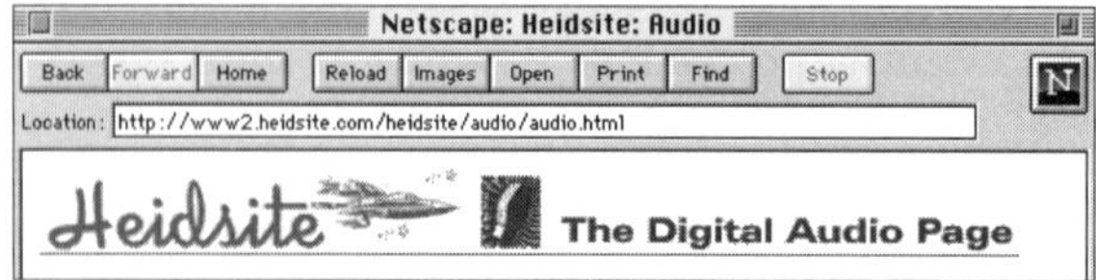

Figure 6-16: A typical banner arrangement. The logo appears on every page, while the material to its right varies from page to page.

Your first inclination might be to create one large graphic that contains the entire banner for each page. But a better approach might be to separate the banner into two graphics: the logo (which appears on every page) and the identification area (which changes from page to page). Because the changing portion of the banner is separate from the logo, it's smaller and loads faster. And because the logo is cached by a visitor's browser, it appears more quickly as the visitor jumps from page to page.

HTML options for a two-graphic banner

You could take any of a few routes to positioning the two graphics that make up the example banner I use here. For instance, you could use the `align=left` and `align=right` attributes:

```
<img src="logo.gif" align=left>
<img src="specific_page.gif align=right>
```

With this approach, the graphics will appear at the left and right edges of the browser window, regardless of the browser window's size.

If you want the graphics to appear in specific locations regardless of the browser window's size, you might put the graphics in a table, such as the following:

```
<TABLE BORDER=0 WIDTH=497>
   <TR>
      <TD>
         <IMG SRC="logo.GIF">
      </TD>
      <TD>
         <IMG SRC="specific_page.GIF">
      </TD>
   </TR>
</TABLE>
```

Preloading graphics for other pages

A particularly cool way to take advantage of caching is to preload graphics that are used on other pages of your site. Here's how: At the bottom of a given page, include `<IMG>` tags for the graphics you want to preload, and specify a `height` and `width` attribute of 1. The graphics will load but each will be displayed as a single pixel — chances are your visitors won't even notice them. But the full-sized versions of the graphics will be stored in the visitors' browser caches. When the visitors go to the pages where the full-sized graphics appear, the images will snap to the screen instantly. If you use this technique, be sure to use `height` and `width` attributes for all of the graphics on the page. Otherwise, the text display will be delayed while the graphics download.

Graphics and hyperlink buttons

Graphics are often used as navigation buttons on a Web site. Instead of clicking on words to activate a link, visitors click on a graphic. Many sites take advantage of the fact that a graphic can be used as a hyperlink to create attractive user interfaces that have a "multimedia CD-ROM" look.

To make a graphic a hyperlink, simply include an `<IMG>` tag within the `<HREF>` tag:

```
<a href="contents.html"><img src="contents_button.gif"
alt="Contents"></a>
```

Notice I provided `alt` text for those visitors who have turned off their browsers' graphics loading capability.

To border or not to border?

When a graphic is part of a hyperlink, most browsers enclose the graphic within a rectangular border, as shown in Figure 6-17.

Figure 6-17: A border appears around a hyperlink graphic.

If your graphic isn't rectangular — maybe it's an oval button, for example — you might want to turn this border off by including a `border=0` attribute within the `<IMG>` tag.

SECRET

But if your graphic is rectangular and your site is geared toward the Macintosh versions of Netscape Navigator, you might want to have a border around your graphic. Here's why: The Mac OS versions of Navigator highlight the border when a user clicks on the graphic. This provides a degree of visual feedback to the user.

Why don't the Windows versions of Navigator highlight the border when you click on the graphic? Don't ask me.

A navigation bar made from separate graphics

Many of the graphical navigation bars you see on Web sites are image maps, which are discussed later in this chapter. But image maps don't have a monopoly on navigation bars — it's also possible to create a navigation bar from a series of separate graphics. There are some good reasons for considering this approach, and some potential drawbacks worth thinking about, too.

Figure 6-18 shows a simple navigation bar that contains four buttons, each of which links to a different page. Each of the buttons in this navigation bar is actually a separate graphic.

```
<HTML>
<HEAD>
   <TITLE>Graphical Navigation Bar</TITLE>
```

```
</HEAD>
<BODY>
<P><A HREF="databases.html"><IMG SRC="databases.GIF" WIDTH=100
HEIGHT=30 BORDER=0 ALIGN=bottom></A><A HREF="graphics.html"><IMG
SRC="graphics.GIF" WIDTH=100 HEIGHT=30 BORDER=0 ALIGN=bottom></A><A
HREF="multimedia.html"><IMG SRC="multimedia.GIF" WIDTH=100 HEIGHT=30
BORDER=0 ALIGN=bottom></A><A HREF="html.htm"><IMG SRC="html.GIF"
WIDTH=100 HEIGHT=30 BORDER=0 ALIGN=bottom></A>
</BODY>
</HTML>
```

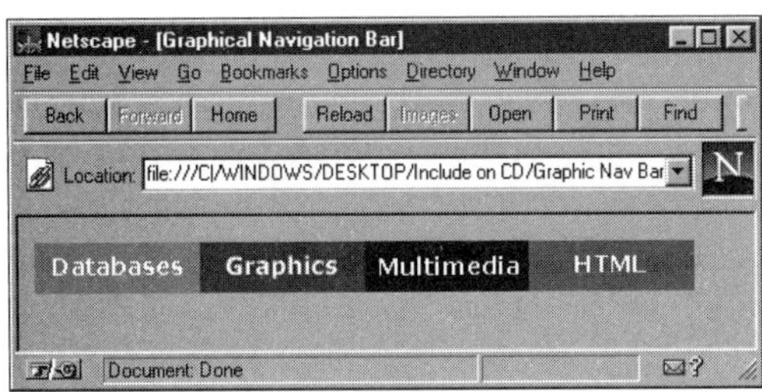

Figure 6-18: Navigation bars can be made from four separate graphics.

Notice that, for this example, I used the <IMG> tag's border=0 attribute to turn off the border that normally appears around a graphic that's part of a hyperlink.

Also notice that I didn't include a return between each <HREF> tag. This makes the HTML a bit more difficult to read, but it enables the graphics to snuggle up against one another. If you separate each <HREF> tag with a return, a thin space appears between each graphic when the navigation bar loads.

Stacking navigation buttons vertically

In the previous example, I arranged the navigation buttons horizontally. You could just as easily stack them vertically — perhaps even in their own frame. If you opt for a vertical arrangement, separate each graphic with a <BR> tag. Or you might want to put each graphic within its own table row.

Advantages of the separate-graphics approach

What does the separate-graphics approach offer that an image map doesn't offer? Several things:

- **It's easy to implement.** You don't have to fuss with image map software or drawing hot spots.
- **You can indicate a visitor's current location.** You can provide a "you are here" indicator to a visitor by swapping the standard version of a specific page's button with an altered version of the same button — perhaps a version that looks as though it was pressed, or perhaps a version that's a different color, or has a border around it. Figure 6-19 shows how you might apply this to the example in Figure 6-18. Notice that the button labeled HTML has a bold white border around it.

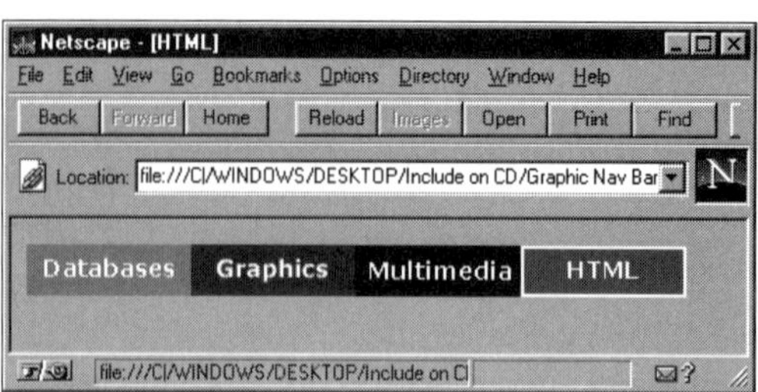

Figure 6-19: A visitor's current location is indicated by swapping a graphical button with an altered version of the same button.

To create this effect, I simply replaced the reference to the button called `html.gif` with a reference to a button called `html_current.gif`. When a visitor arrives at the HTML page, the browser retrieves only the new button from the site; the remaining three buttons are loaded from the browser's disk cache.

- **You can have JavaScript status bar messages.** Chapters 7 and 11 contain a collection of useful JavaScripts that work in any JavaScript-enabled browser (Netscape Navigator 2.0 and later and Microsoft Internet Explorer 3.0 and later). One of my favorite simple JavaScripts is the one-liner that puts a message in the browser's status bar when the mouse pointer is positioned over a hyperlink. By putting this script in each of a navigation bar's `<IMG>` tags, you can provide a status bar message for each link, as shown in Figure 6-20.

```
<HTML>
<HEAD>
   <TITLE>Graphical Navigation Bar</TITLE>
</HEAD>
<BODY>
<P><A HREF="databases.html"
onMouseOver="window.status='Information on Web/database
integration'; return true"><IMG SRC="databases.GIF" WIDTH=100
HEIGHT=30 BORDER=0
ALIGN=bottom></A><A
HREF="graphics.html"onMouseOver="window.status='Tips for creating
Web graphics'; return true"><IMG SRC="graphics.GIF"
WIDTH=100 HEIGHT=30 BORDER=0
ALIGN=bottom></A><A
HREF="multimedia.html"onMouseOver="window.status='Masting Web
multimedia'; return true"><IMG SRC="multimedia.GIF"
WIDTH=100 HEIGHT=30 BORDER=0
ALIGN=bottom></A><A HREF="html.htm"
onMouseOver="window.status='HTML tips and secrets'; return
true"><IMG SRC="html.GIF" WIDTH=100
HEIGHT=30 BORDER=0
ALIGN=bottom></A>
</BODY>
</HTML>
```

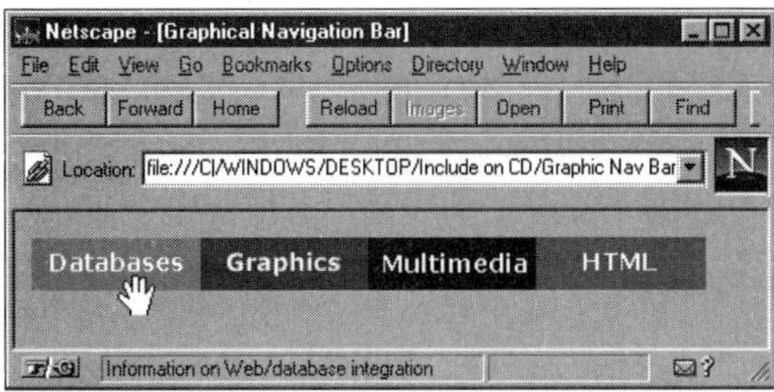

Figure 6-20: When the mouse pointer is positioned over a hyperlink, a JavaScript status bar message appears for each button.

Caution: server overload ahead?

Obviously there are many advantages to creating a navigation bar from discrete graphics. But there's a potential drawback, too: numerous graphics on a page can slow down your server (and, therefore, your site). Most browsers can open multiple connections to a server to retrieve the graphics more or less simultaneously. But if you have more than half a dozen or so graphics on a page, the browser can bog down the server by opening an excessive number of connections. On a server that sees only light or moderate traffic, there won't be much of a performance penalty, but on an extremely busy server, the performance slowdown could be significant. Therefore, if your navigation bar would contain more than six or so graphics, it might be better to set it up as an image map instead.

A word about banner widths

Regardless of whether you implement a banner as an image map or as a series of discrete graphics, it's a good idea to keep the total width of the banner to a maximum of about 470 pixels. That way, the banner will fit within the default size of most browser windows.

If you need a wider banner, consider placing a special sizing graphic on the site's opening page — a graphic that tells visitors to open their browser to the width of the graphic — as described in the previous chapter.

Avoiding the Netscape underscore bug

SECRET

A quirk in Navigator causes an underscore character (_) to appear immediately after a hyperlink graphic under specific circumstances. The underscore isn't a serious problem, but it is an annoying cosmetic flaw (see Figure 6-21).

Figure 6-21: The dreaded Netscape underscore (just off the lower-right corner of the button's rectangle)

You will encounter this problem if

- you put a carriage return after the graphic's <IMG> tag and before the </A> tag *and*
- the <IMG> tag does not contain an align=left or align=right attribute.

The following HTML will cause the underscore to appear:

```
<a href="weirdbug.html">
<img src="bug_button.gif" height=30 width=120>
</a>
```

This HTML will also yield the dreaded underscore:

```
<a href="weirdbug.html">
<img src="bug_button.gif" height=30 width=120 align=top>
</a>
```

But this HTML will *not* cause the underscore to appear:

```
<a href="weirdbug.html">
<img src="bug_button.gif" height=30 width=120></a>
```

This HTML won't cause any problems, either:

```
<a href="weirdbug.html">
<img src="bug_button.gif" height=30 width=120 align=left>
</a>
```

Squirrelly, isn't it? Fortunately, it's easy to avoid: just don't put a return before the </A> tag; instead, put the </A> immediately after the <IMG> tag.

By the way, Internet Explorer doesn't have the same quirk.

More fun with single-pixel GIFs

In the previous chapter, I showed how to use a transparent single-pixel GIF image along with the <IMG> tag's hspace and vspace attributes to control horizontal and vertical spacing.

The value of single-pixel GIFs goes way beyond spacing control, though. By using colored single-pixel GIFs along with the <IMG> tag's height and width attributes, you can create wide bars, thin rules, dotted rules, and everything in between.

ON CD-ROM

A collection of single-pixel GIFs is included on the *HTML & Web Publishing SECRETS* CD-ROM.

Making big bars out of small dots

A colored single-pixel GIF is commonly used to fill a large area with color. Say you want the top of a page to have a bold blue bar that's 40 pixels high and runs from one end of the screen to the other. Don't create a 640×40-pixel GIF; use a single-pixel GIF and scale it to the size you need (see Figure 6-22).

```
<IMG SRC="dot_blue.gif" WIDTH=640 HEIGHT=40>
```

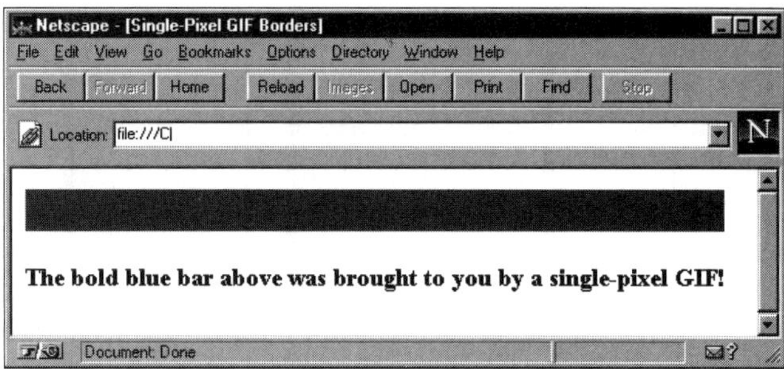

Figure 6-22: Scaling a single-pixel GIF

One big advantage of scaling a single-pixel GIF is bandwidth conservation. It's obvious that a 1×1-pixel GIF downloads a lot faster than a 640×40-pixel one. The other advantage is that you can use the same GIF to create as many borders and dotted lines as you need — the browser loads only one copy from your site, retrieving subsequent copies from its own disk cache.

This technique of filling a large area with a scaled single-pixel GIF is sometimes called *flood filling.*

Creating a dotted rule

Place one single-pixel GIF after another with the `hspace` attribute thrown in for extra horizontal spacing, and you can create a dotted border, as shown in Figure 6-23.

```
<img src="dot_blue.gif" width=10 height=10 hspace=10>
<img src="dot_blue.gif" width=10 height=10 hspace=10>
<img src="dot_blue.gif" width=10 height=10 hspace=10>
<img src="dot_blue.gif" width=10 height=10 hspace=10>
<img src="dot_blue.gif" width=10 height=10 hspace=10>
<img src="dot_blue.gif" width=10 height=10 hspace=10>
```

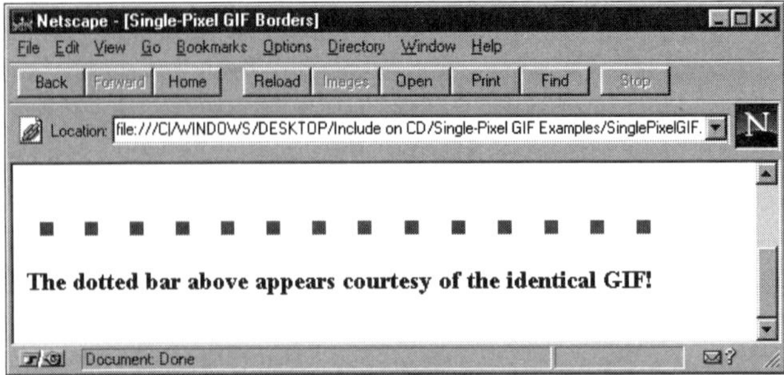

Figure 6-23: A dotted border was created from a single-pixel GIF.

For legibility's sake, I put a return after each `<IMG>` tag in the preceding example. Doing so, however, adds a bit of extra horizontal space between each square. If you want only the amount of space specified by the `hspace` attribute, run all of the `<IMG>` tags together — don't put a return after each one.

One downside to GIF tricks

The only real disadvantage to flood-filling single-pixel GIFs is that older and less-sophisticated browsers either don't support the `<IMG>` tag's `height` and `width` attributes, or deliver awkward results with them. Instead of seeing bars and dotted lines, visitors using these browsers may see a teeny-tiny dot, or they may see an awkward-looking row of dots.

Generally, the single-pixel GIF tricks I described in this section work best in Netscape Navigator and Microsoft Internet Explorer. If you anticipate a great deal of traffic from other browsers — including the old America Online browser — think twice about relying heavily on these tricks.

Background on backgrounds

Netscape pioneered the capability to add a background graphic to a page using the background attribute to the `<BODY>` tag, as in:

```
<body background="my_pattern.gif">
```

Most browsers now support background graphics — for better or for worse. I'm not a big fan of background graphics on Web pages; I think I've been soured on them because too many people use ridiculously busy patterns that make the page's text virtually impossible to read. (I'd hate to see these folks' houses; I imagine their decorating style leans heavily toward a "Late Sixties Bachelor Pad" look.)

ON CD-ROM

It is possible, however, to use background graphics tastefully and create interesting effects with them. The following sections offer a collection of secrets aimed at helping you do exactly this. To help, you'll also find a large collection of background patterns and images on the *HTML & Web Publishing SECRETS* CD-ROM.

Tiling is your friend

Tiling makes many background tricks possible. If a background graphic is smaller than the browser window, the browser *tiles* the graphic: it repeats the graphic so that the graphic fills the browser window.

You can take advantage of tiling to create full-page backgrounds from graphics that are actually very small and therefore fast loading. (But remember to check the page, preferably in a variety of browsers, to verify that the background doesn't render the page's text illegible.)

The vertical bar trick

One common background is a vertical bar that runs along the edge of the page — usually along the left edge. To create such a background, use Photoshop or an equivalent image editing program to create an image that's 1 pixel high and about 1,300 or so pixels wide. Why so wide? So that the bar doesn't repeat when the page is displayed on a large-screen monitor.

Color the left edge of the graphic to create a border with the width you want. (You might find it easier to work if you zoom in several times.) Use the Mode menu to switch to indexed color and to choose a low bit depth, then save the graphic as a GIF file.

Because the browser tiles a graphic to fill the screen, this single-pixel-high graphic becomes a bar, as shown in Figure 6-24.

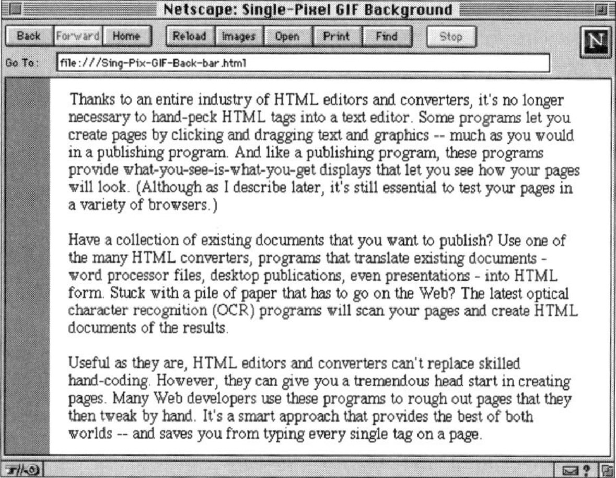

Figure 6-24: A background bar is located on the left edge of the window.

In Figure 6-24, I used an HTML table as described in the previous chapter to indent the page's text so that it isn't superimposed over the bar. You'll probably want to do the same.

A background bar with a feathered edge

Instead of having a background bar with a sharp vertical edge, you might prefer to have a bar that's feathered — that is, its edge blends into the page's background color, as shown in Figure 6-25.

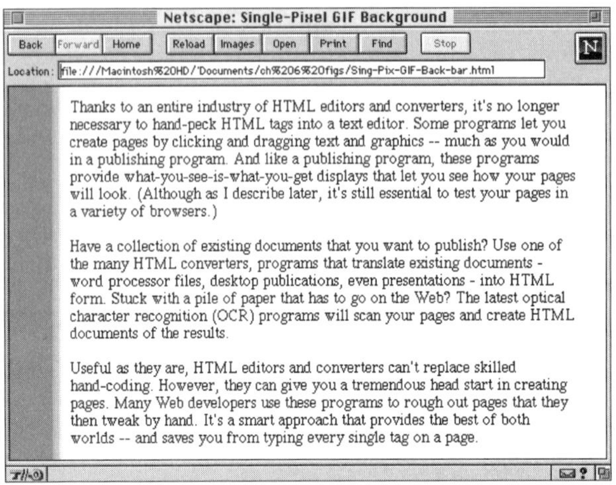

Figure 6-25: This background bar has a feathered edge.

To create this effect in Photoshop, first, make sure the current mode is RGB. (Choose RGB from the Mode menu if necessary.) Next, create the solid color and then select an area that includes several pixels of the color *and* several pixels of the blank area next to the color (see Figure 6-26). Choose Feather from the Select menu, type in a value such as 5, and then click OK. Finally, hit Backspace or Delete. Convert the image to indexed color, and save it as a GIF file.

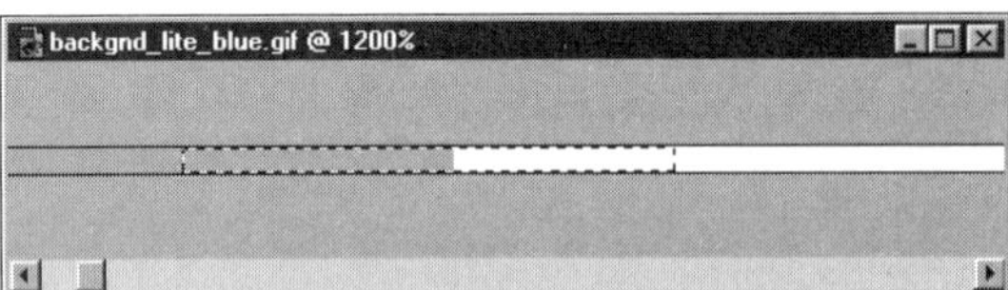

Figure 6-26: To feather an edge in Photoshop, select an area that includes several pixels of the color and several pixels of the blank area next to the color.

On CD-ROM

You can also use Photoshop's gradient tool to create a bar that fades from one color to another, or from one color to the background color of the page. Check out the many examples and samples on the *HTML & Web Publishing SECRETS* CD-ROM to get your creative juices flowing.

Making Image Maps

The maps in your car's glove box help you navigate to a new place. The maps — the image maps, that is — on a Web site enable visitors to do the same. Image maps are among the most popular site-navigation devices; they're right up there with graphical hyperlink buttons and old-fashioned text links.

An image map might look like a set of buttons and icons, a list of text options, or a collage of images. An image map might even look like an actual map: click on a particular city to go to its page, for example.

Under the hood, however, all image maps work in the same way: you create a graphic containing the map's navigation buttons or devices, and then use an image map-creation program to draw hot spots that tie each button to a particular Web page.

But that's the streamlined description. The full story is more complicated, and some of its subtleties can have a big impact on your Web site's performance.

Server-side image maps

Image maps come in two flavors: *server-side* and *client-side*. Server-side image maps are the embodiment of that ugly buzz-phrase *client-server computing*. The operation of a server-side map is a joint effort between the client (a browser) and the Web server software.

How server-side maps work

BACKGROUNDER

When visitors to a Web site click on a server-side image map, their browsers send coordinates to the Web server. These coordinates don't tell the server which navigation option was clicked; they simply specify where the mouse pointer was when the mouse button was pressed. Put another way, instead of telling the server, "the *About This Site* button was clicked," the browser says, "the mouse was clicked 30 pixels to the right and 50 pixels below the image map's upper-left corner."

It's up to the Web server to translate these coordinates into the address (the URL) of the Web page these coordinates correspond to. To do this, the server generally uses a program called a *CGI* application. Short for Common Gateway Interface, CGIs run on a Web server and perform special processing tasks or act as intermediaries between a Web server program and another program. When you fill out an on-screen form to do a search, for example, a CGI takes the information you entered and supplies it to a database manager or search engine.

When you click an image map, a CGI reads the coordinates sent by the browser program and compares them to a *map definition file*. This is a text-only file that contains entries that describe each of the hot spots — the shape and location of the hot spots, as well as the URL to which each one corresponds. The CGI then passes the URL to the server, which transmits it to the browser, which goes to the appropriate address.

The downside of server-side maps

This back-and-forth banter brings up one of the downsides to server-side image maps: they can slow a server and make a site seem less responsive. Consulting a map file and translating coordinates into URLs isn't brain surgery, but it does take time that the server could otherwise spend dishing out Web pages. And when you multiply several image maps by the number of visitors clicking on them — and factor in an increasingly clogged Internet — the processing toll and delays can become significant.

Another drawback to server-side image maps is that they don't provide positive feedback when clicked — a button can't change shape or color, for example. A server-side image map doesn't even provide any clues as to its options' destinations. When you move the mouse pointer over a hypertext link, your browser displays the link's target URL. But when you move the mouse pointer over an image map, all you see is a list of coordinates. Worse, if a visitor clicks part of a map that isn't a hot spot, the back-and-forth communication between the browser and server still takes place. A couple of seconds (or more) elapse and the Web surfer is rewarded with nothing. (See the section, "Image Map Design Secrets" later in this chapter for tips on minimizing this user-interface problem and creating effective maps.)

From a Web developer's perspective, there's one more drawback to server-side image maps: You can't test a map by using a browser to open the HTML file that contains the map. Instead, you must upload the map and its associated map definition file to a Web server that also contains the image map CGI. If your site is hosted by a service provider, this means you'll spend a lot of time uploading as you test and debug your maps.

The client-side alternative

The *client-side* image map is one appealing alternative that addresses almost all of the drawbacks of server-side maps. As the name implies, a client-side map makes the Web browser do the work — no client-server banter is required. Client-side image maps are fairly easy to implement, and they're supported by three top browsers: Netscape Navigator (2.0 and later), Microsoft Internet Explorer (2.0 and later), and Spyglass Enhanced Mosaic (2.0 and later).

Best of all, with a few additional lines of HTML, you can provide a server-side image map to visitors who aren't using one of these browsers. It's a rare moment in Web publishing when you can combine forward-looking design with backward compatibility. Client-side image maps enable this happy combination.

Handling Server-Side Maps Without a CGI

It's worth noting that some Web server software packages can handle server-side image maps without requiring separate CGI software. O'Reilly & Associates' outstanding, Windows-based WebSite series, discussed in Chapter 17, is one such package. With WebSite, you can even store map-definition information in WebSite's Windows registry instead of in a separate map-definition file.

What's more, some servers can accept optional plug-in modules that enable them to handle server-side maps. The Mac OS-based WebStar, from Quarterdeck's StarNine division, is the best-known of this breed (see Chapter 16). Numerous image-map plug-ins have been created for WebStar. You can find a complete list of third-party plug-ins in the WebStar area of StarNine's site (`http://www.starnine.com/`).

In the end, whether a server package requires a CGI to handle server-side image maps or whether a server can handle them internally or through a plug-in module is a minor technical point. It may influence your choice of server software and add-ons — a server that processes maps internally or through a plug-in will generally handle maps a bit faster than one that uses a CGI — but it doesn't change the fact that server-side maps make your server do more work and they don't provide the responsiveness of client-side maps.

How client-side maps work

As the previous section described, server-side maps impose a performance penalty on your server because they require it to translate coordinates that are received from a browser into the address of a specific page.

Client-side maps aren't so lazy. Instead of a browser beaming the server a set of numbers and making it figure out where to go, the browser knows which coordinates correspond to which hot spots. Click on a hot spot, and the browser sends the server a URL. Client-side maps put the smarts in the client, enabling the server to concentrate on, well, serving.

Another benefit: you can test Web pages that contain client-side maps by opening them from a local hard drive — recall from the previous section that to test a server-side map, you must actually upload pages to a Web server and install the CGI application that handles the image map. Because client-side maps work from a local drive, you can use them when creating Web sites that will be distributed on a CD-ROM or floppy disk.

Client-side maps even have a user-interface benefit for Web surfers: instead of simply showing a bunch of numbers in the browser window's status area, a client-side map shows the address of each hot spot as the mouse pointer moves over it.

And I've already mentioned the best part: You can support both client-side and server-side maps in a single HTML document. There's no need to create separate versions of your pages. Browsers that support client-side maps will use them, while browsers that don't support client-side maps will use the server-side map. Thus, there's no excuse to not include support for client-side maps on a Web site.

Software for map-making

A key part of creating a server- or client-side image map involves drawing the hot spots in the graphic and then associating each one with a URL. All of today's WYSIWYG HTML layout programs support both server- and client-side image maps, examples of which include Adobe PageMill, Claris Home Page, NetObjects Fusion, Macromedia Backstage Designer, and Microsoft FrontPage 97. Most HTML editors, including Nesbitt Software's WebEdit Pro and SoftQuad's HoTMetaL Pro 3, also support both server- and client-side maps.

Several shareware or freeware map-making programs are also available. On the Macintosh side, the best of the bunch is Web Map by Rowland Smith, a shareware program available through shareware sites such as `http://www.shareware.com`. Web Map version 2.0b9, the version available at this writing, does not support client-side image maps. However, you can convert Web Map's map-definition files into client-side format by using either one of two free, AppleScript-based programs: Jeff Barnum's MapConvert and Andreas Heissenberger's ClientMap. Both are available for downloading from the *HTML & Web Publishing SECRETS* Web site. Go to `http://websecrets.heidsite.com/`.

Another excellent image-map editor is the freeware Map This!, by Todd C. Wilson. Available only for Windows, Map This! supports both server- and client-side maps and offers a host of slick, time-saving features. You can, for example, define a hot spot's destination by dragging a URL from Netscape Navigator. Map This! is available at `http://galadriel.ecaetc.ohio-state.edu/tc/mt/`. Versions of Map This! are also included with some commercial products, including O'Reilly & Associates' WebSite servers. As I describe later, this version of Map This! is tailored to work with WebSite's built-in image map software.

Map This!'s creator has gone on to create what may be the ultimate map-making utility, LiveImage. This program uses a variety of wizard-like dialog boxes to walk you through the map-making process. You can download a trial version at `http://www.mediatec.com/`.

Making server-side image maps

The steps to create an image map are similar regardless of the program you use.

Create the graphic

An image map begins with a bitmapped graphic. Remember to follow the rules of graphics-optimizing: use a low bit depth, make the graphic no larger than necessary, and choose a compact file format. You can use GIF or JPEG files for image maps.

Open the graphic in the map utility

If you're using an HTML layout tool such as PageMill, import the graphic and position it on the page. If you're using a stand-alone image map utility such as Web Map or Map This!, open the graphic.

Draw the hot spots and tie them to addresses

Image maps support several shapes, including rectangles, ovals, circles, and polygons, and most image map editors provide a tool palette of these shapes. Generally, you draw a hot spot's shape and then use a dialog box or text-entry box to specify the URL that you want to be associated with that hot spot. See Figure 6-27 for an example.

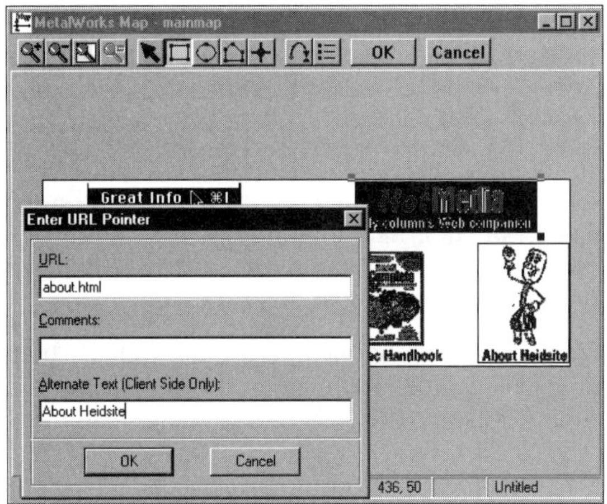

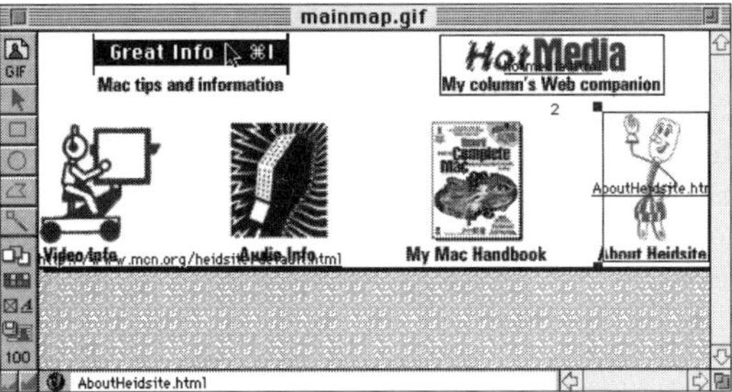

Figure 6-27: These map hot spots were created in SoftQuad's HoTMetaL Pro (top) and Adobe PageMill (bottom).

Each shape attribute requires arguments that describe the shape's coordinates — its location on the map graphic. For example, consider the following hot spot description:

```
rect hotstuff.html 84,25 229,74
```

These arguments indicate that the "Hot Stuff" hot spot's upper-left corner is located 84 pixels to the right of and 25 pixels below the map's upper-left corner, and that its lower-right corner is located 229 pixels to the right of and 74 pixels below the map's upper-left corner. But don't get a migraine: all map-creation tools supply these values for you based on the shapes you draw with their tools.

Save the map-definition file

The end result of a map-making session is a map-definition file — a text file used by the image map CGI that you install on your Web server. The following code illustrates a typical map-definition file:

```
default http://www.heidsite.com/default.html
rect http://www.heidsite.com/AboutHeidsite.html 366,50 436,144
rect http://www.heidsite.com/handbook.html 245,56 320,143
rect http://www.heidsite.com/audio/audio.html 124,56 189,143
rect http://www.heidsite.com/video/video.html 2,56 74,146
rect http://www.heidsite.com/hotmedia/hotmedia.html 261,2 407,40
rect http://www.heidsite.com/generalmac.html 35,1 165,38
```

The <DEFAULT> line at the top of the file tells the CGI or server which page to display if a visitor clicks on an area of the graphic that *isn't* a hot spot. In the example shown above, the page containing the map is redisplayed. Another option is to display a page containing an error message.

Two formats exist for map-definition files: NCSA and CERN. The two formats are similar but arrange the shape attributes and URLs differently. Most servers and image-map CGIs use the NCSA format. If yours is among them, be sure to specify the NCSA format in your map utility's Preferences or Save As dialog box.

Add the map's HTML to your page

If you're using an HTML layout tool, this step is handled for you by the tool. To implement an image map in HTML, create an anchor element (denoted by the <A and </A> codes). Within it, create both an <HREF> tag pointing to the CGI application that will process map requests and the <IMG> tag that points to the map's graphic. The ismap attribute at the end of the <IMG> tag tells a browser to treat the graphic as an image map, as illustrated in the following HTML for a server-side image map:

```
<A HREF="http://www.heidsite.com/cgi-bin/imagemap.cgi$mainmap"> <IMG
SRC="graphics/mainmap.gif"
  WIDTH="437" HEIGHT="148" BORDER="0"
  ALT="No graphics? Click the text labels below instead."
  ISMAP
ALIGN=bottom></A>
```

SECRET

Tips for Image Map-Makers

- An image-map CGI scans the map-definition file from top to bottom. For best performance, prioritize the entries in the file: put the most-often-used hot spot first and the least-often-used last.
- To optimize image-map performance, keep the map simple: avoid using dozens of hot spots and scads of complex polygons.
- Use whatever program you like to create an image map's graphic, but remember to follow the rules of graphics-optimizing: use a low bit depth, make the graphic no larger than necessary, and choose a compact file format.
- Make your hot spots unambiguous — making hot spots look like buttons is a good way to ensure that visitors recognize them as clickable. If visitors aren't sure where to click, they're more likely to click dead spots — which will slow the server and frustrate them. Client-side maps are better in this regard, because they provide some visual feedback in the browser status bar.
- Make your hot spots big and avoid polygons when possible. Say you have an irregularly shaped object — perhaps a house icon representing a home page — that you want to be a hot spot. You might be tempted to create the hot spot using your map program's polygon tool, hugging the shape's contours exactly. But it's better to create a rectangular hot spot that simply encloses the entire shape. For one thing, rectangles are faster to process than polygons. For another, rectangles provide some "fudge factor" space for the site's visitors — they make it less critical for the user to position the mouse pointer *exactly* over the shape when clicking.
- Some Web users are still using text-only browsers such as Lynx. A much larger percentage are using 14.4Kbps modems and have turned off their browsers' graphic-loading option. For these groups, provide text-only navigation options, such as a bar below the image map.

Making client-side image maps

The secret to creating client-side maps is to add some additional HTML tags and attributes to the page that contains the image map. One set of tags defines the coordinates of each hot spot as well as the hot spot's destination. These tags and attributes do the job that, with server-side maps, is performed by a map-definition file.

The following code shows the HTML for a typical client-side image map. Here's a field guide to the tags that make it work.

```
<MAP NAME="mainmap">
  <AREA SHAPE="RECT" COORDS="366,50,436,144"
HREF="AboutHeidsite.html">
  <AREA SHAPE="RECT" COORDS="245,56,320,143" HREF="handbook.html">
  <AREA SHAPE="RECT" COORDS="124,56,189,143"
HREF="audio/audio.html">
  <AREA SHAPE="RECT" COORDS="2,56,74,146" HREF="video/video.html">
  <AREA SHAPE="RECT" COORDS="261,2,407,40"
```

```
HREF="hotmedia/hotmedia.html">
  <AREA SHAPE="RECT" COORDS="35,1,165,38" HREF="generalmac.html">
</MAP>
<CENTER>
<A HREF="http://www.mcn.org/imagemap/imagemap.cgi$mainmap"> <IMG
SRC="graphics/mainmap.gif"
  WIDTH="437" HEIGHT="148" BORDER="0"
  ALT="No graphics? Click the text labels below instead."
  ISMAP
  USEMAP="#mainmap"
  ALIGN=bottom></A>
```

The <MAP> tag

The `<MAP>` tag denotes the beginning of the client-side image map's definition. The `name` attribute that follows gives the definition a name that you'll use when referring to the map.

The list of hot spots and their URLs

In a client-side image map, each hot spot's coordinates and link reside directly within the HTML page, not in a separate map-definition file as they do with server-side maps. Client-side maps support three shapes: polygons (`POLY`), circles (`CIRCLE`), and rectangles (`RECT`). The `<CIRCLE>` tag's three attributes reflect the location of the circle's center point and the circle's radius. The `<SHAPE>` tag is optional; if you eliminate it, the browser assumes the shape is a rectangle (`RECT`).

For clarity, some of the examples in this section contained absolute URLs — URLs that include a full domain name. In the real world, relative URLs — ones that indicate only the path from the current page — are often preferred. As mentioned in Chapter 4, relative URLs make it easier to move your site from one machine or server to another.

The </MAP> tag

After defining each hot spot, end the definition with the `</MAP>` tag.

The usemap attribute

The rest of the HTML code in client-side image maps looks much like its server-side counterpart, and for good reason: this code also supports a server-side map for use with browsers that don't support client-side maps. An anchor element contains both an `<HREF>` tag that points to the server-side CGI and to the map's graphic, and an `ismap` attribute that tells the browser to treat the graphic as an image map. The code also contains a `usemap` attribute, which tells a client-side-aware browser to use the map definition whose name appears after the pound sign (#).

Mixing and Matching Map Types in Adobe PageMill

Adobe PageMill 2.0 was the first PageMill version to support the creation of client-side image maps. But PageMill's approach to client-side maps makes it a bit cumbersome to support both server- and client-side maps in a single page.

Specifically, you must create hot spots and specify their URLs twice: once for each type of image map. Because you create hot spots by clicking and dragging, there's an excellent chance that you won't create hot spots that are the exact same size and in the exact same positions.

One solution to this problem is to create only a server-side map in PageMill, and then convert its coordinates and hand-code the tags for a client-side map. (Or you could reverse this process: Create the client-side map in PageMill and then hand-code a map-definition file.)

The other solution is to create both types of maps in PageMill, and then simply edit one set of coordinates so that it matches the other.

The final solution is to do absolutely nothing. For many image maps, it doesn't really matter whether the client-side and server-side hot spots are *exactly* the same size and in exactly the same location. Most of the time, what's important is that the maps work.

Other graphic navigation strategies

Client-side maps provide a better user interface experience than server-side maps, but they still don't fully address the visual feedback issue. In a CD-ROM title, buttons highlight or otherwise change when a user clicks on them. An image map can't provide this response. Technologies such as Macromedia's Shockwave for Director and Sun's Java allow for multiple-state buttons, but induce their own headaches, such as limited browser support, high memory overheads, and steep learning curves.

As Chapter 7 describes, you can also create "CD-ROM-like" buttons and interfaces through clever use of JavaScript. But again, complexity and browser compatibility rear their ugly heads.

Because of these drawbacks, the best general-purpose navigation device is still the lowly image map — and specifically, one that works from the client or server side. There aren't many areas in Web development where you can support two dramatically different approaches within a single page. This is one of them — take advantage of it.

Summary

- Optimizing Web graphics — adjusting the resolution and bit depth and choosing an appropriate file format — is an extremely important job that has a direct impact on a Web site's performance and appearance.
- GIF files are best for icons, navigation bars, text, and graphics that contain areas of solid colors. JPEG files are best for photographs.
- Issues to consider when optimizing the bit depth of GIF files include browser palettes, bit depth, and dithering. Utilities such as Digital Frontiers' HVS WebFocus and Ulead's PhotoImpact SmartSaver can make the process less painful.
- When combined with the `<IMG>` tag's `height` and `width` attributes, colored, single-pixel GIF files are handy tools for creating bars, buttons, dotted rules, and other graphical elements.
- The Netscape `<LOWSRC>` tag enables you to display a low-resolution image first, and then substitute it with a higher-quality version. You can also use the tag for simple animation.
- You can boost a site's performance by taking advantage of a browser's cache to reuse graphics.
- For navigation, you can use separate graphics or image maps — each has its advantages and drawbacks.
- Server-side image maps are the most widely supported, but client-side maps provide better performance, less server load, and more visual feedback to the visitor. Fortunately, it's easy to support both types in a single page.

Chapter 7

Pushing HTML

In This Chapter

- Dealing with browser compatibility issues — the LCD and HCD methods
- Learn how to use key HTML extensions
- The Tao of tables
- Framing the Web
- JavaScripting your interface
- Getting stylish with style sheets
- Exploring the future of HTML

Pushing HTML is about mastering the subtle uses of HTML tags and about keeping up to speed with its latest developments. By these yardsticks, nobody pushes tags better than Andy King, whose Webreference.com (`http://www.webreference.com/`*) is a must-bookmark site for anyone doing Web development. I asked Andy to share his HTML-pushing strategies, and lucky for all of us, he agreed. — Jim Heid*

HTML's Holy Grail

In earlier chapters, you learned that the Holy Grail of total, pixel-level control over Web pages is not here yet. But it may be approaching. The World Wide Web Consortium (W3C) was formed in part to prevent the balkanization of the Web due to proprietary extensions to HTML. Their crowning achievement will be style sheets, due out in the next version of HTML.

I have more to say about style sheets later in this chapter. First, I describe why the "feature war" brewing between the browser behemoths — Microsoft and Netscape — is actually slowing the growth of the Web. Then I'll show you some key extensions that work on both Navigator and Explorer 3.0 that you can use to jazz up your Web sites.

Headline: Feature wars balkanizing the Web, film at 11

By design, HTML has limited control over page layout. As you learned in Chapter 3, HTML was originally designed to describe the structure, not appearance, of a Web page. That's why HTML is so universal: a few simple tags such as `<P>`, `<H1>`, and `<UL>` can be rendered on a wide variety of output devices, and even be converted into speech or Braille. But pressure from designers who want to distinguish their Web pages has caused a "feature war" between browser companies, mainly Netscape and Microsoft. Thus HTML extensions.

By their very nature, standards take time to become cast in stone. Browser manufacturers have forged ahead to satisfy requests for more appearance and layout control. Netscape pioneered extensions to HTML, some based on HTML drafts and some of their own invention (BLINK <shudder> and FRAMEs). With version 3.0 of Explorer, Microsoft supports or extends most Netscape tags and adds some of their own — for example, `<FLOATING FRAMES>` and `<MARQUEE>`. With Microsoft and Netscape leapfrogging each other, what's a Webmaster to do?

What's the harm with using HTML extensions?

The problem with extending HTML with proprietary extensions is what I call the "balkanization" of the Web. Just as there are different dialects of the same language that can't "interoperate" (for example, the Mandarin and Cantonese dialects of Chinese), there are different dialects in HTML. By making HTML less universal, the browser manufacturers slow the growth of the Web and make it more complex. Many designers now make two or three pages optimized for different browsers and find creative ways to direct or jump users to these pages (see the hidden frame trick later in this chapter for an example). These additional pages take more time to maintain and change.

The solution

The ultimate solution to this complexity conundrum is style sheets. Style sheets separate the presentation (or appearance) of content from its structure. When a new presentation feature comes out, there's no need to recode the HTML; just tweak the style sheet.

An interim solution

Style sheets can now control the appearance and spacing of any HTML tag, and experimental versions can control 2D and even 3D layout. But only a few browsers support style sheets, though they all will eventually. For now, Webmasters must choose their level of HTML support.

Tracking the LCD

Browsercaps at `http://www.browsercaps.com` is a good site to find the current LCD. Short for browser capabilities, Browsercaps is a collaborative effort that tracks the current LCD and offers test pages where you can check your own browser's HTML compliance.

You've probably heard of the *Lowest Common Denominator* (LCD) method, in which your pages are designed to reach the largest number of users. HTML 2.0 was a good choice for a while, but the LCD line keeps rising (the latest America Online and CompuServe browsers now support tables and frames). Finding the LCD is important to larger companies that want to ensure that all of their employees can see their content on the Web.

For some designers, using the LCD approach is too limiting. Pages designed in HTML 2.0 tend to be left-justified, gray, and well, boring. How can you jazz up your page and still make it readable to most users? If you look at the numbers (see Table 7-1), you'll see that 85 to 90 percent of Web browsers use Navigator and Explorer. Many designers now optimize their pages for these two browsers, and offer built-in or alternate pages for older browsers.

Table 7-1 Browser market share

Month	*Navigator*	*Explorer*
December 1996	54.4%	33.0%
November 1996	59.9	31.2
October 1996	61.5	30.0
September 1996	52.3	39.1
August 1996	62.7	29.1
July 1996	72.6	15.8
June 1996	78.2	8.3
May 1996	83.2	7.0

Source: Interse Market Focus (`http://www.interse.com/webtrends/`)

Highest common denominator

I call this, somewhat tongue in cheek, the *Highest Common Denominator* (HCD) method: setting your HTML compliance to tags and attributes common to Navigator and Explorer and still allowing older browsers to see your content. By using features common to both browsers (such as tables, frames, JavaScript 1.0, and Java) and gracefully downgrading for older browsers, you can design one page that looks great to most users. The HCD method uses the following two characteristics of the "well-behaved" Web browser:

- Graceful downgrading (if the browser doesn't recognize a tag, it ignores it)
- Nested tags (for those times when HTML 3.2, Navigator, and Explorer don't agree)

Key Extensions You Should Know

"Okay," you say, "I know the basics but how do I make my site stand out? How can I make it look cool?" Luckily you don't have to dream in C++ or Java to "program" HTML. Second-generation WYSIWYG HTML editors like Adobe PageMill 2.0 and Claris Home Page 2.0 can make creating more complex HTML tags like tables and frames relatively easy. For some of the more advanced tips covered here, such as JavaScript and style sheets, you'll have to do it by hand.

Don't despair — this chapter's code is included on the *HTML & Web Publishing SECRETS* CD-ROM so you can cut and paste it into your pages. You'll also find complete example pages to show you exactly how it works.

The Tao of tables

Chapters 3 and 5 discussed tables, which have become one of the most popular ways to simulate page layout on the Web. Originally intended for tabular or mathematical data, tables have become a designer's best friend for their ability to distribute elements throughout a page. Vertical real estate is at a premium on the Web given the typical aspect ratio of a monitor. Tables allow you to utilize the entire screen. This section shows how to use tables effectively, and points out some bugs to avoid.

Columns and tables

Tables can be used to format multicolumn text and side heads. The computer network, c|net, pioneered the use of tables for finer layout control (`http://www.cnet.com`), and their many spin-off sites (including `shareware.com` and `news.com`) use the same back-end database and template engine that was developed for the c|net site. c|net set a goal of only using 20 to 30K per page, to ensure that each page loads quickly. The site also changes hourly, which makes it an appealing site to visit (see Figure 7-1).

As mentioned in Chapter 5, Sun Microsystems' *Guide to Web Style*, by Rick Levine, (`http://www.sun.com/styleguide/`) is an excellent example of the intelligent use of tables (see Figure 7-2). When visitors enter this page, the server automatically delivers a page optimized for each browser. This is done using browser redirection. The table version uses a simple yet elegant text navigation bar that shows the names of each page in a columnar format. This compound table uses a nested table on top with `TD` tags for each column, and uses the left column for sidehead highlights. The page is clean and designed for quick scanning. The code is included on the *HTML & Web Publishing SECRETS* CD-ROM so you can use this technique on your own pages.

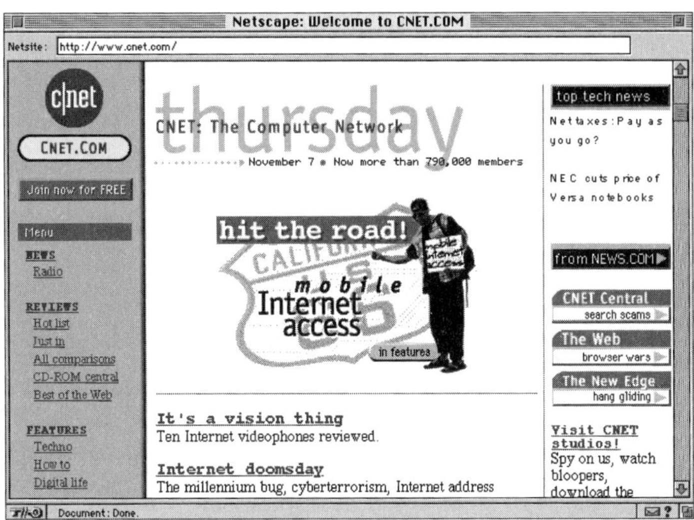

Figure 7-1: The c|net home page

The following code is the HTML for nested tables:

```
<TABLE BORDER=0 CELLSPACING=6>
<TR>
  <TD VALIGN=BOTTOM ALIGN=LEFT>
    <A HREF="/styleguide/tables/Welcome.html">
    <IMG BORDER=1 SRC="/styleguide/images/Web_Style_Small.gif"
WIDTH=127 HEIGHT=52 ALT="GUIDE TO WEB STYLE"></A>
  </TD>
  <TD WIDTH="15%" ALIGN=LEFT VALIGN=BOTTOM>
  <TABLE BORDER=0 CELLSPACING=6>
    <TR VALIGN=TOP>
    <TD>
      <A HREF="/Purposes.html">Purposes</A><BR>
      <A HREF="/Audience.html">Audience</A><BR>
      <A HREF="/Links.html">Links</A><BR>
    </TD>
    <TD>
      <A HREF="/Page_Length.html">Page Length</A><BR>
      <A HREF="/Graphics.html">Graphics</A><BR>
      <A HREF="/Image_Maps.html">Image Maps</A><BR>
    </TD>
    <TD>
      <STRONG>Navigation</STRONG><BR>
      <A HREF="/Security.html">Security</A><BR>
      <A HREF="/Quality.html">Quality</A><BR>
    </TD>
```

```
    <TD>
      <A HREF="/Netiquette.html">Netiquette</A><BR>
      <A HREF="/Content.html">Content</A><BR>
      <A HREF="/Selling.html">Selling</A><BR>
    </TD>
    <TD>
      <A HREF="/Language.html">Language</A><BR>
      <A HREF="/Java.html">Java</A><BR>
    </TD>
    </TR>
  </TABLE>
  </TD>
</TR>
<TR>
  <TD COLSPAN=2><HR></TD>
</TR>
<TR>
  <TD></TD>
  <TD ALIGN=LEFT><H1>Navigation</H1></TD>
</TR>
<TR>
  <TH ALIGN=LEFT VALIGN=TOP>Insert Headling Here</TH>
  <TD VALIGN=TOP>
   Content here...
  </TD>
</TR>
....
</TABLE>
```

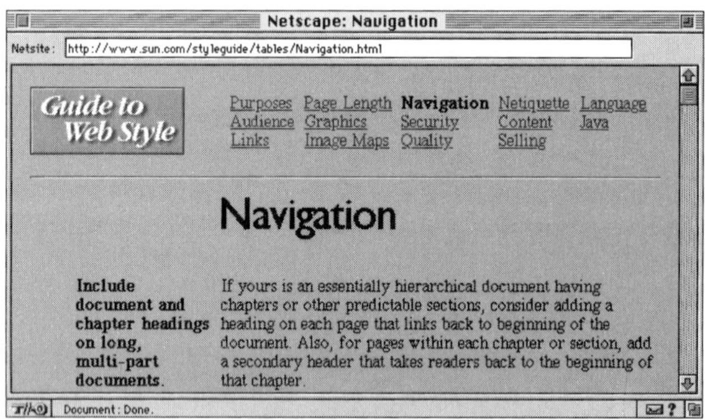

Figure 7-2: Sun Microsystems' *Guide to Web Style*

Terrific Table Tips

JavaScript and Tables. Tables and JavaScript don't mix well in Navigator 2.x. To ensure that they do, use `document.write()` to write out the entire table plus your script, instead of including a script inside a table. You'll avoid bombing Navigator 2 users.

Aligning Tables. HTML 3.2 includes the `align` attribute to the `<TABLE>` tag. The default is `center`. Text flows around a table when left or right aligned, as with the `<IMG>` tag. Navigator 2.0 and Explorer 2.0 support left and right alignment, but not center alignment. For centering tables I recommend using a transition strategy. The most universal way of centering a table is to use the `<CENTER>` tag and the `align=center` attribute of the `<TABLE>` tag (`p align=center` or `right` does not work on tables).

```
<CENTER>
    <TABLE>
      <TR>
        <TD>Centers in Netscape</TD>
        <TD>Datagram</TD>
      </TR>
    </TABLE>
</CENTER> <!-- DISCOURAGED, but now legal in HTML 3.2 -->

<CENTER>
    <TABLE ALIGN=CENTER>
      <TR>
        <TD>Hey, this really works.</TD>
        <TD>Data, Data, where are you Data?</TD>
      </TR>
    </TABLE>
</CENTER> <!-- RIGHT (works for Navigator 1.1+, Explorer 2.0+, and
HTML 3.2)* or -->

<DIV ALIGN=CENTER>
    <TABLE ALIGN=CENTER>
      <TR>
        <TD>da, da, da, dooo</TD>
        <TD>Data, ohhh DATA</TD>
      </TR>
    </TABLE>
</DIV> <!-- RIGHT (works for Navigator 2.0+, Explorer 2.0+, and
HTML 3.2) or -->

<TABLE ALIGN=CENTER>
      <TR>
        <TD>HTML 3.2-only way</TD>
        <TD>Early 1997?</TD>
      </TR>
</TABLE> <!-- RIGHT (works for HTML 3.2-compliant browsers only,
       Netscape or Explorer 4.0?) -->
```

*Recommended until Navigator and Explorer support `table align=center`. You could remove the `<CENTER>` tags after the majority of surfers use these new HTML 3.2-compliant browsers.

(continued)

(continued)

Shorter lines of text are easier to read. Studies by Jan Tschichold, the famous typographer, have shown that the optimum line length is 8 to 12 words. Multiple columns shorten your lines, and create a more magazine-like layout. (For more tips on line length issues, see Chapter 5.)

Close your cells. The closing `<TR>` and `<TD>` tags are technically optional in HTML 3.2, but I've found in practice that it's a good idea to include them. Navigator 1.1 sometimes renders tables incorrectly when you don't use these closing tags.

Showing empty cell borders. With borders on, empty cells appear as raised bumps, which can look a bit strange. By using a non-breaking space or a `<BR>` tag, you can force the borders to show for empty cells. For cells that act as spacers, use the single-pixel GIF trick described in Chapter 5 to hold the cell's width or height.

The Hard Return Bug. In Navigator 1.1 and later there is a little- documented bug that can place extra space between cells. For most tables this isn't a problem, but it can be for precisely aligned tables, especially those with colored backgrounds. Any time you type a hard return after a `<TD>` tag or before a `</TD>` tag, Navigator inserts a small space between cells. To remove this space, remove the returns. For example, `<TD>data</TD>`.

Improving the single-pixel GIF trick

A common mistake designers make is omitting the `width` and `height` attributes when they use the single-pixel GIF trick (see Chapter 5). This causes Explorer to redisplay the page as it calculates the dimensions of your invisible GIF. Be sure to include both the `width` and `height` attributes. When `hspace`, `vspace`, and dimensions are combined, your page will look and act nearly identically in Navigator and Explorer. Here's an example:

```
Wrong:
<IMG SRC="art/1pixel.gif" HSPACE=10 VSPACE=5><IMG
SRC="art/moveme.gif" ALT="">

Right:
<IMG SRC="art/1pixel.gif" WIDTH=1 HEIGHT=1 HSPACE=10 VSPACE=5><IMG
SRC="art/moveme.gif" ALT="">
```

See the Cool Site of the Hour at `http://www.coolcentral.com/hour/` for an example of the use of this table technique.

Advanced tables

Beginning with version 3.0 of each, Navigator and Explorer support background colors for tables and cells, which you can use to create some interesting effects. HTML 3.2 does not include this new feature in the specification, but it is incorporated into style sheets. You can specify the color of individual cells, rows, headers, and entire tables using the `bgcolor` attribute to the `<TD/TH>`, `<TR>`, and `<TABLE>` tags. The color values are set just like the `body bgcolor` attribute; for example:

```
BGCOLOR = "#ff0000" = red
```

Nested tables inherit background table colors. See the following code for an example of the bgcolor attribute and Figure 7-3 for an example of the table cell background colors.

```
<TABLE WIDTH="315" HEIGHT="96" BORDER="0" CELLSPACING="0"
CELLPADDING="0">
   <TR>
     <TD WIDTH="21%" HEIGHT="27" BGCOLOR="#edda1a"><P
ALIGN=RIGHT> Cell </TD>
     <TD COLSPAN="2" BGCOLOR="#ef5cf5"><P ALIGN=CENTER> c r e a
t e</TD>
   </TR>
   <TR>
     <TD HEIGHT="29" BGCOLOR="#edda1a"><P
ALIGN=CENTER> colors</TD>
     <TD ROWSPAN="2" BGCOLOR="#ef5cf5" WIDTH="41%"><P
ALIGN=CENTER>  i n t e r e s t i n g . . .</TD>
     <TD WIDTH="38%" ROWSPAN="2" BGCOLOR="#5ecff2"
ALIGN="CENTER"> effects</TD>
   </TR>
   <TR>
     <TD HEIGHT="29" BGCOLOR="#f45b64"> can</TD>
   </TR>
</TABLE>
```

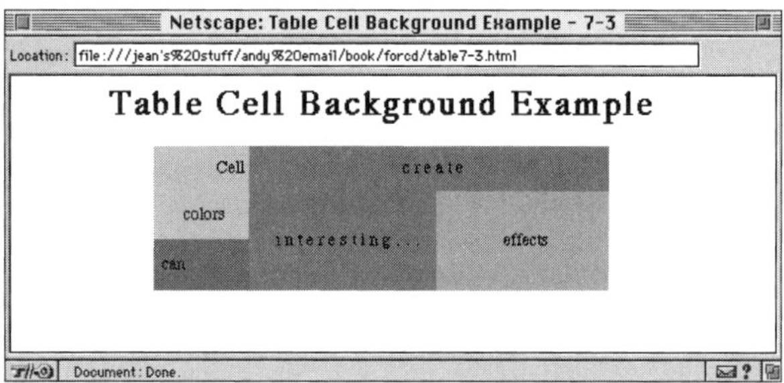

Figure 7-3: An example of table cell background colors

See how the cells are adjacent? The way to do this is to zero out the cellpadding, cellspacing, and border attributes. Used tastefully, table cell background colors can enhance your Web pages. A common use is in sidebars or to highlight phrases. I use a neutral light gray of bgcolor="#ededed" for callouts and sidebars.

Explorer 3.0 also supports table and cell background graphics. The background attribute works as it does with the <BODY> tag, and you can create tables that simulate wooden picture frames with a little ingenuity. Since Navigator 3.0 does not support this tag, HCD designers should avoid this tag for now.

The same rules of text and background contrast that apply to the <BODY> tag also apply to tables. Try to maximize the contrast between your text and background. Dark text on light backgrounds generally works best.

Border patrol

The HTML 3.2 border attribute now works identically in Navigator and Explorer. It can be used alone as a value (<TABLE BORDER>) or as an attribute (<TABLE BORDER=2>) that sets the width, in pixels, of the border drawn around the table's frame. The default is no border.

Explorer 3.0 also includes the rule and frame attributes, which were in the previous table draft, but not included in HTML 3.2. They are in the next version of HTML, however, code-named "Cougar." The rule attribute controls cell interior borders, and the frame attribute controls exterior borders. Both have values of ROWS, COLS, and NONE. You can create interesting magazine-like effects by merging vertical and horizontal cells and raising edges, but again since Navigator 3.0 and HTML 3.2 don't support these attributes, HCD designers should wait for versions that do.

The invisible table trick

When using tables for layout, turn your borders off by setting border=0 or by omitting the border attribute. Bordered tables take up space that could be used by data. And large bordered tables look unsightly.

Relative versus absolute width

The HTML 3.2 width attribute sets the desired relative width of the table as a percentage of the screen width between margins. HTML 3.2 also includes the width attribute (in pixels) for individual cells. These can be used to set the width of individual columns, but in practice it's best to force the cell's width with an invisible GIF and the hspace attribute.

To confuse things, Netscape and Microsoft also allow absolute widths for tables (for example, <TABLE WIDTH="465"> in pixels), and relative widths for cells (<TD WIDTH="40%">). By using the HTML 3.2 relative width (for instance, <TABLE WIDTH="100%">), the table will always be fully visible within the browser's window. Many designers literally live on the edge and use absolute settings for total table widths. Absolute-width tables can extend off of the screen and be partially visible when users shrink their browser windows, but if set wisely they can act as the basis for the structure of your entire page.

If you use fixed-width tables, be sure to take your audience into account. The average monitor works best with a maximum of 600-pixel-wide tables, but the new set-top Web boxes like WebTV use a TV's screen, which is 560 pixels×420 pixels. WebTV doesn't scroll horizontally, and uses an 8-pixel buffer on either edge, so tables wider than 544 pixels will be clipped. The viewable vertical space is 378 pixels. If you're designing a site for TV viewers, keep this width limitation in mind.

Background registration

Registering tables precisely over backgrounds can be a challenge, as different browsers have different margin offsets. Explorer 2.0 solves this problem by including `leftmargin` and `topmargin` attributes to the `<BODY>` tag. Navigator 3.0 does not include these tags. On the Mac OS, Netscape and Explorer 3 both have the same default offset (8 pixels). However, other platforms and browser versions have different offsets so you can't count on everyone seeing your foreground align exactly with your background. In Explorer 2.0 you can set your top and left margins to 0 with the following code:

```
<BODY LEFTMARGIN="0" TOPMARGIN="0"...>
```

Until most browsers support zero offsets, there are only two ways to register backgrounds: browser-optimized pages and frames. Some companies calculated the offsets of many different browsers on different platforms and automatically direct users to perfectly registered pages, no matter who views it. In practice you can design one page with elements that stay well inside different background sections or that span transitions.

Creating tables

Long-time Webmasters like to code everything by hand with a text editor. But for more complex tables and frames, the amount of code and complexity can be daunting. That's where WYSIWYG page layout tools come in. With tools like PageMill 2.0 and Home Page 2.0, you can layout complex tables or frames quickly and tweak the code to fine tune it.

Of the two, I prefer PageMill 2.0. It enables you to merge and split cells easily, and it handles frames better than Home Page 2.0. Creating the nested frame layout for our own Web headlines (`http://www.webreference.com/headlines/`) was a snap in PageMill (see Figure 7-4).

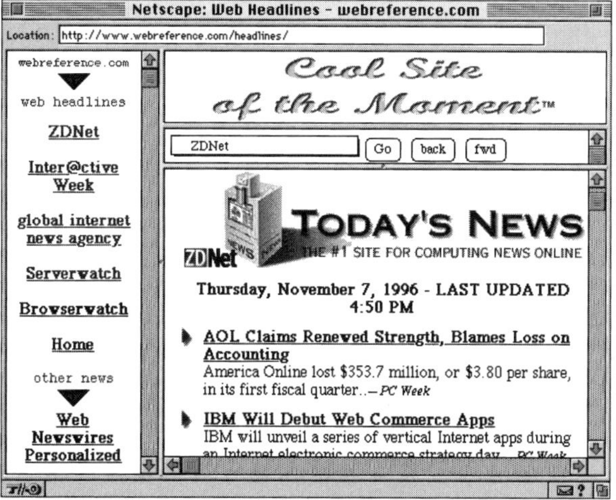

Figure 7-4: Web Headlines nested frame layout in PageMill 2.0

For more details about the <TABLE> tag, consult Appendix A at the end of this book and read "HTML 3.2 and Netscape 3.0 — How to Tame the Wild Mozilla" at http://www.webreference.com/html3andns/.

Framing the Web

Introduced in Navigator 2.0 and supported by Explorer 3.0, frames have taken the Web by storm. But for some, the introduction of frames was a very dark day indeed. This love-hate relationship with frames is caused in part by improper use and overuse. Used without target attributes they can nest indefinitely and cause navigation nightmares. But properly used, they can form the basis of near application-like interfaces. In this section you'll learn the key tips and techniques essential for frame mastery.

Frame syntax basics

To give us a common context for discussing frames, let's be sure we understand the basic syntax used in defining frames within a window.

A window can contain either one or more groups of frames, collectively referred to as a <FRAMESET> and defined with that tag, or a single document contained within the <BODY> and </BODY> tags. If the window uses frames, the skeletal layout for the window's HTML will look something like the following (with lots of variations and extensions omitted in the interest of simplicity):

```
<HTML>
<HEAD>
</HEAD>
<FRAMESET COLS="column  spec" ROWS="row spec">
<FRAME SRC="frame1.html">
<FRAME SRC="frame2.html">
</FRAMESET>
</HTML>
```

The <FRAMESET> defines a number of rows and/or columns and their absolute or relative size with respect to one another. There must be a <FRAME> tag entry for each cell (number of rows times number of columns) in the <FRAMESET>.

The key to getting frames to talk to one another is to name the frames when you create them, like this:

```
<FRAME NAME="mainFrame" SRC="toc.html">
```

The name of the frame doesn't have to be one word as shown here; this is a matter of scripting style. Also, there is no relationship between the name of a frame and the URL to which it is connected, though it's a good idea to use similar names for both because it increases the readability of your JavaScripts and makes it easier to remember later what the frame is supposed to contain.

With frames named, you can use the `target` attribute of an `<HREF>` tag to cause the indicated URL to appear in the named frame, as in the following example:

```
<A HREF="product.html" TARGET="mainFrame">link text</A>
```

When the visitor clicks on the link text in one frame of your window, the browser goes to the URL *product.html* in the frame called *mainFrame* in the same window. If you omit the target, of course, the browser displays the new URL in the frame where the link text was displayed.

All the other `href` attributes and techniques are applicable to frame-based links as well. This means, among other things, that you can use named anchors to force a frame to display its contents scrolled to a specific location at the top of the browser window.

Resizable frames

Navigator and Explorer default to resizable frames. This is a good idea for any frame that could contain content of various sizes. Fixed ad banners or button bars have a known size; for these, you can safely use the `noresize` and `scrolling="no"` attributes to create a "shelf." But navigation popups and other elements can vary in size on different platforms, so give the user control to customize your framesets.

For simple layouts, omit the `noresize` attribute. For more complex layouts in which frames run up against one another, you must nest frame sets to allow resizing.

FrameMaster Tips

Avoid Nesting Nightmares. To ensure external links will jump out of your frames, `use <BASE TARGET="_top">`. This avoids nesting nightmares when a framed site links to another framed site. Local `target`s override this global setting.

Invisible Frame Borders. The good news is that you can now hide frame borders in Navigator and Explorer 3. The bad news is that the browsers use different attributes. Netscape uses the `border` attribute, while Explorer uses the `framespacing` attribute to set frame border widths. Both Explorer and Netscape use `frameborder` to turn borders on and off. However, Netscape uses "NO/YES" while Explorer uses "0/1" or "NO/YES" for the `frameborder` value. The solution is to combine these attributes, as in the following example:

```
<FRAMESET ROWS="60,50,*" FRAMEBORDER="NO" BORDER="0"
FRAMESPACING="0">
```

Figure 7-5 shows a working example of invisible frame borders.

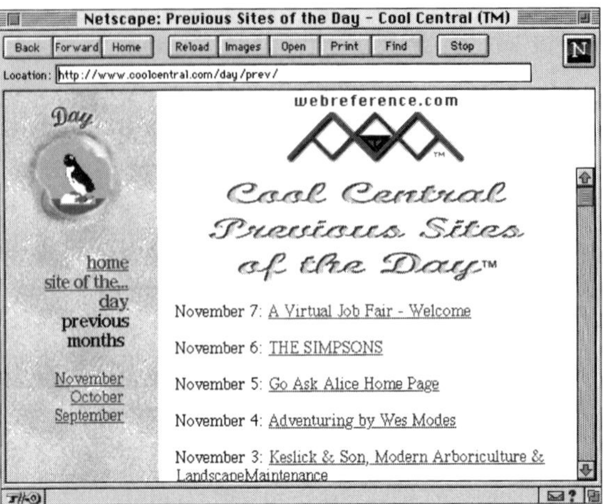

Figure 7-5: Previous Cool Central Sites of the Day (http://www.coolcentral.com/day/prev/)

To allow for older browsers, or users with `frame`s disabled, use the `<NOFRAMES>` tag as shown in the following example:

```
<HTML>
<TITLE>Simple Frame Example with NOFRAME</TITLE>
<FRAMESET COLS="30%,*">
   <FRAME SRC="left.html">
   <FRAME SRC="right.html">
<NOFRAMES>
<BODY>
  <TABLE>
    <TR>
      <TD>Left's content here</TD>
      <TD>Right's content here</TD>
    </TR>
</TABLE>
</BODY>
</NOFRAMES>
</FRAMESET>
</HTML>
```

A common practice on the Web is to use the `<NOFRAME>` tag to scold people who don't have Navigator. A better use is to offer a non-frame alternative so everyone can see your page.

JavaScript and frames

JavaScript is ideal for controlling frames. You can update one or more frames with one link, and create custom frames on the fly. You'll read more about JavaScript later in this chapter and in Chapter 11, but for now, I discuss three useful techniques.

Frame navigation with JavaScript

Navigator 2 jumps to the last page when you press the Back button. This disorients many users who have delved deep into a framed presentation. Navigator 3 fixed this problem, but with JavaScript, you can offer Navigator 2 users navigation aids that enable them to go "back in frame" and "forward in frame."

Because each page is a separate window to Navigator, each frame has a separate history list. The history list keeps track of the URLs of pages you've visited in each session. You can access this list with the history property of each frame. To navigate through a frame's history you only need one line of code:

```
parent.frames[1].history.back() or .forward() or .go(number)
parent.frames[1].history.go(0) - forces the current frame to reload
```

Create two buttons with an `onClick` event that calls the back and forward code as shown in the following example:

```
<HTML>
<HEAD><TITLE>Frame Navigation Example</TITLE>
<SCRIPT LANGUAGE = "JavaScript">
function backInFrame(frameNum){
        parent.frames[frameNum].history.back();
        }
function forwardInFrame(frameNum){
        parent.frames[frameNum].history.forward();
        }
</SCRIPT>
</HEAD>
<BODY BGCOLOR="#FFFFFF">
<FORM NAME="menus">
<INPUT TYPE="button" VALUE="back"
onClick="backInFrame(2)"> <INPUT TYPE="button" VALUE="fwd"
onClick="forwardInFrame(2)"></FORM>
</BODY>
</HTML>
```

For more information on frame navigation see Nick Heinle's JavaScript Tip of the Week (JTOTW) — Moving Around in Frames at `http://www.webreference.com/javascript/960603/index.html`.

The hidden frame redirection trick

SECRET

By combining JavaScript and a hidden frame you can automatically direct users to browser-optimized pages. The trick is to declare two rows (`ROWS="100%,*"`) and define only one frame. This does not cause any errors; it simply displays the frame you define. By dynamically generating the frame set based on the browser type, you can automatically direct users to different pages. The page appears to be a normal HTML page when it is in fact a single frame.

It's a good idea to include `<BASE TARGET="_top">` in the head of your documents so users will clear out of your frame set when they click on a link. Set `SCROLLING` to `AUTO` for an even cleaner look. Another advantage to using frames is that you can set the margin width and height.

We use this trick on the front page of coolcentral.com. Here's the code:

```
<HTML>
<HEAD><TITLE>Cool Central [TM]</TITLE>
<SCRIPT LANGUAGE="JavaScript">
<!--// begin universal browser detection
browser = navigator.appName;
version = parseInt(navigator.appVersion);
if      (browser == "Netscape" && version >= 3) type = "n3";
else if (browser == "Netscape" && version == 2) type = "n2";
else if (browser == "Microsoft Internet Explorer" && version >= 2)
type = "e3";
with (document) {
   if (type == "n2") {
     writeln ('<FRAMESET FRAMEBORDER=NO BORDER=0 ROWS="100%,*">' +
     '<FRAME SRC="indexs.html" NAME="static" MARGINWIDTH="0"
MARGINHEIGHT="0"
      SCROLLING="AUTO">'
     '</FRAMESET>');
 } else { // Netscape 3 or Explorer 3
     writeln ('<FRAMESET FRAMEBORDER=NO BORDER=0 ROWS="100%,*">' +
     '<FRAME SRC="indexa.html" NAME="animated" MARGINWIDTH="0"
MARGINHEIGHT="0"
      SCROLLING="AUTO">' +
     '</FRAMESET>');
 }
}
// end browser detection -->
</SCRIPT>
</HEAD>
<!-- include default frameset for non-javascript but frame-enabled
browsers -->
<FRAMESET FRAMEBORDER="NO" BORDER="0" ROWS="100%,*">
<FRAME SRC="indexs.html" NAME="text" MARGINWIDTH="0" MARGINHEIGHT="0"
SCROLLING="AUTO">
<NOFRAMES>
<BODY>
insert equivalent table code here
</BODY>
</NOFRAMES>
</FRAMESET>
</HEAD>
</HTML>
```

Updating multiple frames

With VBScript or JavaScript, you can update multiple frames with one link. Here's an example in VBScript:

```
<A HREF="" name="ClickHere">Click here!</A>
<SCRIPT Language="VBScript">
<!--
SUB ClickHere_OnClick()
   parent.FrameOne.location.href="ad.gif"
   parent.FrameTwo.location.href="content.html
END SUB
-->
</SCRIPT>
```

In JavaScript you can do the same thing by updating the `href` property of two frames at once, or you can just refer to a link and include an `onClick` call. In the following example I update the main "content" window and the status popup at the same time.

```
function changePopup(i) {
   if (i == 0) return;
top.frames['right'].frames['popup'].document.menus.home.selectedIndex=i;
}
...
<A HREF="zdnet/" TARGET="main"
onClick="changePopup(1)"><B>ZDNet</B></A>
...
```

The advantage to this method is that browsers without JavaScript will still update the main content frame.

Putting it all together

ON CD-ROM

I incorporate many of these techniques into one framed, JavaScript page called Web Headlines (see Figure 7-6). Web Headlines is a front-end to a back-end "newsbot" that copies over special news feeds from various news sources. It utilizes a live popup/status menu that you'll read more about in the next section. You'll find the source code on the *HTML & Web Publishing SECRETS* CD-ROM, or you can go to `http://www.webreference.com/headlines/` for the latest news and code.

Floating frames

Explorer 3.0 introduced a new type of frame that floats in your page. An `IFRAME` acts like an image, but is actually a window to another page. Floating frames combine attributes of images and regular frames. For example, the, `align=left/right` attribute wraps text around a floating frame. The `vspace` and `hspace` attributes work exactly as they do with an image, and specify the margins around the frame.

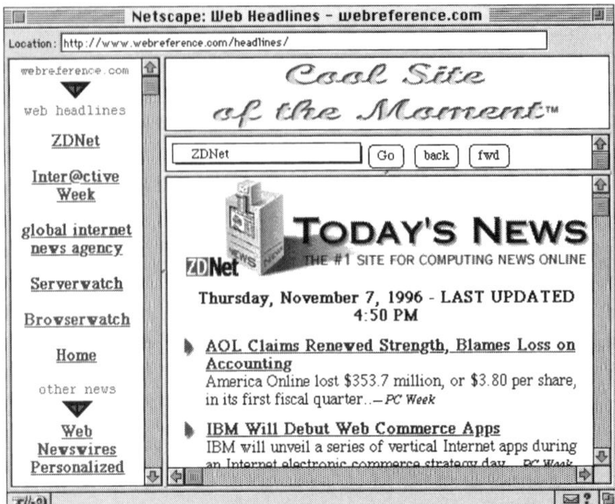

Figure 7-6: Using JavaScript and Frames (Web Headlines)

`IFRAME`s use the same frame attributes included in regular frames (`frameborder`, `marginheight`, `marginwidth`, `name`, `noresize`, `scrolling`, and `src`) plus two more, `width` and `height`. These dimension attributes specify the size of the opening. Here's an example:

```
<BODY>
<IFRAME WIDTH=200 HEIGHT=200 ALIGN=LEFT
SRC="http://www.coolcentral.com">
  <FRAME WIDTH=200 HEIGHT=200 ALIGN=LEFT
SRC="http://www.coolcentral.com">
</IFRAME>
</BODY>
```

Unlike regular frames, `IFRAME`s go inside the `<BODY>` tag. The syntax of floating frames changes from Internet Explorer 3.0 Beta 1 to Beta 2, thus the duplicate tags.

Surf Cam

Like regular frames, `IFRAME`s can be named with the `name` attribute. Target your frame with a link and it will be updated, just like a regular frame. Combined with a "live" page, floating frames can act as a monitor to real-time events. One way to do this is with client-pull. Say you're a surfer, and you want to see the action on the North Shore of Maui, but you don't want to drive all the way out to Hookipa Beach. Fortunately, a Web-savvy friend has set up a Web cam that overlooks the sand and surf. This hypothetical "surf cam" creates a new image every 30 seconds and saves it at `http://www.surfsup.com/hookipa.jpg`.

Create a page that contains the surf image. We'll say the URL is `http://www.surfsup.com/hookipa.html`. Now refresh this page every 30 seconds with a client-pull.

```
<HTML>
<HEAD><TITLE>Surf Watch [TM]</TITLE>
<META HTTP-EQUIV="REFRESH CONTENT=30";
URL="http://www.surfsup.com/hookipa.html">
</HEAD>
<BODY TOPMARGIN=0 LEFTMARGIN=0>
<IMG WIDTH=100 HEIGHT=100 SRC="http://www.surfsup.com/hookipa.jpg">
</BODY>
</HTML>
```

Point to this page inside a floating frame.

```
<IFRAME WIDTH=110 HEIGHT=110 FRAMEBORDER=0
SRC="http://www.surfsup.com/hookipa.html">
  <IFRAME WIDTH=110 HEIGHT=110 FRAMEBORDER=0
SRC="http://www.surfsup.com/hookipa.html">
</IFRAME>
```

You'll be hangin' ten in no time, mon! This technique can be used with any HTML document, and could be used for more practical purposes like stock quotes, video conferencing, and remote security monitors. (For a variation of this technique, see the section on the Heidsite Weathercam in Chapter 8. And if you're sitting near your browser, go to `http://www4.heidsite.com/` and click the Weathercam in a Window box.)

Use JavaScript for Interface Improvements

When I first started working on the Web, I dreamt about completely interactive pages. I imaged Mac OS-like menus that change instantly when other menus change, and automatically perform commands when a visitor selects them and lets go. I fantasized about objects that react to the movement of the mouse and dance around the screen. Clearly this was impossible given the nature of HTML, and when asked I said as much.

JavaScript changed all that. JavaScript, an event-based scripting language, is ideal for improving the Web's interface. You can script HTML pages to "react" to clicks, mouseovers, changes in menus and text areas, and more. Navigator 3 improved JavaScript by making it even more dynamic. You can modify the option text of select menus, and change the source of `<IMG>` tags on the fly. This opens up some intriguing possibilities for visual feedback and popup menus. Three examples of this are live popups, related menus, and "rollovers."

Live popups

CGI-based select menus require two steps to select an option. First, select an option and then click on a submit button. JavaScript can save you that extra click with the `onChange` event. Any time a select menu is changed, it generates an `onChange` event. You can detect that event with some simple code and in effect simulate Mac OS- and Windows-like menus on the Web (see Figure 7-7).

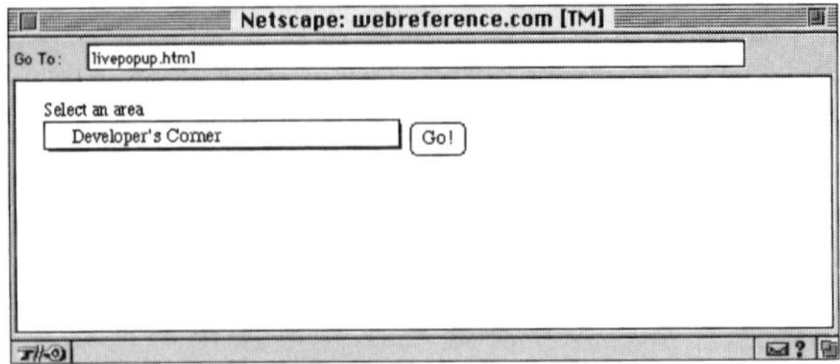

Figure 7-7: Live popup

First define a custom array object, `createArray`. Navigator 3.0 has an Array object but for Version 2 you've got to roll your own. Navigator 2.0 also stores the `length` property in the element 0 of the array, unlike in Navigator 3. That's why `createArray` automatically calculates and stores the array's length and fills the array starting with element number 1.

```
function createArray() {
     this.length = createArray.arguments.length+1
     for (var i = 0; i < this.length-1; i++)
     this[i+1] = createArray.arguments[i]
     }
```

The `this` property is used to refer to the current object. The current object is `createArray`, which has the same name as the function. The `length` property of the array is set with the line:

```
this.length = createArray.arguments.length+1 <!-- which is equivalent to:
createArray.length = createArray.arguments.length+1 -->
```

Then the following line of the function dynamically allocates and fills the array with the passed arguments:

```
this[i+1] = createArray.arguments[i]
```

All you need to do is pass the `createArray` function a delimited list of arguments and `createArray` dynamically allocates an array of the appropriate length and then fills it.

ON CD-ROM

```
<HTML>
<HEAD>
<TITLE>Live Popup Example</TITLE>
<BASE HREF="http://www.webreference.com">
<SCRIPT LANGUAGE="JavaScript">
<!--// hide
/*
Live popup example - for HTML & Web Publishing Secrets
This code is Copyright (c) 1996 by by Andy King
(aking@webreference.com)
and may be reused if these two lines are included. */
```

```
function createArray() {
      this.length = createArray.arguments.length+1
      for (var i = 0; i < this.length-1; i++)
      this[i+1] = createArray.arguments[i]
      }

var siteopt = new createArray("Developer's Corner", "Feature
Articles", "Forum", "JavaScript Tip of the Week", "Jobs", "ROADMAP",
"Table of Contents", "Web Headlines", "Web Wizard", "What's New",
"Cool Central");

var url = new createArray("/dev/", "/articles.html",
"/protect/forum", "/javascript/", "/jobs/", "/roadmap/",
"/index2.html", "/headlines/", "/wizard/", "/new/",
"http://www.coolcentral.com");
var catopt = new createArray("Features", "Beginner", "Webmaster",
"About");

function jumpPage() {
      menuNum = document.menu.primary.selectedIndex;
      window.location.href = url[menuNum+1];
}

// -->
</SCRIPT>
</HEAD>
<BODY BGCOLOR="#ffffff" TEXT="#000000" LINK="#0000ff"
VLINK="#ff0000">
<SCRIPT LANGUAGE = "JavaScript">
<!--
with (document) {
write('<CENTER><TABLE WIDTH=465 BORDER=0 CELLPADDING=5
CELLSPACING=0>');
write('<FORM NAME = "menu"><TR>');
writeln('<TD VALIGN=TOP COLSPAN=2>');
writeln('<FONT SIZE = -1 FACE = ARIAL>Select an area</FONT><BR>');
writeln('<SELECT NAME="primary" onChange="jumpPage()">');
tot = siteopt.length;
for (var i = 1; i < tot; i++)
writeln("<OPTION>" +siteopt[i]);
writeln('</SELECT>');
write('<INPUT TYPE = BUTTON VALUE = "Go!" onClick ="jumpPage()">');
write('</TD></TR></FORM></TABLE></CENTER>');
}
// -->
</SCRIPT>
</BODY>
</HTML>
```

The `jumpPage` function changes the URL of the current window, and is called any time the primary popup changes. The function first finds which menu item is selected by detecting the `selectedIndex` of the primary menu.

```
menuNum= document.menu.primary.selectedIndex;
```

The function then simply changes the URL of the current window by assigning the `menuNum+1` element of your URL array:

```
window.location.href = url[menuNum+1];
```

Related menus

Beginning with Navigator 3, you can modify the option text to select menus on the fly. This makes it possible for one menu to control the content of another. By making both menus live you can compress two levels of site hierarchy into one line.

The following code builds on the live popup example above, and uses two live popups with the left-hand, "primary" menu controlling the content of the right-hand, "secondary" menu (see Figure 7-8).

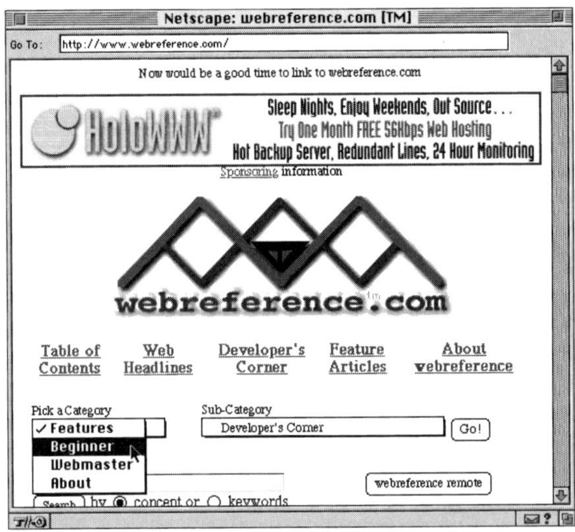

Figure 7-8: Related menus — when the left-hand menu changes, the right-hand one does, too.

How the code works

The code's first job is to check the browser type. This script only creates related menus for Navigator 3 or later; all other browsers get the secondary menu, which is a live popup and works on Navigator 2 and Explorer 3.

ON CD-ROM

```
/*
Dynamically modifiable menu example - for HTML Publishing Secrets
This code is Copyright (c) 1996 by Andy King (aking@webreference.com)
and Nick Heinle of webreference.com
and may be reused if these four lines are included.
*/
// begin universal browser detection
```

```
browser = navigator.appName;
version = parseInt(navigator.appVersion);

if      (browser == "Netscape" && version >= 3) type = "n3";
else if (browser == "Netscape" && version == 2) type = "n2";
else if (browser == "Microsoft Internet Explorer" && version >= 2)
type = "e3";
```

Next, the script defines its default arrays. The script uses the `createArray` function you saw earlier. The primary "category" menu is formed by the array `catopt`. The secondary "sub-category" menu is formed by the array `siteopt`. I've found it necessary to declare the `siteopt` array to be the length of the longest `siteopt` array used (in this case, 8 elements). By filling in the unused elements of the default `siteopt` array with blanks, you reserve these spaces for future use. True dynamically allocated arrays would not need this step. The `URL` array stores the relative or absolute URLs that correspond to the options in the `siteopt` array.

```
function createArray() {
     this.length = createArray.arguments.length+1
     for (var i = 0; i < this.length-1; i++)
     this[i+1] = createArray.arguments[i]
     }

if (type == "n3") {
var siteopt = new Array(8); // 8 elements because arrays start at 0
siteopt[1]  = "Developer's Corner";
siteopt[2]  = "Feature Articles";
siteopt[3]  = "JavaScript Tip of the Week";
siteopt[4]  = "Table of Contents";
siteopt[5]  = "Web Headlines";
siteopt[6]  = "";
siteopt[7]  = "";
var catopt = new Array(4);
catopt[1] = "Features";
catopt[2] = "Beginner";
catopt[3] = "Webmaster";
lst = siteopt.length;
trueLength = 6; // for first iteration;
}
else var siteopt = new createArray("Developer's Corner", "Feature
Articles", "JavaScript Tip of the Week", "Table of Contents", "Web
Headlines");

var url = new createArray("/dev/", "articles.html", "/javascript/",
"/index2.html", "/headlines/");
```

`JumpPage` is used for the right-hand, secondary menu. This function is identical to the one you saw in the Live Popup example, except that it refers to the secondary menu.

```
function jumpPage(form) {
        menuNum = document.menu.secondary.selectedIndex;
        window.location.href = url[menuNum+1];
}
```

The magic begins

The `ChangeMenu` function is where the magic happens. Called by the left-hand, primary menu, `changeMenu` redefines the secondary menu depending on which category is chosen (`menuNum`). `ChangeMenu` uses the `new Option` command to redefine the text in the `option` attribute of the secondary menu, modifying it on the fly.

```
function changeMenu() {
menuNum = document.menu.primary.selectedIndex;
        if (menuNum == 0) {
        siteopt = new Array(6);
        siteopt[1] = new Option("Developer's Corner");
        siteopt[2] = new Option("Feature Articles");
        siteopt[3] = new Option("JavaScript Tip of the Week");
        siteopt[4] = new Option("TOC");
        siteopt[5] = new Option("Web Headlines");

        url = new Array(6);
        url[1] = "/dev/";
        url[2] = "/articles.html";
        url[3] = "/javascript/";
        url[4] = "/index2.html";
        url[5] = "/headlines/";
        }
        if (menuNum == 1) {
         siteopt = new Array(8);
         siteopt[1] = new Option("Books");
         siteopt[2] = new Option("Browsers");
         siteopt[3] = new Option("Collections");
         siteopt[4] = new Option("Conferences");
         siteopt[5] = new Option("FAQs");
         siteopt[6] = new Option("Glossaries");
         siteopt[7] = new Option("History");

         url = new Array(8);
         url[1] = "/books/";
         url[2] = "/browsers.html";
         url[3] = "/collections.html";
         url[4] = "/conferences.html";
         url[5] = "/faqs.html";
         url[6] = "/glossaries.html";
         url[7] = "/history.html";
        }
         if (menuNum == 2) {
         siteopt = new Array(8);
         siteopt[1] = new Option("Agents");
         siteopt[2] = new Option("Announcing");
         siteopt[3] = new Option("Collections");
         siteopt[4] = new Option("File Format");
         siteopt[5] = new Option("Graphics");
         siteopt[6] = new Option("Guides");
         siteopt[7] = new Option("HTML");
```

```
        url = new Array(8);
        url[1] = "/agents.html";
        url[2] = "/announcing.html";
        url[3] = "/similar.html";
        url[4] = "/formats.html";
        url[5] = "/graphics/";
        url[6] = "/guides.html";
        url[7] = "/html/";
        }
tot2 = siteopt.length;
        for (i = lst - 1; i > 0 ; i--)
document.menu.secondary.options[i] = null;
        for (j = 1; j < tot2; j++)
document.menu.secondary.options[j-1] = siteopt[j];
document.menu.secondary.options[0].selected = true;
lst = siteopt.length;
}
// -->
</SCRIPT>
</HEAD>
```

A look at the workarounds

It's worth noting that this script contains a couple of workarounds for JavaScript bugs. First, I zero out all the current options in *reverse order*. Zeroing them in ascending order can cause some menu items to overflow into other menus (they may appear appended to another secondary menu).

```
for (i = lst - 1; i > 0 ; i--) document.menu.secondary.options[i] = null;
```

Then, I fill in the secondary menu with the newly defined `siteopt` array.

```
for (j = 1; j < tot2; j++) document.menu.secondary.options[j-1] =
siteopt[j];
```

The second workaround is for the Windows platform. On Windows when you redefine an entire select menu, it doesn't seem to know which one is the default, although the Mac OS does. I force the first option to be the default.

```
document.menu.secondary.options[0].selected = true;
```

Displaying the menus

The code I discussed so far creates the related menus. Now we have to display them. I write the primary menu for Navigator 3 and later versions only, and write the secondary menu for browsers that support JavaScript 1.0.

```
<BODY BGCOLOR="#ffffff" TEXT="#000000" LINK="#0000ff"
VLINK="#ff0000">
<H1 ALIGN=CENTER>Related Menus Example</H1>
<SCRIPT LANGUAGE = "JavaScript">
<!-- // hid
document.write('<CENTER><TABLE WIDTH=465 BORDER=0 CELLPADDING=5
CELLSPACING=0>');
document.write('<FORM NAME = "menu"><TR>');
if (type == "n3") {
```

```
document.writeln('<TD VALIGN=TOP ALIGN=LEFT>');
document.writeln('<FONT SIZE = -1 FACE = ARIAL>Pick a
Category</FONT><BR>');
document.writeln('<SELECT NAME="primary" onChange="changeMenu()">');
tot = catopt.length;
        for (var i = 1; i < tot; i++)
        document.writeln('<OPTION>' +catopt[i]);
document.writeln('</SELECT>');
document.writeln('</TD>');
document.writeln('<TD VALIGN=TOP ALIGN=LEFT>');
document.writeln('<FONT SIZE = -1 FACE = ARIAL>Sub-
Category</FONT><BR>');
} else {
document.writeln('<TD VALIGN=TOP COLSPAN=2>');
document.writeln('<FONT SIZE = -1 FACE = ARIAL>Select an
area</FONT><BR>');
}
document.writeln('<SELECT NAME="secondary" onChange="jumpPage()">');
tot2 = siteopt.length;
for (var i = 1; i < tot2; i++)
document.writeln("<OPTION>" +siteopt[i]);
document.writeln('</SELECT>');
document.write('<INPUT TYPE = BUTTON VALUE = "Go!" onClick
="jumpPage()">');
document.write('</TD></TR></FORM></TABLE></CENTER>');
       if (type == "n3") {
       for (var i = tot2 - 1; i >= trueLength-1; i--)
       document.menu.secondary.options[i] = null;
       changeMenu();
       }
// -->
</SCRIPT>
</BODY>
</HTML>
```

(*Note:* As this book went to press, Nick Heinle has developed a universal related menu script that works on both Netscape and Explorer 3, which utilizes both JavaScript and ActiveX. See http://www.webreference.com/javascript/ for details.)

Using rollovers for visual feedback

A *rollover* is an image that changes when the mouse pointer passes over it. In Navigator 3, you can dynamically redefine the source for an <IMG> tag when a user rolls his or her mouse over an image. Rollovers use the onMouseOver event handler, which triggers when the mouse passes over a link.

A popular use of rollovers is on an interactive graphic menu. Examples abound on the Web, and you can find two great ones at the JavaScript Tip of the Week home page (http://www.webreference.com/javascript/) and at America Online's home page (http://www.aol.com). We used the same principle with an experimental version of Cool Central's home page (see Figure 7-9 and the *HTML & Web Publishing SECRETS* CD-ROM for a complete working example).

Figure 7-9: Rollover demo — the experimental Cool Central home page

```
<HTML>
<HEAD><TITLE>Cool Central (TM) - Rollover example page</TITLE>
<SCRIPT LANGUAGE="JavaScript">
<!--//
function preloadImage (name, width, height) {
this.on = new Image (width, height);
this.on.src = name + "_on.gif"
this.off = new Image (width, height);
this.off.src = name + "_off.gif"
}
function new_image (name, width, height) {
preloadImage [name] = new preloadImage (name, width, height);
}
```

First, preload all of your images. Instead of checking for the browser type, I use a more universal way to filter browsers — checking the capability of the browser to reference images:

```
if (document.images) {
new_image ("hole_upl",83,83);
new_image ("hole_upr",83,83);
new_image ("hole_lwl",101,95);
new_image ("hole_lwr",99,89);
}
```

The `activate` and `deactivate` functions redefine the image's `src` to `xxx_on.gif` and `xxx_off.gif`. This improved version of the rollover script uses named images, instead of indexed images (1, 2, and so on) for easier referencing.

```
function activate(name) {
  if (document.images) {  // checks for browser capability, not vers
      var src = document [name].src;
```

```
        var off = src.lastIndexOf("off");
          if (off != -1) {
                  var newsrc = src.substring(0,off) + "on";
                  document [name].src = newsrc + ".gif";
          }
      }
}
function deactivate(name) {
  if (document.images) {
       var src = document [name].src;
        var on = src.lastIndexOf("on");
            if (on != -1) {
               var newsrc = src.substring(0,on) + "off";
          document [name].src = newsrc + ".gif";
          }
      }
}
//-->
</SCRIPT>
```

That's it! The steps are: preload, activate, and deactivate. The live popup menu code is identical to that of the previous section. Now we just have to insert `onMouseover` and `onMouseout` events that call the `activate` and `deactivate` functions respectively. I also threw in a status bar message, which you can also use on its own without the rollover.

```
</HEAD>
<BODY BACKGROUND="art/bg_cc.jpg" TEXT="#000000"" LINK="#0000ff"
VLINK="#cc0099">
<CENTER><SMALL>Link to coolcentral.com now, or we ice the
penguin.</SMALL></CENTER>
<CENTER><TABLE ALIGN=CENTER WIDTH=465>
<TR>
   <TD ALIGN=CENTER><A HREF="about.html" TARGET="_top"
onMouseover="activate('hole_upl'); window.status = 'Go to About Cool
Central'; return true;" onMouseout="deactivate('hole_upl')"><IMG
SRC="art/hole_upl_off.gif" NAME="hole_upl" WIDTH=83 HEIGHT=83
ALT="about" BORDER=0></TD>
   <TD></TD>
   <TD ALIGN=CENTER><A HREF="advertising.html" TARGET="_top"
onMouseover="activate('hole_upr'); window.status = 'Go to Sponsorship
Information'; return true;" onMouseout="deactivate('hole_upr')"><IMG
SRC="art/hole_upr_off.gif" NAME="hole_upr" WIDTH=83 HEIGHT=83
ALT="ad" BORDER=0></TD>
</TR>
<TR>
   <TD></TD>
   <TD ALIGN=CENTER><A HREF="index2.html" TARGET="_top"><IMG
SRC="art/hole_ctr.gif" WIDTH=116 HEIGHT=112 ALT="site of the"
BORDER=0></TD>
   <TD></TD>
</TR>
<TR>
```

```
   <TD ALIGN=CENTER><A HREF="picks/" TARGET="_top"
ONMOUSEOVER="activate ('hole_lwl'); window.status = 'Go to Nick\'s
Picks'; return true;" ONMOUSEOUT="deactivate ('hole_lwl')"><IMG
SRC="art/hole_lwl_off.gif" NAME="hole_lwl" WIDTH=101 HEIGHT=95
ALT="Nick's Picks" BORDER=0></TD>
   <TD ALIGN=CENTER>Learn how to make a site <A
HREF="http://www.webreference.com" TARGET="_top">this cool</A></TD>
   <TD ALIGN=CENTER><A HREF="nick/" TARGET="_top"
ONMOUSEOVER="activate ('hole_lwr'); window.status = 'Go to Nick
Click, Private... Eye'; return true;" ONMOUSEOUT="deactivate
('hole_lwr')"><IMG SRC="art/hole_lwr_off.gif" NAME="hole_lwr"
WIDTH=99 HEIGHT=89 ALT="Nick Click" BORDER=0></TD>
</TR>
</TABLE></CENTER>
</BODY>
</HTML>
```

We really liked the effect this had — stopping the default animated GIF and popping up a message — but we discovered that we had pushed HTML a bit too far. We combined LiveConnect, rollovers, animated GIFs, and JavaScript on one page. Apparently we were trying to be too cool, as we started experiencing bombs in Navigator 2 and 3. It turns out there are bugs in LiveConnect (we also used an Embedded sound that played when you clicked on a button) when used with other JavaScript features. Using rollovers with animated GIFs bombs Navigator 3. Using rollovers with static images works fine, but we decided that this would slow the static page too much to include it.

Getting Stylish: Style Sheets

Imagine a World (Wide Web) where all browsers spoke the same language and there were no proprietary extensions. Where Bill Gates and Jim Clark regularly treat each other for lunch and talk shop together. Where browsers compete in speed and utility, not by the number of new HTML extensions they have. Where designers have complete control over the layout and style of every element in their Web pages and one change can affect thousands of pages instantly. That's the promise of style sheets.

While this Web utopia won't exist tomorrow, it is coming. The World Wide Web Consortium recently agreed on a proposed recommendation for the first version of style sheets, CSS1(Cascading Style Sheets One). CSS1, a simplified version of the full specifications, extends HTML to provide support for separate style rules that suggest formatting for HTML elements. Explorer 3 supports a subset of the CSS1 spec, and Netscape 4 and other browsers are expected to follow.

Explorer 3.0 also supports (through an ActiveX control called HTML Layout Control) the *next* version of style sheets, CSS2. Based on the draft W3C note, "Frame-based layout via Style Sheets," CSS2 adds layout capabilities to style sheets, neatly incorporating frames into style sheets that content can flow into.

HTML Standards and the W3C (Or Is It the ERB)?

The W3C, one of the standard-setting bodies of the Web, changed its tune with the introduction of the HTML 3.2 specification. Previously, the W3C attempted to dictate its evolution through the HTML specs. HTML 3.2 adopts a more realistic approach and incorporates many of the popular Navigator 2.0 and Explorer 2.1 extensions.

To quote the HTML 3.2 Document Type Definition (DTD) (emphasis added), "HTML 3.2 aims to capture recommended practice as of early '96 and as such to be used as a replacement for HTML 2.0 (RFC 1866). Widely deployed rendering attributes are included where they have been shown to be interoperable. SCRIPT and STYLE are included to smooth the introduction of client-side scripts and style sheets."

A primary goal of the W3C Internet Engineering Task Force HTML Working Group (IETF HTML WG) was to promote HTML standards for interoperability, specifically style sheets. Style sheets eliminate the need for proprietary appearance extensions as they separate presentation from structure. The pace of innovation on the Web has been so great, however, that the WG has struggled to reach consensus on concise standards that describe the new tags, such as tables and other widely-used features. Dave Raggett, lead architect of the W3C's HTML activity, admitted that "IETF HTML WG has had relatively little effect" and that works in progress would be finished and the working group disbanded.

A new body called the Editorial Review Board (ERB) will replace the WG. The ERB will be composed of industry leaders IBM, Microsoft, Netscape, SoftQuad, Novell, and Spyglass. These companies set de facto standards now so the ERB will thus be better equipped to set HTML standards. The W3C will continue to work together with the ERB to ensure consensus and backward compatibility with HTML 2.0, but will no longer battle over tags. The W3C, however, will finally realize its initial goal of style sheets in their final HTML 4.0 spec, code-named "Cougar." Cougar will include style sheets and probably frames.

How style sheets work: an overview

Style sheets work by separating style (CSS1) and layout (CSS2) from the structure of content. Style rules can be embedded inside a page, but are ideally stored in a separate referenced HTML document — a style sheet. It is this separation that gives style sheets their power. You can change the overall look of an entire page or even entire Web sites by changing one style rule or sheet.

Style sheets are engineered with the future in mind. As the Web spreads across the world's appliances, devices other than browsers (referred to in the specification as user agents, or UA) will enable viewing, hearing, and even *feeling* on the Web. Style sheets' independence of style from structure makes it easier to adapt the Web to different technologies and ways of experiencing those technologies. The blind, for instance, could have a special sound-oriented style sheet that specifies speech parameters, intonation, reader style, and preferred speech plug-in. Set-top Net boxes like WebTV (`http://www.webtv.net`) could invoke special, TV-optimized style sheets that enlarge letters, shrink wide tables, and simplify layouts.

Desktop publishing meets the Web

Style sheets work on the Web like desktop publishing programs do now. Documents can be instructed to take most of their formatting instructions — fonts, spacing, margins — from a separate document. The idea is that by separating style from structure, either can be changed without affecting the other.

Style sheets use common desktop publishing terminology. You can precisely set margins; leading; typefaces and sizes; backgrounds for any element; spacing around elements; and x, y, and even z positioning (CSS2). No more crude workarounds for HTML's limitations — style sheets allow designers much more control over the look and layout of their pages.

Follow the rules

Style sheets *influence* or suggest how HTML documents should be rendered through style *rules*. The rules specify how to render HTML elements `<P>`, `<H1>`, and `<TABLE>`. Each of these rules can be grouped together to form a style sheet — a group of one or more style rules. Each HTML page can be influenced by one or more style sheets.

Styles rules can be embedded inside a page or referenced in a separate file. You can attach multiple style sheets to influence a single HTML document; these multiple style sheets can "cascade" according to additional rules — hence the term *Cascading* Style Sheets.

SECRET

Advantages of Style Sheets

- A company-wide standard style sheet can preserve a uniform look and feel.
- More control with less maintenance costs; one change can affect many pages.
- Older browsers can still read your content.
- Indexing is easier, as software only has to read the structural tags.

For more information on style sheets check out the following sites:

- `http://www.webreference.com/dev/style/` (Cascading Style Sheet Tutorial — an expanded version of this section)
- `http://www.w3.org/pub/WWW/TR/` (all specs)
- `http://www.w3.org/pub/WWW/Style/` (general information)
- `http://www.microsoft.com/workshop/` (a great developer's resource)

Style syntax

Style sheets are composed of simple CSS rules. A rule consists of two main parts: a selector (H1) and declaration (color: blue). The declaration has two parts: property (color) and value (blue).

```
H1       { color    : blue  }
Selector { property : value }
```

This simple example influences only one property of one HTML element, but it still qualifies as a style sheet. Combined with other rules and style sheets, it will determine how the document appears.

The selector is a link between the HTML document and the style, and all HTML tags are potential selectors. Every browser has its own default style sheet, so designers need to create their own style sheets only if they want to suggest a specific style for their documents.

Grouping

You can group selectors and declarations to save space.

```
H1, H2, H3 { font-family: Arial }
H1 { font-weight: bold; font-size: 14pt; line-height: 16pt; font-
family: Arial }
```

Class selectors

To increase the level of control over elements, use the class attribute. All of the elements inside the <BODY> tag can be classed, and you define the class in the style sheet.

```
<HTML>
 <HEAD><TITLE>Class Example</TITLE>
  <STYLE TYPE="text/css">
   H1.artdeco { color: #00FFFF }
  </STYLE>
 </HEAD>
<BODY>
 <H1 CLASS=artdeco>Boy, that's a loud color!</H1>
</BODY>
</HTML>
```

You can also define an entirely new class by omitting the tag name.

```
.artdeco { color: #00FFFF; font-family: geneva; font-size: 14pt }
```

This can be used with the <DIV> tag, to group art deco style content together.

Contextual selectors

You can use inheritance to save even more typing. Instead of setting all style properties, you can create defaults and list the exceptions. To give EM elements within H2 a different color and render them as italic, do the following:

```
H2 EM { color: red; font-style: italic }
```

Pseudo-classes and pseudo-elements

Normally, style is attached to an element based on its type or class. For even finer control, you can use pseudo-classes and pseudo-elements. Pseudo-elements are used to address sub-parts of elements, and pseudo-classes address different element types. In the pseudo-class below, different types of anchors are addressed:

```
A:link { color: red }       /* unvisited links */
A:visited { color: blue }  /* visited links */
A:active { color: yellow }   /* active links */
```

Pseudo-elements are used for common typographic effects such as initial caps and drop caps. These effects cannot be accomplished with structural elements alone, but the `SPAN` element could also be used (for example, `.dropcap { font-size: 200%; float: left }` and use `SPAN CLASS=dropcap` to surround the character).

```
<HTML>
 <HEAD><TITLE>Pseudo-element example</TITLE>
  <STYLE TYPE="text/css">
    P { font-size: 14pt; line-height:16pt; font-family: helvetica }
    P:first-letter { font-size: 200%; float: left }
  </STYLE>
 </HEAD>
<BODY>
 <P>This sentence will have a drop cap. And look, Ma: no FONT
tag!</P>
</BODY>
</HTML>
```

The problem with this method is that all paragraphs would start with a drop cap. A better way is to combine a pseudo-element with a class.

```
P.initial:first-letter { font-size: 200%; float: left }
<P CLASS=initial>First paragraph</P>
```

Applying styles in the real world

Now that you've taken a crash course in style syntax, how do you actually apply this new-found knowledge in the real world? Fear not, stylewalker. The following HTML shows the four ways to attach style to a document:

```
<HTML>
  <HEAD>
    <TITLE>title</TITLE>
    <LINK REL=STYLESHEET TYPE="text/css"
      HREF="http://style.com/elaborate" TITLE="elaborate">
    <STYLE TYPE="text/css">
```

```
      @import url(http://style.com/corporate);
          @import url(http://style.com/division);
      H1 { color: blue }
    </STYLE>
  </HEAD>
  <BODY>
    <H1>Headline is blue</H1>
    <P STYLE="color: green">While the paragraph is green.
  </BODY>
</HTML>
```

These four ways are the following:

- Local (specific to one tag in a page, using the `style` attribute)
- Global (specific to an entire page, using the `STYLE` element inside the `<HEAD>` tag)
- Linked (used across multiple pages, using the `LINK` element)
- Imported (allows multiple style sheets to influence one page)

Local style with the style attribute

Using the `style` attribute to an HTML tag mixes style with content and loses the advantages of style sheets. For quick and dirty styles it is supported but discouraged. Here's an example:

```
<P STYLE="font-size: 18pt">This paragraph is in 18-point text. Yes, I
know it's a kludge but I'm just illustrating a point (size)
here.</P>
```

The DIV and SPAN elements

You can also include the `style` attribute in the new `DIV` and `SPAN` elements. The `DIV` element is used to enclose a DIVision (chapter, section, and so on) of a document that you want to give a distinctive style. The `SPAN` element is generally used within paragraphs, when none of the other HTML elements (`EM`, `STRONG`, `VAR`, `CODE`, and so on) apply.

```
<P><SPAN STYLE="font-size: 14pt">T</SPAN>his is an example of a drop
cap using the STYLE attribute to the SPAN tag. See above for a
better way.</P>
```

As you can see, it's easy to add local style rules. But it's harder to go through a document and change a large number of these attributes than it is to change a few of them at the top of a document. That's where the `STYLE` element comes in.

Global style with the STYLE element

A better way to standardize the look of a few Web pages is to insert a style sheet at the top of each page. This will ensure that different elements of your document, paragraphs, headers, lists, will look the same throughout each page.

To include style rules within an HTML page you just add one or more `STYLE` elements in the head or body:

```
<HEAD>
<TITLE>Style Element Example</TITLE>
 <STYLE TYPE="text/css">
  H1 { color: blue}
  P  { color: green}
 </STYLE>
</HEAD>
```

This simple style sheet sets all H1 headings to blue and all paragraphs to green. You can begin to see the power of style sheets: one change and everything on the page changes.

Older browsers ignore the <STYLE> tags but print the style statements. To avoid this, enclose them in a comment:

```
<HEAD>
<TITLE>Style Element Example - with alternative fonts</TITLE>
 <STYLE TYPE="text/css">
 <!--
  H1  { color: blue; font: 18pt Arial bold }
  P   { color: green;
        font-size: 12pt;
        font-family: Arial, Geneva, Helvetica, sans-serif;
        text-indent: 0.5in }
A  { text-decoration: none; color: red }
 -->
 </STYLE>
</HEAD>
```

You can group style rules with the semicolon. Here I defined H1 headings to be blue, 18-point Arial bold and paragraphs to be green, 12-point Arial, and indented one-half inch. Note that I also defined fall-back fonts: while Windows users will have the Arial font, Mac OS users probably won't. You can specify alternative fonts, separated by commas, to make sure your text renders similarly. Note the `sans-serif`, used as a last resort. Links will appear red and not underlined (no `text decoration`). Navigator 2.0 and above will hide the contents of style elements provided no (non-white) text occurs before the element.

External style sheets

The real power of style sheets comes when you link to an external file. The file contains the same rules you'd normally place in the `STYLE` block at the top of a page.

```
BODY { background: white; color: brown }
H1 { font: 18pt Arial bold  }
P   { font: 12pt Arial; text-indent: 0.5in }
P.initial:first-letter { font-size: 200%; float: left }
A:link { color: red }       /* unvisited links */
A:visited { color: blue }  /* visited links */
A:active { color: yellow }   /* active links */
```

Say you placed these rules in a file at `http://www.surfsup.com/style.css`. To link a page to this style sheet just place the following line in the `HEAD` element:

```
<LINK TITLE="new" REL=stylesheet HREF="http://www.surfsup.com/style.
css" TYPE="text/css">
```

In the `LINK` element, the `rel` attribute defines the type of link. The `REL=stylesheet` is the key: it links the current page to the referenced file. The beauty of linked style sheets is that you can change the look of thousands of pages by changing one file. This is a big time-saver for intranet or large-site Webmasters.

Imported style sheets

You can import multiple style sheets by using the @import command within the `STYLE` element — for example, `@import url(http://www.yoursite.com/funky)`. With the import command, you can use multiple style sheets to affect the same document simultaneously.

Enjoying your inheritance

Now that you know the syntax and how to apply it, it's time to learn about *inheritance*. Suppose you have an HTML document that refers to a linked style sheet. It's perfectly legal to add other global, local, linked, or imported style sheet definitions to this page. The basic rule is that the most specific setting wins, and weights are used in conflicts. Global takes precedence over linked, and local takes precedence over global and linked style sheets. Also, all elements inherit style from their "parents" in the document. The `<HTML>` tag is followed by the `<BODY>` tag and so on.

This can come in handy in corporate settings, where the chief Webmaster can set colors in a corporate-approved sheet, while division Webmasters can set header and font sizes in a divisional style sheet.

Cascading styles

Since multiple style sheets can influence the presentation simultaneously, conflicts can arise. Conflict resolution is an integral part of the CSS spec, and is based on each style rule having a weight. *Cascading* refers to the order in which these conflicting styles are resolved.

At press time Adobe had not yet decided to include style sheet support into the next version of PageMill, though they admit they received a lot of calls about them. Claris says they plan to include style sheets in the next version of Home Page. FrameMaker can now export HTML+CSS with HoTaMaLe and other editors are expected to follow suit.

The next style

The W3C has already started on the next version of style sheets, which extends the CSS1 spec to include full two-dimensional layout capabilities. The preliminary spec, "Frame-based Layout via Style Sheets" (`http://www.w3.org/pub/WWW/TR/`), extends CSS1 to incorporate nested frames, tables, z-axis layering, and precise positioning. This CSS2 specification approaches the holy grail of total control we talked about at the beginning of this chapter. Designers can precisely position frames, layer frames and objects along the *z* axis, set transparency, and attach scripts to objects. Here's an example:

```
<HTML>
 <HEAD><TITLE>Example "CSS2" Style Sheet</TITLE>
  <STYLE TYPE="text/css">
   @page { layout: column }
   @frame toc { width: 20% }
   @frame main { width: 80%; }
   UL.toc { flow: toc; target: main }
   BODY { flow: main }
  </STYLE>
<BODY>
 <UL CLASS=toc>
  <LI><A HREF="about.html">About Yoyodyne</A>
  <LI><A HREF="products.html">Products</A>
  <LI><A HREF="clients.html">Clients</A>
 </UL>
<P>Yoyodyne is a world-class maker of high-tech yoyos...</P>
</BODY>
</HTML>
```

You can see that this version of CSS incorporated frames neatly into style sheets. The `@page` command defines the properties of the outermost frame. The layout can be `fill`, `fixed`, `row`, and `column`. `Fill` is like a normal HTML page, `fixed` gives precise positioning control, and `row` or `column` acts just like Navigator frames. The `@frame <name>` command defines a nested frame. To associate HTML elements with frames you use the `flow: <frame-name>` property to name the frame, as in:

```
P { flow: main }
```

This causes the contents of all paragraphs to flow into the frame named `main`. The targets act just as they did before, but are much easier to code. The following line defines a `toc` class of unordered lists and targets everything within that class to the `main` frame.

```
UL.toc { flow: toc; target: main }
```

Microsoft Explorer 3 supports this new style spec in its HTML Layout Control. Their initial version is an ActiveX control you can download from Microsoft's Web site at `http://www.microsoft.com/`.

The Future of HTML

The ERB, Netscape, and Microsoft are hard at work on future versions of HTML. Navigator 4 supports CSS1 style sheets and JavaScript style sheets. As this book went to press, Microsoft unveiled Dynamic HTML, which is based on preliminary W3C open standards. Dynamic HTML will enable any "object" — a table, frame, image, style sheet, script, you name it — to be modified on the fly. This will allow CD-ROM-type interactivity. Dynamic HTML is a central feature of the Active Desktop, first delivered to users with Microsoft Internet Explorer version 4.0. The Active Desktop is the client side of Microsoft's Active Platform.

So the future of HTML appears to a place where Web designers will have far more control over the elements on a page without having to sacrifice the structure-oriented advantages that make HTML so appealing to begin with. With any luck, it will also be a place where Microsoft and Netscape extensions can coexist. But even if this rosy world comes to pass, there will still be older browsers and limited Web devices (such as WebTV) that will require Web developers to continue to walk the tightrope, balancing themselves between innovation and broad compatibility.

Summary

- HTML extensions can work similarly on both Navigator and Explorer, if common or equivalent attributes are used. When you have a choice, use the HTML 3.2 version.
- Make sure you take older browsers into account by gracefully downgrading or providing alternatives for non-HTML 3.2 tags and attributes.
- PageMill 2.0 makes short work of tables and frames. Tweak manually to refine.
- Tables can simulate crude page layout with fixed widths and 1-pixel invisible GIFs. Be sure to turn off those borders.
- Use frames with care. Avoid nesting nightmares with the `<BASE TARGET="top">` tag. For a more seamless look, try turning off frame borders.
- JavaScript is wonderful for interface improvements and frames, but contains some bugs. Make sure you test on different platforms, browsers, and versions, and offer alternatives for other browsers.
- Style sheets suggest formatting to one or more HTML documents. Style sheets offer more control with less maintenance costs and represent the future of HTML.

Chapter 8

A Cookbook of Cool Things: Immediacy, Interactivity, Community, and Commerce

In This Chapter

- Tips on how to be a Web reporter
- Setting up a Web cam and using a digital camera
- Promoting your site with an e-mail newsletter, and other ways to publicize your Web effort
- An overview of Web commerce options

"Cool things" — you can't define them, but you know them when you see them. The thousands of people who visit Macworld Online (`http://www.macworld.com/`) see them every day. One of the people responsible for Macworld Online's cool things is Online Producer Karen Liberatore, who contributed some of her favorite recipes to this chapter.
— Jim Heid

It is one thing to attract visitors to your site; it is another to keep them coming back for more. Everyone knows by now that competition for a repeat, loyal audience is fierce. So how do you encourage return visits? How do you position your Web site to compete in this field of New Media dreams? Nobody knows, at least not yet. That's the reality of the Web today: Everyone is scrambling to find a niche in this emerging multimedia medium. That's not necessarily bad news. It simply means the playing field is level — creativity and imagination count.

Still, there are a few known elements to master as you venture forth. First, you must provide content that changes on a regular basis. If your site is commercially focused, avoid falling into the pit of simply "repurposing" (reprinting) your company's brochure or catalog, and leaving it at that. Web site critics, and there are many, term this sort of one-shot content (and they're not being kind when they do so), *brochure-ware*. There is nothing more deadly than a static Web site: Go ahead, use your company brochure for the meat of your site, but offer content appetizers and desserts frequently. As one Web developer for a software company said recently, "I put the page up, and was so excited. Then a week later I started getting e-mail from people complaining there was nothing new on the page. I didn't realize it was a full-time job!"

Second, a successful Web site takes advantage of what the medium is all about: immediacy, interactivity, and community.

On the surface, these two keys to the Web kingdom may seem daunting. They are. But anything worthwhile takes time and effort. The good news is that the tools you need to provide immediacy, interactivity, and community are readily available. Implementing these applications is simply a matter of patience and concentration, and those old standbys, trial and error. Once you learn the basics, you can take the knowledge as far and wide as you want. That's the beauty of the Web.

As far as content goes, well, you decide. How impassioned are you about the subject matter of your Web site? How much time do you have to spend on your site? A Web site is a commitment; without that dedication, your site could become what some researchers are calling the "ghost towns" of this new frontier — the vacated ruins of deserted hobbyist home pages.

That said, in this chapter we take a look at a few of the cool things you can do to place your Web site at the forefront of this rapidly developing new communications medium.

SECRET

Remember, though, all the advice in the world cannot replace the most crucial element for successful Web site development: personality. Information may be the cornerstone of the Web, but the human touch is what makes the medium go 'round. How that personality is translated is, of course, up to you.

Adding Immediacy to Your Site

One of the many great things about the Web is its potential for immediacy. Like radio and television, the Web can be a real-time medium. As the popularity of the Web grows, so too grows the public's interest in sites that incorporate the elements of immediacy and timeliness. After all, we are an information-driven society, and the people who use the Web have voracious appetites for information. Tap into this passion for knowledge by adding real-time pizzazz to your site. In this section I take a look at two ways of creating immediacy:

- **Covering live events, including the use of digital cameras.** By covering an event of interest as the event happens, you turn your site into a source for current news and information.
- **Setting up a Web cam: a frequently updated video view of your office, the outdoors, or the company fish tank.** Okay, so a view of the company water cooler may not exactly satisfy a surfer's thirst for information, but it does add its own appealing flavor of immediacy to a site.

You, too, can be a reporter

The Web may have real-time potential in common with radio and television, but it is also a publishing medium. That makes you the editor and publisher of your own electronic journal. Never in the history of publishing have the reins of information been more accessible to the public-at-large than they are today. That fact has not been lost on the traditional print media. More than 400 worldwide daily and weekly newspapers and hundreds of magazines are currently online. Journalism schools are offering New Media and New Technology courses. The esteemed Columbia University School of Journalism has spent millions of dollars to establish its New Media Center, a state-of-the-art "newsroom of the future" designed to educate the next generation of electronic-savvy reporters.

"More changes have taken place in the past five years than in the previous 50 in all three stages of news production: gathering information, producing the package, and distributing the finished product," reads the introduction to a series of seminars on New Media/New Technology offered by the Poynter Institute, a St. Petersburg, Florida-based school for journalists founded by the late Nelson Poynter, publisher of the *St. Petersburg Times*.

In some respects, the traditional media playing catch-up to the thousands of computer savvy laypeople like you. If you have a Web site, or are getting ready to set one up, you already constitute competition to the "professionals." You have the power and ability to report on and disseminate information about a topic or an issue of your choosing, as the story unfolds.

Say that you live in a large city and a computer or Internet convention comes to town. You can add immediacy to your site — and gain a reputation as a source of information — by covering the convention and posting the news generated there.

The possibilities are practically endless: Depending on the theme of your Web site and your interests, you could cover everything from a dog show to an antique fair or a rock concert. You could write book or movie reviews. You could interview noteworthy people in your community, from local chefs to a sports hero.

If your Web site is for family only, as are an increasing number of home pages on commercial services such as CompuServe and America Online, your news could be coverage of your son or daughter's graduation or first prom for the rest of the clan to see.

Even if your Web site is business-oriented, you can take the daily news plunge. If it is computer-based, go to the conventions and report on products that augment your point-of-sale. If you are a professional, cover (or hire someone to cover) seminars that focus on your specialty. There is a gold-mine of information available at these seminars, and your site will benefit by getting the latest word out.

Obviously, the fact that you have an electronic publication does not mean you are a journalist, in the true sense of the profession. Nor does it ensure that you can write a coherent news or feature story. People study journalism and get advanced degrees in this liberal-arts discipline. They learn how to write a news story and how to sift through facts and figures to sort out the meaning of the information thrown at them. They learn about legal issues, such as libel and copyright laws. They also have good editors who make sure that the stories they file make sense and are grammatically and factually correct.

But it does mean you have at your disposal the means to try — and to grow into the role if the process entices you. Certainly there is nothing preventing you from taking a stab at daily journalism. After all, Benjamin Franklin began his career as a printer.

Tips for budding journalists

Teaching someone how to be a good writer and journalist is beyond the scope of this chapter, obviously. However, there are basic and common sense rules to journalism that will serve you well. Here I talk about gathering information and synthesizing it into readable, accurate, crisp copy.

Gathering Information

Let's use as our example an upcoming convention of any kind that you feel would be of interest to you and your readers. Remember, the more interesting a subject is to you, the more enthusiasm you will have when it comes to the hard work of producing the copy.

If you don't already have them, get business cards made up that prominently advertise your Web address and your title.

- Contact the public relations or press relations department/person handling the convention. Tell them who you are and what you want to do. Let them know you have the means (and an audience) to get the word out. Publicity, after all, is what their job is about.
- Collect as much advance information as you can. Ask the public relations people for press releases and other relevant information. You can never have too much advance material.
- Organize your coverage beforehand. Don't go unprepared. Covering an event is hectic at best. The more you plan, the smoother the process. Learn everything you can, from who is speaking and when, to any special seminars or panel discussions. Make a list of what you want to see and who you want to talk to. Check with the public relations people. They may help set up a private interview.
- Hit the floor running. With your homework done, jump into the fray. Don't waste time. Conventions are busy; people are easily distracted and their attention spans are short. Know what you want to ask and ask it succinctly. Don't hem and haw; get to the point. Don't be shy, and if you are, don't cover conventions. It requires assertiveness to get the story and a certain amount of courage to walk up to strangers and start asking questions.

- Get a lot of quotes. Interview more people than you need to; like advance information, the more information you get "on the floor" the better when the time comes to write your story. That includes, depending on the theme of the convention, collecting handouts on products or services.
- The cardinal rule of journalism: Make sure you have the full names and titles, when applicable, of the people you interview. And make sure you spell the names correctly. Remember, Smith can be spelled Smyth and Peterson, Petersen, even Pederson.
- Be prepared. Have plenty of pens or pencils. Bring a couple notebooks (reporters often use steno pads); you'll be surprised how quickly they fill up. Make sure your tape recorder works, and never rely solely on a recorder: Take notes as well. When using a tape recorder, precede the interview with the name of the interviewee, for later reference.

Writing the Story

The hard part is over. Now comes the tough part: synthesizing all the information you gathered. Take a deep breath. Read through your notes. Try to decipher your handwriting. Transcribe your tape. Make sure you have all the names matched to the quotes, and the names spelled correctly. If it's any comfort, even seasoned reporters often dread the next step, which is to put the pieces together in a readable form. One award-winning journalist likens writing a story to building a wall — brick by brick, beginning with the basics.

- After going over your notes, decide what the story is: Just covering a convention isn't enough. The idea is to give people new information. What happened at the convention to make it newsworthy? Was there a particular product that made waves? Did one of the keynote speakers say something intriguing about the future? Don't be, as one city editor used to call his cub reporters, "a myna bird" who just recites the facts.
- Once you know what your story is, synthesize the information in one or two paragraphs. Newspapers call the set-up graphs the "lead" or "nut graf." They tell the readers what to expect. They also should establish a sense of place — the who, what, where, and when. And they should do the above in a crisp and (if the subject allows) entertaining fashion. For example, say you went to a local dog show and one interesting aspect was a purported cure for fleas. Your two-graph lead could be something such as the following:

  > Dog lovers can stop scratching their heads over what to do about fleas — at least that's the word from a Cincinnati firm that jumped at the chance to promote its new cure for flea Ctenocephalides at the Kansas City Dog Show, September 12-14.
  >
  > The results are still out. Said Bob Brown, who was adjusting the flea collar on his golden retriever, Buster, one of 185 dogs strutting their stuff at the annual event, "I'm from Missouri, remember. You gotta show me the proof before I'll take this thing off my dog."

- Stories have a beginning, a middle, and an end. The beginning is the lead and subsequent set-up graphs, the middle is the body of the work, and the end is a subtle summation, or wind down. Reporters often like to save the most pithy quote or comment for the last graph, what they call "the tag line."
- Don't overwrite. Try to strike a conversational tone. Pretend you're telling a friend what you saw and heard at the convention. Don't try to impress people with "big" words or heavy-handed opinions.
- Keep yourself out of the story. You aren't the story — the event or someone else is. Keep first-person references out of a news or feature story altogether; make minimal use of *I* or *me* in book and movie reviews as well. First-person stories are difficult to master; in the hands of an amateur, the result can be off-putting or, worse, can end up sounding pretentious.
- In keeping with the above, let other people tell the story. Use many quotes and make sure every quote is attributed to someone with a first and last name. Add titles when appropriate, and hometowns and ages (if that information is applicable or helps illustrate your story).
- Write in the present tense when possible. Use the active, not passive, voice.
- If you include facts and figures that are not yours, identify the source of the information.
- Don't be sloppy. Use the spelling checker. Even better, ask someone to read your story for grammatical errors. All good writers are better writers when they have a copy editor. Too many errors and you'll lose your audience.
- Have fun when you write, or at least try to. The cool thing about writing a news story or feature is that you are the conduit through which something new or interesting is imparted. It's the old "you are there" syndrome initiated by veteran newscaster Walter Cronkite.
- If all fails and you absolutely hate to report and write, but still want to add immediacy to your Web site, hire a journalism student. Be the assignment editor rather than the reporter.

SECRET

Don't Hide: Identify Yourself

Always sign and date your stories. It's also a good idea to offer your readers an e-mail address so they can respond to your efforts. Be forewarned that by doing so you open yourself up to two possibilities. One, people will send you kudos. That's the good news. The bad news is that people won't hesitate to let you know when they disagree with what you've written, or when you have made an error. Among the most vociferous critics: the Grammar Police.

SECRET

A Word About Appetizers

The work you do to generate your copy will mean nothing unless you advertise the fact of your labor on your home page. After all, the idea is to let readers know that your Web site is "hot," as in timely and informational.

You can do this in one of two ways: either as a link to a story already written, or as an announcement that a story is forthcoming. The latter is the most dangerous for beginners: Your goal, after all, is credibility. If you announce that you are going to provide information, you better deliver.

Announcing an upcoming story, however, is the best policy, for an obvious reason: It gives people a reason to return to your site. If you provide coverage on a routine basis, the number of return visits will increase as your audience anticipates the ever-changing nature of your site.

Digital cameras: adding immediacy with images

Immediacy is not just the province of words. In the emerging world of quick-bake Web publishing, photographs can be served up direct from camera to computer, without the need for film or paper.

Imagine the possibilities: You come back from a birthday outing at the zoo and, before the kids reduce the cake to a pile of crumbs, you've got a slide-show running on the computer to the delight of the now sugar-enabled guests. Or you have a Web site and you're putting together a report from a computer conference. With a digital camera, you can add pictures of new products or celebrity speakers to augment your text. Even in the world of the Web, a picture is worth a thousand (or less) words. Besides, the addition of photographs gives your Web efforts that much more credibility for being hot, as in immediate and cutting-edge.

Digital cameras are not a new phenomenon. They have been in use through the 1990s, mostly in the newspaper and commercial printing industries, both of which embraced the time-saving technology from the beginning. Until recently, good digital camera systems cost thousands of dollars. The best still do. But a new market is opening up — the home consumer. As a result, more cameras are available, and the prices are going down. Apple, Kodak, Olympus, Canon, Epson, Casio, and other companies now offer consumer-side cameras ranging in price from $350 to under $1,000.

Is a digital camera for you? Yes, if your medium of choice for these images is computer- or Web-based. For computer use, a digital camera can be cost effective, if you are serious about the endeavor. First, there is no need to buy film. There is no need to have that film developed. And there is no need to scan the developed print into your computer.

Note, though, that a consumer-priced digital camera can still be more expensive than a good 35mm model. The desktop photography market is in its infancy. Image quality is spotty; features such as built-in flash vary from camera to camera. Caveat emptor: Like everything else electronic, digital cameras will improve over time.

If you are inclined to wait a while before taking the digital camera plunge, and prefer to use your trusty 35mm, companies such as Storm/Primax, Kodak, and Polaroid offer low-cost photo scanners designed just for uploading snapshots. Computer makers such as Hewlett-Packard are adding built-in snapshot scanners. And you can always have your film processed onto floppies for computer-based viewing. Most photo labs provide the service for approximately $10. PhotoCD from Kodak takes this concept a big step further: It puts your photos on a compact disc. The cost is approximately $40.

How a digital camera works

Digital cameras, like all cameras, use light to record the images you want to capture. In normal cameras, light is recorded on silver-based film. In digital camera technology, that light is recorded by a charge-coupled device (CCD), a solid-state chip made up of light-sensitive cells called *photosites*. CCDs come in various sizes. The smallest is 1/8 the size of a frame of 35mm film. The largest CCD is the same size as a 35mm frame. The latter, for professional use, is of course the best in terms of resolution: High-end CCDs hold upwards of 6 million photosites. Smaller CCDs are aimed at the lower-end market; their photosites number 180,000 and up.

These photosites convert light into electrons; the electrons are then converted into digital information that is stored in the camera's electronic memory until you download the images to your computer. The amount of memory a camera provides is one feature that sets digital cameras apart. Generally, the more memory a camera provides, the more pictures it can hold. But I say "generally" because other factors affect image capacity, including the size of the images (in pixels) and the kind of image compression the camera uses. Bottom line: Don't buy based on memory specs alone; also look at image dimensions and quality.

Some cameras accept plug-in memory cards, which can be extremely useful for extended photo shoots — when one card fills, eject it and insert another. Note, though, that most of these memory cards are about the size of a credit card; their addition increases the size and weight of a camera. And some of these memory cards are permanent additions, not add-ons.

To transfer the images from the digital camera to your computer, use the cable and image-transfer software that come with the camera.

Once the images are downloaded, you can use the software bundled with the camera to process, view, and save them. If you're serious about setting up a digital darkroom, you may need to get out your checkbook. Working with photographic-quality images demands a computer with at least 16-bit (thousands of colors) video circuitry, 32MB or more of memory, and a high-capacity hard drive.

What's Out There

Memory and resolution vary from camera to camera, based on price, as do features such as auto focus and built-in flash. Listed here is a sampling of recent contenders in the entry-level market. Note that the prices listed here are rough approximations, but they will give you an idea of what kinds of features each price tier provides.

- **The Kodak DC20.** This is the least expensive digital camera to date with a price of less than $350. Memory: 1MB. No expandable storage. It holds eight images. Resolution: 493×373 pixels. Fixed focus; no built-in flash. (`http://www.kodak.com/`)
- **The Epson PhotoPC.** This camera is under $400. Memory: 1MB, with expandable storage to 4MB (approximately $250 extra). It holds 80 images with expanded memory. Resolution: 640×480. Auto focus; no built-in flash. (`http://www.epson.com/`)
- **Casio QV-10A** or **QV-100.** QV-10A is under $400. Memory: 2MB. No expandable memory. It holds 96 images. Resolution: 320×240 pixels. QV-100 is under $600. Memory: 4MB. No expandable storage. It holds 64 images. Resolution: 640×480. Both feature fixed focus; no built-in flash. (`http://www.casio.com/`)
- **The Olympus D-200L.** This camera is priced under $600. Memory: 2MB. No expandable storage. Holds 20 images. Resolution: 640×480 pixels. Fixed focus; built-in flash. (`http://www.olympusamerica.com/index.html`)
- **Apple QuickTake 200.** This camera is priced around $600. Memory: 1MB. Expandable storage. Holds 20-30 images, depending on quality settings. Resolution: 640×480 pixels. Fixed focus; built-in flash. Also works as a video camera for videoconferencing or Web-cam use. (`http://www.quicktake.com/`)

Digital camera eccentricities

Using a digital camera for the first time is a learning experience. Some include different lenses and offer fixed or automatic focus; some offer zoom functions. Others come with LCD preview and playback (a battery-intensive feature). But no matter how loaded these early models may be in terms of features and functions, like anything else you have to get a feel for what the equipment can do.

There are also certain eccentricities to master. Primarily, you may notice a brief delay between the time you press the shutter release button and the actual capture of the image. This has to do with a number of factors, including clearing the CCD and then correcting for color, exposure, and focus, and, if available and in use, firing the flash. There is a longer delay after the photo is taken, during which the image is stored. During this process, the camera compresses the image so that it takes less space. Alas, compression often introduces undesirable artifacts, such as chunky-looking details. Compression takes up to several seconds, depending on the camera. You can't take another picture during this period, so don't think about using a consumer digital camera to capture fast-moving events.

You'll also play the waiting game when transferring the images to your computer. Again, specifics depend on the camera, but you can expect to wait a half a minute or more when downloading a collection of images.

Preparing digital snapshots for the Web

As with all computer graphics, you must fine-tune digital camera images before posting them on your site. To allow for fast downloads — particularly with the still-popular 14.4Kbps modem — you'll probably want to crop your images, omitting extraneous areas that not only increase file size but also distract from the main subject. You may also want to reduce the size of your final image. A 640×480-pixel image, for example, is too big for a Web page. It's better to reduce such an image to a smaller size, such as 320×240 pixels. If you want to give visitors the option to view a large version, create a link to it. And remember to include the file size of the linked image so that visitors have an idea of what they're in for.

And then there's the file-format issue. As mentioned earlier, digital cameras come with software that enables you to view and save the images in a variety of file formats, including the JPEG format, which for now at least, is the Web's preferred format for continuous-tone (photographic) images.

In general, the software that accompanies most digital cameras doesn't have a sufficient array of features for optimizing images for the Web. If you plan to post digital camera images frequently, you'd do well to invest in an image-editing application such as Adobe Photoshop or Ulead's PhotoImpact with Web Extensions. Happily, Adobe recognized that the consumer market is the wave of the future and released in 1996 a high-quality cousin of Photoshop: PhotoDeluxe, which sells for approximately $89 compared to $600 for the professional version.

In short, images on the Web need to be small, not only proportionally, but in terms of file size. A Web image as it unfolds on a page is measured in "K's" or kilobytes. Each K takes a second to download with a 14.4 modem. A 30K image takes half a minute to download, in other words. For the full scoop on choosing file formats and optimizing images for the Web, refer back to Chapter 6.

Updating your Web page from afar (how to e-mail digital images)

Okay, so you have a digital camera. You mastered the ins and outs of optimizing your images for Web use. Now you're ready to play Superman, or, rather, a super Jimmy Olson.

Newspapers, as mentioned, were among the early adopters of digital cameras. When they return to the paper, newspaper photographers can download photos from a sporting or news event directly into the computer, circumventing the darkroom-to-photo-engraving process. But even more to the point of meeting deadlines, photographers can also send in their photos remotely via modem, even, in a pinch, from locations as quaint as a phone booth.

You can do the same in one of two ways: either by e-mailing the images to your Webmaster or doing the work yourself via FTP. Of course in both of these instances, it goes without saying that you have access to a computer, either a friend's desktop or your handy portable, which is outfitted with the software needed to process your digital images, per the tips in Chapter 6. This scenario also requires that you have access to an e-mail service and that you have FTP software installed, such as Fetch for the Mac OS or NetLoad for Windows, as well as the ability to access your site's server.

This scenario also makes the assumption that you are not doing this for the first time. In the case of FTP, you are doing basically what you do may already do at the home base — uploading new content to your server.

That said, let's pretend that you have a Web site whose focus is antique radios. You're on a buying trip and stumble across a guy who has a store filled with vintage plastic radios from the 1950s. You talk to him and take some great photos of the boxy, colorful radios. It's just the thing you need to liven up your Web site.

You've got two ways to go to get this information to your site. The first is to e-mail the story and images to someone back at the Web site, who can then take the information and ready it for publication. In this case, the text is sent as you normally send a document through an e-mail system. Your production crew can then take the text and put it into HTML form for the Web.

Photos are a little trickier. Every e-mail program has its peculiarities; and, too, every e-mail server can be set up differently, depending on the needs of its network. Add to that the fact that the Internet, by its very nature, is a jerky jump from one server to another, and you've got a bit of a sticky wicket when it comes to e-mail standards, especially for large binary files. The truth is: images don't, in general, "mail" that well, and are easily corrupted by the variety of aforementioned eccentricities. Graphic artists who work remotely tend to favor the commercial services, such as America Online, when they transfer photographic files. You simply send a photo as an e-mail attachment.

If you have a production person who will be optimizing the image for fast downloading, you may want to send the images using your camera's native file format, relying on a compression program such as StuffIt (Mac OS) or WinZip (Windows) to compress the files for faster e-mailing. Avoid using JPEG compression on an image that may be compressed again — you'll introduce ugly artifacts. On the other hand, if you're doing the optimizing yourself, go ahead and save the final image as a compressed JPEG file, using the rules of thumb described in Chapter 6.

FTP is the more direct way to go. In this case, you transfer your images and text as you would from your home base. The only difference is distance, and possibly either a long distance or toll charge. (Hopefully, if phone costs are to be incurred, your host computer sports a 28.8Kbps or faster modem.) In this scenario, you would need to connect to an Internet service provider, log onto your Web site's server, and upload the appropriate files from your hard disk, using the formats called for — either text or binary.

Web cams: sites with cool sights

If you really want to add immediacy to your Web site, a *Web cam* is the way to go. Also called *spy cams*, Web cams are cameras that record and playback for the Web-viewing audience the comings and goings of anything — people, pets, clouds, crowds, ocean waves, traffic on a bridge...

Web cams are often educational, but mostly they are whimsical — and very popular. There are hundreds and hundreds of Web sites with Web cams. Just check out the listing on Yahoo! (`http://search.yahoo.com/bin/search?p=spy+cam`). You will find sites that document just about anything you can think of — people's feet (Feet Cam at `http://www.dcs.qmw.ac/uk/~nickbk/web_camera/`) to the goings-on in the America Online parking lot to weather conditions at the South Pole. There are Web cams aimed at views of and from the St. Louis Arch; the San Francisco Bay Bridge; Venice Beach, California; golfers in San Diego, California; the Empire State Building in New York City; the courthouse at Morgantown, West Virginia; the Space Needle in Seattle, Washington;...you get the picture.

Jim Heid, primary author of this book, has a Web cam set up on his Web site (`http://www.heidsite.com`). It records, from the window in his home office, the weather conditions where he lives in Albion, a village far from the maddening crowd along the wild and scenic coastal region of Northern California (see Figure 8-1).

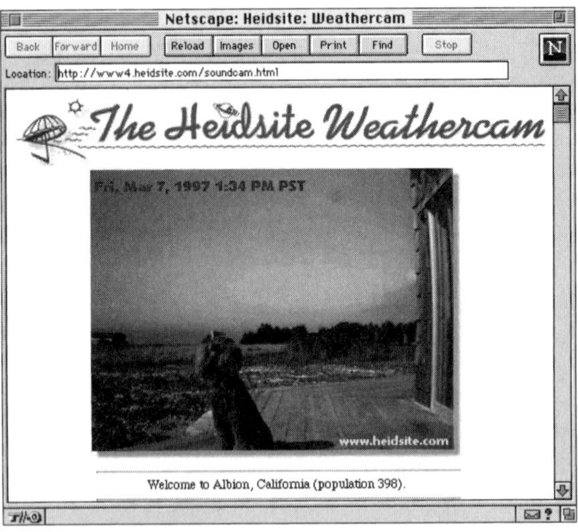

Figure 8-1: Welcome to Albion, California — home of the Heidsite Weathercam.

Now you might suppose that a camera that looks out on a remotely situated front yard would be, well, not that exciting — even if the Pacific Ocean is visible in the distance. How many people do you think want to know if it's foggy or sunny, raining or dry in Albion? As it turns out, quite a few. Months after he put up his Web cam, Heid received an e-mail message from the

National Weather Service office in nearby Eureka. It turns out that his cam is the only such eye on the sky in the region. The Weather Service folks check out his site regularly to gather data for their marine fog forecasts.

Local small-plane pilots in the area also drop by Heid's site before they take off to see what the conditions are. And in the summer, when the California coast is shrouded in fog while inland areas swelter, inland residents check the view to see if they need to wear a sweater before coming to the coast. As Heid says, "Web cams can have fun ancillary benefits."

Call it the "you never know" aspect of the Web: People love to see what's going on, even if it has nothing to do with their lives. And that's exactly what all Web site creators want to see — visitors who find value in their site beyond the obvious. Serendipity and whimsy, in this case, pay good dividends by drawing an audience.

Web cams also help contribute to that all-important personality factor discussed at the beginning of the chapter. A shot of a company lunchroom, a parking lot, or a lowly cubicle helps add a human touch to a site — it reminds visitors that there are people and places behind the pages. And finally, Web cams illustrate — literally — the Web's global nature. It's just plain fun to look at nearly live pictures of people and places located thousands of miles away.

A high-end Web cam site (go ahead, drool)

Web cams come in a variety of packages, but there are standard requirements: A video camera, a machine with video-digitizing features, the correct cable, and commercial software and/or a CGI script to put the images in a readable format, normally JPEG, and on your server. From that point all it takes is the HTML image tag (`<img src="mywebcam.jpeg">`) for your results to be seen by visitors.

SECRET

FTP with Netscape

OK, so you're stuck somewhere hoping to send in an up-to-the-minute dispatch for posting on your Web site and there's not an FTP program to be found. Good news: You can use Netscape Navigator instead.

All you do is type in the same information that you would use in a program like Fetch, doing so in the Location (URL) field. That means entering `ftp://yourname@something.something.com/`. You will be prompted for your password. Fill that in and there you are — in the topmost directory on your server. You can, of course, also type in the full path to a specific directory, such as `ftp://yourname@something.something.com/data/coffee/`. And you can even type in your password and bypass the prompt by the addition of a colon and your password, as in: `ftp://yourname:password@something.something.com/data/coffee/`.

Be careful about the latter approach. The URL goes into Netscape's history file, which means it is available to anyone using Navigator after you on that machine or linked to it via a network.

Some Web cams are state-of-the-art, like the KPIX-TV Live Camera (http://www.kpix.com) on the roof of the Fairmont Hotel atop Nob Hill in downtown San Francisco (see Figure 8-2). Developed in-house and used primarily by the CBS-affiliate's news and weather teams, the camera scans for sunrise and sunset as well as overview shots of the city — from the Bay Bridge to the Golden Gate Bridge, with Coit Tower, Fisherman's Wharf, and Alcatraz Island in sight along the way.

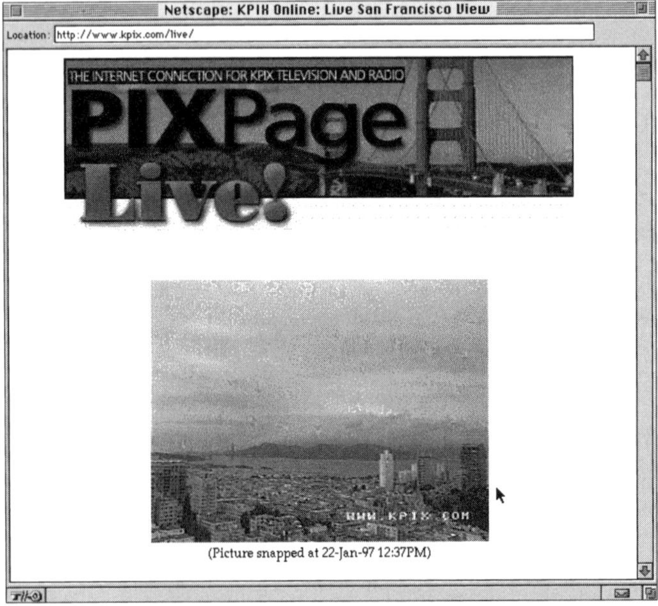

Figure 8-2: The KPIX-TV Web cam, at http://www.kpix.com/live/

The KPIX camera is an expensive, remote-controlled studio camera mounted in a weatherproof shelter. The images are transmitted via microwave to the TV studio located one mile away; the staff uses a Touch-Tone telephone interface to control such things as camera pan, tilt, and focus, and even to "windshield wipe" the lens. The images are snatched at five-minute intervals, and time-lapse views that combine multiple images are also available.

The good news today is that the majority of the Web cams online are the products of amateurs. Remember that level playing field? Even less-sophisticated Web cams can strike a chord with viewers. In other words, there are simpler, less expensive ways of presenting whatever it is you feel is worth focusing your camera on — like the view from your home office. (No need for microwave transmission here — a six-foot cable works fine.)

Creating a Web cam with a Mac OS

The Heidsite Weathercam is a good example of a well-designed Web cam that anyone with the inclination and the right equipment can duplicate. Heid uses a video camera connected to the S-video port of a Macintosh Quadra 840AV, one of many Mac models that contain built-in video digitizing circuitry. The Quadra 840AV, in turn, is networked via Ethernet to an Apple Internet Server 6150 running WebSTAR. The images are taken automatically by a program called MacWebCam (from Rearden Technology, `http://www.rearden.com/`) and saved on the server. His server is connected to a local Internet service provider through a dual-channel ISDN line.

MacWebCam, available at `http://www.rearden.com/`, can save images in a variety of formats, including JPEG. MacWebCam includes features that enable Heid to add captions to his Weathercam images — time and date, for instance — and it allows him to change the capture intervals. MacWebCam also provides time-lapse and even live-video modes; to see the Heidsite Weathercam's time-lapse mode, visit `http://www4.heidsite.com/fastforwardcam.html`. Another Mac-based shareware program, WebCamToo (`http://www.mmcorp.com/~binky/webcamtoo/index.html`), provides similar features.

Rearden Technology is working on some impressive new features for MacWebCam, including a remote-control tripod head that will allow Web surfers to aim the camera in the direction of their choice. For the latest, visit the company's Web site at `http://www.rearden.com/`.

Web cam secrets

Heid uses some cool tricks to set his Weathercam apart from the pack. One of them is what he calls the "Weathercam in a window," and it's shown in Figure 8-3.

Keep a Weathercam image on your screen! If you're using Netscape Navigator 2.0 or later and you have a continuous Internet connection (or you're just going to be surfing for a while), you can keep a current Weathercam image on your screen. The image will be updated every five minutes. To open your Weathercam-in-a-window, just click the button below.

Weathercam in a Window

Figure 8-3: The Heidsite Weathercam in a window. Top: The button that visitors click to open the Weathercam in a window. Bottom: The window, which is updated every five minutes.

Using the JavaScript code shown below, Heid creates a second browser window that contains only his Weathercam — there is nothing else in the window but the image generated by the Web cam.

This second window stays on the screen even when people visiting his site leave to go somewhere else (they can, of course, close it). Think of it as a "constant eye on the cam." Think, too, of the uses you could find for this clever, unobtrusive program. The following code is the JavaScript for the second window.

```
<script language="JavaScript">
<!--
function HeidsiteFrame() {
var isMac = navigator.userAgent.indexOf("Mac") !=-1
msg=open("http://www4.heidsite.com/weather.html","HeidsiteWeathercam","
toolbar=no,width=330,height=250,directories=no,status=no,scrollbars=no,
resize=no,menubar=no");
if (isMac){
msg=open("http://www4.heidsite.com/weather.html","HeidsiteWeathercam","
toolbar=no,width=330,height=250,directories=no,status=no,scrollbars=no,
resize=no,menubar=no");
}}
// the end -->
</script>
```

To activate this JavaScript, you must include a button on your Web cam page. The following HTML does the job. When a visitor clicks the button labeled *Weathercam in a Window,* the function called `HeidsiteFrame` executes, which opens the new window:

```
<form>
<input type=button name="quarter" value="Weathercam in a Window"
onClick=HeidsiteFrame()>
</form>
```

There's one more piece to the Weathercam in a window: the HTML page that's called by the JavaScript, that follows. In Heid's case, the page is named `weather.html`. Its HTML code appears below:

```
<html>
<head>
<meta http-equiv="Refresh" content=300>
<title>Heidsite: www.heidsite.com</title>
<body background="http://www4.heidsite.com/images/image.jpg">
</body>
</html>
```

This code uses the `<META>` tag with a `refresh` attribute that causes the page to reload itself every 300 seconds (every 5 minutes). The cam's image is displayed as a background image.

Heid also added a soundtrack to his Weathercam. The sounds correspond to the time of day — birds singing in the morning, crickets chirping at dusk, in tune with the crashing waves. The sound-effects, available to users of Netscape 3.x and later, are actually audio-only QuickTime movies that loop so that they repeat continuously. This enables small sound files — in the 30K ballpark. (For details on working with QuickTime movies, see Chapter 13.)

To have different sounds play at different times of the day, Heid uses a Mac-based server plug-in called NetCloak, from Maxum Development (http://www.maxum.com/). NetCloak provides HTML-like tags that enable the creation of dynamic Web pages. The following code produces the Heidsite Weathercam's soundtracks.

```
<hide>
<show_time 21 22 23 00 01 02 03 04>
<embed src="http://www.heidsite.com/movies/night.mov" width=100
height=20 autoplay=true controller=true loop=true>
<show>
<hide><show_time 05 06 07 08 09 10><embed
src="http://www.heidsite.com/movies/OceanBirds.mov" width=100
height=20 autoplay=true controller=true loop=true>
<show>
<hide><show_time 11 12 13 14 15 16 17 18><embed
src="http://www.heidsite.com/movies/Birdsongs.mov" width=100
height=20 autoplay=true controller=true loop=true>
<show>
<hide><show_time 19 20><embed
src="http://www.heidsite.com/movies/OceanBirds.mov" width=100
height=20 autoplay=true controller=true loop=true>
<show>
```

The NetCloak tags here cause a different sound to be played depending on when a user visits. For example, the sound named night.mov plays between 9 p.m. and 4 a.m.

Is a soundtrack an essential feature for a Web cam? Of course not. But it does add an interesting twist. And Heid has a folder full of e-mail messages from surprised visitors who wondered where the bird songs were coming from until they realized they were coming from their computer speakers!

Color QuickCam: a Web cam for everyone

As I mentioned, the Heidsite Weathercam is a Mac OS-based beast. Indeed, the Macintosh is the ideal platform for creating a Web cam — a great many Mac models include built-in video digitizers, so all you need to add is a video camera and a program such as MacWebCam. (Mac models that include digitizing features, by the way, include the Centris/Quadra 660AV and 840AV, the Power Mac 6100AV, 7100AV, and 8100AV, and the Power Mac 7500, 7600, and 8500, and 8600.)

But if you live in a world of Windows — or if you have a Mac OS machine that lacks a built-in video digitizer — don't give up hope. You can create a Web cam with just about any Mac OS or Windows machine using the inexpensive and popular Color QuickCam video camera from Connectix Corporation (http://www.connectix.com/ or http://www.quickcam.com/).

QuickCam is an all-in-one color camera package. It plugs directly into your computer and comes with the software you need to get your Web cam up and running. It is about four inches tall and looks like something from outer space — or an eyeball sitting on a triangle base. And at a cost of about $299, it can't be beat. Its QuickPICT software includes auto-capture for updating your scene-of-choice for Web viewing, and it captures those pictures in .PICT, .TIFF, and JPEG formats for the Mac OS and .BMP, .TIFF, and JPEG for Windows.

QuickCam is not just for Web cam use. With optional software, QuickCam can also be used to set up video conferences. Connectix offers its own videoconference software, for both Windows and Macintosh. Another popular videoconference program is CU-SeeMe (freeware from Cornell University, `ftp://gated.cornell.edu/pub/video/Fetch/`, or licensed Enhanced CU-SeeMe from White Pine, `http://goliath.wpine.com/cu-seeme.html`).

Of course, you can also use the Color QuickCam as a *camera,* to take and send pictures. As mentioned in the preceding section, digital cameras are still on the expensive side. For the price, QuickCam hopes to be a contender in this fast-growing market. America Online is betting on the QuickCam solution: In October of 1996, AOL incorporated QuickCam technology into its e-mail service, which means AOL members with QuickCams can send friends and family the pictures the cameras take with just a click of a button.

A fairly high-end Web cam option for Windows-based sites is Perceptual Robotics' InterCam, which provides remote-control panning and zooming. For details, visit the company's Web site at `http://www.nethomes.com/intercam/`.

Adding Interactivity and Community to Your Site

Interactivity and community are one in the same in the world of the Web.

What is interactivity? Like community, it is an exchange between individuals, whether a sharing of information or opinion, simple greetings, even jokes. Interactivity on a Web site is an open-door policy for the cybercommunity that intimates a number of things: "Talk to me." "Tell me who you are." "Your opinions count here."

Interactivity and community can be expressed in a number of ways, but the key point remains the same in all cases: to generate an exchange between you (via your Web site) and your hoped-for audience. The more lively or informative this exchange, the more likely people will return for more.

One easy and satisfying way to promote both interactivity and community on your Web site is through that old standby — the mail, though in this case we're talking electronic (not snail) mail. And we're talking specifically about an e-mail newsletter. It is definitely the way to go if you want to reach out and touch a repeat audience.

The e-mail newsletter

E-mail is the hottest thing on the Internet. Consider the figures offered in a study on electronic mail usage conducted by the investment banking firm Morgan Stanley: 35 million people in 1995 used e-mail, compared to 9 million who surfed the Web. That's impressive on its own, but there's more. The study went on to predict that when the figures for 1996 are in, 23 million people will have browsed the Web, but a staggering 60 percent used cyberspace to send and receive e-mail. And the trend will continue. Even though the number of Web surfers will grow five-fold from 1996 figures, in the year 2000, e-mail users will still out-number surfers: 200 million to 152 million.

Savvy Web site administrators are hip to this trend. Adam Engst, author of the *Internet Starter Kit*, uses e-mail to deliver his popular newsletter, TidBits. The computer network c|net (`http://www.cnet.com`) offers a newsletter. The *New York Times* (`http://www.nytimes.com`) sends out occasional updates to registered users. So do HotWired (`http://www.hotwired.com`), MS-NBC's The Site (`http://www.thesite.com`), Salon Magazine (`http://www.salon1999.com`),...the list goes on.

At Macworld Online (`http://www.macworld.com`), two newsletters are sent out each month to more than 50,000 readers each. One newsletter lists free software and other goodies from such megavendors as Microsoft and Adobe. The other highlights what's new and hot on the site. Both are aimed at enticing the recipients to drop by Macworld Online. It works. The day after the newsletters go out, usage at the site jumps dramatically.

Get the picture? Newsletters, if done well, are welcome aids for people who do not have the time or the money to idly surf the Web. Newsletters are, in essence, the simplest of "personal agents," as automated programs that search Web sites are called. People appreciate the updates that newsletters provide: Newsletters let them know it's time to drop by to see or read something new. Besides, unlike personal agents or 'bots (short for robots), as the search application is known, a newsletter is truly personal. Wrote one correspondent to Macworld Online: "For Mac users with too little time to surf all over the place for answers to their needs, MW Express is a welcome help."

How to promote your newsletter

SECRET

Obviously, you advertise your newsletter and generate your e-mailing list on your Web site. Add a button to your home page that identifies the service and that links to a page that describes what you are offering: a monthly or bimonthly or periodic update to what's new and hot on your site.

On this page include a sign-up form (see Chapter 9). All of the information you really need from this form is a name and e-mail address. Anything more might make people wary. An e-mail address is a lot less intimidating to give out than a street address or phone number.

If you have a robust Web site that includes a registration area, you will automatically collect e-mail addresses from the registration process. That's a heady situation: After all, e-mail addresses, like phone numbers, are powerful solicitation tools. *Be careful and be considerate with this information.* Always state clearly that if you fill out this form, you will receive a newsletter. Or provide that information with the caveat that a newsletter will be sent *unless* the reader objects — in this case, include a "Don't Send Me a Newsletter" checkbox. And respect your registrant's wishes.

If you send out an e-mail newsletter without prior notification that you plan to do so, or if you ignore the "Don't Send Me a Newsletter" checkbox, you are asking for some very unpleasant responses from your hoped-for repeat audience.

As far as mailing your newsletter, that depends, of course, on the length of your e-mailing list. In the beginning, you can probably do the posting by hand, or set up a simple script to automate the process (or hire someone to do it for you). As your list grows — be positive, it will — check out commercial programs that manage mailing lists. For details on the technicalities behind setting up a list server, see Chapter 9.

Be selective

Newsletters are appropriate only if you have content that changes. If your Web site is (heaven forbid!) static, forget the e-mail newsletter. Its appearance in electronic mail boxes will only irritate the cyberoccupant. After all, the idea here is to stimulate interest in your site because it has something fresh to offer. A newsletter with no purpose is junk mail.

What constitutes change? Well, that depends on your site. Say you have a home page that deals with antique and collectible dolls, and you just got in a vintage 1959 Barbie doll. That's worthy of note. Someone out there in cyberspace — probably a lot of people — will want to know she's available. Or you have a Web site that deals with your passion for the St. Louis Cardinals. They win the National League Pennant and you've got the scoop on the stats. That's worthy of note.

Think of your newsletter as a postcard to a friend or associate. All you are doing is communicating a simple fact: "Having a great time. Wish you were here."

Keep it short and sweet

In most cases, a newsletter should be a short and sweet announcement that something worthwhile has been added to your Web site. Don't confuse a newsletter with a feature story. The idea here is to be concise and succinct — "just the facts, ma'am," in other words. Go ahead, use jargon if you want: Newsletters are, like the postcard analogy we used above, casual reminders not formal letters.

In terms of length, one or two paragraphs can suffice. Think of them as your "lead" or "nut graf," as we discussed in the "You, too, can be a reporter" section, earlier in this chapter. In the case of a newsletter, your goal is to give people the who, what, and where. If you give them too much information, they won't do what a newsletter is supposed to encourage: make a return visit to your site. Too much talk in your newsletter could translate into no repeat action on your site.

For example, say your home page is an adjunct to your business, which is a coffeehouse named Joltin' Joe's Coffee Club. The idea of the Web site is to promote your latest venture: mail-order beans. A newsletter is a natural for you. It's a perfect vehicle for announcing your "Java of the Month" selection. Your nut graf, then, might read something like the following:

```
Joltin' Joe's Java of the Month Club

Hello from Joltin' Joe's. New this month: The Grand Slam,
a blend of rich Colombian and flavorful Ethiopian beans
guaranteed to get you up and out in record time. Drop by
Joltin' Joe's (www.joltin.com) for a virtual tasting: Read
the scoop on how best to brew this exotic combo. And have it
delivered to your door for only $9.95, plus shipping and
handling.
```

Designing your newsletter

We've already mentioned length: one or two paragraphs are often fine for your newsletter. If you have more to say (and only if your Web site is jam-packed with new content on a regular basis), think in terms of screen length.

In the old days of print communication, editors measured stories by word count, or, in the case of newspapers, in inches. In the electronic publishing world, the measurement is by screen size, as in one or two screenfuls of copy.

The screen analogy is also the way to measure the width of your newsletter. Remember that a newsletter is in ASCII (plain text) only: it is being sent through the mail, not posted via HTML on a Web page. With the latter, you can control design. With a newsletter, you have to be careful to manipulate your copy based on the nonstandard whimsy of the e-mail services and varying screen sizes of your audience.

There is also the limitation of special characters to consider. A special box character or other graphical dingbat that appears on your computer is unlikely to survive the journey to another platform. Happily, though, there are universals, such as equal signs (====), dashes (----), asterisks (***), and, of course, the "at" symbol, @. While the @ symbol is crucial for purposes of e-mail addressing, the other symbols are of importance when it comes to designing your newsletter. Use the ==== or ---- to break up topics, for example. The * can be used for emphasis or to indicate and separate items in a list. Note, too, that boldface and italic attributes are not translatable in text-only documents. If you feel that you must give extra weight to a word or two in you copy, use uppercase letters — but use them sparingly. Uppercase SCREAMS.

It is also important to remember screen-character width when you create your newsletter. Depending on the e-mail program your subscribers use, text can wrap to the next line if your newsletter default is wider. Wraps like these are not only unattractive, but it makes for difficult, choppy reading. A good rule of thumb is to keep your screen measure at a maximum of 80 characters.

Use extra carriage returns as a design element. Extra line spaces between elements adds a nice touch of what designers call *air* or *white space,* and *rom* helps set off lines of text.

Before you begin your newsletter in earnest, send trial copies to friends who use different operating systems to see how the spacing, the characters, and so on, translate. Rework your newsletter based on this information until you have found a clean-looking, easy-to-read common denominator.

Always sign and date your newsletter, and include an e-mail address along with your Web address. Honesty is the very best policy in electronic newsletters.

Let's take a look at the Joltin' Joe's newsletter again, using the above design elements.

```
=================J O L T I N'  J O E ' S=================

April, 1997

http://www.joltin.com

joltin@swell.com

Joltin' Joe's Java of the Month Club

Hello from Joltin' Joe's. New this month: The *Grand Slam,* a
blend of rich Colombian and flavorful Ethiopian beans
guaranteed to get you up and out in record time. Drop by
Joltin' Joe's (www.joltin.com) for a virtual tasting: Read the
scoop on how best to brew this exotic combo. And have it
delivered to your door for only $9.95, plus shipping and
handling.

-------- Hey, there's more!

Drop by www.jolt.com and check out our *blasts from the past,*
including:

**Mad Dog Morning Bark ($7.95)

**Mid-Day Perk ($6.95)

**Espresso for You ($7.95)

--------
```

```
All prices plus shipping and handling. Whole beans or ground to
order. Buy direct from www.joltin.com, or call 1-800-JOLTING.

Joltin' Joe's Java House

Springfield, Missouri, USA

Joe Costanza, proprietor

joe@swell.com

====================================================
```

Using your newsletter to promote interactivity and community

Okay, so far I've talked about how you can interact with a community of like-minded folks via an e-mail newsletter. So far, though, it has been a one-way communication: you to them. Now for the fun part.

As I mentioned, it is good policy to include your name and e-mail address on your newsletter. It is even better policy to add a line asking for comments from your readers. Be forewarned that you may not like every response that you get, but all responses, good or bad, provide lessons in communication. Take the comments to heart. Learn from your mistakes. Incorporate suggestions.

The idea is to let people know that you asked for, and are listening to, their opinions. Those opinions can be put to good use: Add them to your newsletter, sparingly, of course, as a kind of "Letters to the Editor" forum. People love to see their names in print. Even more to the point, their comments can provide an outlet for establishing your expertise, and, as a side benefit, can create content for your Web site. For example, Joltin' Joe's incorporated a "letter to the editor" in the following version of the newsletter:

```
==================J O L T I N'  J O E ' S==================

April, 1997

http://www.joltin.com

joltin@swell.com

Joltin' Joe's Java of the Month Club

Hello from Joltin' Joe's. New this month: The *Grand Slam,* a
blend of rich Colombian and flavorful Ethiopian beans
guaranteed to get you up and out in record time. Drop by
Joltin' Joe's (www.joltin.com) for a virtual tasting: Read the
scoop on how best to brew this exotic combo. And have it
delivered to your door for only $9.95, plus shipping and
handling.

-------- Hey, there's more!
```

```
Drop by www.jolt.com and check out our *blasts from the past,*
including:

**Mad Dog Morning Bark ($7.95)

**Mid-Day Perk ($6.95)

**Espresso for You ($7.95)

--------

All prices plus shipping and handling. Whole beans or ground to
order. Buy direct from www.joltin.com, or call 1-800-JOLTING.

==================B E A N  T A L K==================

Got an e-mail letter the other day from Sue Woods of Omaha,
Nebraska. Sue is confused about grind: fine or coarse, which is
which and what's what?

Well, simply stated, the finer the grind, the darker and
stronger the brew. Espresso is a fine-grind coffee: it has
nothing to do with the bean variety. Medium grind is the most
common to use for a good cup of java brewed in a drip coffee-
maker.

Got questions? Joe has answers. Send 'em to javatalk@swell.com.
And drop by our Virtual Koffee Klatch Page
(www.joltin.com/beantalk) for more Bean Talk.

Joltin' Joe's Java House

Springfield, Missouri, USA

Joe Costanza, proprietor

joe@swell.com

=======================================================
```

As illustrated in this example, Joltin' Joe established himself as an expert on coffee, simply because someone asked him for advice and he answered. Now he's got he best of both worlds: a business and a growing reputation as Mr. Virtual Coffee.

Newsletters, of course, need to stay true to their form — they are updates, not packages in and of themselves. But as the Joltin' Joe's example illustrates, newsletters can be used to generate dialogue and content for a Web site.

Here's another way to use a newsletter to stimulate return visits: the "collaborative" document.

Let's say that the theme of your Web site is mountain biking (you sell mountain bike accessories, helmets, seat covers, and so on). The fact that your site represents an activity that many people enjoy and that represents adventure makes it a natural for the collaborative process. There is nothing a thrill-seeker likes more than to swap tales. The idea is to use that natural human inclination and set up a page that features your readers' contributions. Not only will people visit your site to see if their tale is posted, they will tell their friends about it and they'll want to participate. The only danger in all this: You might be overwhelmed by the outpourings of readers. What a shame! And you might even find that other bike sites begin linking to your page — that's how communities on the Web get together, after all.

To get the wheels turning, let people know you are interested in hearing about their adventures by saying so in your newsletter. Maybe this month's newsletter talked about some new, improved helmets you just received. Use that as a jumping off point. For example:

```
================ B I K E  W R I T E R S=================

*Dirt Tales Wanted*

Hey, helmets are no laughing matter. We all know how important
they are to good biking safety. Let's not be flip (excuse the
pun), but let's get down and dirty: Tell me about your most
hair-raising biking experience. I'll put your stories on my
upcoming Dirt Tales Page (www.mountainbikes.com/dirt.html).
C'mon. Share your adventures... and advice. Novices need to
know what they're getting into! Send them to
tales@mountainbikes.com. Please add your name and hometown
(e-mail addresses and Web site addresses welcome, too).

================================================
```

As the stories come in, simply post them on an appropriate page — make sure it is advertised on and linked from your home page.

Advice and collaborative documents are just two of many ways you can use a newsletter to encourage interactivity and community. Set up a trivia game. Consider a contest with company T-shirts or products as the prizes. The beauty in all of this is its simplicity. People, as the statistics show, love to send and receive e-mail. You're just finding ways to direct that flow to your Web site.

Publicizing Your Web Site

You've got your Web site set up; you've incorporated immediacy, interactivity, and community into your pages; you're planning to send out a monthly newsletter. Now what? Where do you go from here? Publicizing your site is one of the most important things you can do to get noticed initially. From there, staying "noticed" is up to you.

Registering with site directories

It goes without saying, though I will do so here in some detail, that you need to get your Web site publicized. Yahoo! remains the most visited directory of Web pages, and it is where you want to be listed, too. Yahoo! makes it easy. Just go to the section called Add to Yahoo! (`http://add.yahoo.com/fast/add?+`). All of the information you need to know to add your wonderful Web site to the Yahoo! pool is there, plus a form to submit.

That's the first step. The second is to do your homework. You need to find all of the services on the Web that either list new Web sites or help with that listing process. The best place to start is again at Yahoo! Check out `http://www.yahoo.com/Computers_and_Internet/World_Wide_Web/Announcement_Services/`.

This URL gives you a huge directory of such services, including `comp.infosystems.www.announce`, a Usenet newsgroup whose sole purpose is to announce new Web happenings.

As you will see when you fill out the Yahoo! submission form to add new Web pages, it is imperative that you know exactly what your site is about. The more succinct you are in your description, the better. Pretend you are a librarian who, without the benefit of the Dewey decimal classification, must collate a huge collection of information based solely on key words.

Actually, this is not a pretend situation — it is the reality of the Web. There is no system per se for collecting Web pages and sorting them in easy-to-reference virtual "card catalogues." And note that this electronic-based library is a massive one. One commercial directory reported that it had identified more than four million individual Web pages, and the number keeps growing. Since no one person is in charge of this global repository of information, the job of seeking and seizing information is left to *robots* also known as *spiders* and *crawlers*. Robots are automated for page search and seize. They do not do so, as it may sound, by going out on the Web for an information treasure hunt. Robots and their crew are programmed to "read" hypertext documents and the hyperlinks on these individual pages. Huge directories such as WebCrawler, AltaVista, and InfoSeek employ robots and spiders. When people go to these search services, they fill out forms that are based on the Web's version of Dewey's decimal collection — key words, like, say, *coffee*, *mountain bikes*, *dolls*, *dogs*.

Helping the spiders crawl

Robots and spiders read HTML tags to collect information that is translated into key words for searching. For example, spiders look at the `<TITLE>` tag. So make sure that every one of your `<TITLE>` tags contains "key" descriptives of what your page contains. Forget cuteness and adjectives. When Web surfers request information on a topic of interest, they use a key word. The more often that exact word appears in a robot `<TITLE>` search-and-seize, the higher the page will appear when the results are returned to the surfer. For example, in the Joltin' Joe's newsletter example, a good "title" for the coffee talk page would be, simply, `<TITLE>Coffee Talk</TITLE>`. Using `<TITLE>Bean Talk</TITLE>`, however, would confuse — and diffuse — matters. Joltin' Joe's could find itself mingled in with the chili, jelly beans, even part of a search-return for "bean bag" furniture. (For more tips on titling, see Chapter 2.)

Robots and spiders also read the HTML `<META>` tag, which is used to describe "metainformation" about a Web document. `<META>` tags are placed at the top of a document, usually within the `<HEAD>` information. (Note that `<META>` tags are used similarly to the `name` attribute and require a key/value pair.) Again, since the purposes of using this tag is to attract spiders, keep the information clear and concise.

For example, you could give the spider key words that you choose on your own (note the use of commas and quotes):

```
<META NAME="keys" CONTENT="dogs, retrievers, fleas">.
```

Another use of the `<META>` tag:

```
<META NAME="description" CONTENT="Add a description of your site here.">
```

Note in the preceding example that while you can write a fairly long description, keep it pointedly to the point. The idea is to use as many "key" key words as you can. Let's use Joltin' Joe's as an example:

```
<META  NAME="description" CONTENT="Coffee beans, coffee talk, and
coffee news are brewing at Joltin' Joe's Java of the Month Club, an
e-mail mail-order coffeehouse on the Web.">
```

You'll find more details on the `<META>` tag in Chapter 10.

How to keep pesky robots at bay

Not everyone is happy to see robots knocking at their virtual door. The number of search engines is growing; as a consequence, the number of robots deployed to collect information is also on the rise. Sometimes people just don't like seeing them. As one Webmaster said, "I looked in the log and there were spiders everywhere." The image is as creepy as it would be if in fact he meant the real things were scurrying across his desk.

But usually the distaste for robots has to do with their origins: Robots are created by people, and people sometimes make mistakes. A poorly created robot can create traffic jams, particularly if it comes up against a page that confounds its programming in some way, such as, preventing it from collecting the information because of a glitch in its code. In these cases, the robot won't go away — it will keep trying to accomplish its (incorrectly) programmed task, even if that means tying up access to the server in question.

There are two ways to keep robots at bay. The first is with a file called `robots.txt`, which is placed at the top level of a Web site. Robots are programmed to check for `robots.txt`, and then follow the instructions that are contained within it.

With robots.txt you can exclude robots and spiders from all or some of your directories. To exclude them from your entire site, the robots.txt file should read (# being a comment):

```
# Excluding all robots from joltin' joe's:
User-agent: *
Disallow: /
```

To exclude them from one directory:

```
# Excluding robots from joltin' joe's images directory:
User-agent: *
Disallow: /images/
```

The robots.txt file, as mentioned, needs to go at the top level of a Web site. That's easy enough if you administer your own server. If you don't, you can use the HTML <META> tag to do the job. NOINDEX prevents the robot from indexing the page; NOARCHIVE prevents the robot from archiving the page; and NOFOLLOW stops the robot in its tracks — it will not follow any links in the document.

The <META> information is placed in the <HEAD> area of your HTML document:

```
<META NAME="ROBOTS" CONTENT="NOINDEX">
<META NAME="ROBOTS" CONTENT="NOARCHIVE">
<META NAME="ROBOTS" CONTENT="NOFOLLOW">
```

Note that at this writing, not all robots support these attributes. For the latest scoop and for more information on robots and robot-prevention in general, see The Web Robots Pages at http://info.webcrawler.com/mak/projects/robots/robots.html.

Promoting your site the old-fashioned way

A year ago, the Web was the new kid on the media block. Now it has gone mainstream. That's good news for you when it comes time to publicize your site. Since newspapers and television are covering the Web with ardor, they need all the help they can get to tell their stories. Don't believe for a minute that reporters are sitting around surfing the Web all day to come up with ideas — they rely heavily on press releases to help them find something new and noteworthy.

Check your local daily or weekly newspapers. Many daily papers now have Web-specific pages, usually in the business section. Many also carry a local Web site of the Week column. And all newspaper feature sections like to find interesting people or things to write about. Let them know you exist by sending the editors in charge a press release announcing the birth of your site (and send one out whenever you update your pages). But keep the release short. Use all of the tips you learned in this chapter to make your press release as professional as possible. (Always include your phone number and, of course, your Web address and e-mail address.) As you compose your press release, think of yourself as a Web surfer — what sets your Web page apart from the others? What makes it unique or fun or timely? Be enthusiastic, but keep in mind that to entice a newspaper editor, you need a "hook." A hook is what the term implies — something that grabs attention beyond the simple fact that your Web site exists.

Because the Web is a global medium, you don't have to stick close to home in your search for publicity. Depending on the topic of your site, contact related periodicals, magazines, journals, and so on. Again, do your homework: research pays.

Doing Web Business: An Overview

Some people say that you can tell when a medium has reached critical mass when the entrepreneurs start showing up. A lot of people say that a better way to tell is when Hugh Hefner shows up, but that's a discussion for a different book.

If either of these rules is true, then the Web has definitely reached mass-medium status. Internet old-timers may whine about the commercialization of the Net, but they can't reverse the tide. Thousands of businesses, large and small, have set up shop to sell products ranging from software to clothing to books to... well, that's a discussion for a different book.

The issues, options, and technicalities behind Web commerce are far too complex to cover in a single chapter — and they're evolving so quickly that it'd be difficult to write anything that would have a shelf life longer than a carton of milk's. So in this section, I'll provide a brief overview of Web commerce issues and options, and then take a look at some relatively painless ways to integrate commerce into your site.

Security is the key

No matter what you want to sell and how you intend to sell it, one of the most important issues in Web commerce is security: specifically, the security of credit card information supplied by your customers and sent over the Internet.

From a technical standpoint, security is an issue because it's possible for cyberthieves to obtain credit card information as it traverses the 'net. You could accept orders via e-mail, but a customer's credit card data would be accessible to any hacker with the skill and determination to look for it.

How serious is the risk? Some people say you're more at risk when you hand your credit card to clerk at a store or allow a waiter or waitress to carry it away on a little plastic tray. When you think about it, these folks have a point — and as the haystack that is Internet e-mail grows larger, finding those needles that contain credit card information becomes harder and harder. Still, it is possible.

Ultimately, the greatest threat is one of perception: people aren't going to beam their credit card information into cyberspace if they perceive a risk of theft. And if that prevents them from clicking your Order Now button, it's a problem, no matter how real the risk.

The secure server route

One common solution to the security problem is a *secure server* — a Web server that works together with a supporting browser to transfer sensitive information in a scrambled, or *encrypted,* form. Secure servers rely on technique called *public-key* encryption, in which the merchant has a mathematical formula (the public key), that can be used to encrypt messages. Anybody can use this key, but only the merchant who has the private key can open the message.

Virtually all major server vendors — from Netscape to Microsoft to O'Reilly to StarNine Technologies — offer secure server options for their Web server packages. Some also offer turnkey Web commerce products that go well beyond just accepting scrambled credit card numbers. Netscape's Netscape Merchant System and Microsoft's Merchant Server each provide a database system for storing information about products and generating appropriate HTML pages; a search engine that enables shoppers to locate items of interest; a *shopping basket* feature that enables them to indicate which items they want; and a transaction server that accepts credit card information and handles the details behind the transaction (see Figure 8-4).

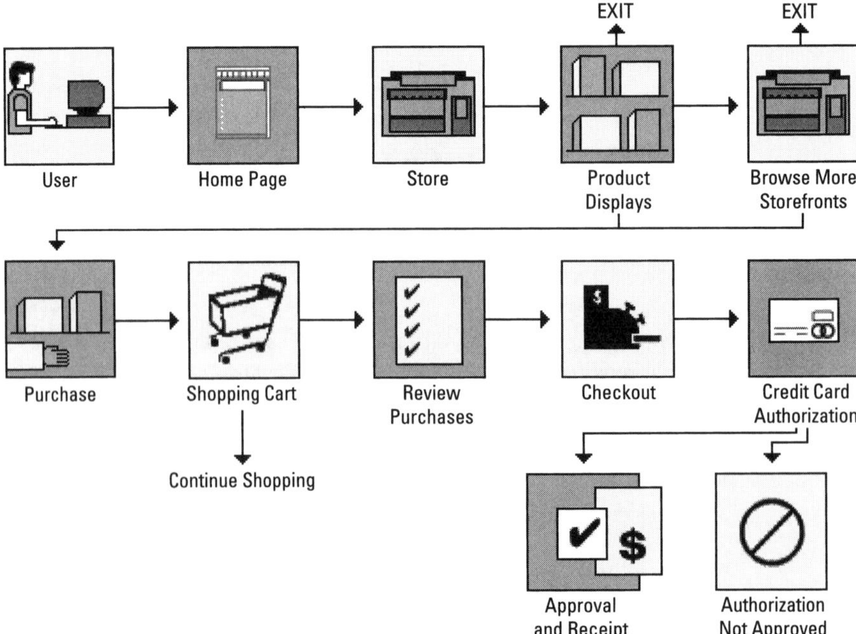

Figure 8-4: Anatomy of an online shopping expedition (source: Netscape Communications)

A large number of Internet service providers and site-hosting services provide secure server services, and many of these provide shopping basket and other commerce-related features. If you're contemplating commerce and you're creating a site that will be hosted by an ISP, you'll want to inquire about the availability of secure servers. (See Chapter 15 for more questions to ask a potential service provider and for tips on locating a provider.)

How secure servers work

Secure servers generally use the Secure Sockets Layer (SSL) protocol, developed by Netscape based on encryption technology developed by RSA Data Security, Inc. For details on SSL and encryption in general, see the Secrets sidebar, "For More Details on E-Commerce, Click Here," later in this section.

BACKGROUNDER

Anatomy of a Secure Link

When visitors click a link to enter a secure area of a site, their browsers begin an exchange with the secure server that goes something like this:

1. The browser sends a request to connect to the secure server.
2. The server sends a signed digital certificate to the browser. The server uses the certificate it acquired from the certification authority. The certificate contains several tidbits of information, including the name of the server, its public key, and a digital signature.
3. The browser *authenticates* the server — that is, it verifies that it's dealing with the server that the visitor really wants to be dealing with and not some impostor. It does so by decrypting the digital signature and matching it with the certificate information. If the certificate was tampered with during transmission, the digital signature won't match, and the browser terminates the connection to the server. If the certificate checks out, the server is authenticated and things move along to the next step.
4. The browser generates a *session key* and encrypts it using the server's public key, which it obtained from the certificate that it received in Step 2. The browser sends the encrypted session key to the server.
5. The server receives the session key, which it uses to encrypt and decrypt the data that will subsequently be sent and received from and to the browser during this surfing session. At this stage, the browser's window changes to indicate a secure connection. In Netscape Navigator, for example, a small key icon appears in the lower-left corner of the browser window. (With conventional connections, this key appears broken to indicate a connection that isn't secure.)

Whew — that's a lot of back-and-forth effort to prevent some dweeb from scarfing up a credit card number. Fortunately, you don't have memorize the ugly technicalities in order to use a secure server — especially if you contract with a service provider who has one.

Before you can use a secure server, you need to purchase a digital ID, also called a *certificate,* from a company called a *certification authority*. One such outfit is VeriSign, Inc. (`http://www.verisign.com/`). At this writing, VeriSign charges approximately $290 for a one-year, one-server certificate, and approximately $95 for each additional server within an organization.

After you install the secure server software and your digital certificate (a process that varies depending on the server software you use), you can dish out pages requiring security. Generally, these will be pages containing forms that visitors will use to provide credit-card and ordering information. To dish out such pages, begin their URLs with HTTPS instead of HTTP — for example, https://www.your_domain.com/orderform.html.

The Web payment route

When you long to join the frequent buyer club at the local TrinketWorld, chances are you apply for a TrinketWorld credit card that you can use at TrinketWorlds across the globe. The Web's variation on this theme involves what's often called *digital money* or even *e-cash.*

In a nutshell, it works like this. Sam and Susie Surfer are eager to become cyberconsumers but are wary of sending credit card information over the Internet. So they establish an account with a third-party payment service — for the examples in this section, I'll use one of the first and largest, First Virtual Holdings (`http://www.firstvirtual.com/`).

To establish this account, they fill out a form on First Virtual's Web site that includes name, address, and e-mail information — but no credit card numbers. After they submit the form, they'll receive an e-mail telling them how to use old-fashioned (and arguably theft-prone) technologies such as the mail or telephone to contact First Virtual and provide their credit card information. When they're done, they get a personal identification number (PIN) that they can use at any on-line merchant that accepts payments from the service they chose.

When Sam and Susie buy a product from a site that supports First Virtual, they simply supply their PIN, not their credit card information. First Virtual then sends them an e-mail asking if they really want to make the purchase. They can respond with one of three replies: *yes*, *no*, or *fraud*. They'd use the last option if their PIN had been used without their consent.

Assuming they answer *yes,* First Virtual charges their credit card and then transfers the funds into the site owner's bank account, after taking a cut off the top for their trouble. (This is a simplified description; there's more to the actual funds-transfer process, and you can read all the gory details on First Virtual's Web site.)

But there's a drawback. If the Surfer family wants to buy a widget from http://www.widgetsworld.com and widgetsworld.com doesn't accept First Virtual payments, Sam and Susie are out of luck. It's the "we take VISA but not American Express" concept extended to the Web, and it's going to take some time before the major players establish themselves. And in fact, the

Big Guns aren't standing still. Visa and MasterCard have teamed up to develop their own standard for secure transactions. You can read about their initiatives at http://www.visa.com/ and http://www.mastercard.com/.

Becoming a First Virtual merchant

First Virtual offers a variety of options for would-be cybermerchants. The Pioneer Seller option costs a mere $10 for initial sign-up, but payments from First Virtual to you can be delayed up to 90 days. (Again, visit the company's Web site for the full — and current — scoop.) The Express Seller option has a $350 application fee, requires credit checks and other red tape, but has numerous advantages, including a delay of only four days until you get your bucks.

When you become a First Virtual merchant, you add a graphic to your site indicating that you accept First Virtual PINs. First Virtual also adds your site to its shopping directory, a list of First Virtual merchants (http://www.firstvirtual.com/shop/index.html).

Other electronic commerce options

First Virtual isn't the only pioneer blazing the electronic commerce trail — far from it. Another major player is CyberCash (http://www.cybercash.com/). CyberCash's approach differs from First Virtual's. Rather than signing up with a credit card and getting a PIN, CyberCash consumers make payments from the CyberCash Wallet — a program that runs on their computers.

SECRET

For More Details on E-Commerce, Click Here

If you're serious about setting up an online cash register, here are a few on-line resources you may want to consult.

- **Yahoo's Internet commerce index (http://www.yahoo.com/Business/Electronic_Commerce/).** This is a good jumping-off point for learning about all aspects of Web commerce, from conducting transactions to advertising.
- **The EFF's "Digital Money and Transactions" archive (http://www.eff.org/pub/Privacy/Digital_money/).** The Electronic Frontier Foundation has compiled an extensive list of links to articles and papers discussing various electronic commerce technologies and their privacy ramifications.
- **First Virtual's "Perils and Pitfalls of Practical Internet Commerce" (http://www.firstvirtual.com/company/index.html).** You'll find a fascinating report from the front lines of Internet commerce in the Company Information area of First Virtual's site.
- **RSA Data Security's Cryptography FAQ (http://www.rsa.com/rsalabs/faq/).** This site is a superb resource for background into cryptography issues and technologies.
- **Netscape's SSL home page (http://home.netscape.com/newsref/std/SSL.html).** This page is a good starting point for information on Netscape's SSL initiatives.

When starting out with CyberCash, a consumer downloads and then runs the Wallet application, which uses a wizard-like series of dialog boxes to obtain credit-card or checking account information. Next, the consumer transfers some money into his or her CyberCash account. Then he or she goes shopping at merchants who accept CyberCash.

Amsterdam-based DigiCash (`http://www.digicash.com/`) takes a similar approach. One potential advantage to this approach is that it offers consumers a bit more privacy: no one is keeping track of what consumers buy and where. With the First Virtual approach, purchases are ultimately charged to a consumer's credit card, creating a record of buying habits.

Selling information: the pay-per-surf approach

Maybe you don't want to sell trinkets, but information: market research reports, industry-specific news, astrology forecasts. As you probably know, the notion of selling information doesn't really fly all that well on today's Web, where you'll sometimes hear netizens blather things like, "Information wants to be free." (Tell that to my publisher. For that matter, tell it to anyone who works his or her hands numb creating information and also has bills to pay.)

One problem has been the Web world's resistance to the notion of paying for a subscription to a Web site. A variation on the electronic commerce theme, sometimes called *micromoney*, aims to work around this resistance. It does so by charging not a relatively high flat subscription fee for access to information, but a relatively low per-use charge each time a visitor requests a specific piece of information. Rather than paying $19.95 a year for access to an entire site, visitors might pay a dime or a dollar to read an article or report. It's the TV industry's pay-per-view concept extended to the Web. Call it pay-per-surf.

First Virtual has set up a virtual information mall called InfoHaus (`http://www.infohaus.com/`) where information publishers can offer their wares to visitors. At this writing, much of InfoHaus's content leans toward "how to get rich" articles and astrology reports. And it's too early to say whether Web consumers will embrace the pay-per-surf concept. But it's worth visiting the site to get a look at one potential outlet for selling information in a way that doesn't involve subscriptions. DigiCash and CyberCash also have pay-per-surf mechanisms in place.

The old-fashioned route

If you don't want to tread on the edge of digital commerce — or even if you do — there are simple ways to enable visitors to your site to buy products. One way is to post a telephone number for visitors to call and order products by phone. Another is to provide an on-screen form that visitors can print, fill out, and fax. These options enable folks who don't trust Web-based commerce to buy your stuff. And they enable you to offer reasonably painless payment opportunities to your visitors without grappling with secure servers or third-party payment vendors.

Summary

- Change is good, especially for a Web site. Make your site stand out in the maddening URL crowd by using basic "human" tools — your own creativity and imagination — augmented by updates of old standards, notably the use of photographs as produced by digital cameras and video as captured by Webcams.
- Immediacy is accomplished by updating your Web site at regular intervals, using photos and video but also the written word. Become a true Web publisher by creating dynamic content based on the focus of your Web site; in short, by doing what a successful publisher does best — seek out and report on the news, trends, and issues of interest to a target audience.
- One way to stimulate both interactivity and community on your Web site is to communicate with your audience through an e-mail newsletter. A newsletter, if produced well, stimulates interest in your Web site. Even better, a newsletter can encourage return visits to your site by publicizing your dedication to change, such as through regular notices of content updates.
- Change means nothing unless your Web site is duly noted. To this end, this chapter discusses ways of publicizing your site on popular Web directories like Yahoo!. It also discusses Web robots, which index the vast Web library, and how to get and, if needed, discourage, these Web page search-and-seize programs.
- Electronic commerce options range from setting up your own secure server to using a third-party payment vendor such as First Virtual. Or just create a form that visitors can fill out and fax.

Part II

Advanced Interactivity Secrets

Chapter 9

Can We Talk? Conferencing, Chatting, and List Serving

In This Chapter

- Virtual communities and the benefits of visitor interaction
- Setting up and maintaining conferencing areas
- Surveying Windows and Mac OS conferencing and list-server products
- Setting up live chat rooms
- Protocol and e-etiquette: to moderate or not to moderate?
- E-mail list servers: "push" delivery for the rest of us

As the previous chapter discussed, interactivity is a key element of a successful Web site. No matter what the topic, the best Web sites attract and engage audiences through an active exchange of information, ideas, and opinions.

Three tools can help make your site a lively communication center: conferencing areas, real-time chat rooms, and e-mail list servers. With these tools, you can encourage traffic to your site, involve visitors in your content-creation process, and establish a community centered around your site, your company, or your cause.

This chapter explains how to set up and use these community-building tools, and provides tips and techniques to help you get the most out of the tools you decide to use on your site.

Talk About Cool Software: Try These Interaction Tools

The *HTML & Web Publishing SECRETS* CD-ROM includes trial versions of some of the best conferencing, chatting, and e-mail serving tools available for the Windows and Mac OS platforms, including the following:

WebBoard 2.0 (Windows). With its attractive conferencing interface, easy setup, great documentation, and low price, WebBoard from O'Reilly & Associates is a superb choice for Windows-based conferencing. The version on the CD-ROM is fully functional for 30 days.

Allaire Forums (Windows). Allaire Forums builds on the company's Cold Fusion database-integration technology (described in the next chapter) to provide conferencing features.

Web Crossing (Windows and Mac OS). Lundeen & Associates's Web Crossing is an industrial strength conferencing system whose users include the *New York Times* and Salon 1999. The versions on the CD-ROM are fully functional. (If you're interested in buying Web Crossing, be sure to check out Lundeen's special offer in the back of this book. When you buy the software, you can unlock the trial version included on the CD-ROM and be up and running.)

ListSTAR (Mac OS). StarNine's mailing list server software is one of the most popular commercial list servers in the Mac OS world. (If you're thinking of buying ListSTAR, be sure to check out StarNine's special offer in the back of this book.)

LetterRip (Mac OS). Fog City Software's list server software is extremely easy to use but powerful, too. It's a relative newcomer to the list-server scene but promises to be a major contender.

Virtual Bulletin Boards: Conferencing Areas

A conferencing area is a virtual bulletin board, a place where people can post messages that others can read and respond to. Conferencing areas enable people with different schedules to communicate. By contrast, participants in a real-time chat must be at the same virtual location at the same time in order to communicate.

When visitors see a post that they want to respond to, they can do so either through private e-mail or by posting publicly to the conferencing forum. These replies to the conferencing area form *threads* (see the following Backgrounder sidebar, "Nice Threads: Understanding Multithreaded Conferencing").

A conferencing area is also a great communication tool for an intranet. You might use an intranet-based conferencing area to post memos, announcements, and policy information. Employees can comment on and ask questions about the postings. You might also use a conferencing area to help teams communicate. Each team might have its own discussion corner within a conferencing area where its members can post and discuss project status and timeline information. This allows others inside the company to check the status of the project and allows team members to keep tabs on each others' progress.

Nice Threads: Understanding Multithreaded Conferencing

In the operating system world, you'll often hear the jargon term *multithreaded,* which refers to a program's or operating system's ability to divide a task into separate chunks, or threads, each of which the computer can execute independently of other threads.

Conferencing areas can also be multithreaded, but the jargon term means something different here. In the conferencing world, threads are groups of messages on the same subject. Imagine a discussion group with eight messages in it. Messages 1, 3, and 6 are connected — message 1 was posted as a new message to the discussion, and messages 3 and 6 where posted as replies to message 1. This group of messages is a thread. Threads tie a set of posts together, enabling a reader to follow a discussion.

When evaluating conferencing software, assess the support it provides for threaded discussions. How easy is it for visitors to follow the trail of postings on a specific topic and add to the thread by posting replies of their own? How are the threads displayed, and can you customize the way threads are displayed? Address these questions and you'll make it easier for your visitors to navigate your discussion threads — without getting tangled.

Through a conferencing area, visitors can have their problems solved and their questions answered. Once your visitors discover what your conferencing area can do for them, they'll return again and again.

What are your conferencing options?

So you're sold on the benefits of a conferencing area. What options are available? As I describe in this section, there are quite a few, and they run the gamut from tried-and-true but somewhat cumbersome Internet technologies to proprietary conferencing software that you can set up within minutes.

A news server

One of the oldest ways to communicate on the Internet is through Usenet news groups. Usenet relies on the Network News Transport Protocol (NNTP). There are now over 10,000 public news groups on the Internet, accounting for more than 10 percent of its total communications traffic. By setting up a news server, you can join in this cacophony, creating your own public news groups or creating private ones for use within your organization.

All major operating systems support NNTP server software that you need to set up a news server. Table 9-1 is a listing of some news servers for the Windows and Mac OS platforms.

Table 9-1 A sampling of NNTP servers

Name	*Platform*	*URL*
MCIS News Server	Windows NT	`http://backoffice.microsoft.com/`
DNEWS News Server	Windows 95, NT, Mac OS, others	`http://netwinsite.com/`
RumorMill	Mac OS	`http://www.share.com/peterlewis/rumormill/index.html`
Newstand	Mac OS	`http://www.imagina.com/`

One advantage to using a news server for conferencing is that visitors can leverage their existing knowledge of Usenet news: if they've wasted — er, I mean spent — thousands of hours in public news groups, they'll feel right at home navigating your own news groups. Of course, if they're news newbies (newsbies?), they'll be at the bottom of what can be a steep learning curve.

One drawback to using a news server, however, is that visitors must use a separate news client (or the news client built into Netscape Navigator and Microsoft Internet Explorer) to read and participate in your conferences. Your discussions don't appear to be as tightly integrated into your Web site as they do if you use one of the Web-based conferencing products covered in the next section.

Also, news-based conferences lack some of the convenience features that Web-based conferencing products provide, such as the ability to search for specific terms or for postings made on certain dates or by certain people. Unless you want to create a conferencing system that's integrated into the wild, wonderful world of Usenet, I recommend opting for a dedicated conferencing product rather than a news server.

Web-based conferencing: slick and powerful

Web-based conferencing products go well beyond the basic threaded discussions that news servers make possible. For an overview of the kinds of features they provide, see the Backgrounder sidebar, "What Kinds of Features Do Conferencing Products Provide?"

Here's a look at two of my favorite Web conferencing products.

O'Reilly & Associates's WebBoard (Windows)

O'Reilly & Associates's WebBoard (`http://webboard.ora.com/`) is a first-rate conferencing system that runs under Windows 95 and NT. That is, the conferencing software runs under Windows 95 or NT; any Web client can, of course, participate in conferences.

What Kinds of Features Do Conferencing Products Provide?

Some of the slick features you might find in a conferencing product include the following:

Registration. Visitors can register, giving themselves user names and passwords and optionally specifying personal information, such as their e-mail addresses and home page URLs. One benefit of registration is that the conferencing software can keep track of their visits and show only those messages that have been added since the last time they stopped in. Registration also enables you to compile a database of your site's participants, which can be valuable for marketing and research purposes. All conference packages also enable you to allow people to log in as guests — that is, without having to first register. You can also provide various levels of guest access. For instance, you might want to allow guests to browse conferences but require that they register in order to post messages.

Public and private conferences. You can designate some conferences as public or private. Any guest or registered user can participate in a public conference, but private conferences are restricted to only those users whose names you (or the conference administrator) specify. You can mix and match both types of conferences with a single product. You might have public conferences for your customers and private ones for your employees — or even for specific departments or work teams.

Read-only conferences. You can set up conferences in which anyone can read messages but only a certain person or group of people can post them. You might use a read-only conference to provide a daily news announcement or to post policy information.

Moderated conferences. You can configure a conference so that incoming messages have to be screened and approved by a moderator before they become available to everyone — handy for keeping a conference focused on its topic and for keeping out undesirable posts or posters.

Search features. Conferencing products provide search features that enable visitors to locate posts by typing words they're looking for or names of participants.

Logs and usage statistics. Enter the administration mode that conferencing products provide, and you can view statistics showing which discussions are attracting the most visitors. As with any log data, this information is priceless — you can use it to determine which topics your visitors are interested in and fine-tune your discussions accordingly.

Embedded HTML support. Most products enable visitors to include HTML tags in their postings so that HTML-savvy visitors can create their own formatting or include links to other sites. Most products also enable you to control which HTML tags you will allow in postings, so you can, for example, allow visitors to format their text but not include links to other sites.

WebBoard contains a built-in server, so you don't even need to buy or install an HTTP server to set up a conferencing area. If you already have a Windows server, you can also use it instead of WebBoard's built-in server.

WebBoard provides powerful, multithreaded conferencing features and all the niceties described in the preceding Backgrounder sidebar. But WebBoard doesn't stop there. It also provides such goodies as the following:

- "Top Ten" links that display a list of the top ten most popular topics and most active participates
- A "today's messages" link that displays those messages added on the current day
- An e-mail notification feature that enables visitors to receive an e-mail notifying them when new messages are added
- Support for file enclosures along with messages — a terrific feature for workgroup collaboration.

One of the things I like the most about WebBoard is the attractive user interface that it presents to visitors. Conferences, postings, and replies appear in a Windows Explorer-like outline format. For example, reply posts are indented from the post to which they reply, and you can expand and collapse the outline by clicking on tiny plus (+) and minus (-) signs, as shown in Figure 9-1.

WebBoard also provides real-time chat features that work with any JavaScript-compatible browser; I discuss these features in the section "Build Your Own Chat Rooms," later in this chapter.

Web Crossing (Windows and Mac OS)

Lundeen & Associates's Web Crossing is another powerful conferencing system. And it's a popular one — among the high-profile sites using Web Crossing are the *New York Times* (`http://forums.nytimes.com/comment/`), Salon 1999 (`http://tabletalk.salon1999.com/webx`), and Excite (`http://talk.excite.com/`). I also use Web Crossing for my own site's conferencing area, which I call "The Back Room."

Like O'Reilly's WebBoard, Web Crossing provides all the necessities outlined in the Backgrounder sidebar, "What Kinds of Features Do Conferencing Products Provide?" — and then some. A few of Web Crossing's unique talents — features it provides that WebBoard lacks — include the following:

- **Subscriptions.** Visitors can subscribe to specific conferences by tweaking their registration settings. Each time they visit, they can click on a Check Subscriptions buttons to see what's new in their favorite forums.

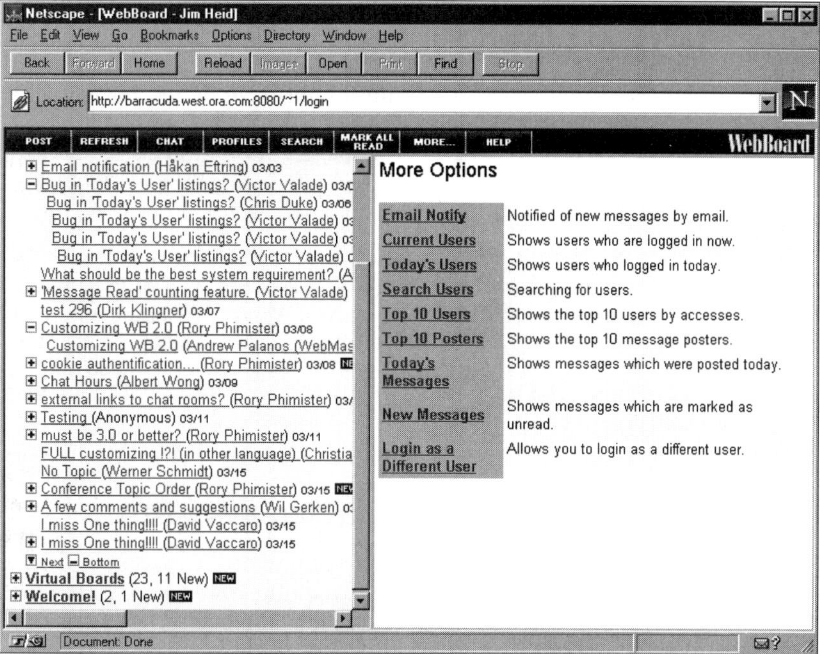

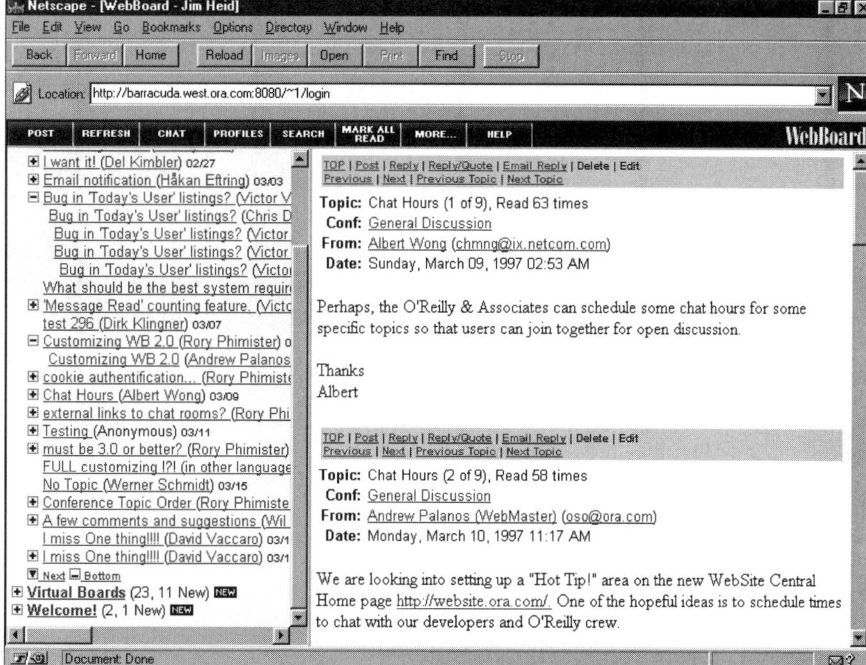

Figure 9-1: Conferencing with O'Reilly's WebBoard

- **A formatting and scripting language.** Web Crossing's Web Crossing Template Language (WCTL) is a simple scripting language that enables you to customize the appearance of your discussion area and more. WCTL provides `IF-THEN` conditional statements that you can use to test and respond to certain conditions — for example, if it's past noon but before 6:00 p.m., you can display a "Good afternoon!" message when visitors log in. You can also use WCTL to process and store data that visitors enter into HTML forms — to compile surveys, for example.
- **User pictures.** Visitors can upload their pictures and specify that they appear alongside their postings. It's a cute way of personalizing a discussion board. And who knows? Maybe arrogant users will be less likely to turn on the flames when they can see who's at the receiving end.

Web Crossing also provides a real-time chat feature; I'll have more to say about it later in this chapter.

Other conferencing alternatives

It's worth noting that several site-building products also enable you to create conferencing areas. Such products include Macromedia's Backstage family, Microsoft FrontPage 97, and NetObjects Fusion. To use these products' conferencing features, you must install their server extensions on your Web server.

The conferencing features these products provide generally fall short of their counterparts in dedicated conferencing products such as WebBoard and Web Crossing. And they require you to work within the site-building program's structure and limitations. Still, if you're already building a site with one of these products and if you don't need high-octane conferencing features or real-time chatting, it's worth trying out the conferencing features your site-building program provides.

And when you think about it, a discussion board is really a database that visitors are accessing and adding to. It stands to reason, then, that you can also create conferencing areas using the database-integration packages covered in the next chapter — products such as Cold Fusion from Allaire Corporation (`http://www.allaire.com/`) and Tango from EveryWare Development (`http://www.everyware.com/`).

On CD-ROM

Allaire has taken this concept to its logical conclusion by developing Allaire Forums, a conferencing system that runs under Cold Fusion. Allaire Forums is a full-blown conferencing system, sporting features such as conference subscriptions, e-mail notification, document attachments, and thread searching. A trial version is included on this book's CD-ROM.

On the Mac OS side, you can also create rudimentary conferencing areas with Maxum Development's NetForms forms-handling package, also included on this book's CD-ROM.

Secrets for Web conferencing software

Regardless of which conferencing software you use, there are ways you can make it better. This section is a collection of tips and secrets that apply to all conferencing packages. I've also tossed in some tips that show how to apply these tips to some of the products I've discussed so far.

Customize your conference area

All conferencing products provide predesigned pages that display the conferences, enable visitors to search, and so on. All conferencing products also enable you to customize the appearance of these pages. Do it! Give your conferencing pages a look and feel that's consistent with that of the rest of your site.

Simple customizing jobs might involve adding a company logo or site banner to the top of certain pages and changing the conferencing pages's background colors to be consistent with the rest of your site. More ambitious customizing projects might involve creating your own navigation buttons to replace the ones that come with the product, or even redesigning the way conference threads are presented.

Customizing WebBoard

O'Reilly's WebBoard provides such an attractive user interface that you just want to use it as-is. But there are a few customizing tweaks you might want to make.

WeBoard relies on a large collection of HTML files that control the appearance of its various screens. These files live in WebBoard's HTML directory (c:\WebBoard\Html), and are thoroughly documented in WebBoard's top-notch manual. You can open them in your favorite text editor and customize to your heart's content. But think twice about editing these files in a WYSIWYG text editor such as Claris Home Page or Adobe PageMill. Many of WebBoard's HTML files contain specialized WebBoard tags and scripts, and a WYSIWYG editor may corrupt these nonstandard codes, causing WebBoard to operate incorrectly. Before editing any WebBoard file, make a backup copy of a file and perform your surgery on the backup.

One simple change you might consider making to WebBoard's HTML files will make WebBoard's conferences a bit more attractive when viewed on Mac OS machines. WebBoard's HTML files use the `<FONT FACE>` tag to format conferences in the Arial font. (Specifically, the tag reads `<font face=Arial,Helv>`.) There's just one problem: There are no Mac OS fonts that go by the name Arial or Helv, so on Mac OS machines, conferences appear in the ubiquitous Times font. The fix: edit the tag to read: `<font face=Arial,Helv,Helvetica>`. This will cause Mac OS machines to format the text in Helvetica — another standard font on Mac OS systems. The benefit: The conference displays will look more similar across platforms. (See Chapter 5 for more details on the `<FONT FACE>` tag.)

Customizing Web Crossing

Lundeen's Web Crossing offers numerous customizing opportunities, most of which you can access through Web Crossing's browser-based control panel (see Figure 9-2).

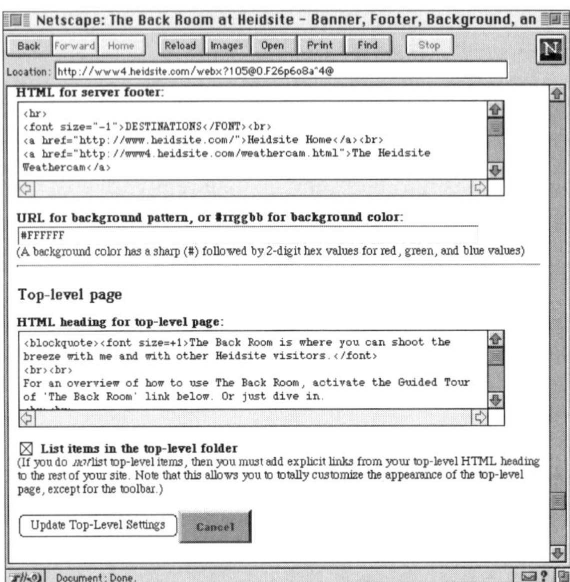

Figure 9-2: You can customize Web Crossing from any Web browser.

Some of the most basic tweaks you can (and should) make are available through the control panel link named "Banner, footer, background, and top-level page appearance." Click this link to add a graphic to the Web Crossing home page, to add navigation buttons to the bottom of each conferencing page, and to change the background color or add a background image for each conferencing page.

The fact that Web Crossing lets you make these tweaks from any Web browser is a plus when you're covering a live event from a remote location. For example, if you're covering a convention or event of some kind, you might create a new front-page greeting — complete with graphic — on each day of the convention, with links to conferences that relate to that day's events.

With Web Crossing's template language, you can completely reformat the appearance of conferences and discussions. You'll find all the details on the Web Crossing documentation (which is included, along with the trial version of the software, on the *HTML & Web Publishing SECRETS* CD-ROM).

Web Crossing is an ideal candidate for navigation button customizing; although it's an awesome conferencing product, its buttons aren't exactly fashion statements. Fortunately, a session with a graphics program such as Photoshop is all it takes to replace Web Crossing's stock buttons with your own. But note that it may be a long session — Web Crossing has nearly 50 buttons. Table 9-2 lists their file names, their alternate text (which appears on browsers whose image-loading option is turned off), and their purpose. All of these files are stored in the Images folder.

Table 9-2 Graphic-customizing opportunities in Web Crossing

File Name	*Alternate Text*	*Purpose*
access.gif	Access List	Create or change the access list
addcat.gif	Add Folder	Add a folder
addforum.gif	Add Discussion	Add a discussion
addlink.gif	Add Link	Add a link
addlive.gif	Add Chat	Add a chat area
cancel.gif	Cancel	Cancel
cancelsb.gif	Cancel Subscripts.	Cancel subscription (in this folder or discussion)
chkmoder.gif	Check Moderated	Check for messages to moderate
chksubs.gif	Check Subscripts.	Check for new messages
cnclsbtp.gif	Cancel All Subscripts.	Cancel all subscription
confernc.gif	Conference	Return to the conference (from a sysop area)
delcat.gif	Delete Folder	Delete a folder
delete.gif	Delete	Confirm deletion of a folder or discussion
delfrm.gif	Delete Discussion	Delete a discussion
editcat.gif	Edit Folder	Edit a folder
editfrm.gif	Edit Discussion	Edit a discussion
emlsysop.gif	E-mail to Sysop	Send e-mail to sysop
export.gif	Export	Export
gstlgin.gif	Guest Access	Request guest access
import.gif	Import	Import
login.gif	Login	Login as a user
lstpswd.gif	Lost Password	Send e-mail to sysop about lost password
newuser.gif	Register	Register as a user

(continued)

Table 9-2 (Continued)

File Name	Alternate Text	Purpose
nrwhelp.gif	?	Help (question mark)
ok.gif	OK	Accept
prefs.gif	Preferences	Change user preferences
pstmsg.gif	Post Message	Post a message (toolbar button)
pstmymsg.gif	Post My Message	Submit the message
search.gif	Search	Search for text
setprefs.gif	Set Preference	Confirm preference changes
smdel.gif	Delete	Small delete button for messages
smedit.gif	Edit	Small edit button for messages
smmore.gif	More	Small button to show more messages
smprev.gif	Previous	Small button to show previous messages
smrecent.gif	Recent	Small button to show recent messages
smtolast.gif	To Last	Small button to show last message
smtotop.gif	To Top	Small button to show first message
subscrib.gif	Subscribe	Subscribe (to this folder or discussion)
subscrtp.gif	Subscribe To All	Subscribe to everything
toctrl.gif	Control Panel	View control panel (visible to sysop only)

If you opt to perform this interface lift, be sure to keep all toolbar buttons the same size; ditto for all small in-line buttons (the ones Web Crossing displays next to messages, such as the Edit and Delete buttons).

And if your new buttons are larger or smaller than Web Crossing's originals, be sure to specify the new size in the sysop Custom buttons and Icons form. If you don't, the new buttons will appear distorted.

Web Crossing relies on several additional graphics that you might also want to customize; they're listed in Table 9-3.

Table 9-3 Web Crossing's miscellaneous graphics

File Name	Purpose
converse.gif	The discussion icon
guest.gif	Default image for guest posts
live.gif	The chat icon
link.gif	The hyperlink icon
pathdiv.gif	The path divider icon
site.gif	Icon for backpath display
topic.gif	The folder icon

Back up your conference databases

Of *course* you back up your server frequently. Sure you do. Backing up HTML files is important, but it's utterly essential to back up the databases that conferencing products use to store user information and the conferences themselves. If you don't back up for a week and then the product's database is corrupted, you risk losing not only a week's worth of postings but also registration information for visitors who joined up during that period. You'll get e-mail from confused visitors who wonder why the system isn't accepting their passwords (answer: because it no longer knows about them). You'll get e-mail from irate visitors who will complain that several day's worth of interesting discussion has vanished. You'll spend a lot of time apologizing. Take it from someone who's been there: back up your conferencing product's databases *often*.

Each conferencing product takes its own approach to storing user information and conferences. For example, Lundeen's Web Crossing stores both user registrations and conferences in a single file named webx.db. You can have Web Crossing automatically make a backup copy of this file by using the Backup option in the Web Crossing control panel. But be sure to copy this backup file to another disk — it won't do you any good if your conference server's hard disk dies.

How much power should users have?

All conferencing products enable you to specify the degree of privileges that registered visitors have. For example, you can enable registered users and/or guests to create their own conference topics, or you can prohibit this and enable them to only participate in existing topics.

Think twice about enabling users to add their own discussion topics. In my experience, when people can create their own topics, they're less likely to post questions and comments in existing topics that may well be more appropriate locations. For instance, I have one conference topic on my site entitled Digital Video, in which people discuss all matters relating to —

yes! — digital video. But I found that visitors were creating new topics relating to digital video in *other* areas of my conferencing board, even in areas that had nothing to do with digital video. So, I tweaked Web Crossing so that users could only add to existing conferences, not create their own.

The moral: You can't force people to adhere to the structure of your conferences, but you can steer them in the right direction.

Should you allow links?

A related issue concerns the use of HTML within conference text. Most conferencing products support embedded HTML: conference participants can do rudimentary text formatting, create hypertext links to other sites, and even embed graphics. Is this a good thing? It depends. When you open up a conferencing topic and find a raunchy picture whose link was added by a mischievous 15-year-old, the answer is probably no. (If it's yes, then I don't want to know what your conferencing topic is.)

And even if your visitors aren't the type who would create links to alt.binaries.nasty.raunchy, you might not want them creating links to external sites whose content you can't control. Links to external images can even slow down the perceived performance of your conferencing area — if an external site is offline, busy, or otherwise unavailable, visitors will experience delays while their browsers attempt to contact it.

The answer: configure your conferencing software so that embedded HTML tags or external links aren't permitted. In WebBoard, you can use the Allow Active Links and Images step in the Add Conference wizard. Or, you can use the Manage Conferences window to change the settings of an existing conference. In Web Crossing, you can set separate link privileges for registered users and guests. Use the Web Crossing control panel's Registered User Access and Guest User Access options to set these privileges.

Creating links to your conferences

Once you've created your conferencing area, modify your home page and your navigation bars to include a link to the conferencing area's main page.

But don't stop there. Consider creating links to *specific* conferences in relevant places throughout your site. For example, each month on Heidsite (`http://www.heidsite.com/`), I post a new installment of a section I call HotMedia, which is a Web-based companion to the monthly "Media" column I write for *Macworld* magazine. In each HotMedia page, I include a link to a discussion area that I create for whatever topic I've covered in my column. This enables visitors who want to discuss or ask questions about the topic to go directly to its conference (see Figure 9-3).

This technique has paid off in a larger number of conferencing participants. The moral: Make it easy to people to get to a specific conference topic. Rather than simply linking to your conference area's front page, put links to specific conference topics on any pages that relate to that topic.

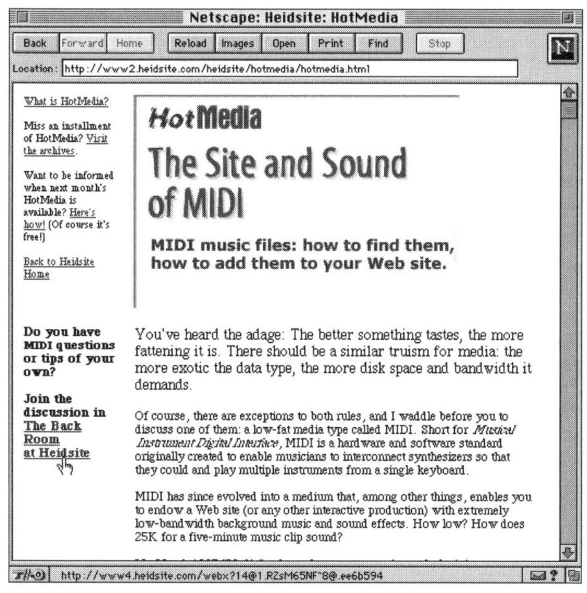

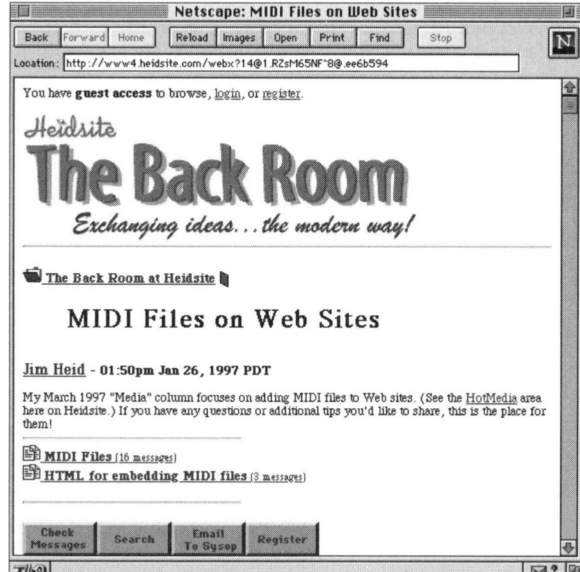

Figure 9-3: Each HotMedia page (top) contains a link to its related conference topic (bottom).

Creating these topic-specific links isn't exactly straightforward. The problem is that conferencing products assign their own URLs when you create a new conference topic, and these URLs aren't what you'd call reader-friendly. A typical Web Crossing URL might read `http://www4.heidsite.com/webx?13@1.fcFw8rhP^78@.ee6b379/151`. I'd like to hear one of MSNBC's anchors rattle *that* off on the air.

The solution: Create your conference topic, and then use your Web browser to copy its link location. Go to the conference topic, select the URL in the Location box at the top of the browser window, and then choose Copy from the Edit menu. Next, go into your HTML editor and paste the URL.

Register your conferencing area

If your conferencing area is on a publicly accessible Web site, consider registering it with Forum One (`http://www.forumone.com/`). Forum One is a Web site search engine devoted specifically to Web conferencing — think of it as the Yahoo! of conferencing areas. On Forum One's Web site, visitors can search for forums by entering keywords, or they can browse a directory of forums organized into categories: current events, entertainment, sports, and so on.

Lundeen & Associates has a special partnership with Forum One whereby participants in Web Crossing-based conferences can automatically search Forum One from within Web Crossing's Search page. It's a cool feature that enhances Web Crossing's already considerable appeal.

The secrets of moderation

You've shopped around, you've bought a conferencing product, and you've installed it on your server. Now comes the hard part: creating a virtual meeting place that people will want to visit not once, but over and over again.

The key to success with a conferencing area is to keep the discussion alive. The best way to do that, of course, is to discuss interesting topics. But it also helps to have a good *moderator.*

Moderation basics

If you're just getting started, there's a good chance that you'll be doing your own moderation. As the moderator, you have several duties, which include the following:

- Keeping the conversation going
- Seeding the discussion when it slows down
- Refocusing the group if the discussion gets off the topic
- Creating the board's sense of community by making visitors feel welcome to participate in the discussion

Do you have to have a moderator? Of course not — you could just let things take their own course, but this could lead to discussions petering out or diverging to topics that have nothing to do with you or your site. This could destroy the sense of community you're trying to achieve. A moderator can help to set the tone and keep people interested and the discussions focused.

A forum moderator must also be part diplomat. If one person is dominating the discussion or discouraging people from participating, you may want to step in and give others a chance to throw in their two-cents' worth.

A moderator can also be a traffic cop. In both WebBoard and Web Crossing, you can set up a conference as moderated, which means that new postings must be approved by the moderator before being available to everyone. In Web Crossing, you can even specify a list of objectionable words — any posting containing one or more of them is automatically not posted, but first routed to the moderator.

Sometimes the discussion may wander off the topic, but some members of the group will want to participate in the new topic. When this occurs, you have three choices: start a thread on this new topic, start a new discussion for this topic, or ban the off-topic material. The third choice is the riskiest one of the three — it risks annoying the board's participants by making them feel censored or constrained. A moderator who annoys visitors risks lose visitors.

How to handle anarchists

A common challenge involves people who decide to pursue their own topics in a conferencing area. You need to gently uproot these anarchists so the other participants can continue to discuss the board topic. To do so, you can simply suggest a more appropriate discussion group for the current topic, or maybe a private discussion on the topic rather than a public one.

There often seem to be a few people who try to dominate a discussion. When faced with a domineering person, try using the following strategy. First, take that person aside and privately ask him or her to let others into the discussion. If this doesn't work, you may have to resort to removing the perpetrator from the discussion altogether. A moderator can forcibly remove the person by deleting all the messages posted by the offending party. All commercial conferencing products also allow you to deny access by login name, e-mail address, or IP address.

When you remove a person from a discussion, it's best to do it privately. It's not a good idea to get into a shouting match in public. This just diminishes your credibility and bolsters the power of the offending party.

Discussion group maintenance (or, keeping the flames turned down)

As the moderator, you need to watch over the discussion group by keeping track of its messages. You will decide when to post related messages to the board and when to remove undesirable messages. As I mentioned previously, you can have boards without moderators, but this “anything goes” approach can lead to anarchy.

Alas, in the world of online conversation, anarchy can often lead to *flame wars:* volleys of less-than-kind messages often containing words you probably wouldn’t want Mom to read. Here’s where your diplomat’s hat will earn its keep, and where that old summer job as a tightrope walker will come in handy. You need to carefully balance the importance of free speech with the need for common decency.

So how much of your life will discussion-moderation consume? You can expect to spend a few minutes per day moderating a single discussion group. As groups grow and become more active this may become more time consuming, but generally you shouldn’t have to spend hours moderating a discussion.

Encouraging etiquette

Useless or tasteless messages do more than destroy your online community — they take up resources on your server. Your job as moderator is to keep this junk out. Occasionally you need to remind visitors of basic board etiquette. You might want to advise visitors in private, or you might prefer to post a generic message than any newcomer can read. In either case, be gentle. It’s easy to forget that a lot people are new to this technology and don’t know the correct etiquette. Be a mentor to new visitors, teaching them the rules and etiquette without embarrassing them.

Build Your Own Chat Rooms

In a conferencing area, conversations between participants take place over time. In a chat room, participants talk with each other in real time. Real-time chatting allows people to have live conversations about a topic. Like a party, a real-time chat can be very intense — or very boring. It all depends on who’s gathered together and on what they’re talking about.

Low-cost chat options

There are several high-end chat servers available for high-volume, industrial-strength chat applications. But most of us don’t need chat servers capable of handling hundreds of rooms containing thousands of chatterboxes. Most of us need a simple chat facility that can handle modest traffic and is easy to implement and inexpensive.

The good news is that several such options are available. As I mentioned earlier, O’Reilly’s WebBoard and Lundeen’s Web Crossing both provide real-time features. There’s also a completely free option called EarthWeb Chat.

All three options rely on Java applets or JavaScript to provide real-time chatting without requiring a specialized chat server. Given that both Netscape Navigator and Microsoft Internet Explorer support Java and JavaScript, these options give you access to most of the people on the Web today.

Let's take a closer look at what each has to offer.

WebBoard chatting

When setting up a WebBoard conference, you can designate that chatting be available for that conference. (You can also enable or disable chatting for existing conferences by using the WebBoard administration mode.) When setting up a chat room, you can choose whether to allow active links and images in the chat stream. For some advice on whether to choose this option, see the section "Should you allow links?", earlier in this chapter.

WebBoard also provides an optional chat-logging feature that lets you create disk-based record of everything that happens in the chat room. This can be very useful for recording brainstorming sessions or chats with celebrities or industry luminaries, but it might not be appropriate for chats that deal with, shall we say, more personal themes. WebBoard's manual wisely recommends that you inform visitors if you activate chat logging.

WebBoard provides a useful feature that lets you insert HTML documents, called *chat spots,* into the chat stream at regular intervals or at random intervals. You might use chat spots to provide regular reminders of chat rules or upcoming events to chat participants, or you might use them to provide advertisements. Because chat spots are based on HTML files, they can include graphics. WebBoard enables you to serve up to 255 different chat spot documents.

Web Crossing chatting

In the base version of Web Crossing, only five users can chat simultaneously — that's more of a chat closet than a chat room. You can buy a license for up to 100 simultaneous chat users or up to 250 simultaneous users. By setting up optional *fanout* servers, you can create industrial-strength chat areas that, according to Lundeen & Associates, can handle 100,000 simultaneous users. See the company's Web site (`http://www.lundeen.com/`) for pricing details.

As mentioned earlier, Web Crossing relies on a Java applet for real-time chats. As Figure 9-4 shows, the applet displays chat room participants and text in a format that's very similar to that used by online services such as America Online as well as Internet Relay Chat (IRC) clients.

True to the chat room metaphor, Web Crossing enables you to set up rooms with multiple "tables." Each table appears as a separate list of users on the right-hand side of the chat applet. Visitors to a multitable chat room can table-hop — move from one table to another in search of a discussion that's of interest to them.

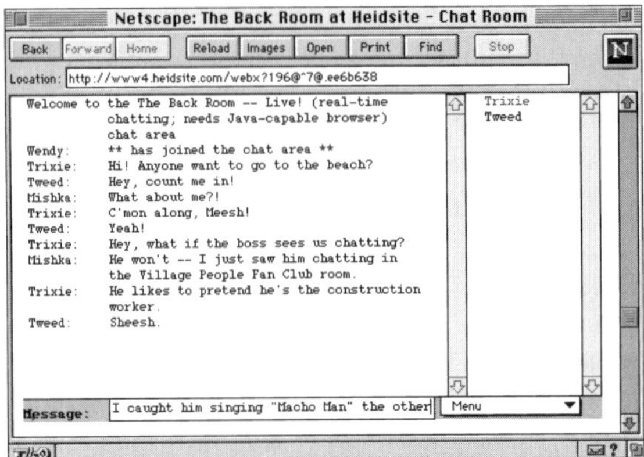

Figure 9-4: Chatting with Web Crossing

Web Crossing also enables you to set up auditorium-style events, in which a host and selected participants can broadcast to an audience. And you can apply Web Crossing's user-registration and access-privilege features to, for example, make real-time chatting available only to people who have registered in your Web Crossing-based conferencing area.

EarthWeb Chat

The easiest and cheapest way to add chat capabilities to a Web site is to use EarthWeb's Java-based EarthWeb Chat (`http://chat.earthweb.com/`). To implement EarthWeb Chat on your site, go to `http://www.chatplanet.com/` and click the Start Your Own Chat Room link. From there, you must fill out a licensing form containing your e-mail address, the name of the proposed chat room, and a brief description of the chat room. This information goes into a database that visitors to the ChatPlanet Web site can search.

After you supply the required information, EarthWeb sends you an e-mail containing HTML code that you paste into the page where you want your chat room to appear. This HTML code will resemble that shown in the following source code:

```
<APPLET CODEBASE="http://c1555.channels.chatplanet.com/chatplanet-
codebase" CODE="eweb.chat.ChatApplet.class" WIDTH="640" HEIGHT="400">
<PARAM NAME="boot" VALUE="NULL">
<PARAM NAME="channel" VALUE="My Chat Room">
<PARAM NAME="host" VALUE="c1555.channels.chatplanet.com">
<PARAM NAME="port" VALUE="5030">
<PARAM NAME="style" VALUE="default.style">
</APPLET>
```

After you paste this code into a page, your chat room is ready to go.

How can EarthWeb offer free chatting? For one thing, your chat page will have EarthWeb's advertisements on it. For another, EarthWeb would like to become so fond of its chat features that you purchase one of the fee-based chat options that the company offers, options that provide for custom logos and graphics and no advertising. And maybe you will. But even if you don't, it's worth exploring EarthWeb's free chat service. It doesn't offer all the control that you get in products such as WebBoard and Web Crossing, but as the old saying goes, you can't beat the price.

How to keep the conversation flowing

Once you've set up your chat room you must decide on topics for your chats. As with a conferencing area, you want topics of interest to your site's visitors and that help build a sense of community. Setting up a Web site to support a product? Schedule real-time chats with support engineers or the product's designers. Covering an event such as a convention? Consider scheduling chats with exhibitors and keynote speakers.

Inviting experts or celebrities to your chat room is a great way to entice visitors to stop by and ask questions or just listen in. Michael Jackson brought in an all-time high of roughly 16,000 visitors during his appearance in an America Online chat room. Doing these types of events once a month or so will generate repeat traffic. But note that Michael's schedule is busy, so book him early!

If your chat area is successful, your visitors will get to know one another over time, and you will have a living, breathing community on the Internet. But remember: content is king, and it's up to you to keep conversations going. If no one is talking in your virtual party, your guests will fetch their virtual coats and head for the virtual door. As with discussion groups, it helps to have somebody seeding the discussions, getting people involved in conversations, and pulling the shy ones out of their shells. One way to do this is to have a greeter in each chat room that types out a "Hi!" every time somebody enters the room. A friendly greeting helps breaks the ice and invites the visitor to respond in some way.

VR chat: the next generation

The most exotic of the new communications media combine interaction and exploration by providing chat features within virtual reality spaces. Several companies have developed 3D chat technologies that create virtual meeting places: you can enter a representation of a 3D space, navigate toward a group of people, and start typing or even talking. This is not your father's chat room — it's George Jetson's.

Like so many Web technologies, many VR chat tools are a bit rough around the edges, and both the tools and the technologies are evolving faster than a time-lapse movie. And as is often the case, the coolest tools can have discouragingly stiff connection-speed or hardware requirements. Still, we're on the cusp of a brave new online world, one where pages are being joined by places.

How VR chat works

From its terminology to its implementation, VR chat is delightfully futuristic. Before entering a VR space, you choose an *avatar*, an on-screen character whose image represents you in cyberspace. Upon entering a VRML chat space, you see the avatars for other people in that space. Approach them, and you can begin chatting.

OnLive! Technologies' OnLive! Traveler

The most drop-dead impressive VR chat browser is OnLive! Technologies' (`http://www.onlive.com/`) OnLive! Traveler, which supports voice-based chat: no typing, just talking — and as you speak, your avatar's mouth moves (see Figure 9-5). OnLive! Traveler provides dimensional stereo sound: if a group of avatars is chatting to your left, their voices come from your left-hand speaker. And as you approach the group, their voices get louder.

Figure 9-5: Face to...face? Chatting with OnLive! Traveler.

OnLive! spaces also make great use of graphics and background sound to create dangerously addictive virtual worlds. When working on this chapter, I used OnLive! Traveler to conduct some virtual interviews with OnLive! support technicians. I knew a new era had arrived when, in a follow-up call to the company, I heard myself saying, "I just wanted to confirm some things that a tech-support avatar told me."

To set up a OnLive! chat world of your own, you need the OnLive! Community Server, which is currently available for Windows NT 3.51 and 4.0 (as well as several variants of UNIX). The Community Server supports up to five simultaneous chatters when connected to an ISDN line, and up to 75 when connected to a dedicated T1 line. But don't worry — your visitors don't need fat pipes to connect. OnLive! supports two-way voice chat on connections as slow as 14.4Kbps.

There is one piece of bad news about OnLive! Traveler — it's available for Windows only, and runs only on Pentium-based machines. (OnLive! says that its voice-compression technology uses floating-point math routines that are specific to the Pentium chip.) OnLive! says they may do a Mac OS version someday, but hasn't committed to a specific timetable. Thus, by setting up an OnLive! Traveler-based VR chat area, you're leaving out a significant percentage of the Web-surfing public.

OnLive! Text Server

It's worth mentioning that OnLive! also provides a text-based chat server that doesn't discriminate against Mac OS machines. OnLive! Text Server runs on the Windows 95 and NT platforms and provides real-time, text-based chatting as well as a conferencing board system. The real-time chat window works on any Java-supporting browser, and provides a cute little array of icons that chat participants can insert into the text stream (see Figure 9-6).

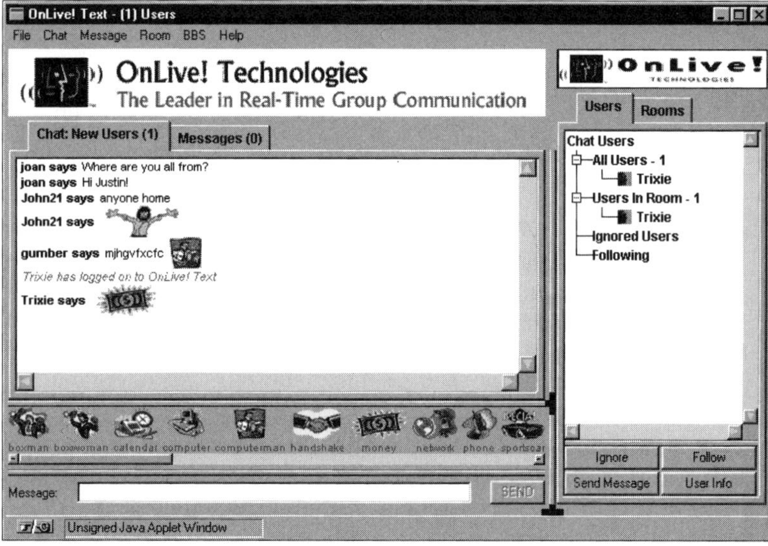

Figure 9-6: Express yourself with icons with OnLive! Text Server's real-time chat features.

Other VR chat contenders

I'm fondest of OnLive! Traveler's approach to VR chat, but OnLive! isn't alone in the VR chat world. If you're interested in pursuing the leading edge in chat, you might also want to investigate the following:

- **Black Sun Interactive's Cybergate** (`http://www.blacksun.com/`). Cybergate relies on a Netscape Navigator plug-in module called Passport to provide VRML-based worlds with text-based chatting. Passport also enables surfers to explore other VRML-based sites. The server software runs under Windows NT and UNIX.
- **The Palace** (`http://www.thepalace.com/`). The Palace uses two-dimensional avatars and text-based chatting. Each chatter's text appears in a little, cartoon-like balloon adjacent to its avatar. Inexpensive personal servers supporting up to 50 simultaneous are available for the Windows, Mac OS, and UNIX platforms. Commercial servers require UNIX.
- **Fujitsu Software Corporation's WorldsAway WebWorlds** (`http://www.worldsaway.com/`). WorldsAway WebWorlds is a relative newcomer to the Web-based VR chat scene. WorldsAway was originally developed to be a service within the CompuServe online service; WorldsAway WebWorlds is the technology's Web variant. WorldsAway. WebWorlds chatting is text-based, but enhanced with 3D avatars that can "pick up" objects and give (or sell) them to each other.
- **Worlds Inc.'s Active Worlds** (`http://www.worlds.net/`). Active Worlds is a set of VRML-based development tools for creating and serving 3D interactive spaces. The server runs under Windows NT and is available in configurations supporting between 20 and 1,000 simultaneous users. A free, three-user trial version is available from the company's Web site.

A Simple 'Push' — E-mail List Servers

The problem with living on the edge is that it's easy to fall over the edge — that is, to fall victim to a brand-new technology's drawbacks, such as stiff system requirements or proprietary browsers or plug-ins. With this in mind, let's step back from the precipice and end our tour of community-building techniques with a simple technology that, strictly speaking, doesn't even have anything to do with the Web.

I'm talking about e-mail list servers. A list server is a program that automatically broadcasts e-mail to people who sign up, or *subscribe,* to a given mailing list. People subscribe to the list server by sending an e-mail containing a `subscribe` command, as shown in Figure 9-7.

You might set up a mailing list to enable people to share ideas and tips about a particular product or technology, or you might set up one in order to transmit a weekly newsletter or send out announcements. Chapter 8 contains more examples of ways to use a mailing list; in this section, I'll describe the technical and administrative issues behind list serving and describe some Windows and Mac OS list server software.

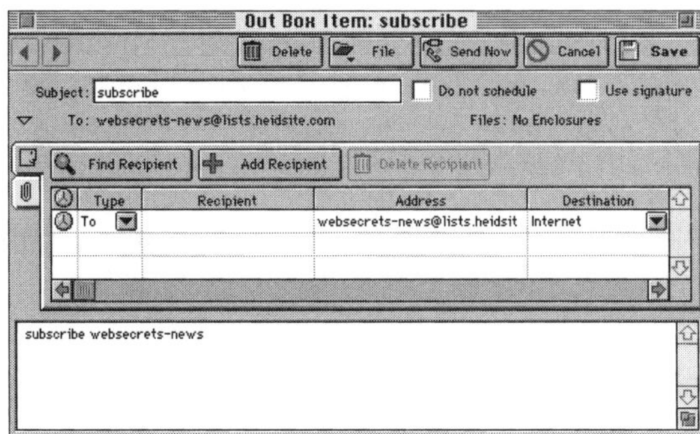

Figure 9-7: Subscribing to a mailing list. The subscribe command is typically put in the body of the message.

One-way versus two-way lists

There are two basic flavors of mailing list:

- **One-way.** Also called a *broadcast list*, an *announcement list,* or a *one-to-many* list, a one-way list permits postings only by the list administrator. Subscribers aren't permitted to post messages.
- **Two-way.** With a two-way list, anybody on the list can send messages to the entire list. Some list servers even enable non-subscribers to make postings.

Each flavor of list has its own applications.

When to use one-way lists

One-way lists are great for announcements, news releases, newsletters, and other instances when you want to control content and don't need or want a response. Indeed, one-way lists are an easy, low-cost form of "push" technology — one of today's hot buzzwords and markets. It remains to be seen how the heavily hyped push market will evolve, but you can have the basic benefit of push technology — delivering content to people instead of making them come to you for it — through one-way mailing lists.

How a one-way list works

In a one-way list, the administrator is the only person who can actually send messages to the subscriber list. The administrator sends a message addressed to the list name or to a private e-mail account associated with the list, and the list server automatically forwards it via e-mail to all of the subscribers to the list.

When to use two-way lists

Two-way mail lists resemble conferencing areas. Two-way lists are used for technical support and discussion forums of all kinds.

How a two-way list works

In a two-way list, any subscriber can post a message to the list; he or she does so by sending the e-mail to a list's address, which might be something like `websecrets-talk@lists.heidsite.com`. (That is, in fact, the address of a two-way mailing list that I've set up for this book. I invite you to join it; see the section, "So Can *We* Talk?", later in this chapter.) When the list server receives the message, it rebroadcasts it to all of the list's subscribers. Subscribers can then comment on the posting by sending e-mail to the list address, and the whole process repeats.

A busy mailing list can result in a large number of individual e-mails cluttering up subscriber's mail boxes. For this reason, most lists also offer a *digest* subscription option, which subscribers can join by sending a subscribe digest command to the list server. With a digest, the list server compiles all postings into a single e-mail and then sends it to all subscribers at a specified interval, such as once a day. A digest makes for less clutter in subscribers' e-mail boxes and can also make it a bit easier to follow the trail of a conversation. On the downside, because a digest is usually sent only once a day, it lacks the immediacy of a conventional subscription.

How to run a mailing list

Here's a collection of tips and secrets for running an effective mailing list.

Naming your list

One of your first decisions is what to name your mailing list. It's common, though by no means required, to include the word *talk* in a mailing list — for example, `websecrets-talk` (this book's two-way list). Many listmasters prefer the letter *L* — for example, `Direct-L` (a terrific list for Macromedia Director users; to subscribe, send `SUBSCRIBE DIRECT-L your-full-name` to the address, `listserv@uafsysb.uark.edu`).

In any event, keep the list name short, sweet, and to the point. List names appear in an e-mail program's From field and column, and a long-winded name won't appear in its entirety.

Building a subscriber list

You can build a list in two ways: people can sign up themselves, or, as the list moderator, you can manually add them.

Most mailing lists are of the first variety. A person signs up to the list by sending an e-mail message addressed to the list name; for example `websecrets-news@lists.heidsite.com`, including the word *subscribe* in the body or subject of the message. The list server then sends an automated response to the sender informing him or her that he or she has been added to the list. This automated response usually also includes basic information on how to send posts to the list and how to cancel a subscription.

To cancel his or her subscription, the person sends another e-mail, this time putting the word *unsubscribe* in the subject or body of the message.

Making Sign-Up Easier with Subscription Forms

Imagine if, to subscribe to a magazine, you had to write a letter containing specific words in specific places. If that's how the publishing industry worked, you can bet *TV Guide* wouldn't be the well-read publication that it is. No, magazines are easy to subscribe to because all you have to do is fill out a simple form — you know, the kind that fall out of a new issue and litter the library floor.

You can make your mailing list easier to subscribe to by providing an HTML form for visitors to fill out. Such a form might look like the one in Figure 9-8.

One way to process a form such as this is with a server CGI that takes form input and then transmits its contents as an e-mail. Set up the CGI to transmit an e-mail to your list server, which will think that the e-mail is coming directly from the would-be subscriber.

On the Mac OS side, several CGIs can turn form-submitted data into an e-mail; two examples are Net.Dream's FlexMail (`http://www.netdreams.com/net.dreams/software/index.html`) and Maxum's NetForms (a trial version of which is included on the CD-ROM that accompanies this book). On the Windows side, O'Reilly & Associates's outstanding PolyForm, also included in trial form on this book's CD-ROM, can have you up and running in a few minutes.

If you're feeling ambitious, you might want to create a form that enables visitors to subscribe to the digest version of a list, to unsubscribe, and to get help. Use radio buttons to provide these options, and then have your forms-handling CGI e-mail the appropriate results to your list server.

If you don't want to futz with forms, here's an easier way. Most list servers accept commands located in either the main body of the message or in its Subject field. Create a Web page containing a collection of `mailto` tags, one for each list available. Append the `subject` attribute to the `mailto` tag, and the subject — in this case, the command that you want to send to the list — will automatically be inserted into the Subject field. The code below creates a `mailto` link that enables visitors to subscribe to this book's discussion list.

```
<a href="mailto:requests@
lists.heidsite.com?subject=
subscribe websecrets-talk">
Subscribe to the WebSecrets-
Talk list</a>
```

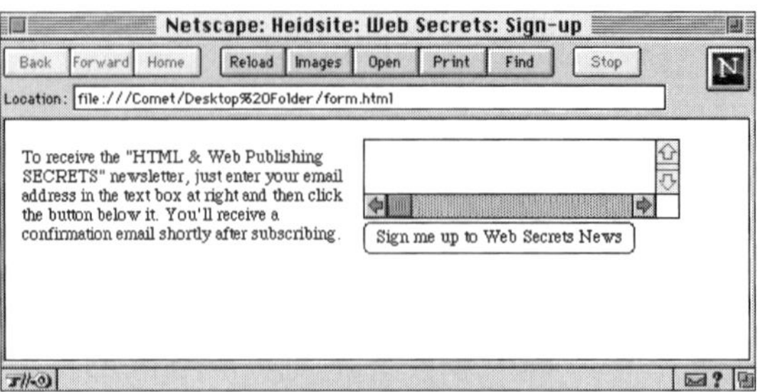

Figure 9-8: A simple list server subscription form. Top: the HTML source. Bottom: the result.

To moderate or not?

Like conferencing boards, two-way mailing lists can be moderated or unmoderated. The moderator, also called the *administrator* or more informally the *list mom,* performs the same basic job that a discussion moderator performs: screening incoming messages and then either posting them to the list or sending them to that great Recycle Bin (Windows) or Trash can (Mac OS) in the sky.

Moderating a small mailing list doesn't take up much of your time, but moderating an active list can. And you don't want to ignore this duty — if you wait too long before posting subscribers' messages, the messages will get stale and the subscribers will lose interest.

Providing confirmation, help, and other hand-holding

All list servers enable you to set up a variety of confirmation, information, and help files that subscribers or would-be subscribers can receive by e-mailing special commands, such as `info websecrets-talk`. These files are often called *auto-responder* files or *auto-replies.*

The confirmation and help files are the most useful — to your subscribers and to you. By containing essential information on a list's purpose, its rules and regulations, and its commands, confirmation and help files can streamline a list's operation and spare you many an e-mail from confused subscribers.

A confirmation e-mail is what subscribers receive after signing up for the list. It should start out with a welcome message and then briefly summarize the list's purpose and its rules and regulations. It should also include a sentence suggesting that the subscriber keep a copy of the confirmation e-mail for future reference. You might also want to include instructions for subscribing to the digest version of the list and for unsubscribing.

As for the help file, it should contain instructions for subscribing to the list's normal and digest modes; for posting messages to the list; and for unsubscribing. You might also want to include a frequently asked questions (FAQ) list that succinctly summarizes the list's operation and contains other information you think subscribers should have (see the Backgrounder sidebar, "How to Give Your Subscribers the FAQs").

While it's important to include essential information in your auto-reply files, brevity is also a good idea. The shorter your replies are, the more likely it is that people will take the time to read them.

How to Give Your Subscribers the FAQs

To explain the ins and outs of your list to new subscribers, consider including a frequently asked questions (FAQ) list in your subscription confirmation, help, or information files.

FAQ Style

Keep it concise. People look to FAQs for quick answers to common problems. Keep the questions and answers short and concise. This is not the place for press releases or hype.

Make it complete. The information in a FAQ should stand alone. It's okay to include references to your Web site in your FAQ, but try to provide an answer in the FAQ itself if possible.

FAQ Questions

Where do you get the questions? Any common question that gets sent to the Webmaster is a good candidate — remember, it's a list of *frequently* asked questions. The FAQ might also contain answer to questions you receive in your non-Web service areas as well — for example, questions that your telephone support or field-service representatives might receive.

There's also a place for some infrequently asked questions, too — queries that may not directly concern the topic of the mailing list or Web site. Such off-topic questions and their answers might resemble the following:

Q: I found your site while looking for company XYZ's site. Do you know where it is?

A: The XYZ site can be found at http://www.xyz-co.com. We are sorry for the misunderstanding. But please remember us if you find yourself in the market for a left-handed smoke shifter.

Q: I was very impressed by the fast-loading graphics on your site. Could I ask who created them?

A: Photography was by XYZ photography with image processing and compression by our talented in-house design staff.

You can also use a FAQ to provide diplomatic but deliberately vague answers to questions that, for one reason or another, you don't really want to answer.

Q: Who is the model on the front of your catalog and where does she live? I'm in love!

A: The ABC Agency provided the models for our catalog photos.

Q: What is the company president's home phone number?

A: In order to protect the privacy of our employees, we do not give out personal information.

Make your FAQ detailed, but don't try to anticipate every possible question. Don't bother writing questions and answers for arcane topics that have never come up. Take a page from a politician's play book: if someone isn't asking a question, don't volunteer an answer. You'll make your job a lot easier.

Getting the word out

After your mailing list is up and running, tell people about it so they can subscribe. Add a page advertising the list to your site and put links to this page on appropriate Web pages. If you've created a list to support a commercial product, consider adding a mention of the list to your print advertising and even your letterhead.

If there's a certain group of people who you think will benefit from the list, you might want to send e-mail to let them know about it. You might even want to send a message to an existing list to spread the word even further. But be careful — send such e-mails indiscriminately, and you might be accused of *spamming* — the justifiably despised act of sending junk e-mails or cross-posting a message to numerous newsgroups regardless of its relevance.

L-Soft, makers of a highly regarded list server package I'll describe shortly, has a great backgrounder on the evils of spamming; you can read it at `http://www.lsoft.com/spamorama.html`.

Creating a list archive

In a conferencing system, messages are stored and newcomers can pick up on a discussion thread by working their way back in time through existing messages. A mailing list doesn't offer this permanence. But you can provide it by creating an archive of the mailing list's contents and making it available for searching on your site.

To create an archive of a mailing list, import the list's postings into a database manager, and then tie that database to your Web site using one of the database-publishing products described in the next chapter. You can import each individual posting to the database as a separate record, or create a daily digest of the list and import that. Importing individual postings provides more flexibility, as it enables visitors to your site to locate and follow discussion threads by searching for all postings containing a particular set of characters in their Subject field.

On the Mac OS side, Blue World Communications's (`http://www.blueworld.com/`) MailArchiver is a terrific tool for creating a database archive of e-mail. MailArchiver automatically archives e-mail into a FileMaker Pro database, and works with all popular e-mail programs, including Claris Emailer and Qualcomm's Eudora. MailArchiver even includes a template that lets you set up searchable mail archives.

Give me that document: e-mail on demand

A variation on the mailing list theme involves using a list server to enable people to request that text or binary documents (photographs, formatted word processor files, spreadsheets, and so on) be e-mailed to them. Called *e-mail on demand*, it's a convenient way to enable people to request and obtain documents.

You've probably used a fax-on-demand system at least once. You dial a phone number and then use a menu to request that a document be faxed to you. You enter your fax number and a while later, your fax machine starts its warbling song.

E-mail on demand works similarly. To request documents, people send e-mail to your e-mail-on-demand server, which then replies with an e-mail accompanied by the document attached as an enclosure.

To set up an e-mail-on-demand server, you need a list server package that supports auto-replies containing enclosures. Not all list servers are up to the task. For example, StarNine's ListSTAR enables you to create as many auto-reply messages as you need, and each have its own enclosure. Fog City's LetterRip doesn't provide these features.

E-mail on demand is a simple solution to document or even software distribution. Many companies are finding that e-mail on demand is ideal for internal document distribution. A company might use e-mail on demand to enable employees to retrieve policy papers, technical documents, and template files. An employee sends e-mail to the intranet's list server, and a few moments later, a Microsoft Word document arrives in his or her mailbox. It's an ideal way to deliver frequently updated documents without printing costs and without having to discard an inventory of outdated printed material.

Making it easier to request documents

As an alternative to making people send e-mail to receive documents from the e-mail-on-demand server, consider creating a Web page containing a form that enables visitors to choose documents by clicking on check boxes. This is the slickest way to enable people to request documents via e-mail, but making life easier for them does mean more work for you: you must set up a CGI of some kind to act on the choices that visitors make in the form. For an overview of some CGIs that can handle this sort of task, see the Secrets sidebar "Making Sign-Up Easier with Subscription Forms," earlier in this chapter.

The `mailto` tag tip that I described in that sidebar also applies nicely to e-mail on demand. You can set up a Web page containing a collection of `mailto` links, one for each document available through the e-mail-on-demand server. Figure 9-9 shows a sample.

```
The following documents are available for your enjoyment.<BR>
<BR>
<A HREF="mailto:lists@heidsite.com?subject=cats">Why Cats Will Lose
the Battle for
Global Domination</A> (24K Microsoft Word file)<BR>
<A HREF="mailto:lists@heidsite.com?subject=beans">Lima Beans:
Nutritional Goldmine
or Evil Plot?</A> (14K Microsoft Word file)<BR>
<A HREF="mailto:lists@heidsite.com?subject=calories">Your Hourly
Calorie Intake Planner</A>
(54K Microsoft Excel file)<BR>
<A HREF="mailto:lists@heidsite.com?subject=teri">Teri Hatcher versus
Eva LaRue</A>
```

```
(439K Photoshop file)<BR>
<A HREF="mailto:lists@heidsite.com?subject=trixie">Trixie at the
Beach</A> (1.4MB
QuickTime movie).
```

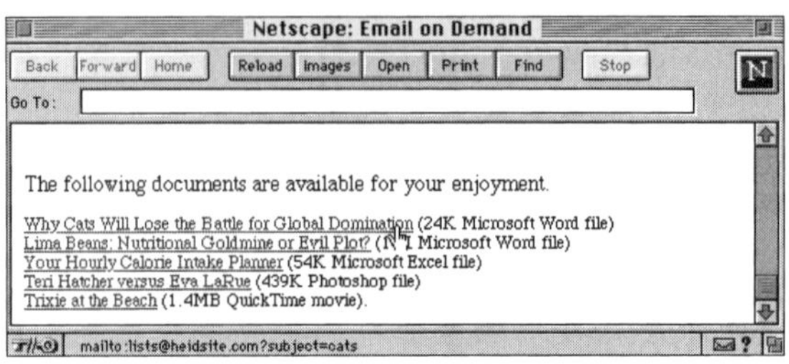

Figure 9-9: Using mailto tags to present a catalog of available documents. Top: The HTML source. Bottom: The result.

Surveying list server software

Numerous list server packages are available for both the Windows and Mac OS platforms. In this section, I'll spotlight some free as well as commercial offerings.

L-Soft's LISTSERV family (Windows)

L-Soft International's (`http://www.lsoft.com/`) LISTSERV is a popular family of list servers available for Windows 95 and Windows NT and also most flavors of UNIX (a Mac OS version is also in the works). The head of the family is LISTSERV Classic, which traces its origins back to 1986. Among its users thousands of users is c|net (`http://www.cnet.com/`), which runs LISTSERV Classic under Windows NT to delivers over 200,000 e-mail messages per day to over 1.7 million subscribers. Now *that's* a mailing list. (To see a full database of publicly accessible lists that are served by LISTSERV, visit `http://www.lsoft.com/lists/listref.html`.)

LISTSERV Lite is an entry-level list server for small to mid-size sites that want to host a mailing list but don't need the industrial-strength features that LISTSERV Classic provides. Two versions of LISTSERV Lite are available: a commercial product and a freeware version for non-commercial use. The Free Edition offers the same features as the commercial product but supports a maximum of 10 mailing lists containing up to 500 subscribers each. You can use the Free Edition provided you don't derive a profit, directly or indirectly, from doing so. (L-Soft's Web site describes the company's policy on this in detail.)

LISTSERV is powerful, but it isn't pretty. Although the LISTSERV programs run under Windows 95 and NT, they don't provide graphical user interfaces. You create and manage lists by typing commands in a DOS window, as shown in Figure 9-10.

```
SMTPW
Auto
28 Mar 1997 08:33:01 From LISTSERV@WWW3.HEIDSITE.COM: help
*
* LISTSERV(R) version 1.8c - most commonly used commands
*
* Info       <topic|listname>         Order documentation
* Lists      <Detail|Short|Global>    Get a description of all lists
* SUBscribe  listname <full name>     Subscribe to a list
* SIGNOFF    listname                 Sign off from a list
* SIGNOFF    * (NETWIDE               - from all lists on all servers
* REView     listname <options>       Review a list
* Query      listname                 Query your subscription options
* SET        listname  options        Update your subscription options
* INDex      <filelist_name>          Order a list of LISTSERV files
* GET        filename filetype        Order a file from LISTSERV
* REGister   full_name|OFF            Tell LISTSERV about your name
*
* There are more commands (AFD, FUI, PW, etc). Send an INFO REFCARD for a
* comprehensive  reference card,  or just  INFO for  a list  of available
* documentation files.
*
* This server is managed by:
*   jim@heidsite.com

Enter your command:
lists
```

Figure 9-10: What year is this? L-Soft's LISTSERV's command-line interface.

If you don't relish a journey back in user-interface time, you might consider Shelby Group's Lyris or one of the Mac OS-based list servers I discuss later in this section.

SECRET

Running a Mailing List Without a List Server

A list server's ability to automatically add and remove subscribers and broadcast e-mails is a tremendous time-saver, but you can run a small list without one. If your subscriber base is fairly stable, you can use your e-mail program. The address book features in most of today's e-mail programs enable you lump collections of individual e-mail addresses into *groups*. Simply create a group containing your subscribers' e-mail addresses. When it's time to send out a new edition of your Village People Fan Club Zine, just specify the group as the addressee.

Many e-mail programs provide sophisticated mail filtering features that enable the program to automatically perform specified activities when certain criteria are met — such as when a Subject line contains a specific piece of text. You can use mail filters to automate the aspects of list serving that would otherwise be handled by a list server. For instance, you could set up a filter so that when a message starts with the word "help," your e-mail program replies with your list's help file.

But even the most sophisticated mail filters can't handle the grunt work of adding and removing subscribers to a list or of compiling a digest. A list server is still the only choice for extremely active, rapidly evolving mailing lists. But an e-mail program is a great way to test the waters of light-duty list serving.

Shelby Group's Lyris (Windows)

Lyris lacks many of the industrial-strength features that LISTSERV provides, but it atones by wrapping its list-serve features around a nicely designed, browser-based user interface. Indeed, Lyris is unique among list servers in that it provides a Web-based front end that enables visitors to subscribe to mailing lists, contribute to them, and read messages sent by other members (see Figure 9-11).

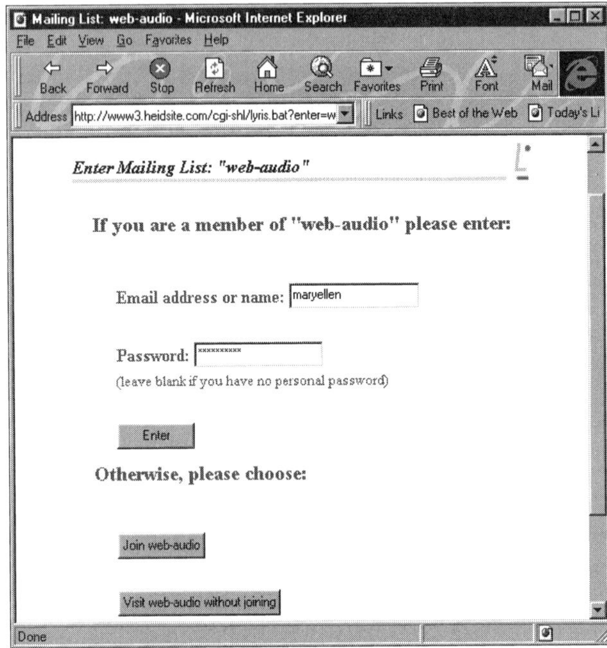

Figure 9-11: The Lyris browser-based user interface.

At this writing, the Lyris server is available for Windows 95, Windows NT, and IBM's OS/2. Versions for the Mac OS and several UNIX variants are in the works.

A freeware version of Lyris supports up to two mailing lists containing up to 50 members each. You can download this version at `http://www.lyris.com/`. Commercial versions that support more users and provide more features are available; you can find current pricing information and other details at the Lyris Web site.

StarNine's ListSTAR (Mac OS)

StarNine's ListSTAR is a full-featured list server for Mac OS machines; a trial version is included on the CD-ROM that accompanied this book. ListSTAR is an industrial-strength list server, and can be correspondingly difficult to set up. ListSTAR relies on a series of *rules* — sets of actions and results that control what ListSTAR does when it receives commands and postings. For example, one rule handles subscriptions, another handles postings, while still another handles digests.

Because creating and working with rules can be difficult, ListSTAR includes several list configurations that you can duplicate and then modify to suit your needs. Even so, don't expect to be up and running within minutes.

But there is a payoff for climbing ListSTAR's learning curve: the program provides features that no other Mac OS-based list server can match. One example is ListSTAR's excellent support for Apple's AppleScript system-level scripting technology. You can set up a ListSTAR rule so that it runs an AppleScript routine upon receipt of a command, a capability that comes in handy for advanced e-mail-on-demand applications. For instance, you could use AppleScript in conjunction with a database manager to create a real-time report-on-demand feature: a visitor could request a current inventory report, and through AppleScript, ListSTAR would run a database manager, retrieve the requested data, and send that data back to ListSTAR to send, via e-mail, to the person who requested the information.

Hardware for Serving Your Mailing List

Regardless of the list server software you use, it's a good idea to run the list server on a separate machine other than your primary Web server. Besides simplifying setup and eliminating a possible security risk (the mail socket), doing so eliminates the performance and resource drag the list server might otherwise impose on your Web server.

What kind of computer does a list server need? The answer depends in part on the volume of traffic your list receives, but generally, you don't need a high-performance speed demon to run a list server. In fact, you can manage a modest set of lists using an old 80486 box or a Mac IIcx.

The Mac OS platform is particularly flexible in this regard. You couldn't hope to boot Windows 95 or NT on an old, 80386-based PC, but Mac OS 7.5.5 runs (or at least trots) on a 16MHz, 68030-based Mac IIcx. Take my word for it: I serve the mailing lists for this book and my Web site using a rusty but trusty IIcx and Fog City Software's LetterRip list server.

Fog City's LetterRip (Mac OS)

Fog City Software is the creator of Claris Emailer, one of the most popular e-mail client programs in the Mac OS world. (A Windows version of Emailer is in the under development, and anyone using Windows should take a look at it. Visit Claris' Web site at `http://www.claris.com/` for details.)

One of the things that makes Claris Emailer so wonderful is its combination of powerful and an attractive, approachable user interface. Fog City has applied this same happy formula to its list server package, LetterRip. The name may be a bit corny, but the software is outstanding, a breath of fresh air in a software category where cumbersome user interfaces and complex setup routines are common.

You can perform nearly every aspect of list management using the four commands in LetterRip's Setup menu. The Mail Lists command enables you to set up new mailing lists and subscriber lists. Within this window's four tabbed dialog boxes, you can specify general list settings, edit auto-reply responses, specify that a digest be created, and activate or deactivate moderation (see Figure 9-12).

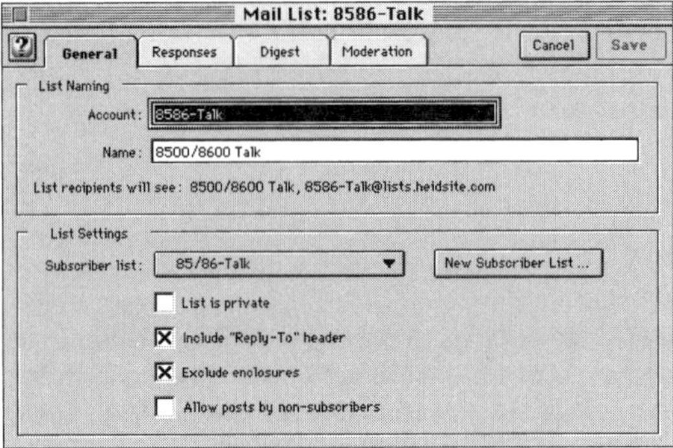

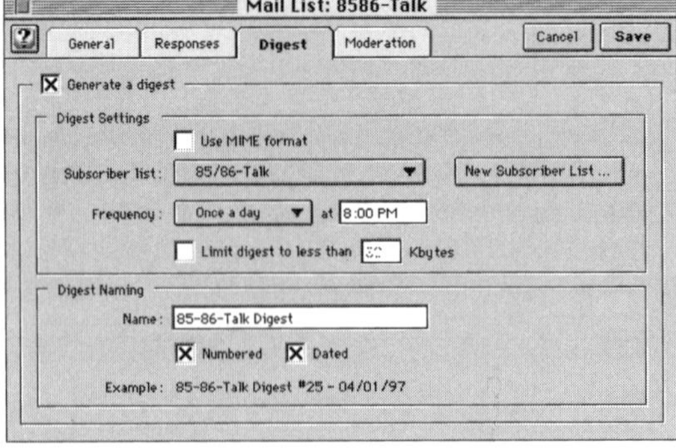

Figure 9-12: One-stop shopping: setting up a list in LetterRip

With the LetterRip Administrator utility, you can administer a LetterRip server from a remote machine, creating new lists, managing existing ones, and working with the server log. On my network, I run the LetterRip server on an ancient Mac IIcx that doesn't have a monitor or keyboard connected, handling administration by running the LetterRip Administrator on a remote machine.

LetterRip doesn't have all the high-octane list server features of ListSTAR. It can't, for example, include an enclosure with an auto-reply response, so it isn't suitable for creating an e-mail-on-demand service. Nor does LetterRip allow you to create additional auto-replies; you're limited to the basic ones built into the program.

But what LetterRip lacks in high-end features, it more than makes up for in ease of use and low cost (at $295, LetterRip is less than half the cost of ListSTAR). It's the easiest list server available — for any platform.

Two freeware Mac OS list servers

On a tight budget? Want to set up a simple list server for personal use? Here are two freeware Mac OS-based list servers you might want to try.

Note, however, that both of these programs require that you also run mail server software, such as Apple's free Apple Internet Mail Server, or AIMS (available at `http://applenet.apple.com/`). AIMS runs on any 68040 or PowerPC-based Mac OS system. By comparison, ListSTAR and LetterRip don't require a separate mail server; each provides a built-in SMTP (Simple Mail Transport Protocol) server.

MacjorDomo

Michele Fuortes' MacjorDomo is available for downloading at `http://leuca.med.cornell.edu/Macjordomo`. (If that URL gets you nowhere, try `http://hofdi.med.cornell.edu/Macjordomo`.) Although Macjordomo's name sounds a bit like Majordomo, the Perl- and UNIX-based granddaddy of Internet list servers, it isn't a Mac OS port of Majordomo. Rather, it's an honest-to-goodness Mac OS application that provides all the basics you'd want in a list server, including customizable auto-responders, the ability to import and export subscriber lists, and complete logging features.

AutoShare

Mikael Hansen's AutoShare is available for downloading at `http://www.dnai.com/~meh/autoshare` and also through Mac freeware and shareware distribution sites. AutoShare packs a broader array of features than does Macjordomo, including full AppleScript and Frontier scripting support, remote administration via e-mail, and support for enclosures.

So Can *We* Talk?

Conference areas, real-time chat rooms, list servers — there's no shortage of ways to establish a two-way dialog with your site's visitors. I'm trying to practice what I've preached in this chapter by setting up a conferencing area and a mailing list for this book. I encourage you to visit this book's Web site (`http://websecrets.heidsite.com/`) and check them out — or better yet, start a conversation.

See you in cyberspace.

Summary

- Conferencing areas, chat rooms, list servers, and e-mail on demand are powerful tools for building an online community.
- Discussions boards are great for on-going discussions, for technical support, and for inter-office communications.
- Real-time chat rooms have the advantage of immediacy. But like a party, whether they're interesting or not depends on who's in attendance and on what they're discussing.
- List servers provide a simple, low-cost way of implementing conferencing and providing "push" delivery of news and announcements. With e-mail on demand, list servers also enable you to make documents available via e-mail.
- Online communities are prone to the same personality conflicts and disputes that can arise in real communities. As a moderator for a conference, mailing list, or real-time chat, you often have to wear a diplomat's hat to deal with difficult personalities, to steer the discussion in a particular direction, and to make sure that everyone gets a chance to be heard.

Chapter 10

Dialing for Data: Searching and Database Publishing

In This Chapter

- How to make your Web site searchable
- Databases and Web sites: a marriage made in heaven
- Choosing and using Web database publishing tools
- Performance secrets for creating fast Web database applications
- Converting graphics stored in a database — on the fly

Next-generation Web sites go beyond static HTML pages to provide timely, dynamically updated, searchable content — which is often stored in databases. This chapter discusses how to enable your site's visitors to dial for data. Much of the Windows-related insights come from Adam Block of PC World Online, a site whose underlying databases dish out daily news, tips, and stories from the magazine. — Jim Heid

Previous chapters stressed the importance of good site planning and design: creating a sensible site hierarchy, creating navigation bars and buttons, and so on. All of this is important, but one day the site will reach the point where navigation buttons and site maps just aren't enough. Visitors will wear out their mouse buttons and their patience as they click their way through the site in search of that single tidbit of information that brought them there in the first place.

When that moment comes — or better yet, *before* it comes — it's time to think about adding a search facility. Search features enable visitors to locate information on their own terms. Rather than haplessly clicking until they either stumble on the page they need or they give up and go elsewhere, visitors can type in a few keywords or a phrase, click a Search button, and view a list of pages that (hopefully) contain relevant information.

This chapter addresses site searching from two perspectives. First, I'll look at the issues, programs, and techniques involved in adding a search feature to a site. Then I'll move on to address the "dialing for data" issue from a different angle: linking a database manager to a Web site to enable visitors to browse, locate, update, and enter information stored in a database such as Microsoft Access or Claris FileMaker Pro.

How Search Software Works

There are many different products and techniques behind making a site searchable. But most search strategies have two key components in common. One is a search CGI application, a program that accepts text that visitors enter into browser forms, conducts the search, and returns the results to a visitor's browser. Each possible find, or *hit,* is displayed as a hyperlink, enabling a visitor to go directly to that particular page. One visit to a major search site such as Yahoo! or AltaVista is all it takes to see this process in action.

For a search CGI to work its magic, another component must first come into play: an *indexer.* This is a program that scans all of the pages that make up the site and creates a compact database containing keywords from each page. When visitors conduct a search, the search CGI searches this index, not the original HTML pages. This enables much faster, more accurate searches.

Many Windows and Mac OS Web server packages include indexing and searching software; many additional products are available from third-party developers. Some are even free — one excellent Mac OS search CGI, Apple's awkwardly named Apple e.g., costs nothing more than a download. I'll have more to say about Apple e.g. later in this chapter.

ON CD-ROM

Searching for Something? Start Here

The *HTML & Web Publishing SECRETS* CD-ROM contains multiple searching and database-publishing utilities and demo packages, including the following:

- **Allaire's Cold Fusion (Windows).** A trial version of the outstanding Web database-publishing tool.
- **iHound (Mac OS).** One of the best Mac OS Web-searching tools available.
- **FlatFiler and FindFile (Mac OS).** FlatFiler is a freeware WebSTAR plug-in that makes it easy to Web-publish data stored in tab-delimited text files. FindFile lets visitors search for and download files stored on your server.
- **Tango for FileMaker Pro (Mac OS).** From zero to Web in under a minute: There isn't a faster way to Web-enable a FileMaker Pro database. Try dancing the Tango for yourself.
- **Phantom (Mac OS).** Try out the Mac OS world's best Web robot.
- **Lasso (Mac OS).** The fast and free Lasso Lite WebSTAR-format plug-in lets you search FileMaker Pro databases. Its commercial cousin, Lasso, adds database-modification features.

Four steps to searching

Each of these searching tools has its own operating style, but the basic steps you perform to implement a search facility are the same regardless of the one you choose.

1. **Run the indexer to generate an index of the site's pages.** Some indexers have options that enable you to specify what types of documents you want to index and how you want to index them. For example, it's pointless to index the contents of graphics files on your site, because a text display of them would look like gibberish. Many indexers also enable you to specify that some directories or folders be omitted from the index. And because your Web site's contents are changing as pages are added and updated, many indexers also have options that let you specify that the index be automatically updated at regular intervals — such as at 2:00 a.m. each morning, when your site's traffic is probably low.
2. **Design the HTML form that visitors will use to enter the text they're looking for.** Most indexing tools include a canned form design that you can modify by adding your own custom headers, footers, and navigation elements. Or you might create your forms in an HTML editor and then import them.
3. **Test the form, the CGI, and the index.** Before you make your search facility available to visitors, you want to make sure it's working. You do so by installing the CGI on your server and trying out a few searches using the form you created in the previous step. When you're convinced that everything is working properly, you're ready to...

4. **Add a link to your site's pages that enables visitors to access the search form.** Where should you put a link to the search page? Everywhere! Make the link a standard part of every navigation banner or bar, and put one in a prominent place on the home page, too. It's also a nice idea to put one on the error page that your server returns when a visitor requests an nonexistent URL. This lets visitors who get a "file not found" error message to jump directly to the search page.

Building a Search Feature: Windows

Let's take a look at the process of adding a search feature to a Windows-based site — specifically, to one being served by O'Reilly & Associates's outstanding WebSite or WebSite Professional packages. (You can learn more about the WebSite family in Chapter 17.)

If you're going to be using a different Windows-based server package, you might still want to read this section to get a feel for the process and to pick up some tips that apply regardless of the server software you use. And if you're a Mac Webmaster, feel free to skip on to the section "Building a Search Feature: Mac OS," later in this chapter.

WebSite includes two programs that address each of the two phases involved in building a search facility. For indexing, WebSite includes a program named WebIndex. For searching, WebSite includes a CGI called WebFind.

Building an index with WebIndex

Building an index with WebIndex is a breeze. You simply specify the directories you want to index and click OK, as shown in Figure 10-1.

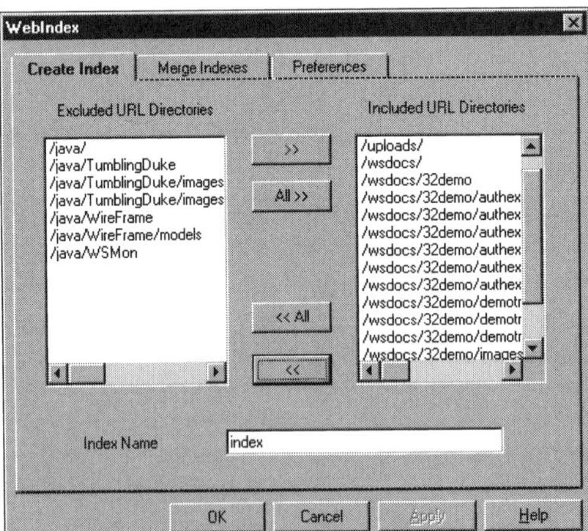

Figure 10-1: Choosing directories for indexing in O'Reilly's WebIndex

You might be tempted to click the All button and index every single directory in the site. Resist the urge. Think about the way you've structured the site's directories. If you're storing images in a directory named Graphics, for instance, omit it from the index.

And before you generate the index, you might want to click the Preferences tab and tweak WebIndex's preferences settings (see Figure 10-2). Think about the documents your directories contain. Are there file types that you want to omit from the index? Might you want to tweak the list of words to omit?

Testing your search feature

After you generate the index, you can test it out. Start up WebSite and type `http://www.your_domain_here/cgi-bin/webfind.exe`. The canned search form built into WebSite's WebFind program appears, as shown in Figure 10-3.

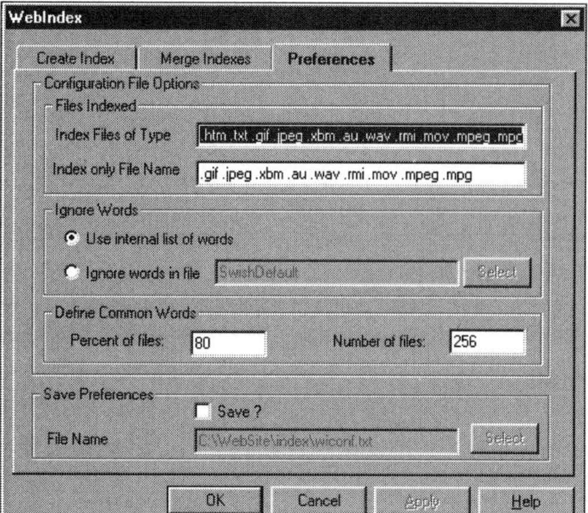

Figure 10-2: Fine-tuning the WebIndex preferences

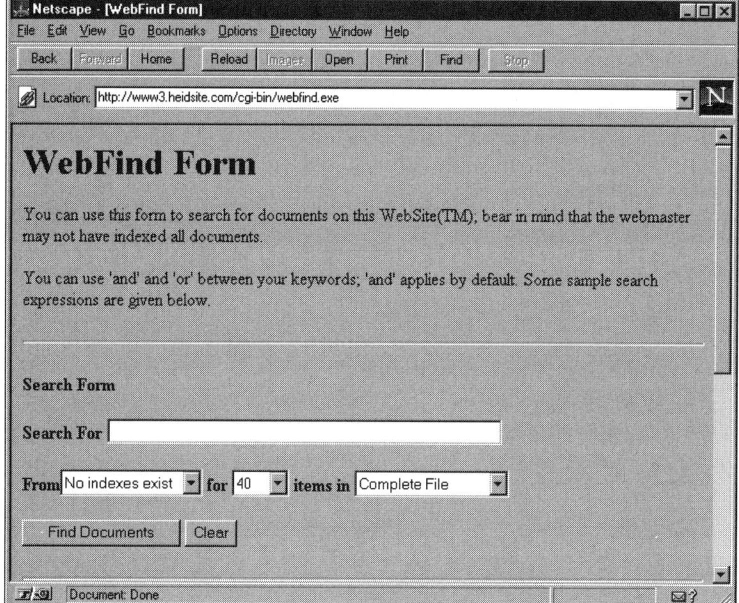

Figure 10-3: WebFind's canned search form

Type a word or phrase that you know is present somewhere in the site and click Find Documents. If everything is working, you will get a list of pages containing the search text. You can jump to a specific page by clicking its link.

Building a custom search form

WebFind's canned search form is fine for testing, but it isn't exactly gorgeous. You'll want to create your own customized search form, one whose appearance is consistent with the rest of your site — similar banner graphics, background color, navigation devices, and so on.

To create your own search page, you can use the Form Wizard that accompanies WebSite's WebView program. Here's how:

1. Use your favorite HTML editor to open the page on which you want the link to the search page to appear. (For instance, if you want to add a search link to a page named *index.html*, open the file named *index.html*.)
2. Navigate to the spot where you want the link to appear, and then create it. For example:

```
<a href="search.html">Search this site</a>
```

3. Use WebView's Find command to locate broken links. (In the Find Node dialog box, clear any text from the text area and then check the Broken check box.) WebView will place an X adjacent to the page named search.html.
4. Select this page, right-click on it, and then choose Wizards from the pop-up menu. The Select Wizards dialog box appears.
5. Click the FindForm wizard and then click OK. The dialog box shown in Figure 10-4 appears.

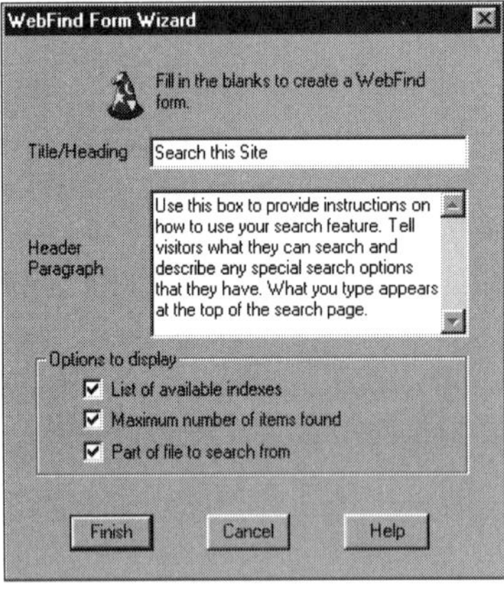

Figure 10-4: The WebFind Form Wizard's dialog box

6. Type some text that will help visitors understand how to use your search feature. If you include additional options that enable them to select which index they want to search, describe what those indexes are.
7. Configure the check boxes at the bottom of the wizard's dialog box as appropriate for your site. If your site has only one index, uncheck the List of Available Indexes box — there's no reason to clutter up the page and confuse visitors by providing a pop-up menu with just one option.

Similarly, if you expect that most visitors will want to search the complete document (as opposed to just its heading or title), uncheck the Part of File to Search From box. As for the Maximum Number of Items Found box, I recommend always leaving it checked — let your visitors decide how many search hits they want to see.

8. After you've tweaked the wizard's dialog box to your heart's content, click Finish. WebView creates the search form (see Figure 10-5).

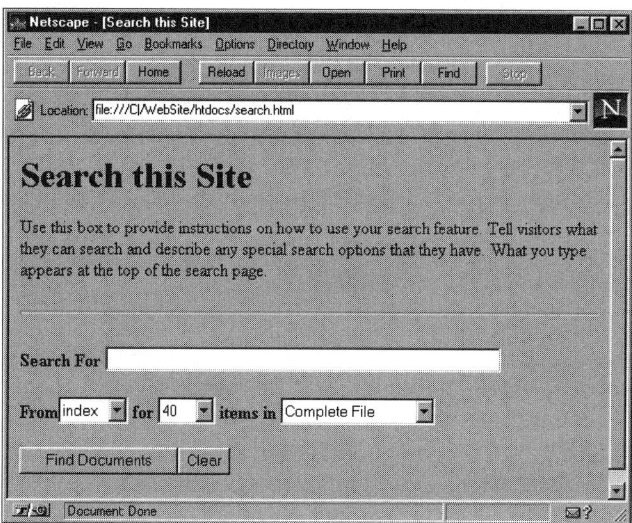

Figure 10-5: A completed WebView search form

Customizing the search form

You've created a search form containing your own help text, but it still isn't exactly a visual masterpiece. To fix that, open up the search form using your favorite HTML editor and customize it. Add some graphics consistent with your site's design, and change the background color to the same color you use for your other pages. Add some navigation links that enable visitors to go elsewhere if they decide not to conduct a search after all.

To give your site a polished look, go beyond the canned search form that a search engine creates for you. Take the time to customize the page so that its appearance is consistent with the rest of the site's.

Adding a search capability to other pages

Creating a search page and putting a link to it is a great idea, but you might want to go a step further: add a search field directly to certain pages, such as the site's main home page and key section home pages.

Here's how: Use an HTML editor to open the search page that you created in the previous step, and then select all of the HTML code between the <FORM> and </FORMS> tag, including those tags themselves (see Figure 10-6).

Copy this text to the Clipboard, and then paste it into the HTML pages on which you want it to appear. Now your visitors will be able to conduct searches without having to click their way to a separate search page.

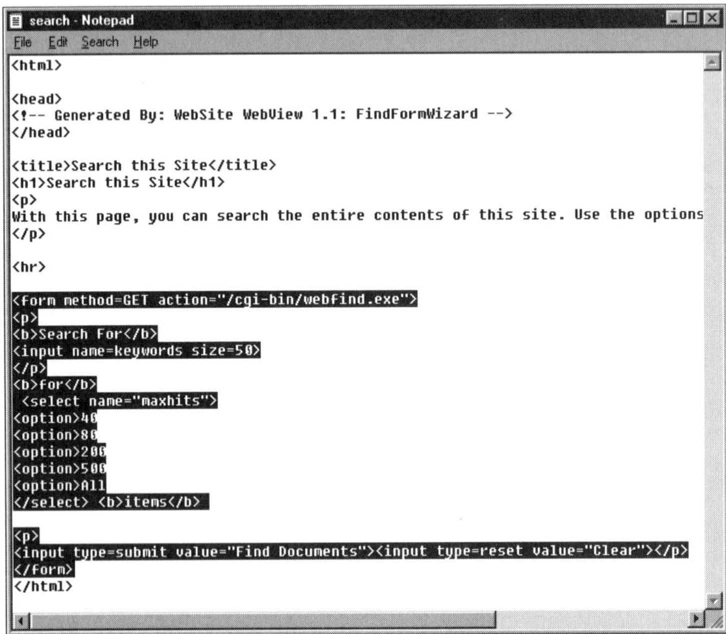

Figure 10-6: Select the search form's HTML before copying it to the Clipboard.

More Windows search tools

The previous section highlighted WebSite's search and indexing tools because they're easy to use and because the WebSite family is popular among Windows Webmasters. But for all its popularity, WebSite shares the Windows server market with some big companions, including Microsoft and Netscape. This section spotlights the search tools you'll find in Netscape's and Microsoft's servers.

Netscape's search alternatives

Netscape Enterprise Server includes a version of Verity's well-regarded Information Server search engine. You can create a search collection — a group of documents reviewed by the software and ready to be searched — by simply clicking the Index Documents button in the Administration Server.

Fill in the appropriate fields to determine which directories are assigned to the named collection; you should set the Insert Documents box to *.html if you only want to index your HTML files. Once indexing is complete, you can access your search page at `http://www.mycompany.com/search/iaquery`.

The Administration Server also provides a tool to schedule regular reindexing of your documents; this feature is useful if the contents of your site change frequently. Instructions for customizing search forms and the output of the results set can be found in the Enterprise Server manuals. (See Chapter 17 for more information on Netscape Enterprise and Administration Servers.)

Microsoft's Index Server

Microsoft's Internet Information Server (IIS) does not come packaged with a search system, but you can download Index Server for Windows NT from Microsoft's Web site at `http://www.microsoft.com/ntserver/info/indexserver.htm`.

Index Server sets itself apart from the other search engines by enabling you to catalog not only HTML documents, but also formatted Microsoft Word and Excel files. This functionality might enable visitors to your site to search through sales information spreadsheets by specifying the selling region that they are interested in, for example, or select a Word file based on its author.

Index Server uses a special scripting language and so-called Internet Data Query files to define these searchable elements. Installation is straightforward and includes a number of examples; if you wish to review the documentation before downloading Index Server, you can find it at `http://www.microsoft.com/ntserver/search/docs`.

Maxum Development's Phantom

Later in this chapter, I describe Maxum Development's Phantom, a Mac OS-based Web robot that can index not only your own site but any other site on the Web as well. As this book was going to press, Maxum shipped a Windows 95/NT version of Phantom. If you're interested in setting up your own equivalent to Digital's AltaVista — albeit perhaps on a smaller scale — you might want to jump forward to the section "Maxum's Phantom: a Web robot." The Windows version is identical to its Mac counterpart.

Commercial search technologies for hire (or for free!)

Search sites such as Digital Equipment Corporation's AltaVista (`http://altavista.digital.com/`) and Excite Inc.'s Excite (`http://www.excite.com/`) have become essential stopping places for Web surfers on the prowl for information. There's good news: Both companies have made their search technologies available to Web developers who want to incorporate searching into their sites.

Exciting searches from Excite

Excite Inc.'s search software is called Excite for Web Servers (EWS), and runs on Windows NT-based servers. And get this: it's free. Excite Inc. requires that you include a link to its site somewhere on your site, and it offers a variety of fee-based support programs.

Excite Inc. touts EWS's "concept-based searching" features. To quote the company, "When EWS goes through its indexing process, it uses probabilistic techniques to analyze the interrelationships between words within a collection of documents." Oh. While that concept may not be crystal clear, EWS has become a popular search tool for Windows NT-based sites. To see EWS in action, visit the EWS home page at `http://www.excite.com/navigate/`. Or check out any of the many sites that are using it, including *InfoWorld* magazine's InfoWorld Electric site, at `http://www.infoworld.com/`. You can also see a complete directory of sites that use EWS at `http://www.excite.com/navigate/community.html`.

The view from AltaVista

AltaVista's commercial search products include the AltaVista Search Intranet Private eXtension, a search engine geared toward intranet applications. This product, which runs on Windows NT servers (as well as under Digital's UNIX for Alpha workstations) indexes all of the HTML and plain-text files on an intranet site, making them available for searching. To learn more about it, visit `http://altavista.software.digital.com/`.

Building a Search Feature: Mac OS

There's a healthy selection of search software available for Mac OS machines. I'll start out this section with a look at a package that I've been using on Heidsite for some time with excellent results: Apple's free Apple e.g. Then, I'll provide an overview of some other search options.

An overview of Apple e.g.

Apple e.g. is available for downloading from the Apple e.g. Web site at `http://www.cybertech.apple.com/apple_eg.html`. Apple e.g. runs on PowerPC- and 680X0-based Mac OS machines. Note that at this writing, Apple considers Apple e.g. a beta-release product and doesn't provide any support for it. However, there is an Apple e.g. mailing list; you can join by sending e-mail to `listserv@cybertech.apple.com`. Put the following text into the body of your e-mail: `subscribe egg-list your-real-name`; for example, `subscribe egg-list Jim Heid`.

Apple e.g. uses an Apple-developed search technology called V-Twin. Developed in Apple's Advanced Technology Group, V-Twin was designed to perform lightning-fast searches within a small memory footprint. (Apple e.g.

requires about 2.6MB of RAM.) V-Twin is also used by Apple's CyberDog Internet-access software, and is expected to make its way into a future version of the Mac OS, where it will enable Macintosh users to search for and locate documents on their hard drives and on network file servers.

V-Twin's searching engine delivers relevance-ranked results — Apple e.g. lists hits in an order that reflects the program's best guess as to how relevant it thinks the hit is to your query. Apple e.g. also provides a slick option, called More Like This, that lets visitors essentially tell the program, "Try and find documents that are similar to this one." Figure 10-7 shows a typical search session with Apple e.g.

Why is it called e.g.?

What's the matter — did you forget your Latin? The abbreviation *e.g.* is short for *exempli gratia,* which means *for example*. Apple e.g. lets you search *by example.* Get it? Yes, I know — it's a stretch. But hey, who are we to complain? It's a free program.

Setting up Apple e.g.

After you've downloaded and unstuffed Apple e.g., copy the entire contents of its folder to your WebSTAR folder. (I assume you're using WebSTAR; if you're using a different server package, just substitute its name where you see *WebSTAR*. The Apple e.g. setup procedures are identical regardless of your server software.) The files named *0.GIF* and *1.GIF* are graphics that Apple e.g. uses to draw the little relevance graphs that appear next to each hit (refer back to Figure 10-7). The file named *EGTemplate.html* is, as its name implies, a template file that controls the appearance of your search page.

After you've copied Apple e.g.'s files to your WebSTAR folder, start up WebSTAR and then start up Apple e.g. by double-clicking on the file named *eg.acgi*.

Apple e.g. has an automatic setup mode in which the program will automatically set the Apple e.g. root folder to the WebSTAR folder, set the automatic indexing interval and time to once a day at midnight, and index the entire contents of the WebSTAR folder. If you click the Setup button, Apple e.g. will set itself up using these defaults.

But depending on how you've set up your Web site, you might not want to index the entire contents of the WebSTAR folder. Perhaps you're serving multiple sites and you just want to index a specific folder within the WebSTAR folder. Or perhaps your site doesn't change once a day and therefore you don't want Apple e.g. to automatically update its index when the clock strikes midnight. For these and other specialized tasks, you'll want to click Cancel in the Auto Setup dialog box and instead use Apple e.g.'s Settings menu as described in the following sections.

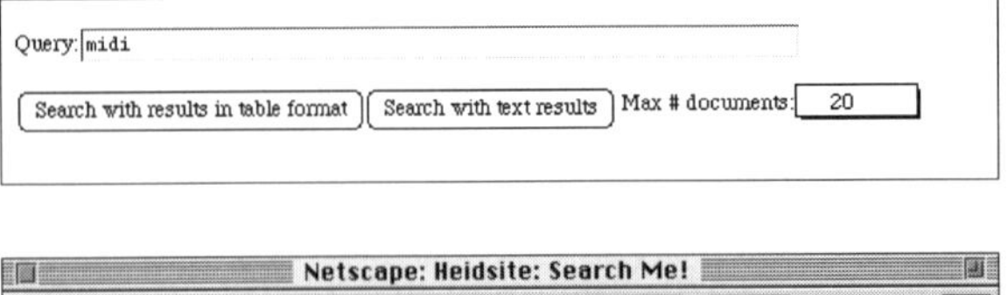

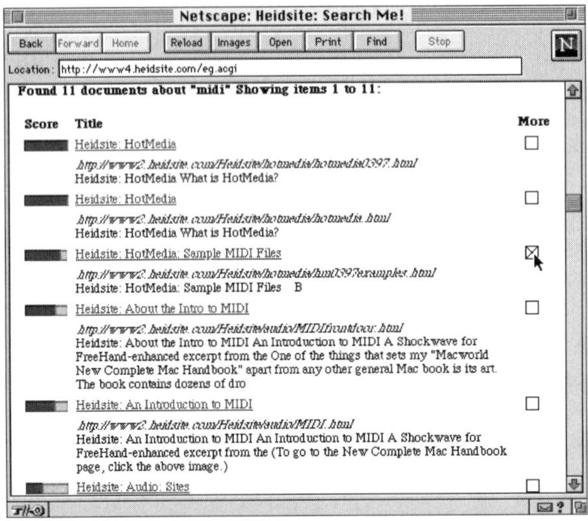

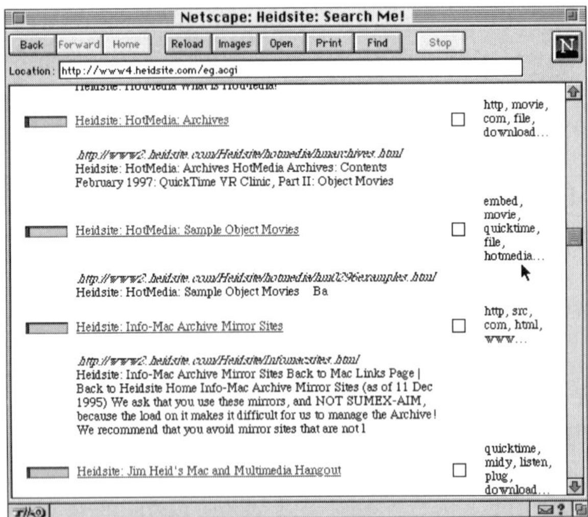

Figure 10-7: Searching with Apple e.g. Top: Typing the search query. Middle: Apple e.g.'s list of results. Note the More check box at the right edge of each hit listing. Bottom: A refined search. Notice how Apple e.g. lists the words it finds.

Specifying which folders to index

To specify that Apple e.g. index only certain folders, choose Edit Folder Settings from the Settings menu. In the Folder Settings dialog box, use the Add button in the Folders to index area to specify which folders you want to index (see Figure 10-8).

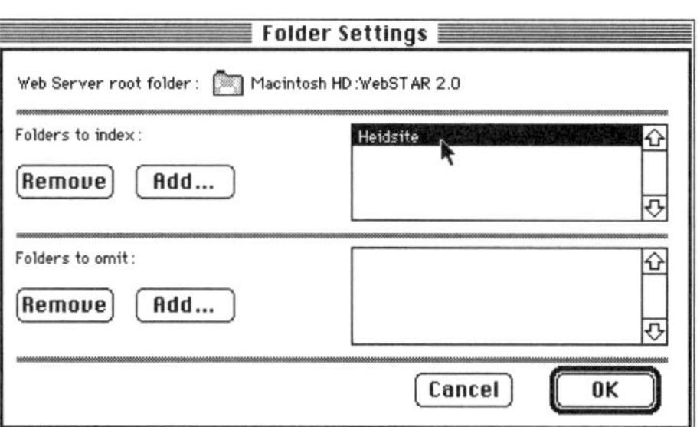

Figure 10-8: Specifying folders to index

As I described in the section "Building a Search Feature: Windows," resist the urge to index every single folder in the site. Think about the way you've structured the site's folders. If you're storing images in a folder named Graphics, for instance, omit it from the index.

Omitting some folders from the index

To exclude specific folders from your index, you use the same Folder Settings dialog box described in Figure 10-8. This time, though, use the Add button in the Folders to Omit area to specify folders that you do not want to index.

Specifying the types of files to index

To specify which types of files you do and don't want to index, choose the Edit File Settings dialog box. Apple e.g. indexes only text files, so you can speed up the indexing process by omitting other types of files, such as Adobe Acrobat PDF files. To specify that Apple e.g. not index a certain type of file, choose Edit File Settings and be sure the button named "Do not index documents ending with:" is selected. Next, type the extension of the file whose type you don't want to index, and click Add (see Figure 10-9).

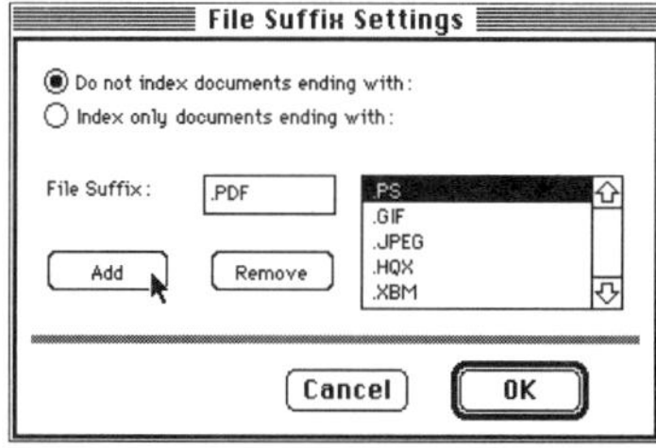

Figure 10-9: Setting up Apple e.g. to omit PDF files from the index

Generating the index

After you've specified your folders and file types, you're ready to generate the index. To do so, choose Update Index Now from Apple e.g.'s Settings menu. A status dialog box appears, your hard disk grinds away for a minute or so, and an index is born.

Apple e.g. stores the index in a file named eg.acgi Index. This file is located in your server's root folder. If you're ever having problems with Apple e.g. — it crashes, for example, or doesn't return the results you'd expect — quit Apple e.g. and throw away the eg.acgi Index file. Then restart Apple e.g. and generate a new index.

Here's a secret that can help yield more reliable results when generating a new index: use the Finder's Get Info command to boost Apple e.g.'s memory allocation by a few megabytes. After you've generated the index, quit Apple e.g. and use the Get Info command to reduce its memory size to the recommended amount.

Linking to Apple e.g.

To create a link to Apple e.g. and its search page, simply create a link that references the eg.acgi application file, like so:

```
<a href="http://www.your_site.com/eg.acgi">Search this site.</a>
```

When a visitor activates this link, Apple e.g. displays its canned search page.

Customizing the Apple e.g. search page

Apple e.g.'s canned search page isn't ready for prime time. Instead of a real header and footer, it displays the text *Add your header here* and *Add your footer here.* I'll just bet that you want something a bit more personal.

It's easy to customize the Apple e.g. search page to add your own header and footer. Use your favorite HTML editor to open the file named EGTemplate.html. Add banner graphics, descriptive text, and navigation devices. Just be sure that the `<EGCONTENT>` tag appears within the `<BODY>` section of the document. This special tag tells the Apple e.g. CGI to display its search field.

When you edit the EGTemplate.html page, be sure to choose Apple e.g.'s Reload Template command as soon as you've finished your edits. This command tells the CGI to reload the current version of the template file into memory. If you don't perform this step, Apple e.g. will continue to dish out the previous template file.

The bad news about Apple e.g.

Apple e.g. is fast, easy to use, and free — what more could a Webmaster ask for?

How about reliability?

The sad thing is, Apple e.g. can crash over time and take your server down with it. The problem is apparently a memory leak — with each search, Apple e.g. gobbles up a bit of memory that it doesn't release after the search has been completed. The problem, obviously, is more acute on sites that see a great deal of searching.

Many Apple e.g. users have worked around this problem by simply restarting their servers once a day. If you're running a lot of CGIs on the server, clearing the machines head by restarting it now and then isn't a bad idea anyway. Other users report success by simply boosting Apple e.g.'s memory allocation by a few megabytes.

Another alternative is to run Apple e.g. on a dedicated machine — maybe an old Mac IIcx or Quadra 700 that's been collecting dust in the equipment closet. With this approach, if Apple e.g. crashes, it doesn't take down your Web server.

The ultimate solution, of course, is to turn to one of the commercial search tools I describe later in this chapter. For high-profile, high-traffic sites, that's definitely the safest route.

Running multiple copies of Apple e.g.

If you want to index two different areas of a site — say, a private area available only to your intranet and a public area available to the rest of the world — you need to run two copies of Apple e.g. Rename one of the copies, and it will create index and preferences files that correspond to the new name.

Because this effectively doubles the amount of RAM you need for searching — and because of Apple e.g.'s tendency to go south now and then — it's probably time to consider a commercial search tool. I describe a few such programs later in this section.

A look at Apple e.g.'s support files

Apple e.g. maintains a few additional files as it does its thing. Here's a look at the files and what they do.

- **eg.acgi Settings.** This file stores the folder- and document-indexing settings that you specify using Apple e.g.'s Settings menu.
- **eg_index_info.html.** This file stores summary information about the index: its size, the most common words it contains, and more. As you can tell by the file's .html extension, it's coded in HTML so you can open it with a browser or even make it available to visitors. (Its contents aren't all that informative, though, so there isn't a particularly good reason to make it publicly available on your site.)

- **EG log.** This file is a bare-bones log that stores time and date information for each search request. Apple e.g. stores this information only if you choose the Verbose Messages command in the Settings menu.
- **eg._query_log.html.** This very valuable file stores a log of all search queries that visitors make. To learn why it's so very valuable, see the following Secrets sidebar, "The Hidden Value of Your Search Software's Log."

More Mac OS Search Tools

I highlighted Apple e.g. in this chapter because it's fast, easy to use, free, and delivers fine results. But Apple e.g. isn't the only Mac OS-based searching software — far from it. Here's a survey of some alternative Mac search tools. For a comprehensive list, visit StarNine's Extending WebSTAR page, at `http://www.starnine.com/development/extendingWebSTAR.html`. Or visit the *HTML & Web Publishing SECRETS* Web site (`http://websecrets.heidsite.com/`) to learn about tools I've played with since this book went to press.

Virginia Systems has taken Sonar to the Web. One key strength of WebSonar is its ability to index just about any kind of document that contains text, including formatted word processor files or QuarkXPress or PageMaker publications. This enables you to make a large library of documents available on a Web site without having to convert the documents into HTML. Just index them with WebSonar's indexer, and the WebSonar CGI displays their text. WebSonar doesn't convert graphics on the fly or mimic the formatting of the original document — you get plain text and nothing but. Still, for many applications, that's perfectly adequate.

Like its siblings in the Sonar family, WebSonar also enables extremely precise searches. Take a gander at Figure 10-10, which illustrates the specifics WebSonar lets you apply.

SECRET

The Hidden Value of Your Search Software's Log

Some search software packages, including Apple e.g., maintain a log file that contains a list of the searches visitors performed: what they were looking for, whether it was found, and so on. A search log is an extremely valuable piece of intelligence: it gives you a glimpse of what the site's visitors are interested in.

If the log contains numerous entries for a particular subject, it's telling you that visitors are interested in that topic. If you don't have much coverage of that topic, you might consider beefing up your coverage of it. If you do cover the topic extensively, you might consider highlighting it on the home page so that visitors can get to it quickly.

It's a subject repeated in later chapters, but it's so important that it's worth mentioning here: logs contain priceless information about how a site is being used. Learn how to listen to what they're telling you.

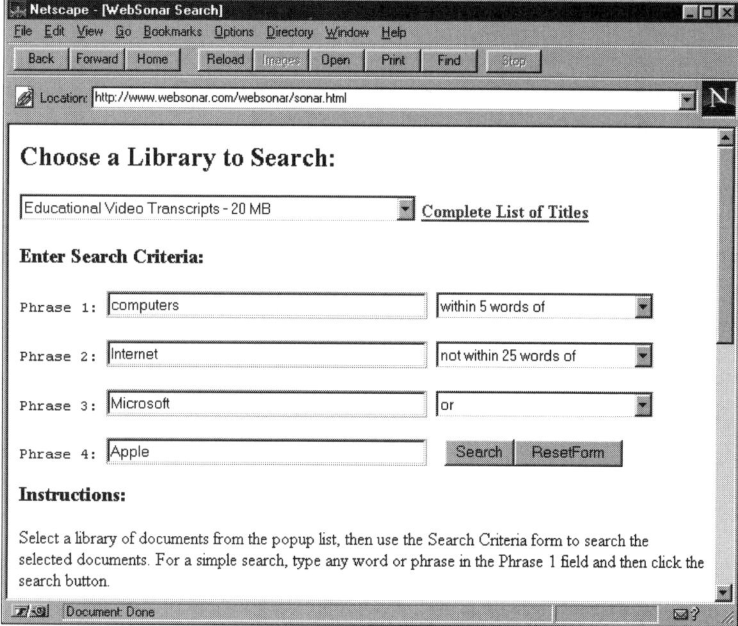

Figure 10-10: Searching with specifics: Virginia's Systems's WebSonar

WebSonar: Fast, versatile document searching

Virginia Systems's Sonar has long been a popular high-end text-retrieval package in the Mac OS world. Sonar has more recently become available for Windows 95 machines, too.

With WebSonar, a Mac OS-based CGI and indexing program, WebSonar even supports phonetic searching: Type `Mac/in/tosh/`, and WebSonar will find *Macintosh*, *McIntosh*, or *McIntauch*.

You can try out WebSonar at `http://www.websonar.com/`. Virginia Systems has set up an impressive demo that lets you search the collected works of Shakespeare, the Bible, the CIA World Factbook, and half a *gigabyte* of additional literature.

Maxum's Phantom: a Web robot

You may recall from Chapter 8 that a robot is an automated Web-surfing program that scans sites and indexes them for searching. Robots, also called spiders and crawlers, are the key to search sites such as AltaVista and WebCrawler.

Maxum Development's Phantom is, as of this writing at least, the only commercially available robot for the Mac OS platform. (A version of Phantom is also available for Windows 95/NT.) With Phantom, you can index not only your site but also any other site on the Web, enabling you to create a powerful search facility that's customized to address the needs of your visitors.

Say you operate a site about microbreweries and there are several other sites that deal with the same subject. With Phantom, you can index not only your own site but the others as well. By enabling your visitors to search many sites, you turn your site into a central clearinghouse for information on microbreweries. You can become your own specialized AltaVista — and even attract advertisers. Indeed, Phantom has features that enable it to display advertising banners and keep track of advertiser hit counts (the number of times visitors clicked on a specific ad).

Phantom is a cinch to use: you simply specify the URLs of the sites you want to index and specify other optional settings, such as how often you'd like Phantom to update its indexes. Phantom provides a remote-administration feature that lets you set up crawling sessions and adjust settings from any Web browser, as shown in Figure 10-11.

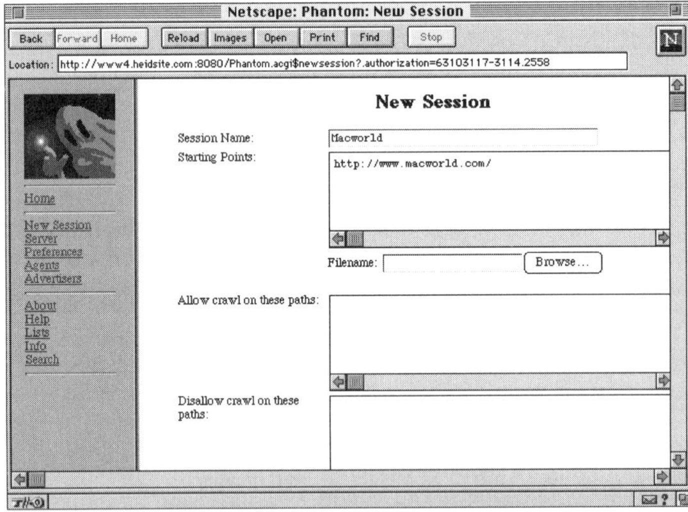

Figure 10-11: Get ready to crawl! Setting up Maxum's Phantom.

Setting up searches for Phantom

Like most all search packages, Phantom includes canned HTML pages for searches and results, and as I've mentioned elsewhere in this chapter, you should always edit a search program's default page to make its appearance and navigation options consistent with the rest of your site. The default search page appears when you call Phantom through the URL `http://www.yoursite.com:8080/Phantom.acgi`. To customize Phantom's built-in search page, use the HTML Header and HTML Footer links in the Preferences window to create your own header and footer for the page.

You can also create a search page from scratch. A handy way to do this is to use a browser to bring up Phantom's canned search page, and then choose the View Source command and copy the HTML to your favorite HTML editor. Now edit the page's header and footer areas to your heart's content. The advantage of this approach is that there's no risk of mistyping the many form-related tags that make up the Phantom search page.

Speaking of those many form-related tags, Phantom's default search page provides options that let visitors tap all of Phantom's power: using phonetic searching; choosing what to search (URL, title, header); choosing a specific crawling session; and much more. You might consider borrowing a page from AltaVista and similar sites: create a simplified search page that lets visitors search only for text contained in the document, and then create a separate advanced search page that lets visitors search for every darn thing. Put a link on the simple search page that lets visitors get to the advanced one.

iHound: fast and powerful in any language

iHound, from Amsterdam-based ICATT (`http://valley.interact.nl/ICATT_TOOLS/ihound/home.html`), is a commercial search package that includes an indexing utility and a search CGI and plug-in. iHound enables you to use logical operators (such as *and* and *or*) in searches and also provides powerful multilingual support.

Using Phantom to Back Up and Mirror Sites

Phantom's primary job description is that of a site-crawling robot, but it has some additional talents, too. Specifically, you can use Phantom to create a backup of a site by downloading the HTML pages and even the graphics, audio files, and QuickTime movies that Phantom encounters as it crawls a site.

To use Phantom to create a backup or mirror of a site, create a new session and navigate your way to the Preferences area of the New Session page. Next, check the box labeled Copy Files to "Downloads" Folder. If you also want to copy graphics, sound files, and movies, check the box labeled Include Graphics and Other Binaries. (In the binaries realm, Phantom can download GIF and JPEG images; QuickTime, MPEG, and AVI movies; and AU and WAV audio files.) For faster performance, check the Disable Indexing box.

After you make these settings and run a Phantom session, you'll find on your server a folder named Downloads. Inside, Phantom reproduces the folder structure of the site it crawled.

iHound tips and secrets

iHound abounds with customizing opportunities. Here are a few ways you can tailor it to your needs:

- **Customizing its words-to-omit lists.** To determine which words should be omitted from its index, iHound uses plain-text files called *filters,* which are stored in the folder named Filters, within another folder named iHoundDir. A file named Filters English contains lists of common English words to omit — *the*, *and*, *if,* and so on. (As becoming a multilingual product, another file named Filters Dutch contains common Dutch words.)

  iHound also relies on another file, named *filters-bad words*, that contains words that the program will not index. If you want a glimpse into ICATT's attitudes, open up this file. You'll find words like *Microsoft*, *Windows*, *Pentium*, *Bill*, and *Gates*! Feel free to tweak this file to match your own digital religious beliefs.

- **Boosting iHound's performance.** iHound is fast by any measure, but if you have a huge site with thousands of pages, you can make it even faster by storing the index on a fast external hard drive. Then, make an alias of the index file and move the alias to the iHoundDir folder.
- **Updating the index automatically.** iHound doesn't provide a feature that enables you to update its index automatically at specified intervals. However, you can still have automatic updating by using any utility that can start applications at regular intervals. One example is CE Software's Quickeys. Another is the PowerKey software that accompanies Sophisticated Circuits' PowerKey Pro (discussed in Chapter 16). And still another is Chron, by Chris Johnson (available at `http://gargravarr.cc.utexas.edu/cron/cron.html`).
- **Customizing iHound's search page.** The appearance of iHound's search page is determined by a file named iHound.html. You can (and should) customize this page to make its appearance consistent with that of the rest of your site. But be careful — iHound requires that its keywords *(INDEX, HEADER,* and so on) be formatted in all-uppercase characters. If you retype them as lowercase, the search page won't work.

FindFile: a different kind of searching

Every Mac OS veteran is familiar with the Find File command, which lets you locate files on your system's storage devices. MacXperts' FindFile is a freeware plug-in for WebSTAR that lets you locate files over the Web. Install FindFile, and you can search for and locate files located on any volume that appears on your server's desktop. Run FindFile along with an FTP server such as Stairways Shareware's NetPresenz, and visitors can download the files they find. FindFile respects any Mac OS access privileges that you specify for files, so you can designate certain folders as off limits if you like.

Secrets for search features

You can build a workable search facility by doing nothing more than using the default options provided by your search software. But why stop there? Take the time to fine-tune your search facility, and you'll make it easier for visitors to locate what they need.

The secrets behind creating a first-rate search facility are the same regardless of whether you're using a Mac- or Windows-based server. Here's a look at the most common issues and their solutions.

Problem: Visitors want to conduct multiple searches

Sometimes visitors will find what they were looking for on the first try, but many times they'll want to try again.

Solution: Provide a link back to the search form

In the page containing the list of hits, include a link that enables visitors to jump back to the search form to conduct another search. Or better still, add a search text box to the hit list page itself, as shown in Figure 10-12.

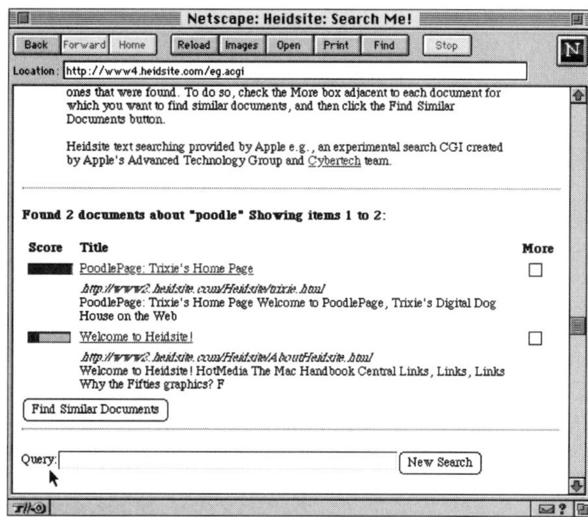

Figure 10-12: A search box on the hit-list page enables visitors to conduct another search without having to go to a different page.

If you use Apple e.g., you don't have any extra work to do. Apple e.g. automatically includes a search text box at the bottom of its hit list pages.

Problem: Common words yield too many hits

Visitors type common words like *the* and *it* in their search specifications, causing your search engine to return dozens of documents, many of which have nothing to do with what the visitors are looking for.

Solution: Omit common words from the index

Most search indexers automatically ignore common words in their searches. Some also let you create your own list of words to ignore. Your list of common words should include the ones listed previously along with *and*, *but*, *nor*, *for*, *yet*, and any others that occur often in your documents.

As discussed earlier in this chapter, many search indexers, including O'Reilly's WebIndex and ICATT's iHound, enable you to fine-tune the list of words that will not be indexed.

Problem: Visitors might search for nonexistent words

You may have pages that do not contain the word or string that the visitor is searching for, but are nonetheless related to the word or string. For example, let's say your site contains a page about poodles, but that page doesn't contain the word *dog*. (That may be hard to imagine, but it's a known fact that poodles don't consider themselves dogs.) As a result, someone conducting a search for pages containing the word *dog* would come up empty.

Solution: Use the <META> tag

When you want visitors to be able to locate pages using words that might not actually be present in those pages, you need to use the `<META>` tag. A `<META>` tag, as you may recall from Chapter 8, enables you to embed meta-information not defined by other HTML elements. This information can include instructions to browsers or indexing engines.

In the Great Poodle Hunt example I mentioned, you'd want to create a tag similar to the one shown in the code below, which uses the `<META>` tag's `keywords` attribute:

```
<META NAME="keywords" CONTENT="dog, dogs, puppy, puppies, canine">
```

For more secrets of the `<META>` tag, see the following Secrets sidebar, "Mysteries of the <META> Tag."

Problem: The scope of a search may be too broad

Usually, a search engine is set up to search every facet of a document — from titles to `<META>` tags to the headings to the actual body of the document. For a very large site, you might want to enable visitors to focus their searches on specific items, such as keywords. This will cut down on the number of hits returned, yielding more-efficient searches.

SECRET

Mysteries of the <META> Tag

The `<META>` tag accepts a `name` attribute that provides several search-related options. Many of these options are used by the indexers that accompany Web servers as well as by large search engines such as AltaVista. Here's the lowdown on how they work:

Site Description. You can provide a description of your site for search engines and indexers by including the `description` attribute.

```
<META NAME="description"
CONTENT="This is a statement or
description that you want search
engines to read when they search
your site. Most search engines
allow around 200 characters for
this field, so don't be shy.">
```

Keywords: Many of the big search sites use keyword information when cataloging a site. From what I've been able to gather, the commas are required by some indexers and ignored by others, so I always include them.

```
<META NAME="keywords" CONTENT="dogs,
puppies, curs, mutts">
```

Author: Another use of `<META>` is to denote the author of a document. This information isn't used by many indexers, but it doesn't hurt to include it.

```
<META NAME="author" CONTENT="Jim
Heid">
```

Solution: Enable visitors to focus their searches

Many search CGIs provide options that you can use to enable your visitors to select specific areas they want to search in the document by limiting their search to the following:

- **Titles.** This is the most specific and searches just document titles.
- **Title and Keywords.** This searches the document titles and also the `<META>` tags.
- **Title, Keywords, and Body.** This searches the document titles, the `<META>` tags, and the document itself.

If your search software provides this or a similar capability, consider making it available to your visitors, perhaps on an "advanced search" page.

The Web-Database Connection

Searching for information within a Web site is only one half of the "dialing for data" equation. The other half deals with searching for — and modifying — information stored within a database.

As it turns out, databases and Web sites are a marriage made in heaven. Think about it: databases store information, and Web sites deliver it. Databases enable people to search for tidbits that are relevant to them, while the most appealing Web sites are timely and customized to meet visitors' needs and tastes.

Is your Web site a candidate for the Web-database connection? The answer is yes if you're currently using a database to store anything that your customers or coworkers might find useful: price lists, catalogs, employee directories, inventory records, softball-team schedules. By tying your database to an Internet or intranet Web site, you enable people to access it directly: there's no need to export information from the database and then manually create HTML pages. You can also enable users to delete, update, and add records to the database.

On a company intranet, Web database publishing can also save money. Rather than buying a copy of the database manager for every employee, you buy one for only those employees who need the program's rich report-printing features and the fastest performance. Casual users access the database through a Web browser.

Pardon the pun, but Web database publishing is a hot field. More and more sites are relying on databases that work together with a CGI program to whip up HTML pages on the fly — pages whose contents are tailored for each visitor. This on-the-fly page generation enables the ultimate in timeliness, and it avoids the ugly chore of constantly revising pages by hand and then posting them on a server.

This section is a guide to Web-enabling databases. I'll start out with an overview of what you need to Web-publish a database, and then I'll explore the Windows and Mac OS products and techniques available for doing so. Along the way, I'll pass along some secrets for getting the best performance from your Web/database application.

In the Windows world, most of the database-publishing action centers around what I call *alphabet soup* database technologies: ones built around SQL (Structured Query Language, an industry-standard language for structuring and accessing relational databases) and ODBC (Open Database Connectivity, a Microsoft-created standard for database access).

In the Mac OS world, the action centers around Claris FileMaker Pro (`http://www.claris.com/`). This is partly because of FileMaker Pro's dominance among Mac database managers: Web database publishing requires third-party products, and developers of these products want the largest possible market. But FileMaker Pro is also the Web database of choice for the same reasons it's the Mac database of choice: it's easy to use, reasonably priced, and powerful. (There are also some "different strokes for different folks" Web database options for Mac OS Webmasters; I'll describe some of them later in this chapter.)

Assembling the pieces

The marriage of a database and a Web site may be a happy one, but like any union, it requires advance planning and cooperation. And there's a dowry: the lovebirds won't talk to each other unless you invest some time and additional software. Let's run down the bridal registry to see what you need.

Which database manager?

For starters, of course, you need the database-management software that's currently holding your data. On the Windows side, you might be using Microsoft Access or Borland's Paradox, two popular and inexpensive ODBC-compliant desktop database managers. Or your company may have a more sophisticated Windows NT-based relational database system in place, such as Microsoft's SQL Server or a product from Oracle, Sybase, or Informix.

On the Mac OS, if you want to publish a FileMaker Pro database, you need a copy of FileMaker Pro to run on your server. At this writing, the latest version is 3.0v4. Be sure to use *v4* — it contains some fixes that relate specifically to Web database publishing. (You can download a free updater for any FileMaker Pro 3.0 version from the Claris Web site at `http://www.claris.com/`.)

The CGI connection

The key component in the Web-database connection is a CGI program — the intermediary that enables Web surfers to search your database. The CGI processes data that users enter into browser-based forms; it finds, deletes, and adds records; and it routes found records to the Web server, which blasts them to the user's browser. (Most Mac OS database publishing products also ship as WebSTAR- format plug-in modules. But for simplicity's sake, I'll use the term *CGI* throughout this section.)

It's possible to write your own Web-database CGI in languages such as Perl, AppleScript, or Frontier, and many Webmasters have done exactly that. But the good news is that a new generation of database-publishing products has appeared that enables you to Web-publish a database without having to program. In some products, such as Allaire's ColdFusion (Windows) and EveryWare Development's Tango (Windows and Mac OS), you can use wizard-like windows to publish a database within minutes. I'll have more to say about these and other products later in this chapter.

The Web-database two-step

From a Web-surfer's perspective, accessing information in a database through a Web site is similar to performing a search on a site such as AltaVista or Yahoo!. It's a two-step process that first involves specifying what to search for. In this step, the visitor pecks text into an on-screen form and may use pop-up menus to choose options that refine the search.

After filling out the browser form, the visitor clicks a Submit or Search button, and the server's database-publishing CGI kicks in. If it locates some data that meet the search criteria, it returns a *search results* page to the visitor. This page lists just a few fields from the records that meet the visitor's criteria. One field in each record is formatted as a hyperlink, enabling the visitor to view a specific record by clicking on the hyperlink. The page containing the specific record is often called a *detail page*. This process of clicking on a summary field to view a specific record is often called *drilling down*. Figure 10-13 illustrates the drill-down process.

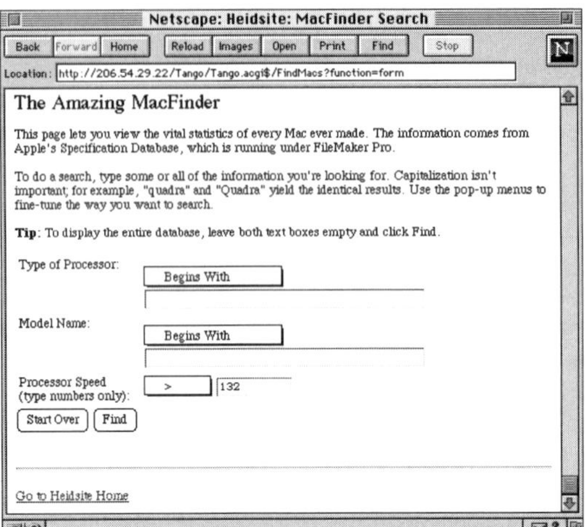

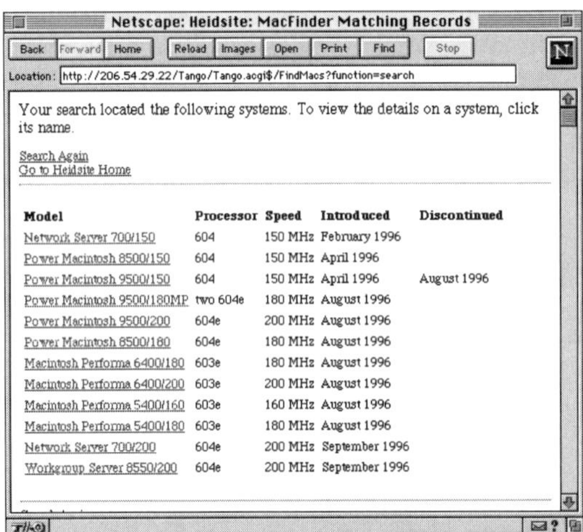

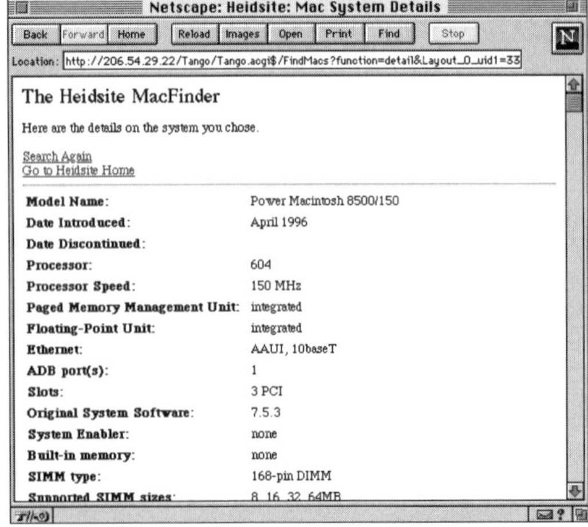

Figure 10-13: A typical database drill-down. Top: Specifying search criteria. Middle: A search results page. Bottom: A detail page showing a single record.

Windows Database Publishing Tools

FileMaker Pro dominates among Mac OS database publishing applications, but the Windows platform sports a wide variety of competing packages. Thus, the first step in tying your database (or RDBMS, for relational database management system) to the Web is to determine which such product you will be using. You can link virtually any database product to a Web server through the use of ODBC drivers. As mentioned earlier, ODBC (Open Database Connectivity) is a Microsoft standard that enables the exchange of information between RDBMSs and data-access components such as Web-integration tools, report generators, and application construction kits (Delphi and Visual Basic, for example). The majority of database products available for Windows are shipped with matching ODBC software.

SECRET

If you have an enterprise RDBMS like Sybase, Oracle, or Informix, you may find that ODBC does not give you the performance that you want. This is because the internal translations that ODBC performs introduce delays — or latency — into the database transactions. Under these circumstances, you should choose a database-publishing tool that supports so-called *native* connections to your database.

Total Access

In early 1996, Microsoft publicly announced that — in conjunction with a company-wide move to focus on the Internet — they were going to Web-enable the forthcoming versions of all Microsoft Office applications, including Word, Excel, PowerPoint, and Access. The company has made good on its promise, and Access 97 — Microsoft's very flexible desktop database manager — offers a set of valuable resources that enables anyone using Microsoft's Internet Information Server to construct a database-supported site with remarkable ease. If you are not using IIS, you might want to skip down to the section on third party data-integration products from Allaire, SoftQuad, Bluestone, and NetDynamics.

If you are already using Microsoft Access but do not have the Office 97 version, it pays to upgrade if you want to publish your data to the Internet; the upgrade is probably cheaper than a standalone package, and certainly offers the quickest route to Internet distribution of database content. If you are using another desktop database, you might consider "side-grading" — you might find that Microsoft offers a special price on Access to owners of a competing product.

Once you've installed Access, constructed your database model, and entered your data — or imported content from an older version — the Internet publishing action centers on the Save as HTML command in Access's File menu. This menu activates a wizard that gathers all of the information Access needs to automatically publish your database information in a Web-compatible format. The wizard offers three different approaches to distributing your data through a Web site:

- **Publish your data as static HTML text.** This option is fine if you have a lot of material that you want online, but that doesn't need to be changed or updated frequently. As noted above, while static data exports save redundant HTML coding — and reduce error rates — they are not particularly useful if you want to enable visitors to update database information or customize their view of your data. Also, remember that databases published statically represent a *snapshot* of your information at one point in time; you must update the snapshot by re-exporting to reflect any changes.
- **Publish your data dynamically using the Internet Data Connector (IDC).** The first way to display live information from your database is to employ a database-publishing tool, called the Internet Data Connector, that ships with IIS 3. Access can create the data files that the IDC uses to construct a page on the fly. The first of these files is called an .idc file; it contains a reference to the information in your database that you want to show on the page. The .idc file works in tandem with an HTML template document — the .htx file — that contains Web page formatting instructions. In place of data, the .htx template includes special placeholder instructions that describe where in the .idc file to insert the information returned from the database query. When a Web visitor requests an .idc page from your site, the Web server calls the IDC server module, which opens a connection to the specified data source, reads the data from that source, and inserts it into the .htx template. The server then sends the completed HTML document to the visitor's browser.
- **Publish your data using Active Server Pages.** The second dynamic database-presentation method that Access supports is called Active Server Pages (ASP). There a number of reasons you may wish to use ASP in place of the Internet Database Connector to deliver dynamic information. For example, you should use ASP if you want to create a data entry form on your Web page, because IDC only supports the display (not the input) of database information.

  If you are a programmer, ASP also offers you more flexible output options. Unlike IDC, ASP uses a single file, with the extension — surprise! — .asp. The .asp file contains both the query information used to locate and extract the data you wish to publish as well as the HTML template into which the content is to be inserted. Access automatically writes the query portion of an .asp document in VBScript, Microsoft's preferred language for client and server scripting. VBScript is syntactically nearly identical to Visual Basic — hence the name — so if you are a VB programmer you should have no trouble modifying the VBScript if you choose to do so. Active Server Pages requires a server plug-in component freely available from Microsoft at `http://www.microsoft.com/iis/LearnAboutIIS/ActiveServer/default.asp`. I cover ASP in more detail later.

Access 97's strong database capabilities and Web publishing features make it the most valuable single tool that a Windows Webmaster can buy. Using a combination of Windows NT 4.0 (including Internet Information Server and Active Server Pages) and Access 97, a beginning Web developer can establish an Internet presence with a feature set equal to or better than all but the most advanced commercial sites.

Activating your Microsoft-based site

What if you are using Microsoft IIS, but need to connect to a database other than Access? Or perhaps you want to have more direct control over the look of the content output from your database and presented by your Web server. If so, you should know that both of the dynamic page-generation options that Access 97 supports (and which are described in the previous sections) work with database systems other than Access. In fact, an IIS server using either the Internet Data Connector DLL or Active Server Pages technology can query any database that supports ODBC — in other words, nearly every product on the market.

The difference is that Access creates the necessary data and template files for you; if you choose to use a different database product you'll have to roll your own. This is not as difficult as it sounds; IDC in particular is fairly straightforward (though, as mentioned, it is far less flexible than ASP and cannot be used if you want to add database *input* capabilities to your Web site).

SECRET

One option might be to replicate the data structure that you maintain in a corporate RDBMS system such as Oracle within Access 97 itself. Use Access simply to generate the constructor files you need for Web integration. Then simply make a few changes to the lines that the Web server uses to find your database (inserting the Oracle server references, for example), and you're on your way. Or you might try using Access-created IDC or ASP data files as a template from which to build your own custom pages.

You can write Active Server Pages documents in any scripting language you choose, including VBScript, Jscript (Microsoft's implementation of JavaScript), or a language such as Tcl or Perl that is supported by an ASP plug-in. Because ASP uses a data-access server object called the ADO to communicate with your ODBC database, your data access capability is preserved no matter what server-side development language you select. This flexibility makes ASP an extremely functional tool — you can leverage your existing skills to rapidly build highly interactive Web sites with remarkably little effort.

Allaire Cold Fusion

ON CD-ROM

Despite all this discussion of Microsoft products, I realize that IIS is not the only Windows Web server available. In Chapter 17 I look at IIS, Netscape's server offerings, and O'Reilly's WebSite. In addition to these market leaders, there are a large number of other contenders available, each with their own particular strengths. If you are using FastTrack, WebSite Pro, EMWAC or Purveyor, or even if you use IIS but want to look beyond Microsoft for connectivity tools, you should definitely examine Cold Fusion, one of the first players in the Web-database integration market. Cold Fusion uses a separate *application server* to manage database queries coming from the Web. Here's how it works:

1. A user requests a dynamically generated page from the Web server, specifying a Cold Fusion template file (with the extension .cfml).

2. The Web server passes the request to the Cold Fusion Application Server, either through CGI or via one of the Windows server programming interfaces.
3. The Cold Fusion Application Server (CFAS) locates the appropriate template, constructs and executes a database query, and then fills in the template with the data returned from the database.
4. The CFAS returns the assembled document to the Web server, which forwards it to the visitor's browser.

Note that because Cold Fusion supports both CGI and three popular Windows server application programming interfaces (Netscape Server API, Microsoft's Internet Server API, and the O'Reilly WebSite API), it is optimized for speed when used with the most widely deployed Web servers but remains compatible with virtually every server on the market.

Cold Fusion uses a single-page template approach, much like Microsoft's Active Server Pages. However, instead of taking advantage of a standard scripting language, Allaire has developed its own set of proprietary codes, called the Cold Fusion Markup Language (or CFML). A CFML page looks just like plain-vanilla HTML, with two exceptions. First, the CFML page contains an ODBC database query stored in the HTML header, within a `<CFQUERY>` tag. The following sample query would load into memory all of the information in the data table called CourseList:

```
<CFQUERY NAME="CourseListQuery" DATASOURCE="Cold Fusion Examples">
SELECT * FROM CourseList
</CFQUERY>
```

The second feature that differentiates HTML from CFML pages is that in the latter, much of the document's actual content is replaced with placeholders (designated with `<CFOUTPUT>` tags) that indicate to the Application Server where to insert the information returned from the query. So in this example, the following text might appear somewhere within the body of the CFML file:

```
<CFOUTPUT QUERY="CourseListQuery">
<B>#Course_ID#</B> #CourseName#<BR>
</CFOUTPUT>
```

When the Application Server parses the page, these Cold Fusion tags will be replaced with the data returned by the CourseList query, with the course ID presented in bold (specified by the HTML `<B>` element). Note that the `<CFOUTPUT>` tag identifies which query should provide the output content; you may have multiple database queries (directed against separate databases, if desired) within a single CFML page.

Cold Fusion compares favorably against Microsoft's ASP. For example, both offer features that enable you to create Web sites that maintain so-called *client state* information, keeping track of a visitor's identity as he or she moves from page to page. Such tracking is critical for applications like online shopping, in which visitors might explore dozens of pages while stocking their personal shopping carts.

Cold Fusion also offers a couple of excellent visual tools to assist a Webmaster who is just getting started with database publishing. The first is a set of application development wizards — interview-driven dialog boxes — which create the necessary Cold Fusion Markup Language files for you. These wizards offer functionality similar to that of Access's Save as HTML command; you can rapidly create CFML pages that support user data entry or Web-based reporting and filtering of the information in your database.

Cold Fusion also includes a specially integrated copy of Crystal Reports 5, a popular Windows database reporting tool. Using Crystal Reports, you can point and click to design the format in which you wish your data to be presented; the application will then automatically create the CFML template required to duplicate your formatting in a dynamic Web document.

Cold Fusion is an excellent choice for a wide variety of database publishing tasks. Since it debuted in 1994, the product has evolved into a mature, robust development tool that is widely employed by Windows Webmasters. O'Reilly bundles a copy of Cold Fusion with its WebSite Professional server product, a testament to Cold Fusion's popularity.

A trial version of Cold Fusion is included on the *HTML & Web Publishing SECRETS* CD-ROM. You can purchase Cold Fusion online directly from Allaire's web site at: `http://www.allaire.com/`.

Netscape LiveWire

Netscape offers a proprietary server-side programming environment called LiveWire that includes database access features. LiveWire competes directly with Microsoft's Active Server Pages (described earlier in this section), but is less robust and significantly more complex to use.

LiveWire offers only a single development language — JavaScript — compared to the open architecture of ASP. Even more limiting is the requirement that you must recompile your program and restart the server every time you modify a LiveWire application. This process can significantly increase the time it takes to debug or modify your programs. By contrast, ASP dynamically recompiles programs as needed. Furthermore, while you can insert an ASP-built document anywhere in your site (simply by suffixing the document with the .asp extension), LiveWire requires you to store all dynamic pages in special "applications directories."

These restrictions can be frustrating; having to work around a development system's quirks consumes resources and time that could be more appropriately used for database design and construction. If you own Netscape Enterprise server (which comes bundled with LiveWire) or if your company compels you to use only Netscape products, you may wish to evaluate this development tool, but due to its unintuitive behavior and lack of flexibility, LiveWire simply doesn't measure up to the challengers. However, the Web server tools market shifts constantly, and Netscape's next version may prove to be a winner.

Just the basics

One other option to consider if you are just getting started with Web databases is WebFiler, from SoftQuad. Unlike standard desktop databases such as Access, WebFiler does not have a Windows-based front-end tool. You create and manipulate your data using a Web browser. So while the other tools I've discussed in this section have focused around linking database products to Web servers, the WebFiler database may be thought of as part of the Web server, inaccessible on its own.

However, the forthcoming Professional version of WebFiler *will* offer ODBC connectivity to existing RDBMs. SoftQuad has made an effort to simplify all aspects of WebFiler, from creating tables to entering data. As such, WebFiler is not the right tool for users demanding sophisticated functionality or high performance. But if you simply want to maintain an online phone list for publication on your company intranet, or even just want to publish a searchable list of your favorite recipes, WebFiler's simple installation and straightforward operation may make it the product you have been looking for. You can learn more about it and download a sample copy from `http://www.webfiler.com/`.

High-end development systems

If you are developing a corporate intranet focused around a database-enabled Web site, or if your company has specific enterprise compatibility requirements, the packages that I've looked at so far may be too simplistic for your needs. For example, suppose you have to support Web servers running on both the UNIX and Windows operating systems; you would ideally assemble database applications that work seamlessly on either platform. Or your database application needs may be so grand as to exceed the performance capabilities of a single hardware server. Requirements like these call for a scaleable, cross-platform, high-performance answer to Web-database integration problems.

NetDynamics (`http://netdynamics.com`) and Bluestone (`http://bluestone.com`) offer solutions to address the needs of more advanced Webmasters. NetDynamics 3.0 is a Java-based database integration tool that offers developers a visual environment in which to create applications. NetDynamics Studio provides a graphical workspace — reminiscent of the Windows Explorer — within which programmers can assign queries and their results to HTML pages using the built-in database access objects. Users may customize these objects' internal Java code to extend the system's native capabilities. NetDynamics Studio automatically generates and compiles Java code when the application is ready for testing. The NetDynamics Application Server uses the information stored within this code to deliver the appropriate data to the Web server as site visitors request pages.

Bluestone Software's Sapphire/Web offers a similar construction model, but does not force developers to implement their code in server-side Java. Sapphire/Web does support Java, but in addition can automatically construct CGIs (using C++), or Netscape API or Internet Information Server API modules — each with the appropriate database access specifications stored internally. Furthermore, Bluestone enables developers to select the format of their database output; whereas all of the products I've looked at so far can generate only HTML pages on the fly, Sapphire/Web has the capability to present information in Java or ActiveX form as well.

SECRET

The flexibility of these products comes at the expense of a steep learning curve. While you may relish the power provided by a cross-platform C++ generation tool, it is important to remember that at their core, NetDynamics and Sapphire/Web are based on languages that are fundamentally far more complex than the script-based tools I described earlier. When your database application demands that you extend the capabilities of the built-in objects, you will most likely find yourself confronting some pretty ugly Java or C code. If you're a skilled programmer, or if your company maintains a fleet of developers on hand to assist with RDBMS integration projects, then the NetDynamics or Bluestone offerings may be for you. But if you are responsible for setting up your company's Web site single-handedly and have little formal programming education, you will be far better off with Active Server Pages, Cold Fusion, or WebFiler.

Mac OS database publishing tools

The FileMaker Pro database-publishing camp is divided equally among freeware and commercial products. The freeware offerings include Russell Owens's (`http://rowen.astro.washington.edu/`) ROFM 4.1, Blue World Communications's (`http://www.blueworld.com/`) Lasso Lite, and Claris's own FileMaker Pro CGI. Each has its strengths, but all force you to sacrifice either performance or features.

ON CD-ROM

The three commercial CGIs are EveryWare Development's (`http://www.everyware.com`) Tango for FileMaker Pro, Blue World Communications' (`http://www.blueworld.com/`) Lasso, and Web Broadcasting Company's (`http://www.macweb.com/`) Web FM. Competition among these three is furious; new versions of all three products appear frequently as each developer attempts to leapfrog the competition.

Database modification required?

Every marriage ceremony is different, and every FileMaker Pro database-publishing product takes a unique path down the aisle. The most dramatic differences between products lie in the steps you take to unite database and Web site.

Some CGIs require you to modify your database in order to Web-enable it — specifically, by adding calculation fields containing HTML that the CGI uses to process and format data. CGIs that take this approach include Web FM and the freeware ROFM and Claris FileMaker Pro CGI. Lasso, Lasso Lite, and Tango don't require database modifications, and instead rely on separate files that control formatting.

FlatFiler: Bare-Bones Database Publishing

If your data doesn't change all that often, one option you might consider is a freeware WebSTAR plug-in called FlatFiler, from MacXperts. (FlatFiler is included on the *HTML & Web Publishing SECRETS* CD-ROM.) FlatFiler lets you merge the contents of a tab-delimited text file with an HTML template. You export your data to a tab-delimited text file (that is, a file in which each record ends with a carriage return, and each field is separated by a tab code; all database managers and most spreadsheet programs can export to tab-delimited text files). Then, create a FlatFiler template that refers to the fields in the text file.

The drawback of this approach is that each time your original database changes, you have to export a new tab-delimited text file in order to keep the Web-published version of the database current. But for databases that change infrequently, FlatFiler is a terrific option. And you can't beat the price!

Each approach has its strengths. Calculation fields are fast and using them enables you to tap FileMaker Pro's array of text-handling and number-crunching functions. Using calculation fields also helps keep your site cleaner — there are fewer files to keep track of and back up.

But calculation fields aren't for the faint of FileMaker — if you haven't mastered them, use a product that relies on external format files, such as Lasso or Tango for FileMaker. Also, in institutional settings, individuals may not be permitted to modify a database's structure. And even if yours is a one-person shop, you might simply prefer to keep your database files pure rather than blurring the lines between FileMaker Pro's duties and the CGI's.

Comparing development features

A database-publishing package's development features are what you use to Web-enable a specific database: to specify which fields you want to be Web-searchable, whether surfers can add, modify or delete records, and how the data that surfers locate appears on their browsers.

For fast development and a gentle learning curve, you can't beat EveryWare Development's Tango for FileMaker. Its Tango Editor utility makes database publishing a click-and-drag proposition (see Figure 10-14).

You use Tango Editor to build *query documents,* which the Tango CGI uses to display search forms and found records. To help you build the most common types of query documents, Tango Editor provides wizard-like windows called Query Builders. With the Query Builders, you can put a database on the Web in less than a minute — I've timed it.

The resulting screens aren't visual feasts, but windows that hold custom HTML for headers, footers, and overall page formatting are a click away. And here's a cool tip: if you use an HTML editor such as Adobe PageMill, use it to design page elements and then drag and drop their HTML into Tango Editor.

Figure 10-14: Three steps to the Tango: publishing a FileMaker Pro database with Tango for FileMaker.

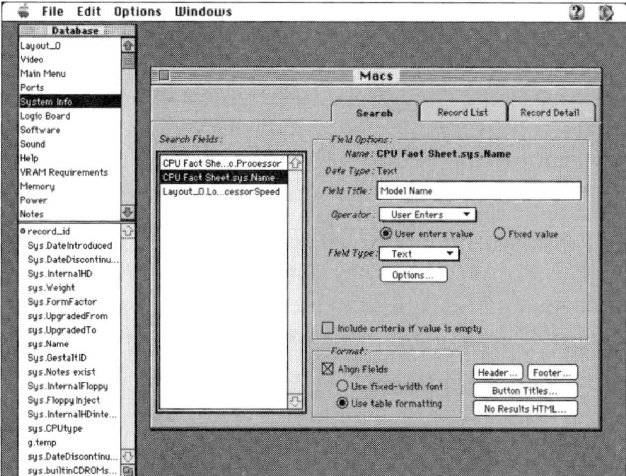

Creating a search server

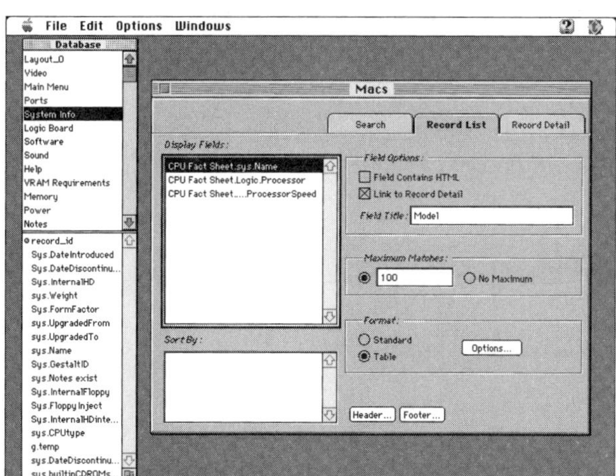

Creating a record list, which shows found records

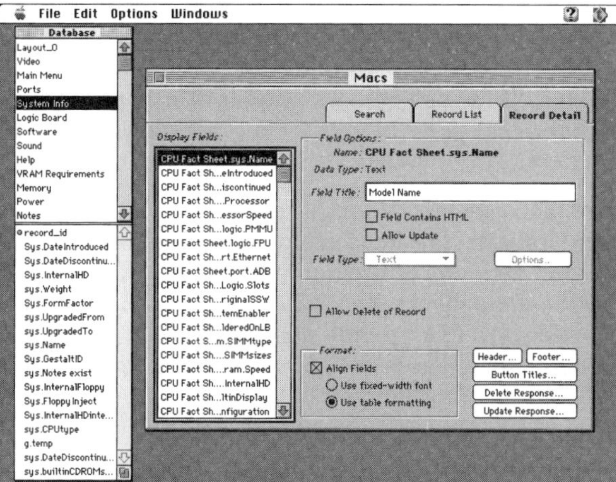

Creating a detail page, which shows a specific record

When you need more sophisticated query documents, such as ones that perform calculations on database information or that perform different activities depending on a condition, you use Tango Editor's visual programming mode. Tango's gentle learning curve becomes a much steeper slope here. You'll need to learn a new vocabulary of Tango-specific tags and master a flock of option dialog boxes.

Tango's query documents also work with EveryWare's Tango Enterprise, which Web-enables high-end, client-server databases as well as FileMaker Pro. This not only gives you a growth path to the enterprise databases that many big businesses and institutions use, it also enables you to mix and match data from disparate data sources on a single screen.

Neither Lasso nor Web FM offers the immediate gratification of Tango Editor. With Lasso, you create format files containing Lasso-specific tags and commands that control the CGI (see Figure 10-15). A separate format file is required for each page that presents data from the database; this contrasts with Tango, in which one query document can handle both search summaries and search details.

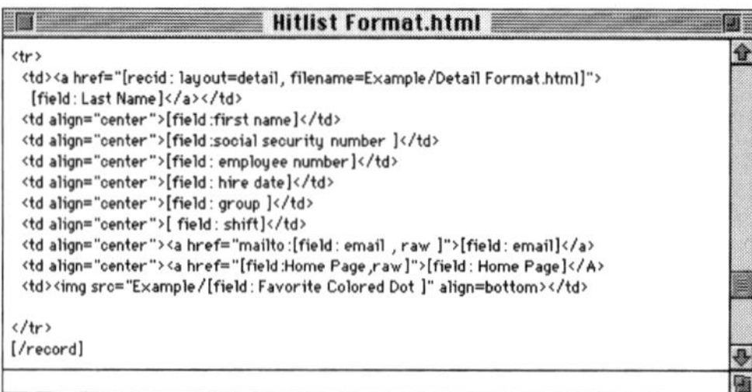

```
Hitlist Format.html

<tr>
  <td><a href="[recid: layout=detail, filename=Example/Detail Format.html]">
   [field: Last Name]</a></td>
  <td align="center">[field:first name]</td>
  <td align="center">[field:social security number ]</td>
  <td align="center">[field: employee number]</td>
  <td align="center">[field: hire date]</td>
  <td align="center">[field: group ]</td>
  <td align="center">[ field: shift]</td>
  <td align="center"><a href="mailto:[field: email , raw ]">[field: email]</a>
  <td align="center"><a href="[field:Home Page,raw]">[field: Home Page]</A>
  <td><img src="Example/[field: Favorite Colored Dot ]" align=bottom></td>

</tr>
[/record]
```

Figure 10-15: A typical Lasso format file. Note the specialized tags, which display data from the FileMaker Pro database.

You create Lasso format files using any HTML or text editor. Lasso includes a utility, FM Link, that provides palettes from which you can drag and drop Lasso tags, database field names, and so on. But FM Link doesn't provide the hand-holding of Tango's Query Builders; it just cuts down on typing. Version 2.0 of Lasso, which was in development as this book went to press, will provide a Java applet that makes working with Lasso dramatically easier. Check out Blue World's Lasso Web site (`http://www.blueworld.com/lasso/`) to get the latest on the new version — and to download templates created by other Lasso users.

And the freeware packages? ROFM require you to edit the database file. For each field in the database, you must create a calculation field that will hold the HTML-formatted versions of the data that ROFM will return. Click-and-drag database publishing it isn't. Lasso Lite works with Blue World's FM Link. Claris FileMaker Pro CGI provide no development-streamlining aids; indeed, it's sparsely documented and requires you to do some AppleScript programming. ROFM or Lasso Lite are better alternatives.

FileMaker advanced feature support

Getting up to speed is one thing; what you can do when you get there is another. If you're a FileMaker Pro guru, you might be using scripts to automate tasks, and you might be linking FileMaker Pro with other programs via AppleEvents. Many CGIs enable you to extend these advanced features to a Web site. Similarly, if your database relies on FileMaker Pro's repeating or picture fields or on relations and portals, you'll want a CGI that supports the features you need.

Of the commercial offerings, Lasso and Web FM provide the best support for advanced FileMaker Pro features. Both programs enable you to display, update, and add to repeating fields. Both also support FileMaker Pro relations and portals, but Web FM edges out Lasso by enabling you to add and update related records; the current version of Lasso doesn't enable you to add or update related records within portals. Tango doesn't support relations or portals at all.

All three programs support FileMaker Pro scripts. Tango and Web FM can also send AppleEvents to other applications. Lasso can't.

Among the freeware CGIs, you don't get what you don't pay for: none of the freeware programs support the features I've discussed in this section.

Safe and sound

Security is a common concern in the database world. You may want to give some users modification privileges and others browse-only privileges. Or, you may want to hide some fields (such as a personnel database's salary field) from unauthorized eyes.

Most FileMaker Pro Web-publishing tools support these as well as a variety of Web-specific security features. In all three commercial programs, you can specify whether visitors can update or delete a found record. Controlling updates and deletions is easiest in Tango for FileMaker Pro, where you can simply check a box in Tango Editor to designate whether users can delete or update a record.

But Web FM and Lasso provide a more complete array of security features than does Tango. With Tango, you can't specify that some users be allowed to browse and others be allowed to modify. In Web FM and Lasso, you can.

Bells and whistles

Most CGIs also provide features specific to the Web world. *User identification* features enable the CGI to keep track of users as they access the database — to track the kinds of information they're requesting or maintain security logs. Lasso, Web FM, and Tango all provide logging features.

All three products also enable you to retrieve and store information received by a user's browser, such as the browser name and version and the user's IP address or domain name. You can combine this capability with the IF...THEN conditional features all three programs provide to, for example, tailor page display to take advantage of browser-specific features or to control which fields are displayed based on a visitor's domain address.

All three programs also provide *variables*, which enable you to store and track information as a user navigates a database application. Variables, also called tokens or cookies, are important ingredients in online shopping cart applications, where you might use them to store order numbers or customer IDs as visitors shop.

SECRET

Picture This: Serving Graphics Stored in Databases

FileMaker Pro provides *container fields* that enable you to store graphics in a database: for example, pictures of products in a catalog or inventory database, pictures of people in a personnel database, or pictures of places in a travel database.

In the past, Web developers who wanted to display graphics along with database data had to go through some special gyrations. Rather than just using picture fields, they had to store graphics in separate GIF or JPEG files, and then create a field to hold the URL for each graphic. When it came time to dish out a particular record, the Web server would read that record's URL field and go out and grab the appropriate graphic.

This roundabout technique was required because FileMaker Pro stores graphics as PICT images, which Web browsers don't recognize. The good news is there's now an easier way: Beginning with version 2.1, EveryWare Development's Tango can serve up PICT images stored in a FileMaker Pro database by converting them into JPEG images on the fly.

But there are some caveats to keep in mind. For starters, Tango is limited to retrieving a maximum of 64K from a single field. That's more than adequate for text fields, of course, but it might not be enough for large graphics. To increase the maximum supported field size, use the Tango query document named Settings; it's located in the folder named Admin, within the Tango folder on your Web server. Open this query document and assign a larger value to the system global named sys$itemBufferSize. You should also boost the memory allocations of FileMaker Pro and the Tango CGI or, if you're using the Tango plug-in, WebSTAR itself. You'll need to experiment to find a memory size that handles your graphics without devouring too much of your server's RAM.

Also note that you'll need to have Apple's QuickTime 2.0 or later installed on the server. This is because Tango uses QuickTime to perform the conversion from PICT to JPEG. This isn't a drawback by any means, but you'll want to make sure your server is properly configured before putting your application into service.

If you use Lasso or Web FM instead of Tango, you can add graphics-conversion features using Web Broadcasting's PICT FM utility. PICT FM is a WebSTAR-format plug-in module that performs on-the-fly conversion of PICT images to JPEG format.

PICT FM also includes a terrific plug-in called PicturePlug, which converts a standalone PICT file to JPEG format. PicturePlug can be a tremendous time-saver if you have a lot of PICT files that you'd like to serve. Rather than convert them all to JPEG format, install PicturePlug on your server and then simply reference the PICT files in your HTML documents (for example, `<img src="dogphoto.pict">`). PicturePlug will convert the PICT image to JPEG on the fly.

The FileMaker Pro graphics-conversion features I've described here are terrific, but if you have a large library of pictures you want to serve, you might consider using a database designed specifically for image serving, such as Canto's Cumulus. See the Backgrounder sidebar, "Different Strokes: Alternative Mac OS Database Publishing Tools," later in this chapter.

For some tasks, you might want to have a copy of a newly entered record e-mailed to a specified address — for order verification, for example. Among the commercial database publishing packages, only Blue World's Lasso provides built-in e-mail forwarding features; you can graft e-mail forwarding onto Web FM with a free Web Broadcasting utility, FMailer. Russell Owens' freeware ROFM also provides e-mail forwarding.

Speed counts: tips for fast FileMaker Pro publishing

Ultimately, your site's users don't care how long it took *you* to Web-enable your database. They care about how long it takes *them* to work with it: how quickly they see the records they're looking for and how quickly your site responds when they delete, update, or add records.

As with any Web or network application, much of the performance equation is out of your hands. You can't control a dial-in visitor's modem speed or the traffic on the Internet or an office network.

But there are some performance aspects that are under your control. Here are some tips for optimizing the performance of a Web-enabled FileMaker Pro database:

- **Create simple search summaries.** Search summaries are those lists of records that meet a user's criteria and enable a user to drill down to view an individual record. Never include more fields in this summary than are necessary for a user to identify which specific record he or she wants to view. This minimizes network traffic and lessens the load on your server software and on FileMaker Pro.

  Also, all FileMaker Pro database-publishing CGIs except for the Claris FileMaker Pro CGI enable you to return found records in small chunks — say, ten records at a time. You've seen this scheme in search sites such as Yahoo!: only 10 or 15 hits appear on a page, and hyperlinks let you view the next or previous batch. Returning data in an easily digestible — and downloadable — chunks scheme improves perceived performance and avoids clogging the network by transmitting data users may never need.

- **Hide FileMaker Pro.** Hide FileMaker Pro so that its windows aren't open as it runs. (Choose Hide FileMaker Pro from the application menu at the right edge of the menu bar.) FileMaker Pro updates its screen to reflect users' activities; by hiding the program, you save time that would be spent on these updates. Another option is to use the Mac OS's WindowShade control panel to hide FileMaker Pro's window.

- **Compress your database now and then.** Use FileMaker Pro's Save a Compressed Copy option (in the Save dialog box) to save your database. This rearranges the database file, making it smaller — and therefore, faster to search.

- **Make sure you have enough RAM.** Because you will be running FileMaker Pro and your Web server software on the same Mac, you'll need plenty of memory: at least 32MB, and more if you'll be running other CGIs, too.
- **Avoid sorting found records if possible.** The less work you give FileMaker Pro, the faster your visitors will see their results.
- **Run WebSTAR as the front-most application.** Choose WebSTAR's name from the application menu so that it has a check mark next to it. This gives WebSTAR the lion's share of the Mac OS's time, boosting performance. See Chapter 16 for more tips on boosting WebSTAR's performance.

BACKGROUNDER

Different Strokes: Alternative Mac OS Database Publishing Tools

Although FileMaker Pro's popularity and simplicity make it the ideal Web database publishing foundation for the Mac OS, there's also the "different strokes" crowd: products that put their own spin on the database-Web connection.

Provue Development's (`http://www.provue.com/`) WebView is a database-publishing add-on for Provue's Panorama database manager, which has long been known for its speed. (Unlike most database managers, Panorama keeps an entire database in RAM, so it doesn't have to access the disk to find and modify records.) WebView sports an approachable user interface and some unique features, including the capability to preview search and results forms without having to run a server — something no FileMaker Pro database-publishing tool permits.

Purity Software's (`http://www.purity.com/`) WebSiphon uses a proprietary scripting language to tie into an included database manager called Verona, which is optimized for Web serving. WebSiphon is an excellent tool for creating dynamic site features such as shopping carts, online polls, and conferencing boards, as well as for workaday jobs such as delivering browser-optimized pages, generating page counters, and password-protecting portions of a site.

Canto (`http://www.canto-software.com`) offers a CGI that Web-enables databases stored in Canto's Cumulus media database. With the Cumulus Internet Image Server, you can enable Web users to search and download from databases containing stock photography, clip art, music clips, Adobe Acrobat documents, and other media types. You must also own the Cumulus Network Image Database.

TECSoft (`http://www.tecny.com/`) has created a unique application, called HTMLGenerator, that links FileMaker Pro and Canto's Cumulus multimedia-database application, which stores images as well as audio files, QuickTime movies, and other media types. With HTMLGenerator, you can build the kind of dynamic Web sites that were formerly the province of high-end, object-oriented databases.

Pacific Coast Software's (`http://www.pacific-coast.com`) WebCatalog is a solid package for creating online shopping systems. WebCatalog provides shopping cart features and can also display rotating advertising banners. (EveryWare Development also offers an online shopping system called Tango Merchant.)

Summary

- Adding a search feature to a Web site enables visitors to locate pages of interest by typing search criteria.
- A variety of search tools exist, but most work similarly: by indexing the site's pages, and then providing a CGI or server plug-in that enables visitors to search that index.
- Use `<META>` tags on your pages to enable search sites such as AltaVista to index your site accurately.
- All search packages provide canned search forms and results pages, but you should customize these pages to create ones whose look and feel are consistent with the rest of your site.
- Make a link to your search page a standard part of every navigation banner or bar, and put one in a prominent place on the home page, too. Also consider putting one on the error page that your server returns when a visitor requests a nonexistent URL.
- The logs that search programs maintain provide valuable information about your visitors' interests. Take the time to study these logs and adapt your site's structure and content to give visitors more of what they're looking for.
- Web-enabling a database makes it possible for visitors to search for records and, if you allow it, add to and modify the database.
- A variety of commercial and even freeware packages exist for Web-enabling Windows and Mac OS databases. These packages eliminate the need to write custom CGI programs for database publishing.
- To optimize your database-publishing application, design search summary and detail record pages carefully.
- For databases that don't change often, you might find it easiest to export the data to tab-delimited text files and then use a CGI that merges this file with an HTML template.

Chapter 11

JavaScript and Java Secrets

In This Chapter

- Often overlooked basics of JavaScript
- Cool tricks, tips, and secrets of JavaScript, including a method of managing the creation, opening, and closing of new windows on the fly
- Known bugs and workarounds that often trip up even experienced JavaScripters
- The basics of how to call Java applets from within your JavaScripts
- Where to find ready-to-use JavaScripts and Java applets

Learning JavaScript is like climbing a mountain: it helps to take along an expert guide who can show you the ropes. That's why I asked Dan Shafer to share his experience in this chapter. Much of this material is not for JavaScript neophytes, but for people who have experimented with some canned JavaScripts — maybe the ones presented in earlier chapters — and are now trying to learn the language's subtleties. After we look at the finer points of JavaScript, Dan and I hit the basics of Java applets: how to find them, how to roll your own, and how to add them to your site. — Jim Heid

JavaScript, the scripting language developed by Netscape to include in its browsers, can be used to add an amazing array of features to a Web site. Previous chapters showcased several of the most common applications of JavaScript. For example, as described in Chapter 7, you can create cool user interfaces and navigation aids, such as pop-up menus and status bar messages. Chapter 8 illustrated how to use JavaScript to enhance a Web cam. You can also use JavaScript to perform calculations and check form entries for accuracy. In short, JavaScript is a powerful tool for adding smarts to a Web page.

This chapter isn't a beginner's tutorial on the scripting language, however. Many such guides already exist. Rather, this chapter is a collection of JavaScript insights, and tips, and pitfalls to avoid. Consider it a memoir of a veteran who descended into the JavaScript trenches and lived to tell the tale. (For a list of online JavaScript resources, see the following Secrets sidebar, "Essential JavaScript Resources.")

The information in this chapter applies specifically to the JavaScript implementations in Netscape Navigator. Microsoft incorporated JavaScript into Internet Explorer under the name JScript. The Internet Explorer implementation is not identical to the Netscape implementation, however, and differences are often quite annoying. In fact, Version 3.0 of Internet Explorer for the Macintosh doesn't even implement JavaScript or JScript. Microsoft promises to fix this problem, but at this writing, you can't be sure that Macintosh visitors to your site will be able to appreciate your JavaScripting prowess.

SECRET

Essential JavaScript Resources

As with so many things relating to the Net, some of the best JavaScript resources are online. Here are a few sites worth bookmarking:

- **JavaScript Authoring Guide** (`http://home.netscape.com/eng/mozilla/3.0/handbook/javascript/index.html`) Straight from Mozilla's mouth, this is Netscape's official documentation for the Navigator 3.x implementation of JavaScript.
- **The JavaScript Index** (`http://www.c2.org/~andreww/javascript/`) This site, maintained by Andrew Wooldridge, is a comprehensive list of JavaScript resources: books, sites, mailing lists, news groups, and much more.
- **Gamelan** (`http://www.gamelan.com`) Gamelan (pronounced gamma-lon) is one of the most popular and most comprehensive collections of JavaScript and Java information.
- **JavaScript Tip of the Week** (`http://webreference.com/javascript/`) True to its name, this terrific site provides a slick new JavaScript tip every week.
- **JavaWorld** (`http://www.javaworld.com/`) This monthly magazine includes a JavaScript column written by Gordon McComb, author of the *JavaScript Sourcebook* (Wiley Computer Publishing). McComb's own site at `http://www.gmccomb.com/` contains material to support his book.
- **My Web site** (`http://www.gui.com`) My site contains updates to my JavaScript book, documentation of new features of the language as they develop, and sample scripts that emerge from my day job as the Director of Technology and Senior Webmaster at Salon Magazine (`http://www.salonmagazine.com`).
- **Danny Goodman's JavaScript pages** (`http://www.dannyg.com/`) Veteran computer writer Danny Goodman's *JavaScript Bible, 2nd Edition* (IDG Books Worldwide, 1996) is an outstanding source of scripts and insights. His Web site contains examples from his book and more.
- **JavaScript: Simple Little Things to Add to Your Pages** (`http://tanega.com/java/java.html`) This site's name says it all — it's a collection of simple but useful JavaScripts that you can cut-and-paste into your own pages.
- **Yahoo!'s JavaScript Index** (`http://www.yahoo.com/Computers_and_Internet/Programming_Languages/JavaScript/`) Go here for a list of more JavaScript sites than you probably have time to explore.

Some of the subtle and not-so-subtle differences between JavaScript and JScript are discussed at several points in this chapter. A complete discussion of the differences is beyond the scope of this book, however. And such a list would quickly become obsolete anyway as soon as Microsoft or Netscape released new versions of their browsers.

Often Overlooked Basics

There are numerous subtleties in JavaScript that are important to master. Unfortunately, documentation on these nuances isn't always easy to find. In this section, I look at several of the basic issues that will help make your JavaScripting experience a little more smooth.

<HEIGHT> and <WIDTH> tags required

Many beginning JavaScripters encounter situations in which their scripts fail to execute without any apparent reason. The scripts are correct, properly placed, and properly called, but they don't run.

This problem, oddly enough, usually turns out to be related to the *images* on the page where the scripts appear.

Here's why. If you create pages that include images, forms, and JavaScripts, you must include `<HEIGHT>` and `<WIDTH>` tags in each of the page's `<IMG>` tags. If you omit `<HEIGHT>` and `<WIDTH>` tags, the JavaScripts on that page won't execute. Since JavaScripts don't take up display space, it's hard to see the connection between the absence of one or both of these tags and the failure of JavaScripts to execute, but that's the reality.

Actually, there is another way to avoid this problem, although it is a method I don't recommend. (You may hear others suggest the following approach, so I'll discuss it and then explain why it isn't a great idea.) You can put a blank script at the end of the HTML page before the `</BODY>` and `</HTML>` tags and the scripts will execute properly. The last lines of your page would then look like this:

```
<SCRIPT LANGUAGE="JavaScript">
</SCRIPT>
</BODY>
</HTML>
```

This approach may enable you to get away without using `<HEIGHT>` and `<WIDTH>` attributes, but is that really such a good thing? No it isn't. As Chapter 6 described, `<HEIGHT>` and `<WIDTH>` attributes enable a browser to lay out a page and display its text before the page's images have finished downloading. This boosts the perceived performance of a site, particularly for visitors with slow connections.

Another downside to this approach concerns compatibility. Adding a blank JavaScript to the end of a page may work with today's browsers, but it may cause tomorrows' to crash in flames.

Here's the bottom line: get into the habit of including `<HEIGHT>` and `<WIDTH>` tags in all of your images. Your pages will display faster, and you'll have one less JavaScript-related issue to troubleshoot.

Dates use zero-indexed months

Date-related functions and operations in JavaScript can be confusing. For example, you might expect this line of JavaScript:

```
theDate = new Date(96,03,10)
```

to end up placing the date, March 10, 1996, into the variable `theDate`. But you'd be wrong.

Months in JavaScript are zero-indexed. January is not month 1 as you'd expect, but rather month 0. The above line, then, would actually put the date April 10, 1996, into the variable `theDate`.

It is also worth noting that the Date activities in Netscape Navigator are quite buggy; I'll have more to say about this later in this chapter.

Arguments should be strings

Most of the time, arguments to JavaScripts need to be text strings. Where it seems logical that a number is appropriate, a string is often required. If you run into odd error messages and scripts that don't work or don't perform as expected, check your arguments and try converting them to strings. When in doubt, use strings.

A common example of overlooking this requirement involves the `window.setTimeout()` function. The basic syntax of this function is:

```
window.setTimeout ("JavaScript to execute", "delay in milliseconds");
```

For example, if you want a window to close after 10 seconds, you would write a line of JavaScript like this:

Right: `window.setTimeout ("window.close()", "10000");`

Because the second argument is a time in milliseconds, you might be tempted to write this call as:

Wrong: `window.setTimeout ("window.close()", 10000);`

But that would not work. At least it wouldn't work reliably on all platforms and with all versions of Netscape Navigator or Internet Explorer and JavaScript.

Working with frames

A good bit of controversy surrounds the question of whether frames are a good idea. People who object to the use of frames express concern about slower page load times and about what happens to frame-based layouts when they are viewed with browsers that don't support frames. Aesthetically, it is also pretty easy to come up with complex and cobbled-together frame layouts that are quite ugly. But frames are not in and of themselves bad; they are simply one technique. And, like all techniques, they can be used incorrectly.

As Andy King described in Chapter 7, frames allow you to divide a single browser window into discrete rectangular regions, each of which may or may not have scrollbars, the ability to be resized, or display its own URL. Whether you love frames or hate them, you can't deny that many site developers have put them to use since Netscape introduced them with Version 2.0 of the Navigator browser.

Figure 11-1 shows a typical navigation bar approach to a frame-based window. The top frame contains information that stays the same throughout the navigation process. For example, this site displays a banner that contains the name of the site that is unchanging. The left frame contains a table of contents, and when a visitor clicks on linked text or buttons, the contents of the right frame changes.

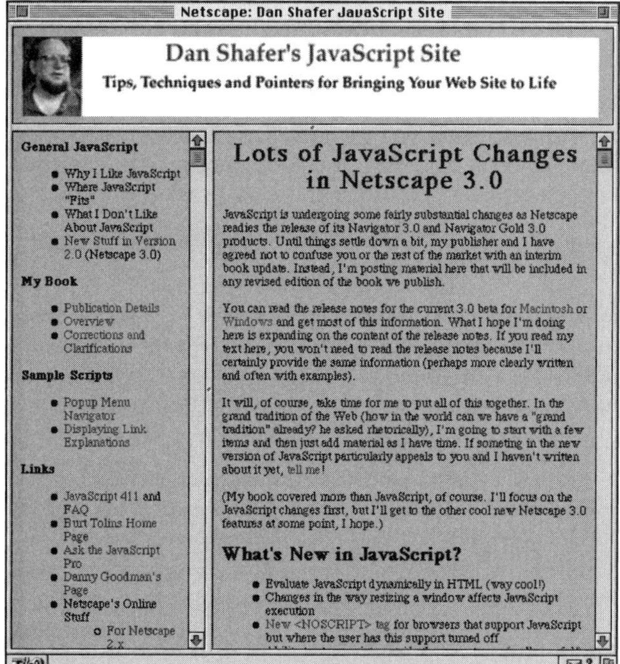

Figure 11-1: A typical multiframe navigation window

Using standard <HREF> tag terminology, you can allow the visitor's mouse-clicks in the left frame to alter the contents of the right frame. Adding JavaScript makes it possible to extend this interactivity in a number of interesting directions. To use either of these approaches in inter-frame communication, however, you must understand two basic ideas: frame names and the special variables that define specific uses of frames.

Special variable usage

Several specially defined JavaScript variables help you deal with frame interaction with greater flexibility than what is allowed by named frames. The most important of these special variables is `_top`.

If you have been displaying the visitor information in a frame-based window and you want to switch to a conventional, unframed window, you can set the `target` attribute's value to `_top` as shown in this example:

```
<A HREF="newstuff.html" TARGET="_top">link text</A>
```

Depending on the version of the browser the visitor is using, this may close the current, frame-based window. In any case, it opens a new window with no frames and displays the URL in the new window.

Calling scripts in other windows and frames

As you become more experienced with JavaScript, you'll eventually want to use a script that exists in a window other than the current one. Doing so isn't difficult; it's just not very clearly explained in documentation.

Consider a scenario in which you opened a window called "Main Window" and renamed it "main." This window has a number of links, one of which opens a window titled "Employee Detail." You open this window with a line like this:

```
<A HREF="#" onClick="newWindow('Employee Detail", "empdetail")>link
text</A>
```

Let's say that the Main window contains several JavaScript functions in its <HEAD> section, one of which is called `calculateSalary`. You want to use this function in the Employee Detail window. To do so, you need to only supply a full path name to the script. Rather than calling the function in the usual way by using:

```
calculateSalary(this.form1.jobLevel.value)
```

you would prefix the function name with the path to its location in the current environment. Something like this:

```
main.calculateSalary(this.form1.jobLevel.value)
```

This same approach works with scripts that appear in other frames in the current window or even in a frame in another window. Just work out the full path to the frame starting at the browser's viewpoint and you'll be just fine.

This problem is solved in Netscape 3.x and JavaScript 1.1. This release added an `src` attribute to the `<SCRIPT>` tag that lets you store your JavaScripts in a file that is completely outside the page or pages from which they are called. Unfortunately, this trick isn't supported in earlier versions of Netscape Navigator in recent releases of Microsoft Internet Explorer, but if you are in an environment such as an intranet where you can control the browser your users run, you might find this trick quite useful. You can also implement this technique if you have a way of determining which browser a visitor is using and then routing him or her to the right page. This is becoming increasingly common and necessary as the Browser Wars continue to accelerate.

Avoiding the mysterious User Directory quirk

Sooner or later, you'll be testing some code and write a line like this:

```
<A HREF="" onClick="...some JavaScript...">text to click</A>
```

You'll click on the text and the original window will fill with a directory listing of your local disk's directory. If you're like me, you'll be a tad surprised at that turn of events.

It isn't clear if this is a bug, but there's a simple way of dealing with the need to supply an empty or dummy `<HREF>` during JavaScript testing. Rather than an empty string, use a pound sign (anchor link tag) as a value for the `href` attribute:

```
<A HREF="#" onClick="...some JavaScript...">text to click</A>
```

All will now be well.

Cool Tricks, Tips, and Secrets

JavaScript has myriad uses. In this section, I look at how to use it to carry out interesting and useful tasks.

Rounding numbers

If you create HTML pages that use JavaScript to perform calculations, you probably want those calculated figures to be rounded off to some reasonable number of decimal places. By default, JavaScript in Netscape produces numerical results to 16 decimal places (on the Macintosh; other platforms may vary), which is rarely — if ever — what you want.

Here is a script that rounds values to the number of decimal places you provide as an argument to the function:

```
function roundOff (val, places) {
    whole = Math.floor(val)
    val = "" + Math.round(val * (Math.pow(10,places)))
```

```
    decimal = val.substring (val.length-places, val.length)
    return (whole + "." + decimal);
}
```

You could easily extend this script so that it returns a formatted US dollar amount to two places:

```
function roundDollars (val) {
    whole = Math.floor(val)
    val = "" + Math.round(val * 100)
    decimal = val.substring (val.length-places, val.length)
    return ("$" + whole + "." + decimal);
}
```

Creating read-only form fields

You may find yourself in an interesting dilemma if you make extensive use of forms on your HTML pages. Let's say you have some data that you don't want the visitor to be able to change but that you need to submit when the visitor submits the form. There are at least two ways to accomplish this.

First, you can use a hidden field and set its value. The values of hidden fields are submitted along with the values of visible form elements when the visitor clicks on the form's Submit button or its equivalent. This is the most common technique.

But what if you want users to see the information so that they can cancel the submission if the information is wrong or causes them to change their minds about submitting the form? One way to accomplish this is to create a read-only Text object in the form.

You can make a Text object read-only by intercepting the `onFocus` event when the field receives it, and have that event trigger a script that simply selects the next field on the form (any other object that can be selected, for that matter).

Here's a simple example. The form in Figure 11-2 is created by the following HTML:

```
<HTML>
<HEAD>
<TITLE>Sample Form</TITLE>
<BODY>
This form demonstrates a read-only Text object.<P>
<FORM NAME="testForm" ACTION="" METHOD="POST">
This field is read-only: <INPUT TYPE="text" NAME="field1" VALUE="This
is a test" LENGTH="30" onFocus="document.testForm.field2.select();
document.testForm.field2.focus()"><P>
This field accepts user input: <INPUT TYPE="text" NAME="field2"
VALUE="" LENGTH="30"><P>
<INPUT TYPE="submit" NAME="" VALUE="Submit">
</FORM>
</BODY>
</HTML>
```

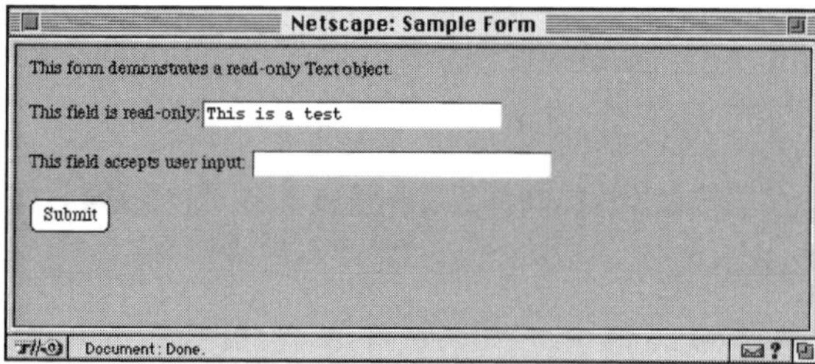

Figure 11-2: A simple form with read-only field

When users try to click or tab into the first field, the insertion point immediately appears in the second field. No amount of chicanery (at least no reasonable amount of chicanery) will circumvent this behavior.

Executing single-line scripts interactively

When you just want to find out what a particular JavaScript statement or operation might do, or you want to test a statement to see why it's not working in a full script as expected, you can use a nearly hidden trick. In Navigator, click within the Location field, type **javascript:** (don't forget the colon), and then type the script and press Return.

Here's an example. Type the following text into the Location field of your Netscape Navigator window:

```
javascript:alert("The answer is: " + 13 * 39)
```

The result is a by-now-familiar JavaScript dialog like the one shown in Figure 11-3.

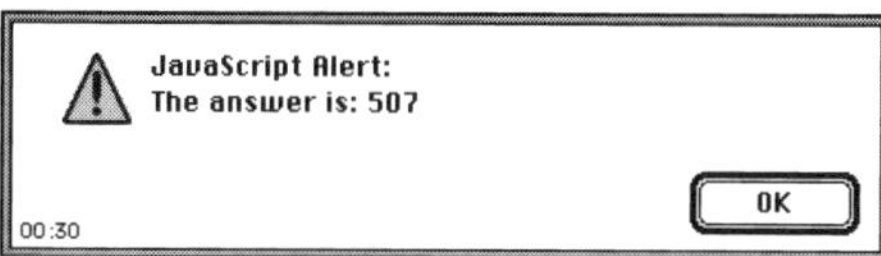

Figure 11-3: Dialog produced by single-line JavaScript

For historical reasons, you can substitute either *livescript* or *mocha* for the word *javascript* in this example and the results will be identical. LiveScript is what JavaScript was called before the marketing people at Netscape got into the loop. Presumably, "mocha" was an internal code word or shorthand term for the scripting language. Or maybe it was just some engineer's favorite beverage.

You can also use this notation — placing the language name and a colon before a script — in the event-driven scripts you include in your HTML pages. Doing so isn't necessary if you are using JavaScript because Navigator defaults to that language. However, other browsers might not always do so.

Carrying out multiple tasks in a single event handler

Often the need arises to carry out two or more tasks as a result of a single event. To do so requires an understanding of the way events are processed by Navigator via JavaScript.

Assume you want to create a Submit button on a form that submits the form and then takes the visitor to a new location using a JavaScript function you defined and called `goToIndex()`. We won't concern ourselves here with the code in the function itself; rather, our focus is getting the visitor's click of the Submit button to instigate two tasks.

As you know, when someone clicks a button whose type is defined as *submit,* Navigator calls the function or CGI defined as the value of the `action` attribute of the form object to which the button belongs. If you want an additional task performed, you might think that you could just define an onClick handler for the submit button, as shown here:

```
<INPUT TYPE="submit" NAME="Submit Form" onClick="goToIndex()">
```

This approach will not work, however. The reason: a form submission isn't handled in the same way as a normal JavaScript. Even if the form's `action` attribute has a value that is the name of a JavaScript function, the submission process will occur but the function called in the `onClick` event handler will never execute.

The problem is that Navigator calls the `submit` function and then immediately calls the `onClick` handler's event script. But because the form has not been submitted yet — the process has been initiated but not completed — the second process ends up in a state of suspended animation.

To solve this problem, insert a `setTimeout()` function call ahead of the function you want called in the `onClick` handler. The number of milliseconds you supply as the second parameter to this function is largely a matter of trial and error, and depends to a great extent on how much time the form submission process requires. Start with 2000 (which pauses for two seconds) and increase gradually until you find a value that works for a given form.

Here's the HTML that would have this effect:

```
<INPUT TYPE="button" NAME="Submit Form" onClick=" window.setTimeout
('goToIndex()',2000)">
```

This scheme — inserting a `window.setTimeout()` function before functions that are to be called in a sequence — often works in other situations as well. If you find that your JavaScripts behave somewhat erratically when they follow one another, try this technique. It may save you quite a bit of hair.

Adding information to a mailto: link

One of the most useful HREF links you can use in a Web page is the mailto: link, which generates an e-mail message addressed to the e-mail address specified in the link. For example, this link would send an e-mail message to the sales department at the (hypothetical) Smith Co.:

```
<A HREF="mailto:info@smith.com">Contact Smith Co. Sales</A>
```

Occasionally you may want to create a link that generates an e-mail message with a pre-determined subject line so that you can appropriately screen incoming mail. Or you may want to send one or more carbon copies (CCs) of the message. You can do either or both of these from a mailto: link. (Strictly speaking, of course, none of this has anything to do with JavaScript. But since you're likely to use the mailto: tag in conjunction with a button on a form where JavaScripts are used, it seems to make sense to include this discussion here.)

To add a subject line to an e-mail message using this technique, use the question mark separator and then add a subject= attribute followed by the subject you want to use, as in the following example:

```
<A HREF="mailto:info@smith.com?subject=Widget Inquiry">Contact Smith
Co. Sales</A>
```

Similarly, you can add one or more CCs to an e-mail message generated this way:

```
<A HREF="mailto:info@smith.com?CC=pres@smith.com,
support@smith.com">Contact Smith Co. Sales</A>
```

You can add either a subject line or a CC line with this technique, but you can't add both, nor can you add e-mail content using this technique. (As with many such techniques, you'll want to test this in any browser you want to support on your site. With some versions of Internet Explorer, for example, adding information after the mailing address can result in the mail being addressed incorrectly.)

Keeping browsing context

Normally, when surfers activate a link, the browser takes them to a new location by replacing the contents of the window with the contents of the destination URL. In the process, the original contents of the window or frame are hidden. (Actually, they're placed into the document's history so that the user can navigate back and forth among recently visited pages.) However, you might find that it is useful for the original window to remain visible when the user navigates off of your site. Keeping the original window visible enables the visitor to quickly and easily return to your site after a side trip — instead of having to click the Back button, the visitor can simply activate the window that contains your site. This scheme also helps give the visitor some context (a way of remembering) where he or she was before traveling to a new location.

There are several ways to accomplish this, both with and without JavaScript. The JavaScript method is to use an `onClick` handler for the link and return a value of `false` instead of `true` at the end of the handler.

Here's an example:

```
Open the <A HREF="#"
onClick='window.open("http://www.gui.com/","");return false'>GUI
window</A>
```

Normally, JavaScript returns a value of `true` to let the browser know that the event has been handled and normal processing can resume. By returning `false`, we essentially suspend normal processing on the browser's part. In this example, the result is that the window in which this link appears remains open after opening my personal home page at `http://www.gui.com/`.

Referring to another window

As you create more complex Web sites with many pages, you will undoubtedly encounter situations in which you'd like one window to refer to something in another window. Doing so isn't difficult, but it's not entirely self-evident, either.

To avoid confusion in this example, let's call the first window "Window A" and the second window "Window B." Now let's say that some action a visitor takes in Window A causes Window B to open. Window A is also presumably one that the user opened (or that you opened for the user) so that you are in control of its contents, including its JavaScripts.

The method for this inter-window communication is considerably simpler with JavaScript 1.1 (which debuted in Navigator 3.0) than it was with JavaScript 1.0, so let's look at the two versions separately.

Referencing another window in JavaScript 1.0

In JavaScript 1.0, you need to provide some way for Window B to "know" about Window A. The only way to do this is to define a new property for Window B that contains Window A's identity. You can then use the new property to refer back to Window A.

To do this, you have to open Window B from Window A with a JavaScript, not with a standard HREF link, which is pretty straightforward. Here's what the basic link text and its associated anchor would look like:

```
<A HREF="#" onClick="openNewWindow('newLocation.html');return
false">Open the new window by clicking here.</A>
```

Notice that we call a function named `openNewWindow` and give it an argument that is the URL of the desired destination. Also notice that we returned a value of `false` (rather than the usual `true`) so that Window A remains open, as discussed earlier in this section.

Here's what the minimal JavaScript called `openNewWindow` might look like:

```
<SCRIPT LANGUAGE="JavaScript">
<!--Hide from non-JavaScript browsers
function openNewWin (destURL) {
winB=window.open(destURL)
winB.opener=self //This is the key idea
return false
}
//-->End hiding
</SCRIPT>
```

In the fifth line of the script, I create a new property for the new window. The property is called "opener" but it could have been called "Fred" for all JavaScript cares. (You'll see in a little while why I chose the name *opener*.) This places the identifier of the current window (Window A) into the opener property of Window B.

Now in Window B, where you want to refer to something in Window A, you simply use the `opener` property to do so. For example, let's say you wanted to get the value of a text field called `username` from the form in Window A. You could use this reference:

```
opener.theForm.username.value
```

JavaScript would translate this as meaning the form called `theForm` in the window identified in the `opener` property (in this case, Window A).

Referencing another window in JavaScript 1.1

With the release of JavaScript 1.1, Netscape's engineers decided to make our lives a little easier. Each time you create a window with an `open()` function in JavaScript 1.1, JavaScript automatically creates a property for the newly opened window called (as you might have guessed) *opener*. You can use this property as described in the previous section to refer to any property or content of the originating window.

Compatibility techniques

Until you can be sure that all of your visitors are using a browser that supports the JavaScript 1.1 extensions (in other words, Netscape 3.0 or later at the moment), you can use conditional logic in the JavaScript in Window A that opens another window to ensure that the new window contains an `opener` property, regardless of which JavaScript version it runs under. The code fragment looks like this:

```
var windowB = window.open("URL")
if (windowB != null && windowB.opener == null) // Netscape 2.0 in use
windowB.opener=self
```

You can now be sure that each of the windows opened by your window will have an opener property that can be used to refer back to the original window.

Bringing a different window to the front

You can't use a graphical user interface for very long without falling victim to window clutter: multiple overlapping windows littering your digital desktop. (And if Murphy's Law has any say in it, the window you want is buried beneath them all.) In the Web world, window clutter can be a problem if you've created a small navigation window, sometimes called a remote control, that enables visitors to navigate through your site. If this window gets buried beneath other browser windows, it's almost as bad as losing the remote control under the couch cushions. What you need (for your virtual remote control, anyway) is a way to force a window back to the top of the stack.

By using the `focus()` method associated with a Window object in Navigator 3.x and with form objects in Navigator 2.x, you can force a window that may be behind the current window (even several levels behind it) to become the topmost window.

In JavaScript 1.1, the code is simple:

```
opener.focus()
```

In JavaScript 1.0, windows don't understand the `focus()` function. As a result, you have to have a form object to which to give the focus:

```
opener.document.formName.elementName.focus()
```

This latter technique is not completely reliable. In some situations, particularly on Macintosh and UNIX platforms, this approach works sporadically. Experimenting with different approaches to the form contents may help you work out a way that is reliable in your situation.

Taking full advantage of mouse movements

Virtually anyone who has written a handful of JavaScripts is familiar with the `mouseOver` event, which is triggered when a visitor positions the mouse pointer over a link. It is common to use this technique to display text descriptions of what the link does in the browser window's status bar. (Chapter 7 contains an example of this technique in action.)

A new mouse event was introduced in JavaScript 1.1, but it's not clearly documented and it requires a small workaround, which I shortly describe. This event is called `mouseOut`. It is triggered when the user positions the cursor over a piece of text that responds to `mouseOver`, and then moves the cursor away from that text. Here's a simple example of its use:

```
<A HREF="#" onMouseOver="status='You are over me!';return true"
onMouseOut = "alert('You left me!')">The text for the status
update.</A><P>
```

This link displays the text, "You are over me" in the status bar when the user moves the pointer over the link text, and then displays an alert box containing the message "You left me!" when the user moves the pointer outside of the link text.

You can use `onMouseOver` and `onMouseOut` to create user interfaces that approach those of a CD-ROM title — with buttons that change shape when pointed to, for example. For details on this and other user-interface magic that JavaScript makes possible, refer back to Chapter 7.

SECRET

If you want the `mouseOut` event to update the status bar, be sure to insert a `window.setTimeout` call before attempting to change the status bar. If you don't insert this delay, the script will appear not to work. This is because there is a delay in execution involved in changing the status bar's contents.

Bugs and Workarounds

This final section describes some of the peskiest bugs in Version 3.x of Navigator and, where possible, how to work around them. New bugs are found and fixed all the time, so before you assume these bugs are valid in the version of JavaScript you're using, check them out. The release notes furnished by Netscape with each new version of Navigator generally document known bugs and workarounds.

Also note that some of the bugs in this section aren't strictly bugs, but fall into that weird category known as the "unexpected behavior." That is, they may work as intended by JavaScript's developers, but they still do things that some script authors find to be unusual.

document.clear() broken

On all platforms, the `clear()` function associated with the `document` object does not work as expected. Since Netscape indicated that it will remove this function at some point, you should avoid using it.

For what it's worth, when you do use `document.clear()`, the apparent erasure of the document in the window is just that: apparent. If the window is obscured and then brought back to the top, for example, the document contents mysteriously reappear.

As a rule, you don't want to clear the document in any case. Modifying the contents of a window after it's been displayed isn't possible in JavaScript. Although some techniques may appear to work now, they're unlikely to work in the future as JavaScript matures.

If you really want to substitute a new document in a window, close the window and open a new one. It's a good idea to perform the tasks in this order. If you open the new one and then close the old one, the visitor may not see as obvious a visual change.

window.open() flawed on non-Windows platforms

The `open()` function associated with Window objects is broken on all platforms other than all versions of Microsoft Windows. This is one of the most annoying bugs in JavaScript because of the following:

- It appears to indicate that Netscape engineers working on JavaScript are more interested in getting it right on Windows than in doing it correctly on all platforms.
- It has been a problem from the first version.
- By all accounts, it shouldn't be hard to fix.
- Working around it is a hassle.

With that venting out of the way, what exactly is the problem? On all non-Windows platforms, if you want to open a new window with a URL in it, you must call the `open()` method *twice*. Failing to do so opens an empty window. (There are other solutions, including setting a newly opened window's location property, but using the same call twice is foolproof.)

Unfortunately, calling the `open()` method twice on a Windows system opens two identical windows. As a result, JavaScripters adopted the practice of determining whether the script is running under the Windows platform, and then acting accordingly. The following function illustrates one way to accomplish this:

```
var isWinUser = navigator.userAgent.indexOf("Win") != -1
newWin = window.open ("newURL.html")
if !isWinUser {
newWin = window.open ("newURL.html")
}
//rest of the function
}
```

If the first line results in a value other than –1, the substring "Win" is contained in the identification of the user's browser, so we can be sure the user is running a Windows browser. Next, the script tests the value of this variable and decides whether to call the `open()` method a second time.

Executing "changed" code

Every JavaScripter has encountered this bug. You edit a Web page containing one or more JavaScripts, save it, then tell your HTML editor to preview the page in Navigator for you. The error you just thought you fixed shows up again. You click the Reload button but the result is identical. You have fallen victim to the fact that Navigator's caching algorithm sometimes fails to refresh a page in memory as it should.

If this happens to you, two solutions seem to work.

First, you can order Navigator to do a *super reload*. You can do this by pressing the Shift (Windows) or Option (Mac OS) key while clicking on the Reload button in the browser toolbar.

Second, you can place the insertion point in the browser window's location-editing box and then press Return.

Either of these techniques properly refreshes the page so that the most recently saved version of the page and the JavaScripts on it are loaded and executed.

Hiding your JavaScript source

One of the problems many JavaScripters saw in Version 1.0 was the inability to hide their source code. If the user chooses one of the source-viewing options from the View menu, the JavaScript code is immediately readable. There are many reasons you might wish to protect your JavaScripts from prying eyes, but in JavaScript 1.0, you simply cannot do it.

With the release of Navigator 3.0 and JavaScript 1.1, Netscape added a new attribute to the `<SCRIPT>` tag. The `<SRC>` tag is used to point to a local file containing JavaScript code, which the browser loads and includes in the document dynamically. The user viewing the source of the page sees only the `<SCRIPT>` tag with the `src` attribute:

```
<SCRIPT SRC="../jssource/tools.js">
```

The JavaScript file must end with the suffix ".js" for this to work.

How'd that directory get in there?

You've seen in a number of places in this chapter where I've used `HREF` values that consisted of a single "#" character. You may have wondered why I did that.

If you supply an empty `HREF` in an anchor link, Netscape will create a URL that results in it displaying the contents of the current directory. This is not only ugly and unexpected, it has the potential of revealing information not intended for public consumption.

By using "#" as the `HREF` link, you tell Netscape Navigator to go to an anchor whose name is empty. And the result is that the browser stays on the current page.

Where did that field value go?

JavaScripters who build forms on their pages often use hidden objects to contain data they need but don't wish the user to see. The generic tag for such objects is the following:

```
<INPUT TYPE="hidden" NAME="StartTime" VALUE="0915">
```

When a Web page is reloaded, however, the values of these hidden objects are forgotten — that is, they revert to the values they had when the page was loaded. The values in visible objects do not get reset. It's important, therefore, that you not store any information in hidden objects that will be modified dynamically.

Why did Navigator quit?

On Windows platforms, if the user or a script closes the last window on the screen, Netscape Navigator simply quits. (On Macintosh and UNIX platforms, this problem does not arise.)

To avoid this problem, you have to ensure that any JavaScript you include on a page that is designed to close a window checks the window's name first. A top-level window you didn't create will have no name and should therefore not be closed by your scripts.

The following code fragment addresses the problem:

```
if (window.name != null) {
    window.close()
}
```

This implies, of course, the necessity that you name all windows your scripts open, but that's good JavaScripting practice anyway.

In Navigator 3.x, if a script attempts to close a window it did not create, a dialog box appears asking if the user really wants to close the window. This confirmation dialog box is a pain for the user, who not only has to answer the question but also probably has no clue why the question is being posed in the first place. Unfortunately there is no way to avoid it. And in any case, users will probably come to appreciate it once they understand its purpose.

Watch text size limits on scripts

Each of the platforms on which Netscape Navigator is available has its own built-in system limitation on how large a text document it can deal with. If your pages or scripts exceed this limit, strange things can happen.

The most common evidence of this arises when a complex JavaScript fails to execute as expected or generates strange syntax errors. When you open the script in your favorite editor, it may look fine, but if you choose View Source from within Navigator and then scroll to the bottom, you may be surprised to see that the last portion of the file failed to load. The only way to solve this problem is to break your scripts into pieces that fit within each system's limitations.

While reliable data is not available (apparently because of a number of system interaction issues), Windows platform JavaScripters report problems when a script exceeds 20 to 40K. On the Macintosh, the limit is approximately 32K. (UNIX platform limitations vary widely.)

Problems with less-than signs

If a very old browser is browsing your JavaScript-enhanced page, JavaScript errors may arise even though you've carefully hidden the script from view with comments. Some of the older browsers recognize a comment as beginning with the <!-- sequence but expect the comment to be terminated not by the standard --> combination but by a single greater-than sign (>). This won't cause a problem unless your JavaScript contains a greater-than sign as part of its code, in which case the old browser sees the next character as valid text to render. To get around this one, reverse the logic of the comparison operator. Instead of `a>b`, for example, use the logically equivalent `b<=a`.

Dates border on unusable

In Netscape Navigator 2.x and JavaScript 1.0, the Date object's methods have so many bugs that the object is considered all but unusable. A complete list of all of the bugs would be many pages long; suffice it to say that you should either avoid using the Date and Time objects altogether or thoroughly test your code if you must use them.

Netscape promised to fix these problems in a later release of Navigator. Indeed, some of the problems are fixed in Navigator 3.0, but some persist. My advice is to ignore date and time functions and use a Java applet to deal with these issues, at least until Netscape gets these bugs straightened out.

Incorporating Java Applets in Your Pages

There has been a good deal of confusion in the market between JavaScript and Java. It didn't help matters when Netscape renamed LiveScript to JavaScript in an attempt to capitalize on the burgeoning fame of the Java programming language. But there are a number of key differences between Java applets and JavaScripts. For our purposes, the most important differences include the following:

- JavaScript is a reasonably easy-to-use language that non-programmers can master, while Java is a full-blown, modern programming language that requires programming skills to use effectively.

- JavaScripts are generally written directly into a Web page, while Java applets are never stored on the page itself. Instead, a Java applet is invoked from a Web page by an `<APPLET>` tag.
- JavaScripts, for the most part, only can deal with the information contained within the HTML page to which they are related. This limits their capabilities considerably. A Java applet can be aware of anything that exists on the server from which it is served to the visitor, giving it far broader powers.
- JavaScripts typically wait for an event to take place before they begin to execute, while Java applets tend to begin loading and running as soon as the page on which they are included has finished transferring to the visitor's browser.

Calling an applet from your Web page

To call a Java applet from your Web page, simply insert an `<APPLET>` tag where you want the applet to appear on the page. This tag requires three parameters:

- `CODE`, which tells the browser the file name for the Java class that constitutes the applet
- `HEIGHT`, which tells the browser how much vertical space to set aside for the applet's display
- `WIDTH`, which tells the browser how much horizontal space to set aside for the applet's display

A typical call to a Java applet, then, might look something like this:

```
<APPLET CODE="D:\MySite\applets\HelloApplet.class" HEIGHT="50"
WIDTH="100">
```

In case you're curious, the class is created by the Java compiler when the Java programmer finishes writing and testing a program and then tells the compiler to generate the application for use in a browser. The names of such objects, which can include full-blown programs in addition to applets, always end with the word *class* preceded by a period.

You may wish to separate the path name of your applets from the names of the applets themselves; doing so gives you some flexibility in locating your applets. If you move them, you can just change a parameter. You can also use conditional processing to define the base path (for example, depending on which browser the visitor is using or on which server the visitor is logged into) and still be required to provide just a single `<APPLET>` tag. In this case, use the `CODEBASE` parameter, as shown here:

```
<APPLET CODEBASE="D:\MySite\applets\" CODE="HelloApplet.class"
HEIGHT="50" WIDTH="100">
```

Passing parameters to applets

Most Java applets require some information to operate. For example, an applet designed to look up an employee record in a database might expect to be told the employee's ID number so it can find the employee. You can pass parameters to Java applets by using the <PARAM> tag. In the case of this fictitious database applet, you might write the code like this:

```
<APPLET CODEBASE="D:\MySite\applets" CODE="FindEmployee.class"
HEIGHT="250" WIDTH="350">
<PARAM NAME="EmployeeID" VALUE="14923">
</APPLET>
```

This example demonstrates how to pass parameters to an applet and points out that the <APPLET> tag is a container tag — that is, it is non-empty and requires a closing </APPLET> tag.

Dealing with browsers that don't drink Java

Dressing up a site with Java applets isn't exactly developing for the lowest common denominator. What do you do about the millions of Web surfers who don't have Java-capable browsers?

One alternative is to create non-Java versions of your applet-enhanced pages and redirect Java-ignorant browsers to those pages. (See Part IV for details on browser redirection.) With this scheme, surfers using Java-capable browsers get the applets, and everyone else gets applet-free pages.

An easier alternative is to create your applet-enhanced pages so that they display an error message or alternate text when viewed on a Java-dumb browser. Simply place the error message between the <APPLET> and </APPLET> tags, like so:

```
<APPLET CODEBASE="D:\MySite\applets" CODE="FindEmployee.class"
HEIGHT="250" WIDTH="350">
<PARAM NAME="EmployeeID" VALUE="14923">
<H2>Sorry, you must use a Java-supporting browser in order to view
employee data</H2>
</APPLET>
```

When this page is viewed with a browser that doesn't support Java, this tag displays the error message. On a browser that does support Java, the applet runs.

Easy ways to sample some Java

Although Java is a complex programming language, you don't have to own a beanie with a propeller on top of it in order to incorporate applets into your site. A large selection of ready-to-use applets is available online.

Macromedia's AppletAce

The folks at Macromedia, the company responsible for the Shockwave family of Web multimedia technologies, created a family of useful applets called PowerApplets, all of which are available free from Macromedia's Web site at `http://www.macromedia.com/`.

Within the PowerApplets clan is an applet that creates animated text and graphics displays. Another applet generates charts based on data in a text file. Still another creates sophisticated image maps that can contain graphics that change when the mouse pointer moves over them.

You can download and customize the applets individually, but a better approach is to download them all along with Macromedia's free AppletAce, a Windows-based utility that makes it easy to customize the PowerApplets. AppleAce runs under Windows 95/NT only, but the PowerApplets work on any Java-supporting platform. AppletAce even generates the HTML needed to call the applet. In all, it's a great way to test the waters of Java.

Figure 11-4 illustrates AppletAce being used to set up a text animation.

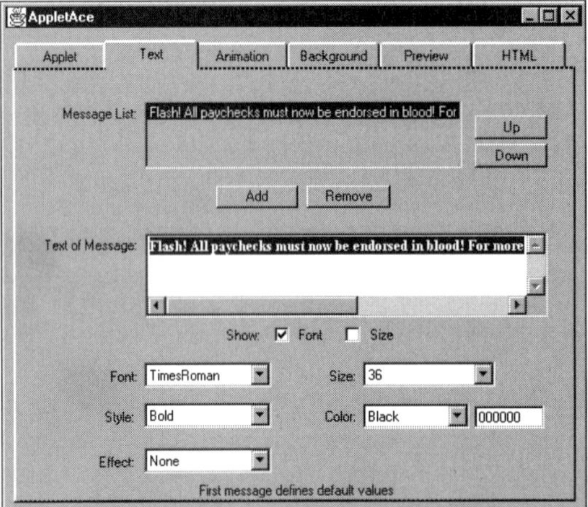

Figure 11-4: Macromedia's AppletAce in action. Here, an animated text banner is being created.

The banner's text and text formatting are specified here.

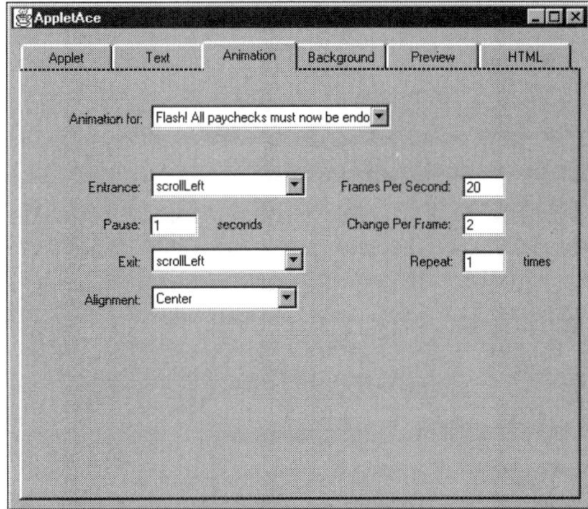

You can choose from a variety of animation styles.

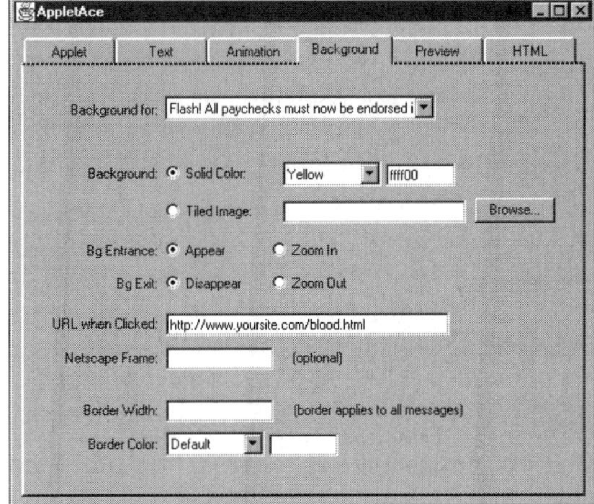

You can specify a background color and a URL to be opened when a visitor clicks on the banner.

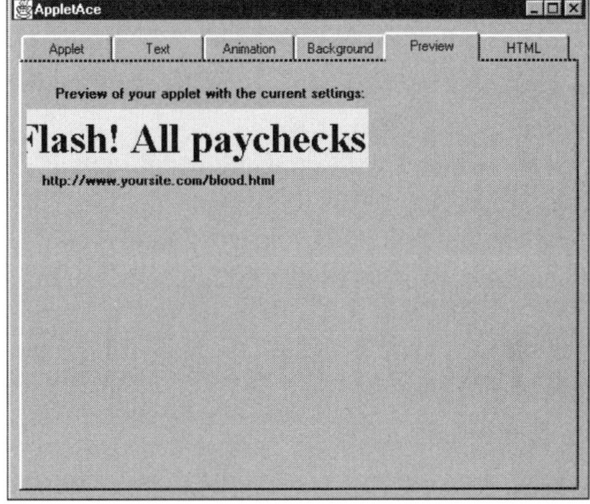

A preview mode shows what the final product will look like.

Other sources for Java applets

The Gamelan site (http://www.gamelan.com/) mentioned at the beginning of this chapter is another superb source for Java applets. Grab a cub of java and spend a few hours exploring it. You're bound to find some applets that have a place on your Web site.

You might also consider creating your own Java applets — no, not by buying a compiler and pecking out your own source code, but by using one of the growing number of multimedia authoring tools that enable you to save your efforts as Java applets. One such tool on the Mac OS side is ActionLine, from Interactive Media Corporation (http://www.imcinfo.com/). Within ActionLine's simple authoring environment, you can build interactive image maps, animations, and presentations, and then save them as Java applets. Another such product is Astound's (http://www.astound.com/) WebMotion, which is available for Mac OS and Windows machines alike.

Some observers believe that it remains to be seen what Java's ultimate impact on the Web — and on the computer world as a whole — will be. I happen to be a member of the school of thought that holds Java as a serious world-changer. The longer it is used and the more it is extended, the more convinced of that I become. But in the near term, there's no question that Java applets have the potential to enhance a Web site — provided you address the thorny issues of browser compatibility and provide alternatives for visitors who don't have Java-savvy browsers.

Summary

- You must include `<HEIGHT>` and `<WIDTH>` tags on all images you place on pages that also contain JavaScripts or the scripts may fail to execute.
- JavaScript defines dates so that January is month 0 instead of month 1.
- Most of the time, you should use strings as arguments to your JavaScripts even when you are passing numeric values. This will become increasingly unnecessary over time, but for the moment it does no harm and is a good idea.
- Use specially defined variables such as "_top" to manage the interaction among frames.
- By supplying the full path name to an open window containing a JavaScript, you can execute that script from another window.
- Supply an unnamed anchor tag in an `HREF` link when using an `onClick` handler to avoid having the user presented with a list of the files in the Web site directory.
- You can intercept the `onFocus` event for a field to make it read-only so that its value can be submitted with the form but not edited by the visitor.

- Test your simple JavaScript one-liners by typing them in the Location field in the Navigator window, preceding them with the label `javascript:`.
- Use `window.setTimeout()` to provide a needed pause between two processes to be carried out in one event handler function.
- You can add a subject line and a CC line to an e-mail message you send with a `mailto:` link, but this doesn't work in all browsers so you should test it before publishing a page that uses it.
- Sometimes it helps to retain some navigational context for your visitors by opening new pages in a new window rather than simply replacing window contents. You can use `window.open()` to accomplish this.
- When a window is opened by a script in Navigator 3.x, it carries with it a property called `opener` that defines the window from which it was launched. Navigator 2.x omitted this feature but you can emulate it with a user-defined variable. This allows you to carry out inter-window communication.
- Take advantage of the `mouseOut` event introduced in Navigator 3.x (JavaScript 1.1) to add even more interactivity to your pages.
- Among the most annoying bugs to watch for in JavaScript are the fact that the `document.clear()` function is broken on all platforms, the `window.open()` function doesn't work correctly on any non-Windows system, and your Navigator browser doesn't always load the latest version of your script even when you tell it to reload the page. In addition, the values of hidden fields are reset when the page is reloaded, Navigator can be accidentally quit if the last window is closed, and date and time arithmetic is so buggy it's unusable.
- Calling a Java applet from your Web page requires the `<APPLET>` tag and a minimum of three parameters: `CODE` (which is where the class to be loaded and run is found), `HEIGHT` and `WIDTH` (which describe the size of the region in the browser document to set aside for the applet).
- Passing parameters to a Java applet uses a `<PARAM>` tag with two properties called NAME and VALUE.
- Any valid HTML placed between an `<APPLET>` and a `</APPLET>` tag will not be executed by a Java-aware browser, but will be seen and treated as expected by a Java-ignorant browser. This provides a good way to let visitors without Java-enabled browsers know what they're missing.
- Macromedia's AppletAce is one of the best online sources for sample Java applets that you can incorporate in your site without learning a lick of Java.

Part III

Web Multimedia Secrets

Chapter 12

Make it Move: Web Animation

In This Chapter

- The promise and pitfalls of animation plug-ins
- Secrets of the animated GIF
- Ready-made motion: where to find canned animation for your site
- Avoid motion sickness: guidelines for using animation on Web pages
- Web-animation techniques and technologies compared
- Push me, pull you: client and server animation schemes

Web technologies tend to change faster than the minds of politicians, and one of the fastest-moving targets is motion itself: animation. Numerous commercial products that enable you to create animations that play back with browser plug-ins are available. The best known is Macromedia's Shockwave for Director, which lets Director projects play over the Web. Sun Microsystems's Java programming language is also frequently touted as an animation medium, although as described in Chapter 11, its capabilities go well beyond bouncing buttons.

But there are problems with commercial Web-animation technologies. One is that they require browser plug-ins, which only more-recent versions of Netscape Navigator and Microsoft Internet Explorer can use. This narrows the audience of a site — not only because millions of people access the Web with other browsers, but also because even Navigator and Explorer users may lack the particular plug-in your animation requires. While most of these plug-ins are free and widely available, users may not want to download and install them. And if they do, the high memory overhead imposed by many plug-ins may make their browsers unreliable. A gracious host doesn't make visitors jump through hoops just to get in the door, nor does a Web site trying to attract visitors or customers.

Another problem with commercial animation products is that they generally require you to fine-tune the Web server software so that it recognizes the animation format. Technically speaking, you must set up a *content map* that enables the server to tell a browser how to handle the incoming data. The content map associates a particular file extension, such as Shockwave for

Director's .dcr, with a particular plug-in. When the browser sees an incoming file with that extension, it knows which plug-in to use. That's a two-minute tweak if you're operating your own server, but it can be a drama if an Internet service provider is hosting the site. And if you're running a small site through an online service such as America Online, it's downright impossible.

One form of Web animation doesn't require a plug-in, works with both Netscape Navigator and Microsoft Internet Explorer, and needs no server tweaking. It's the animated GIF, and you've undoubtedly seen them popping up and moving around on Web sites. This chapter is a guide to creating animated GIFs and also compares some alternative animation options.

ON CD-ROM

Make Some Moving Experiences of Your Own

The *HTML & Web Publishing SECRETS* CD-ROM contains a full selection of top animation tools for Mac OS and Windows machines alike.

- **GifBuilder (Mac OS).** Yves Piguet's legendary utility is the program that started the animated GIF craze, and it remains one of the premier GIF animation tools.
- **Gif-glF-giF (Mac OS and Windows).** This utility from Pedagoguery Software enables you to create animated GIFs of Mac OS or Windows screen activity — great for online training applications or, if you're a software developer, for creating animations that illustrate your product in action.
- **Ulead's PhotoImpact GIF Animator (Windows).** My favorite Windows GIF animator, PhotoImpact GIF Animator combines powerful features with an attractive, easy-to-use interface.
- **Sizzler** and **WebPainter (Mac OS and Windows).** These hot animation utilities from Totally Hip Software enable you to create and view Sizzler-format animations as well as animated GIFs.
- **WebPainter (Mac OS and Windows).** This hot animation utility from Totally Hip Software enables you to create and view animated GIFs as well as animations in Totally Hip's Sizzler format. (Check out Totally Hip's ad at the back of this book to learn how you can pick up the program at a discount.)
- **Microsoft GIF Animator (Windows).** Microsoft's GIF Animator is a simple utility that enables you to import existing images and create an animated GIF. It doesn't provide WebPainter's painting tools or PhotoImpact GIF Animator's array of fine-tuning options, but it's adequate for basic tasks.
- **A Smaller GIF (Mac OS and Windows).** Also from Pedagoguery Software, A Smaller GIF is obviously a utility that makes smaller GIFs. Specifically, A Smaller GIF analyzes an animated GIF and then employs a variety of compression techniques to decrease its size. Apply this trial version to your animated GIFs and see if it makes a difference.

The Animated GIF Story

As their name implies, animated GIFs are a variant of CompuServe's Graphics Interchange Format, which Chapter 6 covered in detail. In 1987, the GIF specification was enhanced, enabling GIFs to contain multiple images that can be played back sequentially to provide flip-book-style animation. In 1989, another amendment provided additional controls, such as an optional delay between frames. Thus the GIF89a format was born — another moniker often used for animated GIFs.

GIF89a's animation format remained in a state of suspended animation until Netscape Communications added support for animated GIFs to Navigator 2.0. Microsoft followed suit and now supports the format in its Internet Explorer browser.

In addition to the advantages I outlined earlier, animated GIFs are easy to create. You can create an animated GIF from any series of images, including

- Images created with a paint or imaging program such as Fractal Design's Painter, Adobe Photoshop, or Ulead's PhotoImpact
- Images drawn from scratch using an animated GIF utility such as Totally Hip Software's WebPainter
- Images rendered by a 3D package such as Specular International's Infini-D or LogoMotion
- Animation frames exported from Macromedia Director
- QuickTime or Video for Windows video frames exported from a video editor such as Adobe Premiere or Ulead's Media Studio Pro

All you need is a series of images in the appropriate format (more on this later) and a program that combines them into an animated GIF.

Numerous commercial, freeware, and shareware programs that create animated GIFs are available for Windows and Mac OS machines. Each program has its own operating style, but creating animations is usually a matter of dragging and dropping the image files created in other programs. After you've created the animated GIF, a standard `<IMG>` tag is all it takes to put your pages in motion.

Another nicety: you can create *looping* animations — ones that play over and over. Once a browser has loaded the GIF, the animation plays back from the browser's disk cache; no additional communication between browser and server takes place.

Now the bad news

For all their advantages, animated GIFs aren't the perfect medium for digital Disneys.

Limited color palettes

Because animated GIFs *are* GIFs, they're limited to a maximum of 256 colors (jump back to Chapter 6 if you need a refresher on color palette issues). This means animated GIFs aren't exactly ideal for photographic images, such as a time-lapse view of a sunset. Although you can get good results with the palette optimizing tricks I describe later in this chapter, animated GIFs are best suited for moving banners or text, buttons, or line-art-style animations.

Limited playback control

You can stop a looping GIF animation by using a browser's Stop button and you can resume it by reloading the image, but you can't stop and resume playback halfway through the animation. If you need VCR-like playback control, a commercial animation program is a better bet.

The loopy status bar

A looping animation causes Netscape Navigator 2.x to display a "loading" message in its status bar over and over again. Besides being distracting, this message obscures the URL that normally appears in the status bar when the mouse pointer is over a link. Fortunately, Netscape fixed this problem in Navigator 3.

Frame woes on other browsers

An animated GIF appears in browsers that don't support GIF animation, but *how* it appears depends on the browser. The old America Online browser displays only the last frame of the animation, but most other browsers, including Navigator 1.x and Internet Explorer 1.x, display only the first frame. The latter approach complicates life if you want to create, say, an animated logo that assembles itself. All that appears on first-frame-only browsers is a disassembled logo — probably not the corporate image you want to project.

SECRET

To ensure an animated GIF looks presentable on a browser that won't animate it, create it on the assumption that some visitors will see only the first or last frame. This doesn't apply, of course, if you're creating separate pages for separate browsers and your server uses redirection to automatically route visitors to the appropriate pages based on the browsers they're using. In this case, use static GIFs for the browsers that require them.

No talkies

Animated GIFs are silent movies. To mix sound and animation, use QuickTime or Video for Windows movies, Macromedia's Shockwave for Director, or DeltaPoint's WebAnimator.

'Tis a GIF to be simple

Despite its shortcomings, the animated GIF is the best medium for simple Web animation: no plug-ins, no server tweaking, and relatively mild browser-compatibility headaches. The animated GIF is one of those simple technologies that has come to dominate its field exactly because it's simple. In a Web world increasingly obsessed with bells and whistles, that's an important lesson.

Making an Animated GIF

With the background out of the way, let's take a look at the tools and techniques behind creating animated GIFs. Many of the tools I describe in this section are included on the *HTML & Web Publishing SECRETS* CD-ROM (see the "On the CD-ROM" sidebar at the beginning of this chapter).

Tools for making animated GIFs

Whether you use a Windows or a Mac OS machine, there's a fine selection of programs for making animated GIFs. Here's a summary of the best offerings.

GifBuilder (Mac OS)

ON CD-ROM

The program that started the animated GIF craze is free and included on the *HTML & Web Publishing SECRETS* CD-ROM. (It's also available at `http://iawww.epfl.ch/Staff/Yves.Piguet/clip2gif-home/GifBuilder.html`, and at a US-based mirror site at `http://www.pascal.com/mirrors/gifbuilder/`.) GifBuilder's creator, Yves Piguet, releases revisions frequently and always makes outstanding enhancements. The latest GifBuilder versions sport outstanding AppleScript support, enabling experienced users to automate the production process.

Smart Dubbing (Mac OS)

This freeware program from Netherlands-based Maatschap Blom/Verweij (`http://www.xs4all.nl/~polder`), converts QuickTime movies and PICS animations into animated GIFs. A commercial version, Smart Dubbing Pro, includes a Java applet that provides rudimentary sound support.

GIFmation (Mac OS)

This program from BoxTop Software (`http://www.boxtopsoft.com/`) doesn't provide built-in painting features as WebPainter does, but it does provide excellent color-reduction and palette-management features, as well as image-alignment niceties.

PhotoImpact GIF Animator (Windows)

ON CD-ROM

This program from Ulead Systems (`http://www.ulead.com/`) lacks built-in painting features, but provides excellent palette-management and image-optimizing features. It's included with Ulead's PhotoImpact with Web Extensions and also available separately. (And it's on the *HTML & Web Publishing SECRETS* CD-ROM.)

WebPainter (Mac OS and Windows)

This program, from Totally Hip Software (`http://www.totallyhip.com`), provides solid painting and animation features, including an onion-skin mode that shows adjacent frames, simplifying the process of positioning images within each frame (see Figure 12-1). WebPainter can also convert QuickTime and Video for Windows movies into animated GIFs. You can save animations in GIF format as well as in Totally Hip's Sizzler plug-in format, which is discussed later in this chapter.

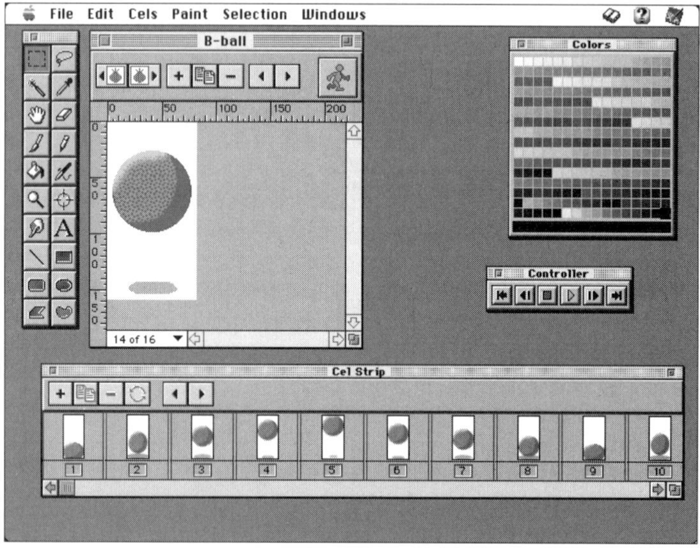

Figure 12-1: Totally Hip Software's totally hip WebPainter program

GIF Construction Set (Windows)

This shareware package from Alchemy Mindworks (`http://www.mindworkshop.com`) was the first GIF animation utility for Windows. You won't find painting features here, either, but you will find solid palette- and image-optimizing features.

Gif-gIf-giF (Mac OS and Windows)

This utility from Pedagoguery Software (`www.peda.com/`) has a strange name that's spelled even more strangely. But the program is a winner — it records screen activity and then creates an animated GIF of the result. You specify an area to record and the number of frames per second that you want to record (see Figure 12-2). You then start recording, perform the tasks you want to record, and then stop. It's a terrific tool for computer training.

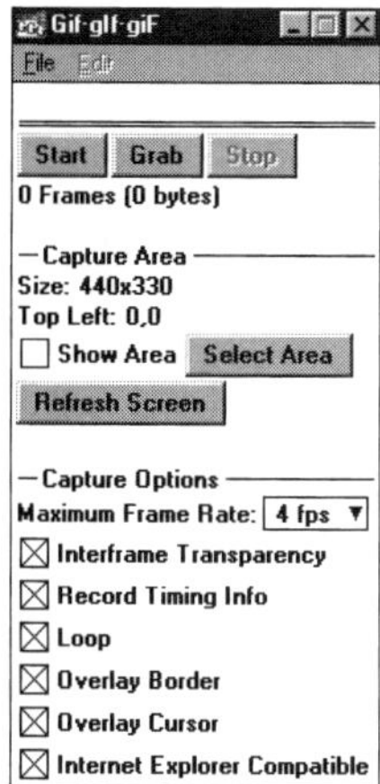

Figure 12-2: Pedagoguery Software's Gif-glF-giF utility

An overview of the process

The process of creating an animated GIF is similar regardless of the program you use. The following overview assumes you're creating an animated GIF from files you created in other programs and then exported or saved in a format that your GIF utility can handle.

Step 1: Get your frames in order

Most programs with animation features can export an animation as a series of image files. You import these files into an animated GIF utility. Most animation-oriented programs — for example, 3D modeling and rendering applications — provide automatic-naming features that number frames appropriately. As I describe in the next step, naming files appropriately can save you a lot of time when creating GIFs that contain numerous frames.

And now a word about file formats. Most animated GIF utilities can import their platform's most popular formats — for example, PICT on the Mac OS side, BMP on the Windows side, and TIFF on both sides. Table 12-1 lists the formats supported by the programs covered in this chapter.

Table 12-1 Import file formats supported by GIF animation utilities

Program	*Formats Supported*
GIFBuilder (Mac OS)	PICT, GIF, TIFF, Photoshop 2.5/3.x, QuickTime, PICS, Adobe Premiere Filmstrip
Smart Dubbing (Mac OS)	QuickTime, PICS
GIFmation	GIF, JPEG, TIFF, Photoshop, PhotoCD, ScitexCT, PCX, and BMP

(continued)

Table 12-1 *(continued)*

Program	*Formats Supported*
WebPainter (Mac OS and Windows)	GIF, PICS, PICT, BMP, QuickTime
GIF Construction Set (Windows)	BMP, TIFF, GIF, PCX, JPEG, PNG, and many others
PhotoImpact GIF Animator (Windows)	BMP, GIF, JPEG

Step 2: Import the images

Most GIF animation utilities enable you to import a flock of images in one fell swoop, either by dragging and dropping them or by using an Open dialog box. Be sure you name your image files in a way that enables the utility to import them in the correct order — that way, you won't have to do a lot of manual reordering. GifBuilder, for example, arranges the files in alphabetical order (see Figure 12-3).

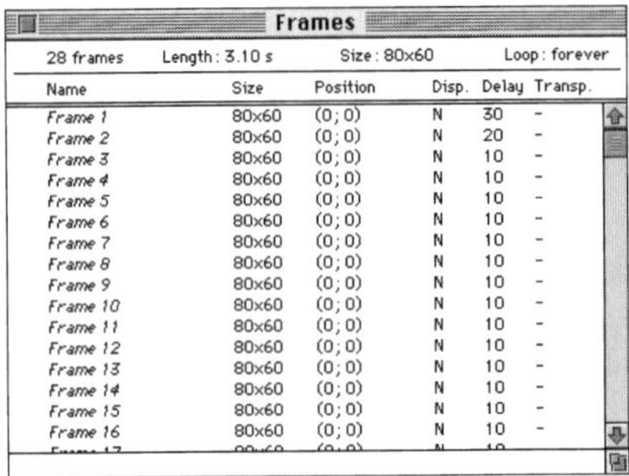

Figure 12-3: GifBuilder's Frames window shows the frames in an animation.

Step 3: Fine-tune your 'toon

After importing frames, you can fine-tune the animation: specifying its timing, the way frames are displayed, whether the animation loops or plays just once, and more. Here are some of the ways you can tweak a 'toon; Figure 12-4 shows the tweaking options that several GIF animation utilities provide.

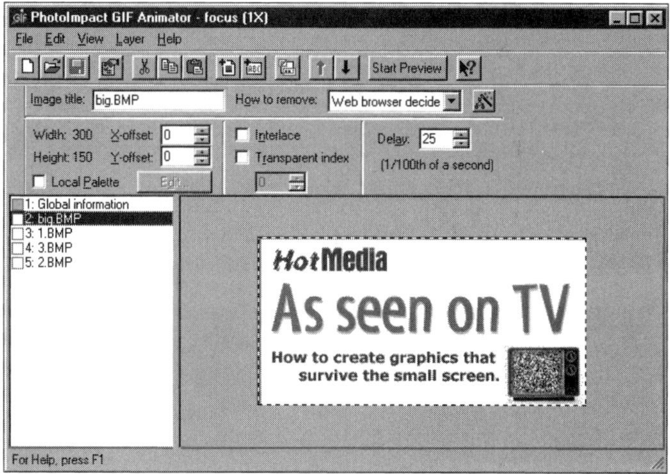

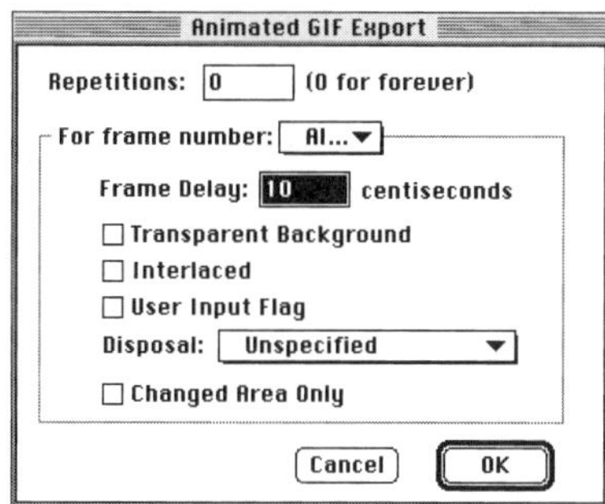

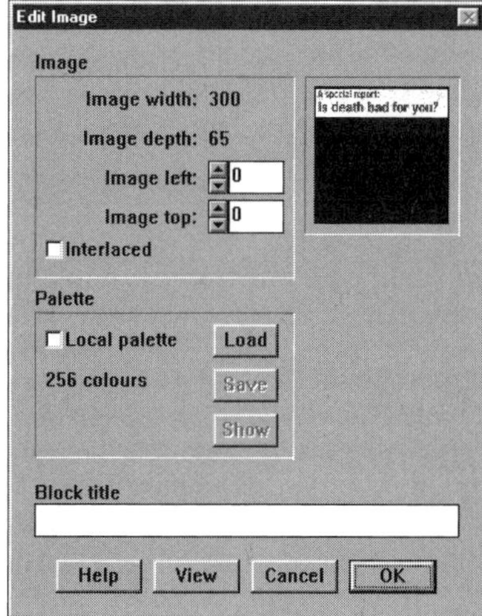

Figure 12-4: In the editing room: GIF fine-tuning options in Ulead's PhotoImpact GIF Animator (top), Totally Hip's WebPainter (middle), and Alchemy Mindworks' GIF Construction Set (bottom).

SECRET

Turning Video into Animated GIFs

Several of the programs discussed in this chapter can directly open QuickTime or Video for Windows movies. If you're creating an animated GIF from either of these formats, you don't have to go through the extra step of exporting the video's frames with a video editor. Instead, you can simply open the video file with the GIF animation program, and then fine-tune it as described in this chapter.

But you should note that this direct-import technique often doesn't allow as much control over the final animation. For example, unless a movie has a very low frame rate (such as five frames per second), you probably won't want to import every single frame — doing so would create a huge GIF that would download slowly.

When you want the most control over the conversion process, it's best to export a movie to individual files. If you're using Adobe Premiere, you can do this using the Make menu's Output Options command. Choose Output Options, and from the Output As pop-up menu, choose Bitmap Sequence (Windows) or PICT Sequence (Mac OS). When you use the Make Movie command, Premiere creates a separate file for each frame.

You can also convert a video into a series of frames using Equilibrium's DeBabelizer utility.

To make the animated GIF, import the frame files into your animation utility. After you save the animated GIF, examine its file size. If it's too large for your liking, consider going back and deleting frames — say, every third frame for a minor size reduction, or every other frame for more significant shrinkage. Deleting frames will make playback jumpier, of course, but it will also yield a smaller file that more people will be willing to wait for.

Position

You can specify the position of each frame within the animation by dragging the frame's contents. You might combine this option with a static image to create the illusion of movement, say a ball bouncing. Make the frames containing the ball image only as large as the ball itself, then change the position of each frame within the movie to create the bouncing effect.

Disposal

The disposal method specifies how or whether a frame is removed after it is displayed. You can, for example, specify that one frame completely cover the previous frame or be superimposed over it.

For GIFs converted from digital video movies or exported from a 3D animation program, you can generally use either the Do Not Dispose or Unspecified options — because all frames are the same size, each new frame will cover up the previous one. If you're moving frames within a larger animation, use the Restore to Background option to avoid having each frame remain visible.

Note that some GIF animation utilities may use slightly different terminology than the lingo I've used here, which corresponds to the disposal options in GifBuilder. For example, Ulead's PhotoImpact GIF Animator uses the phrase Web Browser Decide instead of Unspecified.

Delay

The animated GIF specification enables you to specify a delay — a time during which a specific frame remains visible. The GIF89a specification measures delays in 100ths of a second. You can also specify a delay of 0, in which case a visitor's browser plays the animation as quickly as the computer allows. (This can result in some mighty speedy animations on fast PowerPC or Pentium computers.)

The capability to display a specific frame for a longer period of time is extremely useful. Just a few of the possibilities it introduces include

- **A slide show.** Make each frame a different picture and specify a delay of, say, five seconds for each frame. When the GIF displays, each picture will appear for five seconds.
- **A looping, two-frame text advertisement.** You see this frequently in Web ads: a banner might cycle between two phrases, such as, "It's the most exciting thing you'll ever see..." and "...and it's free! (Click here for details)." I'll have more to say about this type of animation later in this chapter.
- **Simulate a movie coming up to speed.** Give the first few frames a progressively shorter delay — $^{40}/_{100}$ of a second for frame 1, $^{30}/_{100}$ for frame 2, $^{20}/_{100}$ for frame 3, $^{10}/_{100}$ for frame 4.

To have an animation play back as quickly as possible, specify a delay of zero. The speed with which the animation plays for the first time depends on the speed of a visitor's Internet connection. Fortunately, browsers that support animated GIFs display each frame as soon as it's received, so even large animations don't force visitors to stare at a static screen. For looping animations, subsequent plays are much faster because the browser loads each frame from the browser's disk cache.

Interlacing

Just as you can interlace a conventional GIF, you can specify that frames be interlaced. I think interlacing tends to look odd in animated GIFs, however — especially looping ones. I say leave it off.

Palettes

Oh, no — not palettes again! I'm afraid so. Being limited to a maximum of 256 colors (8-bit), animated GIFs impose the same palette issues that their static counterparts do: when optimizing a GIF, you must choose between a system palette, a browser palette, or an adaptive palette. And for the smallest file size, you should choose the smallest number of colors that still delivers acceptable quality. This is particularly important with animated GIFs — because they're comprised of many images instead of just one, their size can balloon quickly.

An animated GIF can have two types of palettes: *local* and *global.* A global palette is one that applies to every frame in the animation, while a local palette is one that pertains to only one specific frame. Each frame can have its own local palette.

Now, your finely-tuned sense of logic might be telling you that giving each frame its own palette is the best way to optimize image quality and file size. Sorry, Mr. Spock. Because video displays can work with only one palette at a time, giving each frame its own local palette yields less-than-ideal results. To quote from the documentation that accompanies Alchemy Mindworks' GIF Construction Set, "Attempting to display multiple GIF images, each with its own local palette, will usually leave you with something that looks like bad abstract art or the aftermath of an all you can eat spaghetti dinner."

It's best to create a single global palette for the GIF. Most GIF animation utilities contain features for creating a global palette that is optimized for all of the frames in the animation.

Background color

The background color is the color of the area around the animation's frames, and appears only when a frame's image doesn't actually fill the size of the GIF. The background is one of the colors in the global color palette; if you change the global palette, the background color may change accordingly.

Step 4: Add the GIF to a page

To include the animated GIF in an HTML page, use a standard `<IMG>` tag. As with any image, using the optional `<HEIGHT>` and `<WIDTH>` helps the browser format the page faster.

You can display the animation in more than one place on the same page by simply copying and pasting the GIF's `<IMG>` tag. There's no performance penalty for repeating an animation; the browser loads the image only once. In most HTML layout programs, you can make a duplicate of an image by pressing the Option (Mac OS) or Ctrl (Windows) key while dragging the image.

Where to Find Ready-Made Animated GIFs

If you want to dress up a page with animated buttons, borders, icons, or photos, you don't have to start from scratch. Several Web sites contain free animated GIFs that you can copy and reuse.

Actually, there are more than several. At this writing, Yahoo!'s GIF animation collection category lists 42 sites containing ready-to-use animations. I don't list any specific sites here because in my experience, these sites tend to come and go. For a current list, visit `http://www.yahoo.com/Computers_and_Internet/Graphics/Computer_Animation/Animated_GIFs/Collections/`.

Some clip-art and stock photography houses are also now selling animated GIF collections — and many of these are far more polished and professional-looking than the ones you find on "Karl's Killer Kollection of Kartoons"-type sites. I'm particularly impressed with the offerings from PhotoDisc (`http://www.photodisc.com/`). Visit the company's Web site to see examples, which are available in GIF as well as Shockwave formats.

Some animated GIF projects

ON CD-ROM

This section is a cookbook of animated GIF projects you might want to try. The sample files I used for these projects are included on the *HTML & Web Publishing SECRETS* CD-ROM.

Text messages dissolving into each other

You see this technique used often in animated GIFs that contain text banners (see Figure 12-5).

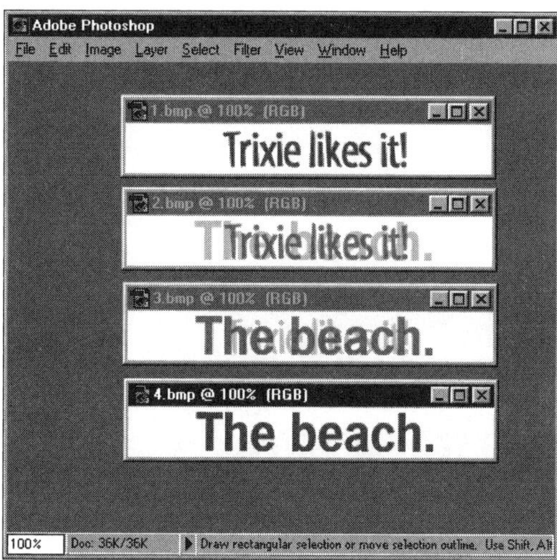

Figure 12-5: In this animated text banner, one message dissolves into another.

Here's how to create this effect in Adobe Photoshop 4. (The basic concepts also apply to Photoshop 3.) I used text in this example, but there's no reason you can't substitute images.

1. Create a new, untitled document and make its dimensions large enough to accommodate the largest element in the animation.
2. Use the Layers palette to create two layers. Name them *First Message* and *Second Message*, or something similar.
3. Type the first message's text in the layer named *First Message*.
4. Hide the *First Message* layer by clicking the layer's show/hide icon (the little eye).
5. Activate the *Second Message* layer by clicking its name.
6. Type the second message's text in this layer.

At this point, you have a two-layer file, with each layer containing a different message. In the next steps, you create the individual images that you then import into an animated GIF utility.

1. Show the *First Message* layer and hide the *Second Message* layer.
2. Choose Save a Copy from the File menu.
3. Choose an appropriate file format (for example, BMP for Windows or PICT for Mac OS), give the frame a name, and save. (You might want to pick a name that will make it easy to sort your frames later, such as *1.BMP* or *1.PICT*.)
4. Show the *Second Message* layer by clicking its show/hide icon. At this point, you should see both layers superimposed over one another.
5. Activate the *First Message* layer by clicking on its name in the Layers palette.
6. Adjust the Opacity slider to about 70 percent.
7. Activate the *Second Message* layer by clicking on its name in the Layers palette.
8. Adjust the Opacity slider to about 30 percent. Your image should resemble Figure 12-6.

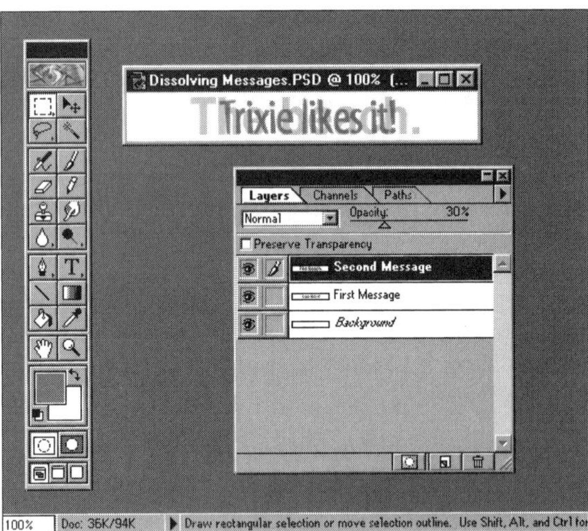

Figure 12-6: The dissolve begins!

9. Choose Save a Copy and create another image, giving it a name such as *2.BMP* or *2.PICT*.
10. Repeat Steps 5-8, changing the *First Message* opacity to about 30 and the *Second Message* opacity to about 70.
11. Choose Save a Copy and create another image, giving a name such as *3.BMP* or *3.PICT*.
12. Hide the *First Message* layer. You should see only the contents of the *Second Message* layer.

13. Choose Save a Copy and create another image, giving it a name such as *4.BMP* or *4.PICT.*

You now have four frames ready to import into a GIF animation utility. Do so, and set the delay for each frame appropriately. For example, you might want the first and last frames to appear for a second or two, and the middle two (the dissolve) to appear for only $^{10}/_{100}$ of a second or so. Save the animated GIF and add it to a page using the `<IMG>` tag.

A variation: A fade-in layer

Figure 12-7 illustrates a variation of the preceding project: A two-message banner in which the second message fades in for a dramatic effect.

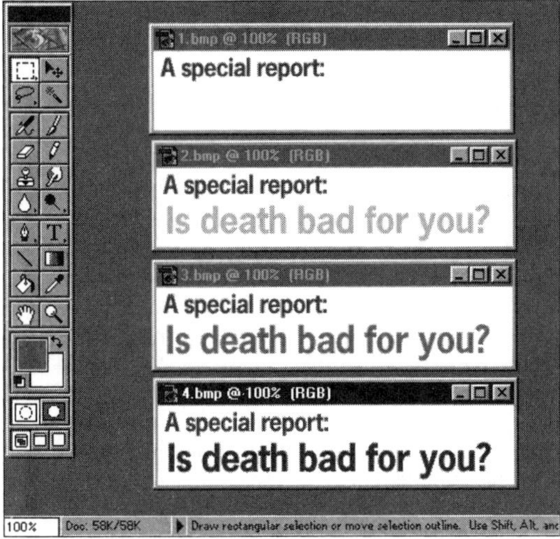

Figure 12-7: A fade-in effect

To create this effect, leave the first layer's opacity at 100 percent for each frame, and vary only the second layer's opacity, increasing it for each frame until it's at 100 percent, too.

And needless to say, there's a variation of this variation. Fade out a layer by starting with an opacity of 100 percent, and then decrease the opacity for each frame until it's at 0.

A motion blurring effect

With Photoshop's Motion Blur filter, you can create text titles that appear to vibrate (see Figure 12-8).

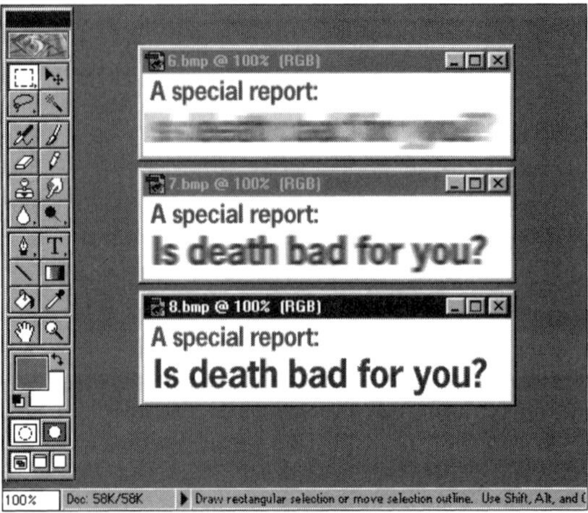

Figure 12-8: A vibrating text title

To create this effect, first create the unblurred version of the text, and then save the document as a Photoshop file. It's important to save the document in Photoshop format before proceeding.

Next, choose Motion Blur from the Filter menu's Blur submenu. In the Motion Blur dialog box, choose an amount and an angle for the blur (see Figure 12-9). Click OK or press Return when you're done.

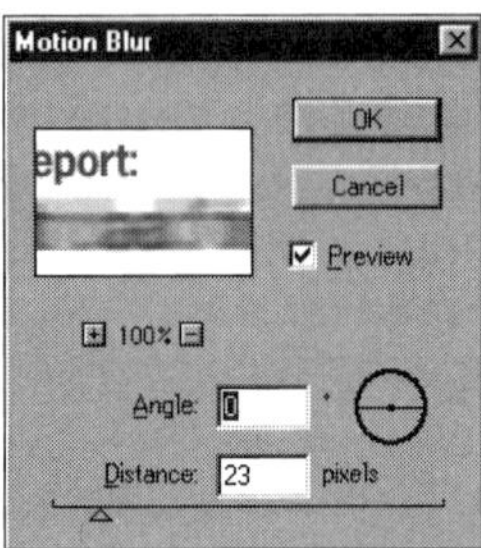

Figure 12-9: Specifying motion blur in Photoshop

Use Save a Copy to save a bitmapped file. Next, you need to restore the text to its unblurred state — otherwise, you would be blurring already-blurred text, and the effect wouldn't look right.

To restore the text, choose Revert from the File menu and click Revert or press Return when Photoshop asks you to confirm the command. Now you know why it was so important to save the file in Photoshop format before you blurred its text!

After the file reopens, choose Motion Blur again, specify a different blur amount, and use Save a Copy to create another frame.

Repeat these steps as many times as desired to get the number of frames and the effect that you want.

A variation: Text that comes into focus

To have a text headline or a graphic start out blurred and gradually come into focus, use the Gaussian Blur filter. Start with a setting of about 15 pixels, and then create successively sharper frames by decreasing this amount (see Figure 12-10).

One potential problem with this effect: As I noted early on in this chapter, Navigator 1.x and Internet Explorer 1.x show only the first frame of an animated GIF, so visitors using those browsers will see only the fuzziest version of the graphic.

Other Animation Techniques

Animated GIFs are by far the most popular animation medium on the Web, and as this chapter has shown, for good reasons. But there are other techniques.

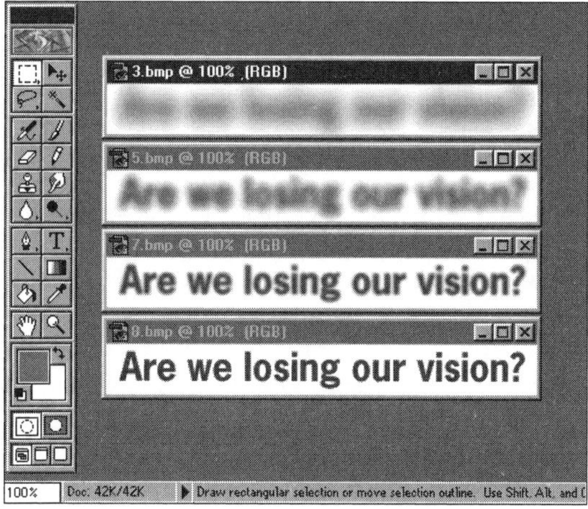

Figure 12-10: This text heading comes into focus, thanks to the Gaussian Blur filter.

Plug-in-based animation products

Details on plug-in-based animation products could fill an entire book. Rather than spin-off a second volume to this tome, I summarized the key points of today's most popular plug-in-based animation products in this section. The best source for more information is each company's Web site.

Macromedia Flash

Company: Macromedia (`http://www.macromedia.com/`)

Pros: Transmits vectors (compact drawing instructions) rather than bitmaps, which yields compact, fast-loading animation files. Supports streaming (files play as they download). Provides anti-aliased text. Powerful, well-designed animation environment. Animations can be saved as QuickTime (Mac OS) or Video for Windows (Windows) formats and as animated GIFs.

Cons: Its vector orientation makes it unsuitable for converting QuickTime movies or PICS-based animation. No sound support (planned for future versions).

Emblaze

Company: Geo (`http://www.geo.inter.net/Welcome.html`)

Pros: Supports streaming and sound. Java applet version enables playback on Java-supporting browsers without having to download and install plug-in.

Cons: Animations are limited to a maximum of 256 colors. Minimal interactivity within animations — you can specify an entire animation as a hot spot, but not elements within one, as with most other packages.

Sizzler

Company: Totally Hip Software (`http://www.totallyhip.com/`)

Pros: Easy, drag-and-drop conversion of PICS files, QuickTime, and Video for Windows movies. Works with Totally Hip's WebPainter. Supports sound and streaming. Sizzler for Java version enables playback with no plug-in required on Java-supporting browsers. An ActiveX control is also available.

Cons: Minimal interactivity within animations. (Enhanced interactivity is in the works.)

Shockwave for Director

Company: Macromedia (`http://www.macromedia.com/`)

Pros: Superb animation controls. Full sound support. Full interactivity within animations. Plug-in is bundled with Netscape Navigator Personal Edition.

Cons: Steep learning curve. Relatively expensive authoring software. Fairly high memory overhead for plug-in.

Special comment: Although vector-oriented animation products (such as Macromedia's own Flash) have file-size advantages, Shockwave for Director is the best overall plug-in based animation technology. And of course, Shockwave for Director goes well beyond just animation. With it, you can create sophisticated user interfaces that resemble those of a CD-ROM:

buttons that highlight when the mouse pointer moves over them, background audio, and much more. Macromedia knows multimedia, and with Shockwave, it has taken Web multimedia further than any other company.

In early 1997, Macromedia released Director 6 and a new version of Shockwave, one that supports streaming animations as well as sound, making larger, more ambitious Shockwave productions far more practical. Macromedia has also partnered with Narrative (`http://www.narrative.com/`) to develop a special server for streaming Shockwave media. These developments indicate that Shockwave's lead in high-end Web animation is likely to last for some time.

If you want to learn more about Shockwave for Director, sprint to your bookstore and pick up a copy of *60 Minute Guide to Shockwave* (IDG Books Worldwide, 1996). A more hands-on, in-depth guide is *Shockwave Studio: Designing Multimedia for the Web,* by Bob Schmitt (O'Reilly & Associates, 1997).

WebAnimator

Company: DeltaPoint (`http://www.deltapoint.com/`)

Pros: Supports vectors and bitmaps alike. Imports PICS animations and QuickTime movies. Supports sound and interactivity within animations.

Cons: Windows version of the authoring tool was unavailable at this writing.

Server-push/Client-pull

Some of the earliest Web animations were created with server-push and client-pull. With server-push, the server spews streams of data that represents the animation. With client-pull, the browser requests — or pulls — successive pages from the server.

Client-pull and server-push animations are supported by Netscape 1.1 and later versions, and in Microsoft Internet Explorer.

Client-pull: Give me that page

Client-pull animations are much easier to create than server-push animations. Client-pull involves using the HTML `<META>` tag in the header of an HTML page. The tag contains a special HTTP header field called *Refresh*, which tells the browser to go to a different page after a certain amount of time has elapsed. By creating several pages and doing a client-pull from one page to the next, you can create a simple animation.

For example, say you have three images that you'd like to display one after another, with a five second pause between images. Put each image on its own page, and in the header area of each page — the area sandwiched between the `<HEAD>` and `</HEAD>` tags — include a `<META>` tag as follows.

In the first page of the animation:

```
<meta http-equiv="Refresh" content="5;
URL=http://www.yoursite.com/pagetwo.html">
```

In the second page of the animation:

```
<meta http-equiv="Refresh" content="5;
URL=http://www.yoursite.com/pagethree.html">
```

See how it works? After five seconds (the value specified in first part of the `content` attribute) the browser retrieves and displays the page referenced in the second part of the `content` attribute.

If a page contains a hyperlink of any kind, a visitor can abort the animation by activating the link — activating a link always overrides the timer value specified in the `<META>` tag. Give your visitors the flexibility to stop an animation or go elsewhere by including a hyperlink on each of the pages in your client-pull animations.

The downside of client-pull

One big drawback to client-pull animations is that they don't enable you to update only a portion of a page. Each entire page is, in essence, a frame of the animation. Thus, client-pull animations lack the flexibility of animated GIFs or plug-in-based animations.

Another drawback concerns performance. Because displaying a new frame requires a new connection to the server, a client-pull animation will never provide the fast, fluid motion of an animated GIF, a video clip, or a plug-in-based animation. Combine a slow modem, a clogged Internet, and a busy server, and you could be looking at delays of several seconds or more between each frame.

Cool ways to use client-pull

Still, client-pull animations have their place. Here are several potential applications.

A slide show

Put each image on its own page and use client-pull to switch between them. Want the slide show to loop? Have the last image's page call up the first one. Throw in a RealAudio-based soundtrack (discussed in Chapter 13) for extra spice.

A kiosk

Setting up a Web kiosk for a library, school, or trade show? Consider using client-pull to create a couple of "hey, try me!" screens. Alternate between the two screens, and put a hyperlink on each one that enables a visitor who has taken the bait to begin doing something useful.

A splash screen

Many CD-ROM titles open with a flashy welcoming screen that serves to welcome users and draw them in. You can use client-pull to do the same thing for a Web site. Have a flashy opening screen that appears for a few seconds before surrendering to a home page. Be sure to put a hyperlink on the screen that gives repeat visitors the option to skip past the glitz and go directly to the glory.

A regularly updating page

If you've set up a Web cam, you can create a page that updates its image at regular intervals — great for those virtual voyeurs who want to keep a constant eye on your cam's image. The secret to this application is to not specify a different page in the `<META>` tag. For example, the following tag updates the page every 60 seconds:

```
<meta http-equiv="Refresh" content="60">
```

I use client-pull with my Weathercam in the Window page, which displays an updated view of the scene outside my office window every five minutes. For more details, see Chapter 8.

This regularly updating page technique is also useful for a page that displays data obtained from a hardware device that is connected to the server, such as a weather system, an electronic thermometer, a piece of lab equipment, or a security system.

Server-push: Take that, browser!

Server-push animations are driven from the opposite side of the connection: the server. Implementing a server-push animation generally requires installing a CGI on the server.

In conventional HTTP communications, the connection between client and server is opened and closed as needed to retrieve data. (You can see this connection process taking place if you watch a browser's status bar when a page containing several different elements is coming in.) With a server-push animation, the connection between the server and client remains open as data is spewed from the server to the client.

There's little to recommend the server-push approach to animation. It is useful for creating a continuously updating display — for example, of a Web cam image or of a series of images taken over the last several hours — but its bandwidth demands are significant.

Summary

- Numerous animation techniques and technologies are available, but animated GIFs are the most popular and the most versatile.
- Many of the same issues behind static GIFs, such as a 256-color limitation and transparency, also apply to animated GIFs.
- Of the plug-in-based animation products, Macromedia's Shockwave for Director is the most versatile and popular.
- Vector-based animation products such as Macromedia's Flash and DeltaPoint's WebAnimator have potential file-size advantages over other products because they rely on transmitting compact drawing instructions (vectors) rather than large bitmapped images.
- Client-pull animations make the browser request a different page (or the same page) at a specified interval. They're useful for simple slide shows, splash screens, or kiosk screens.
- With server-push animations, the connection between client and server remains open as data is transmitted from the server. Server-push animations can gobble up network bandwidth; other animation schemes generally deliver better results with a lower bandwidth budget.

Chapter 13

Listen and Watch: Web Audio and Video

In This Chapter

- Just how practical are audio and video on Web sites?
- Secrets for choosing audio formats and optimizing quality
- HTML and media: the tags you need to know
- Streaming audio with RealAudio and Shockwave Audio
- Creating Web-page soundtracks with MIDI
- Compressing video clips so they download within a lifetime
- Streaming video with VivoActive Producer and RealVideo

Way back in this book's preface, I said that one of the exciting things about the Web is its support for multiple media — not just text and graphics but also audio, video, and animation.

Alas, anyone who gets fired up about the Web's multimedia capabilities quickly gets hosed down by today's bandwidth limitations. Sure, you can post CD-quality sounds on a Web site, but your listeners had better have ISDN lines or better, or downloading takes forever. Audio-streaming technologies such as Progressive Networks's RealAudio eliminate lengthy downloads, but they do so by compressing and processing audio to low fidelity levels. Video's demands are even higher.

Still, it is possible to enhance a Web site with audio and video clips and not clog your connection, cripple your server, or cause download times that exceed today's average life span. Today's Internet pipes rule out any surround-sound, high-resolution, audio-video extravaganzas, but they can certainly accommodate some audio-video seasoning. And if the experts are right — if several years down the road we will have virtually unlimited bandwidth — now is the time to start learning how to apply audio and video.

This chapter is a guide to putting audio and video on a Web site. There are innumerable technicalities behind audio and video production, ranging from choosing microphones to lighting a scene to buying sound cards and video-digitizing hardware for your computer. I touch on those production-oriented points in this chapter, but I concentrate primarily on the technicalities that are specific to Web-based audio and video: file formats, quality optimizing, compression, and HTML. If you don't have any audio or video experience, I recommend consulting the additional resources I list in this chapter to learn more about the production process. Because the quality of your end product hinges on the quality of the raw material.

Sound on Your Site

Audio's bandwidth demands are significant, but they're a pittance compared to those of video. That's one good reason to start our tour in the audio realm. Here's another reason: unless you're posting silent movies on your Web site, you're going to need a solid grounding in audio concepts when you move up to video.

How digital audio works

BACKGROUNDER

To understand how a computer can record and play back sound, think of a movie. By taking 24 photographs per second, a movie camera captures a reasonably accurate sampling of the action in front of it. When those samples are played back, the illusion of smooth motion is created.

Digital audio also samples motion, the moving air molecules that make up sounds. Vibrating objects — whether strings, saxophone reeds, vocal chords, or slamming car doors — produce *sound waves,* variations in air pressure that travel outward from the sound source like the ripples from a stone dropped into a pond.

ON CD-ROM

Listen and Look Here

The best way to appreciate Web audio and video is to listen to it and watch it. The *HTML & Web Publishing SECRETS* CD-ROM contains several items that let you do just that.

- **Audio sample files.** Just how good do various audio technologies sound? Hear the difference between CD-quality and, well, Web quality.
- **Video sample files.** See what kinds of movie sizes, frame rates, and quality two streaming video technologies, Vivo's VivoActive and Progressive Networks' RealVideo, provide at both 28.8Kbps and ISDN speeds.
- **HTML example files.** Use and adapt the sample code in this chapter for your own needs.

A computer equipped with sound-recording circuitry can sample these sound waves thousands of times per second. Each sample is a digital reproduction of the sound at a given instant. The samples, each recorded as a series of bits, are stored in memory and can be manipulated. Bits can be added or removed, their order can be altered, or their values changed. Each modification alters the overall image of the sound wave, so when the samples are played back, you hear a different sound.

Sampling rate

With movies, taking too few pictures per second results in jittery, unrealistic motion. With sound, taking too few samples per second results in a distorted recording that doesn't faithfully convey all the frequencies present in the original sound. The faster the *sampling rate,* the more accurate the recording, and the better the recorder is able to capture the highest frequencies.

Compact discs are recorded at a rate of 44,100 samples per second, or 44.1KHz. Most current Mac OS computers can record at 44.1KHz with no additional hardware. Most of the sound cards available for Windows machines can also record at 44.1KHz.

Sampling resolution

Another factor that influences digital sound quality is the *sampling resolution* — the number of bits assigned to each sample. These bits store information about the sample's amplitude, or loudness. The more bits assigned to each sample, the more accurately the recorder can store and re-create the original sound's variations in loudness.

A compact disc player has a 16-bit sampling resolution, enabling it to reproduce thousands of distinct volume levels. Most Windows sound cards also support 16-bit audio, as do most current Mac OS machines. (Some older or less-expensive Mac models support only 8-bit audio; they re-create only 256 volume levels. When a given sample's amplitude lies between two levels, the amplitude is rounded to the nearest level. This rounding of amplitude information, called quantization, causes distortion. I have more to say about 8-bit distortion later in this chapter.)

It's the bandwidth, stupid

44.1KHz, 16-bit sound — so-called *CD-quality* audio — may be commonplace in music stores and even within computers, but it's a rarity on the Web. The reason? Bandwidth. One minute of 16-bit, 44.1KHz stereo audio uses 10MB — *ten megabytes!* — of disk space. A Web surfer with a 14.4Kbps modem would get old waiting to hear that clip.

ON CD-ROM

As a Web audio producer, you must compress and compromise your audio tracks in order to reduce download times and bandwidth demands. The result is something a great deal less than CD quality. But as this chapter describes, there are techniques for minimizing quality loss. You can hear examples illustrating these methods on the *HTML & Web Publishing SECRETS* CD-ROM.

Audio Production Secrets

Recording secrets

Getting good Web audio requires starting with the highest-quality audio possible. And that means following the tips in this section.

Use the best microphone you can afford

A $1,000 AKG C-414 microphone will do admirably, but you don't have to spend that much — Shure Brothers, Audio Technica, and AKG each have excellent offerings that sell for under $150. Even a $39 public address mike from Radio Shack is far better than the bargain-basement mike that comes with some Mac OS machines and Windows sound cards. A tie-clip mike works very well for recording voice.

Use more than one mike for multiple subjects

If you're recording a roundtable or music group, dedicate a mike to each participant. Use a mixer to adjust volume levels and combine the signals into one track (for mono recording) or two (for stereo). (The Mackie Designs MS-1202LZ mixer is hard to beat and costs only a few hundred dollars.)

Position mikes properly

If you're recording to the Mac's hard drive (rather than to a video recorder, for example), move the mike away so it doesn't pick up hard drive and fan noise. Record in an acoustically dry room; spread some carpets and hang some drapes or blankets on the walls to deaden echoes. (To size up a room's dryness, clap once and listen.) If you're recording a narration, position the mike a few inches from the narrator's mouth to avoid breathy results. (As a test, record the phrase "pretty poppies." If the result sounds like a hurricane, move away from the mike.)

SECRET

Where to Shop for Audio Gear on the Web

RF Specialties Group is a large dealer of professional audio and radio-broadcasting equipment with eight US-based offices. The company now operates an impressive Web site containing product information on hundreds of audio products. Located at `http://www.rfspec.com/index.htm`, it's a great resource for audio product information.

Another terrific resource is Sweetwater Sound's Web site, at `http://www.sweetwater.com/`. Sweetwater Sound is a major retailer of not only audio equipment, but also electronic musical instruments and music software and hardware products.

Set levels properly

Adjust your recording software's levels so the on-screen volume meter reaches the upper end of its range during loud passages. To avoid distortion, however, the meter's clipping indicator should never illuminate. Figure 13-1 shows how a recording in a digital audio program looks when the recording is too soft, too loud, or just right.

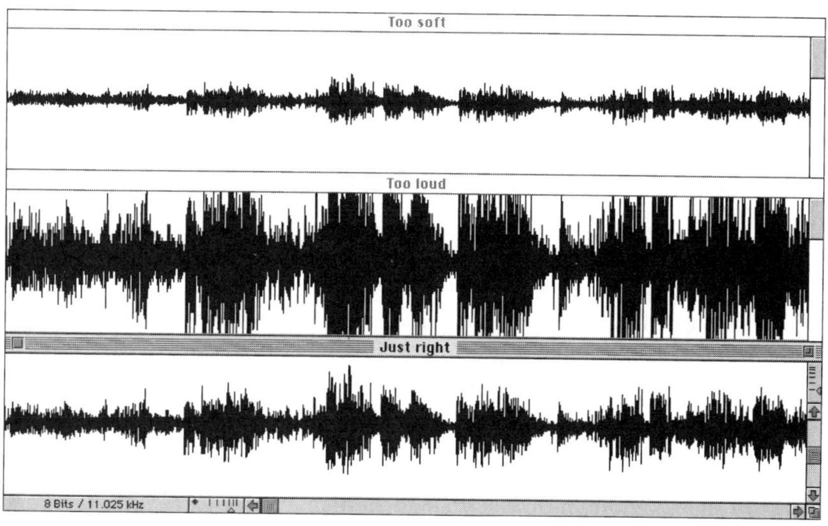

Figure 13-1: The same clip three ways: too soft (top), too loud (middle), and just right (bottom)

The sound in the top window is too quiet: notice that the loudest portions of the waveform aren't that much louder than the background noise. The sound in the middle window was recorded at too high a volume setting: note how the waveform seems to crash into the upper and lower edges of the display. The sound in the bottom window was properly recorded: the waveform peaks almost reach the top and bottom of the display.

All audio programs I'm aware of provide a Normalize command that automatically maximizes the sound's volume. Using Normalize isn't a substitute for good recording techniques and proper levels, but it can help dramatically.

Record at your machine's highest-quality setting

If your computer supports it, record at 44KHz, 16-bit, with no compression. As mentioned earlier, you can do so using any PowerPC-based Mac OS machine or 680X0 AV Mac, or using most current Windows sound cards.

Editing sound

Following the advice in the aforementioned section yields a clean, crisp recording. But you've only just begun. If you recorded a narration or interview, you'll want to delete awkward pauses and flubbed words. If you're creating a music sound-effect clip, you may need to edit the sound — to shorten it, for example, or to extract a particular segment.

Editing tools

To perform sound edits like these, you need a sound-editing program. On the Mac OS side, Macromedia's SoundEdit 16 (`http://www.macromedia.com/`) and Bias Systems's Peak (`http://www.bias-inc.com/`) are excellent editing tools. Macromedia's Deck II is a great program, too, but it's better suited to multitrack recording than waveform editing.

On the Windows side, Sonic Foundry's Sound Forge (`http://www.sfoundry.com/`), Steinberg's WaveLab (`http://www.steinberg-us.com/`), and Syntrillium's CoolEdit 96 (`http://www.syntrillium.com`) all pack impressive audio-editing features. CoolEdit is the most reasonably priced and has some features that make it particularly well suited to Web-audio work. (You learn more about CoolEdit later in this chapter.)

All waveform-editing programs display a recorded sound as a waveform (see Figure 13-2).

You can zoom in on the waveform display to look at an individual cycle (one back-and-forth phase of the sound's vibration), or zoom out to see the entire recording. You can select part or all of the waveform and cut or copy it to the Clipboard to rearrange the notes in a musical passage or the words in a phrase.

You can also modify the sound, adding reverb to simulate a concert hall, or filtering certain frequencies to improve the sound quality. You can even reverse the sound to make it play backwards.

Preparing Clips for the Web

You should perform all your edits at the 44KHz, 16-bit level. Use whatever native file format your editing application uses. (In the Windows world, most audio programs save files in the Windows WAV format. On the Mac OS side, many programs — including SoundEdit 16, Sound Designer II, and Bias Peak — use proprietary formats but also support a wide variety of standard formats.)

Unless you intend to post huge, bandwidth-hungry files, your second-to-last production step involves *downsampling* the audio to a lower sampling rate and perhaps to 8-bit resolution. (I say "perhaps" because 8-bit sound is prone to an annoying hiss. This hiss can be particularly apparent in voice tracks, where its volume pumps along with the speech.) As this section describes, optimizing sound quality while downsampling and converting bit depths requires performing a variety of steps in a specific order.

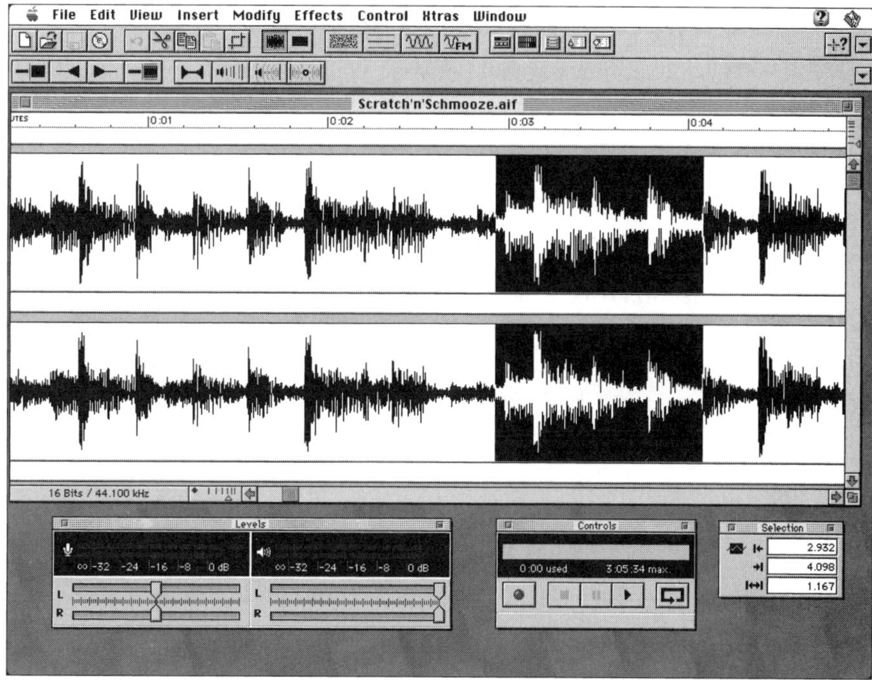

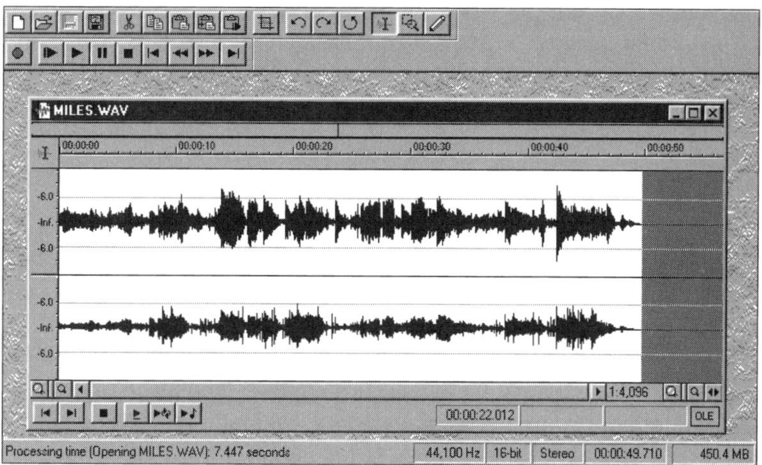

Figure 13-2: The graphic display of a sound is called its waveform. Here are waveform displays in Macromedia's SoundEdit 16 (top) and Sonic Foundry's Sound Forge (bottom).

If downsampling is your second-to-last step, what's the last step? Saving the downsampled clip in a common audio file format. Just as there's a variety of graphics formats — GIF, JPEG, PICT, BMP — there's a large selection of audio file formats, such as WAV, AIFF, and AU. As with graphics, your goal is to choose the format that retains the most quality and assures the broadest compatibility.

Downsampling and processing

There's another parallel between Web graphics and Web audio: the process of slimming down a file for faster downloading always causes an unavoidable loss in quality, but you can minimize the loss if you know what you're doing.

Choosing a sampling rate and bit depth

In what form should you deliver audio? The answer depends on the message and the medium — that is, on the content of the audio clip and the connection over which visitors will be downloading it.

For music, a 22.05KHz sampling rate delivers reasonably good fidelity but fairly large files by Web standards. (Note that's 22,050, not 22,255. The 22,050 rate is exactly half of the CD-quality 44.1KHz rate. The 22,255 rate, while popular in the Mac OS world, isn't supported by some Windows sound cards.)

For voice, an 11.025KHz or even 8KHz sampling rate may be acceptable. Every recording is different, as is every voice; do some tests and let your ears decide.

As for bit depth, 16-bit sounds much cleaner than 8-bit, but 16-bit audio requires twice the storage space as 8-bit sound (unless you use compression — more on this later).

If you do opt to reduce the clip to a depth of 8 bits, you may want to apply your audio program's Normalize command to it first in order to boost its overall level. Whether you should normalize depends on how well the original clip was recorded: If the clip's peaks reach the top and bottom of the waveform display, you may not need to normalize. Again, do some tests and listen.

The right way to downsample

Many sound-editing programs have pop-up menus in their Save dialog boxes that enable you to choose a sampling rate other than the file's current rate. For instance, if you're working with a 44.1KHz/16-bit file, you may think all you need to do is choose the program's 22.050KHz/8-bit options.

To quote a recent presidential candidate, "Just don't do it" — at least not without checking the documentation first. Many programs have commands that perform high-quality downsampling and bit-depth reduction; that is, instead of just lopping off half the bits and slicing the sampling rate in half, they use special optimizing techniques that result in less quality loss.

You've become familiar with one of these techniques already: dithering. Just as dithering can improve a low bit-depth graphic, it can enhance an 8-bit audio recording.

Downsampling in Windows audio programs

SECRET

Here's a guide to the downsampling and bit-rate reduction features in some top Windows audio programs:

- **Sonic Foundry Sound Forge.** To downsample, choose Resample from the Process menu. Be sure the check box labeled *Apply an anti-alias filter during resample* is checked. To reduce the bit depth, choose Convert to 8-bit from the Process menu. In the subsequent dialog box, use either the Round or Dither options, depending on which delivers better quality. (Use the Preview button to hear the effect of each option. While you're at it, preview the clip with the Truncate option selected: this option simply lops off half the bits in each sample. Listen to how much noisier it is.)
- **Steinberg WaveLab.** To downsample, choose Convert Sample Rate from the Process menu. In the Quality area of the subsequent dialog box, be sure the Top (Slower) option is selected. Alas, for bit-depth reduction, WaveLab 1.0 (the version shipping at this writing) does simple truncation — it doesn't provide the higher-quality options that Sound Forge and CoolEdit do.
- **Syntrillium CoolEdit 96.** To downsample and convert bit depth, choose Convert Sample Rate from the Edit menu. (Don't choose Adjust Sample Rate — that isn't the command you want for this job.) In the subsequent dialog box, select the desired sample rate and bit depth. If you're converting to 8-bit, experiment with the options in the Dither area of the dialog box to optimize sound quality.

Downsampling in Mac OS audio programs

SECRET

Here's how to downsample and reduce bit depth in the Mac OS world's two most popular audio packages:

- **Macromedia SoundEdit 16.** Choose Sound Format from the Modify menu. In the subsequent dialog box, select the desired sample rate and bit depth. When downsampling, you may want to check the Boost Highs box to compensate for the loss in high frequencies. If you're converting to 8-bit, check the Use Dither box.
- **Macromedia Deck II.** Choose the Mix to Disk command and select the desired sample rate and bit depth. If you're converting to 8-bit, choose an option *other than* Truncation from the Bit Depth Conv pop-up menu. (There are three additional options; experiment with each to find the best setting for your clip.)

Choosing a file format

As the upcoming Backgrounder sidebar "A Field Guide to Sound File Formats" explains, there are various sound formats in use on the Web. Which should you use?

Riding the Waves to Better Audio

Waves (http://www.waves.com) offers state-of-the-art audio-processing utilities, most of which originally debuted as plug-in modules for high-end audio hardware systems from Digidesign (http://www.digidesign.com/). Good news: Most of the Waves utilities are now available for software-only Mac audio and video applications, including Adobe Premiere, Macromedia's Deck II, and SoundEdit 16.

Waves's L1 Ultramaximizer, a plug-in for Digidesign audio hardware, boosts a soundtrack's volume, shapes its waveform for optimal quality, and optionally reduces its bit depth from 16 to 8. (Always apply L1 as the final step in an audio-processing job.)

Waves's WaveConvert utility (Mac OS and Windows) enables you to provide high-quality downsampling, bit-depth reduction features. This utility also packs sophisticated level-optimization features that yield the best possible audio quality for the sample rate and bit depth you choose. WaveConvert can apply its talents to an entire batch of files, and it provides presets that are optimized for RealAudio. WaveConvert is a terrific tool for optimizing multimedia audio (see Figure 13-3).

You can download trial versions of the entire Waves product line from the Waves Web site (http://www.waves.com/).

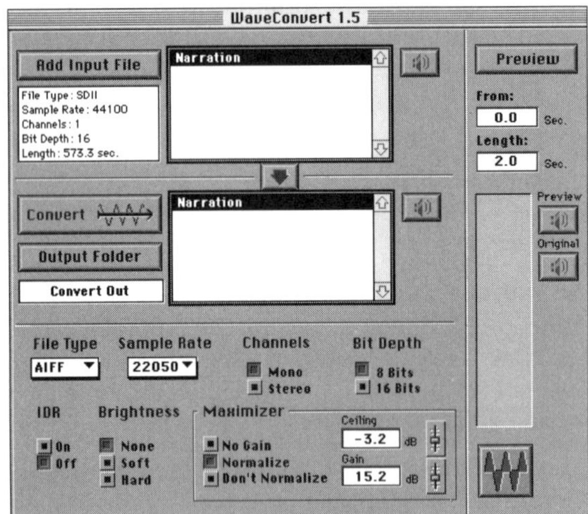

Figure 13-3: Waves's WaveConvert utility in action

The three most popular formats for downloadable Web audio clips are AU, WAV, and AIFF. And guess what? Netscape Navigator and Microsoft Internet Explorer now come equipped to play all three formats — no external helper application is required. Navigator's audio talents come from its LiveAudio technology, which debuted in version 3.0. Microsoft Internet Explorer relies on Microsoft's ActiveMovie technology (which also debuted in Internet Explorer's 3.0 release) to play these formats as well as MPEG clips.

BACKGROUNDER

A Field Guide to Sound File Formats

Here's a field guide to the most popular audio formats in the Web world:

- **AU** Also called uLaw or Sun audio, this is one of the most common audio file formats on the Web. AU files are most commonly delivered with an 8KHz, 8-bit sampling rate and a form of encoding called uLaw. (Technically, AU files encoded under uLaw have an effective depth of 12 bits. In other words, they sound a bit better than other formats' 8-bit audio.) 8KHz AU files have a fidelity — if you can call it that — roughly equivalent to that of a telephone.
- **WAV** The standard file format in the Windows world, WAV files, whose names end with the file extension *.wav* , are also extremely common on the Web. Most Mac OS (and all Windows) sound programs can open and save WAV files.
- **AIFF** The Audio Interchange File Format (commonly referred to as either AIFF or Audio IFF) is the Mac OS world's equivalent to the WAV file. All Mac OS and most Windows audio editors can open and save AIFF files.
- **QuickTime** Strictly speaking, QuickTime isn't an audio file format. But because both Netscape Navigator 3 and Microsoft Internet Explorer 3 (and later versions of both) can play QuickTime movies, you might consider posting audio clips in QuickTime format.
- **RA** This is the format used by Progressive Networks's RealAudio technology, which allows for real-time streaming audio over the Internet. See the section "RealAudio is for real," later in this chapter.
- **MPEG** Short for Motion Picture Experts Group, MPEG is a data-compression standard most commonly associated with digital video. But MPEG is also gaining popularity for distributing audio on the Web.

So which format should you use? For voice, AU is a good bet. For music (or higher-quality voice), either WAV or AIFF is safe. Given that Windows machines make up the majority of computers on the Web, you may want to stick with WAV. Doing so won't lock out any Macintosh users: the Mac versions of Navigator and Microsoft Internet Explorer can play back WAV files, as can popular Mac helper applications for audio, such as SoundApp and SoundMachine.

Naming your audio files

Browsers and helper applications rely on file extensions to identify the audio file format. Table 13-1 lists the extensions you should use for each format.

A parting thought about audio optimizing

Optimizing audio requires some work, but the results are worth the effort. Your site's visitors may forgive slow movie-frame rates or low-resolution graphics, but they'll remember the headaches that bad sound gave them. You'd probably rather be remembered for something else.

Table 13-1 File extensions for the most popular audio file formats

For This Format	*Use This Extension*
AU/uLaw	.au
AIFF	.aiff or .aif
MPEG audio	.mp2
WAV	.wav

Essential HTML for Sound Files

There are several ways to get sound clips from your site's server to your visitors' ears. (HTML files based on these examples are included on the *HTML & Web Publishing SECRETS* CD-ROM.)

- You can create simple hyperlinks to them using the <A> tag, as in:

```
<a href="loudsound.wav">Hold your ears!</a>
```

  This is the simplest method and it provides the broadest browser compatibility. The browser plays the sound directly if it can — or it starts a helper application, such as SoundApp or SoundMachine (Mac OS), or Sound Recorder or Media Player (Windows).

- You can use the <EMBED> tag. The <EMBED> tag gives you much more control over the sound's playback, and it has the additional benefit of enabling the sound's controller (its playback buttons) to appear within a page — that is, with text, graphics, and other elements around it. The downside: visitors who don't have a browser that supports embedded audio won't be able to hear the clip. (You can work around this, though — stay tuned.)

- You can use the <BGSOUND> tag. This tag, which is supported by Microsoft Internet Explorer only, enables you to assign a sound clip to a page to act as a background sound. Its syntax is simple:

```
<bgsound src="sound.wav" loop=5>
```

  The example above plays a sound five times. To have the sound loop continuously until the visitor moves to another page (or unplugs his or her computer in disgust), use `loop=infinite`. To learn how to create a background sound that also works in Netscape Navigator, see the section "Hiding a movie," later in this chapter.

- You can use the <OBJECT> tag. This is another Microsoft Internet Explorer-specific tag. <OBJECT> has a few interesting advantages over <EMBED> but can be tricky to use and lacks solid Netscape Navigator compatibility.

SECRET

Audio Etiquette

Here are a few things to keep in mind regarding Web audio clips:

- **Consider multiple versions.** Because Web surfers may have anything from a 14.4Kbps modem to a 10Mbps cable modem, consider providing each audio file in a compact, low-fidelity form and in a larger, high-fidelity form. Providing both means more work for you and requires more storage on your server, but it will enable visitors to choose the format that best suits their connection speeds.
- **Consider multiple formats.** Most browsers and helper applications can handle the most common formats, so if you stick with AIFF or WAV, you've addressed the majority. But if you also want to address the minority, you might consider posting clips in both formats.
- **Tell 'em what they're in for.** For audio formats that don't stream, always include the file size and format within parentheses near the clip, for example:

  Fingernails on a chalkboard (`45K WAV` file, `50K AIFF` file).

Using the <EMBED> tag

Beginning with version 3 of each, both Netscape Navigator and Microsoft Internet Explorer support the `<EMBED>` tag for adding sounds (and movies) to pages. But don't get the idea that there's peace and harmony between these two battling browsers. Netscape Navigator provides far more attributes for `<EMBED>`, making possible some pretty amazing feats. Microsoft Internet Explorer's `<EMBED>` command is a bit more spartan.

SECRET

What's more, Netscape Navigator requires some attributes that Microsoft Internet Explorer doesn't, and vice versa. So to create an `<EMBED>` tag that works properly in both browsers, you have to mix and match Netscape and Microsoft attributes. It's a bit sloppy, but it works. Each browser acts on the attributes it supports and ignores the others.

A simple playback controller

ON CD-ROM

Figure 13-4 shows the HTML and result for an embedded sound containing a simple playback controller that works in both Netscape Navigator and Microsoft Internet Explorer.

```
<html>
<head>
<title>
Embedded Audio Example #1
</title>
</head>
<body>
Listen to this great clip.
<embed src="sound.wav"
```

```
controls=smallconsole height=15 width=144
controller=true
autostart=false>
</body>
</html>
```

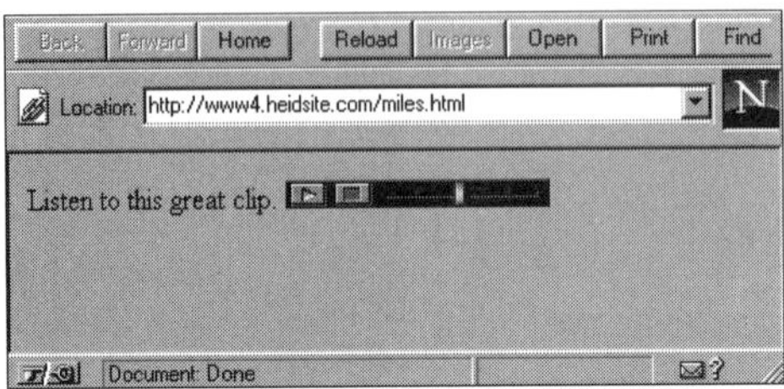

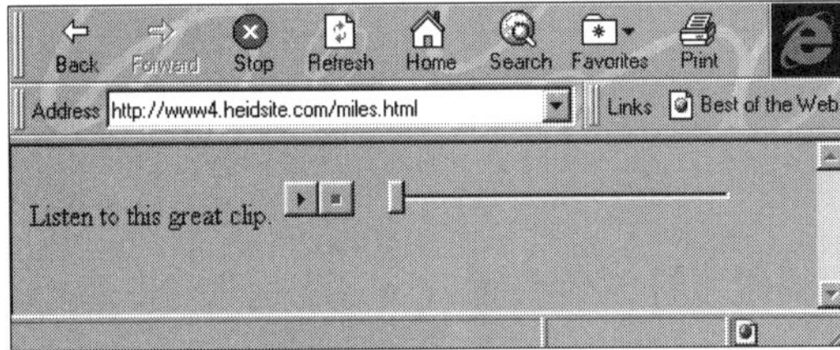

Figure 13-4: Embedding sound for both Netscape Navigator and Microsoft Internet Explorer. Top: The HTML source. Middle: The result in Netscape Navigator. Bottom: The result in Microsoft Internet Explorer.

Here are a few notes about this example:

- The `controls` attribute is Netscape-specific; it determines the type and size of the playback controller bar (the little horizontal scroll bar with the Stop, Play, and Pause buttons). The `smallconsole` parameter gives you the squat playback bar shown in Figure 13-4. For a larger console, use the following:

  ```
  controls=console height=60 width 144
  ```

- The `controller` attribute is Microsoft Internet Explorer-specific; it determines whether or not a controller bar is displayed. If you want a controller, this attribute is optional. If I had left it out of the previous example, the result would have been the same — a controller would have appeared. Note that visitors can customize the appearance of their controllers by right-clicking them and then using the Controls tab of the Properties dialog box.
- The `autostart` attribute applies to both browsers; it determines whether or not the sound begins playing automatically when the page has finished downloading.

Looping sounds

Another attribute supported by both browsers is `loop`; its parameters, `true` or `false`, determine whether the sound repeats continuously:

```
loop=true
```

The default is `false` — if you omit the `loop` attribute, the sound does not loop.

You can use `loop` to repeat a sound, thereby making it seem larger than it really is. This works particularly well for ambient sound effects, such as bird songs, forest noises, and waves crashing. (I use these on my Weathercam page, at `http://www4.heidsite.com/weathercam.html`.) Think twice about using looping for music clips — it can become seriously annoying.

It's worth mentioning that Netscape Navigator supports an additional parameter that lets you loop a sound for a specific number of times. The following `loop` attribute causes a sound to play twice:

```
loop=2
```

When you use an integer value as the parameter for `loop`, Microsoft Internet Explorer ignores the entire attribute and does not loop the sound.

Navigator also provides a `volume` attribute that enables you to set the initial volume for a sound clip.

```
volume=65%
```

As the above example shows, the `volume` attribute's parameter is a percentage, which can be anything from 0 (volume all the way down) to 100 (volume all the way up).

<EMBED> and compatibility with lesser browsers

The problem with embedding sounds is that many older or less-sophisticated browsers don't support the `<EMBED>` tag. The solution: include a conventional link to the sound using the `<NOEMBED>` tag. The following code builds on the example in Figure 13-4, adding a `<NOEMBED>` set of tags for less-sophisticated browsers.

```
<html>
<head>
<title>
Embedded Audio Example #2
</title>
</head>
<body>
Listen to this great clip.

<embed src="sound.wav"
  controls=smallconsole height=15 width=144
```

```
  controller=true
  autostart=false>

<noembed>
  <a href="sound.wav">Click here to hear!</a>
</noembed>

</body>
</html>
```

In this example, if the page is opened on a browser that doesn't support the <EMBED> tag, the visitor can still download and listen to the clip by clicking the Click here to hear! link. Browsers that *do* support <EMBED> ignore the tags that are sandwiched between the <NOEMBED> and </NOEMBED> tag pair.

Advanced <EMBED> tricks for Netscape Navigator

Netscape Navigator's LiveAudio and LiveConnect features can work together, enabling you to combine JavaScript and the <EMBED> tag in some very cool ways. For example, you can create your own custom controller buttons and you can defer the loading of a sound until a visitor clicks on a link. Other functions and statements enable you to gradually fade the volume of sound, determine whether a sound is playing, and more.

SECRET

They Don't Have the Plug-In? Tell Them Where to Go!

The <EMBED> tag accepts an optional attribute, `pluginspage`, that enables you to specify a URL from which a visitor can download a plug-in if he or she doesn't have it. For example, to enable a visitor to go to Apple's QuickTime site if he or she doesn't have the QuickTime plug-in, use:

```
pluginspage="http://quicktime.
apple.com/"
```

And this brings up a good question: which address should you use in a `pluginspage` attribute? The answer: the address that the plug-in's creator tells you to. If the plug-in creator's site has a Webmaster's page, it often lists the recommended URL for the `pluginspage` attribute.

If the site doesn't have a Webmaster's page, don't use the URL where the plug-in is currently located — that address could easily change. Instead, it's safer to use the URL of the plug-in creator's home page. For example:

Risky:

```
plugsinspage="http://www.hotplug.
com/sw/plugin/download.html
```

Safer:

```
pluginspage="http://www.hotplug.
com/"
```

The bad news is that none of these functions work in Microsoft Internet Explorer. (Indeed, getting them to work in Netscape Navigator isn't always straightforward.) In the interest of compatibility, you may want to avoid pushing the LiveAudio/LiveConnect envelope. If you're determined — or you'd just like to see what's possible — visit the Netscape site (`http://home.netscape.com`) and take the tour of LiveAudio features. At present, you can find the tour at `http://home.netscape.com/comprod/products/navigator/version_3.0/index.html`. (As future versions of Navigator appear, however, this location is likely to change.)

Also check out the sample HTML files on the *HTML & Web Publishing SECRETS* CD-ROM. In specific, the file named AUDIOJS.HTML creates a custom LiveAudio controller.

Sound and ActiveMovie: the <OBJECT> tag

Microsoft Internet Explorer's `<OBJECT>` tag enables you to embed an ActiveX control in a Web page. (ActiveX controls are reusable software components that, similar to Java applets and browser plug-ins, enable you to add special features to Web pages. Such features may be simple animations or ticker tape-style text displays, or they may be games or mini-application programs. For the full scoop on ActiveX, read Microsoft's propaganda on the subject, at `http://www.microsoft.com/activex/`.)

Microsoft Internet Explorer includes an ActiveX control that enables the browser to play back audio and video files. This control relies on Microsoft's ActiveMovie media technology, and its name, appropriately enough, is the ActiveMovie control. By using the `<OBJECT>` command to embed the ActiveMovie control in a Web page, you can play audio (or video).

Using the ActiveMovie control to play a sound clip has a couple of interesting advantages. Your sound clip can not only have a controller bar for playing, pausing, and jumping around within the clip, it can also have a read-out that shows the current time within the clip (see Figure 13-5).

```
<HTML>
<HEAD>
<TITLE>ActiveMovie Audio Example</TITLE>
</HEAD>
<BODY>

<OBJECT ID="ActiveMovie1" WIDTH=267 HEIGHT=73
 CLASSID="CLSID:05589FA1-C356-11CE-BF01-00AA0055595A">
    <PARAM NAME="_ExtentX" VALUE="7038">
    <PARAM NAME="_ExtentY" VALUE="1931">
    <PARAM NAME="ShowPositionControls" VALUE="-1">
    <PARAM NAME="ShowSelectionControls" VALUE="-1">
    <PARAM NAME="AllowHideDisplay" VALUE="0">
    <PARAM NAME="FileName" VALUE="sound.wav">
```

```
    <embed src="sound.wav"
      controls=smallconsole height=15 width=144
      autostart=false>
    </embed>
</OBJECT>

</BODY>
</HTML>
```

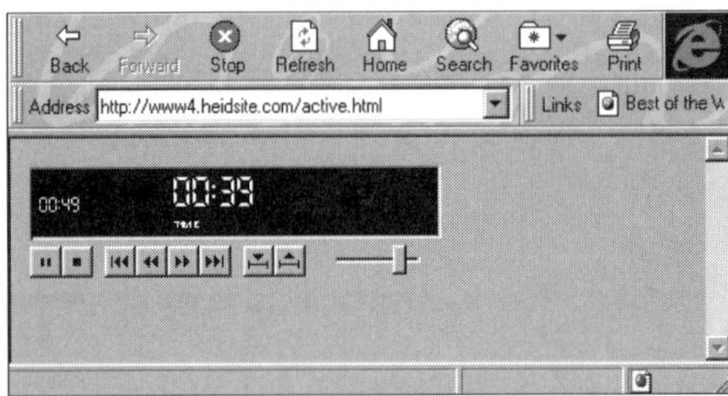

Figure 13-5: A sound clip playing with the ActiveMovie control. Top: The HTML source. Bottom: The result.

ON CD-ROM

As you can see, the HTML for the ActiveMovie control isn't exactly straightforward — all that ActiveX-specific `CLASSID` nonsense doesn't exactly make for clean-reading code. But fortunately, you don't have to hand-peck all that junk into your pages. Simply use Microsoft's ActiveX Control Pad utility (available on the CD-ROM of this book and available from `http://www.microsoft.com/activex`), or any layout tool that supports ActiveX controls (such as SoftQuad's HoTMetaL Pro).

Notice that the HTML in the example also contains an `<EMBED>` tag. This tag enables the code to work in Navigator and other browsers that don't directly support the `<OBJECT>` tag. Unless you're creating separate pages for ActiveX-savvy browsers, it's a good idea to also include an `<EMBED>` tag for broader browser compatibility.

No Waiting: Streaming Audio

Several companies have created technologies that deliver near-real-time audio over the Web: instead of waiting a minute or more while an audio file downloads, visitors begin hearing the audio almost immediately as the rest of the file downloads.

This section covers the two best-known (and in my opinion, the two best) streaming technologies: Progressive Networks's RealAudio (`http://www.realaudio.com`) and Macromedia's Shockwave.

RealAudio is for real

First debuting in 1995, RealAudio was the first streaming audio technology. RealAudio sounded scratchy, but it worked, and the advantage of streaming audio became immediately apparent: major networks and media outlets added RealAudio content to their sites, and newsmagazines ran articles about "Internet radio."

Beginning with version 3.0, RealAudio hit its stride. Not only is its sound quality outstanding, but the ability to serve RealAudio files using a standard Web server package enables you to test the waters of streaming audio (or is it the streaming waters of audio?) without having to buy a RealAudio server package.

Producing for RealAudio

A RealAudio clip begins life like every other sound clip, as an ordinary WAV-, AU-, AIFF-, or PCM-format audio file. (And I mean *ordinary:* to get the best sound quality, never use compression on a clip destined for RealAudio.) You process RealAudio clips into RealAudio format using Progressive Networks's RealAudio Encoder. The encoder applies filtering to the original clip, compresses it, and stores it as a RealAudio RA file. This RealAudio file is downloaded and played on a visitor's system by the RealPlayer application or the RealPlayer plug-in.

BACKGROUNDER

A Snapshot of RealAudio's Evolution

Looking for more proof of how quickly Web technologies evolve? Here's a quick timeline of RealAudio's even quicker evolution:

July 1995. RealAudio 1.0 ships; delivers telephone-quality regardless of connection speed; mono only (no stereo); requires purchase of special server software. (If you want to take a trip — albeit a short one — down memory lane, you can hear the press conference at which RealAudio was announced at `http://www.prognet.com/prognet/pr/launchconf.html`.)

October 1995. RealAudio 2.0 is announced; delivers near-FM quality on 28.8Kbps and faster connections; supports live broadcasts; allows for synchronized multimedia (developers can embed URLs in RealAudio files so that Web pages change during playback); still mono only; still requires purchase of special server software.

January 1996. RealAudio server for the Macintosh ships and is included with Apple's Internet Server Solution models.

September 1996. RealAudio 3.0 appears; delivers near-FM quality stereo on 28.8Kbps connections, and near CD-quality with ISDN and faster connections; no longer requires special server software — sites that don't anticipate heavy RealAudio traffic can serve RealAudio files using a standard HTTP Web server package.

February 1997. RealVideo is introduced; enables streaming video playback. A new helper application, the RealPlayer, replaces the RealAudio helper application and handles both audio and video playback. A companion plug-in, RealPlayer, also debuts.

You'll get the best sound quality if you give the RealAudio Encoder 22.050KHz or 44.1KHz, 16-bit files. Using lower sampling rates or, heaven forbid, an 8-bit resolution yields a noisier RealAudio file. For a detailed look at optimizing for RealAudio, visit this page on the Progressive Networks site: `http://www.realaudio.com/help/content/audiohints.html`.

What kind of compression can you expect? At the beginning of this chapter, I said a minute of CD-quality sound gobbles 10MB. Well, the same minute of audio in RealAudio format uses 60K.

Early RealAudio encoders gave you very little control over sound quality, but the latest versions provide presets for common types of audio content: instrumental music, music that has vocal accompaniments, voice, and more (see Figure 13-6).

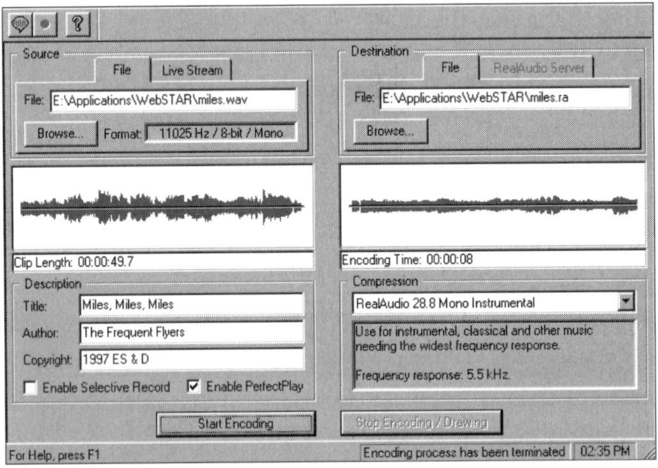

Figure 13-6: The RealAudio Encoder application. The original file appears in the left dialog box, while the settings for the RA file appear on the right.

The Enable Selective Record and Enable PerfectPlay buttons speak to features in Progressive Networks's $29 RealPlayer Plus package. As its name suggests, RealPlayer Plus provides more features than the basic RealAudio Player or RealPlayer applications (both of which are free for the downloading from `http://www.realaudio.com/`). RealPlayer Plus sports preset buttons — like those on a car radio — that let surfers set up to six presets for their favorite RealAudio and RealVideo sites.

RealPlayer Plus also enables visitors to record incoming RealAudio or RealVideo content to their hard drives so they can replay it later — the basic RealAudio Player and RealPlayer don't permit this. This is the *selective record* feature, and you can enable it for a given clip by checking the Encoder's Enable Selective Record button. Note that doing so makes it possible for unscrupulous listeners to pirate your content.

RealPlayer Plus also provides a feature called PerfectPlay, which uses special downloading techniques to enable a 28.8Kbps connection to deliver the sound quality normally associated with an ISDN line. (In a nutshell, Player Plus downloads more of the file at the beginning, enabling it to provide the higher quality audio. The downside: the clip's playback takes longer to start up, and playback may pause in midstream while Player Plus downloads more of the file.)

Alternatives to the RealAudio Encoder

If you spend a lot of time in an audio-editing application, you may prefer to do your RealAudio encoding within the application rather than relying on the RealAudio Encoder. Happily, it has become easy to do just that: most major audio programs now provide support for RealAudio. Some examples:

- **SoundForge (Windows).** SoundForge 4.0a and later versions support RealAudio 3.0 encoding. You can download an update from SoundForge 4.0 from the Sonic Foundry Web site, at `http://www.sfoundry.com/`.
- **CoolEdit 96 (Windows).** Syntrillium's terrific audio editor can directly export RealAudio files.
- **SoundEdit 16 (Mac OS).** Progressive Networks offers a plug-in module that enables you to export RealAudio files from within SoundEdit 16. You can get it from the company's Web site, at `http://www.realaudio.com/`. At present, the plug-in supports RealAudio 2.0 encoding but not 3.0.
- **Bias Systems's Peak (Mac OS).** Beginning with version 1.5, Peak can encode RealAudio 3.0 files.

Adding RealAudio clips to your pages

You can't simply reference a RealAudio clip using the tags that you'd use for a conventional sound clip. If you did, the *entire* RealAudio file would be downloaded to a visitor's hard drive before playback would begin — thus defeating RealAudio's streaming features.

To get a RealAudio file to stream, you must introduce a middleman: a tiny file, called a *metafile,* that references the RA file. You then reference that metafile in your HTML page using a standard `<A>` tag. When a visitor clicks on the link, the metafile causes the visitor's RealPlayer to launch, and the player then accesses the server and begins retrieving and playing the RealAudio file.

It sounds complicated, but it isn't. Say you've encoded a RealAudio file and named it *speech.ra.* To create the metafile, break open your favorite text editor and peck in the following:

```
http://www.your_domain_here.com/speech.ra
```

(In this and the remaining examples in this section, we're using a standard HTTP server, not a RealAudio server, to stream the file. If you were using a RealAudio server, you'd use `prm:` as the URL's locator rather than `http:`.)

You've just created the metafile. Save it on the server as *speech.ram*.

Now, create your HTML page and include in it a link to the metafile:

```
<a href="http://www.your_domain_here.com/speech.ram">Listen to this!</a>
```

That's all there is to it.

Using the RealPlayer plug-in

The vast majority of RealAudio sites rely on the RealAudio Player or the newer RealPlayer for playback, but there's another alternative: a RealPlayer plug-in module. This plug-in is installed automatically whenever someone uses the RealPlayer installer's default installation mode. This means there's a very good chance most current RealPlayer users have the plug-in. If you're interested in taking advantage of the plug-in, here's how.

First, instead of ending the RealAudio metafile's name with .ram, end it with the extension .rpm. Next, use the `<EMBED>` tag in your HTML page, as shown in Figure 13-7.

```
<html>
<head>
<title>
Embedded RealPlayer Plug-in Example
</title>
</head>
<body bgcolor=ffffff>
Listen to this great clip.
<br>
<embed src="http://www.your_domain_here.com/speech.rpm" width=300
height=135>
<noembed>
<a href="http://www.your_domain_here.com/speech.ram">Click here to
listen</a>
</noembed>
</body>
</html>
```

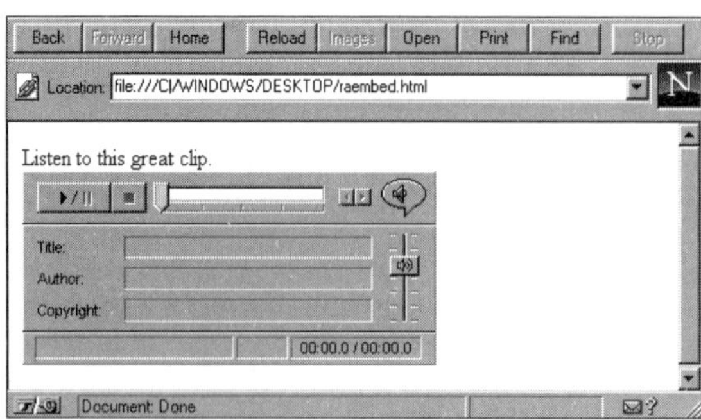

Figure 13-7: Embedding the RealPlayer plug-in. Top: The HTML source. Bottom: The result.

Notice that, for visitors who don't have plug-in-capable browsers, I included a `<NOEMBED>` tag containing an anchor tag that references a .ram file.

Creating custom plug-in interfaces

The HTML in Figure 13-7 simply gives you the standard RealPlayer interface. But the RealPlayer plug-in supports a variety of `<EMBED>` attributes that enable you to create a custom interface. For example, if you just want a Play/Stop button, use the code in Figure 13-8.

```
<html>
<head>
<title>
Embedded RealPlayer Plug-in with Custom Controls
</title>
</head>
<body bgcolor=ffffff>
Listen to this great clip.
<br>
<embed src="http://www.your_domain_here.com/speech.rpm"
  WIDTH=100
  HEIGHT=55
  CONTROLS=playbutton>
<noembed>
<a href="http://www.your_domain_here.com/speech.ram">Click here to
listen</a>
</noembed>
</body>
</html>
```

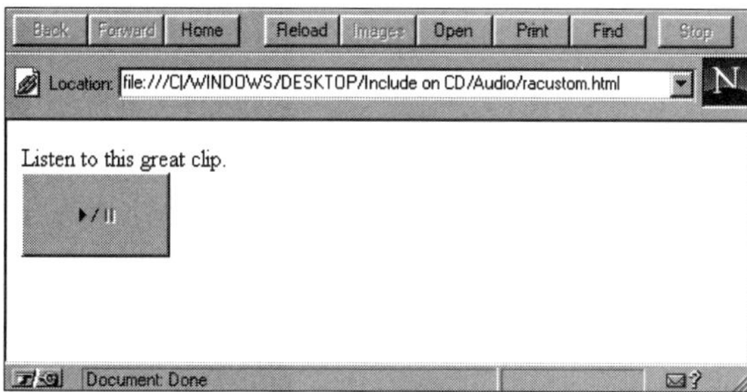

Figure 13-8: A bare-bones RealPlayer interface. Top: The HTML source. Bottom: The result.

You can also have multiple controls — for example, a Play/Stop button and a navigation bar, which lets listeners jump around within a clip. To achieve this, you need to create a "dummy" metafile — an empty text file whose name ends with the extension *.rpm*. Then, you need to use another attribute, the `console` attribute, to group the controls so they all refer to the same RealAudio file. Figure 13-9 shows what I mean.

```
<html>
<head>
<title>
Embedded RealPlayer Plug-in with Custom Controls
</title>
</head>
<body bgcolor=ffffff>
Listen to this great clip.
<br>
<embed src="http://www.your_domain_here.com/speech.rpm"
  width=50
  height=33 controls="PlayButton"
  console="MyConsole">

<embed src="http://www.your_domain_here.com/empty.rpm"
  width=150
  height=33 controls="positionslider"
  console="MyConsole">
<br>
<embed src="http://www.your_domain_here.com/empty.rpm"
  width=210
  height=70
  controls="infopanel"
  nolabels=true
  console="MyConsole">

<noembed>
  <a href="http://www.your_domain_here.com/speech.ram">Click here to
listen</a>
</noembed>
</body>
</html>
```

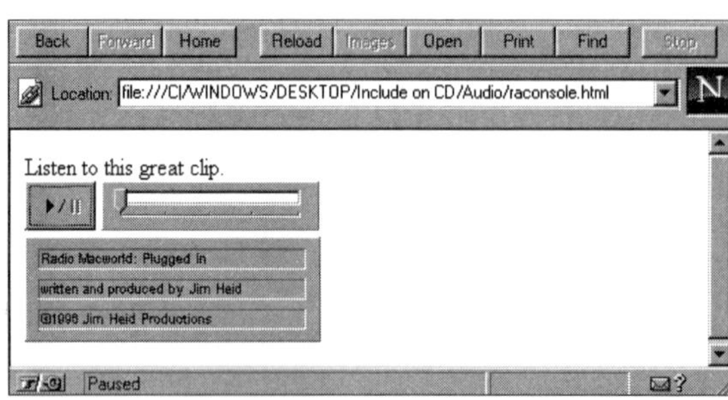

Figure 13-9: Using multiple RealPlayer controls. Top: The HTML source. Bottom: The result.

Notice that I use the `console` attribute in each `<EMBED>` tag, following the attribute with the name `MyConsole`. That's just the name I happened to choose for this example; you can use any name you like.

RealPlayer's plug-in isn't limited to the few custom controls I've shown here. Table 13-2 lists the full family.

Table 13-2 Extended attributes for the RealPlayer plug-in

Attribute	*Description*
`ControlPanel`	Embeds the Play/Pause button, the Stop button, and the position slider
`InfoPanel`	Embeds the title, author, and copyright information
`PlayButton`	Embeds the Play/Pause button only
`VolumeSlider`	Embeds the volume slider only
`PositionField`	Embeds the portion of the status bar that shows current play position and total clip length
`InfoVolumePanel`	Embeds the title, author, copyright information, and a volume slider
`ImageWindow`	Embeds the RealVideo image window
`StatusBar`	Embeds the entire status bar, showing messages, current time position, and clip length
`StopButton`	Embeds the Stop button only
`PositionSlider`	Embeds the position slider (the horizontal scroll bar) only
`StatusField`	Embeds the portion of the status bar that displays message text
`Autostart=true`	Tells the plug-in to begin playing the clip when the page is loaded
`nolabels=true`	Causes the info panel to appear without the title, author, and copyright labels

Playing clips with a hidden plug-in

Want to play RealVideo or RealAudio clips without having a visible plug-in on the page? Hide the control. Embed the plug-in on your page and set its dimensions to `width=2`, `height=0`.

To control the plug-in, you can use JavaScript. For example, the following code works with both Netscape Navigator and Microsoft Internet Explorer.

```
<script Language=JavaScript>
  function playSource()
  {if (navigator.appName == "Netscape")
  {document.javaPlug1.DoPlayPause();}
  else {RAOCX.DoPlayPause();}}
</script>
<A HREF="#" onClick="playSource()">
  <IMG SRC="button.gif"></A>
<OBJECT ID=RAOCX
CLASSID="clsid:CFCDAA03-8BE4-11cf-B84B-0020AFBBCCFA"
WIDTH=2
HEIGHT=0>
```

```
<PARAM NAME="SRC"
VALUE="http://www.your_domain.com/clipname.ra">
<PARAM NAME="CONTROLS" VALUE="PlayButton">
<embed src="start.rpm" width=2 height=0
controls=PlayButton name=javaPlug1>
</OBJECT>
```

Configuring your server for RealAudio

Whether you use a RealAudio server or an HTTP server to dish out, you must configure your HTTP server for RealAudio. In specific, you must set up a content map as follows:

For files with an .ra or .ram file extension: audio/x-pn-realaudio

For files with an .rpm file extension: audio/x-pn-realaudio-plugin

You can find more details on configuring specific Web server packages for RealAudio on the RealAudio site. And if you don't know what a content map is, see the Backgrounder section "Configuring Your Server for Media," at the end of this chapter.

Shockingly good sound: Shockwave Audio

As I described in the previous chapter, Macromedia's Shockwave for Director enables you to embed user interfaces, animations, and full-blown multimedia productions created in Macromedia Director. Macromedia has enhanced Shockwave to support streaming audio, and remarkably good-quality audio at that: near-FM quality for 28.8Kbps connections, and near CD-quality for faster ones.

SECRET

Playing One File After Another

If you've visited some RealAudio sites (if you haven't, you should!), you've probably seen some that play multiple RealAudio files successively: after one has finished playing, the RealPlayer automatically looks for and then starts playing another.

How do they do it? It's easy. Just list each RealAudio file's name in the metafile in the order in which you want them to play:

```
http://www.your_domain_here/file_one.ra
http://www.your_domain_here/file_two.ra
http://www.your_domain_here/file_three.ra
```

Alternatively, if you're using a RealAudio server:

```
prm://www.your_domain_here/file_one.ra
prm://www.your_domain_here/file_two.ra
prm://www.your_domain_here/file_three.ra
```

The RealPlayer will play each of the above files in sequence, and a visitor can use the Clip menu in the Player to move from one clip to the next.

To create Shockwave Audio files on Windows, you must own a copy of Macromedia Director. If you're using Director 5, you also need the Shockwave for Director Afterburner, which is available at `http://www.macromedia.com/shockwave/`. The Afterburner compresses Director movies and converts them into Shockwave format, and it includes an Xtra (Macromedia's term for a plug-in module) that compresses audio clips into Shockwave Audio's SWA format. If you're using Director 6, you don't need Afterburner; Shockwave support is built directly into Director 6.

Now, if you've followed the multimedia authoring scene at all, you probably know that Macromedia Director has a reputation as being powerful but difficult to learn. I call it the Orson Wells of authoring programs: hard to work with, but the best in the business. This reputation may have you a little intimidated about working with Shockwave Audio.

Fear not, audio pioneer. You don't have to be a Director guru to post Shockwave Audio files on your site. In fact, you don't have to know anything about Director except where to buy it and how to launch it. (If you use a Mac OS machine and have Macromedia's SoundEdit 16 audio editor, you don't even need to own Director — more on this later.) The Shockwave Afterburner package includes sample files that you can modify and use on your own pages — and the only modifications you need to make are to substitute a couple of URLs. I'll show you how.

Compressing files using Director

As with their RealAudio counterparts, Shockwave Audio files begin life as ordinary WAV files. To compress a file, launch Director and choose Convert WAV to SWA from the Xtras menu. (If you don't see this command, you don't have the Shockwave Afterburner installed.) The dialog box in Figure 13-10 appears.

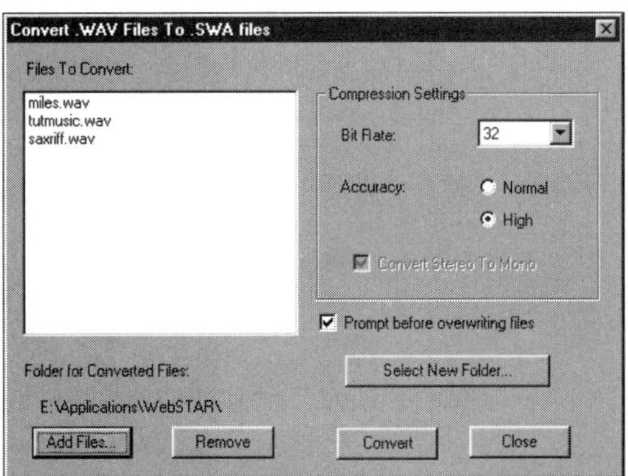

Figure 13-10: The Shockwave Audio compression dialog box

Click the Add Files button to specify the files that you want to convert. Next, choose the desired compression settings in the Compression Settings area of the dialog box. Table 13-3 shows which settings correspond to several common connection speeds.

Table 13-3 Recommended bit-rate settings for Shockwave Audio

For This Connection Speed	*Use This Bit Rate Setting*
14.4Kbps	8Kbps
28.8Kbps	16Kbps
ISDN	32-56Kbps
T1 or local area network	64-128Kbps

For the best sound quality, click the High option in the Accuracy area. If you're just doing some tests and you want compression to take less time, click Normal.

To compress the files, click the Convert button. The Shockwave Audio Xtra compresses each file, giving the new, compressed version the file extension *.swa.*

Compressing files using SoundEdit 16

Open the sound file you want to convert. The sound can be stored in any SoundEdit 16-compatible format; it doesn't have to be a WAV file, as it would with the Director Xtra.

Next, choose Shockwave for Audio Settings from the Xtras menu. (If you don't see this command, you don't have the Xtra installed.) In the subsequent dialog box, choose the desired bit rate and accuracy (see the previous section and Table 13-3 for guidelines). Click OK.

To compress the file you've opened, choose Export from the File menu. From the Export Type pop-up menu, choose SWA File. Type a name for the file, giving it the extension *.swa.* Click Save.

SECRET

How to Get the Best Shockwave Audio

Regardless of which program you use to compress audio for Shockwave, you'll get the best Shockwave Audio quality by following these tips.

- For your original source audio files, use 16-bit, 22.050KHz or 44.1KHz files, preferably 22.050KHz. If you're converting existing 8-bit or 11KHz files, resample them to 16-bit, 22.050KHz.
- Performing some equalization using SoundEdit 16 or another audio program may help improve the quality of files compressed for modem delivery (at, for instance, Shockwave Audio's 8Kbps and 16Kbps settings). For example, if you're working with 22.050KHz files, attenuating the frequencies outside of the 4KHz to 8KHz range may improve quality. Experiment to get the best results.

Embedding Shockwave Audio clips in your pages

To add a Shockwave Audio file to a page, you must embed a Shockwave player that has been created in Director and compressed into Shockwave format. Now, if you're a Director guru, you can create a player from scratch and use Director's Lingo programming language to create your own Play and Volume buttons and other user interface elements.

And if you aren't a Director guru? No problem — Shockwave Audio includes a ready-to-use player. To use it, simply copy the player (its filename is PLAYER.DCR) to the same server directory that contains your SWA files. Then, add the HTML shown in Figure 13-11 to the page where you want to embed the clip.

```
<script language="LiveScript">
<!-- hide this script tag's contents from old browsers
  document.write('<embed  width=416 height=32
SRC="http://your_domain_here/player.dcr" swl=off
swURL="http://your_domain_here/your_clip_name.swa" swText="This text
appears in the player" swPreLoadTime=3 sw2=0 sw3=1>');
<!-- done hiding from old browsers ->
</script>
<noembed>
Sorry, to hear this clip, you need a browser that supports
Shockwave.
</noembed>
```

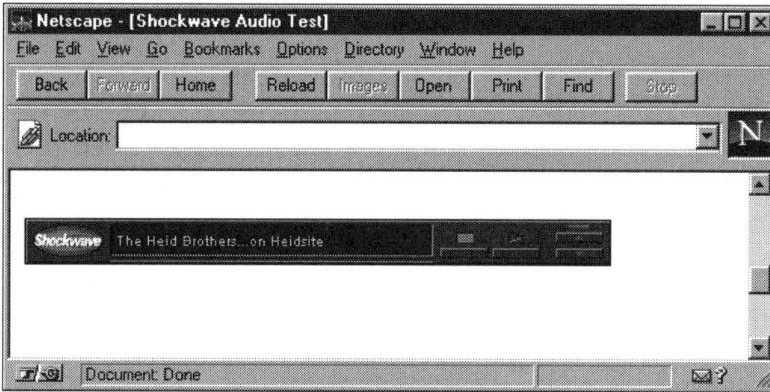

Figure 13-11: Embedding a Shockwave Audio clip. Top: The HTML source. Bottom: The result.

This code works in Netscape Navigator versions 2.0 and later and Microsoft Internet Explorer 3.0 and later. It doesn't, of course, work in browsers that don't support embedding.

A closer look at the Shockwave Audio attributes

If you check out the `<EMBED>` tag in Figure 13-11, you may notice several unique attributes: `sw1`, `sw2`, `sw3`, `swURL`, `swText`, and `swPreLoadTime`. Here's what they do and how you might use them.

- `sw1.` When you use `sw1=1`, debugging information appears. Unless you're debugging a player that you've created, always use `sw=off`.
- `sw2.` To have the clip begin to play automatically, use `sw2=1`. When you use `sw2=0`, the user must click the Play button to activate playback.
- `sw3.` To enable the visitor to play and pause playback by clicking on the Player's Shockwave logo, use `sw3=1`. If you use `sw3=0`, the visitor must use the Play button to begin playback.
- `swURL.` This is the URL of the SWA file — the Shockwave Audio file that you want this player to play.
- `swText.` This attribute enables you to display a short text message in the Shockwave Player. It's an ideal place to display a copyright message.
- `swPreLoadTime.` This attribute determines how much of the audio the Player downloads before beginning playback (if the player is set to automatic play) or before enabling the playback button (if the player isn't set to automatic play). The parameter is in seconds, so if you'd like the Player to download ten seconds of the clip, use `swPreLoadTime=10`. Increasing the preload time can help reduce playback problems with slow connections, but at the expense of making the visitor wait a bit longer before playback begins.

Web Soundtracks with MIDI

MIDI, short for *Musical Instrument Digital Interface,* is a standard that enables musicians to connect electronic instruments to each other and to computers. With a software package called a *sequencer,* musicians can record and play back multiple tracks, building up complete arrangements one instrument at a time. (For more background on MIDI, see the MIDI tutorial on my Web site at `http://www.heidsite.com/audio/MIDIfrontdoor.html`.)

The rise of the MIDI tide has led to a flood of amazing electronic music-makers, and the floodwaters have impacted the personal computer world. Most Windows sound cards have MIDI synthesis features built into them. And on the Mac OS side, QuickTime provides software-only MIDI playback. QuickTime 3.0 for Windows, which was nearing release as this book went to press, will also provide software-only MIDI playback.

One of the things that makes MIDI so powerful is that it deals with extremely compact *note data* instead of actual sounds. When a musician presses a key on a MIDI keyboard for ten seconds, the instrument doesn't send ten seconds' worth of CD-quality audio out of its MIDI jack; it sends a few bytes of data that say, for example, "the middle C key was pressed for ten seconds." MIDI supports up to 16 independent tracks of note data. Other MIDI data specify which of an instrument's sounds are assigned to each of the 16 tracks. When the MIDI sequence is played back, the device — a synthesizer or a sound card — plays the notes using the instruments specified in the MIDI file.

So what's the Web angle? Simply this: by including MIDI sequences in your Web pages, you can create a site soundtrack that will probably take less time to download than a single graphic. MIDI files are that small — a five-minute piece may weigh in at 25K or so. The actual size depends not on the duration of the piece, but on how many notes it contains. And *that* casts a new light on the legend in which Austrian Emperor Franz Joseph II criticizes Mozart's music for having "too many notes."

Every MIDI sequencer program uses its own file format, but as with most other types of software, there's a standard format that all programs support. In MIDI's case, the standard format is called *standard MIDI file,* or simply *MIDI file*. Its file extension is .mid.

The bad news about MIDI

In a world of multimegabyte data types, the compactness of a MIDI file is extremely appealing. Alas, there's a downside: the aural quality of your soundtrack depends on the quality of a visitor's MIDI playback features. High-end Windows sound cards — particularly those from Yamaha, Roland, and Ensoniq — have stunning MIDI synthesis features, but many older or low-end cards sound downright cheesy. Apple's QuickTime MIDI instruments aren't about to be mistaken for the real thing, either.

So that's the problem: embed a MIDI file in a page, and you might treat someone to a delicious aural feast or bag of limp Fritos. A soundtrack, whether it's in a movie or a Web page, sets a tone. Do you really want that tone to be determined by a component that's out of your hands?

There are other problems: many users may not have a sound card or other MIDI playback device, or they may be using a browser that doesn't support MIDI playback (more on this shortly).

And finally, embedded MIDI tracks can be annoying. Playback stops abruptly when you go to a different page but resumes when you return to the page. Consider this: many people may just *prefer* a quiet surfing experience. People are bombarded with unsolicited music everywhere — in stores, in elevators, in TV and radio commercials. Is adding to that cacophony really going to make your site better?

A reasonable compromise: give them a choice

Rather than force a MIDI file on unsuspecting visitors, give them a choice. One simple method may be to include a link in an unobtrusive spot on a page: "A MIDI soundtrack is available."

A more-advanced technique may be to use JavaScript or cookies (no, I don't mean the chocolate chip kind) to enable visitors to set a preference that's used each time they visit. But this seems like overkill for something so basic as Web-page background music.

MIDI playback options

Versions 3 and later of both Microsoft Internet Explorer and Netscape Navigator support MIDI playback. (MIDI plug-ins are also available for Netscape Navigator 2.x.) For sound generation, both use whatever MIDI features a visitor's computer happens to have.

Yamaha (`http://www.yamaha.com/`) has developed a slick plug-in called MidPlug that also provides software-only MIDI sound generation. Its sound quality doesn't measure up to that of high-quality Windows sound cards, but it is dramatically better than the synthesizer built into Apple's QuickTime.

Another MIDI playback alternative is LiveUpdate's Crescendo (`http://www.liveupdate.com/crescendo.html`), which is free and available in plug-in versions for Netscape Navigator and as an ActiveX control for Microsoft Internet Explorer. Crescendo doesn't provide its own sound synthesis. A commercial version, Crescendo Plus, provides MIDI streaming and additional features.

Finally, if you use a Mac OS machine, you can use Apple's Movie Player utility (among others) to convert MIDI files into QuickTime music movies. One advantage to this approach is that any visitor whose browser supports QuickTime playback will be able to hear the music. Another plus is that QuickTime MIDI movies contain a controller bar that enables listeners to move around within a song. Many MIDI plug-ins don't provide this convenience.

Adding MIDI files to pages

As with other audio and video clips, you can use either a conventional hyperlink (the `<A>` tag) or the `<EMBED>` command to add a MIDI file to a Web page. The same advantages and disadvantages of each approach apply to MIDI files.

Netscape Navigator uses LiveAudio to play MIDI, so the same tags and attributes discussed in the audio section of this chapter also apply to MIDI files.

Video on Your Site

Of all the data types that go into a Web site, which imposes the greatest playback demands on a computer, a server, and a network connection: text, graphics, sound, or video?

Those of you who answered *text* are hereby sentenced to a windowless cubicle in the Microsoft Office. The answer is, of course, video. As the previous section has shown, streaming audio is very much a reality now. But audio is easy compared to video, where every second of content is made up of 30 frames, each containing thousands of pixels — *plus* audio.

SECRET

Where to Find MIDI Files on the Web

So you've weighed the drawbacks against the advantages and decided to endow your site with a soundtrack. Great. So where do you get the soundtrack? On the Web, of course.

A vast array of Web sites provide downloadable MIDI files that you can use. (A large array also contain copyrighted material you shouldn't use — be sure to read the site's fine print and honor copyright laws.)

A superb site for classical music clips (many of which are freely useable) is the Classical Music Archives, at `http://www.prs.net/midi.html`. The Archives also contains a list of links to other sources for MIDI files.

Windows users have another source for MIDI files: Microsoft's Music Producer utility, which you can learn about at `http://www.microsoft.com/musicproducer/`. Music Producer uses algorithmic composition techniques to "compose" original music in a variety of styles, from country to New Age to jazz to polka. You can save the resulting files as standard MIDI files and embed them in your Web pages — no need to pay royalties or hire a composer. (Great — another job eliminated by computers.) How well does Music Producer work? My tests yielded results that ranged from bizarre to lame to surprisingly good. Music Producer is a fun program to work with, and definitely worth trying. Just don't tell any composer friends about it — you may ruin their day.

For the vast majority of World Wide Web users, smooth streaming of high-quality digital video just isn't a reality yet. The Internet, the phone system, the modems — the entire Web infrastructure — can't provide the bandwidth of even a double-speed CD-ROM drive. High-speed connections, particularly cable modems and satellite links, have the potential to make high-quality streaming video real, but only for a select few at first. And even a high-speed connection can't overcome the performance vagaries of the Internet itself.

But these are today's limitations. A faster Internet infrastructure, more efficient video-compression techniques, and other advancements *will* make high-quality streaming Web video practical. If you're willing to sacrifice image and sound quality, several low-quality video streaming technologies are available now — I'll spotlight two of them later in this section.

Beyond that, who says video *has* to be streaming? Plenty of Web sites contain downloadable video clips that weigh in at a megabyte or much more, and plenty of Web surfers seem to be willing to download them. The latest video technologies, particularly Apple's QuickTime plug-in for Netscape Navigator and Microsoft's ActiveMovie, can provide some of the immediate-gratification advantages of streaming video. The bottom line: if video clips can enhance the value of the information on your site, you should be using them now.

As with the first half of this chapter, I'm not going to provide a complete primer on digital video in this section. I assume you already have a grounding in video basics, that you've already toyed with a video-editing program such as Adobe Premiere, and that you understand the basics of video-capture devices. If you're a video beginner, you may want to pay a visit to my Web site (`http://www.heidsite.com/`), where you'll find background and tutorials on video (and audio) basics.

Which video format to use?

I suggest using QuickTime. Apple's digital video technology dominates the personal computer world, thanks to its availability on both the Mac and Windows platforms. Using QuickTime for your video clips gives you the broadest platform and browser compatibility. Apple's QuickTime plug-in module for Navigator provides a *fast-start* feature that even provides for *pseudo-streaming*: if the combination of movie size and connection speed allows, the movie plays back while it downloads.

Beyond these advantages, QuickTime is simply superior to Microsoft's Video for Windows (AVI). Basics such as sound synchronization are better, and QuickTime also allows for advanced features, such as text tracks that can display closed-captioning text beneath a video. Microsoft's ActiveMovie shows promise, but for now at least, it's geared more to consumer-level video playback than to video production.

As of early 1997, it's easier to produce QuickTime content on the Mac platform than on Windows. The Windows version of Adobe Premiere lets you output QuickTime movies, but all other current Windows video applications work only with Video for Windows. This is going to change, however: Apple is working on a new version of QuickTime for Windows that will match the features of its Mac OS counterpart, and this will make it easier for Windows software developers to create QuickTime-oriented production software. Look for these developments during 1997, and visit the *HTML & Web Publishing SECRETS* Web site for the latest scoop.

MPEG is another option for Web-based video. Windows and Mac OS machines alike can play back MPEG video with no additional hardware. (Windows machines need Microsoft's ActiveMovie; Power Macs can use Apple's MPEG extension for QuickTime.) But encoding MPEG video is time consuming and difficult, and slower machines may not be able to play it back smoothly. Indeed, 680X0-based Macs can't use the Apple MPEG playback extension. For these reasons, QuickTime is a better format.

A guide to video trade-offs

Making QuickTime movies is all about making trade-offs — between disk space, data-transfer rates, and movie quality. This section outlines the factors that you must weigh against one another when preparing movies for a Web site.

Frame size

The size of the movie window impacts the movie's size. Movie sizes of 320×240 pixels are common on CD-ROM but are impractical for Web sites.

Frame rate

The number of frames displayed per second (fps) also impacts storage requirements and playback quality. A movie with 10 fps uses less disk space than a 15-fps movie, but it looks jerky. 30 fps — the standard television frame rate — yields the smoothest results but uses three times the disk space as 10 fps.

Frame rates of 10 to 15 fps are common on CD-ROM titles, but again, are impractical for the World Wide Web.

Color depth

The higher the bit depth of a movie — the more bits that are assigned to each pixel — the larger the movie. A black-and-white (or, more accurately, grayscale) movie is smaller than a 256-color movie, which is smaller than a 24-bit (millions of colors) movie.

Audio

As with video, however, the higher the quality, the more demanding the movie. A 22KHz, 16-bit soundtrack in stereo makes for a larger movie file than does an 11KHz, 8-bit soundtrack in mono. You need to decide whether a higher-fidelity soundtrack is worth the added baggage.

The key to getting movie files that download within a reasonable amount of time is reducing the frame size, frame rate, color depth, and audio quality to the lowest levels you can stomach, and then compressing the daylights out of the results.

Compression options

QuickTime (and, for that matter, Video for Windows and ActiveMovie) support numerous compression schemes, or *codecs* (short for *compression/decompression*). When you're compressing video for the Web, you generally choose the desired codec from a pop-up menu in your video program's compression dialog box (see Figure 13-12).

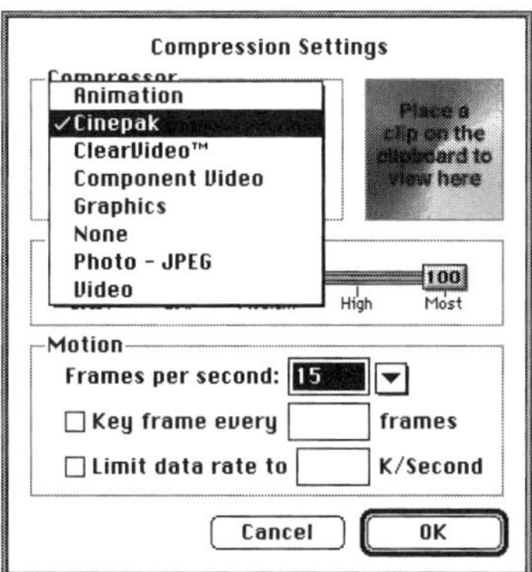

Figure 13-12: Choosing a codec in Adobe Premiere

One of the most popular codecs in the CD-ROM world is Cinepak. Cinepak movies take a long time to compress, but decompression is very fast — fast enough, in fact, for smooth video at high frame rates. Intel's Indeo is another popular codec.

Cinepak is suitable for Web video, too, but there's another alternative: JPEG. I don't mean Motion-JPEG, the enhanced JPEG used by many third-party digital video cards, but good old JPEG — the same JPEG used for photographic-quality still images (see Chapter 6). JPEG is too slow to allow for fluid motion — a computer can't decompress JPEG video frames quickly enough for smooth video without third-party hardware — but this isn't an issue if you're using very slow frame rates, such as 2 or 3 frames per second. (Yes, that's often how low you have to go.)

In addition to these old standbys, there are some up-and-coming compression schemes. A compression technology called ClearVideo from Iterated Systems (`http://www.iterated.com/`) relies on cutting-edge fractal-compression technology and provides excellent quality at low data rates. ClearVideo works with Progressive Networks's RealVideo technology, which I discuss shortly. And a standard called H.263, originally created for videoconferencing, promises to have an impact on Web video.

Compression secrets

Regardless of the compression scheme you use, video compression works best when your video contains simple backgrounds and as little motion and video noise as possible. If you're shooting video that you intend to compress heavily, following a few rules of thumb will help you get the best results.

Shoot in the highest-quality format you can afford

High-end video formats exhibit less video noise than low-end formats. Video noise, which looks like a faint dancing snow, is bad news because it essentially adds motion to the entire frame. In its zeal to retain that motion while crunching down the movie's size, a compressor will degrade the entire frame's appearance. The worst-to-best video formats from a noise perspective are VHS, S-VHS, Hi-8, and Betacam SP. Depending on the camera (and on who you ask), the new digital video cassette recorders provide quality roughly equal to that of Betacam SP.

Light indoor subjects

Today's video cameras are very sensitive to low light, but the dreaded video noise is also far more apparent in low-light shots. Rather than relying on existing room lighting, invest in at least one video light — not a home-movie job that mounts atop the camera, but a high-quality halogen light with a stand and reflective umbrella. The resulting video will be cleaner and free of the odd color casts indoor lighting can produce. I use Omni lights from Lowel-Light Manufacturing; you can find these or similar lights at photography and video supply houses. To learn to use your lights, read Ross Lowell's *Matters of Light and Depth* (Broad Street Books, 1992).

Shoot with compression in mind

Choose plain, solid-colored backgrounds, use a tripod, and avoid excessive panning and zooming. Now, cinematographers might rightfully cringe at the idea of restricting their repertoire to shots that compress well, so take this advice with a pixel of salt. But know that busy backgrounds and lots of movement will cost you in sharpness.

Use Movie Cleaner Pro with Web-Motion

If you're using a Mac OS machine to perform your compression, there's a wonderful utility that will greatly streamline the process of getting Web-ready video. It's Terran Interactive's Movie Cleaner Pro with Web-Motion plug-in. (A basic version called Movie Cleaner Lite is available as freeware. And as I write this, Terran Interactive is working on a significant upgrade of Movie Cleaner Pro, to be called Media Cleaner Pro. Visit the company's Web site at `http://www.terran-int.com/` for the latest news on the new version.)

Movie Cleaner Pro's exquisite interface takes the black art of QuickTime compression and makes it easy. Beginners can use the program's Movie Expert to arrive at the correct compression settings by answering a series of questions. Gurus can hand-tweak compression settings and use the program's batch-processing feature to apply those settings to an entire folder worth of movies.

Movie Cleaner Pro's WebMotion plug-in expands Movie Cleaner Pro's gentle interrogation technique to encompass the Web's bandwidth limitations (see Figure 13-13).

Web-Motion formats the compressed movie to use the QuickTime plug-in's fast-start feature, and it also creates the HTML code that the plug-in requires. Sample audio and video clips let you preview your settings.

A session with Web-Motion can be a bit discouraging. Program Web-Motion to give you a movie that plays smoothly over a 28.8Kbps connection, and you get a jittery postage stamp with garbled sound. But to its credit, Web-Motion lets you explore the full range of quality/performance trade-offs that Web movie moguls face, and by balancing those trade-offs carefully, you can successfully cram QuickTime into the narrow pipe that is the Internet.

Essential HTML for Video Files

As with audio, there are a few ways to get video clips from your site to your visitors:

- You can use conventional anchor tags to enable visitors to download clips to their hard drives.
- You can use the `<EMBED>` tag to embed QuickTime or Video for Windows movies for use with Apple's QuickTime plug-in or Microsoft's ActiveMovie.
- You can use the `<OBJECT>` tag to embed movies for playback using Microsoft ActiveMovie.

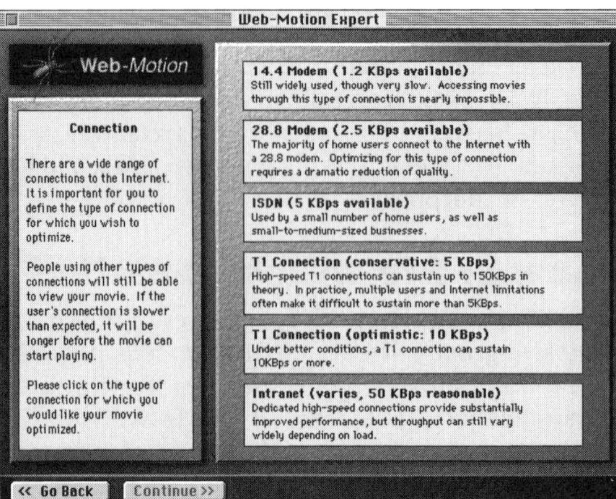

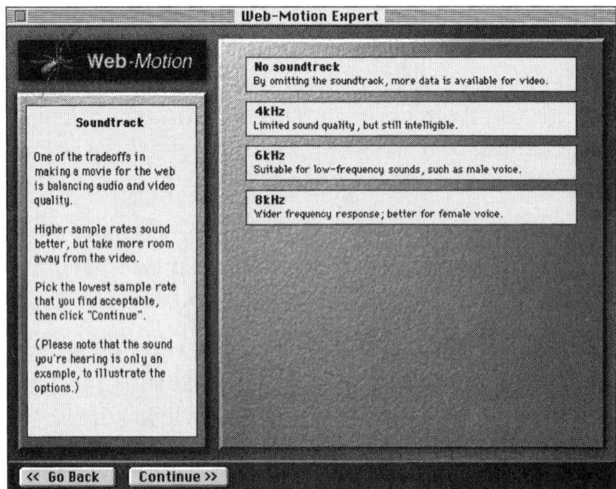

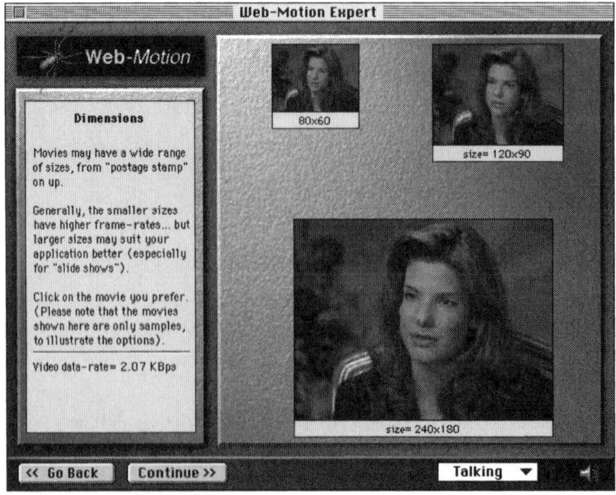

Figure 13-13: With Movie Cleaner Pro's Web-Motion plug-in, you answer a series of questions to arrive at the appropriate connection settings. Each set of questions comes with background information.

Many of the same concepts and tips in the section "Essential HTML for Sound Files," earlier in this chapter, also apply to video clips. You can use the `<NOEMBED>` tag to provide compatibility with browsers that don't support embedding. You can post video clips in both QuickTime and Video for Windows format to improve cross-platform compatibility. And you should *always* tell visitors how large a movie file is before displaying an embedded movie.

Rather than rehash these basics here, I'll just outline some of the points that are specific to Web video clips. Refer back to "Essential HTML for Sound Files" if you need a refresher course.

Video and the <EMBED> tag

The basics of the `<EMBED>` tag are the same for video as they are for audio. But there are some attributes and issues that are specific to video clips and Netscape Navigator.

Specifying height and width

The `height` and `width` attributes are required for embedding video. If you don't know the dimensions of a clip, you can find out using the Apple MoviePlayer utility (included with both the Mac OS and Windows versions of QuickTime). Open the movie and choose Get Info (Mac OS) or Get Movie Info (Windows) from the Movie menu.

If you intend to display the movie's controller bar (a good idea), you must add 24 to the height of the movie. For instance, if the movie is 120 pixels high, its height parameter should be 144.

Hiding and showing the controller

To hide the QuickTime controller that normally appears beneath a movie, add `controller=false` to the `<EMBED>` command. (If you omit the controller attribute, the controller appears.) But think twice about hiding the controller. Showing it not only enables visitors to navigate within the movie and control its volume, it also lets them see the movie's download progress — QuickTime displays a little progress bar in the controller when the movie is downloading.

Getting all loopy

To have a movie repeat continuously, add `loop=true` to the `<EMBED>` command. To have the movie play forward, then backward, then forward again, and so on, use `loop=palindrome`. (Palindrome mode is great for creating that Purina Cat Chow "chow, chow, chow!" effect. Ahem.)

Playing the movie automatically

Normally, a QuickTime movie doesn't begin playback until a visitor explicitly clicks its Play button. If you'd rather have the movie begin playback automatically, add `autoplay=true` to the `<EMBED>` command. As soon as the visitor's QuickTime plug-in determines that enough of the movie has downloaded for smooth playback of the entire movie, it begins playback.

Turning a movie into a URL hot spot

You can have a movie act as a URL hot spot — if a visitor clicks on the movie, he or she will be taken to a different page. To set up a movie as a URL hot spot, add `href="url"` to the `<EMBED>` command (substituting *url* with an actual URL — for example, `href="http://www.heidsite.com/movies.html"`). This attribute works only if you *also* use the `controller=false` attribute.

If you use the `href` attribute, you can also use the `target` attribute to specify the name of a frame that will be the target of the link. For details on working with frames, see Chapter 7.

Hiding a movie (and creating a background sound)

To have a movie open and play but not appear, use the `hidden` attribute, as in:

```
<embed src="backgroundsound.mov" hidden>
```

As the example implies, the `hidden` attribute is a way of including a background sound on a page: make the sound an audio-only QuickTime movie, and then reference it as shown. To have the sound loop, add `loop=true`.

The <EMBED> tag and Microsoft Internet Explorer

As mentioned earlier, Microsoft Internet Explorer can use Microsoft ActiveMovie to play back QuickTime movies (not to mention Video for Windows, MPEG, and other formats). Microsoft Internet Explorer doesn't support the full range of `<EMBED>` attributes that the QuickTime plug-in supports. In specific, Microsoft Internet Explorer supports:

```
controller=true/false
autoplay=true/false
loop=true/false
```

Microsoft Internet Explorer's native `<EMBED>` command doesn't allow for the use of the `href`, `target`, or `hidden` attributes. Or, I should say, they don't *always* allow for these attributes. Let me explain. When you restart a Windows system after installing ActiveMovie, a dialog box appears informing you that ActiveMovie can play a wide variety of digital media files, and asking if you want to associate those file types with ActiveMovie.

If a user has chosen to have ActiveMovie play digital video files, these attributes (`controller`, `autoplay`, and `loop`) do not work. If, however, a visitor has installed Apple's QuickTime plug-in for Netscape Navigator *and* he or she does not choose to have ActiveMovie play digital video files, these attributes *do* work.

Nice and confusing, isn't it? Because you obviously can't be sure how a visitor's system may be configured, you may want to think twice about relying on these attributes on pages that will be viewed with Microsoft Internet Explorer.

Naming your video files

As with audio files, browsers and helper applications rely on file extensions to identify the video file format. Table 13-4 lists the extensions you should use for each format.

Table 13-4 File extensions for the most popular video file formats

For This Format	*Use This Extension*
QuickTime	.mov
Video for Windows	.avi
MPEG	.mpeg or .mpg
VivoActive	.viv
RealVideo	.rm

Streaming Video with VivoActive

Streaming video is worth considering if you're willing to tread the leading edge (and make the corresponding sacrifices in image and sound quality), or if you're putting together video for an intranet site (where your bandwidth constraints aren't as significant). Several streaming video technologies are available, including Xing Technologies's StreamWorks (`http://www.xingtech.com`), VDO's VDOLive (`http://www.vdo.net/`), Vivo's VivoActive (`http://www.vivo.com/`), and Progressive Networks's RealVideo (`http://www.real.com/`).

I'm impressed with VivoActive's features, ease of use, and results. I'm apparently not alone: you can view VivoActive clips on such high-profile sites as CNN's (`http://www.cnn.com/`) and Home Box Office's (`http://www.hbo.com/`). In this section, I examine the process of putting together streaming video clips using VivoActive.

VivoActive at a glance

Here's an overview of VivoActive's features and strengths:

- It's cross-platform. The VivoActive browser plug-in is available for the Windows and Mac (PowerPC only) platforms. (An ActiveX control is also available.) VivoActive Producer, the software you use to compress video into VivoActive format, is also available for both platforms.

- It doesn't require a proprietary server. VivoActive streams video using a standard HTTP server, so you don't have to buy an additional piece of server software. VDOLive and StreamWorks, by comparison, both require proprietary servers.
- It's easy. The VivoActive Producer software makes it easy to compress QuickTime or Video for Windows files into VivoActive format. From there, a simple <EMBED> command puts your video on the Web.

VivoActive Producer

Figure 13-14 shows the Mac OS version of VivoActive Producer in action.

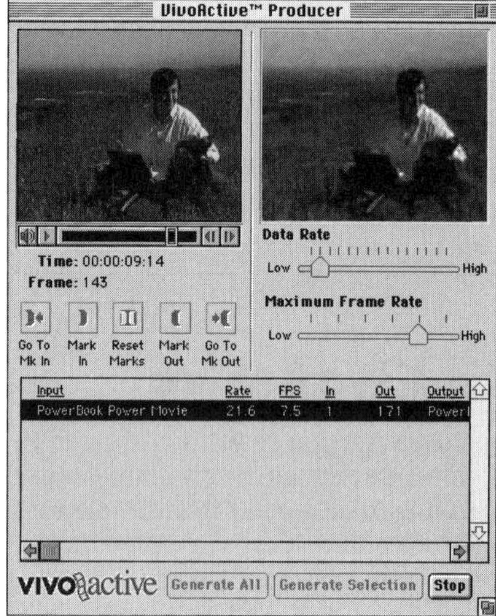

Figure 13-14: Vivo's VivoActive Producer

VivoActive Producer sports a variety of presets for common connection speeds, including 28.8Kbps modems, ISDN connections, and local area networks. Each preset is also provided in two flavors: one for "talking-head" style movies (where there isn't much motion, allowing a faster frame rate) and one for motion-intensive movies (which require slower frame rates, lest quality suffer unacceptably). You can customize the program's existing settings and create new ones of your own. You can also embed copyright information in the clips.

Compressing clips couldn't be easier: open the original QuickTime or Video for Windows clips, specify the desired bandwidth settings, and click a button. As Figure 13-14 shows, VivoActive Producer displays before-and-after views of the clip as it works.

ON CD-ROM

The *HTML & Web Publishing SECRETS* CD-ROM contains two versions of a VivoActive video clip: one compressed for a 28.8Kbps connection and one compressed for ISDN speeds.

Embedding VivoActive clips

To add a VivoActive clip to a Web page, use the <EMBED> command. The following HTML does the job and also supports the VivoActive ActiveX control:

```
<OBJECT CLASSID="clsid:02466323-75ed-11cf-a267-0020af2546ea"
        WIDTH="176" HEIGHT="144"
        CODEBASE="vvweb.cab#Version=1,0,0,0">
        <EMBED SRC="clip_name.viv" WIDTH="176" HEIGHT="144"
AUTOSTART="TRUE" VIDEOCONTROLS="ON">
        <PARAM NAME="URL" VALUE="clip_name.viv ">
        <PARAM NAME="VIDEOCONTROLS" VALUE="ON">
        <PARAM NAME="AUTOSTART" VALUE="TRUE">
</OBJECT>
```

Streaming Video with RealVideo

Given the success with which Progressive Networks launched its RealAudio streaming technology, it was only a matter of time before the company entered the video field. That time has arrived. RealVideo is here, and it's a major contender in streaming video.

RealVideo at a glance

Here's the big picture of RealVideo's features and strengths:

- **It's cross-platform.** Like VivoActive, the RealVideo player is available for Windows and Mac OS computers alike — as is the RealVideo Encoder, the program you use to compress clips for RealVideo delivery.
- **It doesn't require a proprietary server.** Also like VivoActive, you can deliver RealVideo clips using your existing HTTP server software. For high-volume sites, however, Progressive Networks sells a variety of RealVideo servers that deliver more reliable streaming under heavy loads — and that enable you to deliver live video events.
- **It's versatile.** A variety of encoding options enable you to optimize quality for specific applications: talking-head video, music video, 28.8Kbps modem connections, or faster speeds. Another aspect of RealVideo's versatility surfaces at the receiving end of the line: Web surfers can use a single player, called the RealPlayer, to play both RealAudio and RealVideo clips.
- **It looks great.** Progressive Networks has licensed Iterated Systems's ClearVideo compression technology for use in the RealVideo Encoder. The RealVideo Encoder also provides plenty of fine-tuning options that enable you to optimize quality for your content and delivery methods.

- **It's more than just video.** RealVideo allows for video image maps: video clips can have hot spots that, when clicked, take visitors to other pages, open other clips, or jump to a specific part of a clip. (A great program for creating video image maps for RealVideo is Ephyx Technologies' V-Active, a trial version of which you can download from `http://www.ephyx.com/`.) Like RealAudio, RealVideo also allows for synchronized multimedia: you can, for example, set up slide-show-like presentations in which a browser displays a series of Web pages while a video clip plays back.

Encoding for RealVideo: Windows

The RealVideo Encoder is shown in Figure 13-15.

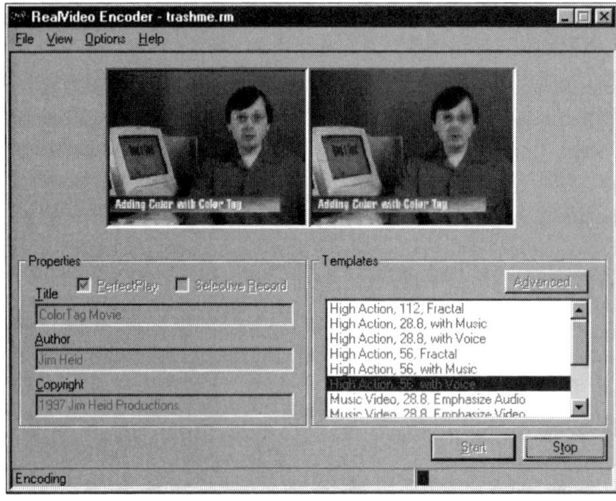

Figure 13-15: The RealVideo Encoder. Note the "before" and "after" displays showing the effects of compression.

ON CD-ROM

The *HTML & Web Publishing SECRETS* CD-ROM contains three versions of a RealVideo clip: one compressed for a 28.8Kbps connection and two compressed for ISDN speeds.

Using the RealVideo Encoder to encode an existing video clip is easy. First, choose Open Session from the File menu and then click the File button in the Open Session dialog box. Click the Add button to specify the files to encode. The RealVideo Encoder can encode Video for Windows (AVI), QuickTime (MOV), and audio (AU) files.

Next, be sure the RealMedia File check box is checked in the Destination area of the dialog box. To specify a name for the encoded file, click the Select button and then type a filename in the Save dialog box that appears.

Figure 13-16 shows the Open Session dialog box configured for a typical encoding project.

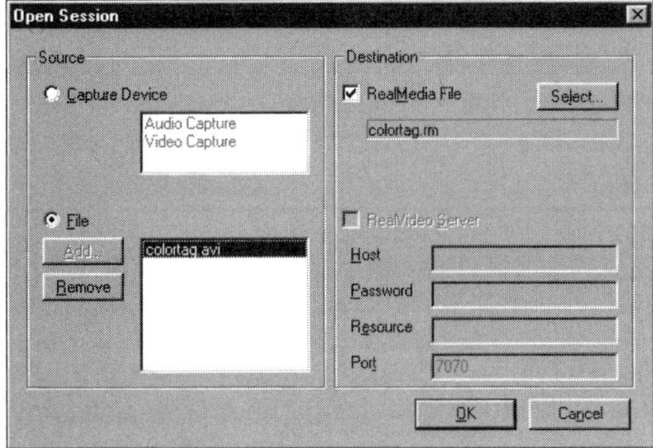

Figure 13-16: Setting up an encoding session

Next, you need to specify the encoding settings. The encoder provides a wide variety of preset templates for common types of content. To examine the specifics behind each template, click the Advanced button. In the Advanced Settings dialog box, you find controls for specifying the frame rate and audio sampling rate and for tweaking quality (see Figure 13-17).

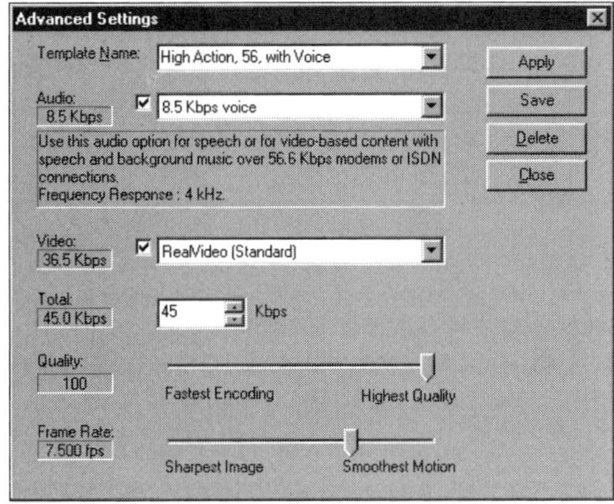

Figure 13-17: The RealVideo Encoder's Advanced Settings dialog box

A closer look at the encoder's settings

As you choose audio settings, the Advanced Settings dialog box displays a brief description of the current setting. To learn about each setting and its best uses, page through each setting and read its description.

Table 13-5 lists the specific settings that the most commonly used templates provide.

Table 13-5 Common RealVideo Encoder template settings

Template Name	*Target Bandwidth (Kbps)*	*Total Data Rate (Kbps)*	*Audio Codec Used*	*Audio Bit Rate (Kbps)*	*Video Bit Rate (Kbps)*	*Frames Per Second*
Talking Heads 28.8	28.8	19	RealMedia 6.5 Kbps	6.5	12.5	7.5
Talking Heads 56	56.0	45	RealMedia 8.5 Kbps	8.5	36.5	7.5
Music Video 28.8, Emphasize Audio	28.8	19	RealMedia 12 Kbps	12.0	7.0	1.0
Music Video 28.8, Emphasize Video	28.8	19	RealMedia 8 Kbps	8.0	11.0	0.25
Music Video 56, Emphasize Audio	56.0	45	RealAudio 3.0-28.8 Mono, full response	16.0	29.0	7.5
Music Video 56, Emphasize Video	56.0	45	RealMedia 12 Kbps	12.0	33.0	7.5
High Action w/ Music, 28.8	28.8	19	RealMedia 8 Kbps	8.0	11.0	0.25
High Action w/ Voice, 28.8	28.8	19	RealMedia 6.5 Kbps	6.5	12.5	0.25
High Action w/ Voice, 56	56.0	45	RealAudio 2.0-28.8	8.5	36.5	7.5
High Action w/ Music, 56	56.0	45	RealAudio 3.0-28.8 Mono, full response	16.0	29.0	7.5

Notice that the total data rate is always below the target bandwidth — for example, when the target bandwidth is a 28.8Kbps modem connection, the total data rate is in the 19Kbps ballpark. This provides a safety margin to allow for poor connections or a busy network. Table 13-6 lists the total data rates that Progressive Networks recommends for each of several common target bandwidths.

Table 13-6 Target bandwidths and their recommended total bit rates

For This Target Bandwidth (Kbps)	*Avoid Exceeding This Total Bit Rate (Kbps)*
28.8	19
56.0	45
64.0	56
128.0	105

SECRET

Choosing Between Standard and Fractal Compression

If you explore the RealVideo Encoder's compression options, you'll notice that two primary types of video compression are available: RealVideo Standard and RealVideo Fractal. Which should you use, and when? Here are some guidelines:

RealVideo Standard. This encoding method is best for most low-bandwidth and Internet uses. RealVideo Standard's decompression is more processor-intensive than RealVideo Fractal's, so clips with fast frame rates may not play smoothly on slower computers. But encoding takes less time with RealVideo Standard than with RealVideo Fractal. Indeed, RealVideo Standard is the only option available for real-time encoding of live events. RealVideo Standard also handles poor connections and packet loss better than does RealVideo Fractal, making it a better choice for environments such as the World Wide Web, where packet loss can often be high.

RealVideo Fractal. RealVideo Fractal encoding is best for high bandwidth and fast-frame-rate applications where packet losses are expected to be low, such as corporate intranets. RealVideo Fractal doesn't perform as well with high-action scenes containing rapid motion and lots of cuts, but it tends to deliver better results with low-action scenes such as talking heads.

RealVideo Fractal's decoding performance is terrific, allowing frame rates of 15 fps on lower end Pentium- and PowerPC-based computers. But encoding is slower than RealVideo Standard — too slow for software-only live encoding.

The bottom line? For Web-based RealVideo clips, RealVideo Standard is generally preferable unless your clips contain a lot of action or rapid cuts. For intranet use, RealVideo Fractal delivers outstanding quality and fast frame rates.

PerfectPlay and Selective Record

In the Properties area of the RealVideo Encoder's window are two check boxes labeled PerfectPlay and Selective Record. These features work similarly to their counterparts in the RealAudio Encoder application discussed earlier in this chapter.

- **PerfectPlay.** Check the PerfectPlay box to enable the PerfectPlay feature in Progressive Networks's RealPlayer Plus package. This feature is particularly valuable for RealVideo, because it enables visitors with slower modems to enjoy clips encoded for higher bandwidths. As with RealAudio, there's a small price to pay: the player must download a larger chunk of the file before playback can begin. But given the dramatic improvements in audio and video quality that higher-bandwidth encoding allows, that's a price many modem users will find worth paying.
- **Selective Record.** As with RealAudio, checking Selective Record enables visitors to save a video clip on their hard drives — and, if they're scumbags, pirate it. Use this option judiciously.

Encoding with Adobe Premiere

If you own Adobe Premiere, you can also encode RealVideo clips using an Adobe Premiere export plug-in. When you install the RealVideo Encoder, the setup program also installs this export plug-in.

The export plug-in works identically to its Mac OS counterpart, which I describe in the next section.

Encoding for RealVideo: Mac OS

If you use a Mac OS machine, you can encode RealVideo clips using Progressive Networks's RealVideo Encoder plug-in for Adobe Premiere. You can also use Terran Interactive's wonderful Media Cleaner or Media Cleaner Lite utilities. This section covers both options.

Encoding with Adobe Premiere

To encode a video or audio clip using Adobe Premiere, open the clip and, from the File menu's Export submenu, choose RealVideo Encoder. The dialog box in Figure 13-18 appears.

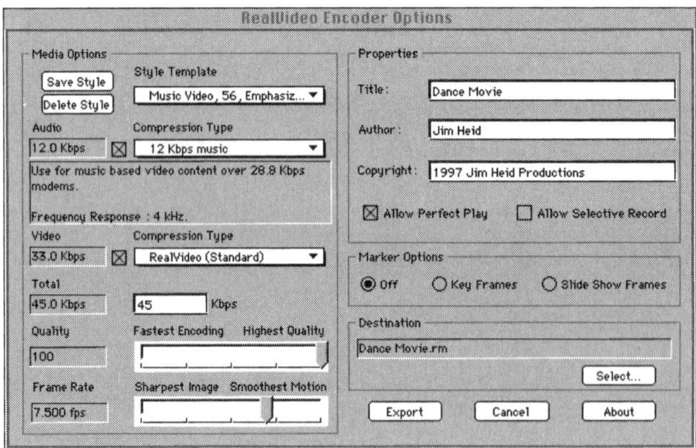

Figure 13-18: The RealVideo Encoder export plug-in for Adobe Premiere

The export plug-in's basic settings are identical to those of the RealVideo Encoder described in the previous section, and all the details in Tables 13-5 and 13-6 apply.

But the Premiere export plug-in provides an additional goodie that allows for some extra finesse. The Marker Options area of the export dialog box contains buttons that let you take advantage of the markers feature in Adobe Premiere. (The markers feature enables you to create electronic bookmarks within clips; when you're working in Premiere, you can use these bookmarks to quickly locate a particular section of a clip or to align clips.)

Where RealVideo encoding is concerned, markers have an additional benefit: they enable you to control exactly which frames of the clip are encoded.

Here's why the export plug-in's marker support is so nifty. As you know from having memorized Table 13-5, most RealVideo encoding settings deliver frame rates that are, shall we say, on the slow side — sometimes as slow as one frame every few seconds. Now, of all the frames in a video clip, chances are that some are more important than others. By setting markers at these frames and then choosing the appropriate settings in the export plug-in, you can ensure that the most important frames are encoded.

If you don't care which frames are encoded, leave the Off button selected in the Marker Options area. Otherwise, choose either Key Frames or Slide Show Frames, as follows:

- **Key Frames.** When you choose Key Frames, the export plug-in encodes every frame to which you've assigned a marker. Other frames in the clip may or may not be encoded, depending on the particular encoding template you set.
- **Slide Show Frames.** When you choose this option, *only* those frames for which you've set markers are encoded. This option enables you to specify exactly which frames should be encoded. For the money, this is the most interesting of the two options. For details on using Slide Show Frames, see the Secrets box "How to Make a RealVideo Slide Show."

Encoding with Media Cleaner

I've already sung the praises of Terran Interactive's Movie Cleaner Pro and Movie Cleaner Lite utilities. Their successor, Media Cleaner Pro and Media Cleaner Lite, are even more powerful — and they support RealVideo encoding.

How to Make a RealVideo Slide Show

As its name implies, the RealVideo export plug-in's Slide Show Frames option is a great way to turn a video clip into a slide show. Here's an example: Say you have a video clip containing a variety of landscape scenes — a wide expanse of prairie, a close-up of a sunflower, a lake and mountain range — and the clip also contains a soundtrack with music and narration.

Now, if you were to encode this normally — that is, allowing the encoder plug-in to choose which frames to encode and which to discard in order to meet a specific frame rate and bit rate — you'd end up with a RealVideo clip containing multiple frames where nothing is really changing, except maybe for some clouds drifting across the sky.

Why waste all that bandwidth by encoding frames in which there's no significant motion? Instead, create one marker for each outdoor scene. Then, encode the clip with the Slide Show Frames option selected. Your resulting RealVideo clip will contain one frame per scene, with plenty of bandwidth left over for a great-sounding soundtrack.

When RealVideo was announced, Terran Interactive shipped a free utility called RealMedia Cleaner Lite, available from Terran's Web site (http://www.terran-int.com/). Figure 13-19 shows RealMedia Cleaner Lite in action.

As Figure 13-19 shows, the best thing about the Media Cleaner family is its array of quality-enhancing options: high-quality scaling, artifact-reducing blurring options, and noise-reduction features work together to deliver terrific results. If you're using a Mac OS machine to prepare video for the Web (or for CD-ROMs), you need this program.

Adding RealVideo clips to your pages

As with RealAudio files, you can't add a RealVideo clip to a page by simply referring to the clip's name in a URL. If you did, the entire clip would download to a visitor's hard drive, thus defeating RealVideo's streaming talents.

As with RealAudio, you must create a text file that references the RealVideo clip, and then call out that text file in your HTML. For example, to make a clip named interview.rm available, create a metafile containing the following:

```
http://www.your_domain_here.com/interview.rm
```

(As with my RealAudio examples earlier in this chapter, this example assumes you'll be streaming your video via HTTP. If you're using a Progressive Networks server to stream the video, substitute http:// with prn://.)

Now save the metafile — let's give it the name interview.ram. Reference this metafile in your HTML page, as in:

```
<a href="http://www.your_domain_here.com/interview.ram">Watch this!</a>
```

You can also use the <EMBED> tag to play back video clips using the RealPlayer plug-in rather than the RealPlayer helper application. For details, see the section "Using the RealPlayer plug-in," earlier in this chapter.

Configuring Your Server for Media

You've come this far, and you have some great audio or video with which to season your site. Now you need to make sure your server knows how to dish out the seasoning.

One of the jobs performed by Web server software involves including a *content type* with every file that it sends to a browser. The browser reads this content-type information and uses it to process the document appropriately. For example, the content type for an HTML file is *text/HTML*. When a browser sees this, it knows it can display the file without a plug-in or helper application.

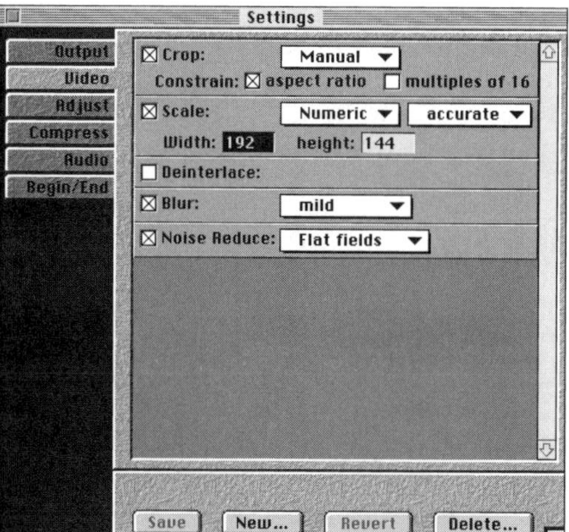

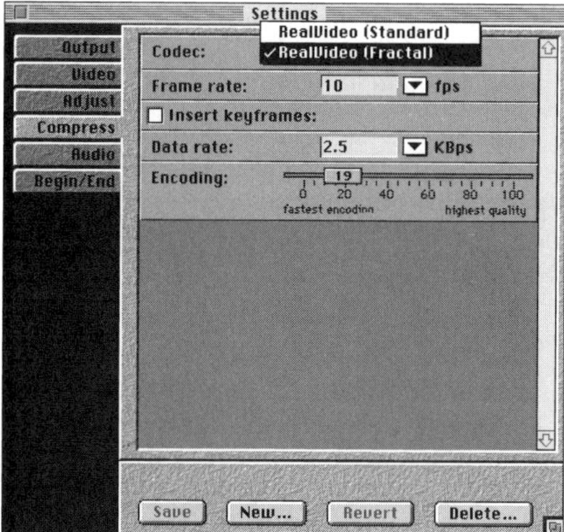

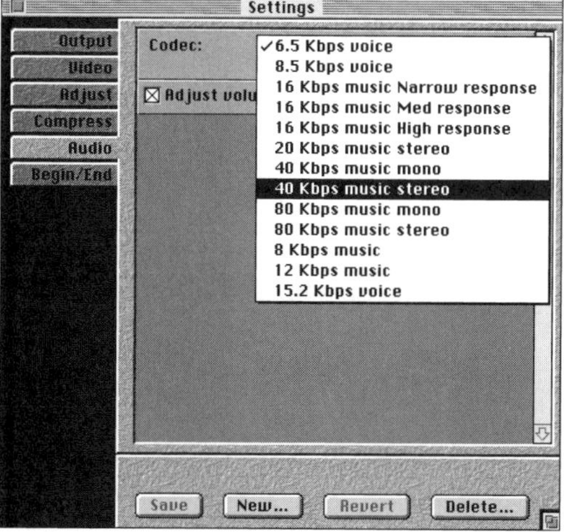

Figure 13-19: Encoding RealVideo with RealMedia Cleaner Lite. Top: Fine-tuning video settings. Middle: Choosing a video codec. Bottom: Choosing an audio codec.

To put all this in conversational terms, the server says: "Hey, here comes an HTML page," and the browser thinks to itself, "OK, I'm going to treat this as an HTML page." At other times, the server may say, "Hey, here comes a WAV audio file," and the browser thinks to itself, "OK, I need to use the WhizzySound helper application to handle this one."

Of Maps and MIME

Of course, the server doesn't say, "Hey, here comes a WAV file." Servers are much too polite to say "hey." Instead, the server transmits the file's MIME type. (MIME, short for *Multipurpose Internet Mail Extensions,* is also what Internet-based e-mail programs use to handle file enclosures.) As mentioned earlier, the MIME type for an HTML page is *text/HTML.* The MIME type for a WAV audio file is *audio/wav.* It's these and all the other MIME types out there that a browser reads in order to determine how to handle an incoming file.

A server relies primarily on a file's extension to determine which MIME type to transmit. The extensions *.htm* or *.html* indicate an HTML page, for instance, while *.wav* denotes a WAV audio file. This association between file extension and file type is called *content mapping* or *suffix mapping:* each extension is associated with — it's mapped to — a specific type of data.

And now — finally — we get to the point: While all server software is preconfigured to handle the most common data types, you may find that some programs don't have a content map for the file format you plan to use. It's easy to set one up — generally, you use the server's Properties dialog box or administration utility to associate the extension with the MIME type, as shown in Figure 13-20.

How do you know what a file's MIME type is? Generally, if you're using a specialized data type — such as Macromedia's Shockwave format — you can find its MIME type in the documentation that comes with whatever program you use to create the data. You can also find lists of standard MIME types at `ftp://venera.isi.edu/in-notes/iana/assignments/media-types/`.

MIME types for sound files

Where sound files are concerned, there's a bit of platform bigotry: Windows-based server programs often don't contain content maps for AIFF files (which are popular on the Mac), and Mac-based servers often don't contain content maps for WAV files (which dominate on Windows).

Two specific examples: WebSTAR (the most popular server on the Mac platform) doesn't contain a content map for WAV files, and O'Reilly and Associates's WebSite, a wonderful server package for Windows 95 and NT machines, doesn't contain a map for AIFF files. Few servers on either platform contain content maps for RealAudio's RA and RAM files or RealVideo's RM files, either.

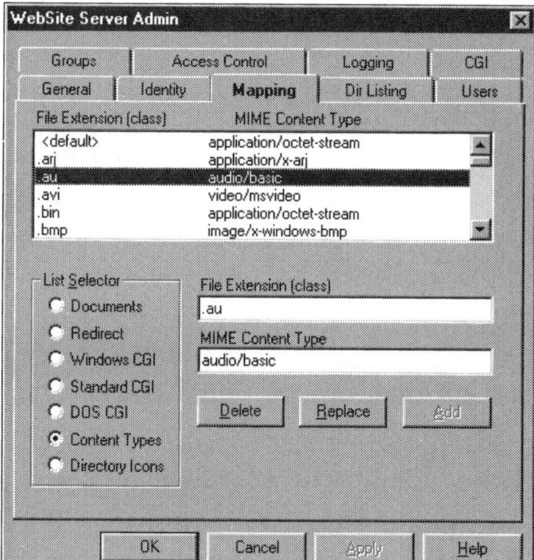

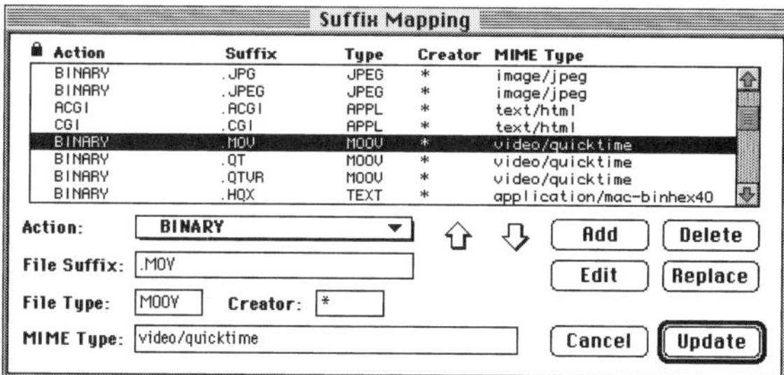

Figure 13-20: Configuring MIME types in O'Reilly's WebSite (top) and Quarterdeck's WebSTAR (bottom)

MIME types for video files

All server packages I'm aware of contain content maps for most video file formats and file extensions discussed in this chapter: QuickTime (.mov or .qt), Video for Windows (.avi), and MPEG (.mpg or .mpeg).

Streaming video technologies such as VivoActive use MIME types of their own. VivoActive's MIME type, for example, is video/vnd.vivo, and VivoActive files end with the extension .viv.

Summary

- Audio and video clips enable a Web site to deliver on the multimedia potential of the Web — but they have stiff bandwidth requirements that limit their practicality.
- In order to yield small file sizes and reasonable download times, you must compress audio and video clips. Compression always means making quality trade-offs, but if you're careful, you can minimize the loss.
- To get the best results, create original audio and video content using the highest-quality equipment and production standards you can afford.
- Streaming audio and video technologies enable visitors to listen and watch content without having to endure lengthy downloads.
- Progressive Networks's RealAudio and RealVideo are the leading streaming audio and video technologies; Vivo's VivoActive is also a strong video streaming contender, and Macromedia's Shockwave also delivers excellent-quality streaming audio.

Chapter 14

You Are (Virtually) Here

In This Chapter

- Why add virtual reality to a Web site?
- Creating QuickTime VR panoramic and object movies
- Essential HTML for embedding and playing QuickTime VR movies
- Comparing QuickTime VR and other VR technologies
- An introduction to the Virtual Reality Modeling Language (VRML)

We humans were exploring new places for thousands of years before we started writing or even drawing pictures. Our need to explore remains strong: we travel to exotic places, we go on Sunday drives, we wander at the mall.

These basic needs are influencing the Web — and the Web's ability to span the globe enhances them in unique ways. The Web world is slowly but steadily moving toward the brave new world of virtual reality. Some forward-looking Web developers are creating everything from virtual cities you can tour to virtual stores you can browse.

There are several routes to Web VR. This chapter concentrates on my personal favorite: Apple's QuickTime VR technology. QuickTime VR brings the best parts of virtual reality — user-controlled exploration and examination — to Windows and Mac OS computers.

Neither QuickTime VR nor other Web VR technologies demand the usual virtual reality garb of goggles and gloves. You view a virtual world on the computer's screen and move around with the mouse. Think of it as virtual VR.

QuickTime VR *panoramic* movies give viewers a 360-degree view of a scene. They're ideal ways to showcase homes for sale, tourist destinations, company's facilities, or your home town. QuickTime VR *object* movies enable viewers to examine things: to pick up and rotate a product for sale, a museum artifact, or an antique doll.

Although QuickTime VR movies can play back on Mac OS and Windows machines alike, creating them requires a Mac OS machine. (If you use only Windows, don't despair: I also describe some QuickTime VR-like technologies that support content creation under Windows.)

This chapter describes the process of creating QuickTime VR movies and provides tips and secrets for optimizing their size and embedding them in Web pages. After our tour of the QuickTime VR world, we'll examine another major player in Web VR: the Virtual Reality Modeling Language, or VRML.

The QuickTime VR Experience

A conventional, or *linear,* QuickTime movie is like a videotape: you can watch it from start to finish or skip around within it, but your view of the subject — say it's of an orchestra on a stage — was cast in stone when the original video was shot.

With a QuickTime VR movie, you can change your view by clicking and dragging within the movie. For example, dragging to the left causes the view to change as if you were turning your head to the left, while dragging up is the equivalent of looking up. You can not only see the orchestra, you can turn around to see who's sitting in the row behind you. You can zoom in on the orchestra for a closer look, or zoom out to see the big picture (see Figure 14-1). As I mentioned in this chapter's introduction, a VR movie that provides this freedom of navigation is called a panoramic movie.

Figure 14-1: QuickTime VR lets you explore locations using the mouse. Here are several views of a single panoramic movie, which you can explore on this book's CD-ROM.

A QuickTime VR movie can actually contain multiple panoramic scenes, each of which is called a *node*. In a virtual house tour, you might have a node for each room. A visitor moves between nodes by clicking hot spots. For instance, the doorway leading from the kitchen into the dining room might be a hot spot: clicking it switches from the panoramic of the kitchen to that of the dining room.

Multiple-node QuickTime VR movies are much more complicated to create than single-node movies, and as you might expect, they're much larger and therefore take longer to download. For these reasons, the majority of QuickTime VR movies on the Web are single-node movies.

QuickTime VR object movies

QuickTime VR panoramic movies enable people to explore places; QuickTime VR *object* movies enable them to examine *things*: to grab them and turn them around, to look at them from above and below (see Figure 14-2).

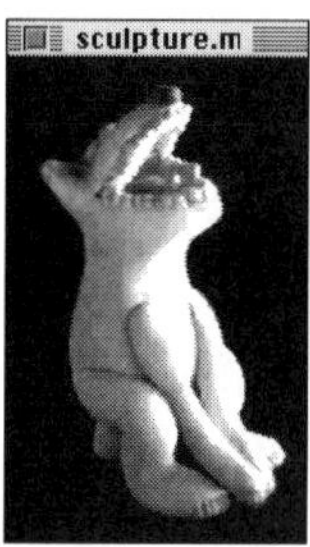

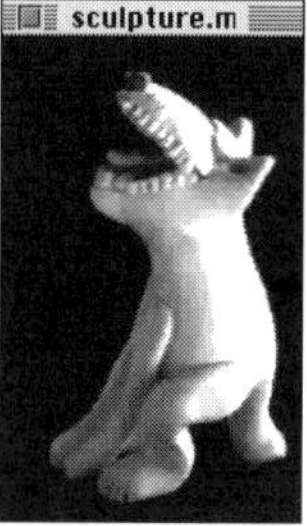

Figure 14-2: The object is the game: Here are three views of a QuickTime VR object movie. Sculpture by Mona Adisa Brooks.

If you're putting together a Web site that showcases objects of any kind, your creative juices are probably flowing already. Just a few of the possibilities for object movies include the following:

- An online catalog that enables visitors to examine items for sale
- A Web museum exhibit that enables visitors to pick up and study ancient artifacts
- A site on antique toy trains that shows the old Lionels from every angle
- An online gallery that showcases sculptures and carvings
- A fashion site that enables visitors to rotate a virtual model wearing the latest threads

Making QuickTime VR Panoramics

Reality is hard enough; virtual reality shouldn't be, too. But alas, it is: making QuickTime VR movies has historically been a black art that requires photographic expertise, a steamer trunk's worth of equipment, and the patience to deal with software whose interface only a programmer could love.

But since QuickTime VR debuted in 1995, the tools *have* improved some. Making movies that contain multiple nodes is still just about as difficult as it was at the beginning, but making single-node panoramics — the kind that are most practical for Web use anyway — has become easier.

Apple released some free utilities that streamline the process of combining a collection of images into a panoramic movie. Getting the best results still means buying Apple's $495 QuickTime VR Authoring Tools package, but if you're willing to tolerate some visible artifacts where the images meet, you can make panoramics by combining one of these free utilities with an image editor such as Adobe Photoshop.

If you prefer your panoramics seamless, you can use another free Apple utility to graft a friendlier face on to the QuickTime VR Authoring Tools. And you can choose from a variety of special tripod adapters that make it easier to position and rotate the camera correctly for each shot.

And in what might be the best news "for the rest of us," third-party QuickTime VR authoring programs are becoming available that are far easier to use than Apple's funky tools. The first such program, Nodester from Panimation (`http://www.panimation.com/`), packs powerful authoring features into an inexpensive, delightfully easy to use program.

ON CD-ROM

After playing with a variety of QuickTime VR accessories, I assembled a gadget bag of Apple and third-party products that deliver consistently high-quality results with few tears. Be sure to check out the samples I've included on the *HTML & Web Publishing SECRETS* CD-ROM. Both the Mac OS and Windows versions of QuickTime and the QuickTime VR playback software are included on the CD-ROM. Also included are two Apple utilities that enable you to try your hand at making your own QuickTime VR movies.

Photographing for QuickTime VR panoramas

If you're into photography, you've probably experimented with panoramic pictures: snap a picture, turn, snap another, and so on until you've photographed a vista too grand for a single picture. When your photos arrive, you arrange them on the dining room table, aligning them where they overlap.

The first steps in creating a QuickTime VR panoramic movie aren't too different from this. Mount a camera on a tripod, orienting it vertically to capture as much of the subject's height as possible. To avoid distortion, the camera must be level and it should be aligned so that it rotates around its *optical center*. Because a camera's tripod mount is on the camera body and not on the lens, a tripod-mounted camera will not rotate around its optical center unless it's offset slightly.

The Truth About Tripods

I mentioned that it's important to mount the camera on a tripod in a way that enables the lens, rather than the camera body, to be at the center of rotation.

The truth is, for outdoor panoramics in which everything is distant, camera alignment isn't that critical. I've even obtained good results by hand-holding the camera and turning in a circle as I shoot. This is particularly practical if you plan to combine the photos by hand using Photoshop or another image editor. If you use Apple's QuickTime VR Authoring Tools, there are additional arguments for precise camera positioning; more on this later in this chapter.

For indoor panoramas — or outdoor scenes that contain subjects close to the camera — it *is* essential to mount the camera so that it's level and rotates around the lens. If you don't, the images don't combine perfectly.

The QuickTime VR Authoring Tools documentation describes a mount you can create with brackets from a photo supply house. But there's a much easier way. Kaidan (`http://www.kaidan.com/`) sells a family of panoramic tripod heads designed specifically for QuickTime VR photography.

I use the QuickPan QP-1, which comprises a panoramic head, a base containing a bubble level and level-adjustment screws, and a wheel calibrated in degrees and notched to make it easy to rotate the camera the same amount for each shot. The QP-1 is well built and a pleasure to work with.

Kaidan also sells a bracket for Kodak's DC-40 digital camera, a universal bracket that can hold just about any kind of camera, and even an underwater photography bracket. Visit the company's Web site to see the full family tree. And if you decide to buy, check out Kaidan's ad page in the back of this book — you'll save some money in the process.

The number of pictures required for a full panorama depends on the camera and lens. Apple recommends using a 35mm camera with a 15mm lens. (A fisheye lens won't work.) Apple also recommends that each image have 25 to 40 percent overlap with the adjacent images. That's more overlap than you'd probably use for tabletop panoramics, but it leads to a better panoramic movie — I'll describe why shortly.

Camera considerations

In the world according to Apple, you use a Nikon N90 with a 15mm lens for your photography, and then transfer the shots to Kodak PhotoCD. PhotoCD scanners yield better images than most desktop scanners, the PhotoCD supplier does the grunt work behind scanning the images, and the discs themselves are an ideal archiving medium.

The Nikon-to-PhotoCD approach is a fine path if you're wearing Bill Gates's money belt, but if you're wearing one like mine, there are cheaper routes.

I've made QuickTime VR panoramics from images shot by a Kodak disposable (oh, sorry — "single-use") panoramic camera. These yield prints that measure 3.5×10 inches; it only takes a few shots to capture a full 360 degrees.

You can also use any 35mm camera, including a low-cost, auto-everything model. As mentioned earlier, you should consider taking the photos in vertical (portrait) orientation, especially if you have a wide-angle lens. This requires taking more images to capture 360 degrees, but the resulting QuickTime VR panoramic will have a wider vertical field of view: users will be able to look up and down more.

Be sure to include some overlap — at least 30 percent — in each image to make it easier to assemble them. Scan your finished prints at 72 dpi and save the images as PICT files.

The easiest way to generate images is with a digital camera such as those offered by Apple, Kodak, Polaroid, and others. A digital camera eliminates the expense of film, processing, and scanning and also saves time.

SECRET

If you use an Apple QuickTake 100 or 150, consider buying Kaidan's WideTake lens, a wide-angle adapter that gives a QuickTake the equivalent of a 28mm lens on a 35mm camera. I was impressed with the WideTake, although I did find it prone to dramatic lens flare. To avoid flare, consider taking outdoor panoramics when the sun is directly overhead or behind clouds.

You can even use a camcorder, capturing images on videotape and then digitizing them using an AV Mac, a Power Mac 7500, 7600, 8500, or 8600, or any Mac equipped with a digitizing card. A camcorder yields grainy panoramas, but it will work.

Combining images by hand

In QuickTime VR parlance, *stitching* is the process of combining your images into a single PICT file, which is then processed into a QuickTime VR panoramic movie.

If you're willing to tolerate some visual flaws — or if you have a panoramic camera — you can make QuickTime VR panoramic movies with a free Apple utility called Make QTVR Panoramic. You can download this utility from `http://qtvr.quicktime.apple.com/`.

Seams like old times

Use Photoshop or another image-editing program to combine each of the images. Because exposure and lighting conditions vary, a seam will appear between each shot, as shown in Figure 14-3.

Figure 14-3: Seams between images

BACKGROUNDER

Panoramic Cameras and Be Here's Portal System

It's worth noting that a variety of companies sell special panoramic cameras that contain motorized mechanisms and special shutters and are capable of capturing a 360-degree image in one fell swoop. One drawback, however, is that panoramic cameras are expensive, ranging in price from $1,000 to over $15,000.

Another drawback is that the resulting image is likely to have areas that are poorly exposed — for example, in a panoramic of a sunrise scene, the area opposite the sun will be too dark. By comparison, if you take individual photos and adjust the exposure for each, the QuickTime VR Authoring Tools or third party stitching software can blend each image to provide a smooth dynamic range across the panorama.

Despite these drawbacks, a panoramic camera is an easy route to 360-degree images. If you're interested in learning more, visit the Black Diamond Consulting site, at `http://www.bkdiamond.com/`. I have more to say about Black Diamond's role in VR later in this chapter.

A fascinating alternative to a panoramic camera is the Portal S1 Capture System from Be Here, Inc. The Portal S1 is a specialized lens that looks like no other lens you've seen. Imagine an upside-down, mirrored mixing bowl with some brackets attached to it, and you'll have the idea. The lens attaches to any camera that accepts Nikon-mount lenses and enables you to take a full 360-degree panoramic in a single shot. One unique advantage the Portal S1 has is its extremely wide vertical field of view: over 100 degrees, much larger than the vertical field of view provided by panoramic cameras or even wide-angle lenses in portrait orientation. (As discussed elsewhere in this chapter, the benefit of a wide vertical field of view is that it enables viewers to "look up" and "look down" to a greater extent, thus enhancing realism.)

But the Portal system isn't cheap. Specific pricing depends on the options you choose, but you can expect to pay several thousand dollars for a complete system, and there's often a per-image royalty charge. System rentals may be available. For the latest scoop, visit Be Here's Web site, at `http://www.behere.com/`.

You're also likely to have gaps at the top or bottom of some shots which are caused by the camera's level varying between images. Apple's QuickTime VR Authoring Tools software automatically blends images to remove seams and can also correct for minor variations in camera level.

This seam's better: touching up the edges

Using Photoshop's editing tools, particularly the smudge, clone, and dodge/burn tools, you can at least minimize seams to make them less jarring (see Figure 14-4).

Figure 14-4: You can minimize seams with careful editing.

When you've finished, remove gaps by selecting the actual image area, copying it to the Clipboard, opening a new, untitled document, and then pasting. Save this new image as a PICT file.

The Windows dimension

If you want a panoramic movie to be playable by QuickTime for Windows, you must resize it so that its horizontal dimension is an even multiple of 4 and its vertical dimension an even multiple of 96. But don't wear out your calculator — the Make QuickTime VR Panorama utility will suggest dimensions for you, as I describe shortly. (The QuickTime VR Authoring Tools package also sizes movies appropriately for Windows.)

Rotating the scene

The Make QuickTime VR Panoramic utility requires that the final PICT file be rotated so that the bottom of the image is to the right. In Photoshop 4, choose 90° CCW from the Rotate Canvas submenu in the Image menu. Save the rotated image.

Making the panoramic

Start the Make QuickTime VR Panoramic utility and choose the image you created. The dialog box shown in Figure 14-5 appears.

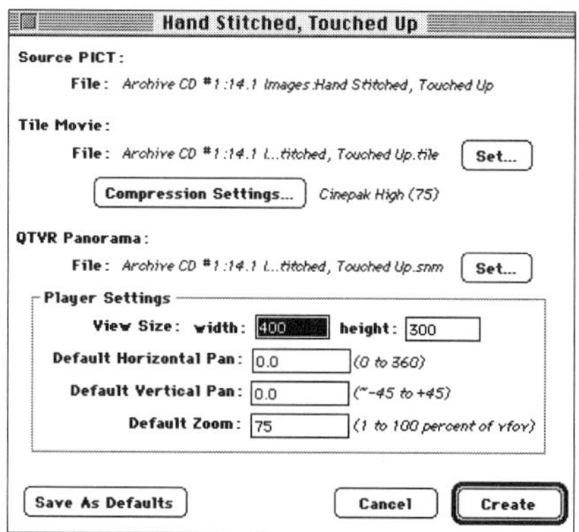

Figure 14-5: The Make QuickTime VR Panoramic utility's settings dialog box

The default settings are good starting points, but if you want to fine-tune them, here are some guidelines:

- **Compression settings.** This button changes the compression settings for the final movie. Cinepak yields the best panning performance and smallest file size. JPEG also works well.
- **View size.** If you want to create a wide-screen, "panavision" look, try a more dramatic aspect ratio, such as 150 pixels high by 400 pixels wide.
- **Default Horizontal Pan.** Normally, the movie opens centered on the left edge of the original image. If you'd like a different portion of the scene to appear when the movie opens, enter a value between 1 and 360 here.
- **Default Vertical Pan.** Normally, the movie opens vertically centered on the middle of the original image. If you'd like a different portion of the image to appear — for example, to see more of the sky or the ground — enter a value between -1 and -45 (to look down) or +1 and +45 (to look up).
- **Default Zoom.** To have the movie open so that it's already zoomed in, enter a value between 1 (slight zoom) and 5 (more zoom).

To make the panoramic, click the Create button. If the original image's dimensions aren't compatible with QuickTime for Windows, a dialog box appears suggesting alternate dimensions and asking if you want to continue (see Figure 14-6).

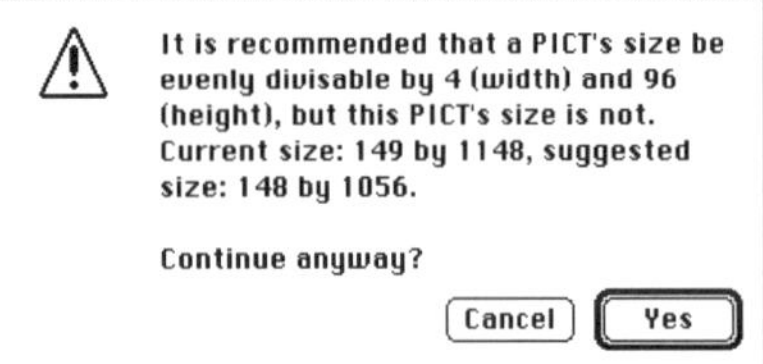

Figure 14-6: If an image isn't compatible with QuickTime for Windows, this dialog box appears. Before you click Cancel, write those values down!

If you don't care about Windows compatibility, click Yes to make the movie. Otherwise, write down the values, click Cancel, and return to Photoshop and resize the image appropriately.

Creating seamless panoramics

Obtaining seamless panoramics requires commercial authoring software such as Panimation's Nodester or Apple's QuickTime VR Authoring Tools software, which you can buy through Apple's developer catalog (visit `http://www.devcatalog.apple.com`). These programs create seamless panoramics by locating the overlap between shots, combining images, and then blending them so that each melds with its neighbor.

In Apple's QuickTime VR Authoring Tools, this job is performed by a component called the Stitcher. Normally, you control the Stitcher by writing arcane scripts for Apple's Macintosh Programming Workshop (MPW), which is included with the Authoring Tools and serves as its control center. But there's now an easier way. Two Apple employees created a free utility, called Sanity SaVR (get it?), that provides a graphical interface to the Stitcher. Sanity SaVR even contains preset values for several common camera configurations.

Painless panoramas: Heid's QuickTime VR Camera Bag

Combine a QuickTake 150, a Kaidan WideTake lens, a Kaidan QP-1 panoramic head, and a tripod, and you have Heid's QuickTime VR Camera Bag: the system I use to create the panoramics on my site (and the samples on the *HTML & Web Publishing SECRETS* CD-ROM).

This section is a step-by-step guide to getting great QuickTime VR panoramas using this system along with two free Apple utilities: QuickNumber and Sanity SaVR, both available from `http://solutions.apple.com/pub/quicktime-vr/jcannon/Workbook.html`. (That site is an unofficial QuickTime VR developer's page maintained by Apple's Joel Cannon. He and Apple's Chuck Wiltgen have been the major forces in the slow-but-steady march toward easier QuickTime VR development.)

How the Stitcher Works

Of all the components comprising QuickTime VR, the Stitcher may be the most magical. And the most important — without it, creating a QuickTime VR panoramic would *require* one of those expensive and inflexible panoramic cameras.

Under the hood, the Stitcher performs what computer graphics gurus call *enviromapping* — it maps, or projects, an environment (such as a beach scene) onto the inside of a shape, such as a cube or a sphere — or, in QuickTime VR's case, a cylinder. When you navigate a QuickTime VR movie, you are in essence moving within a vertically oriented tube whose inner walls contain the panoramic image. The Stitcher's job is to distort the original images — which were intended to appear on a flat surface — and then combine them into a seamless panoramic. In technical terms, the Stitcher mathematically converts an image from a planar projection to a cylindrical projection.

The Stitcher can usually perform its magic automatically by comparing the pixels in each image to locate the points where they overlap. If the images don't overlap neatly — perhaps one was scanned crookedly or the tripod moved during the photo session — you can use a manual stitching mode, which lets you use the keyboard's arrow keys and number pad to move and resize images. But manual intervention is the exception rather than the rule: if you shoot the panoramic the right way to begin with — using plenty of overlap and a properly mounted camera — the Stitcher will be able to work its magic all by itself.

As it combines images, the Stitcher also blends the intensity levels of each one to compensate for differences in lighting or exposure. The more you overlapped the images, the smoother the blends.

Use the QuickTake 150's high-resolution setting. In this mode, the camera holds 16 images, so if you need to capture multiple scenes, tote along a PowerBook and transfer the images after shooting each scene.

1. Shoot 16 images, rotating the camera clockwise by 22.5 degrees between each shot. The click stops in the Kaidan QP-1 head's wheel make it easy to position the camera; just be sure the stop beneath the wheel is set to the 16-shot position.
2. Transfer the images to your Mac and store them in a new folder.
3. Drag the images' folder to the icon of the QuickNumber utility. This utility renames the image files to conform to the Stitcher's requirements (the images are named 01, 02, 03, through 16).
4. Open Sanity SaVR (see Figure 14-7).

   Sanity SaVR includes presets for several common camera rigs. Choose a preset from the pop-up menu at the top of the dialog box, and Sanity SaVR configures the dialog box's options appropriately. (You can also enter your own values.) The version of Sanity SaVR available at this writing included presets for the QuickTake 150 (with and without WideTake lens), the QuickTake 150 in landscape orientation, and the Nikon N90 with 15mm lens.

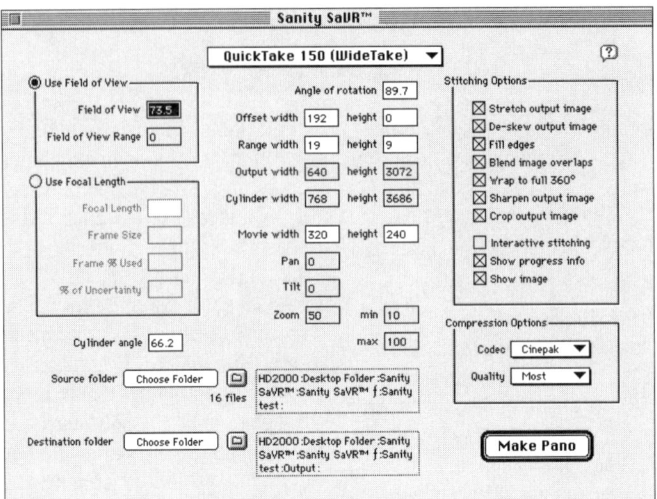

Figure 14-7: The Sanity SaVR dialog box

5. Specify the Source Folder. To specify the folder containing the original images, click Choose Folder. You can also drag a folder icon from the Finder to the Source Files box. (The names of the files to be stitched appear in this box.) If your images' folder happens to contain a non-image file, you can remove it from the list by Command-clicking its name.
6. Specify the Destination Folder. To specify the folder where the stitched PICT file and the final movie will be stored, click Choose Folder.
7. To make the panorama, click the Make Pano button.

QuickTime VR panoramic secrets

SECRET

Here's a collection of tips and secrets for panoramic movie-makers.

Making cross-platform panoramas

Neither the Stitcher nor the Make QTVR Panorama utility create a panoramic that is ready to play under Windows. But it's easy to convert it.

Open the panoramic movie in Apple's Movie Player utility, choose Save As, click the Make Movie Self-Contained and Playable on non-Apple Computers options, and give the movie a new name.

There's an even easier option: a free Apple utility, QuickTime Streamliner, which lets you convert a movie with a single mouse click. Both Movie Player and QuickTime Streamliner are available at `http://www.quicktimefaq.org/`.

Slimming down panoramas

The process I've described here yields a panoramic that uses about 550K of disk space. Here's one way to slim down a movie for faster Web loading: In Photoshop, open the source PICT (its name ends in scrPICT) and reduce it by 50 percent with the Image command. Save the smaller PICT under a different name, and then use the Make QTVR Panoramic utility to create a panoramic movie from it. In my tests, a 550K movie reduced to 156K. The only downside: details break up sooner when a user zooms in.

You can, of course, create even smaller panoramics by reducing the source PICT by even more than 50 percent.

You might consider posting both high- and low-resolution versions on your site; this enables visitors to choose the version that best matches their connection speed and patience.

Stitching and memory

The Stitcher craves memory; indeed, stitching a QuickTake-generated panoramic can require 80MB or more. Fortunately, this is where QuickTime and virtual memory get along beautifully. Turn on VM and boost it up to a hefty value: 130MB or so. Then, select the MPW Shell icon and use the Get Info command to boost its memory allocation to 100,000K or so. Restart to put your changes into effect. Using VM slows stitching, but it's a small price to pay — this technique has enabled me to stitch large panoramas on a machine containing only 24MB of physical RAM.

Printing panorama PICTs

QuickTime VR panoramas look great on paper, too. The PICT files generated by the Stitcher can yield dramatic hard copy when printed on roll-fed, large-format printers such as Encad's NovaJet series, which are popular in service bureaus. Broomall, PA-based Visual Sound (`http://www.visualsound.com/`) printed some beautiful posters for me. The PICT files generated by the rig I've described here measure roughly 7×42 inches.

Adding hot spots to panoramas

At the beginning of this chapter, I mentioned that QuickTime VR movies can contain hot spots upon which users can click. With multiple-scene (also called multinode) QuickTime VR movies, these hot spots take a user from one scene to another — in a VR house tour, for example, from one room to another.

Multiple-node panoramics are usually too huge to be practical for Web sites, but that doesn't mean hot spots don't have a place in Web-based panoramics. Beginning with version 1.1, the QuickTime plug-in supports *URL hot spots* — hot spots that, when clicked, take you to another URL.

URL hot spots have a couple of very cool uses.

- **Simulating multiple node movies.** Create a hot spot and link it to the URL of another QuickTime VR panoramic. With this approach, you eliminate the need to download nodes that a visitor may never go to anyway.
- **Creating panoramic image maps.** URL hot spot support enables QuickTime VR panoramics to become site-navigation devices. A panoramic of a university campus might contain hot spots for each building: clicking on a hot spot could take the visitor to the HTML page for a particular department. Or you might create a non-photographic panoramic using a graphics program, and then assign hot spots to the elements within it.

You can create hot spots with Apple's QuickTime VR Authoring Tools software, but a much easier way is with a free Apple utility named VRL, available from `http://solutions.apple.com/pub/quicktime-vr/Goodies/HotSpots/Hotspots.html`. Figure 14-8 shows VRL in action.

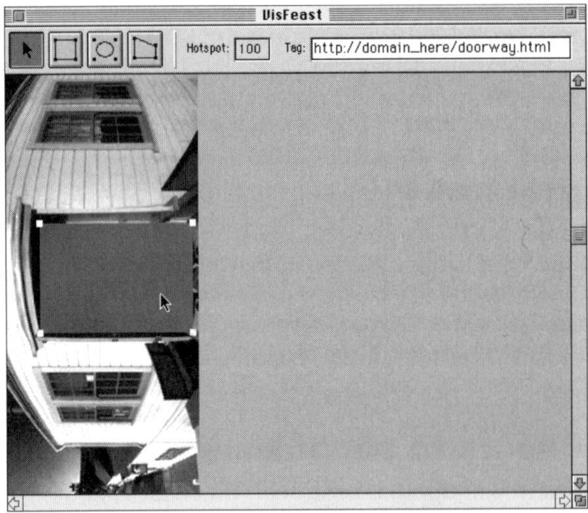

Figure 14-8: Apple's VRL is a tool for creating URL hot spots.

The Read Me file that accompanies VRL contains full details on creating and testing URL hot spots. Here's an overview of the process: To use VRL, first open the source PICT containing your stitched panoramic. Then, draw the hot spots and assign URLs to them. (Tip: You can drag and drop URLs into the Tag text box.) Next, export the hot spots, a process that involves creating a PICT file containing the hot spot locations and a VRL document that contains the URL links.

After performing these steps, use the free Make QTVR Pano utility to generate a QuickTime VR movie that contains the hot spots. (Note that you must use Make QTVR Pano 1.0b5 or later; earlier versions don't support hot spots.) Finally, embed the panoramic in a Web page.

Regardless of how you use URL hot spots, be sure to use the `cache=true` attribute when you embed panoramics that contain URL hot spots. As I explain in the section "Essential HTML for QuickTime VR," later in this chapter, this attribute enables Netscape Navigator 3.0 and later versions to cache the movie, eliminating the need to download it again when a visitor returns to the page containing it.

Virtual competition: QuickTime VR alternatives

The oldest and most mature photographic VR technology, QuickTime VR is also the most popular. The fact that the latest versions of both Microsoft Internet Explorer and Netscape Navigator can play embedded QuickTime VR movies helps ensure QuickTime VR's dominance in its field.

But that doesn't mean it will own the market. At this writing, several competing technologies are vying for a piece of the virtual pie, and if you're serious about putting panoramas on a site, you should investigate the competition. Here's a quick virtual reality check. Note that many of these technologies were still under development at this writing; for the latest on these and other VR technologies, visit the *HTML & Web Publishing SECRETS* Web site; specifically, go to `http://websecrets.heidsite.com/ch14/vrtools.html`.

Omniview's PhotoBubbles

Omniview, Inc. (`http://www.omniview.com`) developed a virtual reality technology called PhotoBubbles. Like QuickTime VR, PhotoBubbles enables you to create navigable panoramas. Also like QuickTime VR, PhotoBubbles supports multiple locations — users can jump from one location to another by clicking a hot spot, such as a doorway.

But unlike QuickTime VR, PhotoBubbles provides a full 180-degree vertical field of view: you can look straight up or straight down. QuickTime VR's vertical field of view is limited to approximately 95 degrees, depending on the lens used to photograph the original scene. QuickTime VR places you within a cylinder whose walls contain a panoramic image. PhotoBubbles, by comparison, places you within a bubble (see Figure 14-9).

PhotoBubbles accomplishes this by requiring the original photographs to be taken using a 35mm camera equipped with a fish-eye lens, which unlike a conventional rectilinear lens, has a 180-degree field of view. On the downside, this requires developers to use a 35mm camera and buy a relatively expensive (approximately $1,500) lens. As this chapter has shown, you can take QuickTime VR images with virtually any type of lens and camera, including digital cameras and even camcorders.

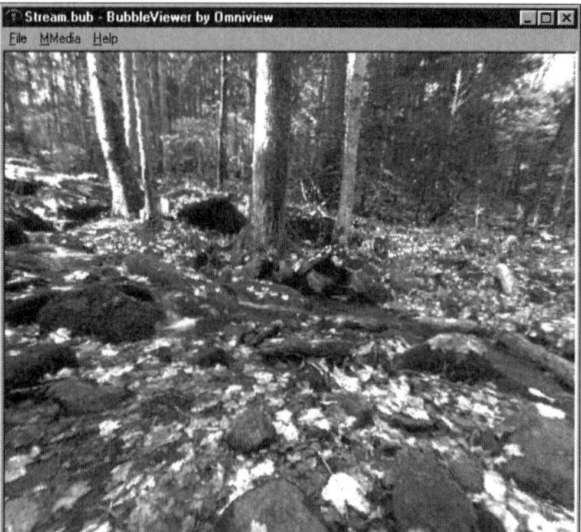

Figure 14-9: The world in a bubble: some views of a PhotoBubble

Because a fish-eye lens can see 180 degrees, a PhotoBubbles photographer need take only two photographs to capture an entire panorama, compared to 8 to 36 photographs for QuickTime VR. Thus, capturing a scene is faster. However, lighting interior spaces can be extremely difficult — and you must use Photoshop or a similar program to remove the tripod from the final image.

At this writing, you can't make PhotoBubbles without Omniview's assistance. The company will sell you its special tripod mount, but it currently isn't selling its processing software — the program that translates the two images you take into a finished bubble. To create a PhotoBubble, you must contract with Omniview's Omniview Studios division. Omniview is in the process of certifying third-party content developers, but by and large, it doesn't appear that PhotoBubbles will reach the do-it-yourself stage any time soon.

Omniview's Web site contains free Windows and Mac OS versions of the PhotoBubbles player and plug-ins as well as sample images and links to sites that contain PhotoBubble views.

RealSpace RealVR

Of all the QuickTime VR competitors out there, RealVR from RealSpace (`http://www.rlspace.com`) is one of the most impressive. Maybe that isn't surprising: The CEO of RealSpace is a fellow named Eric Chen, who used to work at Apple — where he created QuickTime VR. RealVR combines the photorealistic VR advantages of QuickTime VR with the 3D rendering approach of VRML (discussed at the end of this chapter).

Like QuickTime VR, RealVR provides both panoramic and object movies. But where QuickTime VR is currently limited to cylindrical panoramas, RealVR also supports spherical panoramas — the kind Omniview's PhotoBubbles creates. RealVR also supports cubic panoramas, in which an image is projected within the six faces of a cube. Both spherical and cubic panoramas allow for a 180-degree vertical field of view — a viewer can look straight up and straight down. Like many newer VR technologies, RealVR supports progressive downloading.

RealVR's support for VRML 2.0 makes it possible to have 3D-rendered objects within a scene. Apple's QuickDraw 3D technology has the potential to provide the same benefits to QuickTime VR, and indeed, Apple has announced its intent to marry the two. At this writing, however, the ceremony hasn't taken place yet.

RealSpace has also gone further than any other QuickTime VR competitor in providing solid authoring tools. Indeed, it can be easier to stitch a RealVR panoramic than a QuickTime VR one, thanks to RealSpace's Vistagrapher Lite software. This stitching program provides a graphical interface that's much friendlier than that of Apple's tools (see Figure 14-10).

Figure 14-10: Stitching a scene with RealSpace's Vistagrapher Lite

Vistagrapher Lite is included with the RealVR developer's CD-ROM. This CD, available for PowerPC Mac OS machines and for Windows 95/NT, also contains a Macromedia Director Xtra (an extension to Director) that enables you to integrate RealVR scenes and objects into Director productions.

Where does QuickTime VR still have the edge? First, it's available on a broader range of platforms: RealVR works on Windows 95/NT and PowerPC-based Mac OS machines only; QuickTime VR works on these platforms as well as on 680X0 Macs and on Windows 3.1. And the popularity of the QuickTime VR plug-in gives QuickTime VR authors a broader audience. (Playing back RealVR content requires a Web surfer to download the RealVR Traveler plug-in module.)

OLiVR Corporation's OLiVR

Short for *on-line interactive virtual reality,* OLiVR Corporation's (`http://www.OLiVR.com/`) OLiVR was designed specifically for Web-based VR. OLiVR provides streaming and progressive rendering features that QuickTime VR lacks. The company even offers server software that's optimized for downloading OLiVR movies.

OLiVR supports both panoramic and object movies, and anyone familiar with QuickTime VR will feel at home creating them. To create a panoramic movie, you must use a panoramic camera or stitch images using an image editor or Apple's QuickTime VR Authoring Tools. You then supply the panoramic image to the OLiVR authoring tool, which generates the movie. (The company is also working on a QuickTime VR-to-OLiVR translator utility.) To create an object movie, you photograph an object on a turntable and then supply the OLiVR authoring tool with a series of bitmapped images.

At this writing, the OLiVR authoring program is available for Windows platforms only, while the viewer plug-in is available for Windows as well as Mac OS machines.

When I wrote the first draft of this chapter, I ended this section with the following comment: "to me, OLiVR seems less like a competitor to QuickTime VR than a potential companion to it. I can see QuickTime VR developers wanting to experiment with the OLiVR authoring tool and plug-ins to see if they can deliver faster downloads." Well, I must have been on to something, because in early 1997, Apple and OLiVR announced a strategic alliance in which OLiVR's streaming technology would be incorporated into a future version of QuickTime VR. Look for interesting things to come from this relationship.

Black Diamond's Surround Video

When Apple originally announced QuickTime VR, Microsoft announced a similar technology called Surround Video. And then Surround Video went underground, or so it seemed — it was difficult to find information on it, even from Microsoft.

Surround Video lives, but it's no longer a Microsoft initiative; it's now being offered by Black Diamond Consulting (`http://www.bdiamond.com/`).

Surround Video offers many of the same basics as QuickTime VR: navigable panoramics containing hot spots that link to other panoramics or to Web pages.

But there are differences, too. On the downside, Surround Video requires that you shoot original scenes using a panoramic camera; there's no equivalent to the QuickTime VR Stitcher. And because panoramic cameras have a smaller vertical field of view than a portrait-mounted conventional camera, a Surround Video movie doesn't let you look up or down as much as its QuickTime VR equivalent. (The Be Here lens described earlier eliminates this drawback.) Also, Surround Video supports panoramic movies only; it offers no equivalent to QuickTime VR object movies.

On the plus side, Surround Video stores movies in a way that enables them to render progressively. A Surround Video panorama is divided into a series of vertical stripes or slices. A visitor might see only one or two stripes at first, with the rest of the scene filling in as the movie downloads. Surround Video also supports an interlacing scheme similar to that of GIF; you can even navigate a panoramic before it has finished downloading. Another nice feature: If you right-click on a multinode panoramic, a pop-up menu appears listing all of the scenes within that panoramic.

NetVR's Turnado technology

For Web work, there's an object movie-like technology that doesn't use QuickTime at all. NetVR Corporation's (`http://www.netvr.com`) Turnado technology relies on a Java applet to provide object movie-like features. NetVR is also working to provide panoramic features. For each Turnado movie you want to create, you must purchase a license from the company.

Because it relies on Java, Turnado works with Netscape Navigator 3.0 and Microsoft Internet Explorer 3.0. The advantage: no plug-ins are required to view objects. The drawback: visitors who don't use Java-capable browsers can't view objects.

Quicktime VR Object Movies

In the previous section, I showed how to make QuickTime VR panoramics using Apple's latest tools, some of which are free. In this section, I concentrate on the world of object movies, and there's good news: simple object movies are easier to create than panoramics. (I'll describe what I mean by *simple* later.) A tripod-mounted camcorder, a couple of hardware store gimcracks, and still-more free Apple utilities are all you need to create object movies suitable for Web sites.

A different spin

When you take a QuickTime VR panoramic, you rotate the camera, snapping a picture at each stop. Object movies turn this around: the camera remains stationary, and you rotate the object for each shot. You then create a conventional (linear) QuickTime movie from those shots, and convert *that* movie into a QuickTime VR object movie.

Setting up for the shoot

To get the best results, you should use a turntable-style rig that enables you to position and rotate the object for each shot. You can get by without a turntable if you're willing to eyeball the object's positioning, but a turntable allows more precision, and that yields object movies that deliver smoother navigation.

Making your own rig

For smallish objects — vases, small statues, toy cars, small dogs — you can use an initiative-challenged (formerly known as *lazy)* Susan. I use a 12-inch diameter Rubbermaid rotating spice tray that I commandeered from my kitchen cabinet. Calibrate the edges of the turntable to help you rotate it the same distance for each shot.

A vertical extension enables you to shoot the object from below, which is important if you're shooting multiple sets of images. It doesn't have to be fancy: I used a paper towel tube covered with black construction paper. For accurate rotation, be sure the tube is centered on the platform.

Larger objects will tax your spice tray. One option we've used at *Macworld* magazine: a bicycle wheel and an axle vice, which mounts to a table and enables the wheel to rotate horizontally.

Commercial object rigs

Don't happen to have any spare bike wheels handy? Consider a commercial object rig. Kaidan, the company whose panoramic tripod mounts I raved about earlier in this chapter, offers several object-movie rigs. The $399 Magellan QC Object Rig is designed for use with Connectix's Color QuickCam (`http://www.connectix.com/`) and for objects of up to 12 inches across and less than 10 pounds. The Magellan 1000 Object Rig can handle objects of up to 36 inches across and up to 150 pounds, and can hold a camera weighing up to 5 pounds.

What kind of camera?

Speaking of cameras, a video camera and a Mac with video-capture hardware work best. This enables you to see each shot before you take it and to adjust brightness, color balance, and other settings. The object-movie instructions I provide later in this section assume you're using a video camera.

An ideal low-cost option is a Connectix Color QuickCam, which doesn't require a Mac with video-capture hardware. The QuickCam connects directly to a Mac's modem or printer port. If you're using a QuickCam for your site's Web cam as described in Chapter 8, you might consider commandeering it for object-movie sessions.

If you don't have a video camera (or a Mac with video-input features), a digital camera such as an Apple QuickTake or Kodak DC-40 will work, although these cameras' fixed-focus lenses lose focus at distances smaller than four feet.

Some background on backgrounds

Apple recommends photographing an object against a black background: this "gives the feeling that the user is picking up and manipulating the object, rather than just walking around it," to quote the QuickTime VR Authoring Tools documentation.

A jet-black background does yield a dramatic object movie, but might not be practical for all objects and it isn't exactly lively. If you want some color, try to keep the background a consistently lit, solid color. This helps the movie compress efficiently, which helps keep its size down.

Whatever background you use, it's vital that it remain the same for each shot — if you accidentally get your hand in one shot or crease a piece of photographic background paper, the object movie illusion will vanish.

And if you can't control the background — maybe you're shooting the old Chevelle in a parking lot — just shoot away and retouch your shots in Photoshop.

How many shots to take?

Earlier, I said a QuickTime VR object movie enables someone to examine an object from above and from below. It's time to qualify that. An object movie allows this only if you shoot multiple sets of images, changing the camera's *vertical* position between each set.

Shooting multiple image sets is, simply, a bear. Camera positioning and the degree of rotation for each shot are extremely critical. And the movie's size balloons to several megabytes — too big to be practical for Web use.

For Web-based object movies, take only one set of images. To give the object more of a 3D appearance, don't have the camera and the object at the same height; rather, position the camera slightly above the object.

For a Web object movie, take between 8 and 12 shots. If file size is no object, take 36 — the more shots you have, the smaller the degree of movement between each shot, and the smoother the object will appear to turn.

The number of shots you take may also be influenced by the dimensions of your movie. If a small frame size is acceptable, you can include more shots. For Web sites, you might also consider posting low- and high-bandwidth versions.

Making Object Movies with 3D Programs

You can also create object movies from images created by 3D programs — make an object movie of that next-generation toaster you've designed, or of a spaceship, or even of some 3D type.

Render a series of images, rotating the object by the same amount between each one.

Convert the images to a linear QuickTime movie, and then convert that movie into an object movie. If your 3D program can render directly to a QuickTime movie (most Mac OS 3D programs can) you can simply convert that movie into an object movie.

Object lesson: Making a QuickTime VR movie

After you've set up a rig, you're ready to make a QuickTime VR object movie. The following instructions assume you're using a video camera connected to a Mac.

Adobe Premiere has a stop-motion capture feature that's ideal for object movie-making. To use it, choose Stop Motion from the File menu's Capture submenu. (Don't have Premiere? You can also use the Apple Video Player utility that accompanies the Power Mac 7500, 7600, 8500, and 8600, as well as Performas equipped with video-in features; its Copy Video Display command copies the current video signal to the Clipboard. Paste the resulting image into Apple's Movie Player utility. Repeat for each shot. If you're using a Connectix Color QuickCam, use the capture utility that accompanied it.)

Step 1: Setting up

Place the object on the stand, arrange the background and lighting, and point and focus the video camera. Zoom in so that the object fills the frame. To ensure that the entire object will appear in each shot, turn the object one full revolution while looking through the camcorder's viewfinder or at the video window on the Mac.

Step 2: Adjust capture settings

Adjust your capture hardware's brightness and contrast settings for the best picture. If you're using a black background, you can ensure it appears completely black by turning down the brightness and turning up the contrast a bit. But don't go overboard, lest image quality suffer. It's better to retouch the frames later if need be.

As for compression, use a high-quality compressor, such as Component Video, for the initial capture, or even no compression. You're going to compress the movie again later, so you want to start out with the highest-quality image.

Step 3: Capture the frames

Snap each frame, rotating the object counter-clockwise one increment between each one.

Your first shot should be of the back of the object; because of the way object movies are structured, this improves navigation performance. (If you're taking only 10 or so shots for a small object movie, this isn't critical.)

To snap a frame in Premiere's Stop Motion mode, press the spacebar. Premiere shows the number of frames you've snapped above the video window (see Figure 14-11). When you've finished, click Stop. You now have a linear QuickTime movie that contains each shot. Play it if you like: you'll see the object spin once.

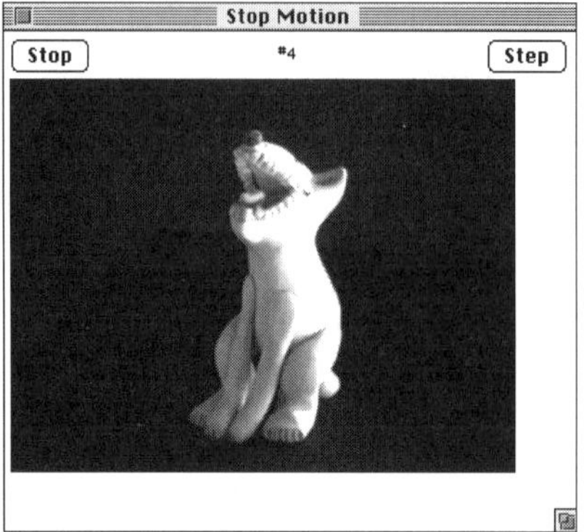

Figure 14-11: Adobe Premiere's Stop Motion window

Step 4: Cropping and compressing

For smaller file size and better composition, crop the movie so that just the object appears. You can do so with Premiere's CD-ROM Movie command or Terran Interactive's Movie Cleaner Pro, shown in Figure 14-12.

Figure 14-12: Cropping a movie in Movie Cleaner Pro

Leave several pixels of space around the object. To make sure you don't cut off part of the object, step through each frame after drawing the crop area and verify that the object fits within it.

For compression, Apple recommends using the Video compressor at a quality setting of 50 or 75.

Step 5: Making the object movie

Creating the object movie involves processing the cropped and compressed linear QuickTime movie you just made using Apple's free Make QTVR Object utility (included on this book's CD-ROM and also available from `http://qtvr.quicktime.apple.com/`). Launch Make QTVR Object and open the movie you want to convert. Choose Add Object Data from the Edit menu and specify the details as shown here (see Figure 14-13).

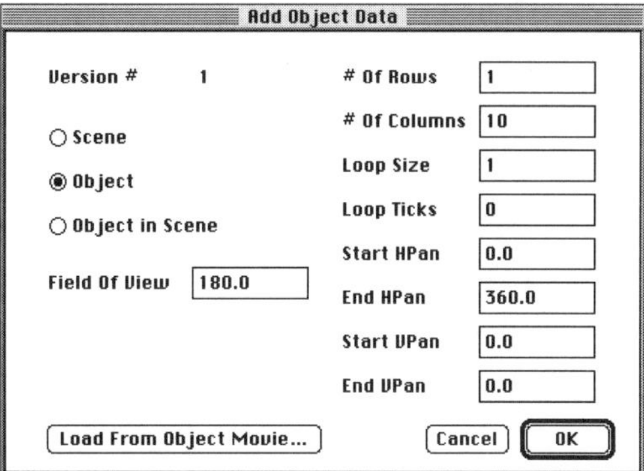

Figure 14-13: The Make QTVR Object utility's dialog box

- **# Of Rows.** If you didn't follow my advice and instead took multiple sets of images, altering the camera's vertical position for each one, enter the number of sets you took here.
- **# Of Columns**. Enter the number of images you took for each horizontal increment here. In other words, if you took 9 shots, enter 9.
- **Loop Size** and **Loop Ticks.** These options deal with an advanced object-movie technique that's rarely used in Web object movies; see the file that accompanies Make QTVR Object.
- **Start HPan.** For a 360-degree rotation, use the default values of 0 and 360. If you shot a 180-degree rotation — perhaps the back of the object just wasn't interesting — specify 180 for the End HPan.
- **Start VPan.** If you took multiple rotation sets, enter the angle of the start and end sets. For example, if the first set was shot looking directly down at the object and the last set was shot looking directly up, enter 90 and -90.
- **The Object radio button.** Select this option to give the movie the standard object-movie user interface.
- **The Object in Scene radio button**. Choose this option to give the movie a different navigation interface that's more suitable for large objects (for example, a car) within a scene.

Object movie tips and secrets

Setting the Poster View

If you'd like a particular view of the object to be visible when the movie opens, navigate to that view and then choose Set Poster View from the Edit menu.

Creating a low-bandwidth version

If you want to create a smaller, faster-downloading version, scale down the original linear movie using Premiere, Movie Cleaner Pro, or any video editor with scaling features. Perform this step at the same time that you crop and compress.

Making a cross-platform movie

To make an object movie that plays under Windows, open the finished object movie in Apple's Movie Player, choose Save As, and check the Playable on non-Apple Computers box.

Objects of the future: QuickTime VR 2.0

QuickTime VR 2.0, which shipped in early 1997, adds enhancements to object movies. For the first time, you can pan across them and zoom in and out on objects — much as you can with QuickTime VR panoramics. In QuickTime VR 2.0, object movies also support hot spots, which enables users to branch to a different movie or to a Web page by clicking on an area within the object movie.

QuickTime VR 2.0 also introduces a new version of the Make QTVR Object utility. Called QTVR Object Maker, the new utility supports the enhanced features of QuickTime VR 2.0 object movies and enables you to convert QuickTime VR 1.0 object movies to the 2.0 format.

Essential HTML for QuickTime VR

After you make your panoramic and object movies, you have to get them onto your site. As with linear QuickTime VR movies, there are two routes to putting QuickTime VR movies on a Web site:

- You can create simple hyperlinks to them using the `<A>` tag. This is the simplest method and it provides the broadest browser compatibility.
- You can use the `<EMBED>` tag. As the previous chapter described, `<EMBED>` provides much more control over the movie's playback, and it has the additional benefit of enabling the movie to appear embedded within a page — that is, with text, graphics, and other elements around it. The downside: Visitors who don't have the QuickTime VR plug-in (or a browser that allows plug-ins) won't be able to view the movie. To work around this, include a `<NOEMBED>` tag that enables them to download it, as described in the previous chapter.

How to prepare your visitors

QuickTime VR is one of those Web enhancements that relies on software a visitor might not have. In QuickTime VR's case, that software includes the following:

- The QuickTime software itself. All of today's Mac OS machines include QuickTime, but as you might guess, Windows does not.
- The QuickTime plug-in. This plug-in module is included with Navigator 3.0, and will presumably be included with future Navigator versions, too. Beginning with version 1.1, the Mac OS version of the QuickTime plug-in can play both linear (conventional) QuickTime movies as well as QuickTime VR movies. Version 1.0 of the plug-in couldn't play back QuickTime VR movies without the addition of a second file, called the QuickTime VR component. This file is still required for the Windows QuickTime plug-in.
- The QuickTime VR component (Windows only). This file enables the playback of QuickTime VR movies on Windows computers; strictly speaking, it isn't a plug-in, but a software extension that adds code necessary to support QuickTime VR playback. It is *not* included with Navigator 3, at least not at this writing. (Apple is negotiating with Netscape to include the QuickTime VR components file, however, so this may change. Visit the *HTML & Web Publishing SECRETS* Web site for updated information.)
- The QuickTime VR Player. This helper application is required only if a visitor does not use the QuickTime plug-in and QuickTime VR component. Visitors who use the QuickTime plug-in do not need the QuickTime VR Player.

Tell them where to get the goods

Because visitors may not have all of the above, it's important to let them know where they can get it. Apple recommends aiming visitors to the main QuickTime VR page: `http://qtvr.quicktime.apple.com/`. From there, they can make their way to the appropriate download page.

There is also a central download page for QuickTime VR software; at this writing, it's located at `http://qtvr.quicktime.apple.com/sw/sw.html`. From this page, visitors can choose to download some or all of the aforementioned QuickTime software for the Mac OS, for Windows 3.1, or for Windows 95/NT. Because the location of the software-download page may change, however, it's probably safer to guide people to `http://qtvr.quicktime.apple.com/`.

SECRET

Another Visit from the MovieStar

In the previous chapter, I mentioned that Intelligence at Large (`http://www.ialsoft.com/`) created its own plug-in for QuickTime and QuickTime VR playback. The MovieStar plug-in is available for Windows 3.1, Windows 95, and Mac OS machines — and unlike Apple's QuickTime plug-in, it works with Netscape Navigator 2.0 as well as the latest versions.

Where QuickTime VR and Windows is concerned, the MovieStar plug-in has an advantage over Apple's software. Specifically, MovieStar doesn't require the separate QuickTime VR components file — MovieStar can play QuickTime VR movies from the get-go. If you recommend that your visitors download and install the MovieStar plug-in, they will have fewer pieces of software to download and install, especially if they use Windows. (The MovieStar download package for Windows also includes the QuickTime for Windows software.)

If you take the MovieStar route, instruct your visitors to go to this page to get the MovieStar plug-in: `http://www.beingthere.com/plugin.html`.

On the downside, version 1.0 of the MovieStar plug-in does not support the QuickTime VR-specific tags that the Apple plug-in can use. (These tags are discussed in the section "Embedding a QuickTime VR movie," later in this chapter.) This gives you a bit less control over the presentation of a QuickTime VR movie.

Tell them how to get around

It's a good idea to include help text somewhere on your site that describes QuickTime VR navigation techniques. Table 14-1 provides a good quick reference.

Table 14-1 Consider including this QuickTime VR quick reference on your site

To...	*Do this...*
Look to the left, right, up or down	Drag to the left, right, up, or down
Zoom in	Press Shift (Windows) or Option (Mac OS)
Zoom out	Press Ctrl (Windows) or Control (Mac OS)

Don't force a QuickTime VR movie down their throats

Because you can't assume that visitors will have everything they need to view QuickTime VR movies, you shouldn't embed a QuickTime VR movie in a page without first presenting some kind of "what you need to view QuickTime VR" page. Don't subject your visitors to an annoying "plug-in not found" error message.

How to name the movie

In order to be recognized by a browser, a QuickTime VR movie, like a linear QuickTime VR movie, must end with a specific filename extension. Netscape Navigator recognizes three possible extensions:

- .mov — as in *bigscene.mov*
- .moov — as in *myobject.moov*
- .qt — as in *panorama.qt*

The .mov extension is the most common; for broadest compatibility, use it.

Linking to a QuickTime VR movie

To create a conventional hyperlink to a movie, use the `<A>` tag, like so:

```
View a <a href="bigscene.mov">panoramic movie</a> of my sock drawer.
```

If a visitor has the necessary plug-ins for Navigator or Internet Explorer, the movie is played by the plug-in. If the visitor doesn't have the plug-in, the movie is played by a helper application — generally, by Apple's QuickTime VR Player or Movie Player utility.

Embedding a QuickTime VR movie

To embed a QuickTime VR movie in a page, you use the same `<EMBED>` tag that the previous chapter introduced. The `<EMBED>` tag supports several additional attributes that are specific to QuickTime VR movies. These attributes and the arguments they accept are listed in this section. Note that every single one of these attributes is optional; if you omit them, QuickTime VR simply uses its own default settings.

Pan

Normally, the movie opens centered on the left edge of the original image. If you'd like a different portion of the scene to appear when the movie opens, specify a pan value of between 1 and 360. For example, `pan=25` opens the movie so that it's rotated 25 degrees from its left edge (see Figure 14-14).

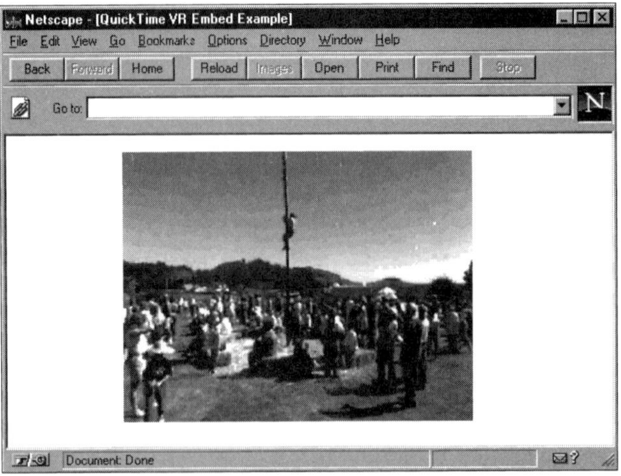

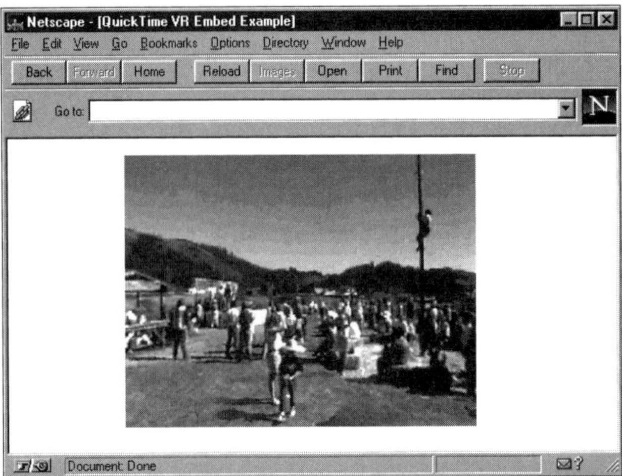

Figure 14-14: Top: Without the pan attribute. Bottom: With a pan attribute of 25.

Tilt

Normally, a movie opens centered on the middle of the original image. If you'd like a different portion of the image to appear — for example, to see more of the sky or the ground — specify a `tilt` attribute of between -42.5 (looking down) to 42.5 degrees (looking up). Figure 14-15 shows an example.

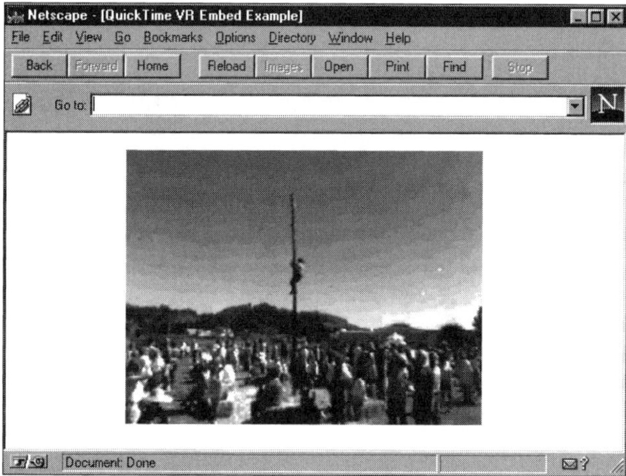

Figure 14-15: Top: Without the tilt attribute. Bottom: With a tilt attribute of 25.

Fov

Short for *field of view*, the `fov` attribute allows you to specify that the movie open zoomed in or zoomed out to other than its default zoom setting. The range of values for a typical movie are 5.0 (zoomed in a great deal) to 85.0 degrees (zoomed all the way out). Figure 14-16 shows an example.

Correction

The `correction` attribute lets you specify the degree of image correction, or dewarping, that QuickTime VR applies to panoramic movies. Possible values are `none`, `partial`, or `full` (the default value).

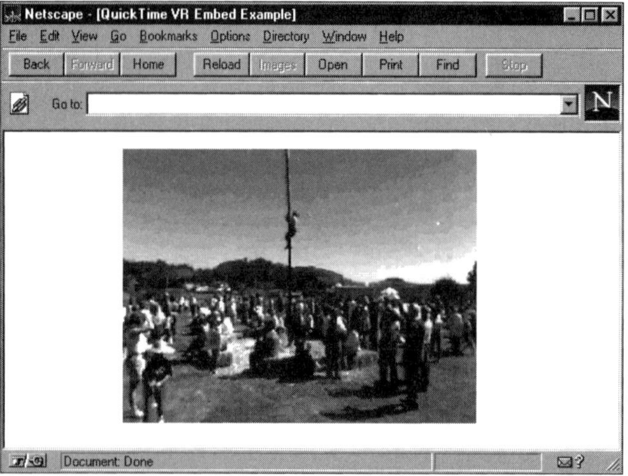

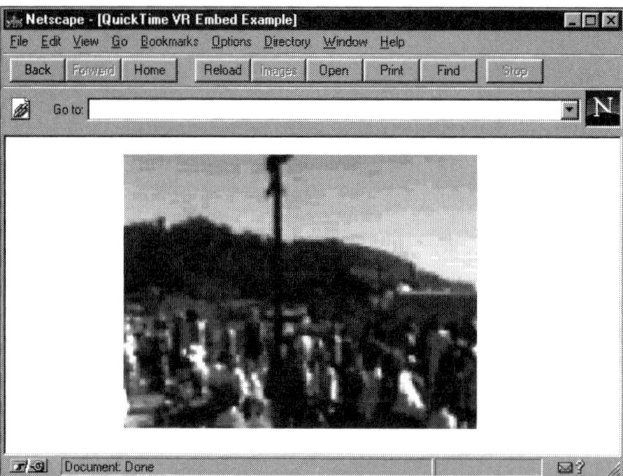

Figure 14-16: Top: Without the fov attribute. Bottom: With a fov attribute of 5.

Node

The `node` attribute lets you specify the initial node for a multinode QuickTime VR movie.

Cache

The `cache` attribute lets you specify whether or not the movie should be saved in the browser's cache. If you use `cache=true` (or just `cache` by itself), the movie is cached; if a visitor moves to a different page and then returns to the page containing the movie, the plug-in retrieves the movie from the cache rather than reloading it.

The `cache` attribute is extremely useful if you've created a QuickTime VR panoramic movie containing hot spots that link to other pages.

Note that at this writing, the `cache` attribute works only with Netscape Navigator 3.0 and later versions, when used with QuickTime plug-in 1.1 or later.

Hotspot

The `hotspot` attribute enables visitors to click on a hot spot in a QuickTime VR panorama to go to a specified URL. The syntax of the attribute is the following:

```
hotspot id = "http://destination_URL_here"
```

In place of *id,* use the ID number of the hot spot you created using the QuickTime VR authoring tools or the VRL utility described earlier in this chapter (see the section "Adding hot spots to panoramas").

Varying the view with the height and width attributes

As I've said in previous chapters, it's always a good idea to use the `height` and `width` attributes when embedding a graphic using the `<IMG>` tag or a movie using the `<EMBED>` tag. Doing so enables the browser to compose the rest of the page instead of having to wait for the image or movie to download.

As the previous chapter discussed, the `<height>` and `<width>` tags work a bit differently where movies are concerned. To recap: With static images, if the height and width you specify differ from the original element's height and width, the browser scales the element to fit the values you specify.

This doesn't happen with QuickTime movies. Instead, if the height and/or width you specify is smaller than the movie's actual dimensions, the browser simply crops the movie. If the height and/or width you specify is larger than the movie's actual dimensions, the browser simply centers the movie within the space — let's call it the viewing area — you specified.

With QuickTime VR panoramics, this behavior makes possible some cool effects. Specifically, you can give a panoramic a completely different look by varying the height and the width of a panoramic's viewing area. An example is worth a thousand words. The following is the HTML source code, and Figure 14-17 shows the resulting views of the *same* QuickTime VR panoramic.

```
<html>
<head>
<title>
QuickTime VR Embedding Examples
</title>
</head>
<body>
Normal Size<br>
```

```
<embed src="Pano.mov" height=240 width=320>
<br><br>
Short Version<br>
<embed src="Pano.mov" height=100 width=320>
<br><br>
Keyhole Version<br>
<embed src="Pano.mov" height=240 width=100>
</body>
</html>
```

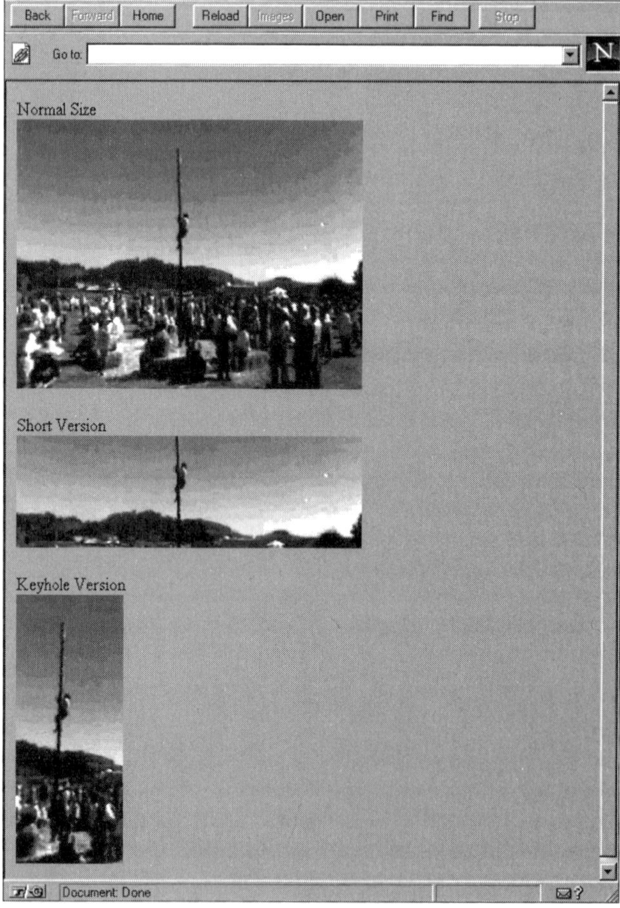

Figure 14-17: Same movie, different-sized viewing areas

To be honest, I'm not sure how useful the short and keyhole versions are for most panoramic movies — maybe you can find a creative way to apply them.

A reminder about the pluginspage attribute

To keep this section's HTML examples small, I deliberately left out the `<EMBED>` tag's `pluginspage` attribute, which, as described in the previous chapter, contains a URL that enables visitors who don't have the required plug-in to go to the page where they can get it.

In the real world, it's a good idea to include this attribute. As described in the previous section, Apple recommends using this address: `http://qtvr.quicktime.apple.com/`. If you want your visitors to use Intelligence at Large's MovieStar plug-in, use this address:
`http://www.beingthere.com/plugin.html`.

VR via VRML

QuickTime VR and technologies like it represent only one facet of the Web VR scene. The other facet is represented by the Virtual Reality Modeling Language (VRML). Often pronounced to rhyme with *thermal,* VRML is a standard command set for describing navigable spaces — just as HTML describes the appearance of pages, VRML describes the appearance of places.

When a visitor clicks on a Web site's hyperlink for a VRML space, the site's server downloads a VRML file to the visitor's computer. The visitor's browser then launches a helper application or a plug-in, which reads the VRML file and then works together with a 3D rendering engine to translate and render the scene described by the file. (Cosmetically speaking, a plug-in delivers a better trip than a helper application, since a plug-in enables the scene to appear directly within the browser window or even within a frame — it doesn't force visitors to switch between programs to browse pages and places.)

VRML versions

There are two versions of the VRML standard, and the VRML sites you may encounter may use either — or they may provide both and let you choose the one to download.

Currently, most VRML worlds are built around the original VRML 1.0 specification, which doesn't allow much beyond simple navigation. VRML 1.0 worlds can provide object URLs that enable you to jump to other scenes or pages by clicking on objects, but VRML 1.0 doesn't allow for animated objects within scenes, it doesn't enable you to pick up an object and examine it, and it doesn't support background sound. In short, VRML 1.0 isn't very real.

Many of these limitations disappeared in August of 1996 when the VRML 2.0 standard appeared. VRML 2.0 does allow for the features I just described — and then some. For example, VRML 2.0 allows for directional sound: if a sound source is to your right, you hear it from your right-hand speaker, and as you move toward the source, it becomes louder. VRML 2.0 also supports animation and something called object behaviors: VRML developers can specify the characteristics of the objects in a scene to create, for example, balls that bounce like Super Balls — or like bowling balls, if that's what the developer wants.

Another VRML variant is Netscape's Live3D, which provides numerous extensions to VRML 1.0. At this writing, Netscape is adapting Live3D to conform to the VRML 2.0 standard. For details on Live3D, visit Netscape's Live3D Web site at `http://home.netscape.com/comprod/products/navigator/live3d/`.

The VRML experience

Regardless of which version a VRML world uses, when you enter it, you can navigate — move forward and backward, to the left and right, up and down — by moving the mouse while pressing its button (see Figure 14-18).

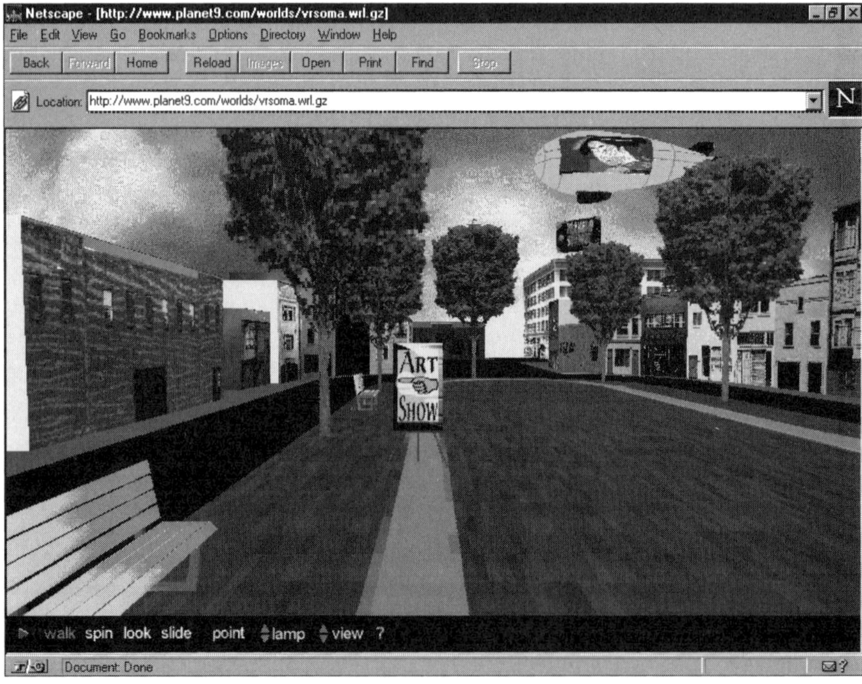

Figure 14-18: Moving in VRML space

As I've mentioned, objects within a VRML world can contain links to other VRML worlds, to HTML pages, or to audio and video clips. It's this object-linking capability that can make a VRML site more than just a 3D walkthrough. Some scene scenarios might include a gallery (click on paintings to learn about their artists), a store (click on products to buy them), a music tutorial (click on instruments to hear them), or a city tour (click on buildings to enter them).

Because VRML scenes are 3D renderings, the speed of a visitor's computer has a major bearing on how quickly he or she can journey through cyberspace. While even a low-end Mac OS or Windows machine can deliver satisfying HTML-browsing performance if it has a speedy modem, VRML benefits from not only a fast Internet connection, but also a fast processor, ideally a Pentium PC or a PowerPC 604-based Mac OS machine. In many ways, a fast computer with a 28.8Kbps modem is a better VRML platform than a slower machine with an ISDN connection.

As with any computer-generated 3D scene, the realism and performance of a VRML scene depends in part on the effort that goes into creating it. For example, VRML objects can contain *texture maps* — bitmapped graphics of surfaces, such as bricks and stucco, that are applied to objects as though decals. Texture maps add realism, but increase download and rendering times.

The objects in a VRML world are comprised of polygons. When creating worlds, smart VRML authors can take steps to minimize download times and maximize navigation performance — for example, by reducing the number of polygons used to describe shapes and by optimizing the scene so that each area's details aren't rendered until you navigate close to them.

Tools for building Web spaces

Whether you use a Windows or Mac OS machine, there's no shortage of VRML authoring tools, although not all current offerings support VRML 2.0. There are two primary categories of VRML tools:

- Programs designed specifically for VRML authoring
- Conventional 3D modeling and rendering packages that have had VRML export or conversion features grafted on to them

If you're a first-time world builder, you might find a VRML-specific tool easier to learn and use. VRML authoring tools provide VRML-specific features, ranging from the ability to attach URLs to objects to implementing VRML's time-saving *level of detail* feature, in which details aren't rendered until a viewer navigates close to them.

In a general-purpose 3D program, accomplishing these tasks is often more cumbersome. Also, many 3D programs provide shapes and geometries that aren't supported in VRML. You'll need to train yourself to use only those features that VRML supports. Still, if you've already invested time and money in a conventional 3D package, you can leverage your investment into the VRML world.

VRML authoring tools

If you're just getting started with VRML, an ideal place to begin is with Virtus Corporation's 3D Website Builder. This straightforward program, which ships on a CD-ROM containing both Mac OS and Windows versions of the program, takes a drag-and-drop approach to VRML authoring. 3D Website Builder includes a huge selection of prebuilt shapes and models — everything from cubes to furniture to space stations to alphabets — all of which live in a variety of gallery files. To add a shape to your world, simply drag it from the gallery window into a design window (see Figure 14-19).

Visit these Places for More VRML Details

There's far more to VRML than I have room to describe in this introduction. For more information, pay a virtual visit to the following Web sites:

- **Black Sun's Travel Guide** (`http://ww3.blacksun.com/cool/guide/`). VRML vendor Black Sun maintains this index of VRML sites in numerous categories, from entertainment to virtual trade shows.
- **Planet9 Studios** (`http://www.planet9.com/`). This pioneering VRML design studio has VRMLized numerous cities, including San Francisco, San Diego, Austin, and Boston. Worlds in VRML 1.0, 1.0 with Live3D extensions, and 2.0 are available.
- **San Diego Supercomputing Center's VRML site** (`http://www.sdsc.edu/vrml/`). This site is an excellent source of information on all VRML authoring matters.
- **Silicon Graphics Moving Worlds** (`http://vrml.sgi.com/worlds/`). Silicon Graphics has been instrumental in promoting VRML and contributing to its evolution. The company's VRML Web site contains hundreds of VRML worlds, including some in VRML 2.0.
- **The VRML Architecture Group** (`http://vag.vrml.org/`). The VRML Architecture Group, or VAG, is the guiding force behind VRML. On this site you can find lists of frequently asked questions, copies of the VRML standard, and links to other VRML sites.

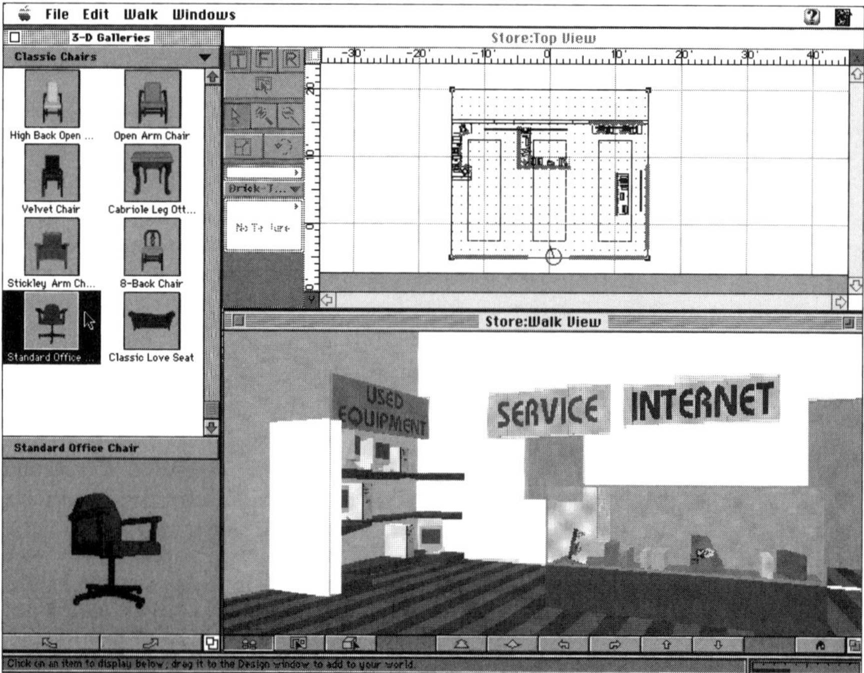

Figure 14-19: Virtus's 3D Website Builder enables you to drag-and-drop your way into VRML. The Walk View window previews the world and lets you navigate through it.

With 3D Website Builder, you can resize, reposition, and reshape objects as well as apply textures. Adding a URL link to an object involves selecting the object, choosing a command, and then typing the URL into a dialog box. When you've finished, you can export the world as a VRML 1.0 file, as a JPEG or PICT image, or as a QuickTime movie. A VRML 2.0 version of 3D Website Builder is scheduled for release in 1997.

Another solid program for VRML beginners is Paragraph International's (`http://www.paragraph.com/`) Virtual Home Space Builder 2.0 (Windows and Mac OS), which supports VRML 2.0 features such as sound, animation, and object behaviors. Paragraph's Internet3D Space Builder (Windows) is a high-end package that builds on Virtual Home Space Builder's basic interface but provides more sophisticated modeling tools.

For a complete and current list of VRML-supporting tools, visit the San Diego Supercomputing Center's VRML site (`http://www.sdsc.edu/vrml/`).

VRML converters

Several mainstream Mac 3D programs can now export VRML files directly or include a converter application.

Fractal Design's (`http://www.fractal.com`) Ray Dream Studio 4.1 (Mac OS) can export VRML 1.0 files. VRML 2.0 support is planned for a future release.

Strata (`http://www.strata3d.com/`) added VRML 2.0 support to its Strata Studio Pro 2.0 (Mac OS).

Macromedia has shipped a free VRML 2.0 converter for its Extreme3D package (Mac OS and Windows). The converter, created for Macromedia by VRML pioneer Intervista, is available for downloading from Macromedia's Web site at `http://www.macromedia.com/`.

Several freeware and shareware VRML converters are also available that convert common 3D and CAD formats (such as DXF) into VRML files. Again, a terrific source of information on this and other VRML authoring matters is the San Diego Supercomputing Center's VRML site at `http://www.sdsc.edu/vrml/`.

Virtual cautions

There's a lot the hype and activity surrounding VRML, but it's been slow to catch on in the real world. This is partially due to the fact that browsers and VRML helper applications haven't always been what you'd call rock-solid. Crashes, flaky screen updates, and slow performance on older computers have soured many Web surfers on VRML sites, and have caused many Web developers to look toward other technologies for delivering VR experiences — technologies such as Apple's QuickTime VR, which is reliable and in many ways, more practical.

Summary

- QuickTime VR and technologies like it enable visitors to explore panoramic images (panoramic movies) and examine objects (object movies).
- You can make a quick-and-dirty QuickTime VR panoramic using just about any kind of camera along with an image-editing program and Apple's free Make QTVR Panoramic utility.
- To get high-quality, seamless panoramics, use Apple's QuickTime VR Authoring Tools software along with the free Sanity SaVR utility.
- You can make object movies using a simple lazy Susan turntable, a camcorder, and Apple's Make QTVR Object utility (or, for QuickTime VR 2.0 object movies, the QTVR Object Maker utility).
- To add a QuickTime VR movie to a Web page, either create a hyperlink to it (best for compatibility) or use the `<EMBED>` tag (best for design flexibility and playback control).
- Be kind to your visitors: tell them where to get the QuickTime VR plug-in, tell them how to navigate within a QuickTime VR movie, and don't present them with a page containing an embedded movie without first letting them know what they need to view it.
- The Virtual Reality Modeling Language, or VRML, is a major force in Web VR. VRML 2.0 allows for sound, animation, object behaviors, and other advanced features.
- VRML authoring tools and VRML converters come in many flavors, with only some supporting VRML 2.0. Visit the VRML sites named in this chapter for more details on VRML development.

Part IV

Web Server Secrets

Chapter 15

To Serve or Be Served?

In This Chapter

- Deciding how to host your site: key hardware and software issues
- Server hosting options and the advantages of each
- Factors to consider when choosing a host service
- Questions to ask prospective site hosts

If you enjoy good reading and you haven't yet visited Salon Magazine (`http://www.salonmagazine.com/`*), set this book down for a while and check it out. That was swell, wasn't it? Salon provides a delightful mix of insight, entertainment, and humor – and unlike other many online magazines, without obsessing on the technology that delivers it.*

And speaking of delivering Salon, that job is the responsibility of this chapter's principal author, Dan Schafer. As Director of Technology and Senior Webmaster at Salon, it's Dan's job to see to it that Salon's servers and surfers are happy. As I edited Dan's first drafts of this chapter, I realized he'd put into words many of the same issues I've struggled with in setting up my own humble Web outpost. So whether you're putting up a big-budget site or a virtual lemonade stand, you will find Dan's from-the-trenches advice to be practical and rock-solid. — Jim Heid

As a Webmaster, one of the most important decisions you will face is whether to host your site's server yourself or whether to trust someone else with that function. If you decide to contract a third party to host your server, as many Web site developers do, it's essential to select the appropriate company and ensure all the important Web-serving issues are addressed.

In this chapter, I address the main issues involved with Web serving. I begin by looking at the difference between hosting your own server and farming out the hosting to a third party. I examine the criteria you should look for when evaluating candidates to host your server. Finally, I focus on some of the subtle issues you should at least discuss before you sign on the dotted line.

To Host or Not to Host?

Webmasters often start out believing the best thing for their site is to host it internally. As Chapter 1 described, this option gives at least the illusion of maximum control over all aspects of the server. But before you jump to that conclusion, there are a number of issues to think about, some of which may not be readily apparent. These issues fall into the following categories:

- Hardware ownership and maintenance
- Software licensing and maintenance
- Security
- Load management
- Monitoring and support

Hardware issues: what you need

What hardware do you need to host your own site? Table 15-1 provides a fairly comprehensive list of the hardware along with some notes that may help you determine where your site stands with respect to each issue.

Table 15-1 Site hardware and common issues

Hardware	*Considerations and Tips*
Computer	This should be a dedicated machine for all but the smallest sites. Get the fastest computer you can afford. On the Mac OS side, a PowerPC-based server is best. Although many server products run on 680X0 Macs — and many small sites are using these elderly machines to dish out pages — some server add-ons demand a PowerPC chip's performance. On the Windows side, think Pentium or Pentium Pro. On either platform, a Level 2 cache can be a big boon as well.
Disk capacity	Don't compromise; the biggest disk you can get will eventually fill up.
Memory	Not as big an issue as most think. Server software typically can't make full use of memory beyond 5–10MB because at that point, RAM isn't the limiting factor; connection speed is. (The exception to this rule: if you plan to run a large number of CGIs along with the server software, you may need a hefty amount of memory.) If RAM is abundant, consider using a RAM disk to serve your most frequently requested files.

Hardware	Considerations and Tips
Internet connection	Some Webmasters successfully serve sites using 28.8Kbps modem connections, but I say don't even think about using less than ISDN. Modem connections are just too slow and unreliable for serious sites. If you expect heavy traffic, a T1 or fractional T1 connection is your best bet.
Monitor, keyboard, mouse	You only need one of each, even for a multiserver setup; you can use a switchbox or remote-access software to access each server using one set of input devices.
Backup device	DAT is the current preference; removable disk media are too easy to forget to put online.
Redundant server	A mirrored drive array is your best bet, but a disk on a second CPU works, albeit less transparently. You may even want both.
Redundant backup	Plan off-site backup regularly as a disaster recovery scheme.
Uninterruptible power supply (UPS)	Having a UPS is essential, particularly if your site is expected to be available at all times. If you live in an area that suffers prolonged power outages, a standby generator may be in order.
Hardware	***Considerations and Tips***
Remote power-cycling device	Unless the server is down the hall from where you live and work, you want to be able to reset it over the telephone.
Mounting rack	A rack is clearly optional, but if your servers are located where nontechnical people may be tempted to poke buttons, get one that locks!

Assuming you can afford to buy — or that you already own — all this hardware, hosting your own server is an option. If the budget for all this hardware (which could approach $15,000 even for a single-server site) is out of reach, then you don't have a decision to make; just skip ahead to the discussion on how to choose a third-party host.

With the right equipment in place, the job is still not done, of course. When planning their sites, many Webmasters forget there is an on-going time commitment and that supporting hardware is not a background task. In addition, Webmasters are often software people with little or no hardware background. Keeping a hardware setup as elaborate as the one I just described running smoothly and efficiently requires effort, and it gets more complex as you add servers. Just as with the computer on your desktop, you need to keep an eye on numerous maintenance issues — but the importance of this maintenance is multiplied many times. Table 15-2 lists some of the most common hardware issues you will need to address.

Table 15-2 Webmaster headaches and their remedies

Headache	*Remedy*
Disk fragmentation	Run disk-optimizing software at regular intervals.
Cable operation and replacement	Keep spare cables on hand and position the cables so they won't be stepped on, kinked, or otherwise abused.
Manual backup of critical data	Build a backup routine into your schedule — and follow it!
Cleaning of cases, display screens, keyboards, mice	Invest in a small vacuum cleaner designed for cleaning electronic equipment (available through most mail-order computer supply houses). Keep equipment, particularly servers, hard drives, and network routers, clean and cool.

What's more, some things you probably never worry about on your own personal system will need attention, including throughput testing and monitoring, Internet connection troubleshooting, and TCP/IP troubleshooting.

You may find yourself spending hours on the phone with the telephone company or your Internet service provider (or any of a surprisingly large array of intermediaries who work their way into the loop without you even knowing!) trying to figure out why nobody in Schenectady can connect to your server.

Software concerns

Although the software side of Web-serving is less expensive, it is more fraught with pitfalls and has the potential of becoming a major time sink. In fact, managing this aspect of server hosting requires far more time and energy than managing the hardware. (And remember, you're still doing infrastructure work here — none of this pertains to the presentation of the site: its page design, structure, and content.)

Table 15-3 shows you the types of software you should purchase or license to host your own successful Web site.

Table 15-3 Site software and common issues

Software	*Considerations and Tips*
HTTP server	This is the brains of the outfit. Learn this program's ins and outs thoroughly.
Server monitoring software	It's a good idea to run this software on a machine other than the server so it can alert you when your server stops working.

Software	Considerations and Tips
Statistics program	Use this software to track hits, errors, timeouts, sources of referral, and myriad other site activities.
Mailing list server	You need this only if you plan to run one or more mailing lists.
Conference, discussion, or real-time chat server	One or more may fit into your site's plans now or in the future.
CGI Scripting/Programming tools	Your choice depends on your skills and tasks that need to be done, but you will almost certainly need this at some point. On the Mac platform, the usual choice is Frontier (from UserLand Software) and/or Apple's AppleScript. Perl, C, C++, and other languages are also usable and are the most common choices on the Windows platform.
Specialty servers	RealAudio, secure commerce, graphics, multimedia, and other server software may be important, or become important, depending on the direction your site takes.
Filters and other programs	Sometimes these can replace or supplement CGIs and make your site more flexible.

Depending on your site's audience and purpose, you may only need the first three or four programs listed in Table 15-3. You may, however, find yourself with a surprisingly staggering array of software to learn and support (and buy).

Deciding which of these programs you need, which specific software meets your needs, and how all these pieces interact with one another is a fairly significant task. Factor in the need to keep current with new products and versions — learning the latest program nuances as your site's needs change and keeping an eye on the technical horizon can eat up an amazing amount of time.

For example, you're cruising along just fine, things have been running smoothly for a few weeks, when one of your content developers comes to you and says, "I'd like to include a Macromedia Shockwave movie with the article I'm doing on the election tomorrow. Any technical problems?" You may or may not already know the answer, but if you don't, you're about to find out how quickly you can research such a question.

Security concerns

There are at least two major security concerns for a Webmaster hosting his or her own site:

- **Access and data security.** This issue deals with controlling and monitoring access to prevent unauthorized use and vandalism of the site content.
- **Physical equipment security.** This issue deals with people stealing equipment.

I can't really say much about the second point here except to warn you not to overlook it. If your company is not located in a secure building, put your server under lock and key inside your facility. Buy a locked mounting rack or put a combination lock on the door to the room or office where the server is housed. (You may want to do both.) If your building is secure, you probably don't need to obsess on this issue. But don't ignore it.

Data access and the attendant issue of data security are issues of increasing concern. Every time you turn around, someone is going to be asking you about them.

SECRET

The degree to which you spend money and time addressing these security issues should relate directly to the intrinsic value of the data at stake. If you're running a Web site and your only fear is that someone may gain access to material for which you normally charge a nominal subscription fee, the downside is fairly small. Likewise, if the only content an intruder can get at is on the Web server and that content isn't mission critical or confidential (you *are* backed up, aren't you?), you don't want to spend huge amounts of time and resources trying to prevent unauthorized access, use, or destruction of information.

INTRANET ANGLE

If, as is often the case with company intranets, the information on the Web server is confidential or intrinsically valuable, you want to spend what it takes to make that data as secure as possible.

Once you've decided the appropriate level of security for your site based on these and other considerations, and you've factored in political concerns among company management, you are ready to examine the issues involved.

Table 15-4 summarizes the main data-security truisms you need to take into account when deciding and implementing data security in your Web server.

Table 15-4 Security truisms

Principle	***Comments***
No security system can be devised that will keep out a determined hacker with plenty of time and technical resources.	Believe it. You can never guarantee security. Period.
Security is heavily dependent on the operating system.	Mac Web servers are the most secure because the Mac OS can limit file access. Windows NT servers are less secure, but UNIX servers are most prone to security breaches due to the openness of the server design.
Security designs often compromise user convenience.	If your site is intended for public use, you may have to compromise on security to prevent potential visitors from becoming discouraged by passwords and other gates.

Load management

When you host your own server, you can manage and control how much load is placed on your system, including its Internet connection. If you start noticing slowdowns, user timeouts, connection refusals, and other indications of a potential overload, you can respond reasonably fast. (I say "reasonably" because you are still often at the mercy of third parties such as the telephone company and your Internet service provider.)

On the other hand, if you farm out server hosting, you may be able to find out what is happening with the server load (through a remote administration and monitoring application, for example), but your ability to influence its status may be limited. For example, many companies that provide hosting services reserve the right to place multiple servers on a single T1 or T3 line. This may be — and often is — just fine. But if your situation suddenly demands a full T1 line, you may have difficulty convincing your service provider to make a quick change, if the provider can acquire the additional capacity at all.

Monitoring and support

Perhaps the most convincing argument against acting as your own server host is the need for quick-response, around-the-clock support. If your business depends heavily on its Web site, the server can't be "off the air" for extended periods. Even a few hours of downtime can cost significant money. And at the very least, turning away visitors during those dark hours doesn't reflect well on the site.

Hosting services generally offer support 24-hours-a-day, seven-days-a-week and guarantee a quick response time — they may ensure that your site is never unreachable for longer than an hour. Many services are fully staffed around the clock, which means you get an almost immediate response to a crash or other server problem.

Providing the same support yourself, even with a moderate staff, is difficult. After all, supporting Web sites probably isn't your company's main business — it's unlikely you can afford to have people on call all the time. You can use monitoring software that alerts you when a server crashes, and you can obtain remote restart capabilities, but every now and then you will likely come across a situation in which you just can't solve a problem in a short time frame.

Some people say that the life of a Webmaster is like that of a commercial airline pilot: hours and hours of routine, punctuated by infrequent moments of stark terror. And this is why the ability to monitor and adjust the server is so important. If you notice, for example, that users are experiencing a 20 percent refusal rate when that value is usually under one percent, you may be able to fix the problem before it takes the system down.

The Flavors of Server Hosting

There are several types of Web server-hosting services available from a staggering array of Internet service providers. This section takes a look at each flavor. (Note that not all ISPs offer all, or even any, of these services.)

The two most common types of service offered by ISPs are *virtual hosting* and server *colocation*. Other alternative services fall between these two extremes.

Virtual hosting: renting space

In virtual hosting arrangements, the ISP owns the equipment and rents you disk space, telecommunications capacity, and other technologies (such as prebuilt libraries of CGI scripts you can use). You create your Web pages on your own computer and then use FTP software to transfer the pages to the ISP's machines.

Such arrangements are generally only useful if you have a fairly small site (under 20MB, or fewer than 100 HTML pages).

Colocation: your hardware, their location

In colocation arrangements, you purchase or lease your own hardware and the ISP gives it a physical home. The ISP provides an Internet connection, support staff, backup facilities, and additional services. Colocation arrangements are often very economical and provide you with peace of mind as well as some other advantages, which I explore throughout this chapter.

Choosing a Host Company

Assuming you've decided not to host your own server, you must identify a company that will provide the kind of service and support you need. You know all the obvious factors to consider — cost, reputation, and capabilities — but in this section I cover a few points that may not be entirely obvious as you start the process. They include ther following:

- Location
- Experience
- CGI accommodation
- Remote administration capability
- Line-capacity guarantees and an above-normal-demand policy

SECRET

How to Find an ISP

How do you find an ISP that provides colocation services? It's not too difficult, thanks to a Web site that exists to provide exactly the kind of information you need to start your search.

The site is called The List, shown in Figure 15-1. The List is located at `http://thelist.iworld.com` and is maintained by Mecklermedia, a major publisher of Internet- and Web-related publications.

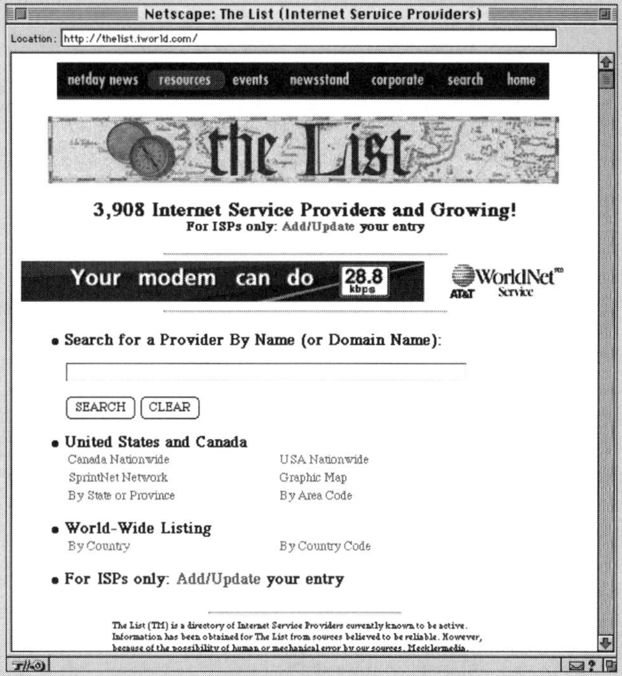

Figure 15-1: The opening screen of The List Web site

You can search The List by area code and geographic location, you can confine the search to ISPs that serve the entire country, and you can even find international support. The List is an invaluable starting point.

Some other good sources are as follows:

- Your local telephone directory
- Internet user groups
- Fellow Webmasters
- The business section of a metropolitan daily newspaper
- The Usenet newsgroup alt.internet.services

Location isn't everything

Real-estate agents, witty folks that they are, often say the three most important factors in determining the value of a property are location, location, and location. In choosing a Web site hosting partner, location may be the least important factor. At the very least, don't consider it a governing factor.

This is, after all, the Internet: You should be able to manage your site regardless of where you are located, particularly if you work with a hosting service that provides good support for remote administration (which I discuss later in this chapter) and you have a decent connection to the Internet. Given the way companies and people move around in today's world, you could begin your server-hosting experience with a local vendor and then find it, or you, moving anyway.

Experience counts

In addition to the basic questions you should ask about the hosting service's business longevity and depth of Internet and Web knowledge, you should also ask questions about specific experience you will require.

If you plan to host your site on Mac OS server hardware, for example, you want to be certain your hosting service is knowledgeable in Mac OS system and software issues. You'll find it quite frustrating to deal with your hosting service's technical support team over the phone in an emergency — you may spend more time explaining how to copy a file on the Mac than getting the solution to your problem. The same principle applies to UNIX and Windows server experience.

Aside from platform- and software-specific experience, you may want to delve into a hosting service's capability to deal with specific aspects of your site. If you will be using a secured online transaction process for ordering merchandise, for example, you want to be sure your host service can support the software and processing. "Support" doesn't mean simply allowing you to do what you want; it means being able to help you with problems when they arise.

If you will be using special software, make sure your hosting service not only allows this use, but is knowledgeable about the server side of the software and can help you. Here's a case study: A colleague of mine runs a Web site that depends heavily on Web Crossing, a cross-platform conferencing tool from Lundeen and Associates (discussed in Chapter 9). She was having problems with the software reliability on her hosting service's UNIX system. She evaluated switching to a Macintosh for conferencing but was able to solve the problem far more efficiently by simply switching hosting services. She found a vendor with experience serving Web Crossing conferences on UNIX, and the problems disappeared.

Often, software upgrades on the server side must be installed by the hosting service's technical staff because over-the-net installation isn't always possible or efficient. Find a hosting service with people who can handle this requirement for you.

Accommodating CGI programs

Occasionally Webmasters sign up with a site-hosting service only to find out the service imposes unacceptable limitations on the site's ability to program and execute CGI programs and scripts.

Except for the most trivial sites, it is safe to say that CGI scripting has become an essential ingredient of up-to-date Web sites. Most often, the Webmaster writes and implements these CGIs or evaluates and purchases off-the-shelf CGIs from third parties. Only rarely does the site-hosting company offer this service.

But CGIs by nature reside and execute on the server, which is physically housed by the hosting service. The hosting service, therefore, takes a proprietary interest in the management of CGI usage on their equipment (or on your equipment which is housed at their location). CGIs, particularly on UNIX and Windows servers (Macs have inherent security in this regard), can wreak havoc if they are allowed to run unchecked.

In addition to researching whether a hosting service allows CGIs, find out how the service handles the following issues:

- **Programming and scripting languages supported.** For example, if the host is running on UNIX, you probably can't expect any Mac-specific scripts written in UserTalk or AppleScript to be executable; you may have to resort to Perl.
- **Security or other restriction issues.** Can you freely upload files? Can you control access to data you place on your site? Are there limits to file storage size or extra charges for exceeding thresholds?
- **Storage and addressing rules.** Do your files have to be stored in certain directories? Do you have access to upper-level directories? Can you create your own subdirectories?

Remote administration: The importance of access

All major (and most minor) hosting services provide you with a way to maintain your site via FTP or another mechanism. Don't even think about working with a hosting service that requires you to e-mail pages to them and places the responsibility of maintaining your site on its staff. You want to be in charge of when and how your site is updated because frequent updates are a critical part of most commercial Web sites' success. If the hosting service's staff is the only group that can store data on your site for you, you will always be at the mercy of their priorities and staffing levels.

Beyond FTP for file upload, however, there are two other aspects of remote site administration you should consider.

Making directories

You will almost certainly want the ability to create new subdirectories (folders) and upload documents. Your site's physical structure should be fluid. You don't want to be locked into someone else's structures or into your original, unchangeable decisions about how the site should be structured.

Remote restarting

You will probably want the ability to restart your server remotely, either over the telephone or by using a TCP/IP connection and software. Again, you don't want to lock yourself into a site-hosting service that makes this kind of task difficult or impossible.

If, on the other hand, the hosting service has really good, reliable, round-the-clock support, perhaps a remote-restart capability isn't crucial. Ultimately, you need to assess just how good the service's support is before making a decision.

Line capacity guarantees

If you spend enough time checking into candidates for server-hosting services, you'll undoubtedly encounter many definitions of various "standard" terms. Line capacity is one of the most common areas of confusion. You may think a T1 line is a T1 line, but you may well be wrong.

Unless your hosting service gives you a *dedicated* T1 line (some do, whether or not you need it), you may find yourself sharing a T1 line with any number of servers — the hosting service may decide to hang 25 different servers on the T1 line. Depending on how busy those other servers are when your server is busy, you can experience some unpleasant performance problems.

The other side of the coin is that you may not always need the full bandwidth of a T1 line. For example, you may be running a site which most people visit between 6 a.m. and 2 p.m. on weekdays. In that case, you wouldn't mind sharing the T1 line (and its associated cost) with other servers, but only during your non-peak usage periods.

SECRET

Some hosting service companies provide graduated line capacity under any of several rubrics. You may pay for the bandwidth you *use* rather than for the use of a T1 line all the time. This approach, in the hands of a well-equipped hosting service, can offer an added benefit: when you need more than one T1 line, the service may be able to give you part of another T1 or even a portion of a T3. Again, you pay for the bandwidth you use and this approach can get expensive — but if it's what you need, it's well worth checking into.

At the very least, I recommend that you obtain a commitment from the hosting service that no more than approximately 12 servers are ever connected to your server's T1 line. If you can afford it, however, a dedicated T1 is your best bet in today's market.

What to Ask: An ISP Checklist

Few Webmasters ever go so far as to prepare a formal Request For Proposal, known in the business world as an RFP. But you should begin the task of identifying and contracting a server-hosting company with a clear set of questions in mind. This section provides a comprehensive set of questions you should raise. (I've provided additional comments on some questions.)

Background

- Name of company
- Address of company
- Location of hosting services, if different
- Years in business
- Name(s) of principal(s)
- Years of experience of each principal — in networking, the Internet, and the computer telecommunications industry in general
- Degrees or certificates held by principal(s)
- Name, title, and qualifications of person responsible for your account

  Comment: It doesn't matter if the CEO is the most knowledgeable programming guru on the planet if your account is going to be in the hands of some recent college grad who majored in cultural anthropology and thinks computers are "okay for some people."
- Number of servers and clients presently hosted at this location
- Contact names and telephone numbers of representative clients
- Internet connections in place

  Comment: You want to know not only what your server's connection will be, but how the host service is connected to the Internet. The key point to determine is how many "hops" between the ISP and the Internet backbone? Efficiency gets lost in these jumps.
- Name of telecommunications provider and phone number of individual contact

  Comment: This question only became necessary recently, as the telephone industry has been deregulated. Dozens of small local exchange carriers (LECs) have cropped up. If your hosting service is using someone other than the predominant local phone company, check out the company it is using. Some LECs are good — even better than the local phone company. But some aren't.

Services provided

- Type of Internet connection your server will have
- Number of servers to share this connection
- Are any of the present servers high-throughput sites (such as adult-oriented and/or heavily multimedia-based sites)?

  Comment: You may share a T1 line with only one other site, but if that site is generating 500,000 hits per day dishing out cheesy pictures, you're better off on a dedicated, lower-speed line. It pays to know who your neighbors are.
- What log reports and statistical analyses will be provided and with what frequency?
- Can you obtain the original log files yourself?

  Comment: Without access to the server log files, you cannot double-check the accuracy of the host service's reports, nor can you generate custom reports of your own. If you can't obtain these logs, be sure that you won't ever need to provide information other than the reports furnished by the host service's standard analysis.
- How often will your server be backed up and to what media?
- Where will backups be stored?
- What are the specifications of the UPS to which your server will be connected?
- How often will routine hardware maintenance, such as disk optimization and memory diagnostics, be performed?
- Do they offer a contingency plan in the event that your hardware must be taken offline for maintenance or other purposes?
- Who has direct access to your hardware and how is that access controlled?
- What, if any, special software will you need to access your server remotely?
- What, if any, restrictions does the hosting service place on your use of CGI scripts and/or applications?
- What, if any, restrictions does the hosting service place on the content you can post on your site?

Comment: For example, some site-hosting services object to sexually explicit material being hosted on systems in their facilities. Others may have competitive concerns.

Support

- What are "normal" working support hours for the site, where "normal" means there is a person physically present and able to respond immediately to a support need?
- During off-hours, what is the guaranteed maximum turnaround time in response to a trouble call?
- How will you contact support personnel during normal working hours and off-hours?
- In the event of a technical support problem that isn't resolved satisfactorily in a timely manner, will you have a pager number or other direct access to the manager responsible for your server?
- Will your servers be supported by a system that will enable you to reset them by telephone if necessary?

Costs

- What, if any, startup costs are involved? What do they cover?
- What are the fixed monthly costs?
- Are there any variable monthly costs? If so, how are they calculated?
- Are there any penalties incurred by the hosting service if it fails to perform support or provide line capacity as outlined in the contract?
- What is the pro rata reduction in fees you earn if your site is unavailable for more than some minimal, agreed-upon time?

Summary

- One of the biggest decisions you face is whether to host your site yourself or contract a service provider.
- Hosting a site yourself gives you more control and enables you to respond to problems immediately but is expensive and a significant responsibility.
- Contracting with a service provider lightens your load, but can mean less control, fewer logging statistics, and its own set of headaches.
- If you decide to host a site yourself, don't consider any connection speed slower than ISDN. If you can afford it, a fractional T1 or dedicated T1 line is your best bet.

- Mecklermedia's The List site is a good place to start a search for a service provider.
- As you narrow down your candidates for a service provider, ask each one about its history, experience, equipment, costs, and service options.
- Remember: the life of a Webmaster is like that of a commercial airline pilot: hours and hours of routine punctuated by infrequent moments of stark terror.

Chapter 16

Mac OS Web Server Secrets

In This Chapter

- Good reasons to use a Mac as your Web server
- Fine-tuning the performance of WebSTAR
- Accessorizing WebSTAR with NetCloak and other add-ons
- Mac-based tools for analyzing your server logs
- Monitoring your server — and keeping it running

While the alleged pundits predict the Mac's demise (again), tens of thousands of sites of all sizes are being served out by the computer platform that popularized graphical computing to begin with. The Mac's popularity among designers guaranteed its success in Web site creation, but its security, machine longevity, and famous ease of use have also made it a force in Web site serving. Dan Shafer knows this — he presides over the Mac servers at the award-winning Salon Magazine (see the previous chapter's introduction). He shares his experience in this chapter, to which I've added some tips of my own — I've long used Macs to serve my site.
— Jim Heid

Despite mountains of evidence to the contrary, many people believe that any Web site served by a Macintosh will be inherently slower and somehow dumber than those served by Windows NT or UNIX systems.

This is simply not true. There may be some highly specialized Internet (as opposed to World Wide Web) tasks for which Windows NT and UNIX are arguably better suited — I'm referring to primary Domain Name Server (DNS) support and bulk e-mail (mailing list) management. But you can always transfer these tasks to a Windows or UNIX system, either through your Internet service provider or perhaps at a publicly accessible server provided by educational or other non-profit institutions. (Be sure to check with the owner of the server before using it for anything if you are not a subscriber or supporter, however.)

On the other hand, there are dozens of valid reasons to prefer the Macintosh as a Web server platform. I discuss these advantages only briefly here because I'm primarily interested in helping you to understand, manage, use, and extend your Mac-based Web server.

ON CD-ROM

Get Your Mac OS Server Tools Here

The *HTML & Web Publishing SECRETS* CD-ROM that accompanies this book contains a full array of first-rate Mac OS server tools, including the following:

WebSTAR. Check out this fully functional trial version of the Mac OS world's top server package. If you decide to buy, see StarNine's special offer in the back of this book.

NetCloak. Energize your site with this terrific tool from Maxum Development. Other Maxum products on the CD-ROM include Phantom (discussed in Chapter 10), NetForms, WebLock, RushHour, and PageSentry.

ServerStat Lite. Kitchen Sink's ServerStat is one of the top commercial log-analysis packages for the Mac. ServerStat Lite is a scaled-down, shareware version.

Also on the CD-ROM are Mac database-publishing and searching tools from Blue World Communications, Everyware Development, and ICATT. For details, see Chapter 10.

If you aren't yet using a Macintosh as a Web server or you're curious about its role as one, check out `http://www.evangelist.macaddict.com/market_internet.html`. This is the Web- and Internet-oriented part of Apple Fellow Guy Kawaski's EvangeList. (The main list at `http://www.evangelist.macaddict.com/` is a great source for positive Mac news and reinforcement.)

A final disclaimer: The Mac OS Web server world is a big place, and there isn't room in a single chapter — or even a single book — to describe every issue and every add-on. In this chapter, I tried to concentrate on the most important issues and the most essential add-ons. Don't forget to visit this book's Web site for updates, more tips, and links to companies and relevant information sources.

Some Good Reasons to Choose the Mac

Here are a few of the most important reasons to consider a Macintosh as your Web server:

- **Ease of management.** Macintoshes are known for their inherent ease of use; this concept extends to their usability as Web servers. You can generally get a Macintosh-based Web server on the air faster and with less technical skill than either a Windows NT or UNIX server.
- **Security.** The Macintosh file system is inherently secure. Because of the way file sharing and access privileges are implemented in the Mac OS, it is all but impossible for anyone who doesn't have direct hardware access or password access to get at any file you don't want to serve as part of your site. This is in direct contrast to UNIX, in particular, and even Windows NT, where security is a fairly complex issue and where holes crop up frequently.

- **Scriptability.** You can create Common Gateway Interface (CGI) applications on the Macintosh in relatively simple, English-like scripting languages such as Frontier's UserTalk and Apple's own AppleScript. A Webmaster with relatively little programming background can extend the server's capabilities in useful and meaningful ways. On Windows NT and UNIX systems, writing CGI applications generally requires considerably more advanced programming skills and complex programming languages.
- **Cost.** Several studies have shown that a Macintosh Web server can be put into place for about 40 percent less money than an equivalent Windows NT server, and less than half the cost of an equivalent UNIX system. When maintenance costs are factored into the equation, the differences are even greater.

If you decide to choose a Macintosh for your Web server, you should know that it's not necessary for you to choose a Mac model that includes the word *server* in its name. Generally speaking, the differences between Mac OS systems specifically sold as servers and "plain" Mac OS machines tend to be relatively insignificant — usually, server models simply include a bundle of server-related software, which you can easily buy on your own.

Depending on the volume of your Web site, you might even find that a fairly old 680X0-based Macintosh might serve your purposes quite well. But the more page views and bytes you expect to transfer in a given period, the more you'll want to invest in machine speed.

SECRET

If you face a trade-off at some point between CPU speed and disk speed, go for the faster disk; the disk will turn out to be the largest single bottleneck in your site's ability to serve information quickly.

BACKGROUNDER

Web Serving on the Cheap

WebSTAR is the most popular and the best of the commercial Mac Web server packages, but at approximately $795, it isn't cheap. Here are a few alternatives that are:

Quid Pro Quo. This freeware Web server package by Social Engineering, Inc., provides reasonably good performance, an easy-to-use interface, and compatibility with WebSTAR-format plug-ins. You can download it from `http://www.slaphappy.com/`.

NetPresenz. This shareware package from Peter Lewis' Stairways Software provides FTP and HTTP serving. It isn't known for its speed, however. NetPresenz is available from `http://www.stairways.com/`.

MacHTTP. This shareware program pioneered Mac Web serving and is still available at `http://www.starnine.com/`. Its feature set is limited, however; if you want a full-featured HTTP server and you're on a budget, Quid Pro Quo is a better bet.

Fine-Tuning WebSTAR Performance

Most Macintosh Web servers — in excess of 80 percent of them at this writing — use WebSTAR as their HTTP server. The brainchild of Chuck Shotton, one of the brightest young programming minds in America today, WebSTAR is marketed by the StarNine Technologies division of Quarterdeck. Chuck originally developed his Web server for the Macintosh as a shareware product called MacHTTP, which remains available from `http://www.starnine.com/`. MacHTTP was so wildly successful that it quickly became the de facto standard. StarNine, later acquired by Quarterdeck, became the marketing vehicle for the commercial product, whose name was then changed to WebSTAR.

With WebSTAR, you can serve Web pages and all their various content types in minutes — literally. It is one of the simplest software installations you may ever perform.

There are some settings available in WebSTAR that can improve the performance of your Web site in sometimes subtle but important ways. In this section, I examine the most important performance-optimizing tricks, which include the following:

- Adjusting maximum users and listens
- Turning off DNS (and what to do when you need it)
- Modifying the timeout period for connections
- Tweaking buffer size
- Fine-tuning WebSTAR's status window

These settings are all adjusted through the WebSTAR Admin program, a companion program to the WebSTAR server. The gateway to most of these settings is the dialog box shown in Figure 16-1. To display this dialog box, choose the Miscellaneous Settings command from the WebSTAR Admin utility's Configure menu.

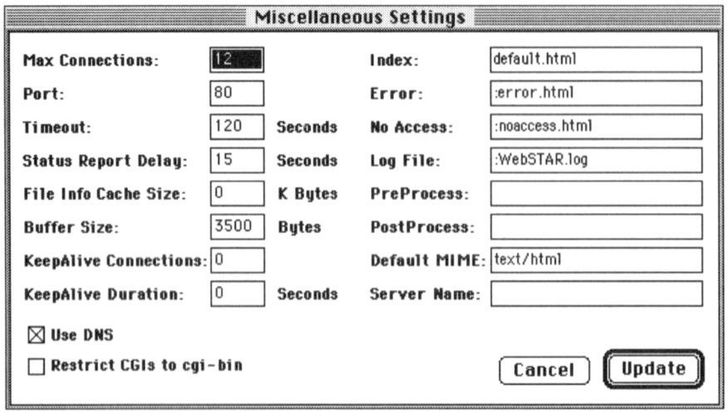

Miscellaneous Settings

Max Connections:	12		Index:	default.html
Port:	80		Error:	:error.html
Timeout:	120	Seconds	No Access:	:noaccess.html
Status Report Delay:	15	Seconds	Log File:	:WebSTAR.log
File Info Cache Size:	0	K Bytes	PreProcess:	
Buffer Size:	3500	Bytes	PostProcess:	
KeepAlive Connections:	0		Default MIME:	text/html
KeepAlive Duration:	0	Seconds	Server Name:	

☒ Use DNS
☐ Restrict CGIs to cgi-bin

Cancel Update

Figure 16-1: WebSTAR Admin's Miscellaneous Settings dialog box

You can also adjust most WebSTAR settings remotely using any Web browser. This is a terrific convenience — whether you're next to the server or on the other side of the world, if you can get yourself to a Web browser, you can fine-tune WebSTAR's performance. Most of WebSTAR's remote-administration features are identical to the administration features provided by the WebSTAR Admin program, so I'll just discuss the latter here.

Adjusting maximum users and listens

Perhaps the largest single factor that affects the performance of WebSTAR is the capacity you provide your visitors for connections to the server. Generally, the more connections you provide, the easier it will be for visitors to connect to your site. The more connections you support, the better your site's overall performance — assuming you allocate adequate memory to WebSTAR (more on this in a moment).

But like all things in life, there are trade-offs. If you provide too many connections than your machine can deal with, users will find themselves either unable to connect or waiting for things to happen. The truth is, they probably won't wait; they'll hit their browsers' Stop buttons and move to a faster site.

Two values affect WebSTAR's capacity: MaxUsers and MaxListens. The former refers to the number of users who can be accessing files on your Web server at one time. The latter determines how many processes WebSTAR will have available to listen for new connection attempts. The interaction of these two values will become clear shortly.

Maxing Out MaxUsers

If your server is running Apple's Open Transport networking software (and it should be), WebSTAR enables you to set a maximum of 150 MaxUsers. If you're running the older and slower MacTCP, WebSTAR limits MaxUsers to a maximum of 50. It's unlikely you'd ever want to set your limit as high as 150, unless you're using a very fast connection (such as a T3 line) to the Internet's backbone and your site is receiving a huge amount of hits. For most sites, I've found that allowing 60 to 80 MaxUsers seems to provide top-end performance with little or no waiting or timeout experiences for users.

Just about every WebSTAR neophyte Webmaster's first impulse is to crank MaxUsers up to 50 or so and never consider the issue again. But this turns out to be a mistake. Not only does 50 connections require considerably more memory than a lower number, but StarNine has calculated that if you are connected to the Internet via a T1 line or anything slower, setting your MaxUsers higher than 35 actually degrades performance. (These calculations were done by Louis P. Slothouber, a StarNine scientist. You can read his paper on this subject in all its gory mathematical detail at `http://www.starnine.com/webstar/summary.html`.)

Unless you're fortunate to be hanging your server directly off of a T3 connection, set MaxUsers to 35 and know that you are providing your users with maximum effective capacity. When I did this on one server where I was Webmaster, I saw an immediate performance improvement I estimated at 20 percent, which is a big step in the right direction for a busy site.

The amount of memory you allocate to WebSTAR must take into account the MaxUsers setting. Fortunately, if you try to launch WebSTAR with insufficient memory allocated for the MaxUsers setting, WebSTAR will behave quite nicely. It will let you know what you've done and then gracefully quit (see Figure 16-2).

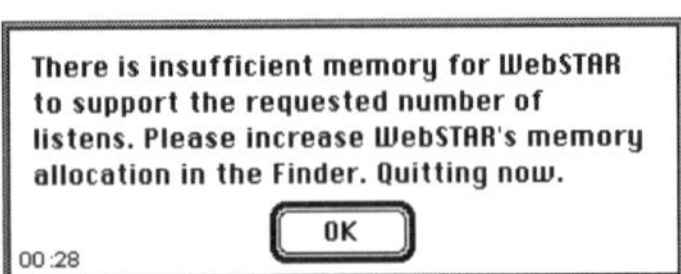

Figure 16-2: Dialog box warning of memory setting too low for MaxUsers

Table 16-1 defines the recommended memory settings for various popular MaxUsers settings. Use this table to arrive at a good memory allocation for your server's MaxUsers setting.

Table 16-1 Memory allocation for MaxUsers settings

MaxUsers	*Recommended Memory Allocation (MB)*
15	1.5
25	3.0
35	4.5
45	6.0

Allocating more memory than Table 16-1 calls for will not, in itself, speed up your server. In fact, it can slow it down because of some of the intricacies of the Mac's memory management techniques that are far too arcane to go into here. Stay with the recommended settings and you can be sure you're optimizing your server's performance.

And by the way, if your server has a very light load, you can reduce WebSTAR's memory appetite by reducing the MaxUsers value. But it's neither possible nor rational to set MaxUsers lower than four. At that setting, you have only one connection available to users because WebSTAR sets aside three connections for error message feedback of various types.

Matching MaxUsers with MaxListens

It turns out that the most effective and efficient setting for MaxListens on WebSTAR 1.3.1 and later is the same setting you are using for MaxUsers. In earlier releases of WebSTAR and its shareware predecessor MacHTTP, this was not the case.

Set MaxListens to the same value as you have MaxUsers and you'll be fine.

Only 35 users at a time!?

By now, you may be wondering if all of this means that your Macintosh Web server running WebSTAR can only handle 35 users at a time. You may trying to calculate how many such servers you'll need to build a site that can handle the millions eager to pay money to visit your Web site and learn how to make award-winning chili.

Not to worry. As it turns out, there's actually no meaningful correlation between connections and users. There are two reasons for this.

First, a single user usually triggers more than one connection when downloading a page from your Web site. Unless the page consists entirely of a single HTML file with no graphics or sound effects or other multimedia doohickeys, the user's browser will at least try to open a separate connection for each object on the current page (until it reaches a typically user-definable maximum for the browser). Sounds like the situation just got worse, doesn't it?

But the second reason there's no real link between users and connections explains why this is merely a matter of false appearance. A connection normally stays "live" for an incredibly brief period, usually considerably less than a second. This means that even though there are only 35 connections, literally hundreds or thousands of users might be trading use of those connections in rapid-fire order. Users may have to wait in line for a few seconds for an open connection when things are really busy, but such delays are hardly noticeable when you consider all the other choke points and delays inherent in Web browsing and Internet usage. In effect, all of the users connected to your server appear to be alone or in very select company when they are actually making use of HTTP connections.

You can look it up — but you shouldn't

By default, WebSTAR performs a Domain Name Server (DNS) lookup on every IP address that makes a request of it. It then dutifully logs this DNS entry so that you can later find out, for example, how many people visit your site from educational institutions or from Iceland.

The process of DNS lookup, however, is slow and at times unreliable. As a result, DNS lookup is a notorious performance destroyer. Every Macintosh Webmaster I know who is running a busy site has long since turned this feature off in WebSTAR.

But if you turn off DNS lookup and then the boss pops into your office and asks you to do a report on how many people are visiting your site from a competitor's network, what are you going to do? Yammer something about how performance is more important than the company's bottom line? Come up with a really buzzword-laden gibberish explanation of why you can't do that? Look for a new job?

You won't have to do any of these things if you buy ServerStat. This wonderful program from Kitchen Sink Software will actually do DNS lookup for you from your WebSTAR log file offline as part of its statistical reporting process. This means that as long as you've preserved your log files, you can do DNS-oriented statistical reports any time you need them without slowing down your Web server to do real-time DNS lookup. I'll have much more to say about ServerStat later in this chapter when I discuss monitoring your Web server.

Adjusting timeouts

The timeout period determines how long WebSTAR will keep a connection open without some activity on the other end of the link. When this time expires, WebSTAR can drop the connection and make it available to others.

Any number of things, from a user cancellation to a crashed system on the user's end to a too-slow network link can cause a connection to drop. When this happens, all WebSTAR knows for sure is that the connection has died. It can't be very accommodating about how it handles such situations, because it doesn't have much information about what has happened.

By default, WebSTAR sets the timeout to 60 seconds, which usually works pretty well. But there are some situations where changing it can help improve performance or make users happier.

If you are running WebSTAR on an intranet where you know everyone connecting to the server is running a reasonably zippy connection, you could set this timeout to something lower, perhaps even 10 to 30 seconds. You should experiment with this setting following the guidelines in the section called "Tools and techniques for server monitoring" later in this chapter to know when you have it set at an effective level.

On the other hand, if your server is acting as an interface to a large database, or if your site is graphically intensive, you might want to bump the timeout to 120 seconds. StarNine doesn't recommend setting the value higher than 120 seconds but WebSTAR permits you to go as high as 600 seconds (10 minutes). If you set it higher than 600, it will revert to a value of 60. And if you find a Web surfer who's willing to wait ten minutes for *anything*, let me know!

Tweaking buffer size

WebSTAR's buffer size determines how much information your server sends to a client in any given chunk. Because the process of assembling this data in the server's memory is obviously much faster than the physical transfer speed between the server and the client, you might conclude that increasing the buffer size would significantly improve your server's performance.

Unfortunately, some implementations of TCP/IP will choke if you feed them data too quickly. Notably, several popular Windows TCP/IP stacks can't deal with data coming in chunks larger than 4K. Some slower modems (those with speeds below 28.8 Kbps) may also have difficulty with the larger buffers of data.

As a rule, then, you should set your buffer size to 4K, which is, conveniently enough, WebSTAR's default setting. If you know that all your users are connecting via Macintoshes running Open Transport and/or over a reasonably high-speed connection, you might consider increasing the buffer size.

The status window and performance

WebSTAR's status window displays incoming hits and other information. That information is handy, but having to display it slows down WebSTAR a bit.

For best performance, keep the status window closed. If you just can't live without it, consider adjusting the delayed-updating feature built into WebSTAR 2.x. Normally, WebSTAR 2.x updates its status window every 15 seconds. If your site is very busy, you might want to increase this interval to lighten WebSTAR's load a bit. Run the WebSTAR Admin program and then choose Miscellaneous Settings from the Configure menu. In the Status Report Delay box, type a time interval. You can increase the delay to a maximum of 60 seconds.

Another way to boost performance without completely sacrificing the status window is to run it in its "iconized" view. Click the zoom box in the window's upper-right corner, and it shrinks to show only connection information.

Squeezing the Most Out of Your Server

Setting up WebSTAR to handle your site's traffic as efficiently as possible is important, but there also are a number of decisions you can make about how content is served that will improve efficiency as well.

These decisions include the following:

- Using a RAM disk or cache to store static and frequently accessed files
- Using a specialized server such as Maxum's RushHour to serve portions of your site
- Adopting Frontier and its object database as a repository for site files

- Using graphics wisely
- Writing HTML with speed in mind

In this section, I look at each of these areas and share some insights into how you can squeeze every drop of performance out of your server.

Using a RAM disk

If you have plenty of RAM (and if you don't, you should remedy that problem immediately!), you might consider using a RAM disk to improve performance. (How much RAM is "plenty?" Making specific RAM recommendations is always risky, but I recommend that you not attempt to run anything but the lowest-volume server in less than 32MB of RAM. 64MB is probably closer to a good baseline. With Web servers and RAM, the phrase "the more, the merrier," applies, so give yourself some room to grow. Someday you'll be glad you did.)

Documents, applications, and CGIs stored in the RAM disk remain in your server's memory. Because it is obviously much faster to transfer information from memory than it is from disk to memory and then to the requester, using a RAM disk can speed things up considerably.

You'll get the largest performance boost if you can identify a small number of files — say 20 or fewer — on your site that account for a substantial portion of your server's load as revealed in your log-analysis program. Each time one of those frequently needed files is requested, the time to serve it up will be substantially less if you store the file in a RAM disk.

Of course, the usual cautions regarding RAM disks apply — a RAM disk loses its contents when your system quits or crashes, so don't use a RAM disk to hold files that change, such as a database that visitors may be modifying. And of course, you shouldn't have your only copy of any document or file stored in the RAM disk; instead, copy those files to the RAM disk when your system starts.

There are a number of utilities (including the widely used RAM Doubler from Connectix, at `http://www.connectix.com/`) that help you manage your RAM disk more or less automatically. There are also a variety of excellent freeware and shareware RAM disk utilities; search for *RAM disk* on `http://www.shareware.com/` for the current crop.

Using a specialized server

A fairly recent development in the battle to make Web servers more efficient is the emergence of special-purpose servers fine-tuned to deal with a particular type of data, or to serve it in a particular way.

One notable example is RushHour from Maxum Development (http://www.maxum.com/). RushHour was specifically designed and optimized to serve graphic images, which it does with amazing alacrity. By storing your graphics on a server that runs RushHour, you can offload a sizable portion of the load your Web server otherwise faces, freeing it up to deal with HTML file transfers, CGIs, and other tasks. You can run RushHour on the same hardware as your main Web server, with a different port number, or, more efficiently, on a separate system altogether.

Learn Frontier and adopt the Frontier ODB

If you're serious about being a Macintosh Webmaster, you should consider becoming familiar with UserTalk and Frontier scripting. Frontier can handle virtually any CGI-related task. While Webmasters on other platforms struggle with arcane languages such as Perl, you can knock out Frontier scripts in a fraction of the time. Seasoned Macintosh Webmasters rely heavily on Frontier and UserTalk to make their lives easier.

Version 4.2 of Frontier includes many commands and capabilities specifically directed at supporting the Web and the Internet. This includes a full set of e-mail-oriented commands as well as a sophisticated database server in the Frontier object database (ODB). You can download the latest version of Frontier from http://www.scripting.com/.

To create CGIs in Frontier, you need Mason Hale's Frontier CGI Framework, a set of scripts and ODB entries designed to facilitate the creation of CGI scripts that can interact with information extracted from the user's browser. You can download the CGI framework from http://www.scripting.com/frontier/cgiframework/.

I have used Frontier to handle such tasks on my servers as

- HTML form parsing and management
- Disk space monitoring and cleanup
- Random generation of banner ads and other content
- Dynamic content generation based on ODB contents using some cleverly designed and eminently usable macro capabilities in Frontier
- Site management and tracking

Performing these tasks in Frontier is typically much faster and easier than writing, compiling, and testing C programs. Besides, you have the advantage of a full development and database environment that you can use for all kinds of purposes as long as it's running your CGI scripts anyway.

To get an idea of all the possibilities for Frontier on your Macintosh-based Web site, check out http://www.scripting.com. A moderate-sized group of Frontier fanatics frequents this site and the associated mailing list so getting started in Frontier is fairly easy.

How Frontier's object database can boost performance

As Macintosh Webmasters throughout the world have studied ways to improve server performance, WebSTAR creator Chuck Shotton and Dave Winer of UserLand Software, the inventor of Frontier and its UserTalk scripting language, looked at the Macintosh file system for some clues.

They found, somewhat to their surprise, that the Macintosh file system itself was a fairly significant bottleneck on busy Web servers. Because of the Macintosh's Hierarchical File System (HFS), accessing files that were several folders deep in the Finder structure required several disk accesses in many cases. This process is, of course, relatively slow compared to the speed of other server activities. It also doesn't help that at this writing, the Mac OS file system is not completely PowerPC-native. As a result, PowerPC-based Mac OS machines must run the file system in emulation mode, thereby hampering performance even more.

Together, Shotton and Winer came up with a powerful and brilliant solution. By extending Frontier's basic capabilities in some simple ways, Shotton created a new set of commands that essentially enable you to store some or all of your Web site's contents in Frontier's immensely capable and very high-speed object database (ODB). Rather than WebSTAR going to the disk to find files to serve or CGIs to execute, it makes a single call to Frontier, which uses its optimized mechanisms to search the ODB, find the desired content, and zip it back to WebSTAR for transmission to the browser.

At this writing, this technique is fairly new, but several sites, including one that I manage, are shifting to the Frontier ODB and extensive reliance on UserTalk scripts to provide significant speed increases. I'll be the first to admit that we're treading on the edge — it's not yet clear how large a site can actually be moved into this environment. The scalability of the Frontier ODB is an unknown quantity past a few megabytes; keep an eye on the Webmaster mailing lists and Web sites listed in this chapter for updates as we struggle with this issue together.

As I write this, Dave Winer has a team working on a port of Frontier to the Windows world. If and when this product becomes a reality, there will be an even greater reason to think about chucking that obscure Perl and C/C++ code and using Frontier and its associated tools to deal with the complexity of Web sites.

Using graphics wisely

Graphics make up at least a portion of most Web pages. But everyone knows that graphics take much longer to download than the text contained in HTML documents. The usual advice is to use graphics sparingly, keep them as small as possible, and always include `width` and `height` attributes with each HTML `<IMG>` tag. All of that advice is sound.

As discussed in Chapter 6, there are two basic types of graphics formats supported on the Web: JPEG and GIF images. You always face a trade-off between image quality and image size, which in turn generally requires that you select both an appropriate graphics format type and an optimum compression ratio or bit depth.

Remember that the larger the graphics files you place on your server, the more time the user spends waiting for the page to download. In an era of 28.8 Kbps modems as the de facto standard, you should probably try to avoid creating a page that contains more than 40 or 50K of graphic images if you can.

Making smart page-design decisions

Some basic page-design decisions can have an interesting impact on server performance. Much of this material is discussed in detail in previous chapters, but it's important enough to repeat here.

Think twice about background images

Stay away from background images unless your site just won't work without them. Using background colors is much more efficient because there's no image to download. As a rule of thumb, a GIF or JPEG image used as a background shouldn't exceed 6K. And remember that your background images may not appear anyway (users can set their browser preferences to not display them) and that using background images in combination with some user preferences for colors and type styles can lead to hard-to-read pages.

Think twice about lowsrc graphics

You may have seen some sites that seem to download graphics in two steps. In the first step, a gray or black-and-white image, usually on the grainy side, appears fairly quickly, and is followed by a color image. The intent is to give the impression of faster download and quicker usability. Chapter 6 showed how to implement this technique, which involves using the `lowsrc` attribute to the `<IMAGE>` tag.

In reality, of course, this double download results in more data served to the browser, which will be inherently slower than downloading only one graphic. Think twice about using this technique unless you're after a special effect, as discussed in Chapter 6.

Don't bother compacting your HTML code.

Some Webmasters go so far as to create two copies of HTML pages: one with comments and nice formatting for editing and readability and the other with comments removed and white space reduced to a bare minimum. My experience is that unless you have a huge number of comments or blank lines, this change produces little or no performance improvement, and at the expense of readable and maintainable pages. I don't advise this trick.

Take the load off with client-side features

Client-side image maps, which are also discussed in Chapter 6, can also save huge amounts of server time by eliminating the need for a CGI application to convert coordinates into URLs. There's no excuse for not using client-side image maps.

While you're offloading work from the server to the client, consider other options that lessen the server's load. For example, consider using JavaScripts to handle form-validation tasks instead of using a CGI to do so. Remember, the fewer chores you give the server, the more time you give it to concentrate on its primary job: dishing out your site's pages.

Essential Accessories for WebSTAR

A universe of third-party software and hardware products has evolved around WebSTAR. This section describes some of the most useful and common server accessories and provides some tips for using them. For an up-to-date list of products that enhance WebSTAR, visit StarNine's Extending WebSTAR page, at `http://www.starnine.com/development/extendingwebstar.html`.

BACKGROUNDER

Plug-ins or CGIs?

As you embark on your search for WebSTAR add-ons, you'll encounter two basic types: plug-in modules and CGI programs. What's the difference, and which should you use?

Plug-in modules reside in WebSTAR's Plug-Ins folder and tap directly into WebSTAR, loading when you launch the program. CGIs, on the other hand, are standalone application programs that are generally launched when called for in a URL.

The primary advantage of a plug-in is speed. CGIs communicate with WebSTAR and with other programs using the Mac OS's Apple Events mechanism, which is powerful but not exactly speedy. Because a plug-in taps directly into WebSTAR, it doesn't have to send and receive Apple Events in order to communicate with the server software.

On the downside, if a plug-in is buggy and crashes, it will take WebSTAR down with it. If a CGI crashes, it may or may not bring the server down, too. Also, the memory that a plug-in requires is unavailable while WebSTAR is running — whether or not the plug-in is actually in use. By comparison, you can often configure a CGI to quit after a certain period of inactivity. Thus, CGIs give you a bit more memory-management flexibility.

Some WebSTAR add-ons ship in both CGI and plug-in form. Given that you have a choice, which should you use? Generally, if performance is paramount, use the plug-in version. If you prefer the memory-handling flexibility that disparate CGIs provide, use the CGIs.

Energizing your site with NetCloak

One of the most widely used and powerful tools available to Macintosh Webmasters is NetCloak from Maxum Development (`http://www.maxum.com/`). (You'll notice that Maxum's name comes up a lot in this book and in discussions with Macintosh Webmasters. That's because this company has earned a sterling reputation for providing world-class tools that help Webmasters do things they have to do every day.)

Although the array of things you can do with NetCloak is staggering and would justify a book in its own right, I'm going to focus on three of its talents:

- Custom page counters
- Altering your pages' appearance based on the browser your visitor is using
- Password protecting pages

Custom page counters

Log-analysis programs like ServerStat, discussed in the next section, provide you with detailed statistics about who is visiting your site and what they are viewing. However, these programs require you to capture a snapshot of a moment in time — for example, a day's or a week's worth of WebSTAR log data.

There are many situations in which you would like to inform, in real time, a visitor or a manager involved with a site how many people have viewed a particular page. On some systems, this requires a special CGI whose sole purpose is providing counters for Web pages. As it happens, one of NetCloak's thousand-and-one talents involves creating page counters.

NetCloak lets you define counters by name and have the counters automatically increment each time a given page is served. You can specify that the counter values be visible to everyone who sees the page, or you can specify that the counters be visible only to certain IP addresses. With this latter option, you can create counters that only you can see.

One effective way I've used this capability is to add incrementing but invisible counters to key pages on a Web site, and then create a single page (password protected, if appropriate) that can be viewed by those with a need to know up-to-the-minute traffic figures.

NetCloak's talents come from custom tags that you add to your pages. When a visitor hits a page, NetCloak scans it, processes the tags, and then passes the results, along with the HTML in the page, to WebSTAR, which beams it out to the Web.

If you're familiar with HTML, it's easy to use NetCloak's most basic tags. For example, the tag `<INSERT_TIME>` tells NetCloak to insert the current time at the tag's location in the page. (To make working with its custom tags easier, Maxum has shipped a freeware utility, TagBuilder, that lets you insert NetCloak tags into any drag-and-drop-compatible editor, including Adobe PageMill and Bare Bones' BBEdit.)

To create a page counter in NetCloak, you would add the following NetCloak tag to the HTML page whose hits you want to count:

```
<INSERT_COUNT homepage>
```

This tag would add 1 to the counter called *homepage* each time the page on which it appears is requested by a visitor. The tag also causes the counter's current value to appear at the tag's location.

You can suppress incrementing and/or displaying the counter with special codes appended to the `<INSERT_COUNT>` tag. For example, if you want the counters to be incremented but not displayed (perhaps because you want to display them on a password-protected page), put an asterisk after the `COUNT` keyword, like so:

```
<INSERT_COUNT* orderpage>
```

Customizing page layout for browser differences

One of NetCloak's most interesting and useful capabilities is its ability to show and hide information based on conditions such as time of day, day of week, user IP address, and other data. Chapter 8 discussed how to use this feature to have a different Web cam soundtrack play back depending on the time of day.

NetCloak's capability to show and hide information based on certain conditions can also help you deal with the rapidly changing world of Web browsers and their differing capabilities and HTML interpretations.

BACKGROUNDER

When a browser and a Web server begin a conversation, the browser sends a piece of information called a *user agent*. The user agent identifies the browser: its name, its version number, and the platform on which it's running. Web servers can keep track of incoming user-agent data in their logs, enabling you to use log-analysis packages to determine which browsers and platforms your visitors are using. NetCloak can use the user-agent data to custom-tailor pages so that they're optimized for a specific browser.

By combining `<SHOW>` and `<HIDE>` tags with the NetCloak `<HIDE_CLIENT>` and `<SHOW_CLIENT>` tags, you can achieve tremendously sophisticated customization for various browser combinations. The following is a simple example of using NetCloak to differentiate between Windows and Macintosh browsers and pointing the user to the right place to download a file appropriate to his or her platform:

```
<HIDE>
<SHOW_CLIENT "Macintosh">
<A HREF="FTP://myftp.macfile.hqx">Download the Mac Version</A>
<HIDE>
<SHOW_CLIENT "Win">
<A HREF="FTP://myftp.winfile.zip">Download the Windows Version</A>
<SHOW>
```

The lines that contain only `<HIDE>` or `<SHOW>` tags are unconditional lines; they are always executed. The other lines are executed only when the condition they contain is true.

The HTML that follows a conditional <HIDE> or <SHOW> tag can be anything. Thus, you can use NetCloak to do the following:

- Display framed versions of a page to browsers that support frames, and unframed versions to other browsers
- Supply JavaScript to Netscape Navigator browsers and JScript to Microsoft Internet Explorer browsers
- Redirect a browser to a different page based on its user agent, its IP address, or even the time of day or the date
- Provide different content depending on the time of day (for an example of this application, see "Web cams: sites with cool sights" in Chapter 8).

Password protecting pages

WebSTAR has built-in security for what it terms *realms*, which are folders contained in your Macintosh's WebSTAR folder. You can create password protection for each realm and achieve a reasonable degree of security.

But sometimes realms are overkill. You may not want to go through the hassle of creating a separate folder for password protection, but you may need to protect one or more pages from prying eyes. NetCloak's <HIDE_PASSWORD>, <SHOW_PASSWORD>, and <REQUEST_PASSWORD> tags are quite handy for this task.

The <REQUEST_PASSWORD> tag displays a dialog box in which the user is requested to supply a user name and a password (whose characters are displayed as bullets for security reasons). You can then use this password to allow or deny access to specific pages based on whether it matches one of the passwords you provide as arguments to the <HIDE> and <SHOW> tags.

BACKGROUNDER

Server-side includes in WebSTAR 2.x

It's worth mentioning that WebSTAR 2.x provides some of the features found in NetCloak. Specifically, WebSTAR 2.x includes a plug-in that implements *server-side includes* (SSI), those HTML-like tags that enable you to create counters, sniff out user agents, and show or hide HTML based on various conditions.

WebSTAR 2.x's support for SSI adheres to the SSI standards proposed by the National Center for Supercomputing Applications (NCSA, at http://www.ncsa.uiuc.edu/). The NCSA SSI standard uses syntax that differs from NetCloak's. NCSA SSI tags take the form of HTML comments, like so:

```
<!--#counter var="homepage"-->
```

The fact that WebSTAR's SSI plug-in relies on a different syntax than NetCloak means you can't easily move from one to the other. For example, if you start with WebSTAR's SSI plug-in and then decide you want to tap into NetCloak, you have to rewrite your SSI tags to conform to NetCloak's syntax. Ultimately, NetCloak provides far more capabilities than does WebSTAR's SSI plug-in, and I recommend it heartily. If your needs are relatively simple, you might find the plug adequate — but remember that you'll have to rewrite your SSI tags if you graduate to NetCloak in the future.

This technique is often useful in designing a Web site with a custom counter setup as described earlier. You can password protect the master page on which the site's current traffic volume — which may be considered proprietary information — is displayed.

Tools and techniques for server monitoring

There are as many tools for monitoring your server's activity as there are activities worth monitoring, and then some. In this section, I take a look at three types of information you will want to track and spotlight the best tools for the jobs. These three monitoring points include the following:

- User timeouts and other unpleasant experiences
- Statistics that help you decide who is using your server and how
- Keeping tabs on the server to make sure it keeps operating when you're away from it

Timeouts and what they mean

One of the most important server statistics to monitor is the number of timeouts visitors experience. This figure is always displayed in the upper right corner of the main WebSTAR status window, as shown in Figure 16-3.

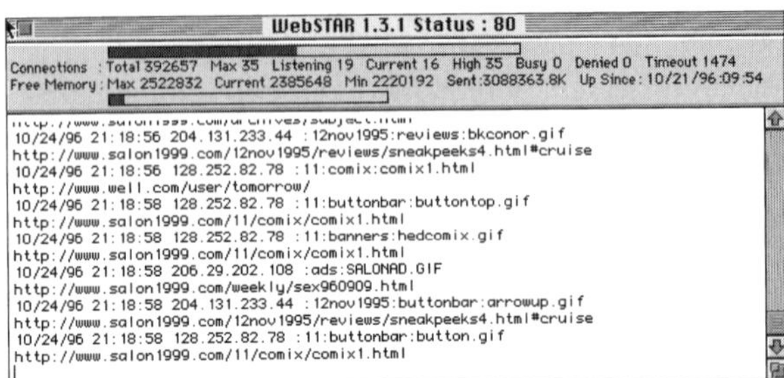

Figure 16-3: Timeouts reported in WebSTAR's status window

By itself, this value doesn't tell you as much as you might think. As I said earlier, there are so many things that can cause a server timeout that drawing major conclusions based solely on this statistic may not make much sense. However, there are some rules of thumb that can help you detect when you probably need to start looking at the issue of what's causing the timeouts.

If a timeout occurs, a visitor has lost his or her connection to your site. Unless they intentionally did so, they are probably at least disappointed. You want to keep your cushy Webmaster's job, so you want to keep visitors from being disappointed.

Experience indicates that if your timeouts stay at or below 0.5 percent of the number of connections (shown at the left side of the same window), you are doing about as good a job as anyone can of serving files on your server. Don't even spend 30 seconds worrying about trying to get the value under 0.5 percent.

On the other hand, if timeouts reach 3 percent of connections, you probably want to start watching the situation to see if you can determine what might be going wrong. And if timeouts hit 5 percent of connections, it's time for some serious analysis and corrective action.

SECRET

The first thing to check if timeouts become excessive is the number of MaxUsers and MaxListens (discussed earlier in this chapter). Then take a look at the timeout setting to see if you have it set too low for the type of material your site is managing. Beyond that, you might have to consider adding speed or capacity to your Macintosh server or to your Internet connection.

Tracking user activity with log-analysis programs

How busy is "busy?" That's a question every Webmaster grapples with. As marketers, advertisers, and other people who want to know about traffic begin to understand the Web site's role in the organization, questions start to flow freely.

To answer these questions, you need to analyze the contents of the WebSTAR log on your server. There are several ways of accomplishing this.

ON CD-ROM

The most popular is to use a program designed to analyze the log for you. At this writing, the most popular such program on the Macintosh is Kitchen Sink Software's ServerStat (`http://www.kitchen-sink.com/`), which I mentioned earlier in this chapter. ServerStat is extremely flexible and only gets better with each revision by its highly committed author, J. Eric Bush. (ServerStat is included with Apple's Internet Server Solution Macintosh models. And a shareware version, ServerStat Lite, is included on the *HTML & Web Publishing SECRETS* CD-ROM.)

SECRET

Create a Better Error Message

WebSTAR includes a file, called Error.html, whose contents are displayed when a visitor attempts to view a page that isn't available on your server. Alas, StarNine didn't exactly put a lot of effort into creating an attractive error message. When a visitor requests a page that doesn't exist, he or she sees a bold message that says, "Error! The file you requested was not found."

Do your visitors a favor and create your own Error.html file that contains a more graceful error message and perhaps a graphic. In this message, include a link that enables visitors to get to the site's home page. Better still, include a set of links that let them get to the key areas of the site — including your search page, if you have one.

Besides ServerStat Lite, there are several other freeware and shareware statistics programs. The most popular is Phil Harvey's WebStat, available at `ftp://ftp.uth.tmc.edu/public/mac/MacHTTP/webstat.sit.hqx`. Another terrific freeware analysis program is Analog. Many commercial programs are also available, including Everyware Development's Bolero (`http://www.everyware.com/`). For a comprehensive list, see StarNine's Extending WebSTAR page, at `http://www.starnine.com/development/extendingwebstar.html`. Like so many Web-development tools, most log-analysis packages are available in free trial versions. Find out what kind of information people in your organization want to see about the site's traffic, how they want it presented, and then pick a statistics package accordingly.

If you don't want to use someone else's program, you can, of course, write your own. The WebSTAR log format is well documented and the file is a plain, text-only file, so parsing it and extracting information from it is a fairly simple programming task. Several Webmasters I know have created custom AppleScript and Frontier scripts for this purpose. The advantage of such an approach is that you can get exactly what you want, the way you want it. The disadvantages, of course, are the same that accompany any custom software project: cost, time, and maintenance (also known as "job security").

Another way to deal with the need for statistics is to farm out the assignment, either to your ISP or to a traffic auditing firm such as A. C. Nielsen, the Audit Bureau of Circulation, or I/PRO (an independent auditing firm). In fact, at this writing, many companies who advertise heavily on the World Wide Web are beginning to insist on such audited figures as the basis for their charges.

SECRET

Using ServerStat's DNS lookup feature

Earlier in this chapter, I indicated that you could improve WebSTAR performance by turning off its DNS lookup feature. I promised that I'd tell you about how to deal with the need for domain information later. Well, later has arrived.

ServerStat has an optional setting that permits you to have it perform DNS lookups on known domain names when it runs its statistics report. Of course, doing so greatly slows down the log analysis, but as a rule you can afford that time, which isn't coming at the expense of your server's performance.

You can also sort your ServerStat reports by domain name. This makes it possible to answer questions about the kinds of sites from which users are accessing your server. Educational sites have domain names ending in *edu,* government office domain names end in *gov,* and international visitors have a country code as part of their domain names. You can also find out things such as how many America Online visitors your site receives because AOL visitors all have "aol.com" in their address.

Knowing when the server is down

If you are hosting your own server — or if you're not but you happen to be particularly paranoid — you'll want to know when the system crashes or a vital piece of software stops running *before* people start screaming at you.

There are a number of ways to accomplish this, but the best tool I've seen is Maxum Development's PageSentry.

Using PageSentry as a monitor

You can set up PageSentry to monitor any number of servers (or any kind of Macintosh system for that matter) to which you have TCP/IP access. Configuring PageSentry is straightforward. Simply supply the URL of a page on the system you want to monitor, a piece of text that the program can look for to know when things are working correctly, and an action to take if a problem arises.

Because PageSentry relies on the server not only responding but responding in a predictable way, it is more effective than more primitive methods that simply ping the server to ensure that it is still on the network. (This method is primitive because a server can be up but not serving pages correctly.) Typically, you have the server look for the `</HTML>` tag that indicates the end of a page. This ensures that the server is operating correctly.

As for the action PageSentry takes when an error occurs, you have a great deal of flexibility. Macintosh Webmasters use PageSentry to do all of the following:

- Display an alert and play a sound when a problem arises
- Send a message to an auto-restart sub-system (discussed later in this chapter) to reboot
- Transmit a message to the Webmaster's pager
- E-mail a notice to the Webmaster and/or system administrator

All of these steps are possible because PageSentry enables you to trigger an AppleScript when an error occurs. Anything you can create an AppleScript to accomplish, therefore, is a candidate for an action to take when the server stops working.

Keep your server up with KeepItUp and AutoBoot

Sometimes, though usually not often, WebSTAR or a vital CGI will stop working even though the server is up and running smoothly.

You can use a simple shareware product called KeepItUp by Belgian developer Karl Pottie to help prevent such software failures from crippling your Web server. KeepItUp has been a life-saver for many Macintosh Webmasters, and you'll find it on the *HTML & Web Publishing SECRETS* CD-ROM.

To use KeepItUp, place aliases of programs that you want to be sure are always running into a KeepItUp folder. Then you launch KeepItUp (which, for obvious reasons, is generally in the Startup Items folder in the System folder). KeepItUp monitors the programs for which it has aliases and if it detects that a program has stopped responding to queries, it restarts the program.

CGIs are generally launched automatically by WebSTAR when they are called by an HTML tag or some other action. Still, if an important CGI quits, you might want to restart it before someone needs it because starting up a CGI can often take some time. If you can restart the program while the user is otherwise occupied or while nothing else is happening on the server, you can increase users' efficiency.

A companion product to KeepItUp, called AutoBoot, is another useful server tool. AutoBoot, as its name implies, automatically restarts the computer if a system error occurs. That's an amazing feat when you think about it, and indeed, AutoBoot may not always be able to restart a machine when a particularly ugly crash occurs. But it works more often than not. AutoBoot is also included on the *HTML & Web Publishing SECRETS* CD-ROM.

Restarting your server by remote control

Despite your best efforts, your server will manage to crash. When this happens, it's a safe bet it will do so while you are not in the office where you could simply restart it from the keyboard.

You can always head into the office to restart the server, but that's hardly convenient, especially if you happen to be on vacation or otherwise out of town. And if do happen to be some distance from your office, the server may be down for an extended period.

Use that Startup Items Folder!

On Mac OS machines, the System Folder contains a folder named Startup Items. When the Mac starts up, it opens anything that you put in the Startup Items folder. By combining the Startup Items folder with AutoBoot, you can ensure that your server will pick itself up and dust itself off after a crash.

Make an alias of your WebSTAR application file and copy the alias to your Startup Items folder. If you're running other applications that you'd like to have start automatically — perhaps a conferencing CGI or a mailing list manager — make an alias of their icons and put them in Startup Items, too.

The Mac OS opens the items in alphabetical order. If you want the applications to load in a specific order, rename the aliases appropriately.

The best solution to this problem is a product called PowerKey Pro from Sophisticated Circuits (`http://www.sophisticated.com/`). PowerKey Pro is a combination hardware-software device: the hardware consists of a very smart power strip and surge protector that also connects to the telephone line; the software enables you to restart up to two servers by simply by making a phone call and entering codes from the telephone keypad.

The PowerKey Pro has two separate circuits in its six-outlet main box, which is only slightly larger than an ordinary six-outlet power strip. One of these circuits is associated with one of the six outlets while the other is connected to four outlets. (The sixth outlet is always on.) You can control each of these two circuits in three ways: with a telephone call, with a keyboard command, or with a script that runs unattended.

The latter two options are useful, but it's the first one that will save you from those middle-of-the-night trips to the office. Connect the PowerKey Pro to a power outlet and a telephone line, and then plug your server and its peripherals into the PowerKey Pro's outlets. If the system hangs or crashes, or if you want to reset the server, call the phone number associated with the PowerKey Pro unit, dial a security code, and then peck in codes that tell PowerKey Pro to turn a given circuit's power off and then back on.

In addition to shutting down and restarting the system and peripheral devices, you can also use the phone to tell the PowerKey Pro to execute a script that performs some action — backing up data, running a log analysis, or performing any other scriptable activity. You can also set up these actions to take place at a specific time or at regular intervals.

SECRET

Using PowerKey Pro with One Phone Line

You'd like to use PowerKey Pro to restart your server by phone, but you don't have a spare phone line to handle incoming calls to the device. Here are a couple of solutions to this problem.

A time qualifier. Use the PowerKey Pro software to create a qualifier for the Phone event, and set up the qualifier so that the PowerKey Pro answers the phone only during certain hours, such as after 11 p.m. and before 8 a.m. — or during any time window you don't expect conventional phone calls.

This approach isn't as convenient as having a dedicated line for the PowerKey Pro, because it eliminates being able to restart the server remotely at any time. But it's better than nothing.

A distinctive ring. Many phone companies offer distinctive ring service, in which you have multiple phone numbers assigned to a single line, and each number has its own unique ring pattern. The PowerKey Pro software supports distinctive ring, so if your phone company offers it, you might consider getting a distinctive-ring number and using it to control the PowerKey Pro.

Timbuktu: More remote-control power

Farallon Computing's Timbuktu remote-control software is another useful Web-server accessory. Timbuktu enables you to control one Macintosh from another over a network: you can choose commands, launch and quit programs, and restart. In fact, you can do anything that doesn't require access to the server's hardware.

In an office setting, Timbuktu gives you the flexibility to monitor and maintain your server from any computer on your network. When you're on the road, you can take advantage of Timbuktu's support for IP connections to connect to your server over the Internet itself. (You'll want a fast modem for this.)

SECRET

Timbuktu can even save you money by enabling you to create what's often called a *headless* server — one without a monitor connected to it. After configuring your server and installing Timbuktu, turn off the server and disconnect its monitor. Then start up the server and use another machine's copy of Timbuktu to control it.

The design of the video circuitry in most current Macs adds a minor complication to this scheme. In order for Timbuktu to work, you need to trick the Mac into thinking that a monitor is attached. The solution: connect a Macintosh-to-VGA adapter to the Mac's video port before booting up. This adapter, which you can get for under $20 from any Macintosh dealer or mail-order house, fools the machine into thinking it has a monitor, enabling Timbuktu to work its magic.

You can download a 30-day trial version of Timbuktu from Farallon's Web site, at `http://www.farallon.com/`.

Summary

- Although Windows and UNIX zealots may tell you otherwise, the Mac OS is a first-rate Web server platform, thanks to its ease of use and low cost; its security; and the ease with which you can write scripts in languages such as AppleScript and UserLand Frontier's UserTalk.
- StarNine's WebSTAR is the fastest, most capable Mac OS server package. Inexpensive alternatives include Social Engineering's Quid Pro Quo and Stairways Software's NetPresenz.
- Take the time to fine-tune WebSTAR's settings to optimize performance given your site's traffic and your connection speed.
- You can boost your server's performance through judicious use of a RAM disk and through careful page design.
- UserLand's Frontier and its object database are powerful tools for CGI scripting and creating dynamically updating Web sites.
- Tools such as Maxum's PageSentry, Sophisticated Circuits' PowerKey Pro, and Farallon Computing's Timbuktu can help you keep your server running reliably.

Chapter 17

Windows on the Web

In This Chapter

- Choosing a Windows platform
- Purchasing the right hardware for your server needs
- Selecting Windows Web server software
- Wringing the best performance from your server
- Organizing and customizing your Web site content
- Adding interactivity to your site with server-side programming
- Understanding and analyzing server log files
- Managing your Web server remotely

The Windows Web server world is a big place filled with big companies, not to mention plenty of acronyms and registry entries. As Director of Product Development for PC World Online, Adam Block keeps tabs on this world in the course of researching and developing new Web sites and electronic publications. He brings this experience to bear in this chapter, a guide to the key players, technologies, and optimizing techniques behind Windows Web serving. — Jim Heid

Wherefore Windows?

It doesn't matter who you tell that you are planning on setting up a Windows Web server; you're going to hear the same comment: "What about UNIX?" From your boss — who thinks his CD-ROM tray is a coffee cup holder — to the Dilbert-reading MIS guru down the hall, everybody seems convinced that a serious Web serving system should be noisy, heavy, and have a Sun Microsystems or Silicon Graphics logo on it. They're right. If, that is, your job description as Webmaster includes the following phrases:

- "Webmaster should frequently type lengthy, obscure commands into the server without having any real understanding of what they mean."
- "Webmaster must not use a handy graphical user interface under any circumstances."
- "Webmaster is expected to stay up nights worrying about which Web server security hole the hackers will locate next."

Now let's be fair. For the biggest sites, UNIX — which is actually a collective name for a dozen similar operating systems that run on hardware from IBM, HP, Sun, SGI, and other manufacturers — offers a number of advantages. UNIX servers *can* be faster and more fault-tolerant (able to withstand the failure of one or more components and keep running) than their Intel-powered siblings. In addition, because UNIX is a multiuser operating system designed to offer networking and remote control capabilities, system administration tasks may be more straightforward.

From the ease-of-use and entry-price perspectives, however, Windows beats UNIX hands down. Instead of fighting UNIX's steep learning curve, users who are comfortable with software installation and basic configuration on desktop PCs can fairly painlessly graduate to managing Windows NT servers. And while a well-equipped Windows NT Web server can be purchased from a top-name manufacturer for around $15,000, you may pay twice that for a midrange UNIX system from a company like Sun Microsystems. This price disparity has led a number of large Internet content providers to replace one or two UNIX servers with farms of inexpensive and identically configured Windows machines. This approach has the additional benefit of fault-tolerance: if one machine stops working, the other servers can pick up the slack.

From a security perspective, Windows is a clear winner. While there are still ways to break into a networked PC, Windows system software generally has far fewer holes that a determined hacker can exploit to damage your system or steal your data. Finally, though in the past new Web products and tools were first available on UNIX platforms and then were slowly ported to Windows, the current popularity of Windows — and Microsoft's vast development and promotional efforts in the Internet market — have reversed this trend. Windows server products and content creation tools are frequently released months before the UNIX versions, which more and more often never see the light of day.

What flavor of Windows do you prefer?

So running your Internet or intranet server on Windows is nothing to be ashamed of. But before you go about selecting the software you want to use, you have to answer one more question: What kind of Windows operating system software will you use? Off the top of your head, you can probably come up with at least five variants:

- Windows 3.1
- Windows for Workgroups
- Windows NT 3.51
- Windows 95
- Windows NT 4.0

Quite frankly, Windows 3.1 and its siblings (like Windows for Workgroups) simply aren't appropriate Web serving platforms. Not only are their networking capabilities unstable and nonstandard, but — unlike Windows 95 and Windows NT — they lack multithreading and protected memory, two OS features that greatly reduce the frequency of complete system lockup, or *hanging*.

The argument for Windows 95

Windows 95, currently the standard desktop operating system for new Intel-based PCs, is an acceptable choice for low-volume Web serving. However, Windows 95 has been tuned as a desktop operating system, which means it is optimized to run business applications (like Microsoft Office) at the expense of networking and file serving performance. In addition, because Microsoft — for compatibility reasons — erected Windows 95 atop some of the core DOS and Windows 3.1 code, Windows 95 is less secure and more crash-prone than Windows NT, which was engineered from the ground up for reliability. More about this shortly.

Windows 95 also has the hardware-compatibility advantage. Windows NT lacks plug-and-play hardware configuration, and although Microsoft has published a long list of NT-certified products, Windows 95 — which supports both 16- and 32-bit drivers — runs happily on virtually every PC system in existence. And while you can install Windows 95 on a 486 PC, Windows NT requires at least a Pentium 60 with 16MB of RAM.

The bottom line: If your server hardware happens to be an older PC (perhaps a 486 box that just can't handle the latest Microsoft Office without breaking into a sweat) or if you have less demanding Web server needs (maybe you're just setting up a small intranet site for a department or workgroup), by all means consider Windows 95 as your Web-server platform.

The argument for Windows NT

Windows NT, with its protective-memory architecture, runs all programs in their own rigidly confined memory space; if one badly behaved application bites the dust, it simply can't crash the system at large. In addition, because each NT driver — software that controls system peripherals such as video cards and CD-ROM drives — must strictly adhere to standards defined by Microsoft, the operating system can continuously monitor all aspects of the server to ensure that no rogue code can bring down the machine. Windows NT 3.51 still sports the ancient File Manager/Program Manager interface pioneered in Windows 3.1. Windows NT 4.0 updates the old look and feel with a Windows 95-style desktop.

In the final analysis, the overall server operating system leader is Windows NT 4.0. It's more expensive than Windows 95, requires more powerful hardware, and is less compatible with obscure peripheral devices. (Microsoft publishes on their Web site at `http://www.microsoft.com/isapi/hwtest/hsearchn4.idc` a list of hardware that is compatible with Windows NT 4.0; you'll want to review this list before you upgrade your operating system.) However, NT's dramatically increased network performance, stability, and security offset these drawbacks. Windows 95 will suffice for low-volume Web serving needs where you can't justify the cost of an NT box, and I'll be calling out Windows 95-specific tips throughout this chapter. But if you want to assemble a robust, dedicated Web server system, NT 4.0 is the platform for you. It's also the OS that the rest of this chapter assumes you are running, unless otherwise stated.

Of course, if you simply can't make up your mind about which Windows to install, or indeed whether to install Windows at all, there are versions of UNIX available that run on your PC: FreeBSD, BSDI, and Linux. Each one will run flawlessly on your desktop system, and each has compatible Web server software, including the free Apache, which by many accounts is the most popular high-end Web server software (for more information, see `http://www.apache.org/`).

If you go the UNIX route, you will have to compile your own operating system. But for the real computer nut who has lots of time to experiment and wants to squeeze the most possible speed out of a Pentium, UNIX may be the way to go.

NT Workstation versus NT Server

One important distinction that begs clarification is the difference between Windows NT 4.0 Workstation and NT 4.0 Server. To the apparent consternation of the majority of people who post messages to Internet newsgroups, Microsoft has deliberately reduced the network performance of NT Workstation, which the company bills as a desktop operating system featuring "high performance, and industrial-strength reliability and security."

Unlike NT 4.0 Server, which can support thousands of simultaneously connected users, Workstation has a hard-coded limit of 10 clients at any one time. This makes NT 4.0 Workstation fundamentally unsuitable for server work, which is exactly what Microsoft wants — NT Server costs about $400 more than NT Workstation (at this writing, the street price for Server is about $700; Workstation goes for approximately $270). NT 4.0 Server has also been internally modified to offer the best network server performance, while Workstation has been adjusted to run applications like spreadsheets and CAD programs more efficiently.

SECRET

The upshot of Microsoft's "de-engineering" of NT Workstation is that the product is actually less suited for Web serving than is Windows 95. If you decide to run an NT server, make sure that it's NT Server.

The Hardware Store

Now that you've selected the OS that is right for you, it's time to determine what kind of hardware you'll need to run your Web server. Assuming that you are starting from scratch (and I am), your first decision to make is what kind of PC system to purchase. The most common advice experts offer to those buying a new desktop PC is "buy as much system as you can afford," and that approach makes a lot of sense when selecting a server as well.

You may be tempted to look in the small ads in the back of your favorite computer magazine to try and sniff out a bargain basement system on which to run your Web site. But before you do so, think about how you want your site to perform. Is zero downtime your goal? Is it acceptable for users or clients to try to reach your site and to get a "Server unavailable" message instead? Experience has borne out the truism that in terms of system reliability, you get what you pay for: if you purchase from a reputable, well-known dealer — Hewlett-Packard, Dell, Compaq, IBM, and Digital come to mind — you will most likely have a much lower incidence of system failure in the future. And the generally excellent service policies of these companies mean that if something does go wrong, it will be fixed faster than if you buy from Larry's Discount Computer Basement. Don't get me wrong: companies other than those I mentioned above do make excellent hardware, and many offer generous support agreements. If you have a local dealer who builds PCs for you and with whom you have an excellent relationship, there may be no reason to look elsewhere for your Web server system. My point is simply that you should be sure to thoroughly analyze whether the money you save on an inexpensive box is worth the potential for long-term hassles.

Hardware configuration

CPU

Windows NT 4.0 Server won't run on anything lower than a Pentium-class machine. That's generally not a problem, because you can't buy a new 486 system today even if you want to. When determining what speed Pentium system you should buy, it helps to think about what services you are going to offer on your site. Are you going to let users post messages to a discussion thread system? Will you offer access to internal databases? Will search engines be available so that users can find exactly what they need among all the documents that you offer online? All of these items require server-side programs — applications that run alongside your Web server software to augment its capabilities; the more server-side programs you are running, the more powerful the processor that you need.

These days it's pretty tough to buy a PC slower than 166MHz from a major vendor; if you have a lot of these server-side programs, you will need a more powerful CPU — go with 200MHz minimum — to handle the load. A Pentium Pro-class machine is warranted for true heavy-duty use, and the price difference over a same-speed Pentium-based machine is often just a few hundred dollars. You will realize the best possible server performance by combining the fully 32-bit Windows NT operating system with Pentium Pro hardware, because Pentium Pro processors are optimized for 32-bit applications. Expect to pay a few hundred dollars more for a Pentium Pro machine versus a Pentium of equivalent processor speed.

Many PC manufacturers sell "server" systems configured with built-in network cards, extra room for multiple hard drives, and beefy power supplies. Do you need one of these systems to run a Web site? Absolutely not. But if you can afford one — they can cost twice as much as desktop systems with equivalent processors — server systems may offer significantly more reliability and better support policies (and the peace of mind that these amenities provide) than the typical desktop PC. I've run Web servers successfully for years on desktop-class machines; whether or not you buy a "server" system may depend on how much you really need space for 10 internal disks or that five-year warranty.

Hard disks

Your hard disk is critical to the health of your site, so don't be frugal when deciding what size and type to purchase. In addition, server add-ons, log analysis tools, and content creation utilities can rapidly gobble gigabytes of disk space.

It's always a good idea to put two or more drives into your server; by putting the server application on one drive and your Web files on another, you will distribute the disk load and speed up data retrieval. In addition, because Web serving is so disk-intensive, you may wish to purchase a SCSI interface and SCSI hard disks instead of the usual IDE or EIDE drives; SCSI has a 10 to 15 percent speed advantage over IDE. Be warned that it may be difficult to find NT 4.0 drivers for your SCSI card unless it comes from a well-known manufacturer like Adaptec; make sure to verify with your dealer that the appropriate software is available.

There are a number of new SCSI standards available, each of which promises improved drive performance. Wide-SCSI provides for data transfer between the hard drives and the server at twice the speed of Fast-SCSI, today's baseline standard. Ultra-SCSI (also called SCSI-3) provides an even greater boost, provided that you use the right cables and SCSI adapter. These SCSI variants *will* enhance the performance of your Web server — to a point. Because most Web servers deliver lots of relatively small documents, your server is unlikely to achieve the very high transfer rates promised by Wide- and Ultra-SCSI. Unless you expect your Web server to support very high traffic volumes, you'll probably see few gains from enhanced SCSI. If you do spend the extra dollars for a SCSI-3 or Wide-SCSI drive, make sure that your other hardware supports the new features, or you'll be throwing away your money (though virtually all SCSI devices are backward compatible with older equipment). Check the manufacturer's Web site to verify that you are buying compatible hardware, or better yet talk to a knowledgeable dealer.

Webmasters who seek true inner peace would be well advised to look into adding a RAID (redundant array of inexpensive disks) device to their server system. As the name suggests, a RAID combines a number of smaller disks (1, 2, or 4GB in general) into one "mega-disk." The advantage that a disk array has is that it can be configured for fault tolerance. In a RAID with three or more physical drives, one drive can be configured as backup; if a disk fails, the backup drive takes over, and the system stays up. You can then replace the failed drive at your leisure. While arrays can be expensive ($8,000 for a 3-disk, 8GB array is reasonable), they offer the ultimate way to guard against disk failure — and hard drives are the devices statistically most likely to give up the ghost. (If you're interested in learning more about RAID, you'll find a fine tutorial on the subject at `http://www.designphase.com/application/design_guides/raid_reference.html`.)

Backup devices

You've heard this advice before: back up your data. Now, backing up the personal information on your desktop PC is certainly important. But if something goes wrong with your Web server, not having a copy of the data stored on that server could cost you your job — or your business. There are a vast number of backup devices available; which type you choose depends on how much data you have on your server and how critical it is to keep it running. If your site is small, a single Iomega Zip or SyQuest EZFlyer cartridge — able to store 100 to 200MB or so — may be all the media you need to keep a duplicate copy of your data. If you accidentally erase a file, or a mischievous hacker messes with your system, you can manually replace the damaged elements from the removable drive.

If you have a larger site, or wish to back up the entire Web server to guard against system crash, you may wish to look at a large removable hard drive (like Iomega's Jaz) or a tape backup system. Travan-based tape drives like Iomega's Ditto are fairly inexpensive, back up 200 to 800MB of information, and are easy to set up and use. DAT (4mm) drives can store up to 8GB, and are popular with IS managers at small to midsize companies. Note that most 4mm drives require a SCSI adapter in your server system. With the right software (one popular option is ArcServe from Cheyenne; you can get more information at `http://www.cheyenne.com`), a server with a 4mm drive can back up multiple systems across your company's internal computer network. Windows NT ships with a simple tape drive-based backup package, which is adequate for single-server backups.

Very large sites may require even more storage horsepower. 8mm or DLT drives can store 20 to 70GB of data on each tape (though tapes can cost upwards of $100). Robotic tape jukeboxes are also available that can automatically eject and insert tapes in your absence. These advanced features make it easy to set up a complex automated backup schedule that will ensure that you always have a copy of your most recent data. It makes sense to talk to an experienced dealer or consultant about your options if you need one of these highly reliable (and expensive) backup systems.

One important point to remember is that hard disk or power supply failures are not the only traumas that could affect your server system. If the worst happens and the building that houses your server burns to the ground, you will kick yourself if your carefully designed backup strategy didn't include moving your backup media (whether it's tape, cartridge, or removable disk) offsite. You should always keep a recent copy of your data located in a different location from the server itself; that way you will be best insured against calamity. Check your yellow pages for the phone numbers of local companies that will perform this offsite-rotation service for a nominal fee. They'll pick up your backups once a week, and bring them back to you a few weeks later. In the interim, you will have copies of your valuable data safely stored in a secured facility away from your offices.

Network cards

Network interface cards (or NICs) are fairly straightforward items. You need to know the speed at which your network runs, and its *media* — the format of the physical cables that have been laid in your building. Most office networks are 10MBps Ethernet, running over either twisted pair (10BaseT) or coaxial (10Base2) cable. You can purchase NICs that support both media types if you prefer; they generally cost about $20 more.

Recently many companies have made the move to Fast Ethernet, which runs at 100MBps. Fast Ethernet cabling is always twisted pair (100BaseTX, usually). Most Fast Ethernet cards support standard 10BaseT Ethernet as well, and they only cost a few dollars more. If you can afford it, go with the 100BaseT card as a hedge against future network upgrades. If your server PC contains PCI expansion slots, make sure that whatever type of NIC you get sports a PCI interface. PCI offers far greater performance than the older ISA slot standard.

RAM

16MB is the minimum amount of RAM that you need to run Windows NT Server; buy at least 32MB. If you are going to run multiple Web servers on one physical machine (for example, if your marketing and HR departments each have their own intranet server), or if you expect to have a lot of server-side programs, spring for a lot more.

At PC World Online, we found that we could run four Netscape FastTrack Web servers on a single PC with no less than 96MB of memory, and that the system was much more comfortable with 128MB.

CD-ROM drive

You'll need a CD-ROM drive to install server and OS software. Period. Don't even think of trying to get by with a floppy drive alone. And don't borrow the CD-ROM from a friend just for the initial installation. All new PCs will come bundled with at least an 8x drive anyway. This is not the place to cut costs.

Monitor, PC, and mouse

This is the place to be frugal. Because the system that you are assembling will most likely sit in a corner somewhere and be touched by human hands only infrequently, feel free to forego buying a new monitor altogether. There is no sense in splurging on an expensive display that no one will spend much time looking at; if you have an old dusty VGA display out in the loading dock that no wants to use on a desktop PC, it may find a happy home atop your server. Or better yet, buy the nice 17-inch monitor with your new Web server, and then when it arrives swap the dim old 14-inch display on your desk with the brand new tube.

You may even be able to get by without a monitor, keyboard, or mouse at all if you are hooking up a number of PC servers. With a KVM (keyboard/video/mouse) switch box, you can hook multiple PCs into a single display, keyboard, and mouse, and switch between them at a keystroke or with the turn of a knob. Look for a switch box that provides a "keyboard signal." Most PCs won't boot correctly unless they sense that a keyboard is installed; switches with this feature send the appropriate electrical pulses to the computer during startup.

Sources for switch boxes include Black Box (`http://www.blackbox.com/`), DataComm Warehouse (`http://www.warehouse.com/`), and Inmac Corporation (`http://www.inmac.com/`).

Uninterruptable power supply

An uninterruptable power supply (UPS) is a big battery and AC inverter that installs between your server system and your building's power. When you have a brownout or suffer complete power loss, the UPS instantly delivers power to your hardware from the battery. You can purchase a very small UPS that gives you just enough time to shut down the server gracefully (it is not good for the system circuitry and components — particularly the hard disks — to suffer instant power loss), or one that will let your Web site stay up and running through an hours-long outage. Remember not to plug your monitor into the UPS; it needlessly drains battery power during a blackout and is not critical to your server's operation. If you need to turn on the display in order to manage the server during an outage, you can temporarily plug the monitor into the UPS by hand.

Shopping for Windows Web Server Software

There are dozens of Windows Web server packages. You probably have never heard of most of them, but they're out there. Languishing on the bottom shelf of computer store racks. Piled high in forgotten warehouses. Offered as free giveaways when you purchase ten dollars worth of gasoline at your local service station. When the Internet boom hit the software market in 1995, company after company thought that they could compete in the new marketplace, and they all rushed server software into development as fast their programmer's fingers could tap out the code.

Of course, as is the case in the browser market, there are many server products, but just a handful of truly successful standouts. In this section, I'll concentrate on Microsoft Internet Information Server, Netscape's FastTrack and Enterprise Servers, and O'Reilly's WebSite. I will also touch on related server products from the aforementioned companies. I focus on these products because they're the most popular and the best overall; if I don't cover your server software of choice, that doesn't mean it's worthless. What's more, many of the principles I'll describe apply to every Windows server package.

It's difficult to pick a clear standout among the three extremely popular server packages I'll be focusing upon; each has its strengths and weaknesses. Microsoft has a particularly strong market position because they bundle their IIS software with NT 4.0 Server. If you want to switch to another manufacturer's product (and you very well may), you'll have to pay the $100 to $500 difference. Thus while IIS is not the most flexible or adaptable Web server available, it is good enough that many NT Server buyers don't feel the need to look any further. Nevertheless, both Netscape and O'Reilly's entries outperform IIS in some ways; given the amount of money that you will invest to launch your site and to keep it up and running, spending a few hundred dollars more to acquire the software that best meets your needs may make good business sense.

Microsoft Internet Information Server

Microsoft's entry into the Web server market is a compact and easy to administer system that is installed automatically when you install Windows NT 4.0 Server. IIS is actually three servers in one: a gopher server for serving up text documents (before the advent of the World Wide Web with its graphical interface, gopher was a popular format for distributing textual information); an FTP (File Transfer Protocol) server to distribute files; and a Web (or HTTP) server. IIS is well integrated into the NT operating system (it uses NT file and directory permissions to control access to Web and FTP content, for example), and performs well in computer publication comparison tests. Microsoft has made a number of additions to IIS freely available at its Web site at `http://www.microsoft.com/ntserver/`. These additions include the following:

- **Active Server Pages** is a server-side scripting language that lets site developers deliver dynamically assembled Web pages customized to individual users.
- **Index Server** is a local search engine component that lets publishers offer users the ability to search the site's content (see Figure 17-1).
- **NetShow** is a multimedia server that can deliver audio and video clips directly into users' Web browsers.

If you're still using Windows NT 3.51, you can download IIS 2.0 from the URL listed above.

Microsoft also offers a limited version of IIS called Peer Web Services (PWS). Individuals within a company or workgroup who want to publish small amount of personal- or business-related content can use PWS to distribute such material locally; PWS is not an Internet server and will not work outside of a single office or network. However, because PWS acts so much like IIS in most respects, it can also be used as an effective test platform for Web site developers. Peer Web Services ships with Windows NT 4.0 Workstation. If you didn't install PWS when you set up Windows NT, you can go back and load it at any time: simply open the Network Control panel and select Add... from the Services tab. The Peer Web Services analog for Windows 95 is called — confusingly — Personal Web Server. You can download it from Microsoft's Web site at `http://www.microsoft.com/ie/download/`.

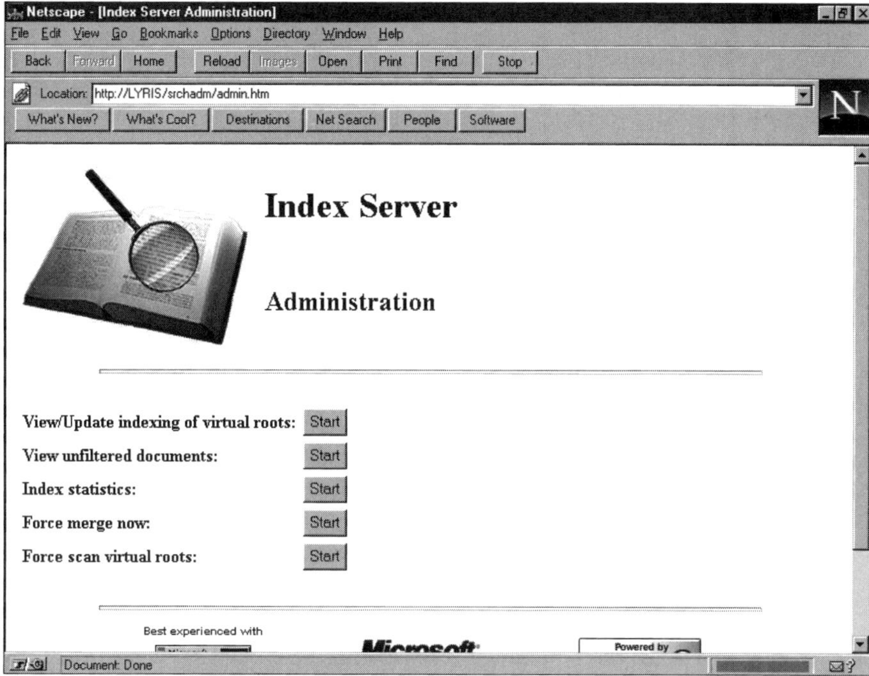

Figure 17-1: Microsoft Index Server's administration page

Netscape FastTrack and Enterprise servers

FastTrack server is Netscape's entry into the midrange server market. FastTrack boasts a Web-based administration tool for straightforward remote control, a management interface identical to its UNIX brethren, and highly customizable behavior. Unlike Microsoft, Netscape has chosen not to integrate FastTrack tightly into the NT operating system; as I'll describe in this section, this decision has both positive and negative ramifications. A version of FastTrack server for Windows 95 is also available.

Enterprise Server upgrades FastTrack by including a built-in search engine, native tools for connecting to enterprise database systems, a content management package, and Simple Network Management Protocol (SNMP) support. SNMP enables the Web server itself to be controlled by centralized network management applications like Hewlett-Packard's OpenView system. In addition, Enterprise Server is faster than FastTrack under heavy loads. An analysis performed by *PC Magazine* found that Enterprise server was able to support twelve simultaneous users before slowing down, whereas FastTrack began to lose steam with six open sessions. Remember that Web sessions open and close very quickly, so six simultaneous connections may equate to fifty users actively browsing your site at the same time. (This concept is explained in detail in the section "Only 35 Users at a Time?!", in the previous chapter.)

The Netscape products share nearly identical management interfaces (Enterprise Server's just has a few more buttons in each section), and all configuration files and setup routines are alike, regardless of product or platform. This approach encourages organizations to standardize on the Netscape Web server product line enterprise-wide.

You can download Netscape servers for evaluation purposes from Netscape's site at `http://www.netscape.com/`.

O'Reilly WebSite and WebSite Professional

O'Reilly & Associates offers a number of Windows-based Internet products, but the company is probably best known for its books on UNIX programming. This editorial strength is ably demonstrated by the manual that O'Reilly ships with its WebSite server; the manual is a 480-page tome that provides complete documentation of all product features as well as such niceties as a CGI programming guide and thorough tutorial. The WebSite application itself is a compact yet full-featured Web server that runs smoothly under either Windows NT or Windows 95.

If IIS provides perhaps too few administrator-controlled options within its sparse interface and Netscape overdelivers a bit within its cluttered Web forms, WebSite achieves a happy medium. The server control panel is a tabbed dialog box that you can call up at any time by clicking on the gear icon WebSite places in the tray area of the NT or Windows 95 task bar when it is running. From this dialog box, the system administrator can access all server functions. Wizards are available to provide step-by-step guidance through complex procedures like setting up multiple servers on different IP addresses (so that one WebSite installation could host servers at both `http://www.daytime.com/` and `http://www.nighttime.com/`, for example). Detailed Windows help is available for all functions.

The Standard version of WebSite is available for free trial download at `http://software.ora.com/download/`.

O'Reilly has addressed the needs of sophisticated Webmasters and large content providers with a more advanced server called WebSite Professional. WebSite Pro is built on WebSite's capable foundation, but extends the package with a host of server-side programming tools that allow Web developers to write high performance Internet applications in a variety of languages, including Perl, Java, and Visual Basic (see the section "Who Is This CGI Guy, Anyway?", later in this chapter).

WebSite Professional supports secure (or encrypted) client-to-server transactions, and ships with a custom version of the Allaire Cold Fusion database access toolkit, which lets Webmasters connect their Web server to corporate database systems on a variety of platforms. (You can read more about Cold Fusion in Chapter 10.)

Which server package is for you?

You may not need to select a Web server at all — Microsoft may have already done it for you. If you've purchased NT 4.0 Server, by all means experiment with the IIS installation that came with it; you may find that it meets your needs completely, or that the additional components that Microsoft offers at its Web site round out their offering sufficiently. However, if the Netscape or O'Reilly (or another manufacturer's) servers sound intriguing — or if you simply don't like the idea of Microsoft making your choices for you — don't hesitate to download these alternate packages and give them a try. All of these servers can actually be running on the same machine at the same time — with the right tweaks to the network settings — so a head-to-head comparison is theoretically possible.

If you find it difficult to decide which product you prefer, consider the following bases for comparison:

- **Management interface.** The controls used to set up and administer the server should be straightforward and intuitive. If you wish to administer your Web server remotely, a Web-based administration tool may be a big plus.
- **Security or access control features.** You may be far more concerned about security features and the ability to block out unwanted users if you are developing a Web site for your company than if you are simply creating a personal home page. Options such as encryption and IP address filtering can help you fend off hackers.
- **Flexibility of content management.** Webmasters spend a lot of time tweaking their server to present content in just the right way. You'll want a package that offers lots of flexibility (such as customized error messages) as well as time-saving features like automatic headers and footers.

You probably needn't worry too much about variations in performance from package to package; all three of these Web servers are well-constructed multithreaded applications, and as such each should be responsive enough to meet your needs unless you place extreme loads on your server.

Secrets of Top Performance

Regardless of which server software you're using, a Web server running on a 200MHz Pentium CPU with 32MB of RAM will be an awfully fast system fresh out of the box. Nevertheless, whatever the size of the site that you manage, sooner or later you'll find yourself saying, "Hmm…I wish our Web site responded more quickly when I click on a link." This desire for better performance is fundamentally a good sign — it means that your site is popular and is generating user traffic from the Internet (or from within your company in the case of an intranet site). Maybe your site is generating more traffic than it can handle.

So how do you address a usage overload — add another PC? Perhaps. But before you spend a lot of money and time researching and installing new hardware, you should ensure that your current server is configured to deliver its maximum potential.

Turn off what you don't need

A valuable bit of general performance-tuning advice is, "If you aren't using it, turn it off." Novice Webmasters frequently leave default system settings in place either because they don't know these parameters exist or because they are afraid of doing some harm to a running application. But these settings — probably dreamed up by some wizard in Microsoft's technical marketing department — tend towards the wasteful side in terms of system resources.

When you install Windows NT, a number of networking protocols you probably don't need are installed by default. To find out which ones, go to the Start menu and choose Settings ➪ Control Panel. In the Control Panel window, double-click on Network. Click on the Protocols tab to see what networking protocols you have enabled (see Figure 17-2). Do you see NetBEUI (used to connect NT servers or Windows 95 machines together) or NWLink IPX/SPX Compatible Transport (used to connect to Novell NetWare servers) in the list? If so, and if you aren't in need of those protocols — ask your network administrator if you are unsure — select them one by one and click Remove.

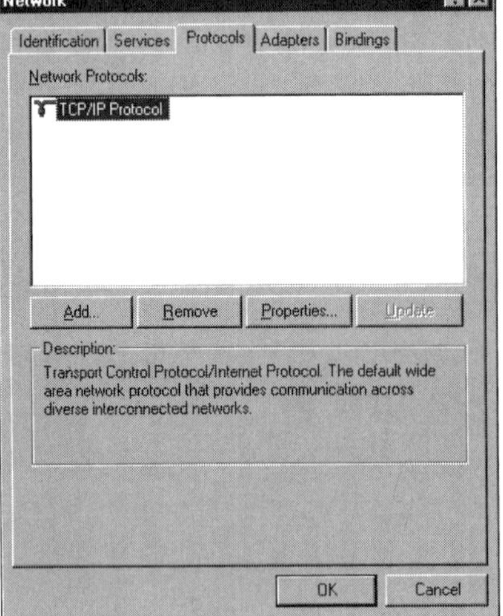

Figure 17-2: Network control panel, showing installed networking protocols

The Novell client protocol in particular is a major resource hog; you may see a fifteen to twenty percent improvement in network performance if you remove the IPX/SPX driver. Just remember not to mess with the TCP/IP driver; you'll need that one for Internet services.

Stay up-to-date

Microsoft constantly updates its system software. In many cases, these updates contain refinements or bug fixes that improve network performance significantly, so it is always a good strategy to keep your operating system software as up-to-date as possible in order to take advantage of these tweaks. If you are using Windows NT 4.0, you can find system patches (called Service Packs) on Microsoft's Web site at `http://www.microsoft.com/ntserversupport/Default-SL.HTM`. Upgrades to Web server software are also released frequently, and may be found at the following sites:

- Microsoft IIS: `http://www.microsoft.com/iis/`
- Netscape FastTrack & Enterprise Servers: `http://help.netscape.com/filelib.html`
- O'Reilly WebSite: `http://software.ora.com/techsupport/software/`

The good old .INI days

If you are a former (or current) Windows 3.1 user, you know about .INI files — text files in which application software and Windows itself maintained system configuration information. SYSTEM.INI and WIN.INI in particular — two essential Windows 3.1 data files — were notorious among system administrators as black holes of obscure system settings and mysterious switches that if disturbed could render a CD-ROM drive, sound card, or entire PC completely unusable.

The good news is that Windows 95 and NT generally forego the use of .INI files to store critical system parameters. The bad news is that this information is now buried even deeper within Windows, and you can wreck your system just as quickly as before if you mess with the wrong bit.

Windows NT stores information about the system and installed software and hardware components in the Registry — an internal database of *keys* (parameters) and *values* (the data associated with those parameters). And while NT itself maintains virtually all critical server settings in the Registry, application vendors such as Netscape and O'Reilly are under no Microsoft mandate to do so — they have the option of storing as many or as few of their configuration switches there as they please.

Thus depending on what server you are using, you may or may not have to go mucking about in the Registry to tune its behavior. If you use IIS, in all likelihood you will want to at some point pop the hood and tinker around — carefully. But I want to stress again that the potential maximum performance gains are probably on the order of 5 percent or less. If you are simply not comfortable with the knowledge that an errant keystroke here or there could (in the absolute worst case) make your system unusable, simply skip over the rest of this section. You aren't likely ever to miss the knowledge. But if you really want to know what Web server settings and switches are hidden from the casual administrator, or if you crave the title "Windows Web Server Guru," read on.

One more thing before we start. All of the information on IIS, Netscape products, and WebSite in this section will let you make incremental adjustments to the server's operation in hopes of improving performance. However, nothing can speed up the display of your pages if you used GIF images when JPEGs were more appropriate, or if every screen has a massive background picture, or if you used a dozen graphical navigation buttons when a single image-map graphic would have been more efficient. Remember that one of the best ways to boost any Web server is to design your pages with bandwidth efficiency in mind. Techniques to improve the overall performance of your pages are covered in Chapter 6 and Chapter 16.

Registry rules

To access the Registry, choose Run from your system's Start menu, and type **regedt32.exe** (in Windows 95, type **regedit.exe**). This will launch the Registry Editor. You will see four windows within the application interface; each window contains a set of keys and values for a specific part of the system (see Figure 17-3). The keys are arranged hierarchically, and the interface operates much like the Windows Explorer. All keys in a given directory are shown in the right hand window along with their associated values; you can double click a key-value pair to edit the value.

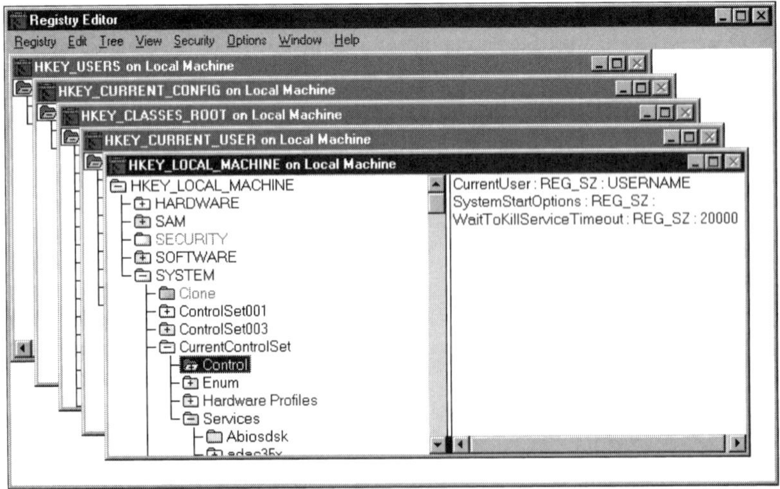

Figure 17-3: The Windows Registry editor

IIS management: Better get used to the Registry

In true Microsoft fashion, the IIS management module — called the Internet Service Manager (ISM) and accessible from the Programs submenu off of the Start menu — offers little control over IIS's internal behavior (see Figure 17-4). As a Webmaster you can bring IIS in line; you will just have to be comfortable with the Registry Editor in order to do so. Table 17-1 describes in detail the different Registry and Internet Service Manager settings that you may wish to adjust to squeeze the maximum performance from your copy of IIS. The entries are arranged with the most important parameters near the top of the table; I've moved the more obscure items towards the bottom.

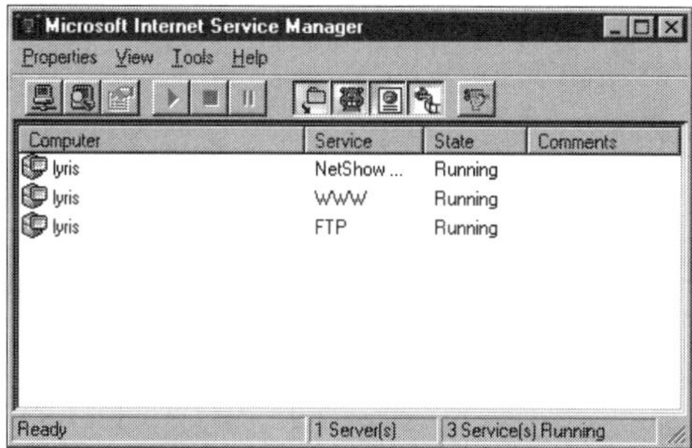

Figure 17-4: Microsoft's Internet Service Manager for IIS

Netscape servers: limited options

The Netscape server management tool is a Web server in its own right, specially configured as an administrative aid. Because it acts like a standard Web server, you can access this so-called Administration Server from anywhere in the world that you have an Internet connection and a Web browser (see Figure 17-5).

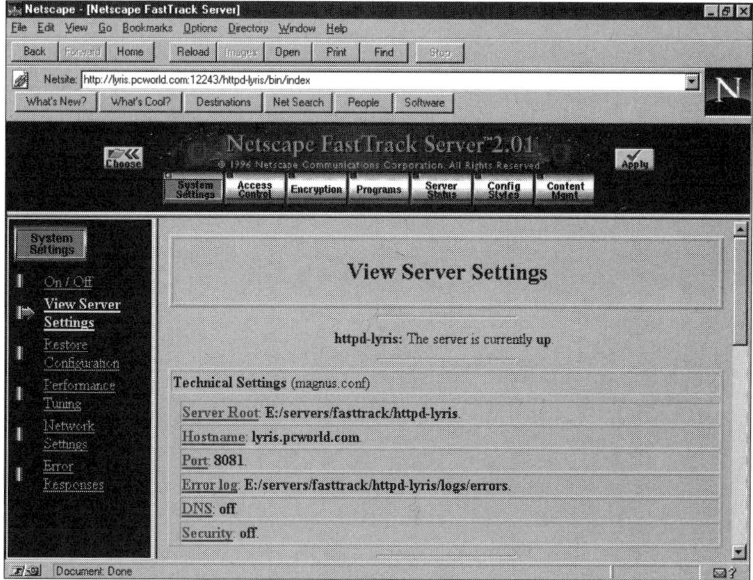

Figure 17-5: The Netscape administration server

Table 17-1 Registry and Internet Service Manager settings

Setting	*What It Does*	*How to Access It*	*What to Set It To*
Internet Connection Timeout	Defines the amount of time that IIS waits before shutting down a connection with a Web browser.	Go to ISM; Double-click on the WWW service; Select the Service tab.	The default setting of 900 seconds (15 minutes) should be fine, unless you have server-side programs on your site that run for a very long time.
Maximum Number of Connections	Defines the total number of simultaneous Web browser connections that IIS will open. Excess connection requests beyond this maximum setting will be queued by the server and handled sequentially.	Go to ISM; Double-click on the WWW service; Select the Service tab.	Web connections generally are opened and closed very quickly (unless the user has a very slow modem), so you don't want to set this number too low. However, setting it too high may reduce the bandwidth available to connected users by allowing too many simultaneous connections. In general, it's safe to set this parameter to the speed of your connection to the Internet (measured in KBbps) divided by five. For example, if you have a frame relay (56 KBbps) connection to your Internet service provider, set the maximum connections to 11 (56 / 5 = about 11).
Limit Network Use By All Internet Services	This setting affects all IIS services (gopher and FTP as well as Web service), and imposes a hard limit on the total amount of your network bandwidth that these services can consume.	Go to ISM; Double-click on the WWW service; Select the Advanced tab.	This setting is designed to artificially limit the amount of network bandwidth that your server consumes. It is useful in a situation where your system shares an Internet connection with other vital services (such as telecommuting workers) and you want to limit your server's impact.

Setting	*What It Does*	*How to Access It*	*What to Set It To*
Listen Backlog	Web servers accept connection requests from browsers even if they cannot service them immediately (they may be busy delivering data to other clients). The listen backlog setting defines how many of these queued requests the system will accept before refusing new connections.	Locate the Registry entry HKEY_LOCAL_MACHINE\System\CurrentControlSet\Services\InetInfo\Parameters\ListenBackLog	IIS does a generally good job of managing the listen backlog setting internally. Heavily used sites may get some performance improvement by setting this number higher than the default of 15. 50 is the maximum size for the listen backlog queue.
Maximum Pool Threads	This entry defines how many system threads (internal processes) are assigned to wait for incoming Web connections.	Locate the Registry entry HKEY_LOCAL_MACHINE\System\CurrentControlSet\Services\InetInfo\Parameters\MaxPoolThreads	The default setting of 10 threads is appropriate for a single-CPU server. If your have a multiprocessor server, set the maximum number of threads to 10 times the number of processors that you have installed.
Maximum Cache Size	IIS uses an internal memory cache to store frequently used data such as the server directory structure. This setting defines the size of that cache.	Locate the Registry entry HKEY_LOCAL_MACHINE\System\CurrentControlSet\Services\InetInfo\Parameters\MaxCacheSize	If you have a lot of system RAM in your Web server (over 80MB), you can increase this parameter from its default of 3072000 bytes (3MB). You won't see much of an increase beyond 5MB (5120000 bytes).
Object Cache Time-To-Live	In addition to the memory cache, the IIS server caches Web objects (such as HTML pages and images) that it delivers frequently. The Time-To-Live setting defines how long those objects stay in the cache before they are erased and reloaded from the hard disk.	Locate the Registry entry HKEY_LOCAL_MACHINE\System\CurrentControlSet\Services\InetInfo\Parameters\ObjectCacheTTL	If you have a large amount of system RAM in your Web server (over 80 MB), and if your pages are largely static and change infrequently, you can disable the process that erases the object cache by setting this parameter to 0xFFFFFFFF.

The Administration Server runs on the same hardware as your regular Web server, but on a different port. (All Internet communications take place on default ports specified by an Internet standards body. Web service, for example, generally runs on port 80, while e-mail is delivered between mail servers on port 25.) Port numbers above 1024 (up to 65,535) are not officially assigned to any service; thus when you install a Netscape Web server, it selects a random port number above 1024 on which you can reach the Admin Server (of course the installation program tells you what port it chose). If the selected port is 1999, for example, in order to access the administration tools from your Web browser you would have to type **http://www.myserver.com:1999** into the Open… dialog box. If you try to connect to the Netscape Administration Server from outside of a corporate firewall, you may find that the admin port selected by the installation software is blocked for security reasons. Speak to your IS manager or system administrator if the Admin Server seems unresponsive.

The first Admin Server screen lets you select from the installed Web servers (see Figure 17-6). You can have many servers running on one machine, as previously mentioned. Click the name of the server you want to manage in order to see its particulars.

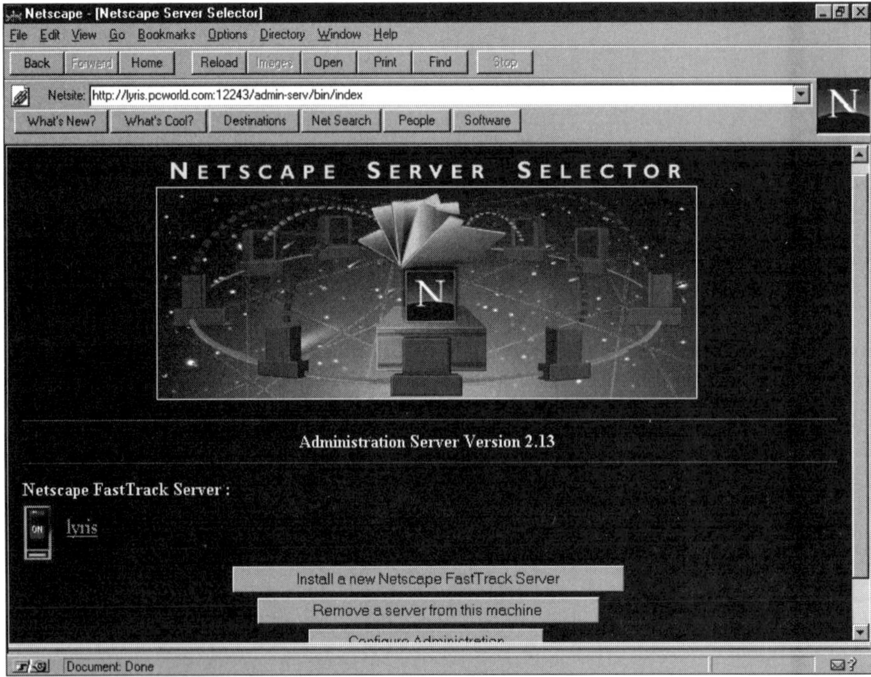

Figure 17-6: The Netscape Server Selector, part of the administration server

The Netscape servers offer only two basic performance enhancement settings, both of which are readily accessible from the Administration Server (see Figure 17-7). Both of these attributes are related to the use of DNS lookup by the Web server (see Table 17-2). As I will explore in detail later (see the section entitled "What is Your Server Doing While You Sleep?"), Web servers generate log files as requests for HTML pages and images come in. These log files contain the IP address (an eight-byte number uniquely identifying each computer on the Internet) of the client's machine.

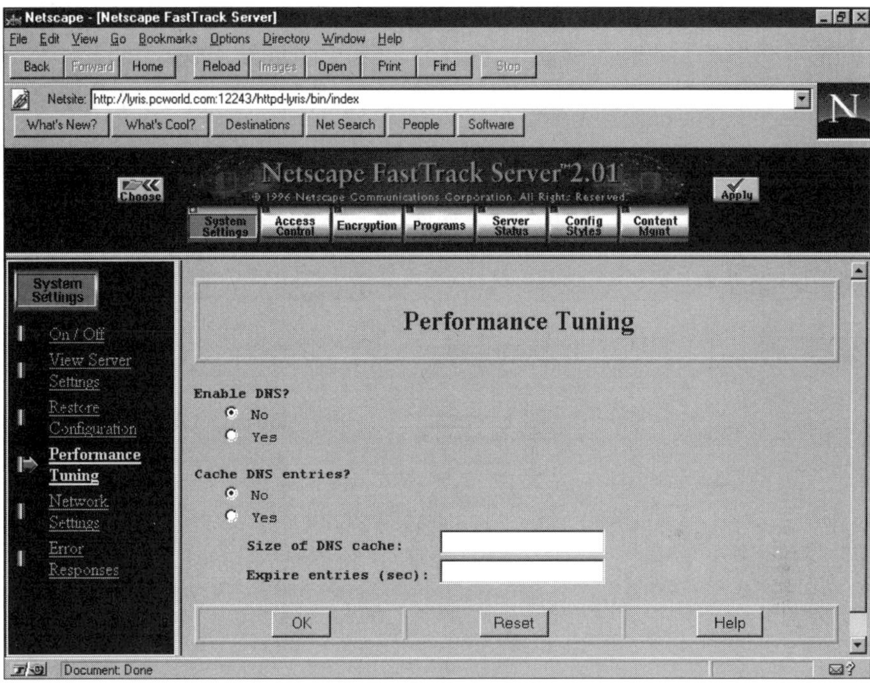

Figure 17-7: Defining DNS settings for best performance on a Netscape server

IP addresses are pretty meaningless in their raw form — they look like this: 131.119.246.8. But your Web server can often convert IP addresses into a more meaningful form (such as `jimheid01.mcn.org`) through a process called DNS (Domain Name Service) lookup. Performing this lookup effort as your log files are written makes them much easier to read. However, because each lookup can take up to fifteen seconds to return an answer, enabling DNS lookup can significantly slow your server's response time. Furthermore, with the appropriate tool you can retroactively perform DNS lookups against your log file data at a later date.

Table 17-2 DNS lookup settings

Setting	*What It Does*	*How to Access It*	*What to Set It To*
Enable DNS Lookup	Turns on DNS lookup for clients accessing your Web site.	In the Admin Server, choose the desired Web server. Select the "System Settings" button in the top frame. Click the Performance Tuning tab in the left frame.	If you have a site with minimal traffic and want as much detail about your visitors as possible, set this attribute to Yes. Set it to No to reduce load on the Web server.
Cache DNS Entries?	If you decide to enable DNS lookups, you should cache these values so that the server does not have to perform multiple lookups for the same user during a given session. You can also define the size of the cache and how long the cache entries persist before they are erased from memory.	In the Admin Server, choose the desired Web server. Select the "System Settings" button in the top frame. Click the Performance Tuning tab in the left frame.	Set this to Yes if you have DNS lookups enabled. The default value for the number of cached DNS entries is 1024; you can increase this if you have a very active site. The default amount of time that cache entries remain in memory is 1200 seconds (20 minutes). This is sufficient for almost any site since the length of a user's session isn't likely to exceed ten minutes or so at any one location.

Table 17-3 WebSite's performance-management parameters

Setting	*What It Does*	*How to Access It*	*What to Set It To*
Maximum Simultaneous Connections	Defines the total number of simultaneous Web browser connections that WebSite will open. Excess connection requests beyond this maximum setting will be queued by the server and handled sequentially.	Go to Server Properties; Select the General tab.	Web connections generally are opened and closed very quickly (unless the user has a very slow modem), so you don't want to set this number too low. However, setting it too high may reduce the bandwidth available to connected users by allowing to many simultaneous connections. In general, it's safe to set this parameter to the speed of your connection to the Internet (measured in KBbps) divided by three. For example, if you

			have a frame relay (56KBbps) connection to your Internet service provider, set the maximum connections to 18 (54 / 3 = about 18). If you are using HTTP Keep-Alive, which enables the server to send multiple items to the browser in one transaction (turn on Keep-Alive by checking the Hold connections open for re-use box), you should divide your bandwidth by five instead of three.
Send and Receive Timeouts	These entries define the maximum amount of time that a connection between server and browser can be held open.	Go to Server Properties; Select the General tab.	If your server's connection to the Internet is slow (56KBbps or less), feel free to increase the timeout to up to 120 seconds to prevent large files from timing out. If you have database access or programs built in to your pages that take a long time to run, you may want to go higher than that. Experiment with your server to see if you are receiving the requested data before the timeout occurs. On a busy server connected to the Internet via a fast line, you should limit timeouts to 30 seconds so that broken connections don't remain open for too long, blocking other transactions from being processed.
Enable DNS Reverse Lookup	Turns on DNS lookup for clients accessing your Web site. (for details, see "Netscape servers: limited options" earlier in this chapter)	Go to Server Properties; Select the Logging tab.	If you have a site with minimal traffic and want as much detail about your visitors as possible, set this attribute to Yes. Set it to No to reduce load on the Web server.

WebSite: just the basics

WebSite offers a few standard performance-management parameters (see Table 17-3), all of which are available through its Server Properties dialog box (see Figure 17-8). To display the Server Properties dialog box, right-click on the gear icon that appears in the Windows task bar's tray area. (If you don't see the gear icon, WebSite isn't running.) You can also open the Server Properties dialog box through the Start menu: choose Server Properties from the WebSite submenu in the Programs submenu.

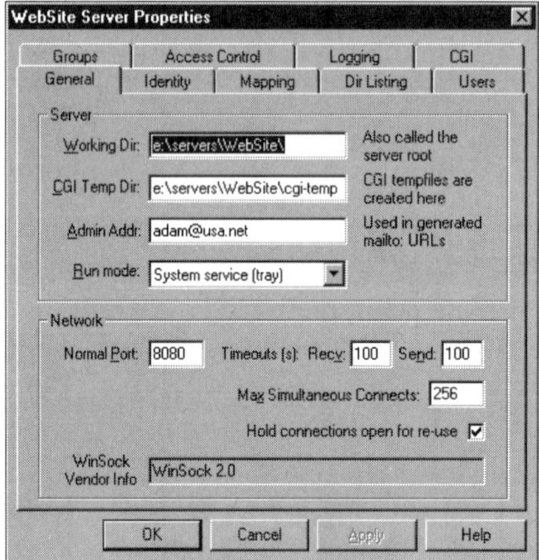

Figure 17-8: Performance tuning with O'Reilly WebSite

Managing Your Web Content

Webmasters must administer dozens, hundreds, or even thousands of HTML pages, images, and server scripts. Keeping track of these files, and controlling how the server displays them — and to whom they get displayed — can be a massively intricate and time-consuming operation. For this reason, developers of Web server software have added various functions to their packages designed to address the complexity of the content-management process. Of course, approaches that simplify management may at the same time reduce flexibility, and Webmasters may find that the software that they selected initially for its straightforward interface proves too restrictive as their Web site matures. As you read the following section, take time to think about your particular needs as a Webmaster and whether the manufacturer of the Web server software you plan to use has addressed the balance between server complexity and server features in a way that meets those needs.

Management tools

Server manufacturers recognize that developing Web content is an involved process, and that keeping track of hundreds of linked elements can be hopelessly difficult. To this end, these companies have developed —

in parallel with the creation of the server software packages themselves — graphical tools that make it easier for Webmasters and HTML producers to oversee entire sites. You can certainly build and administer even a very large online presence without using one of these products — some of the largest and most heavily trafficked sites on the Web are managed completely by hand, sans management tools. However, beginning Webmasters may find that these software packages allow them to create more engaging and interactive online sites — much more quickly and with far less training — than they otherwise could.

Netscape LiveWire

Netscape introduced LiveWire, a suite of tools for creating and publishing online content, which costs approximately $300. It is available bundled with FastTrack server for approximately $500 and is included with Enterprise Server. LiveWire includes the following applications:

- Navigator Gold, Netscape's combination browser and HTML editor (Netscape offers a more advanced page-composition package called Composer, which ships as part of Communicator [also called Navigator 4.0]; Communicator is expected to be released in April 1997).
- Site Manager, a Windows Explorer-like program that displays a graphical overview of how your site is laid out. Site Manager also lets you drag and drop HTML files and directories from one location to another; the program ensures that pages with links are automatically updated so you don't have to make manual corrections.
- JavaScript Compiler, a tool that lets Web developers create custom server applications.
- A data access tool used to tie JavaScript applications into corporate information stores.

The Pro version of LiveWire (which costs approximately $700, versus $300 for the standard version) includes a runtime Informix database license and a reporting tool for analyzing your Web traffic.

Microsoft FrontPage

Microsoft also offers a site management product, called FrontPage, recently updated to FrontPage 97. FrontPage, described briefly in Chapter 4, includes all of the standard site management tools — HTML editor, graphical site overview, and link checking — but also ships with an image editing tool, Internet news and electronic mail clients, and the Internet Explorer Web browser. Because Microsoft has tried to position FrontPage as a complete, standalone tool for Web content creation, it also supports the development of interactive surveys, links to server-side databases, and the creation of client-side ActiveX, VBScript, and JavaScript applets. Tight integration with Microsoft Office enables FrontPage to tie into Office features such as the spelling checker dictionary, thesaurus, and global search and replace without requiring you to switch between programs.

O'Reilly WebView

O'Reilly & Associates's WebSite series include WebView (see Figure 17-9), a basic content management application. WebView enables you to oversee the structure of your site in a hierarchical view similar to the Windows Explorer. It also provides links to the various server and content management tools that ship with WebSite, including the Server Properties administration form, the WebIndex search collection tool, and an imagemap editor. Unfortunately, WebView's interface is confusing and its application fairly limited. If you want to use a management application that provides a graphical overview of your Web site's structure, FrontPage is a better bet and integrates well with WebSite.

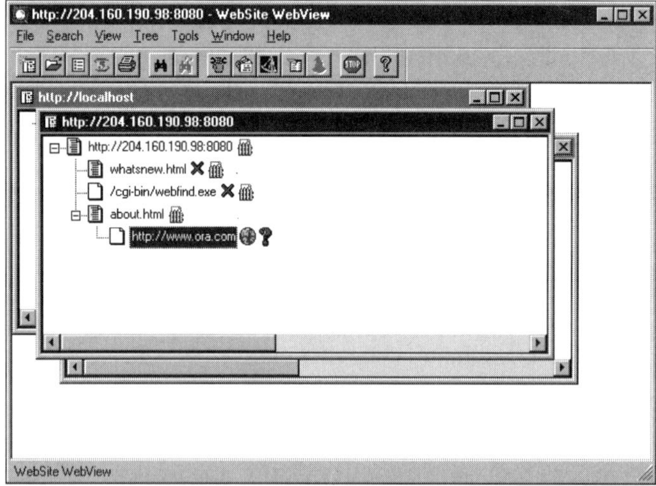

Figure 17-9: O'Reilly WebView

Mastering server content

The concept of Web content management does not refer to any one practice or technique; rather, it suggests the successful organization of a multitude of HTML documents, images, and program files into a cohesive unit — the site in its entirety. As mentioned above, servers offer a variety of built-in tools to help site managers control how their pages are accessed and displayed. While the documentation that comes with your Web server software will cover the basics of setting up your Web site, I've focused below on a number of challenging topics that deserve closer scrutiny by the aspiring Webmaster.

Virtual directories

When you set up a Web server, you must define at least one directory on your PC's hard disk as the Web content directory, or *document root*. This folder can also be thought of as the top-level directory that holds HTML pages and images. As you might imagine, it would be inconvenient to have to serve, say, your entire C: drive; not only would a lot of miscellany in c:\windows\system be open to your users, but you would expose a number of serious system security risks as well. For this reason, all server software lets you specify which directories on your hard drive (or drives if you have more than one) will contain the information that you want to publish on the Internet. When you define more than one directory to store Web content, you have to tell the server how to *map* the real location of the data on your disk to its virtual location on your site. For example, you might define the real and virtual directory pairs that are shown in Table 17-4.

Table 17-4 Setting up virtual directories

Physical Location	*Virtual Directory*	*Notes*
C:\netscape\fasttrack\docs	`http://www.mycompany.com/`	Primary document root
C:\my documents\ spreadsheets\budgets	`http://www.mycompany.com/budgets/`	Secondary document root to hold budgetary data
C:\netscape\scripts	`http://www.mycompany.com/cgi-bin/`	Directory to store server programs
D:\reference\stocksymbols	`http://www.mycompany.com/stocks/`	Secondary document root located on a CD-ROM
X:\office_server\ reports\quarterly	`http://www.mycompany.com/quarterly_reports/`	Secondary document root stored on a network drive

As you can see, the actual names of the directories that hold the files you wish to serve may be very different from the directory names they are mapped to on your Web server. However, all of the data stored in these directories will appear the same to visitors, whether it is viewed through the Windows Explorer or over the Internet. Special virtual directories may be used to store specific kinds of data, such as CGI programs.

Netscape servers

To define the primary document root — remember, that's where most of your Web documents will be stored — for your Netscape server, select the Content Mgmt button in the Administration Server. Click the first item in that section, entitled Primary Document Directory. Then simply enter a complete path name (such as, c:\netscape\fasttrack\docs) into the field provided. Click the OK button when you are finished (see Figure 17-10).

If you want to add additional document directories, click Additional Document Directories. Here you will need to first enter the URL prefix that you want to map, followed by the absolute path to the appropriate content directory on your hard disk. For example, to map "`http://www.mycompany.com/budgetinfo`" to "c:\my documents\budgets," you would type **budgetinfo** into the "URL prefix" field and the complete path information into the Map to directory box.

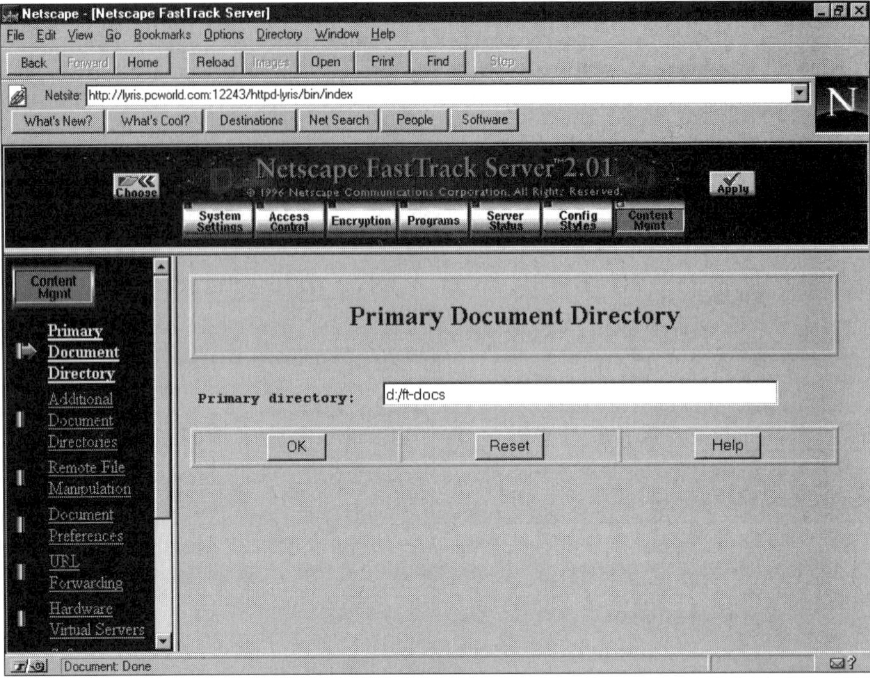

Figure 17-10: Defining a Netscape server's document root

Microsoft IIS

Open the Internet Service Manager and double-click the WWW service. Select the Directories tab. You may edit an existing directory mapping, or click on Add… to create a new one (see Figure 17-11). In the Directory Properties dialog box that pops up, locate the appropriate content directory on your hard disk using the Browse… button (or type in the path directly). If you are specifying the primary document root for your server, click the Home Directory radio button. Otherwise, type the name of the virtual directory you want to map into the Alias field. Remember to precede the virtual directory name with a slash (/).

O'Reilly WebSite

Open the WebSite Server Properties dialog and select the Mapping tab (see Figure 17-12). Make sure that the Documents radio button is selected in the lower left corner of the window. To edit an existing virtual directory mapping, select it from the pick list. Otherwise, simply enter the URL prefix in the Document URL Path field; make sure that the directory name is prefixed *and* followed by a slash (/). You may specify the primary document root here by typing only a slash. Then enter the complete path to the appropriate directory on your hard drive into the Directory box.

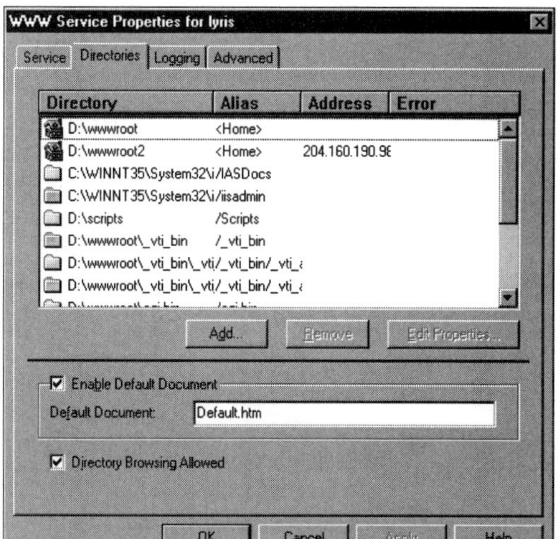

Figure 17-11: Setting up document directories in IIS

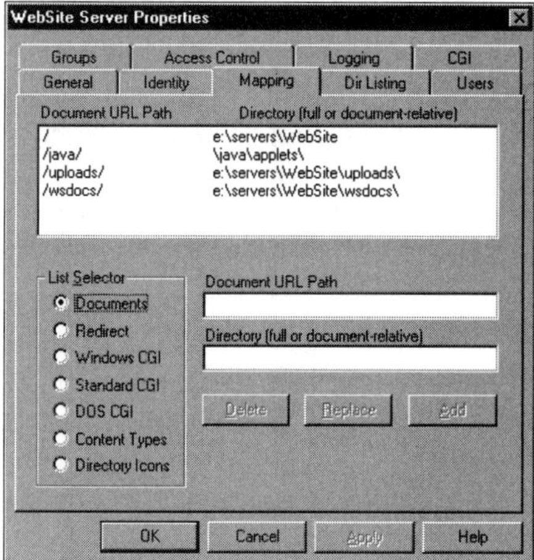

Figure 17-12: Virtual directory mapping with O'Reilly WebSite

Default pages

You are probably aware that `http://www.yourcompany.com/news` is a valid URL, even though the visitor didn't indicate exactly which Web page — *index.html* for example — he or she wished to see. What will the user see when a directory name is specified but the page name is left off? The server will display the *default page* (sometimes called an index page) for the given directory — for example, in this case the user might see `http://www.yourcompany.com/news/index.html`, if index.html was the defined default page. Let's look at a couple more examples of default pages:

DEFAULT PAGE DEFINED AS:	USER TYPES:	PAGE USER GETS:
default.asp	`http://www.slate.com`	`http://www.slate.com/default.asp`
index.html	`http://www.cnn.com/SPORTS/`	`http://www.cnn.com/SPORTS/index.html`

As you can see, default pages may differ between sites; you choose a document name that works well for your particular Web presence. The index page is defined in the Web server's administration tools (or in the Windows Registry, in the case of IIS). The following sections explain how to set one up yourself.

Netscape Servers

Using the Netscape Administration server, select the site that you want to manage. Click the Content Mgmt button and select Document Preferences on the left side of the window. The Index filenames field contains a comma-separated list of default pages; if the server finds more than one matching index page in a given directory (say you have created both an *index.htm* and an *index.html*), the order in which they are listed determines preference.

Microsoft Internet Information Server

Open the Internet Service Manager Application, and double-click the WWW service. From the Directories tab, check the Enable Default Document box if you wish to allow users to access a specific index file (in general you will want to enable this option). You can then edit the file name in the Default Document box; the standard setting is *Default.htm*.

O'Reilly WebSite

Open the Server Properties application, and click on the Dir Listing tab. In the Special Documents section of the window, the field named Default specifies the index page. You can use the Windows wildcard character * (asterisk) to define multiple acceptable default filenames. For example, if you set the value of the Default field to *index.**, the server would accept *index.htm*, *index.html*, or even *index.txt* as the default page.

Customizing error messages

We've all seen it. The dreaded "Document Not Found" message — also known as a 404 for the error code that the server sends to a browser when it can't find the specified page. As a Web content provider, you'll never be able to ensure that every page containing a link to your site is error-free, and you will find that mistakes creep in to even the material that you produce. The result is that visitors will be happily cruising a site when a missing page or an ill-defined link will stop their progress cold.

You can't prevent 404s completely, but there is a solution to the broken-link blues: make sure that if a user somehow finds an error on your site, they will be gracefully fed back into your home page or to other material of interest. This user-friendly site upgrade requires replacing the default "document not found" page with a more sophisticated and informative one. Netscape servers make this easy, but IIS and WebSite don't support this functionality out of the box; I'll tell you the secrets to effecting the four-oh-four fix on Microsoft's and O'Reilly's offerings. Whatever server product you have, definitely *do* install a custom error page; your users will thank you by sending significantly less complaint e-mail.

Netscape servers

Netscape offers the Webmaster lots of error-handling flexibility. While the servers' default error pages are pretty uninformative, it's easy to add unique customized messages for different types of server errors. You can even run a server-side program in the event of an error; we use such a program on our site at PC World Online to notify us of broken links automatically via e-mail, even if the user doesn't file a complaint (see Figure 17-13).

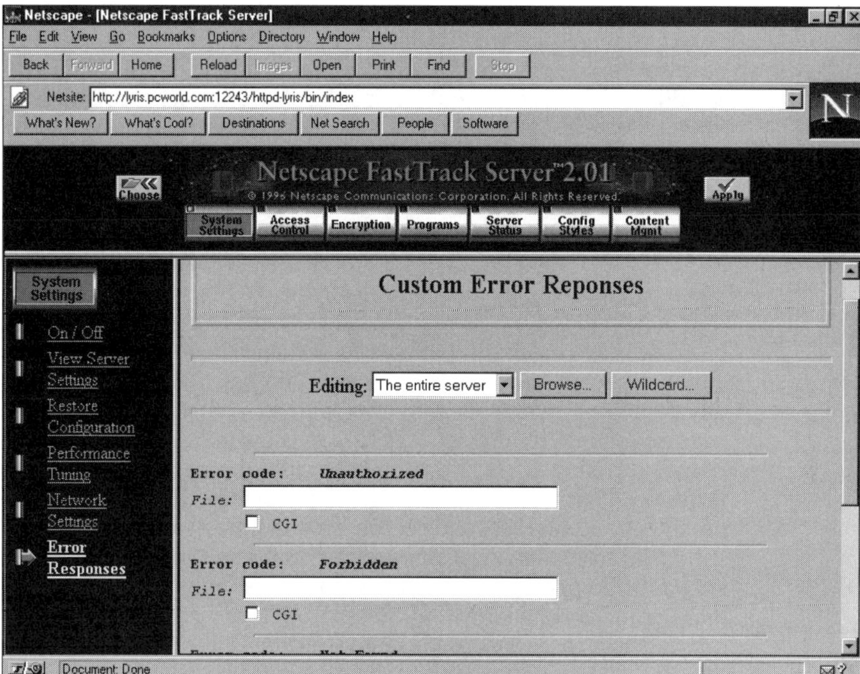

Figure 17-13: Creating custom error responses in the Netscape administration server

To switch on custom error pages, open the Administration Server and click on the System Settings tab after selecting the server that you want to manage. Then choose the Error Responses link. For each type of error, enter the absolute path (starting with c:\) to the text or HTML file that you want the user to see if he or she triggers that error. You will probably want to replace the "Not Found" error at a minimum. If your site requires that users check in with a username and password, the "Unauthorized" error page should contain information about how someone can get an account or subscription. Click the appropriate CGI check box if you want to run a program when an error occurs.

Microsoft IIS

Even though IIS doesn't natively support changing the error response (even for 404s), you can download a special ISAPI plug-in filter that lets you customize your server in this way. An ISAPI Filter is a small program that scans (or preprocesses) each page just before it is delivered by your server. The HTMLEx filter, written by Zoltan Pekic, has a wide array of page customization and dynamic page generation features; flexible custom error handling is just a part of what this terrific preprocessing application can do. You can find HTMLEx at `http://www.riteh.hr/HTMLEx/`; the site includes thorough online documentation and installation directions.

O'Reilly WebSite

Like Microsoft's Web server, WebSite does not support custom error pages. However, it is possible to write one using WebSite's proprietary application programming interface. Thankfully, the good folks at Willow Glen Graphics have saved you the trouble of developing one yourself. Their HAL9000.DLL WSAPI module lets you customize the way your server responds to 401 (unauthorized user), 403 (content access forbidden) and 404 (document not found) errors. You can find HAL at `http://wgg.com/hal.html`. Full installation instructions and release notes are included.

Controlling access to parts of your Web server

You may wish to place all or part of your Web server under *access control*; that is, you may wish to restrict user access to certain pages or directories, or allow only certain individuals to see a given portion of your site. When might you want to use access control? Perhaps you are in the process of developing a newer Web site or expanding your existing one. You may not want the public to have access to your new material until you're ready to release it. Using access control, you could distribute user name and password information to just a few privileged individuals — your company's president and marketing director, for example — while blocking the rest of the world from viewing your work in progress. Or you may want to charge a subscription price for access to your Web site. In such a case, you could make a promotional area of your site open to the general public while offering access passwords only to those users who had paid the monthly fee.

Regardless of which server you use, setting up access control requires the following three steps:

1. You must define users who are permitted access to your server. In many cases, this is similar in theory (if not always in practice) to setting up users for Windows NT or any other network operating system you may have used.
2. You must define the different directories and files on your server that are access-controlled. These protected areas are generally called *realms*.
3. Finally, you must give certain users admission to each realm, as appropriate to your access control model.

Access control in Netscape servers

In FastTrack and Enterprise Server, all access control facilities are managed within from the Administration Server. Once you've selected a Web site to manage, click the Access Control button (see Figure 17-14). From here, you must first define users by selecting the Create Users link. Netscape defines users as existing within both a *group* and a *database* (a database can be thought of as a group of groups).

For the most part you should leave the database popup set to default; there's little reason to create additional databases. You will want to assign the users you create to groups later on; it's easier to specify that the entire marketing group should have access to the "Media Kits" resource, for example, than to uniquely classify each individual user. You can manage the users and groups that you have created with the List, Edit, and Remove tools provided in the Administration Server's Access Control area.

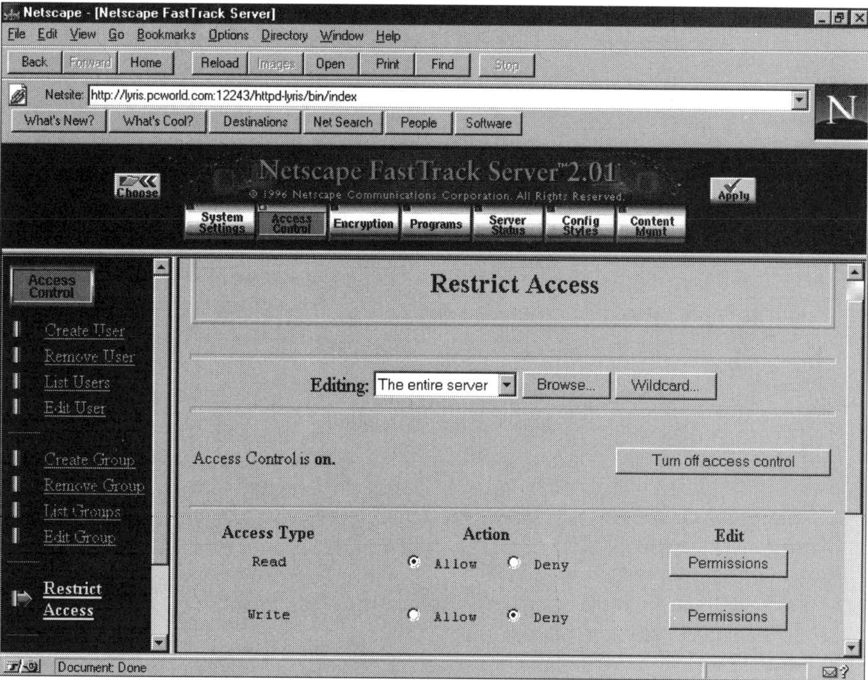

Figure 17-14: Defining access control for a Netscape server

Defining protected realms is a bit trickier than entering users because Netscape's Web-based interface is surprisingly unintuitive. First, select the Restrict Access link, and choose what part of the server you want to secure. You can browse the site's directory structure with the Browse… button. Enable access control by clicking, obviously, Turn on Access Control. Here comes the confusing part. All you care about is the "read" access type ("write" is only used if you are setting up remote HTML page publishing);

Action specifies what the default action for that realm should be. If you want Joe User to be blocked from your site while a small cadre of the elite are allowed entrance, select Deny. If you only want to block access to your site by a few pesky surfers (your competition, say), but want Joe to be able to surf to his heart's content, click Allow. In either case your next step is to define which users are not covered by the default.

In virtually every case (except for the aforementioned competition), you will now go on to specify access to individual users — or groups thereof — by clicking the Permissions button. The window that comes up will allow you to deny access to users from certain Internet domains (competition.com, for example) or specify who has full browsing rights. You may enter a message such as "Enter your user name and password to access the marketing area" in the Login Prompt field; users will see this message in the dialog box that comes up when they try to access the protected part of your site. When you are finished, don't forget to click both the Done button in this window and OK in the previous one (to which you will be returned).

Access control in Microsoft IIS

The beauty of setting up access control in IIS is that the whole application is so tightly integrated with the Windows NT operating system that you need only apply NT file permissions to your files — these rights are then automatically applied to your Web documents. However, in order to apply NT file permissions, your server's drives must use the NT File System (NTFS). For details, see the Backgrounder sidebar, "Dealing with FAT: NT File System Issues."

BACKGROUNDER

Dealing with FAT: NT File System Issues

For compatibility reasons, Windows NT offers two different types of disk file systems. (The file system is the database that keeps track of your files' locations on the hard drive.) If you want to set up access control through NT's file permissions, you'll need to assess and possibly change how your server's hard drives are configured.

Hard disks organized under the older FAT (File Allocation Table) file system do not provide support for file and folder access permissions. Therefore, you can't define Web access control under FAT; you need to use NTFS (NT File System) in order to take advantage of these more advanced security options.

However, your hard drive may have come with FAT preinstalled. If you upgraded from an older operating system, it almost certainly uses the FAT file system.

You can determine a drive's file system type by opening the Windows NT Explorer: select a drive (c:, for example), and then choose Properties from the File menu. If you have a FAT disk, NT comes with a command line utility called CONVERT.EXE that will safely install NTFS on your drive. Simply open a DOS window and type **convert c: /fs:ntfs** (assuming that you want to convert the c: drive); the next time you reboot the machine, your drive will be switched over to the newer file system. Though I've run CONVERT.EXE at least a dozen times without ever losing data, as with any major change to your server it's probably a good ideas to back up your hard disk before converting a drive from FAT to NTFS.

When you install IIS, the installation program creates an anonymous Web-user account (named IUSR_*servername* by default); you can change the account name in the Internet Service Manager. The permissions assigned to this account control the access privileges of the majority of visitors to your Web site. All documents and directories that you want to make publicly available must be readable by IUSR_*servername*, or visitors will receive an "Access Denied" message. In order to protect parts of your Web site with access control, you must first create additional user accounts with the User Manager For Domains, found under the Administrative Tools icon in the Start menu. You can also use the User Manager For Domains to create groups of users to whom you want to allow (or prevent) Web site access.

Once you have assigned the appropriate roles, use the Windows NT Explorer to define file permissions by selecting the items you want to protect and choosing Properties from the Explorer's File menu (see Figure 17-15). Click on the Permissions button located on the Security tab in the dialog box to bring up a second dialog box in which you can define which users and/or groups have read access to the specified content.

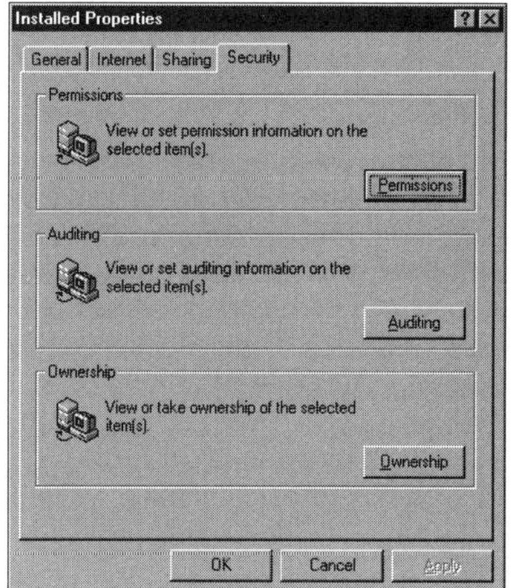

Figure 17-15: Setting file permissions in Windows NT 4.0

Access control in WebSite

As with the other servers, to engage access control in WebSite you must first define users and the groups that they fall into. You may do so in the Server Properties dialog box; there are tabs labeled both Users and Groups (see Figure 17-16). Each user and group that you define falls into a *realm*. Realms are confusing, but you can think of each realm as a collection of user and group entities. You can create a new realm under either the Users tab or the Groups tab, but for simplicity's sake you will most likely only want to maintain a single realm. To add a user or group, click the New... button — if you insert a user you must enter a password for that user as well.

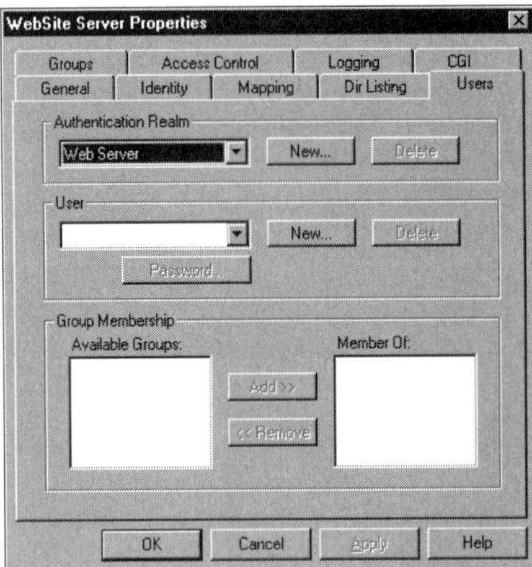

Figure 17-16: Creating users in O'Reilly WebSite

The Group Membership box at the bottom of these tabs enables you to move users back and forth between groups. Groups are handy if you have a very large number of users; when you assign access control to individual directories later, the process will move along much faster if you've grouped your users together by type.

Switch to the Access Control tab when you're ready to password-protect a section of your site (see Figure 17-17). Each directory that you want to place under access control must be assigned a realm. After you've done that, you can select which of the users and groups within that realm should be allowed to read that particular directory by clicking the Add… button in the Authorized Users & Groups box. If you want to restrict access to a particular directory based on the IP address of a user's computer, click in the box beneath …then Deny classes, followed by the Add… button. Enter the IP address or range of addresses you wish to exclude in the appropriate field. For example, you could enter 209.23.17.* to bar any users whose IP addresses begin with 209.23.17.

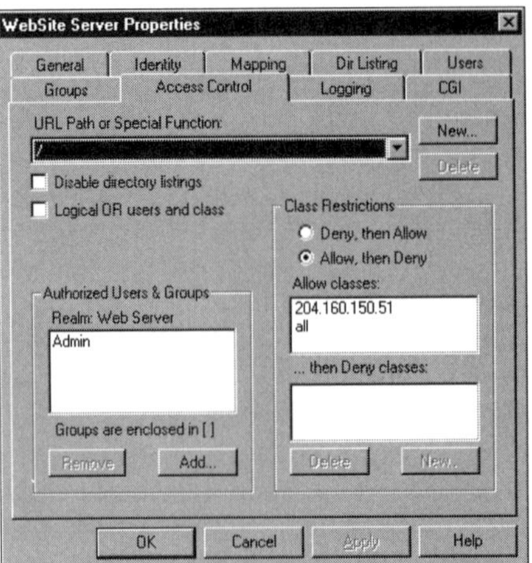

Figure 17-17: Defining access control settings in O'Reilly WebSite

Who Is This CGI Guy, Anyway?

By this time, you've most likely heard mention of CGI, probably in the context of server-based programming. As previous chapters have described, CGI stands for Common Gateway Interface and represents a standard communication method that a Web server can use to exchange data with programs or scripts that run alongside it. These pieces of computer code are often referred to as *CGI scripts*, or — to make things more confusing — simply called *CGIs*.

CGIs are valuable because they enable Web developers to extend the basic document-distribution features of the server in order to create truly interactive sites. For example, you might use a CGI to generate a list of sales leads by letting potential clients browsing your Web site enter their contact information into a form in an HTML page; when visitors submit the form, a CGI script can e-mail the entered data to the appropriate sales rep. Or a CGI might act as the "glue" between your Web server and a corporate database server, passing visitor queries to the database while sending the responses back to the Web server itself. Many of the database-publishing add-ons described in Chapter 10 operate as CGIs.

Unlike in the UNIX world, where CGI is CGI, in Windows there are at least four flavors of the Common Gateway Interface supported by the Web servers I've examined in this chapter (see Table 17-5). Which version you use depends mostly on how your script or program is written.

CGIs are great for increasing the interactivity of your site, but they fall short in one area. Because each call for a CGI requires that a new program be prepared, launched, and run before data can be returned to the user, loading up your site with CGI scripts may slow down your server significantly. For this reason, server developers have come up with a number of additional ways to construct Web pages dynamically.

Server-side includes

Server-side includes are specially formatted tags that can be inserted into regular HTML files. The server scans through the HTML just before delivering the file, and if it finds one of these tags it replaces it with external data. SSIs are generally used to include a small dynamic element, such as the current date or time, into an otherwise static page. They may also be used to insert a common piece of boilerplate text (such as a copyright notice) into every document on your site. If you as the Webmaster wish to modify the boilerplate text, you need only do so in one place instead of editing every one of your HTML files by hand. Let's take a look at a sample include of this type:

```
<!--#include virtual="/notices/copyright_info.txt"-->
```

When an HTML document containing the above line is delivered by the Web server, the <INCLUDE> tag (presumably located at the bottom of the page) will be replaced with the contents of the copyright_info.txt text file.

Table 17-5 Four flavors of Windows CGIs

Type of CGI Interface	*When to Use It*	*Which Servers Support It*
Standard CGI	Appropriate in most cases. Standard environment variables — read from the information that a user enters into a Web form or appended to a URL — pass data to scripts. The server defines these settings just before running the CGI program, and the program can read the variable data when it launches.	All
DOS CGI	Almost identical to standard CGI, DOS CGI is only used when your script is written as a 16-bit DOS application. Because such DOS programs can't read an environment variables defined by a 32-bit Web server, the server must write out a batch file that first explicitly sets the necessary variables before executing the CGI.	WebSite
Shell CGI	Shell CGI is used when you have a programming language interpreter on your server. You can write scripts that are passed to this interpreter for execution at runtime. In this situation, you must map your script's file extension (such as .pl, .py, or .cgi) to the appropriate language interpreter application — Perl is a popular one for Web serving — so that your CGI will be correctly executed. This mapping is generally defined in the Windows Explorer and checked by the server when the CGI is called.	Netscape (both IIS and WebSite support the features of Shell CGI within their standard CGI interfaces)
WinCGI	The Windows CGI specification was drawn up by the developers of WebSite, and addresses an issue similar to the one solved by DOS CGI: Windows applications cannot read data from environment variables. The solution in this case is for the Web server to write out a temporary .INI file containing all of the relevant information. The server then launches the Windows application and passes it the name of the .INI document.	Netscape, WebSite

Advanced SSIs: execs

The most advanced use of SSIs involves executing a CGI that inserts its output directly into the HTML page wherever the `<INCLUDE>` tag is located. For example, if you have a small program called dateprint.exe that outputs the current date and time, you could run that program from an include by inserting the following tag into your HTML page:

```
<!--#exec cgi="/cgi-bin/dateprint.exe"-->
```

This type of include is called an *exec*. It provides a very flexible way to create dynamic pages, but because the server must execute a program every time the page is displayed, the exec include suffers from the same server-load drawbacks as do regular CGIs. Indeed, programmatic SSIs may extract an even greater performance penalty than CGIs if you have more one than such include per page. Because the action of preprocessing a page to look for server-side includes slows down the serving process, Web servers generally only preprocess files specially marked as containing SSIs. Here's how to let your Web server know which pages to parse.

Netscape FastTrack or Enterprise servers

Open the Administration Server and choose a specific site to edit. Then select the Content Mgmt button and click Parse HTML (see Figure 17-18). The set of radio buttons labeled Activate Server-Parsed HTML lets you enable page preprocessing with or without exec includes — Webmasters who run sites with multiple HTML page authors may consider execs a security risk. The lower set of radio buttons enables you to define what kind of pages are parsed: all documents or only pages with the .shtml file extension. While selecting All HTML Files will reduce performance as the server pre-reads all pages before fulfilling browser requests, you gain the flexibility of being able to insert includes anywhere you like.

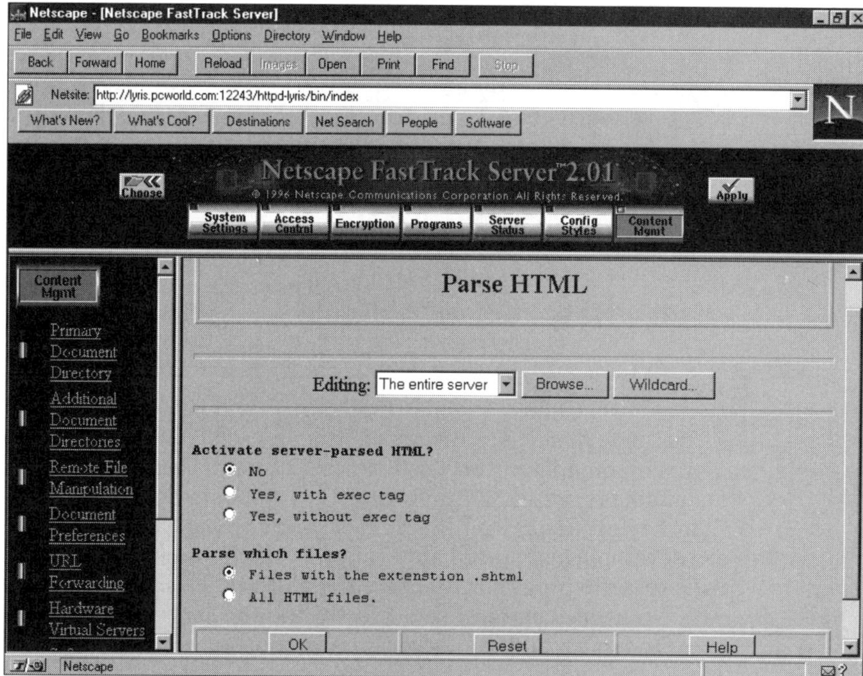

Figure 17-18: Setting up server-side includes for a Netscape Web server

Microsoft IIS

In IIS, a single file extension — the default is .stm — marks pages to be parsed; this extension can be modified only by editing the Windows Registry. To do so, open the regedt32.exe application, and select the HKEY_LOCAL_MACHINE window. Locate the key at SYSTEM/CurrentControlSet/Services/W3SVC/Parameters/ServerSideIncludesExtension, and set the value of this key to the file extension that you wish to be preprocessed.

O'Reilly WebSite series

Using WebSite's Server Properties dialog box, you can define which file extensions should be preprocessed. Simply select the Mapping tab and choose Content Types in the List Selector (see Figure 17-19). You need to map your chosen file extensions to the wwwserver/html-ssi MIME content type. WebSite is preconfigured to associate both the .shtml and .html-ssi file extensions with this MIME type. (For background on MIME types and content maps, see the section "Of Maps and MIME," in Chapter 13.)

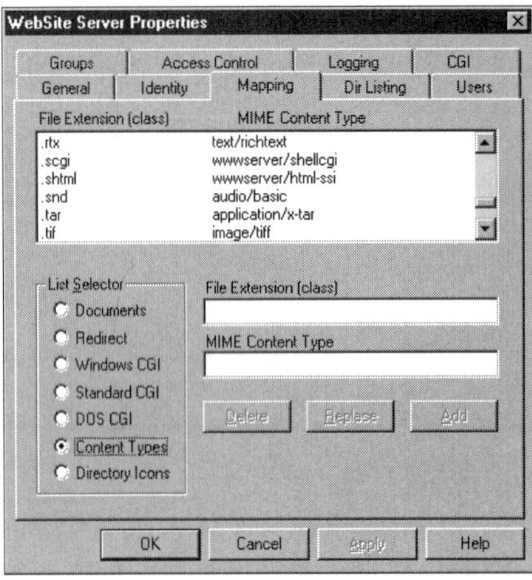

Figure 17-19: Associating a file extension with the server-side include MIME type for a WebSite server

Server APIs

As custom-created and dynamically generated Web pages become more and more commonplace, the server manufacturers are recognizing that CGIs are unsuitable for repetitive delivery of custom data due to the server overhead that they consume. To address this shortcoming, server software companies are developing advanced application programming interfaces that can be used to write programs that take the place of CGIs. Because scripts written as API plug-ins can be linked directly into the server application, the time it takes to launch and run them is reduced by an order of magnitude or more.

However, there are two reasons that APIs are not the answer to every Webmaster's dream. The first is that every major server vendor maintains its own API, and these APIs are not compatible; a program written for one will not run on another. The second problem is that in general API applications are much more difficult to write than a Visual Basic or Perl script. Plug-ins are typically written in C++, and therefore demand sophisticated programming skills on the part of the Web developer.

Server-side scripting

A recently introduced fourth option for custom page builds on the techniques used by Web programmers to construct client-side programs. Both Java and JavaScript — previously relevant only in the Web browser domain — are now supported by servers and allow the development of cross platform back-end applications. Java has the advantage of offering a totally portable runtime environment; if you write all of your CGIs in Java and then switch from a Windows Web server to one running on UNIX or the Mac OS, you should be able to run the same scripts without modification. However, Web developers should take this cross-platform claim with a grain of salt; the application of server-side Java is still in its infancy. Both the Netscape servers and WebSite Professional support server-side Java at this time. On the Mac OS side, StarNine's WebSTAR 2.x also supports server-side Java.

Netscape also offers a version of JavaScript for use on the server. The programming environment for server-side JavaScript is called LiveWire, and it includes a compiler and database access tools. Netscape is attempting to position LiveWire as the premier back-end development environment, but because the implementation of JavaScript is somewhat weak and restrictive, LiveWire has not made significant market headway as of yet.

Microsoft has released its own development system, called Active Server Pages (ASP). ASP uses either VBScript (which is nearly identical in syntax to Visual Basic) or JScript (Microsoft's implementation of JavaScript) to write complete server-based applications that do not require compilation. Like LiveWire, ASP has the advantage of high speed, and offers tight connectivity to the IIS Web server. Active Server Pages is available for free download by IIS users at `http://www.microsoft.com/iis/default.asp`.

What's Your Server Doing While You Sleep?

Once your server is up and running, it's not very interesting to look at. Despite the fact that they may be jumping through digital hoops to serve hundreds of thousands of HTML pages and image files each day, Web servers don't display any fancy graphics on the screen to prove just how darn busy they are.

So how do you know what your server is doing, anyway? In a word: logs. Every time your server answers a request of any type, for an HTML page, a picture, a movie file — even if it doesn't have the asked-for item — an entry is written into the server's access log file. This log includes such information as the time, the IP address of the client, what piece of information was requested, and whether the server could fulfill the request. You can analyze these files to determine who is visiting your site, how often, and when you experience the heaviest usage. If you display advertising on your site, these logs are vital because they to prove to advertisers how often users are seeing their ads.

So while you're sleeping like a log, your server is building one.

Looking inside a log file

The original log format — introduced by the Web server programmers at the National Center for Supercomputing Applications at the University of Illinois Urbana-Champagne, and still supported by most servers — is called the *common log format*, or CLF. Figure 17-20 shows an example of a few lines of a CLF log.

```
access - Notepad
File Edit Search Help
format=%Ses->client.ip% - %Req->vars.auth-user% [%SYSDATE%] "%Req->reqpb.clf-request%"
204.160.190.98 - - [17/Feb/1997:10:50:11 -0800] "GET / HTTP/1.0" 200 2673
204.160.190.98 - - [17/Feb/1997:10:50:11 -0800] "GET /title.gif HTTP/1.0" 200 44263
204.160.190.98 - - [17/Feb/1997:13:01:39 -0800] "GET / HTTP/1.0" 200 2673
204.160.190.98 - - [17/Feb/1997:13:01:40 -0800] "GET /title.gif HTTP/1.0" 200 44263
204.160.190.99 - - [17/Feb/1997:15:33:56 -0800] "GET / HTTP/1.0" 200 2673
204.160.190.99 - - [17/Feb/1997:15:33:57 -0800] "GET /title.gif HTTP/1.0" 200 44263
204.160.190.98 - - [17/Feb/1997:16:29:08 -0800] "GET / HTTP/1.0" 304 0
204.160.190.98 - - [17/Feb/1997:16:29:29 -0800] "GET /title.gif HTTP/1.0" 304 0
204.160.190.98 - - [19/Feb/1997:19:51:32 -0800] "GET / HTTP/1.0" 304 0
204.160.190.99 - - [19/Feb/1997:19:51:45 -0800] "GET / HTTP/1.0" 304 0
204.160.190.99 - - [19/Feb/1997:19:51:45 -0800] "GET /title.gif HTTP/1.0" 304 0
204.160.190.98 - - [19/Feb/1997:19:51:53 -0800] "GET /title.gif HTTP/1.0" 304 0
```

Figure 17-20: Sample log entries in the Common Log Format (CLF)

Each element in each line of CLF is separated by a space. The items are defined as follows (in order from left to right):

- IP address of user's computer
- Username, if authentication is enabled
- More username information, now defunct
- Time stamp, including offset from Greenwich Meridian Time
- The type of request (GET is used to retrieve HTML pages or graphics; POST is used to submit information from a Web form)
- The URL of the requested item
- The HTTP version number supported by the server
- The HTTP status code of the request (some common codes include: 200 — "Transfer OK"; 302 — "Redirect to a different URL"; 404 — "Document not found"; 403 — "Access denied")
- The number of bytes of information sent from the server to the client during the transaction

Customizing your log files

Netscape's Enterprise server lets you customize your log files in a number of ways: you can add additional information — including the type of Web browser the user is running or what page he or she visited just before the one being logged — or define multiple logs in different formats to be written simultaneously.

In typical Microsoft fashion, Microsoft's IIS server uses its own proprietary log format, which offers a few more pieces of information per line than does plain-vanilla CLF. This format is described in full in the IIS documentation. Alternatively, IIS lets you log data directly into an ODBC database, bypassing the normal flat-file log.

O'Reilly's WebSite also offers its own extended log format, but supports CLF-style logging as well.

Analyzing your log files

As previous chapters have already mentioned, your log files can tell you a great deal — if you listen to them. You could clearly answer a number of questions about how people use your server by analyzing and generating summaries from your log files. Results might include the following:

- The percentage of users from outside the United States
- What day of the week or hour of the day is the busiest
- Which of your HTML files is the most popular
- Whether or not people are interested in the chutney recipes you posted

If you were so inclined, you could most likely write your own analysis software — or even use a commercial statistics package — to provide these answers. Those of you who want to take the do-it-yourself path so may put this book down now and retire to your computers. The rest of us will go ahead and take advantage of one of the dozens of terrific bundled, shareware, and commercial analysis packages currently available on the Windows platform that have been written expressly for the purpose of extracting useful information from CLF server logs.

Bundled log-analysis packages

Only the Netscape servers come with log analysis tools included as part of the basic package — two of them, in fact. ANALYZE.EXE and FLEXANLG.EXE — located in the "extras" directory under your server's installation directory — are both command line tools (run from a DOS prompt) that take a log file, or section thereof, and output a report in HTML or text format. You can view the results with a Web browser or an editor such as Notepad (see Figure 17-21).

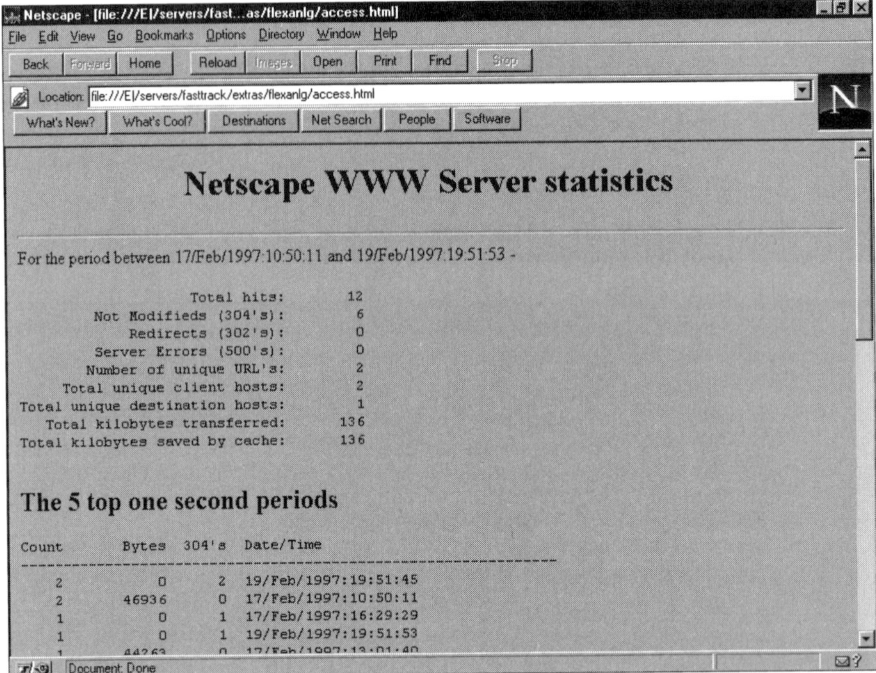

Figure 17-21: Sample output from Netscape's FLEXANLG.EXE command-line log analyzer

The applications — which are nearly identical — have a number of options that control what summary items are included in the log reports. For example, you can see the IP addresses of the most frequent users of your site, or look at how many bytes your server delivered every hour. ANALYZE includes a program that you can place in your server's CGI directory so that you can run analyses from a Web browser. While these programs can generate some fairly sophisticated reports, they are restricted by their clunky interfaces and limited output options.

Shareware log-analysis tools

There are literally dozens of freeware and shareware analysis tools available. If you wish to explore the options yourself, your best bet is to start with Yahoo's Log Analysis Tools page located at `http://www.yahoo.com/Computers_and_Internet/Software/Internet/World_Wide_Web/Servers/Log_Analysis_Tools/`. There you will find links to hundreds of programs, ranging from sophisticated Windows-based tools to simple scripts written in Perl or Visual Basic.

One of the best applications I've found for looking at CLF files is Wusage, written by the prolific Thomas Boutell. Wusage, which also operates from the command line, produces HTML-based reports with colorful graphs that can answer virtually any server use question that you may have. It includes such advanced functionality as support for multiple mirror sites (identical servers used for high-volume Web serving), reads multiple log files at a time while correctly sorting time stamps, and can exclude client entries that you may not wish to report, such as accesses from within your company. The program imports your log entries into its own internal database; if you wish you can extend the program's capabilities by examining this database with a desktop tool such as Excel or Microsoft Access.

Wusage is available for virtually every operating system on the market, and is a steal at a shareware cost of only $75 per server; nonprofits and educational institutions pay only $25 per system analyzed. You can download Wusage from `http://www.boutell.com/`.

Commercial log-analysis applications

The explosion of Web publishing has naturally led to rapid growth in the analysis tool industry. The market itself has undergone a product-line bifurcation. Most companies are either targeting the very high-end publishers with special needs (those delivering 100,000 or more HTML page views per day), or the individual Webmaster who controls a relatively low-traffic site. New products are constantly introduced, and the state of the art six months ago may be gone tomorrow. Here's a quick roundup of the current crop:

- **Market Focus** (previously published by Intersé but acquired in early 1997 by Microsoft) is available in two variants: a Standard Version aimed at small publishers (you can download a trial copy at `http://www.interse.com`), and the Developer Version, which runs in concert with a Microsoft Access, Microsoft SQL Server, or (for extremely large sites) Oracle relational database. Intersé's goal is to provide an analysis product that extends beyond simply reading access logs; in the recently released version 3, Market Focus supports the input and reporting of "metadata" that uniquely identifies and tags every visitor to your site. Version 3 also introduces crosstab features, which let a Webmaster "drill down" into the analysis reports. For example, when viewing a report of user visits by country, the Webmaster could have the system break out that information further by grouping accesses by type of browser used. For high-volume or custom applications, Market Focus is the current leader. Microsoft has stated that they will be integrating many of the capabilities of Market Focus into its server-based BackOffice product line.
- **Net.Genesis Net.Analysis**, also available in a Desktop and an advanced Professional version, offers features similar to Market Focus. However, the Professional version has a unique "logging engine" that runs alongside your Web server and provides real-time reports of system load and usage levels. No other product gives you instant, interactive access to your site's performance. For more information about Net.Genesis products, visit `http://www.netgen.com`.

- Two other products that are worth looking at are: e.g. Software's WebTrends, billed as an easy-to-use CLF log analyzer that produces HTML-based output and includes graphical charting capabilities; and O'Reilly's Statisphere. Statisphere offers a stable of ready-made reports, support for WebSite, CLF, and IIS log formats, and an automated analysis tool that can watch access logs as they are written and update an online report every minute.

It's worth noting that you don't have run a Windows-based log-analysis program. Log files are plain, text-only files, and are easy to zap from one platform to another. Many of the Mac OS log-analysis packages mentioned in the previous chapter can also handle logs created by the servers I've discussed in this chapter.

Log analysis companies

If you have neither the time nor the hardware on which to run your own log analysis, you may wish to contract with an offsite company that will review your logs and provide Web-based reports online. Netcount (`http://www.netcount.com`) and I/Pro (`http://www.ipro.com`) are the big players in this market. To take advantage of one of these services, you must run a small application on your Web server system that periodically (hourly or daily) transmits your log files to the company's remote database over an encrypted link. The analysis company's custom software chews through your logs nightly and you can access an up-to-date report at any time using a Web browser.

The advantage of using an offsite measurement facility is that you do not need to have the storage space or processing power to retain and analyze your own logs. This is particularly valuable if your site is heavily trafficked (a very large site can generate 100MB or more of CLF logs per day). Furthermore, because the analysis firm is nominally a disinterested third party, those who ask to see an audit of your traffic levels may prefer to see an I/Pro or NetCount report rather than an internal accounting. I/Pro, in fact, offers an auditing service — I/Audit — specifically targeted at Internet content providers who must be able to show their advertisers validated usage summaries.

Couch Potato Webmasters: Keeping Your Server Running

Your server will crash. How often this occurs depends on the amount of traffic you have, how much memory is installed in the machine, what type of software (Web server and otherwise) you have loaded, and your general level of good karma.

I'm not referring to a catastrophic crash in which the hard disk catches fire or anything; I simply mean that every once in a while, your Web server will stop responding to requests for HTML pages, and the mouse may freeze up.

Other strange behavior — including the appearance of the Windows NT "blue screen of death" that is never a good sign — may occur as well, but the simple fix in nearly every case is simply to reboot the machine.

Automatically starting system services

Now, rebooting is easy if you happen to be in the same room as the server: simply press Ctrl-Alt-Delete a few times. In the worst freezes you'll have to use the power or reset button to get things moving again. If your Web server software package has been set up as a Windows NT service (all of the servers I've looked at in this chapter support this configuration), it will most likely restart automatically when the system comes up. Check the Services control panel *before* a crash happens to ensure that your server is configured correctly (see Figure 17-22). In the register of system services, you will see your Web server listed. What it's called depends on which product you are using (see Table 17-6).

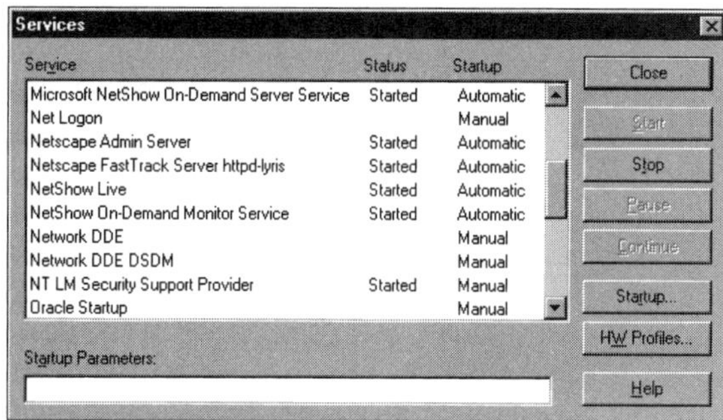

Figure 17-22: The Windows NT Services control panel

Table 17-6 Server product names and corresponding control panel entries

Server Product Name	*Service Control Panel Entry*
Netscape FastTrack Server	Netscape FastTrack Server httpd-servername
Netscape Enterprise Server	Netscape Enterprise Server https-servername
Microsoft IIS	World Wide Web Publishing Service
WebSite	Web Server

Select the appropriate service, and click the Startup... button. In the dialog box that appears, be sure to set the Startup type to Automatic; this ensures that the selected service will launch without user intervention when the system boots.

Remote control software

But what if you're not in the building when the server goes south? I've described at length the Web server administration tools that system managers or Webmasters can use to control a server. Besides configuration options, these tools also allow you to switch the server on and off. However, only the Netscape Administration Server enables you to use a Web browser to start and stop your Web server from anywhere on the Internet (provided that a firewall doesn't get in the way). Microsoft IIS's HTML-based administration tool doesn't support remote server startup and shutdown via the Internet; you must have a Microsoft Networking connection between the server and your local machine. WebSite also provides remote support only via Microsoft Networking.

The remote-sharing workaround

There is a workaround to this problem — a way to fake a Windows 95 or NT client into thinking that a server on a wide-area network (such as the Internet) is really situated locally.

The remote-sharing process basically involves mapping the IP address of your server to the name of a shared drive (called a *share*). This mapping information is stored in a file called LMHOSTS. On Windows NT, you can locate LMHOSTS in:

```
\windows\system32\drivers\etc\
```

In Windows 95, look in:

```
\windows\
```

For each remote share that you want to create, add a line to the LMHOSTS file that consists of the server's IP address followed by a space and then a unique name identifying the machine. For example:

```
209.11.124.56 REMOTEWEBSERVER
```

To force your client PC to reread the LMHOSTS file after you have edited it, type the following command at the DOS prompt:

```
NBTSTAT -R
```

The LMHOSTS file is not enabled by default; you will have to modify your network configuration in the Network Control Panel in order to access a share over the Internet. Open the Network Control Panel, and double-click TCP/IP in the Protocols tab. Under Advanced, click Enable LMHOSTS. If you don't see this entry in the Advanced tab, you may need to reboot your PC. Next, test the changes to the network setup by reading the filesystem of the remote server. For example, if the system's c: drive is shared as DRIVE1, open a DOS window and type:

```
DIR \\REMOTEWEBSERVER\DRIVE1\*.*
```

If you do not see a listing of the selected directory, verify that you have entered the correct IP address data in the LMHOSTS file. You can ping the remote server's IP address to ensure that it is up and listening on the network. In the DOS window, type:

PING 209.11.124.56

(Of course, replace the IP number above with your server's IP number or hostname.) If the ping succeeds, you should be able to access the shared resource over the Internet with the following command:

NET VIEW \\REMOTEWEBSERVER

You will eventually see either an error message or a list of available shares; it may take a while for this information to display. The list should contain the share name that you entered previously; if it is missing, either the server is not properly configured to publish the share, or network configuration is getting in the way.

Don't forget that your local login must match an identical login (both username and password) on the remote server; you will have no opportunity to enter different identification data. If you are consistently rejected from the remote connection for security reasons, check your username and password on both machines to ensure that they are the same.

The remote-control software option

If you're in your office, you may be able to make a network connection to the server system over which you can run your Web server's administration tool. But if you are on the road with a notebook, or working from home, you may desire greater administrative control than that provided by the management program that shipped with your server.

The solution is a remote-control utility — a software package that effectively opens a window on your computer and displays the screen of another PC, right next door or hundreds of miles away. You can use your mouse and keyboard to control this distant system. My favorite PC product in this category is pcANYWHERE 32, and I recommend it highly (see Figure 17-23).

pcANYWHERE is published by Symantec; more information is available at `http://www.symantec.com/`. pcANYWHERE enables you to monitor, manage, and transfer files from a Windows 95 or NT machine using a variety of connection methods, including modem dial-up and TCP/IP networking. The latter facility means that if your desktop PC has a direct or dial-up connection to the Internet, you can monitor and control a properly configured and Internet-connected system anywhere in the world as if it were right in your office. When the system fails in the middle of the night, you can fix the problem from the comfort of your den rather than driving in to work.

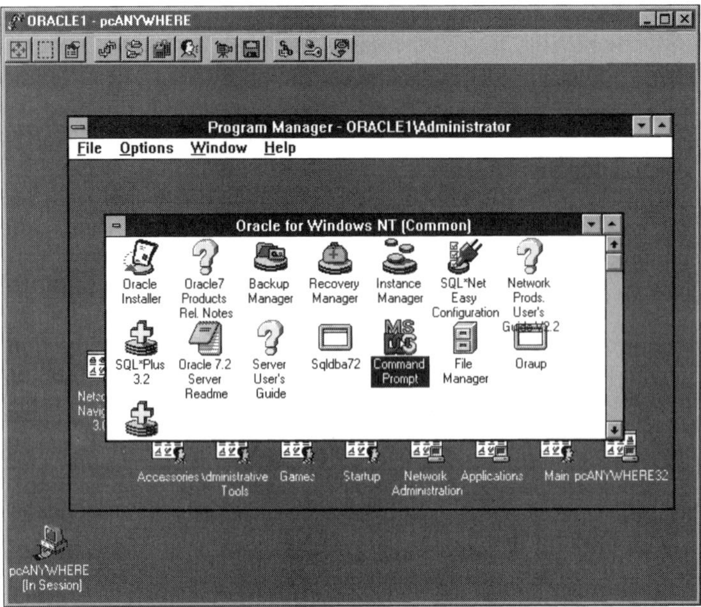

Figure 17-23: An open pcANYWHERE 32 connection

The advantages of remote control clearly go beyond just restarting your server if it stops running. You can set up new products, update software, change server properties, or clean out log files, without ever having to physically touch the machine.

pcANYWHERE and its brethren are even more vital to your server's software stability if you choose to colocate your equipment in an ISP's hosting facility, because limited physical access and a lack of workspace mean that server farms are a rotten place to configure or fix your equipment. A final advantage of remote control software is that it offers you the ability to give complete access to your system to a consultant or technical support technician in the event that you have a problem with your hardware or software.

Let your fingers do the restarting

Sometimes when your Web server software crashes, it takes your server's networking or operating system software down with it. A crash this bad makes the remote management aspects of an application like pcANYWHERE pretty useless. As I mentioned earlier your only option in this situation is to do a "hard reboot" — to reset the server computer with the reset button or power switch. Hard rebooting is virtually impossible to execute remotely; you (or a friendly technician, if your server is colocated) must have direct access to the machine itself.

But there is one piece of hardware that may rescue you from that 3 a.m. trip to the office: the remote-boot box. This handy device, offered by Black Box and other enterprise networking supply companies, plugs into a dedicated phone line, and has power sockets for one or more computer systems. You can program the remote-boot box to cycle power to one or more of the sockets when you dial in and press the appropriate code on your touch-tone phone. After this brief power interruption resets its internals, your server will in all likelihood — if you have defined the automatic start facility for your server service as explained earlier — resume its HTML page delivery chores with no lasting trauma.

Summary

- From the ease-of-use, security, and entry-price perspectives, Windows is preferable to UNIX as a server platform.
- Among the Windows platforms, Windows 95 is suitable for low-volume Web serving, but Windows NT 4.0 Server is the preferred version for high-volume sites.
- A solid configuration for a Windows Web server is a 200MHz Pentium or Pentium Pro with at least 32MB of RAM and a nice, fat hard drive.
- If you are using Windows NT 4.0 Server, Microsoft Internet Information Server may be all the Web server you need. But don't hesitate to download trial versions of O'Reilly and Netscape's offerings if you need more flexibility.
- Removing unnecessary networking protocols is the single most effective software tweak you can make to improve system performance.
- Site management tools can take some of the pain out of managing a vast array of Web content, but be prepared to adapt your work style to the quirks of the software you choose. Microsoft FrontPage 97 is the most full-featured product in this category.
- Placing parts of your site under access control can help you fend off unwanted visitors or keep your Web presence private while it's under development.
- While CGI is a common and easy-to-use way to add interactivity to your Web site, other server-side programming techniques may be more appropriate for high-volume sites.
- You can determine a lot about who is visiting your site by crunching your server log files with a shareware analysis product like Wusage. If you have a large site or desire highly detailed reports, there are a number of strong commercial options to choose from.
- Work with a third-party reporting company if you need to provide audited site traffic information to advertisers or company executives.
- Make sure that you can remotely manage your Web server with a software tool. pcANYWHERE 32 is the premium remote-control product available.

Appendix A

HTML Quick Reference

An Overview of HTML 3.2 Tags and Common Attributes

An HTML 3.2 document has a simple structure consisting of a declaration, a HEAD element, and a BODY element. The HEAD element contains the document head and general information about the document and its origins. The BODY element contains two types of elements: block level elements and text level elements. Standard block level elements such as paragraph breaks, tables, and lists always cause paragraph breaks. Text level elements include other elements for font sizing, text alignment, and basic character formatting. While block level elements generally act as containers for text level elements, text level elements only contain other text level elements.

A standard HTML tag includes the element itself, one or more attributes if any apply, and a value for each attribute. For example, if you want to place a table on your page and align it to the right margin, you type:

```
<TABLE ALIGN=RIGHT>
```

TABLE is the element, ALIGN is its attribute, and RIGHT is the attribute's value. Many elements have more than one attribute, which makes HTML quite versatile.

The Opening and Head Elements

Use the HEAD element to provide general information about the document, its creator, and the document's relationship to other documents.

Tag Element	*Example*	*Description*
!-- ... --	`<!-beginning of section on paintings->`	Use the comment tag to provide notes to yourself or others who may benefit from some comments in your HTML code. The browser ignores text appearing between the dashes.
!DOCTYPE	`<!DOCTYPE...>`	Use !DOCTYPE to distinguish the version and level of your HTML document. This element should appear before the opening <HTML> tag.

(continued)

Tag Element	*Example*	*Description*
BASE	`<BASE HREF=URL>`	Use the <BASE> tag to provide the exact location of the document being viewed. The <BASE> tag defines the absolute URL of the document. This tag is helpful when a site is mirrored.
HTML	`<HTML DIR=LTR></HTML>`	The <HTML> tags open and close the HTML document. They indicate to browsers that the document is in HTML. The DIR attribute (not yet universally recognized) indicates which direction to display text for international documents, with one of two assigned values: LTR (left to right) or RTL (right to left).
ISINDEX	`<ISINDEX>`	The ISINDEX element indicates that the document is a gateway script that enables searches. The FORM element frequently replaces the ISINDEX element in newer documents.
LINK	`<LINK REL=text HREF=URL>`	LINK appears within the HEAD element and indicates relationships between documents, using the REL and REV attributes (explained in the following table). TITLE can be used to suggest a title for the referenced URL.
META	`<META NAME="author" CONTENT="your name">` or `<META NAME= "generator" CONTENT= "your program">` or `<META NAME="keywords" CONTENT="paintings, antiques, masterpieces">` or `<META NAME= "description" CONTENT="We Buy Used Masterpieces">`	Use the <META> tag to display information about an HTML document such as the author, the program or template used to generate the document, keywords to reference it, and descriptions you would like displayed in any search results. You can use the <META> tag to control how your page is indexed in search engines. The last two examples (on the left) would yield the name of your site and the description "We Buy Used Masterpieces."
SCRIPT	`<SCRIPT></SCRIPT>`	Use the SCRIPT element to place inline scripts in your documents in the future. The LANGUAGE attribute enables you to indicate the scripting language used.
STYLE	`<STYLE></STYLE>`	Use the <STYLE> tag to provide inline style information. The TYPE attribute enables you to indicate the language in which the style statements appear.

Tag Element	*Example*	*Description*
TITLE	`<TITLE> The Works of Renoir</TITLE>`	The TITLE element is always contained in the HEAD element. Text in this element appears in the top of the browser window.
Attribute	***Example***	***Description***
REL	`<LINK REL="stylesheet" HREF=URL>`	Use the REL attribute within the <LINK> tag to describe a normal relationship to the document specified in the URL. The value "stylesheet" designates a location for the current document's stylesheet.
REV	`<LINK REV="made" HREF=URL>`	Use the REV attribute in the LINK element to describe a reverse relationship to the document specified in the URL. The value "made" designates the creator of the document and the URL is usually the creator's e-mail address.

The Body Element and Its Attributes

The BODY element encloses the document body. You can place certain attributes in the <BODY> tag to set general defaults for the document, such as background colors, background images, and colors for link text.

Tag Element	*Example*	*Description*
BODY	`<BODY></BODY>`	The <BODY> element tags open and close the main body of the HTML document. The <HTML>, <HEAD>, and <TITLE> tags appear outside of the BODY elements. All other text and block elements appear within the <BODY> tags.
Attribute	***Example***	***Description***
ALINK	`<BODY ALINK= "#FFFFFF">`	Use the ALINK attribute to specify the color that hyperlinks become as you click on them.
BACKGROUND	`<BODY BACKGROUND= "/images/brickwall.gif">`	Use the BACKGROUND attribute to specify the image file you're using as the background for your HTML document.

(continued)

Attribute	Example	Description
BG COLOR	`<BODY BGCOLOR= "#FFFFFF">`	Use the BGCOLOR attribute to specify the color you're using as the background for your HTML document. The color is always described in hexadecimal form, and in quotes. Color values in HTML are given in RGB as hexadecimal numbers (for example, "#C0C0C0"), or as one of 16 color names: aqua, black, blue, fuchsia, gray, green, lime, maroon, navy, olive, purple, red, silver, teal, white, and yellow. (for example, <BODY BGCOLOR="yellow">).
LINK	`<BODY LINK="#FFFFFF">`	Use the LINK attribute within the <BODY> tag to specify the color of link text in your HTML document.
TEXT	`<BODY TEXT="#FFFFFF">`	The TEXT attribute sets the color of nonlinked text in the HTML document.
VLINK	`<BODY BGCOLOR= "#FFFFFF" VLINK= "#000000">`	Use the VLINK attribute to specify the color of visited links in the HTML document.

Block Level Elements

Block level elements fall within the document body. They are containers for most text level elements, and they always cause paragraph breaks. Some block level elements include paragraphs, tables, list items, special formatting for blocks of text, and horizontal rules.

Tag Element	Example	Description
BLOCKQUOTE	`<BLOCKQUOTE> Text </BLOCKQUOTE>`	The BLOCKQUOTE element is used to indent and separate important quotations or sections of the HTML document, for example, in cases of quoting blocks of text from a special source.
CENTER	`<CENTER> Text </CENTER>`	The CENTER element center-aligns any text appearing between its starting and closing tags.
DIV	`<DIV ALIGN=center> </DIV>`	Use the <DIV> tag to set a logical division, or default, for alignment in particular sections of a document. More than one block element can be within a DIV section, but any align attribute within these block elements overrides

Tag Element	Example	Description
		the align value in the DIV element. Values include center, left, or right.
HR	<HR> or <HR ALIGN=left WIDTH="100%" NOSHADE>	Use the <HR> tag to place a distinct horizontal rule between sections of the document. In HTML 3.2, SIZE (in pixels), WIDTH (in pixels or percent), and ALIGN (left, right, or center) attributes can be used to set sizes for the line in certain browsers. You can use the NOSHADE attribute to eliminate shading so the rule appears as a plain line.
ISINDEX	<ISINDEX>	The ISINDEX element indicates the document is a gateway script that enables searches. This older element is frequently replaced by the FORM element in newer documents.
P	<P> or, <P ALIGN=right, left, center, justified>	The P element indicates the beginning of a new paragraph. The ALIGN attribute can be used within the <P> tag to center the paragraph or to give it left or right alignment. If the ALIGN attribute is not present, the paragraph defaults to left alignment.
PRE	<PRE>Preformatted Text</PRE>	Use PRE in sections where you want to maintain the integrity of your text formatting as much as possible, such as columns of numbers or flowcharts. Text inside the <PRE> tag appears in a monospaced font, and line breaks and spaces are rendered as they are in your document source.

Heading Elements

Use heading elements to provide boldface titles for sections of your HTML page. It is best to use these block elements hierarchically for the most effective design. For example, H1 should precede H2, and so forth. While the Level 4 through 6 headings are less commonly used because they are smaller, these headings are useful in documents containing many sections and those requiring a great deal of organization.

Tag Element	Example
H1	`<H1>Level 1 Heading</H1>`
H2	`<H2>Level 2 Heading</H2>`
H3	`<H3>Level 3 Heading</H3>`
H4	`<H4>Level 4 Heading</H4>`
H5	`<H5>Level 5 Heading</H5>`
H6	`<H6>Level 6 Heading</H6>`

List Elements and Attributes

Lists are some of the most useful block level elements. Lists can be ordered with items appearing in numeric or alphanumeric sequence; unordered and appearing beside bullets or other symbols; or they can be menu and directory lists that appear as unordered data, but in a more compact form.

Tag Element	Example	Description
DIR	`<DIR></DIR>`	Use the DIR element to set up compact lists of short items. These items may be arranged in columns.
MENU	`<MENU></MENU>`	Use the MENU list in the same way you would an unordered list (UL). The MENU list displays in a more compact form in some browsers.
OL	`<OL TYPE=1><LI>List Item</LI></OL>`	The OL element encloses an indented list of ordered items (ordered list). The TYPE attribute can be used to indicate which types of numerals or alphanumerics designate list items. Values for the TYPE attribute include: ■ 1 = arabic numbers (this is the default) ■ a = alphanumeric lowercase ■ A = alphanumeric uppercase ■ i = roman number lowercase ■ I = roman number uppercase ■ Use the START attribute to initialize the sequence number and the COMPACT attribute to signify a short list and give the list a more compact format.

Tag Element	Example	Description
UL	`<UL><LI>List Item </LI></UL>`	The UL element indicates an indented list of unordered items (unordered list). The TYPE attribute can be used to indicate which symbols designate list items. Values for the TYPE attribute in an unordered list include disk, square, and circle. Use the START attribute to initialize the sequence number and the COMPACT attribute to give the list a more compact format.
DL	`<DL><DT>Term</DT><DD> Definition</DD></DL>`	Use the DL element to designate a list of terms and their definitions. Within the <DL> tag are tags for individual terms (<DT>) followed by their definitions, which are enclosed in <DD> tags. Definition lists require start and end tags.
LI	`<OL><LI>List Item </LI></OL>`	The LI element indicates individual list items. Use the VALUE attribute to reset the numerical sequence in an ordered list.
Attribute	***Example***	***Description***
COMPACT	`<UL COMPACT></UL>`	The COMPACT attribute displays text and lists in a compact form.

The Form Element and Its Attributes

The block level element FORM has become a commonly used feature in many HTML documents. Forms enable you to collect data from people who visit your site. Using the required attribute, ACTION, the form sends data to a specified URL or to the body of the submission, where a CGI script processes the data entered by a user and returns feedback.

Tag Element	Example	Description
FORM	`<FORM ACTION=URL METHOD= get, post> </FORM>`	Use the FORM element to gather user input. Information the user enters into the form is processed by a CGI script located on the Web sever to retrieve the input information.
INPUT	`<INPUT TYPE=submit NAME= submitform>`	The INPUT element appears in the FORM element to indicate different types of form fields, including password fields, radio buttons, check boxes, submit and reset buttons, image buttons, file upload, hidden fields, and single-line text fields.

(continued)

Tag Element	*Example*	*Description*
SELECT	`<SELECT NAME=x SIZE= MULTIPLE><OPTION> </OPTION></SELECT>`	Use the `<SELECT>` tag around individual `OPTION` elements to format a list of items from which the user can select. The `SIZE` attribute indicates how many list items the user can choose. A value of one generates a drop-down list. Values higher than one produce scrollable lists. The `MULTIPLE` attribute enables the user to select multiple items from the list.
TEXTAREA	`<TEXTAREA NAME= Paintings I'd Like to See ROWS=25 COLS=25> </TEXTAREA>`	Use the `<TEXTAREA>` tag within the `<FORM>` tag to format fields in which the user enters text. The `NAME` attribute gives the area a name for scripting purposes. The `ROWS` and `COLS` attributes specify the area's size in height and width.
Attributes	***Example***	***Description***
ACTION	`<FORM ACTION=INPUT>`	The `ACTION` attribute is used to describe the method of posting a form.
ENCTYPE	`<FORM ACTION=URL ENCTYPE=x></FORM>`	Use the `ENCTYPE` attribute in the `FORM` tag to specify an encoding type for the form data. The only currently supported type is `"application/x-www-form-urlencoded"`; however, as more types become available this tag should gain popularity.
MAX LENGTH	`<INPUT TYPE=text NAME= Your Occupation MAXLENGTH=30>`	Use the `MAXLENGTH` attribute to specify the maximum number of characters the user can enter into a text field in your form. Be advised that before submitting your form, users can edit this area locally to accommodate as many characters as they like.
METHOD	`<FORM ACTION=URL METHOD= get></FORM>`	Use the `METHOD` attribute to describe the way form data is sent to a server. `GET` sends the data to a URL, and `POST` sends it within the body of the submission.

The Table Element and Its Attributes

The block level element `TABLE` is officially recognized in HTML 3.2. Use tables to organize rows of data into cells. When considering using tables for page layout purposes, remember that some browsers do not yet support tables and your data will look drastically different in those browsers. Table cells can contain many block elements, including form fields and nested tables.

Tag Element	*Example*	*Description*
TABLE	`<TABLE ALIGN=LEFT> </TABLE>`	TABLE designates a series of rows as table cells, defined by TR (table row) and TD (table data, or cell) elements. The table can be aligned on the page using the ALIGN attribute with values LEFT, CENTER, or RIGHT. Control the width or height of the table using WIDTH and HEIGHT attributes expressed in pixels or percentages.
CAPTION	`<CAPTION>Conceptual Water Lilies </CAPTION>`	The CAPTION element attaches a label to a figure or table.
TD	`<TD></TD>`	Use the TD element to define an individual cell in a table. Attributes include ALIGN, VALIGN, ROWSPAN, and COLSPAN.
TH	`<TH></TH>`	The TH element, like the TR element, designates an individual table cell. Attributes include ALIGN, VALIGN, ROWSPAN, and COLSPAN.
TR	`<TABLE><TR><TD>table cell</TD><TD>table cell</TD></TR></TABLE>`	<TR> tags enclose individual table rows.

Attribute	*Example*	*Description*
BORDER	`<TABLE BORDER=12> table </TABLE>`	Use the BORDER attribute to specify the thickness (in pixels) of a border around your table.
CELLPADDING	`<TABLE ALIGN="top" COLS=4 WIDTH=40 CELLPADDING=6> Table Here </TABLE>`	The attribute CELLPADDING controls the spacing inside table cells (in pixels).
CELLSPACING	`<TABLE ALIGN="top" COLS=4 WIDTH=40 CELLSPACING=6> Table Here </TABLE>`	Use the CELLSPACING attribute to designate the spacing between table cells (in pixels).
COLSPAN	`<TD ALIGN="center" COLSPAN=4>table cell</TD>`	Use the COLSPAN attribute to indicate the number of columns a table cell (TH or TD) spans across. If the attribute has a value of zero, the cell spans all columns.

(continued)

Attribute	Example	Description
ROWSPAN	<TH ALIGN="center" ROWSPAN=4>Table Cell </TD>	The value ROWSPAN indicates the number of rows a table cell (TH or TD) occupies. If ROWSPAN is assigned a value of zero, the cell spans all rows.
VALIGN	<TD ALIGN=right VALIGN= middle>	The VALIGN attribute indicates the vertical alignment of table cells. Values for VALIGN include baseline, bottom, middle, or top.

Text Level Elements and Attributes

Text level elements are used to format characters. Text level elements can contain other text level elements, but cannot contain block level elements.

Tag Element	Example	Description
A	<A HREF=URL>Link Text </A>	Use the A or ANCHOR element to designate hyperlinks, which, when selected, lead to locations designated in the URL (contained in the tag). The HREF attribute is almost always used in conjunction with the <A> tag to designate the URL location. The NAME attribute designates "name" anchors for specific sections in your current document . Other attributes include REL, REV, and TITLE.
ADDRESS	<ADDRESS></ADDRESS>	The <ADDRESS> tag should enclose pertinent contact information. When formatted in the browser, the text usually appears in an italicized, indented group.
B	<B></B>	The B element displays text in boldface. To indicate strong emphasis, use STRONG instead, because some browsers render these tags differently.
BIG	<BIG></BIG>	The BIG element accomplishes the same thing as <FONT SIZE="+1">, which makes the font larger. If unsupported by a browser, the BIG element is ignored, so the <FONT SIZE="+1"> element may be substituted.
BR	<BR CLEAR=all, left, right, none>	Use the special text level element BR to force a line break. The CLEAR attribute is optional and is used when images accompany your text. If the image is aligned left or right, text flows around it.

Tag Element	Example	Description
		Use <BR CLEAR=LEFT or RIGHT> to align your text below the image and create a clear left or right margin. Using CLEAR=ALL scrolls your text down until both margins are clear.
CITE	<CITE></CITE>	The <CITE> tag indents and italicizes a citation, such as the name of a book.
CODE	<CODE>example code </CODE>	Text between <CODE> element tags formats to look like source code for computer languages.
DFN	<DFN>DaVinci - Painter</DFN>	The DFN element formats text as a description.
EM	<EM></EM>	Use the EM element around words, phrases, or paragraphs you want to emphasize. This element frequently italicizes words; however, make sure to distinguish between <EM>, <I>, and <B> tags, as certain browsers and indexers may interpret them in different ways.
FONT	<FONT SIZE="x"> or <FONT COLOR= "#FFFFFF"></FONT>	Use the FONT element to format characters. The SIZE attribute specifies a particular font size, and the COLOR attribute makes text within the tags a specific color. Color values in HTML are given in RGB as hexadecimal numbers (for example, "#C0C0C0"), or as one of 16 color names: aqua, black, blue, fuchsia, gray, green, lime, maroon, navy, olive, purple, red, silver, teal, white, and yellow (for example, <BODY BGCOLOR="yellow">).
I	<I></I>	The I element italicizes text.
KBD	Type <KBD>cd </KBD> to get to your UNIX home directory.	Text enclosed in the KBD element formats in the browser as keyboard input. This is most useful when you want to clearly state what the user should type into his or her computer.
SAMP	<SAMP></SAMP>	Text in the <SAMP> tag is formatted to indicate sample text, such as an example of programming output. SAMP does not produce a monospace font like KBD.
SMALL	<SMALL></SMALL>	Text within the <SMALL> tag is drawn in a smaller font. The element <FONT SIZE="-1"> achieves the same result.

(continued)

Tag Element	*Example*	*Description*
STRIKE	`<STRIKE></STRIKE>`	Use the `<STRIKE>` tag to render text with a line through the middle of it.
STRONG	`<STRONG></STRONG>`	Text within `<STRONG>` tags is strongly emphasized. Many browsers format `B` (boldface) and `STRONG` in the same way. Still, you should distinguish the two from each other.
SUB	`<SUB></SUB>`	Text inside the `<SUB>` tag is formatted in subscript or is distinctly lower than the surrounding text.
SUP	`<SUP></SUP>`	Text inside the `<SUP>` tag is formatted in superscript or is distinctly higher than the surrounding text.
TT	`<TT></TT>`	Text enclosed in the `<TT>` tag is formatted in a teletype (or monospace) font. The `<KBD>`, `<SAMP>`, and `<CODE>` tags are more specific and thus more likely to produce desired results.
U	`<U></U>`	Text within the `<U>` tag is underlined. This format can be confusing because underlined text usually indicates a hyperlink.
VAR	`<VAR></VAR>`	Use the `<VAR>` tag to format text so it appears like the variables in computer programs. `VAR` formats in a monospace font; however, unlike the `PRE` element, `VAR` collapses multiple spaces.

The Image Element and Its Attributes

Graphics displayed in HTML documents are known as inline images. HTML 3.2 also supports server and client-side image maps, which enable you to click on certain areas of an image to navigate to other URLs or other parts of your HTML document.

Tag Element	*Example*	*Description*
IMG	`<IMG SRC="/images/filename.gif" HEIGHT=120 WIDTH=60 ALIGN=left,>`	Use the `IMG` element to specify the location of an inline image you are displaying in your HTML document. `SRC` indicates the directory location and filename of the image to be displayed. Use the `ALIGN` attribute within the image tag to align the image to accompanying

Tag Element	*Example*	*Description*
		text. Values for this attribute include `left`, `right`, `top`, `middle`, and `bottom`.
AREA	`<MAP NAME=Louvre Museum Image Map> <AREA SHAPE= circle HREF=URL COORDS=10, 10,5 ALT=Link to Renaissance Paintings></MAP>`	Use the `<AREA>` tag to designate each "hotzone" inside the `<MAP>` tags of a client-side image map. `HREF` specifies the URL to which the hotzone links.
MAP	`<MAP NAME= "areas.map"></MAP>`	The `MAP` element contains a client-side image map. The `NAME` attribute assigns a name to the image map.
Attribute	***Example***	***Description***
ALT	`<IMG SRC="monalisa .gif" ALT="Mona Lisa">`	The `ALT` attribute provides text in the place of the image for text-only browsers.
BORDER	`<A HREF=URL><IMG SRC="graphic.gif" HEIGHT=50 WIDTH=70 BORDER=0></A>`	If an image is linked, you may eliminate or adjust the default border around it by using the `BORDER` attribute. In the example to the left, `0` means the link border around the image will be eliminated. Otherwise, you can specify your desired border thickness in pixels.
COORDS	`<AREA SHAPE=circle HREF= URL COORDS= 10,10,5>`	The `COORDS` attribute contains a set of coordinates describing a hotzone in an image map.
HEIGHT	`<IMG SRC=graphic.gif HEIGHT=120 WIDTH=60 ALIGN=LEFT>`	The `HEIGHT` attribute specifies the height of your inline image in pixels.
HSPACE	`<IMG SRC=URL HSPACE=x>`	The `HSPACE` attribute is used within the `<IMG>` tag or the `APPLET` element. `HSPACE` designates, in a numeric value, the number of pixels to be left free horizontally around the object.
ISMAP	`<IMG ISMAP SRC= "graphic.gif">`	Sets the graphic as a server-side image map.
SHAPE	`rect`, `circle`, `poly`, `default`	Use the `SHAPE` attribute to indicate the shape of a hotzone in an image map. Values include `square`, `rect` (rectangle), `poly` (polygon), `circle`, or `default`. `Default` has no coordinates; it usually composes the background of the image map or any areas that aren't specific hotzones.

(continued)

Attribute	*Example*	*Description*
SRC	`<IMG SRC="/images/filename.gif"></A>`	The SRC or "Source" element indicates the location of the file being referenced in an <A> tag. The SRC value can be a filename or a filepath.
USEMAP	`<IMG SRC="URL" USEMAP="areas.map">`	USEMAP sets the graphic as a client-side image map. The USEMAP attribute contains the location of the MAP file.
VSPACE	`<IMG SRC=URL VSPACE=x>`	The VSPACE attribute is used within the <IMG> tag or in the APPLET element. VSPACE designates, in a numeric value, the number of pixels to be left free vertically around the object.
WIDTH	`<IMG SRC="filename" HEIGHT="x" WIDTH="x">`	Use the WIDTH attribute to specify the width of an element, such as an image or a horizontal rule (HR).

Applet Elements and Attributes

The APPLET element is a text level element that is recognized in the HTML 3.2 standard and is supported by all Java-enabled browsers. The APPLET element usually produces an animation.

Tag Element	*Example*	*Description*
APPLET	`<APPLET CODE=code HEIGHT=x WIDTH=x > applet coding </APPLET>`	The APPLET element is supported by Java-enabled browsers. Use it to embed Java applets into HTML documents. ALIGN, WIDTH, HEIGHT, HSPACE, and VSPACE apply within the APPLET element as they do in the IMG element. The ALT attribute can be used to provide alternative text in browsers that don't support Java.
PARAM	`<PARAM NAME=x VALUE=y>`	Use the PARAM element to describe parameters for a Java applet. PARAM provides command-line arguments to the applet, within the APPLET element. The NAME attribute indicates the name of the argument, and the VALUE attribute specifies the value.

Attribute	*Example*	*Description*
CODE	`<APPLET CODE=...>`	Use the CODE attribute to designate the location of the applet class.
CODEBASE	`<APPLET CODEBASE=URL>`	Use the CODEBASE attribute within the APPLET element to specify an absolute URL for the applet.

Unsupported Elements in HTML 3.2

The following Internet Explorer and Netscape Navigator extensions are not currently supported in HTML 3.2.

Tag Element	*Example*	*Description*
BGSOUND	`<BGSOUND SRC= "sound.aiff">`	The BGSOUND element plays a background sound in Internet Explorer.
BLINK	`<BLINK></BLINK>`	One of the more controversial elements, BLINK causes text to blink on the page. BLINK is supported in Netscape Navigator.
EMBED	`<EMBED SRC= "movie.mov">`	Use the <EMBED> tag to specify the location of an embedded object (such as a QuickTime VR movie) to be interpreted by the browser.
FRAME	`<FRAME SRC= "page.html" NAME= "myframe" SCROLLING= "yes" MARGINHEIGHT= "15" NORESIZE>`	Use the <FRAME> tag to describe a single frame within a FRAMESET. Use the SCROLLING attribute to designate a scrollbar for the frame. You can set the margin width and height in pixels using MARGINWIDTH and MARGINHEIGHT attributes. The NORESIZE attribute prevents the user from dragging the frame edge to a different position.
FRAMESET	`<FRAMESET></FRAMESET>`	The <FRAMESET> tag holds FRAME elements, which describe the frames that will make up a page.
MARQUEE	`<MARQUEE></MARQUEE>`	Use the MARQUEE element to insert a scrolling marquee. MARQUEE is supported by Internet Explorer only.

(continued)

Tag Element	*Example*	*Description*
NOFRAMES	`<NOFRAMES></NOFRAMES>`	Use the `<NOFRAMES>` tag within the `BODY` element to provide links to pages that do not use frames, for users with browsers that cannot display frames.
OBJECT	`<OBJECT data= Paris.avi type= "application/avi"> <img src=Paris.gif alt="Paris"></OBJECT>`	The `<OBJECT>` tag provides a richer alternative to the `<IMG>` tag. Use `OBJECT` if you think certain browsers won't support the media you're inserting. In the example to the left, an image will be substituted in the browsers that don't support AVI movies. Use the `TYPE` attribute to tell the browser the filetype, so it doesn't download a noncompatible file.
SOUND	`<SOUND SRC= "sound.aiff">`	The `SOUND` element enables you to insert a background sound in NCSA Mosaic.
Attribute	***Example***	***Description***
COLS	`<FRAMESET COLS="50, *,50">`	Use the `COLS` attribute to describe frames in terms of columns of varying width.
ROWS	`<FRAMESET ROWS="50, *,50">`	Use the `ROW` attribute to describe frames in terms of rows of varying height.
TARGET	`<A HREF="URL" target="_top"></A>`	Use the `TARGET` attribute to direct data to specific frames. The magic target name `"_top"` requests that the document display the referenced URL without any frames. `"_self"` loads the link but maintains the same frame. `"_parent"` loads the document into the same frameset as the link. `"_blank"` results in the document loading into a new, blank window.
VERSION	`<HTML VERSION=3.2> </HTML>`	Use the `VERSION` attribute to indicate the version of HTML you're using in your document.

Special Character Entities in HTML

Certain characters represent attributes in HTML, such as greater- and less-than symbols, which always act as the opening and closing brackets of tags. If you would like to use the actual character, or you want to use a character that does not have a corresponding ASCII value, type the established character "entity" that represents the original character in HTML. Each character entity must start with an ampersand (&) and end with a semicolon (;).

Character	***Appears As***	***Description***
<	<	Less-than sign
>	>	Greater-than sign
&	&	Ampersand sign
"	"	Double quotation mark
		Nonbreaking space

ISO Latin-1 Character Entities

Character	***Appears As***	***Description***
Á	Á	Capital A, acute accent
Â	Â	Capital A, circumflex accent
À	À	Capital A, grave accent
Å	Å	Capital A, ring
Ã	Ã	Capital A, tilde
Ä	Ä	Capital A, dieresis or umlaut
Æ	Æ	Capital AE diphthong ligature
á	á	Small a, acute accent
â	â	Small a, circumflex accent
æ	æ	Small ae diphthong ligature
à	à	Small a, grave accent
å	å	Small a, ring
ã	ã	Small a, tilde
ä	ä	Small a, dieresis or umlaut
Ç	Ç	Capital C, cedilla
Ð	Ð	Capital Eth, Icelandic

(continued)

Character	*Appears As*	*Description*
É	É	Capital E, acute accent
Ê	Ê	Capital E, circumflex accent
È	È	Capital E, grave accent
Ë	Ë	Capital E, dieresis or umlaut
ç	ç	Small c, cedilla
é	é	Small e, acute accent
ê	ê	Small e, circumflex accent
è	è	Small e, grave accent
ð	∂	Small eth, Icelandic
ë	ë	Small e, dieresis or umlaut
í	í	Small i, acute accent
î	î	Small i, circumflex accent
ì	ì	Small i, grave accent
ï	ï	Small i, dieresis or umlaut
Í	Í	Capital I, acute accent
Î	Î	Capital I, circumflex accent
Ì	Ì	Capital I, grave accent
Ï	Ï	Capital I, dieresis or umlaut
Ñ	Ñ	Capital N, tilde
ñ	ñ	Small n, tilde
Ó	Ó	Capital O, acute accent
Ô	Ô	Capital O, circumflex accent
Ò	Ò	Capital O, grave accent
Ø	Ø	Capital O, slash
Õ	Õ	Capital O, tilde
Ö	Ö	Capital O, dieresis or umlaut
ó	ó	Small o, acute accent
ô	ô	Small o, circumflex accent
ò	ò	Small o, grave accent
ø	ø	Small o, slash
õ	õ	Small o, tilde
ö	ö	Small o, dieresis or umlaut mark

Character	*Appears As*	*Description*
Þ	fi	Capital THORN, Icelandic
Ú	Ú	Capital U, acute accent
Û	Û	Capital U, circumflex accent
Ù	Ù	Capital U, grave accent
Ü	Ü	Capital U, dieresis or umlaut
Ý	Y	Capital Y, acute accent
ß	ß	Small sharp s, German sz ligature
þ	fl	Small thorn, Icelandic
ú	ú	Small u, acute accent
û	û	Small u, circumflex accent
ù	ù	Small u, grave accent
ü	ü	Small u, dieresis or umlaut
ý	ý	Small y, acute accent
ÿ	ÿ	Small y, dieresis or umlaut

Appendix B

About the CD-ROM

The *HTML & Web Publishing SECRETS* CD-ROM is a toy box of Web tools: freeware and shareware Web utilities, trial versions of commercial Web-development software, ready-to-use graphics, and the HTML source files for most of the examples that are printed in this book.

The CD-ROM is a Windows/Mac OS hybrid containing a separate partition for each platform. The example HTML files are identical across both platforms, but the software libraries are obviously different. If you're smart enough to be using both platforms in your Web development efforts — or if you have access to both platforms — I encourage you to sample both partitions.

This appendix begins with an overview of the CD-ROM's contents and some tips for working with it. The appendix ends with detailed listings of the goodies that each platform's partition contains. Use this appendix and the "On the CD" sidebars throughout this book as a starting point for your exploration.

How the CD-ROM is Organized

To make it easy to find the software and examples that pertain to each chapter, I've organized the CD-ROM's contents into folders whose names correspond to chapters. Note that there isn't a folder for every single chapter. That isn't a bug — it's just that some chapters don't have any companion software or files on the CD.

Some plug-ins required

Two chapters contain sample HTML files that require you to install browser plug-ins (see Table B-1).

Table B-1 Plug-ins required to view samples

Chapter	Plug-in(s) Required	Where to Get It
13	RealAudio/RealVideo	`http://www.real.com/`
	VivoActive	`http://www.vivo.com/`
	Shockwave	`http://www.macromedia.com/`
14	QuickTime	Included on CD-ROM

About the software

The commercial software on this CD-ROM is either functionally limited or time-dated. A functionally limited program generally has features missing or disabled; a time-dated program is usually fully functional, but for a limited period of time after installation, such as 30 or 60 days.

Many of the functionally limited programs can be unlocked by purchasing a code from the program's developer. Thus, you're getting more than just demoware — you're getting near-instant access to a real, live, commercial product. See each package's electronic documentation or "Read Me" files for details on registering.

Tips for Windows Users

You can install any program on the CD-ROM by double-clicking its Setup application. As with any software installation, it's a good idea to exit any open applications before installing a program.

You can open any of the HTML pages on the CD-ROM by double-clicking them, too. But if you use Netscape Navigator, each time you double-click an HTML file, Windows opens another copy of Navigator. This wastes time and memory. (By contrast, if Microsoft Internet Explorer is your default browser and is running, Windows switches to it rather than launching another copy.)

SECRET

If Navigator is already up and running, there's a better way to open an HTML file: drag and drop its icon onto the browser window. What if you've minimized the browser window? Just drag the HTML file's icon onto the browser's button in the Windows taskbar and continue to hold down the mouse button for a second or two. Windows will restore Navigator's window, and then you can drag the icon into it. It sounds cumbersome, but it becomes second nature after a few tries.

Tips for Mac OS Users

Some of the software on the CD-ROM is ready to run as-is (although you will probably want to use the Finder to copy it to a hard drive first). Other programs have installers that you must run. Each program is accompanied by documentation or "Read Me" files that contain installation details.

If you use Netscape Navigator, you can open any HTML sample file by double-clicking its icon. If you use Microsoft Internet Explorer, you can drag and drop HTML file icons to the Internet Explorer icon to open them.

What's On the Windows CD

Table B-2 is a detailed list of the CD-ROM's Windows partition.

Table B-2 Contents of Windows partition

Path	*What's There*	*Notes/Comments*
\Chap3\Htmltool\	OppoSite HTML PowerTools trial	HTML validation and manipulation utilities; see discount offer in back of book
\Chap4\Homepage\	Claris Home Page 2.0 60-day trial version	HTML layout program
\Chap4\Homepage\ Extras\WebXSamp	Web Explosion art sampler	
\Chap4\Homepage\ Extras\Webart\	Clip art and backgrounds	
\Chap4\AXSetup	Microsoft ActiveX Control Pad	Integrates ActiveX controls into pages and creates scripts — also nice HTML and VBScript command references
\Chap4\Netobjct\ tool	NetObjects Fusion trial version	HTML layout and site-management
\Chap4\Rtf2html\	RTFtoHTML	Shareware Rich-Text Format to HTML converter
\Chap5\	Various Web typography examples — tables, fonts	
\Chap5\1-pixgif\	Single-pixel GIFs and examples	
\Chap6\Itsagif	Pedagoguery Software's It's a GIF trial version	Creates GIF files containing more than 256 colors

(continued)

Table B-2 *(continued)*

Path	*What's There*	*Notes/Comments*
\Chap6\Files\	Various graphics demonstration files — LOWSRC, transparency, navigation bars	Also contains a Netscape color palette for Photoshop
\Chap6\Files\Bakgrnds\	Flood-fill background graphics and examples	
\Chap6\Files\Fig6-10\	JPEG compression examples	
\Chap6\Ulead\	Trial versions of Ulead's PhotoImpact with Web Extensions, GIF Animator, and SmartSaver	Lots of nice clip art and background textures here, too
\Chap7\	Example files from Chapter 7 — frames, JavaScript techniques, navigation pop-ups	
\Chap9\Webxnt20	Lundeen Web Crossing trial version	Conferencing and real-time chat; see discount offer in back of book
\Chap9\Wb2setup\	O'Reilly WebBoard trial version	Conferencing and real-time chat
\Chap10\Allaire\	Trial versions of Allaire Cold Fusion and Allaire Forums	Database integration and conferencing products
\Chap12\Examples\	Animated GIF examples	
\Chap12\Ggg\	Pedagogurry Software's Gif-gIf-giF utility	Records screen activity as an animated GIF
\Chap12\Smallgif\	Pedagoguery Software's A Smaller GIF utility	Optimizes animated GIFs for smaller file sizes
\Chap12\MSGif	Microsoft GIF Animator	
\Chap12\WP10Demo	Trial version of Totally Hip's WebPainter	See discount offer in back of book
\Chap13\Audio\Embedaud\	Embedded audio examples	
\Chap13\Audio\Midi\	Embedded MIDI file example	
\Chap13\Audio\Realaud\	Embedded RealAudio examples	Internet connection required to listen
\Chap13\Audio\Sampdemo\	Examples of different audio sampling rates	
\Chap13\Audio\Shckwave\	Shockwave Audio example	Plug-in required; see Table B-1
\Chap13\Video\Realvid\	RealVideo clip examples	Plug-in or helper application required; see Table B-1

Path	What's There	Notes/Comments
\Chap13\Video\Vivoactv\	VivoActive clip examples	Plug-in required; see Table B-1
\Chap14\Qtvrdemo\	Embedded QuickTime VR examples	Plug-in required; see Table B-1
\Chap18\Pf_setup\	O'Reilly PolyForms trial version	Smart forms-handling CGI
\Chap18\Netload	FTP utility	
\Qtsetup\Qteasy32.exe	Apple QuickTime for Windows and QuickTime browser plug-in	

What's On the Mac OS CD

Table B-3 is a detailed list of the CD-ROM's Mac OS partition.

Table B-3 Contents of Mac OS partition.

Folder/File Name	What's There	Notes/Comments
Chapter 4 — Making Pages		
Claris Home Page 2.0 Trial	Claris Home Page 2.0 60-day trial version	HTML layout program
Premium Web Art	Clip art and backgrounds	
Web Explosion Sampler	Clip art and backgrounds	
TextureMill	Shareware utility for creating seamless backgrounds	
Install Myrmidon 1.2 Demo	Trial version of Terry Morse Software's Myrmidon	HTML conversion utility
RTFtoHTML	RTFtoHTML	Shareware Rich-Text Format to HTML converter
Chapter 5 — Typography	Various Web typography examples — tables, fonts	
Chapter 6 — Graphics		
Files	Single-pixel GIFs and examples; various graphics demonstration files — LOWSRC, transparency, navigation bars	Also contains a Netscape color palette for Photoshop
Premium Web Art	Alias to Web Art sampler (see above)	
Web Explosion Sampler	Alias to Web Explosion sampler folder	

(continued)

Table B-3 *(continued)*

Folder/File Name	***What's There***	***Notes/Comments***
Software		
HTML ColorMeister 1.2.5	HTML ColorMeister	Generates HTML hex codes for colors
Chapter 7 — HTML and JavaScript	Example files from Chapter 7 — frames, JavaScript techniques, navigation pop-ups	
Chapter 8 — Web Cam		
Heidsite Weathercam HTML	Source HTML files for Heidsite Weathercam	
MacWebCam 2.7	Web cam software	
Chapter 9 — Conf/Chat/Listserve		
Install LetterRip 1.1	Trial version of Fog City Software's LetterRip	Mailing list server
ListSTAR/SMTP 1.1 Net Install	Trial version of StarNine's ListSTAR	Mailing list server; see discount offer in back of book
Web Crossing 2.0.1	Lundeen Web Crossing trial version	Conferencing and real-time chat; see discount offer in back of book
Chapter 10 — Search/Database		
FindFile 1.0	Freeware WebSTAR plug-in from MacXperts	Enables file searching over Web sites
FlatFiler 1.0.4	Freeware WebSTAR plug-in	
iHound-demo-1.2.2	Trial version of ICATT's iHound	Web site indexing and searching tool
LassoLite tool	Freeware Web server plug-in	FileMaker Pro database publishing
LassoLite for Home Page 2.0	LassoLite with Claris Home Page libraries	
Lasso	Trial version of Blue World's Lasso	FileMaker Pro database publishing tool; see discount offer in back of book
FM Link 1.0.1	Freeware tag generator	Generates Lasso tags for HTML editors
TangoforFM 2.1.1 Installer	Installs Everyware Development's Tango for FileMaker Pro	FileMaker Pro database publishing tool; see discount offer in back of book

Folder/File Name	***What's There***	***Notes/Comments***
Chapter 12 — Animation		
Examples from the Book	Animated GIF examples	
Software		
A Smaller GIF 1.04	Pedagoguery Software's A Smaller GIF utility	Optimizes animated GIFs for smaller file sizes
GifBuilder 0.5	Yves Piguet's freeware GifBuilder utility	Creates animated GIFs
Gif•glf•giF 1.22	Pedagoguery Software's Gif-glf-giF utility	Records screen activity as an animated GIF
Itsagif 0.94	Pedagoguery Software's It's a GIF trial version	Creates GIF files containing more than 256 colors
Install WebPainter Try Out	Trial version of Totally Hip Software's WebPainter	See discount offer in back of book
Chapter 13 — Audio and Video		
Audio		
Embedded Audio	Embedded audio example	
RealAudio	Embedded RealAudio examples	Internet connection required to listen
MIDI		
Sampling Rate Demos.htm	Examples of different audio sampling rates	
Shockwave Audio	Shockwave Audio example	Plug-in required; see Table B-1
Video		
RealVideo Demo	RealVideo clip examples	Plug-in or helper application required; see Table B-1
VivoActive Demo	VivoActive clip examples	Plug-in required; see Table B-1
Chapter 14 — QuickTime VR		
QTVR Examples	Embedded QuickTime VR examples	Plug-in required; see Table B-1
QTVR Tools	Free Apple utilities for creating QuickTime VR movies	
Chapter 16 — Mac Servers		
AutoBoot 1.5 *f*	Karl Pottie's AutoBoot	Reboots a crashed server
Keep It Up 1.3.1 *f*	Karl Pottie's Keep It Up	Keeps specified applications or CGIs running

(continued)

Table B-3 (continued)

Folder/File Name	What's There	Notes/Comments
Maxum Development	Trial versions of NetCloak, NetForms, PageSentry, Phantom, RushHour, and WebLock	See discount offer in back of book
Search/Database Tools	Alias to Chapter 10 software	
ServerStat Lite ƒ	Kitchen Sink Software's log-analysis tool	
WebSTAR 2.0.2 Install	StarNine's Web server software	See discount offer in back of book
QuickTime 2.5 and Plug-In 1.1		
MoviePlayer 2.5	QuickTime movie-playing and editing utility	
QuickTime™ 1.1 Plug-In	Navigator plug-in for playing embedded QuickTime and QuickTime VR movies	

In Case of Difficulty...

If you have trouble with any of the programs on the CD-ROM, please contact its developer at the address or phone specified in the program's electronic documentation or "Read Me" file. Neither IDG Books nor I can help you out with questions pertaining to the operation of specific programs on the CD-ROM.

Want to Be On the Next CD?

If you're a software developer and you'd like to have your software included on a future edition of this book's CD-ROM, please send me an email at `jim@heidsite.com`.

If you're a Web developer and you've created a particularly cool page, animation, database template, JavaScript, or other element and you'd like to share it with the world, I'd love to hear from you. Please contact me at the email address above.

Keeping Up to Date

Be sure to visit this book's Web site, at `http://websecrets.heidsite.com/`, for information on new versions of the programs on the CD-ROM as well as additional news, tips, and links to relevant information sources.

Enjoy the CD-ROM!

Index

C

G

J

N

Q

S

T

W

(continued)

Y

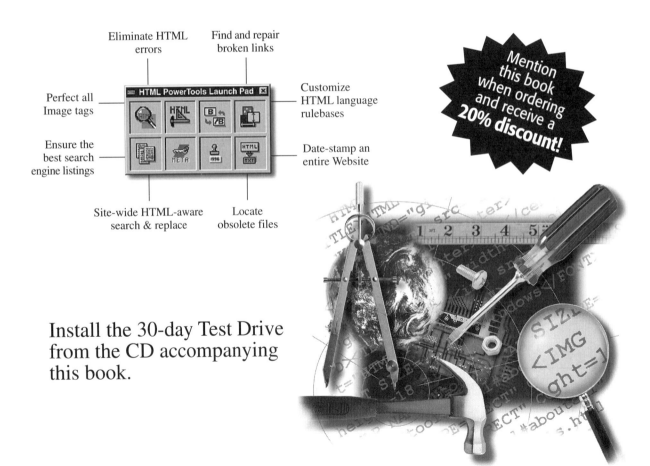

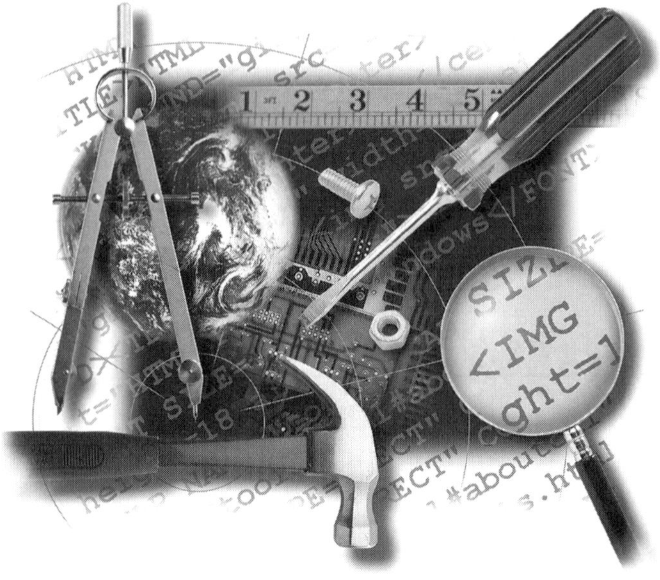

http://www.starnine.com

• Two versions - SMTP or POP
• Templates
• Digests with Table of Contents
• OT Native

Turn your Macintosh into one of the busiest and most productive e-mail hot spots on the internet with ListSTAR's listserver mailing lists and EMail-On-Demand systems.

Do not cut

Save $25 when you return this order form. See details on back.

Do not cut

ORDER FORM

Name ____________________

Organization ____________________

Address ____________________

City ____________________ State ________ Zip Code ____________

Country ____________ Phone # ____________ Fax # ____________

Email address ____________________

Special Pricing for IDG Book Readers ***(Savings are calculated in costs below)***

WebSTAR - # of corporate licenses	_____	x $474	=	________
WebSTAR - # of educational licenses	_____	x $270	=	________
ListSTAR/SMTP - # of corporate licenses	_____	x $474	=	________
ListSTAR/SMTP - # of educational licenses	_____	x $270	=	________
ListSTAR/POP - # of corporate licenses	_____	x $174	=	________
ListSTAR/POP - # of educational licenses	_____	x $ 70	=	________

SUBTOTAL: $____________

Shipping ($6-Continental US; $15-Hawaii, Alaska, & Canada)*: $____________

California Residents Add 8.5% Tax: $____________

TOTAL: $____________

Payment: ☐ Visa ☐ MasterCard ☐ American Express ☐ Check **(see below)****

Card#____________________

Exp. Date____________________

Signature____________________

By signing this order form, I hereby authorize Quarterdeck/StarNine to charge my credit card for the TOTAL amount specified. Prices subject to change without notice.

Name as it appears on card ____________________

Fax this form to 510-548-0393 or
Mail to: StarNine Technologies, Inc.
ATTN: Sales Department
2550 Ninth Street, Suite 112
Berkeley, CA 94710

To contact StarNine by phone, please call 1-800-525-2580.

*** Other countries should contact StarNine Sales at 510-649-4949 or send email to sales@starnine.com***
***** Make checks payable to "StarNine Technologies"***

Special Pricing on Kaidan QuickTime™VR Panoramic Tripod Heads and Object Rigs

The QuickPan Professional (QP-4) is Kaidan's top-of-the-line QTVR panoramic tripod head. It comes with a QP-1B tilt base and QPU-1 universal camera bracket.

QuickPan Pro
***with Tilt* (QP-4): $589.95**
Special Price: <u>$559.95</u>

The QuickPan (QP-5) is Kaidan's standard QTVR panoramic tripod head. It comes with a QP-1C standard base and QPU-1 universal camera bracket.

QuickPan
***w/o Tilt* (QP-5): $399.95**
Special Price: <u>$379.95</u>

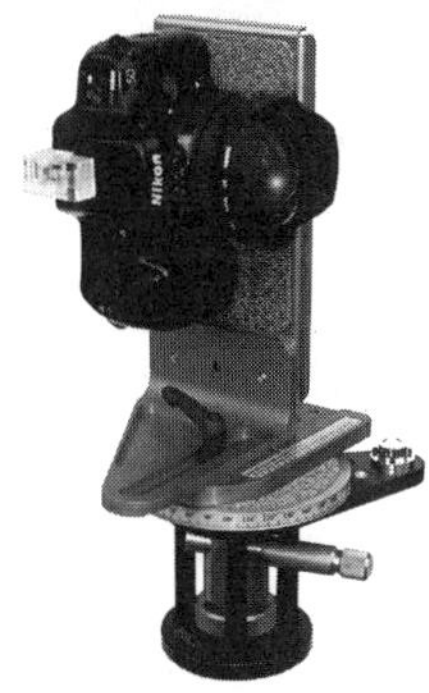

The QuickPan Pro without Tilt (QP-6) relies on our top-of-the-line head mechanism, but in a smaller, lighter package. It comes with a QP-1D base and QPU-1 universal camera bracket.

QuickPan Pro
***w/o Tilt* (QP-6): $489.95**
Special Price: <u>$459.95</u>

For assistance in choosing the tripod head and object rig best suited to your needs or if you need additional information contact Kaidan directly at (215) 364-1778, or visit our website http://www.kaidan.com

The Magellan QC is the smallest and most affordable member of the Magellan family. Capable of handling objects as large as eight inches in diameter and seven pounds in weight, the Magellan QC is the perfect choice for those needing to capture small objects at a reasonable price. The Magellan QC is designed to exploit the capabilities of the recently announced Connectix Color QuickCam digital camera for QTVR object capture.

Magellan QC
(M-QC): $399.95
Special Price: <u>$379.95</u>

The Magellan 1000 (M-1000) is a mid-sized, manually operated rig capable of handling objects as large as 3 feet in diameter and 100 pounds in weight. Sized to fit on a table or desk, the M-1000 employs an adjustable cantilevered arm design with a manually cranked gearbox to position the camera arm, and a click-stop adjustable-height pedestal used to support the object being photographed.

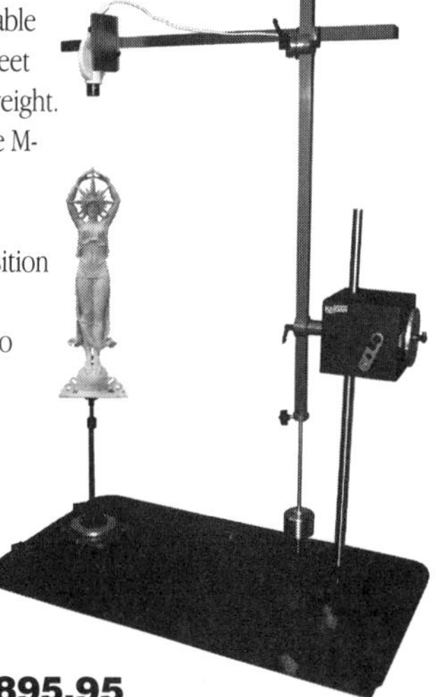

Magellan 1000
(M-1000):
$1995.95
Special Price: <u>$1895.95</u>

Kaidan • 703 E. Pennsylvania Blvd. • Feasterville Business Campus • Feasterville, PA 19053
Phone: 215-364-1778 (9-6 ET) • Fax: 215-322-4186 • WWW: http://www.kaidan.com • info@kaidan.com

Hot topics from IDG Books – Your Competitive Advantage

SECRETS®

Insights from the Experts!

The Award-winning SECRETS series reveals little-known, hard to find, previously undocumented computer tips, techniques, and features. Expert authors share "inside" information and timesaving tricks that sophisticated computer users need today. Whether you're a systems administrator looking to boost the security of your network or a small-business entrepreneur seeking to maximize the productivity of your applications software, you'll uncover a wealth of information in these books!

Access 97 SECRETS®
Cary N. Prague, William C. Amo, and James D. Foxall
0-7645-3043-7
$49.99 U.S./ $69.99 Canada
pp. 1128
Bonus CD-ROM

Office 97 SECRETS®
Steve Cummings & Robert Cowart
0-7645-3015-1
$44.99 U.S./$62.99 Canada
pp. 912
Bonus CD-ROM

Excel 97 SECRETS®
Patrick J. Burns & Alison Barrows
0-7645-3044-5
$49.99 U.S.
$69.99 Canada
pp. 960
Bonus CD-ROM

Visual Basic® 5 SECRETS®
Harold Davis
0-7645-8019-1
$49.99 U.S.
$69.99 Canada
pp. 912
Bonus CD-ROM

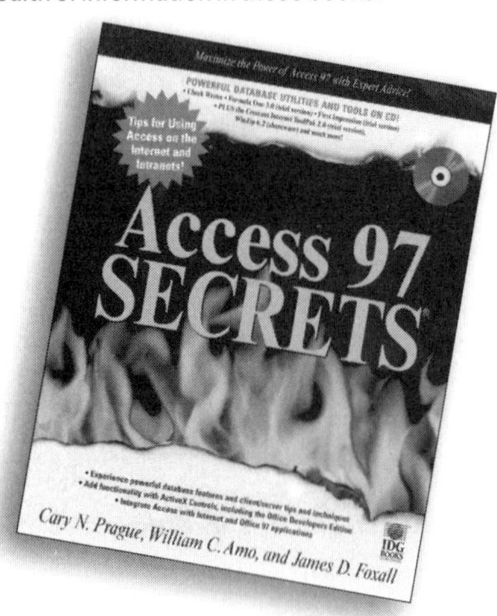

Creating Cool™

The Hottest Topics, The Coolest Results

Learn how to make your web page or presentations stand out in a crowd. Creating Cool™ books provide hands-on examples, practical advice, and step-by-step instructions for putting the latest technologies to work for you, From PageMill to PowerPoint, VBScript to VRML, and JAVA to JAVAscript, Creating Cool books get you productive fast!

Creating Cool™ PowerPoint® 97 Presentations
Glenn E. Weadock & Emily Sherrill Weadock
0-7645-3017-8
$29.99 U.S.
$42.99 Canada
Includes 16 Page Color Insert
Bonus CD-ROM

Creating Cool™ HTML 3.2 Web Pages, 3rd Edition
Dave Taylor
0-7645-3040-2
$29.99 U.S./ $42.99 Canada
pp. 360
Bonus CD-ROM

Creating Cool™ VB Script Web Pages
Bill Hatfield
0-7645-3031-3
$29.99 U.S./ $42.99 Canada
pp. 352
Bonus CD-ROM

Bible Series

Comprehensive Tutorial/Reference Books with 100% of What You Need to Know

Bibles help readers reach higher skill levels by providing comprehensive information on a product or technology. Authors have extensive know-ledge of the topic through years of experience and provide numerous step-by-step examples, real-live uses, and much more.

Office 97 Bible

Ed Jones & Derek Sutton
0-7645-3037-2
$39.99 U.S./$54.99 Canada
pp. 1200

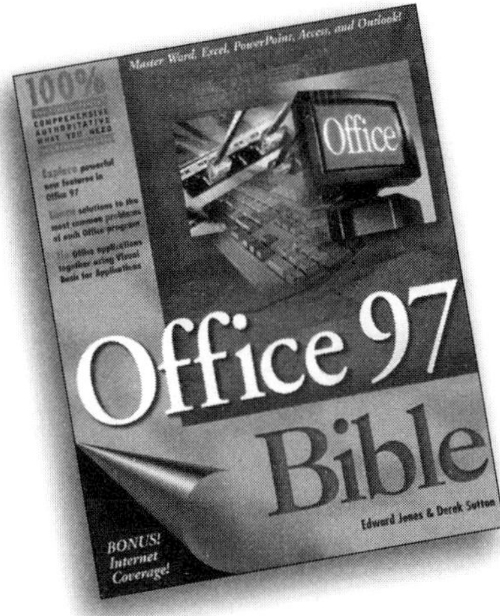

Excel 97 Bible

John Walkenbach
0-7645-3036-4
$34.99 U.S./$48.99 Canada
pp. 944

Word 97 Bible

Brent Heslop & David Angell
0-7645-3038-0
$34.99U.S./$48.99 Canada
pp. 1008

Access 97 Bible

Cary N. Prague &
Michael R. Irwin
0-7645-3035-6
$49.99 U.S.
$69.99 Canada
pp. 1128
Bonus CD-ROM

Updated Bestseller

Intranet Bible

Ed Tittel & James Michael Stewart
0-7645-8013-2
$49.99 U.S.
$69.99 Canada
pp. 912
Bonus CD-ROM

For a FREE catalog listing of all our bestselling titles and series, including Novell Press, ...For Dummies®, Simplified™, and many more, call 800-762-2974

IDG BOOKS WORLDWIDE, INC.
END-USER LICENSE AGREEMENT

READ THIS. You should carefully read these terms and conditions before opening the software packet(s) included with this book ("Book"). This is a license agreement ("Agreement") between you and IDG Books Worldwide, Inc. ("IDGB"). By opening the accompanying software packet(s), you acknowledge that you have read and accept the following terms and conditions. If you do not agree and do not want to be bound by such terms and conditions, promptly return the Book and the unopened software packet(s) to the place you obtained them for a full refund.

1. **License Grant.** IDGB grants to you (either an individual or entity) a nonexclusive license to use one copy of the enclosed software program(s) (collectively, the "Software") solely for your own personal or business purposes on a single computer (whether a standard computer or a workstation component of a multiuser network). The Software is in use on a computer when it is loaded into temporary memory (RAM) or installed into permanent memory (hard disk, CD-ROM, or other storage device). IDGB reserves all rights not expressly granted herein.

2. **Ownership.** IDGB is the owner of all right, title, and interest, including copyright, in and to the compilation of the Software recorded on the disk(s) or CD-ROM ("Software Media"). Copyright to the individual programs recorded on the Software Media is owned by the author or other authorized copyright owner of each program. Ownership of the Software and all proprietary rights relating thereto remain with IDGB and its licensers.

3. **Restrictions On Use and Transfer.**

(a) You may only (i) make one copy of the Software for backup or archival purposes, or (ii) transfer the Software to a single hard disk, provided that you keep the original for backup or archival purposes. You may not (i) rent or lease the Software, (ii) copy or reproduce the Software through a LAN or other network system or through any computer subscriber system or bulletin-board system, or (iii) modify, adapt, or create derivative works based on the Software.

(b) You may not reverse engineer, decompile, or disassemble the Software. You may transfer the Software and user documentation on a permanent basis, provided that the transferee agrees to accept the terms and conditions of this Agreement and you retain no copies. If the Software is an update or has been updated, any transfer must include the most recent update and all prior versions.

4. **Restrictions On Use of Individual Programs.** You must follow the individual requirements and restrictions detailed for each individual program in Appendix B of this Book. These limitations are also contained in the individual license agreements recorded on the Software Media. These limitations may include a requirement that after using the program for a specified period of time, the user must pay a registration fee or discontinue use. By opening the Software packet(s), you will be agreeing to abide by the licenses and restrictions for these individual programs that are detailed in Appendix B and on the Software Media. None of the material on this Software Media or listed in this Book may ever be redistributed, in original or modified form, for commercial purposes.

5. Limited Warranty.

(a) IDGB warrants that the Software and Software Media are free from defects in materials and workmanship under normal use for a period of sixty (60) days from the date of purchase of this Book. If IDGB receives notification within the warranty period of defects in materials or workmanship, IDGB will replace the defective Software Media.

(b) IDGB AND THE AUTHORS OF THE BOOK DISCLAIM ALL OTHER WARRANTIES, EXPRESS OR IMPLIED, INCLUDING WITHOUT LIMITATION IMPLIED WARRANTIES OF MERCHANTABILITY AND FITNESS FOR A PARTICULAR PURPOSE, WITH RESPECT TO THE SOFTWARE, THE PROGRAMS, THE SOURCE CODE CONTAINED THEREIN, AND/OR THE TECHNIQUES DESCRIBED IN THIS BOOK. IDGB DOES NOT WARRANT THAT THE FUNCTIONS CONTAINED IN THE SOFTWARE WILL MEET YOUR REQUIREMENTS OR THAT THE OPERATION OF THE SOFTWARE WILL BE ERROR FREE.

(c) This limited warranty gives you specific legal rights, and you may have other rights that vary from jurisdiction to jurisdiction.

6. Remedies.

(a) IDGB's entire liability and your exclusive remedy for defects in materials and workmanship shall be limited to replacement of the Software Media, which may be returned to IDGB with a copy of your receipt at the following address: Software Media Fulfillment Department, Attn.: *HTML & Web Publishing SECRETS*, IDG Books Worldwide, Inc., 7260 Shadeland Station, Ste. 100, Indianapolis, IN 46256, or call 1-800-762-2974. Please allow three to four weeks for delivery. This Limited Warranty is void if failure of the Software Media has resulted from accident, abuse, or misapplication. Any replacement Software Media will be warranted for the remainder of the original warranty period or thirty (30) days, whichever is longer.

(b) In no event shall IDGB or the authors be liable for any damages whatsoever (including without limitation damages for loss of business profits, business interruption, loss of business information, or any other pecuniary loss) arising from the use of or inability to use the Book or the Software, even if IDGB has been advised of the possibility of such damages.

(c) Because some jurisdictions do not allow the exclusion or limitation of liability for consequential or incidental damages, the above limitation or exclusion may not apply to you.

7. U.S. Government Restricted Rights. Use, duplication, or disclosure of the Software by the U.S. Government is subject to restrictions stated in paragraph (c)(1)(ii) of the Rights in Technical Data and Computer Software clause of DFARS 252.227-7013, and in subparagraphs (a) through (d) of the Commercial Computer@mdRestricted Rights clause at FAR 52.227-19, and in similar clauses in the NASA FAR supplement, when applicable.

8. General. This Agreement constitutes the entire understanding of the parties and revokes and supersedes all prior agreements, oral or written, between them and may not be modified or amended except in a writing signed by both parties hereto that specifically refers to this Agreement. This Agreement shall take precedence over any other documents that may be in conflict herewith. If any one or more provisions contained in this Agreement are held by any court or tribunal to be invalid, illegal, or otherwise unenforceable, each and every other provision shall remain in full force and effect.

CD-ROM Installation Instructions

See Appendix B, "About the CD-ROM" for complete installation instructions and information about the files on the CD-ROM.